WMD Terrorism

WMD Terrorism
Science and Policy Choices

edited by Stephen M. Maurer

The MIT Press
Cambridge, Massachusetts
London, England

MIT Press books may be purchased at special quantity discounts for business or sales promotional use. For information, please e-mail special_sales@mitpress.mit.edu or write to Special Sales Department, The MIT Press, 55 Hayward Street, Cambridge, MA 02142.

This book was set in Sabon on 3B2 by Asco Typesetters, Hong Kong and was printed and bound in the United States of America.

Library of Congress Cataloging-in-Publication Data

WMD terrorism : science and policy choices / edited by Stephen M. Maurer.
    p.   cm.
Includes bibliographical references and index.
ISBN 978-0-262-01298-0 (hardcover : alk. paper) — ISBN 978-0-262-51285-5 (pbk. : alk. paper)
1. Weapons of mass destruction. 2. Weapons of mass destruction—Government policy—United States. 3. Terrorism—United States—Prevention. 4. Terrorism—Government policy—United States. 5. National security—United States. I. Maurer, Stephen M. II. Title: Weapons of mass destruction terrorism.
U793.W2   2009
363.325′3—dc22   2008044225

10 9 8 7 6 5 4 3 2 1

For Suzanne

Contents

Preface

By now, the country ought to know a great deal about WMD terrorism. For one thing, people have studied it for decades. Indeed, the Cold War started with obsessive fears of saboteurs carrying suitcase-sized atomic bombs, and most of what we know about nuclear, chemical, biological, and radiological weapons dates from the 1950s and 1960s. For another, research on WMD terrorism has expanded exponentially since September 11, 2001. Lawrence Livermore National Laboratory alone spent more than $100 million on the topic last year. Anyone who has visited the national labs can appreciate how specialists' talks on, for example, cargo screening have proliferated. And universities are similarly awash in homeland security papers on everything from game theory to improved tort incentives.

And yet it is not enough. The hallmark of a mature academic subject—from chemistry to sociology—is a simple, standard, and above all shared way of looking at things. As the physicist Richard Feynman pointed out more than forty years ago, you do not really understand a subject until you can give a freshman talk. Measured by that deceptively simple criterion, the proliferation of specialist seminars and clever papers falls short. Eight years after September 11, speakers at homeland security conferences routinely begin their talks by admitting how little they know about each other's disciplines. Without a common intellectual framework, new scholars find it hard to get started and established researchers talk past each other. Most importantly, new insights either go unnoticed or are discovered over and over again.

Worse, society ignores what academics already know. When a well-known scholar complains that U.S. policymakers are "deliberately ignoring behavioral research" and "preferring hunches to science," his frustration and anger are easy to see (Fischhoff 2006). Yet academics have not done nearly enough to present the logic and evidence that the Beltway needs. The consequence, inevitably, is that politicians are thrown back on intuition. Given that none of us has ever experienced a WMD attack, intuition has nothing to feed on. Or more accurately, nothing except popular culture's long line of imagined WMD terrorists from *Thunderball* to *True Lies*.

This book is designed to give the interested reader a thorough grounding in WMD terrorism and show her where to learn more. This happens to be a particularly good time for such a project. Much has been learned over the past eight years, and our authors have worked hard to pull this information together. There are also much older currents to draw on. For the national labs, WMD terrorism recalls more than sixty years of previous work on nuclear weapons and deterrence. Universities can similarly offer powerful tools ranging from economics to social psychology to political science. The reader can judge for herself how much has been done to mine these traditions, and how much remains.

1

Introduction: Worrying about WMD Terrorism

Stephen M. Maurer

The idea that terrorists would soon acquire nuclear, chemical, and biological weapons was widespread by the late 1940s. Since then, generations of novelists and film-makers have popularized the idea (see, e.g., Fleming [1959] 2002). Sixty years later, however, very little has happened. Given this evidence, it is only fair to ask whether WMD terrorism is worth worrying about.

The question is further confused by definitions. Since the Iraq War, the always-elastic phrase "weapons of mass destruction" or "WMD" has stretched to the point where it includes a single artillery shell of mustard gas (Fox News, 2004). This usage was, of course, inevitable given the Bush administration's after-the-fact efforts to show that its Iraq War arguments were correct. There is also a certain verbal appeal: if WMD is conventionally divided into chemical, biological, radiological, and nuclear (collectively, "CBRN") categories, then it is surely tempting—though not, strictly speaking, logical—to reverse the definition by saying that any weapon based on these principles qualifies as "WMD." Finally, it makes a kind of legal sense. Nation-states have tried to limit the spread of new weapons technologies through norms and (more fitfully) treaties since the late nineteenth century. But what, exactly, qualifies as a violation? In this environment, it may be acceptable and even desirable to keep the outer limits of WMD vague. At the same time, none of this is satisfying. A term invented to describe nuclear explosions is now used to describe weapons that may be less lethal than high explosives. Worse, it rewrites history. Sixty-six million chemical weapons shells were fired during the First World War. Does it really add anything to call these "weapons of mass destruction," particularly when "ordinary" high explosives seem to have been slightly more lethal? (Harris and Paxman 2002).

Clearly, there is nothing to stop us from saying with Humpty Dumpty that WMD "means what I choose it to mean" (Carroll [1872] 2000). But we should at least choose a meaning that is useful. For purposes of this book, at least, we return to our original instinct that "WMD" is qualitatively different from ordinary weapons.

This immediately suggests violence on a dramatically larger scale than the 2,752 deaths caused by hijacked airliners on September 11 (9/11 Commission 2004). This benchmark is already useful to the extent that it suggests casualties (or at least psychological impacts) much larger than those that precipitated the War on Terror. Nevertheless, it is possible to sharpen the intuition still further. This is, after all, a book about WMD *terrorism*. At what level does the ability to practice violence produce a qualitative change in terrorism itself?

1.1   The Old Terrorism

In the broadest sense, terrorism is not new. There have always been small groups like the Sicarii (first century), Assassins (eleventh to the thirteenth centuries), and Thugs (seventeenth to the nineteenth centuries) who used the threat of violence to intimidate much larger opponents. Calling these groups terrorists, however, is not really accurate. Their understanding of violence was limited to relatively simple strategies like carrying out tit-for-tat threats or pursuing religious goals that transcended politics altogether. What they did not do—what no one seems to have even imagined before the eighteenth century—was to understand that terror could become a social phenomenon in its own right, separate and apart from the violence that spawned it. Still less could they have imagined the example of the French Revolution, in which a carefully manipulated Terror achieved political goals out of all proportion to the number of actual victims.

Even then, such tactics—like all large-scale violence—seemed to be a state monopoly. The idea that small groups could also practice terror required a further act of imagination. The first theoretical suggestion that small groups could amplify their influence through terrorism dates to Karl Heinzen in 1848. Actual efforts to practice terrorism began a generation later with the People's Will in Russia (1870s) and various European anarchist groups (1890s). Even if terror could be achieved, however, it was never entirely clear how groups could use it to achieve their ends. Nineteenth-century terrorists assumed, somewhat doubtfully, that assassinating perhaps a dozen key leaders would destroy the state and allow a new and better order to spring up. Actual experience was, to say the least, discouraging. For one thing, ministers showed an astonishing willingness to replace their assassinated colleagues. More fundamentally, even successful efforts to topple governments (e.g., Russia) invariably ended by installing more reactionary regimes. By the early twentieth century, terrorism had largely fallen out of favor with orthodox Marxists and even anarchists. For modern revolutionaries, terrorism—when mentioned at all—is almost always subservient to political agitation (Laqueur 2002).

Table 1.1
Terrorist strategies (1870–1990)

Announced strategy	Examples	Success
Destroying the state by attacking the government	Russia (1870s)	Poor
Destroying the state by attacking the economy	Italy (1970s), Germany (1970s)	Poor
Publicizing ideology	Germany (1970s), Italy (1970s)	Moderate
Extorting concessions	Russia (1870s)	Moderate
Forcing foreign occupier to withdraw from region	Cyprus (1950s), Palestine (1940s), Aden (1960s)	Moderate
Provoking a crackdown and resulting backlash	Germany (1970s), Italy (1970s)	Poor
Provoking foreign diplomatic intervention	Armenia (1890s)	Poor
Catalyzing conventional diplomacy	Middle East (1970s)	Moderate
Ancillary to traditional military operations	Vietnam (1960s), Turkey (1980s)	Moderate
Blocking political solutions	Russia (1917), Palestine (1970s–), Ireland (1990s)	Moderate
Obtaining operating funds and attracting recruits	Russia (about 1905), South America (1990s)	Moderate
Holding territory against conventional military forces	Algeria (1950s), Peru (1970s)	Poor
Labor disputes with private employers	U.S., Spain (early 1900s)	Moderate

Sources: Laqueur 2002, Carr 2006

If terrorism cannot plausibly topple the state, however, it remains possible that it could achieve less spectacular aims. Twentieth-century terrorist groups have followed many different strategies, although usually without success (table 1.1).

The really striking thing about these diverse strategies is that none of them requires violence on anything like the scale normally reserved to state actors. Indeed, for many purposes—for example, publicizing a cause or garnering international sympathy—mass violence is counterproductive. By the late 1980s, scholars overwhelmingly agreed that terrorists had no real interest in causing large-scale casualties. This comforting assessment was also reasonable. As early as 1973, at least one group of Palestinian terrorists understood that it might be possible to fly a hijacked Boeing 747 jetliner into cities—and even mounted an abortive plot to implement it

(Tinnin 1977). Remarkably, the attempt was never repeated. Instead of encouraging their followers to try again, terrorist leaders stepped back from the abyss.

1.2   Al Qaeda and the New Terrorism

Clearly, Al Qaeda is different. The question is how. Here, it is probably better to start by saying what is *not* new. To begin with, the change is not a matter of rhetoric, even including Al Qaeda's celebrated 1997 "declaration of war" against the United States. Terrorist groups have always invoked the symbolism of "war" and "combat." Nor is it about capability. Technically, at least, the IRA was almost certainly better organized to bomb trains and motorways and set off 2,000-pound truck bombs (Coogan 2000). Nor, finally, is it even about WMD. In the popular imagination, at least, terrorists have sought WMD for years. At the wilder fringes, it is almost impossible to say where journalistic claims that, say, Aum Shinrikyo tested a nuclear weapon in the Australian outback (Pinkney 2006) or the Baader-Meinhof group tried to steal a U.S. nuclear warhead (Harclerode 2000) end and *Goldfinger* begins.

And yet, Al Qaeda *is* different. The IRA may have been able to kill people, but it was signally reluctant to do so and in some cases even apologized afterward (Coogan 2000). Al Qaeda's demonstrated record of mass violence is qualitatively different. Given recent history, we have to take its stated desire to kill tens and even hundreds of thousands with atomic (9/11 Commission 2004) and germ weapons (Leitenberg 2005) seriously.[1] What has changed?

1.2.1   Limited Wars

Perhaps nothing. Some accounts argue that Al Qaeda mounted the September 11 attacks because it wanted to draw the United States into an Afghan War like the one that it claims destroyed the USSR. In this telling, Al Qaeda only mounted the September 11 attacks because the United States had—against all expectation—ignored its earlier provocations (9/11 Commission 2004). Despite unprecedented casualties, the logic for such an attack is not much different from traditional terrorist strategies of using attacks to force nation-state opponents into overreaction up to and including wars. Two wars later, there can be little doubt that the provocation did indeed draw a U.S. military response. In this sense, Al Qaeda's September 11 strategy was rational and traditional.

The jury is, of course, still out on whether it will achieve the broader strategic goal of weakening U.S. influence in the Middle East. That will ultimately depend on the American public's willingness to prosecute two wars where national survival is not at stake. History suggests great powers may be deflected by even moderate numbers (tens of thousands) of casualties. During the Boer War, the British Empire suffered 21,000 soldiers killed. This figure—roughly 0.5 percent of the population at the time—was sufficient to bring about a negotiated peace. The lessons of Vietnam (58,000 killed, 0.03 percent of the U.S. population) are similar. Recent experience in Iraq suggests that even smaller numbers (4,000 killed as this book goes to press, 0.004 percent of the U.S. population) may be sufficient in some circumstances. Significantly, Al Qaeda does not really need WMD to inflict such casualties. Indeed, one of the main virtues of a terrorism-as-provocation strategy from Al Qaeda's standpoint is that most of the killing (and dying) will be done by others. Nevertheless, Al Qaeda could reasonably conclude that possession and/or use of WMD on U.S. soil could help it win a limited war.

There are, however, at least two problems with this scenario. The first involves a kind of Catch-22. To attain its goals, it is not enough for Al Qaeda to cause casualties. It must also be able to *stop* causing casualties if and when its demands are met. Such discipline might not be possible for an organization as decentralized and ill-defined as Al Qaeda. Historically, of course, perfect discipline has not been necessary. Instead, it has usually been enough for terrorists to show that they could significantly reduce the violence even though some splinter groups remained.[2] If Al Qaeda limited WMD knowledge to a tight inner circle, Western governments could decide that the prospect of conventionally armed splinter groups did not matter. In this case, WMD would make Al Qaeda a *more* plausible negotiating partner than traditional groups like the IRA. The situation would be very different, however, if WMD knowledge was known to be widely distributed. In that case, the leadership's willingness to negotiate would mean very little and hostilities would continue.[3]

The second reason Al Qaeda might not be able to exploit WMD in a limited war is more fundamental. At least publicly, there is very little indication that Al Qaeda's goals are limited to Iraq and Afghanistan. To the contrary, it claims to want a "caliphate" that stretches from Afghanistan to North Africa. Of course, this could be rhetoric and prolonged warfare might in any case change Al Qaeda's mind. To the extent that the position is serious, however, U.S. leaders would almost certainly make the judgment—just as they did with Nazi Germany[4]—that something like national survival was at stake. In this case, the concept of a "limited war" would become irrelevant and Al Qaeda would need to inflict enormously more casualties to achieve its goals. In this environment a WMD capability would become not just useful but essential.

1.2.2 Total War
In the weeks following September 11, there were frequent suggestions that Al Qaeda might be able to mount follow-up attacks every few months. Eight years later, this

Table 1.2
Nation-state casualties (1789–1945)

Conflict	Nation	Deaths (including civilians)
Napoleonic Wars (1789–1815)	France	1.4 million—5% of total population
American Civil War (1861–1865)	Union	360,000—1.4%
	Confederacy	200,000—2.5%
World War I (1914–1918)	France	1.4 million—3.6%
	British Empire	0.8 million—1.9%
	Germany (including civilians)	1.7 million—3.1%
	Austria	1.5 million—2.9%
World War II (1939–1945)	United States	405,000—0.4%
	United Kingdom	300,000—0.6%
	USSR	25+ million—15%
	Germany	4.5 million—6%
	Japan	2 million—2.7%

Sources: Merridale 2000; White 2005, 2006; Keegan 1998

fear was clearly unreasonable. One can still imagine conventional attacks killing thousands of people but not tens of thousands. We have seen that such casualties are only marginally useful in the context of limited wars. They seem wholly inadequate for larger projects, including Al Qaeda's stated goal of reorganizing the Middle East.

The question remains how many casualties Al Qaeda would have to inflict to fill this gap. If history teaches anything in this regard, it is that modern nation states are astonishingly resilient. A casual look at modern history (table 1.2) suggests that nation-states can routinely absorb casualties amounting to 2 or 3 percent of their total population and in most cases continue fighting. Indeed, the fact that most wars end not with political collapse but with physical occupation of the losing state suggests that even higher rates are possible.[5] Simple casualty figures do not, of course, tell the whole story—the extraordinary losses suffered by the USSR in World War II reflect many intangible factors too, not least fear of extermination—but these figures do provide a useful benchmark. In American terms this implies that a population bent on total war could continue to function up to perhaps ten million casualties.[6] While this number is much lower than Cold War estimates, it is nearly four orders of magnitude higher than September 11. If Al Qaeda means to prosecute and win a war, WMD is the only option.

Indeed, Al Qaeda cannot survive in its present form without it. In the long run—admittedly decades[7]—terrorist groups need to show results. Otherwise, demonstrated futility will eventually choke off recruits. Al Qaeda cannot afford a stalemate. Even if successful, additional September 11 attacks are not enough to change the game. Only WMD can do that.

1.3 Irrationality

To this point, I have discussed terrorism as if it were a rational means to a rational end. However well this works as an approximation, it is surely not the whole truth. From the beginning, practically all terrorist groups have shared strikingly generic features:

- Terrorists view violence as a symbolic statement rather than as a rational instrument for achieving specific goals.
- Terrorists are almost never recruited from people over thirty and are usually much younger.
- Terrorists attract disproportionate numbers of criminals and the mentally ill (Laqueur 1999, 2004).[8]
- Terrorists hold unusual, extreme, and millenarian beliefs.
- Terrorist groups, like cults, enforce beliefs through incessant indoctrination.
- Terrorists' internal politics are fractious, bitter, and frequently bloody.
- Terrorism—like suicide—follows a "Werther syndrome"[9] in which initial, spectacular acts generate waves of imitators.

It is not hard to see signs of madness in this evidence. At the very least, such regularities suggest that terrorism's psychological roots are important. If so, it is not hard to take the next step by asking whether Al Qaeda's interest in WMD is based on something more than rational calculation. Certainly, technological gimmicks have long fired terrorist imaginations. The prototypical example was, of course, dynamite—a reaction perhaps best exemplified by a radical Brooklyn newspaper's decision to call itself *The Ireland's Liberator and Dynamite Monthly* (Laqueur 2002). But it did not end there. Nineteenth-century terrorists also placed orders for submarines well before the U.S. Navy did (Coogan 2000), dreamed of attacking the Houses of Parliament with osmium gas, debated the merits of James Bond–style poisoned stilettos and, in 1906, talked of inventing airplanes to carry out attacks (Laqueur 2002). Even including dynamite, none of these technologies ever came close to justifying terrorists' hopes.

It is not hard to see how the pursuit and very possibly the use of WMD could possess a similar glamour in the twenty-first century—and could even become an end in itself. Indeed, something like this seems to have happened to Aum Shinrikyo, the Japanese extremist sect that tried to acquire anthrax and chemical weapons less for political reasons than because it thought that WMD attacks would usher in the millennium (Tucker 2000a). The nexus between madness and WMD may be hard to quantify, but it clearly exists.

1.4   Conclusion

Over the past decade, it has become common to predict that biological, chemical, and radiological attacks will eventually occur on U.S. soil. While this seems a safe bet, scale also matters. On the one hand, policy interventions can do little to prevent trivial attacks and there is not much point in thinking about them. On the other hand, we have argued that WMD is unlikely to make a qualitative geopolitical difference unless it causes casualties that are at least an order of magnitude larger than September 11.[10] Succeeding chapters will almost always adopt this definition of WMD.

Readers will have to judge for themselves whether and to what extent WMD terrorism is feasible and, if so, where it should rank on America's list of priorities. WMD terrorism may have low probability, but that does not relieve of us of the obligation to think about the threat and take sensible measures to meet it.

Notes

1. The 9/11 Commission reports that Bin Laden lost $1.5 million in an attempt to purchase weapons-grade uranium from the Sudan. Bin Ladin reportedly talked of wanting a "Hiroshima" with at least 10,000 casualties. Many within the CIA similarly point to a Khartoum soil sample as evidence that Al Qaeda tried to make nerve gas (9/11 Commission 2005).

2. The point is well illustrated by the Belfast conflict, in which the United Kingdom repeatedly demanded—and received—temporary "cease-fires" from the IRA (Coogan 2000). Clearly, the IRA's ability to mount attacks was not enough. It also had to show that it could stop all, or at least most, of the violence if it wanted to. For its part, the British government clearly understood that no IRA cease-fire would ever be perfect and that a negotiated solution was bound to produce splinter groups. Negotiations might still be worthwhile, however, if IRA leaders spoke for enough members to significantly reduce the level of violence.

3. During the Cold War, NATO buttressed deterrence by deliberately placing physical control of nuclear weapons in the hands of low-level commanders. Its goal was to persuade the Soviets that Western governments could not prevent a conventional war from turning nuclear. This made the otherwise implausible threat that NATO countries would use atomic weapons on their own soil credible (Bracken 1983).

4. German policy between the fall of France and the invasion of Russia clearly assumed that the world would not be neatly partitioned into two hemispheres and that further conflict with

the United States was unavoidable (Goda 1998). American elites were therefore justified in thinking that national survival was at stake. Total war also required that the American people to understand and accept the argument. President Franklin D. Roosevelt made the case on December 12, 1940, famously arguing that "if Great Britain goes down, the Axis powers will control the continents of Europe, Asia, Africa, Australasia and the high seas—and they will be in a position to bring enormous military and naval resources against this hemisphere. It is no exaggeration to say that all of us in the Americas would be living at the point of a gun" (Kennedy 1999).

5. Of the thirteen states listed in table 1.2, only three (World War I–era Germany, Austria, and Russia) suffered a political collapse. World War II–era Japan surrendered before being occupied. The French Army suffered widespread mutinies in 1917 but subsequently recovered.

6. Estimates by politicians are instructive. When three nights of RAF bombing killed 60,000 to 100,000 Hamburg residents, Hitler reportedly speculated that further, similar attacks might force Germany out of the war (USSBS 1945). U.S. leaders in the final year of the war similarly seem to have thought that the public would accept an additional 100,000 to 300,000 battle deaths (Frank 1999).

7. Once started, terrorism is notoriously long-lived. Remnants of 1970s-era Marxist groups like Germany's Red Army Faction and Italy's Red Brigades continued to mount sporadic attacks well into the 1990s. Even if Al Qaeda is destroyed its remnants and imitators will continue to mount attacks for years.

8. Easily the most obvious example involves the Socialists' Patients Collective, which seized Germany's Stockholm Embassy in 1975. The terrorists had previously been treated by a Heidelberg psychiatrist who believed that violence could cure mental illness.

9. The term *Werther syndrome* refers to the wave of suicides that followed the publication of Goethe's novel *The Sorrows of Young Werther* in 1774 (Phillips 1974).

10. Chapter 16 does, however, examine the common argument that even a small-scale chemical, biological, or radiological attack would inflict a debilitating psychological impact.

2

Profiling the WMD Terrorist Threat

Jeffrey M. Bale and Gary A. Ackerman

For more than two decades, policymakers and academics have become steadily more concerned about the threat posed by WMD terrorism. This concern became even more acute in the wake of the March 20, 1995, sarin nerve agent attack on the Tokyo subway system by an apocalyptic millenarian religious group known as Oumu (or Aum). Shinrikyō (Aum Supreme Truth), an event that has been described as the "first major sub-state use" of such a weapon (Cameron 1999b).[1] Many experts argued that Aum's blatant and indeed traumatic violation of long-standing societal taboos against the use of WMD by nonstate actors represented a "qualitative leap" that would soon inspire other terrorist groups to employ these weapons, whereas other specialists instead insisted that terrorists were likely to continue to rely on tried-and-true conventional weapons.[2] As it turned out, neither of these positions was entirely warranted (Jenkins 1997). Although no significant spike in actual incidents of WMD terrorism has yet occurred, there are increasing indications that certain types of terrorist groups are planning WMD attacks and, more worrisome still, several apparent WMD plots have already been interdicted. There is therefore an urgent need to separate fact from fiction by examining, synthesizing, and critically evaluating the existing scholarly and policy-oriented literature that addresses WMD terrorism.

This chapter examines this literature in an effort to identify broader trends and assess the current WMD terrorism threat. Section 2.1 clarifies key basic concepts, including both "terrorism" and "WMD." Section 2.2 describes the various motivations that might lead a terrorist group to try to acquire and employ WMD and identifies the types of organizations most likely to be tempted to do so. Section 2.3 examines the organizational and social capabilities that a terrorist group would need to support a credible WMD program. Section 2.4 reviews the specialized assets and technical skills that would be needed to create WMD. Section 2.5 builds on this analysis to consider how likely WMD terrorism currently is and what the trends are for the immediate future. Finally, section 2.6 presents a brief conclusion.

2.1   Basic Concepts and Definitions

Governments and citizens are presently concerned about any and all subnational groups that may end up carrying out acts of WMD violence. For this reason, this chapter will consider all violent nonstate actors who might acquire WMD, including those who might not qualify as terrorists in the strict sense of the term. Similarly, the terms *WMD* and *WMD terrorism* will only be applied to large-scale, high-impact uses of chemical, biological, radiological, and nuclear (collectively, CBRN) weapons that have the potential to cause substantial numbers of casualties.[3] As we will see, however, there are several reasons why terrorists and other violent groups might decide to carry out CBRN attacks that do not inflict enough casualties or damage to fit the criteria of "mass destruction" (Bale 2004b). We will therefore consider the prospects of both "WMD terrorism" and "CBRN terrorism," with the understanding that the latter phrase may apply to attacks that inflict limited (or, in the case of radiological weapons, possibly zero) casualties or damage.

Given such terminological problems, it is hard to analyze the literature without first saying a few words about the meaning of fundamental concepts like "terrorism" and "WMD." Indeed, widespread confusion about those terms routinely hampers analysis and policy formulation. Such a discussion is not a trivial exercise, since these terms are associated with a number of conceptual problems that policymakers often nimbly circumvent or exploit for their own ends. This almost inevitably occurs at the expense of an adequate assessment of the potential for WMD terrorism.

2.1.1   Terrorism

Terrorism is a term that has a great deal of emotional resonance and is often used in a blatantly partisan fashion. A more neutral definition is therefore required. Perhaps the best way to distinguish between terrorism and other forms of violence is to recognize that most acts of violence are dyadic—that is, they involve only two parties or protagonists, the perpetrator(s) and the victim(s). In contrast, all bona fide acts of terrorism are triadic, in that they involve not just perpetrator(s) and victim(s) but also wider target audience(s) whose attitudes and behavior the terrorists are consciously seeking to influence. Terrorism is, as Brian Jenkins (1997) and others have aptly pointed out, violence for psychological effect.[4] Here, the most important nexus is between the perpetrator(s) and the target audience(s) they are trying to influence. For this reason, targeted assassinations as an end in themselves (e.g., murders of particularly effective or brutal policemen) or attacks solely designed to kill large numbers of people (e.g., massacres) are not, strictly speaking, acts of terrorism.

According to this definition, terrorism is nothing more than a violent technique of psychological manipulation and, like other techniques or tactics, it can be used by virtually anyone. It can be employed by states or in opposition to state power; by left-wingers, right-wingers, or centrists; by the irreligious or the religious; and for an almost infinite variety of potential causes. It is therefore not true, as many assert, that "one person's terrorist is another person's freedom fighter." Instead—and regardless of whether one sympathizes with or abhors the underlying motives or proclaimed causes—a terrorist can be identified purely by the methods he or she employs.

2.1.2   Weapons of Mass Destruction

Unlike the word *terrorism*, the use of the term *WMD* in popular discourse is generally misleading rather than polemical. Traditionally, the WMD label has normally been confined to CBRN weapons. This usage is still standard in international academic practice, and hence we will employ it here.[5] However, the usage is imprecise in that the term can encompass both agents that are specifically designed for use in warfare (e.g., nuclear warheads, sarin nerve agent) and toxic materials that are developed for nonmilitary purposes but can be misused in ways that cause significant harm (e.g., pesticides, radioactive isotopes used for industry or research).

Current U.S. military usage is considerably broader. It defines WMD as weapons that can cause "a high order of destruction" and/or "destroy large numbers of people." This can potentially include high-consequence conventional weapons other than CBRN.[6] Further, the military's definition "excludes the means of transporting or propelling the weapon where such means is a separable and divisible part of the weapon" (DoD 2008). This would, for example, exclude a missile or artillery tube that launched a chemical shell. This usage is unfortunate inasmuch as it obscures the fundamental point that a CBRN agent must not only be capable of inflicting harm, but also be deliverable to its intended target before it can qualify as a practical WMD. Indeed, except for nuclear weapons, the efficacy of WMD depends almost entirely on delivery.[7]

The notion of "mass" casualties also leads to difficulties. How many people must a weapon be capable of injuring, and does it matter if the answer depends on how it is used?[8] The answer to many of these questions is subjective, making attempts at quantification seem arbitrary. While some CBRN (nuclear warheads, nerve agents) can cause thousands of casualties and therefore unequivocally qualify as "WMD," smaller-scale terrorist attacks using other CBR materials do not. Similarly, the term *WMD* is especially deceptive to the extent that it obscures differences between the various agents and the effects they cause. The problem is rooted in the word *destruction*, which traditionally connotes annihilation and physical ruin. Unlike a nuclear weapon, a release of *Bacillus anthracis* bacteria would not leave a large crater. Moreover, since nuclear devices are the hardest of all weapons to acquire or manufacture, many scholars and policymakers tend to bundle all CBR weapons as "low-probability, high-consequence" events (Falkenrath 1998a). It is often more illuminating to emphasize these distinctions by pointing out, say, that crude attacks with toxic chemicals are "higher-probability, lower-consequence" events than a nuclear attack (Pilat 1998).

The distinction between WMD and other weapons does, of course, contain an element of truth. Obviously, all true WMD have the potential for relatively high casualties, and it might be more accurate to call them "mass casualty weapons." They also share a generic potential for disruption, both psychological and in terms of affecting existing infrastructure. For instance, a chemical weapons attack would immediately contaminate an area and hinder the functioning of essential services. Also, CBRN agents are inherently more frightening than guns and bombs. There are many reasons for this phenomenon, including a natural human fear of contamination and the invasiveness of many agents, particularly biological organisms. A key anxiety-provoking factor is also the intangible nature of most of these agents, which can lead both to gnawing doubts over whether one has been exposed and a sense of powerlessness against an unseen hazard. The 1995 Tokyo subway attack killed twelve people, but over 4,400 of the 5,510 ostensible casualties who reported to medical facilities showed no symptoms of nerve agent exposure and were classified as the "worried well" (Smithson and Levy 2000). That same year, the bombing of the federal building in Oklahoma City killed 168 people and injured more than 500. Yet there were no "worried well," indicating the greater psychological impact of WMD relative to comparably lethal conventional weapons. In principle, this impact could be blunted through education. In practice, constant misuse of the WMD concept actually *increases* public anxiety so that even small-scale CBR attacks become increasingly attractive to terrorists.[9]

2.1.3   Analytic Framework

Beyond these conceptual difficulties, the current WMD terrorism discussion has frequently been marred by hasty evaluations and colored by public and political anxiety. This has led to threat evaluations that too often exclude key aspects from consideration. A basic threat assessment includes establishing the value and vulnerability of the asset under threat (here, American lives), as well as the capability and motivation of the potential attacker. Yet most current discussions focus almost exclusively on terrorist capabilities for deploying CBRN or on our physical vulnerability to those agents. This obscures the fact that less quantifiable aspects, including the strength of the terrorists' motivation to use such weapons, are equally if not more important. One cannot simply assume that because terrorists hate us and want to attack us that they will necessarily choose WMD, even when their aim is to cause large numbers of casualties. The various branches of a threat assessment interact in several ways, and by concentrating disproportionately on only one or two of these, we may well miss synergies that can help reduce the threat.[10]

This chapter seeks to present a more balanced assessment of the WMD threat posed by particular types of terrorist groups. In particular, we consider both their objectives (ideological and operational) and capabilities (operational and technical). According to this analytic approach, the likelihood of a WMD attack is represented as the product of terrorists' motivations and their capabilities. Furthermore, the term *motivations* can be further subdivided into three interrelated elements. First, there is a group's *ideological agenda*, which we define broadly as its complex of fundamental political, social, cultural, and/or religious beliefs. Second, there are its overall and specific *operational objectives*, which refer to all of those results that terrorists seek to achieve by carrying out a particular attack, both in the short term and in the longer term. And finally, there are the group's *psychological propensities*, though these are rarely noticed, much less explicitly analyzed by the terrorists themselves. These include the individual and collective psychology of its members and, above all, of its leaders. These propensities, in turn, influence (and are influenced by) the group's organizational dynamics.

2.2   Terrorist Motivations for Using WMD

One of the peculiarities of the "WMD terrorism" literature is the disparity between the large amount of attention paid to terrorist capabilities and the relatively small amount of attention paid to terrorist motivations. Indeed, "absent a clear understanding of the adversary's intentions, the strategies and tactics developed [to counter them] are based primarily on knowledge of terrorists' technological capabilities and give insufficient weight to psychological motivations" (Post 1987). The same observation is likewise true with respect to the ideological motivations and operational objectives of different types of terrorists.

2.2.1   Motivations

As we saw in section 2.1, attacks that are solely designed to kill large numbers of people are better described as acts of mass murder (or perhaps as acts of war, if one takes the hyperbolic and often metaphorical rhetoric of terrorists and law enforcement agencies at face value). In contrast, the phrase "mass casualty terrorism" refers to attacks that intentionally inflict large numbers of casualties primarily in order to affect a wider target audience. Both types of motives seem to have been involved on September 11. In this instance al-Qā'ida apparently had multiple aims, none of which were mutually exclusive—to destroy the physical symbols of

American power, to damage the U.S. economy, to kill military personnel in the Pentagon, to commit mass murder, and/or to commit a traumatic act of mass casualty terrorism (Bale 2004b).[11] Of course, September 11 was carried out using more or less conventional means. However, it is not hard to see how CBRN weapons could likewise be employed for these—and many other—material and psychological reasons. Nor would CBR necessarily be used to inflict mass casualties. Indeed, in the past CBR materials have most often been used to target specific individuals.[12]

In short, the objectives for carrying out CBR attacks can vary greatly, both in terms of the actual impact sought and the political or religious goals being pursued.[13] In terms of impact, they could be seen as a means to various ends, including small or large numbers of casualties, minor or severe material damage, or varying levels of psychological trauma. Alternatively, they could conceivably be carried out as an end in themselves, especially if the perpetrator(s) had some sort of technological fetish or were otherwise driven by an inner compulsion to utilize unconventional weapons, in the same way that setting fires appeals to certain types of arsonists for idiosyncratic, psychological reasons rather than rational, instrumental ones (e.g., cheating insurance companies, getting revenge, and so on).

Although most analysts mention possible terrorist motives for employing CBRN in an ad hoc way, there have been few attempts to enumerate and evaluate these motives systematically.[14] This section begins that process. We have already explained that motivation can be further subdivided into operational objectives and ideological/psychological factors. We examine each in turn.

2.2.2   Operational Factors

The most obvious—and to casual observers, seemingly the only—operational reason to acquire CBRN is to inflict mass casualties on declared enemies. Certainly, terrorist groups that wish to kill large numbers of people might well be interested in acquiring CBRN because they believe—rightly or wrongly—that such weapons would help them reach their goal (Falkenrath, Newman, and Thayer 1998).

Some observers simply assume that since "new" types of subnational groups increasingly seem to be interested in mass casualty attacks, and since the required technological information is increasingly public, CBR—if not N—attacks are inevitable (Falkenrath, Newman, and Thayer 1998; Foxell 1999; Marlo 1999). Even apart from the difficulties involved in overcoming technical hurdles or transgressing long-standing moral taboos, there are serious problems with this assumption. The most obvious issue is whether violence-prone groups really need CBRN to inflict "mass casualties," however defined. If terrorists are satisfied with killing "only" dozens or hundreds of people, they will likely find it both easier and less risky to continue employing powerful conventional weapons (above all military-grade explosives) to carry out attacks.[15] On the other hand, if terrorists hope to kill hundreds of thousands or millions of people, they will almost certainly turn to WMD. In that case, however, a violence-prone nonstate group might well seek to acquire a nuclear or high-end biological weapon but be relatively uninterested in other, much less powerful forms of CBR.

Nuclear and (perhaps) some biological weapons apart, the single most important factor motivating terrorists to employ CBRN weapons could be the desire to exert a disproportionate psychological impact. In principle, such an attack might stun if not cow enemies while impressing and inspiring supporters (Falkenrath 1998a; McCormick 2003; Claridge 1999; Gurr and Cole 2002). If the primary aim is to traumatize a wider target audience (or multiple audiences) psychologically, terrorists may prefer to use CBR provided that they have the technical capacity to do so and the cost is not too great. Due to the lay public's primal fears of contamination and infection from unseen agents, a CBR terrorist attack that "only" caused several dozen deaths would probably have a more traumatic and terrifying impact than a conventional terrorist attack that killed hundreds (Tucker and Sands 1999; Falkenrath 1998b). This is certainly the lesson of both Aum Shinrikyō, which attracted inordinate attention by using CBW agents, and the 2001 *B. anthracis* letters in the United States. Given the growing frequency of mass casualty Islamist terrorist bombings, it could be argued that conventional attacks must nowadays produce thousands of deaths to match the psychological impact of these relatively isolated examples of CBR terrorism.[16]

These are not the only possible operational motives for carrying out WMD terrorism. For example, a subnational group may wish to contaminate key areas or facilities within the target nation's "critical infrastructure," economy, and political system (Falkenrath 1998b; Gurr and Cole 2002). Certain especially persistent CBR materials such as *B. anthracis* and Cesium–137 would be particularly useful in this context. Similarly, certain CBRN agents are unusually well suited for covert delivery (Falkenrath 1998a, 1998b; Cameron 2000; Tucker and Sands 1999). A small vial of biological pathogens or a small container of toxic chemicals could easily be transported to a crowded location and released, allowing the bearer to depart unnoticed. Indeed, a sudden outbreak of disease might initially be regarded as natural, enabling the perpetrators and/or their covert sponsors to maintain "plausible deniability"— assuming that they actually want to keep their involvement secret instead of boasting about the attack (Claridge 1999). This might occur, for instance, where terrorists seek only temporary deniability to ensure a safe escape or want to make the intentional character of the attack known—and thus cause generalized fear— without revealing their identities.[17]

Although terrorists and other nonstate actors rarely if ever engage in the sort of formal "cost-benefit" analyses that social scientists seek to model, and their "rationality" may not be comprehensible to outsiders, they normally carry out violence to achieve more or less calculated operational objectives (Crenshaw 1998; McCormick 2003). To the extent that this is true, terrorists' interest in CBRN weapons will largely depend on whether "the operational advantages that their use might be perceived to confer" seem to outweigh "the operational disadvantages that their use might incur" (Gurr and Cole 2002). From this perspective, a group's decision to use CBRN, like its other decisions concerning targeting, weaponry, and tactics, will often be based on some degree of rational strategic calculation or choice.

2.2.3 Ideological and Psychological Factors

That said, terrorist motivations also derive from vitally important ideological and psychological factors. In addition to acts that can be characterized as broadly rational, extremist groups tend to inflict violence because of more arcane ideological, subjective, impulsive, or partially conscious and hence ostensibly less rational needs.[18] These latter "expressive" motives include doctrinal obsessions (e.g., compulsions to attack designated "evildoers," longings to precipitate a prophesied Armageddon, a desire for individual or collective martyrdom, or technological fetishism), group pathologies (e.g., excessive insularity, charismatic and/or authoritarian leadership, extreme peer pressure, the promotion of "groupthink," and outright suppression of internal dissent), and collective emotional impulses (e.g., a burning desire for revenge, glory, or publicity, the chance to demonstrate prowess or outdo rival groups, or a desire to evoke past triumphs or tragedies). For "lone wolf" terrorists, potential motivations can encompass an unusually wide range of personal idiosyncrasies.[19]

Ideology plays a decisive, and perhaps even preeminent, role in the selection of targets, tactical methods, and weapons by terrorist groups. Most importantly for current purposes, the "philosophical and ideological views of a group—including both the espoused philosophy of the organization and the 'actual' philosophy revealed by the group's actions—are . . . critical in determining whether it will seek out new technology" (Jackson 2001). The way groups select targets is an involved process that necessarily varies somewhat from group to group, but can generally be characterized as a progressive narrowing of possibilities. First, a group's ideology, by explicitly establishing what the group is for and against, essentially delimits the outside range of legitimate possible human and nonhuman targets. This list is then further limited by the group's specific operational objectives for launching an attack, its operational capabilities, and the results of close surveillance to determine which targets are most vulnerable. All of these processes will be heavily influenced in particular cases both by the nature of the group and its internal dynamics, above all the characteristics of its leaders and their style and method of making decisions, as well as by external factors such as changes in the security environment and the group's links to other actors offering assistance (WMD Terrorism Research Program 2004).

In considering why certain types of terrorist groups might be more inclined to carry out CBRN or WMD attacks than others, it is useful to divide postwar history into (1) an earlier era dominated by secular (or at least secularized) political terrorist organizations demanding political independence or espousing utopian revolutionary ideologies, whether of the left or right; and (2) a more recent period dominated by groups inspired by religious doctrines and imperatives. We will see that the factors inhibiting and facilitating the use of CBR have changed significantly over time.

The first of these two periods, which lasted roughly from the early 1960s to the early 1980s, was dominated by ethnonationalist terrorism on the one hand and ideological left- and right-wing terrorism on the other. As far as ethnonationalist groups are concerned, there were generally two factors that seem to have especially militated against the use of WMD:

• They and their ethnic group occupied a relatively vulnerable piece of territory and were potentially subject to harsh retaliation.
• They hoped to elicit broader international support for their causes, which would have been significantly eroded by crossing the WMD threshold.

One may object that ethnic hatreds (especially those infused with religious sectarianism) often lead to atrocities against designated "out-groups" and that there are several instances of ethnonationalist groups carrying out or threatening to carry out CBR attacks.[20] Furthermore, a number of these groups, including radical factions of the Palestine Liberation Organization and Irish Republican Army, did conduct cold-blooded, brutal actions that proved counterproductive in the sense of alienating potential international sympathizers, if not always their own constituents. But it remains true that cases involving CBR actions by such groups have been extraordinarily rare.

The desire for international sympathy and support may similarly have put a brake on Cold War–era ideological terrorists' ambitions to commit WMD and CBRN terrorism. Here a distinction should probably be drawn between groups that embraced Marxist or anarchist doctrines, and those that adhered to neofascist or neo-Nazi doctrines,[21] even though both displayed utopian revolutionary ideologies with quasi-religious overtones. The former generally targeted specific "class enemies" or representatives of the "imperialist state of the multinationals," claimed responsibility for their attacks, and eschewed both WMD terrorism and CBR terrorism, whether for moral or purely instrumental political reasons.[22] In general their right-wing counterparts were more likely to carry out mass casualty attacks (such as bombings of banks, public squares, commuter trains, and train stations) but were also less likely to claim responsibility and at times tried to implicate the far left by conducting covert "false flag" operations.[23] Despite this, they too rarely displayed any serious interest in CBR terrorism.[24] These last remarks are clearly applicable to the veteran neofascist terrorists in Europe, but are not nearly as applicable to right-wing radicals elsewhere, who have often been driven by markedly less secular worldviews (e.g., idiosyncratic Christian paramilitary groups in the United States).

There are, of course, a wide variety of internal and external factors that might cause secular terrorist groups to risk alienating their proclaimed constituencies and would-be sympathizers. These potentially include a perceived need to demonstrate continued operational effectiveness, rally the spirits of disillusioned members and hardcore supporters, or teach a pointed lesson to their opponents. Nevertheless, the foregoing discussion strongly suggests that they have historically considered—and will likely continue to consider—certain types of actions to be "beyond the pale," whether for principled moral reasons or because they tend to have a rational under-standing of cause-and-effect relationships no matter how Manichaean their world-views or utopian their ultimate political goals may be.[25]

Things have been rather different since the 1980s. During this latter period, "a surge of religious fanaticism has manifested itself in spectacular acts of terrorism all across the globe . . . [a] wave of violence that is unprecedented, not only in its scope and the selection of targets, but also in its lethality and indiscriminate character" (Ranstorp 1996).[26] The factors that have so far kept the "new" religious terrorists from deploying WMD have sometimes been similar and at other times radically dif-ferent from those which inhibited earlier groups. Some analysts have suggested that religious terrorists are markedly less constrained, seeking "to appeal to no other constituency than themselves," (Hoffman 1998) or having a primary "constituency" limited to the god(s) they choose to worship and seek to please (Jenkins 1997). Cer-tain such groups, given their seeming lack of concern about the psychological and practical effects of their actions in the profane world, are likely to be particularly dangerous because they are more or less unconstrained by external forces. Not surprisingly, Jackson (2001) argues that highly destructive CB weapons would be particularly appealing to a group "seeking maximal destruction for the benefit of a divine audience."

This concern can be overstated. In practice, most religious groups are at least partially concerned with events on the terrestrial plane, and some may be as sensi-tive to the effects of their actions on wider audiences as secular terrorists (Dolnik and Gunaratna 2006). For example, a significant number of Islamist terrorists seek to convert other Muslims to their own radical brand of Islam in the hopes of recruit-ing new members. In certain contexts, this has probably persuaded them to refrain from carrying out "beyond the pale" actions that would have very likely alienated large numbers of recruits. Furthermore, groups that fail to consider potential supporters' views are often self-limiting. One excellent illustration of this can be observed in Algeria, where certain Islamist terrorists became so appalled by the Groupe Islamique Armé's (GIA: Armed Islamic Group) systematic atrocities that they broke away from that organization, formed their own rival group, the Groupe Salafiste pour la Prédication et le Combat (GSPC: Salafist Group for Preaching and Fighting), and then forged an alliance with al-Qā'ida (Gunaratna 2003; Burke 2003).[27]

That said, the general consensus among experts seems to be that religious terrorists are more willing—and therefore likely—to violate traditional moral taboos against the use of CBRN weapons than their secular counterparts (Hoffman 1993a, 1997, 1998; Cameron 2000; Campbell 2000; Gurr and Cole 2002; Tucker 2000a; Zaman 2002; Marlo 1999; Ronfeldt and Sater 1981).[28] This distinction between religious and secular groups does not mean that every violence-prone "religious" group is equally likely to pursue mass violence.[29] Theological, historical, and cultural distinctions also matter.[30] In this regard, groups motivated by apocalyptic millenarian religious doctrines seem to be particularly dangerous, since such doctrines postulate (1) the imminent destruction of the existing world order, which is viewed as thoroughly and irremediably "evil"; (2) a terrible fate for the immoral, unenlightened majority; (3) a key role for a select group of very special people—the true followers of the doctrine, namely, themselves—who will be spared the fate of others; and (4) the collapse of the existing order followed by the creation of a worldly paradise in which the same special people will be freed from want, hardship, suffering, strife, oppression, immorality, and everything else that is "evil" (Daniels 1999). Although some adherents will wait passively for the fulfillment of prophecy, others may decide that it is better to hasten the destruction by attacking the "satanic" forces that rule the world. This was certainly the case with groups such as Aum Shinrikyō and the Covenant, the Sword, and the Arm of the Lord (CSA).[31]

Religious communities that believe that self-sacrifice can atone for earthly sins and lead to a heavenly paradise are likewise more prone to extreme violence. This can easily lead to the commission of horrific acts, including suicide bombings. For example, dedicated members of both Sunnī and Shī'ī Islamist groups now routinely carry out martyrdom attacks in the belief that dying while waging *jihād* will guarantee them immediate entry to paradise, thereby bypassing the Muslim equivalent of purgatory. On the other hand, believers' violence does not necessarily take the form of attacks on external enemies. Instead, it may be directed inward, as happened with the Heaven's Gate UFO cult (Balch 1995; Balch and Taylor 2002; Hall 2000; Wessinger 2000; Perkins and Jackson 1997; Partridge 2006).

However, religious groups are not the only types of extremists that might be attracted to using CBRN materials. Some analysts have argued that groups bent on revenge, assorted right-wing extremists, ad hoc groups of like-minded people, and disturbed lone individuals are also especially prone to adopting such weapons. In truth, however, this observation is largely speculative and rests on only a handful of cases (Tucker and Sands 1999; Falkenrath 1998b). Terrorist organizations with scientific and technological pretensions or even fetishes might be more apt to employ high-tech weapons like CBRN, assuming that they could actually acquire or develop them.[32] Whether such a technofetish is the product of a secular or religious ideology may not matter much.

2.2.4   Ideology vs. Deterrence

As in earlier eras, even very extreme religious impulses will normally be moderated somewhat where groups are firmly ensconced within an exposed, vulnerable piece of territory or actively engaged in a broader array of conventional political activities. However fanatical some of their cadre may be, it would be extremely risky for established Islamist groups like Hizballāh (the Party of God), the Harakāt al-Muqāwwama al-Islāmī (HAMĀS: Islamic Resistance Movement), and al-Jihād al-Islāmī al-Filastīnī (Palestinian Islamic Jihad) to engage in WMD attacks, whether against Israel or the United States, since their entire lands could conceivably be occupied or physically destroyed in response.[33] In this sense, it may well be possible to deter such groups from carrying out WMD attacks in the same way that "rogue" nation-states are. However, this could change quickly if the groups decided that the time had come to launch a global jihād, that it was impossible to achieve their goals using conventional means, or that their existence was threatened.

These restraining factors are significantly weaker for other types of religious groups. First, transnational Islamist groups like al-Qā'ida are spread across the globe, and their survival does not depend on the continued occupation or control of specific territories. In recent years several leaders of al-Qā'ida and its affiliated groups have openly boasted of their intent to acquire such weapons. For example, Bin Lādin himself has said that acquiring weapons of all types, including CBRN, is a Muslim "religious duty."[34] Moreover, evidence found in al-Qā'ida camps and inside information provided by jihadists captured in Afghanistan both indicated that the group had acquired and tested chemical agents and also planned to produce various biological agents including *B. anthracis*, botulinum toxin, plague, and hepatitis A and C.[35]

A second major category of religious (and also political) organizations that are relatively immune to external factors are insular cultlike groups. Such groups typically view external events as signs and portents of prophesied cosmic events, and are likely to become even more paranoid and apocalyptic in the face of hostility from mainstream society or repressive state action. However, they seem to be driven primarily by their own internal imperatives, and often their acts have little or nothing to do with specific developments in the outside world. Instead, they frequently display a combination of idiosyncratic theological conceptions and authoritarian intragroup dynamics. For groups like the Ordre du Temple Solaire (OTS: Order of the Solar Temple) in Switzerland and Quebec or the Movement for the Restoration of the Ten Commandments of God in Uganda, sudden acts of horrific violence seem to be triggered mainly by internal processes and mechanisms.[36]

2.2.5 Warning Signs?

Finally, Campbell (2000) and Tucker (2000a) have pointed to various organizational and behavioral warning signs which could indicate that a particular group was inclined to produce or use WMD. A combined list of these signs includes groups that

• Have sadistic, megalomaniacal, or delusional but nonetheless charismatic and authoritarian leaders
• Are socially isolated, do not seriously aim to appeal to—much less claim to represent—a broader constituency, and are therefore relatively unconcerned about the "blowback" from their actions
• Insistently urge their members and supporters to carry out unrestrained violence against demonized and dehumanized collective enemies
• Employ levels of actual violence that have progressively escalated over time
• Consistently display innovation in their use of weapons and/or tactics, or at least a willingness to take higher-than-normal risks (Jackson 2001)
• Go out of their way to recruit people with relatively advanced technical or scientific skills
• Have sufficient financial resources to subsidize the acquisition or development of CBRN weapons
• Have relatively easy access to WMD-related materials; and/or
• Are in such desperate straits, real or imagined, that they feel they have nothing to lose by employing every means at their disposal (Sprinzak 2000)

Needless to say, terrorist groups that display several of these characteristics are particularly worrisome.

2.2.6 Why Hasn't It Happened?

Given that several types of subnational groups seem interested in using CBRN and/or WMD, the obvious question is why so few attacks have occurred thus far. Here, the primary argument is that the rarity of catastrophic mass casualty attacks reflects the difficulties of carrying them out successfully, which are especially acute in the case of WMD (section 2.3). It is less clear, however, why we have not seen many more cases of cruder, small-scale CBR attacks, which should be feasible for almost any reasonably professional terrorist group that was really determined to execute them. Several analysts have explained this by claiming that terrorists, whatever their ideological predispositions, tend to be "conservative" in adopting new techniques and technologies (Jenkins 1986; Hoffman 1993b; Clutterbuck 1993). The evidence for this is debatable. Even if true, however, one would expect that offsetting incentives to acquire WMD would eventually overcome this conservatism for at least one group. Once this happened, it might be expected that other groups would follow suit if the tactic was shown to be feasible, especially if they felt a perceived need to mimic rivals or even states (Falkenrath 1998b).

There seem to be three main motivational reasons why these types of low-grade but nonetheless fear-inducing attacks have been relatively rare. First, we have already explained that groups may be reluctant to alienate constituents and international support. Second, conventional weapons remain a much more efficient way to damage human beings and property (in terms of harm caused per unit of limited resources) than primitive CBR attacks, and hence will normally be relied on unless the creation of a disproportionate psychological impact is the goal. Finally, terrorist group members—like the general public—may lack the specialized scientific knowledge needed to distinguish CBRN realities from their own phobias about contamination, infection, and disease. This reluctance is reinforced by popular culture, with its gruesome Ebola coverage from Africa and fictional WMD accounts. Suicide terrorists may also have an aesthetic preference for explosives, which allow them to go out in a sudden, painless, and seemingly glorious bang rather than, as with certain germs, a lingering, painful, and inglorious whimper (Dolnik 2004). Then, too, suicide bombing is often imitative. Even assuming that a few volunteers could be persuaded to contract and thereafter spread, say, smallpox, their gruesome ensuing deaths would likely act as a deterrent for other prospective, self-styled "martyrs."

Unfortunately, all three of these restraining factors may be gradually breaking down. As noted above, certain "new" categories of terrorists are seemingly less concerned about local or world opinion than their traditional counterparts, and the bigger psychological payoff that would surely result from even a small-scale CBR attack may increasingly appeal to today's terrorists, especially given the temporary panics that followed the 1995 Tokyo subway attacks and 2001 *B. anthracis* letter mailings. After all, al-Qā'ida only began to look seriously at WMD after the Tokyo subway attacks.[37] Finally, greater levels of scientific and technological literacy could gradually reduce terrorists' phobias (not to mention the technical obstacles they face), increasing their readiness to assume CBR-related risks.

2.2.7   Limits of Analysis

The operational methods, tactics, and weapons used by terrorists in the past cannot, in and of themselves, allow us to predict their future behavior with any certainty. They provide, at best, an indication of the many factors that influence terrorists' choices. Furthermore, history does not really repeat itself, and it will be very hard to say how today's terrorists differ from earlier ones unless we insert informants into their ranks or interrogate captured members. Finally, the history of warfare has repeatedly demonstrated how weapons and tactics that have been standard for long periods can be suddenly and unexpectedly transformed, sometimes for reasons that only make sense in hindsight.[38] These forecasting problems are bound to be compounded in our current era of rapid technological change.

2.3   Capabilities: Social and Organizational

WMD development requires both a large supporting organization and a small-but-skilled R&D team. Here, we review the general social and organizational capabilities that a terrorist organization would need to support a plausible R&D effort. We defer discussion of the skills that an R&D team would need to section 2.4.

2.3.1   Organization

The ability to mount a credible R&D program depends on multiple factors, including group size; leadership mechanisms, centralized authority, and internal dynamics; and the ability to innovate and absorb new technologies. Because of the technical and tactical sophistication associated with WMD, an effective group would most likely require a *substantial membership*, a *central leadership* to coordinate R&D and acquisition, and sufficient *discipline* to maintain secrecy (Zanders 1999). Discipline would also be needed to maintain focus over the long planning horizons associated with WMD. For example, action-oriented groups that depend on constant operations to maintain cohesion are unlikely to maintain a WMD program that takes months or years to bear fruit (Jackson 2001). Zanders argues that religious sects are most likely to display the "vertically organized, highly integrated and ideologically uniform" structures needed to produce clandestine CBW in bulk (Zanders 1999). That said, it is prudent to think that some other groups, including certain ethnonationalist terrorist groups, might also qualify.

2.3.2   Logistics

Credible R&D would also need reasonable *logistics*, including the ability to acquire raw materials and equipment, transport the completed weapon to its target, and maintain communications. There would also need to be a *development site* either beyond the reach of Western security forces or, at a minimum, in a place where covert activities could proceed with only a small chance of detection. Unfortunately, this is not a particularly high barrier for chemical or biological agents, since small-scale production can take place in a sizable basement. Continued production over many months could then yield large quantities of agent, although this would put additional, nontrivial demands on process safety and agent storability.

Several modern terrorist groupings have plausibly demonstrated that they can meet these criteria. For example, various organizations have successfully maintained *covert facilities*, including al-Qāʿida, which reportedly maintained several small-scale biological and chemical weapons–related production facilities in Afghanistan under the Talibān, and Aum, which built and operated a clandestine, state-of-the-art laboratory near Mount Fuji. Similarly, the *clandestine networks* needed to acquire and transport materials across borders have been demonstrated by multiple organizations, including Pakistan's A. Q. Khān network, Russia's illicit nuclear materials trafficking networks, and Mexico's smuggling networks that routinely move people and matériel into the United States. That said, CBR activities would become increasingly difficult to hide as production became larger and more sophisticated (Gurr and Cole 2002). Historically, law enforcement has a good track record of infiltrating groups trying to develop CBR weapons inside the United States (Tucker 2000a).

Finally, demands on logistics would be especially great to the extent that a WMD plot required terrorists to operate and blend into the target society. This was a nontrivial hurdle for the September 11 plotters (9/11 Commission 2004), and terrorists might not be so lucky a second time. The problem would be particularly acute for plots that were complex and/or required terrorists to operate for long periods of time in the West.

2.3.3   Financing

A credible WMD development program would need substantial funding to buy materials and equipment, train would-be designers and workers, operate facilities, and/or pay personnel. Some observers argue that this funding is prohibitive (Cameron 2000), but this seems doubtful. Estimates from the literature (table 2.1) suggest that typical costs would run into hundreds of thousands of dollars for CBR and millions of dollars for a nuclear weapon—not terribly different from the estimated budget for September 11. In principle, terrorists could also cut corners by renting and/or stealing materials and equipment, or receiving in-kind donations from supporters. However, most of these options would increase the risk of detection.

Table 2.1
Estimated cost of acquiring CBRN weapons

Weapon type	Cost
Nuclear	Fissile material—likely to cost $1 million per kilogram or more). Other costs for a crude weapon—a few hundred thousand dollars.
Radiological	Radiological material—unknown cost on the black market.
Biological	Less than a few hundred thousand dollars (e.g., the production of botulinum toxin for $400 per kilogram).
Chemical	Less than $10,000 for a basic production capability. More expensive agents like sarin could be produced for approximately $200 per kilogram.

Source: Falkenrath et al. 1999b; Purver 1996

Financial resources do not, of course, guarantee success. Aum Shinrikyō possessed between $300 million and $1 billion in assets but still failed to develop a viable biological weapon or to produce chemical weapons in bulk. Nevertheless, strong financing allowed both Aum and al-Qā'ida to pursue parallel weapons programs as a hedge against failure and to set up front companies to "buy their way out of technical difficulties" (Cameron 1999a). In addition to al-Qā'ida, a handful of other groups have sufficient resources to mount a credible WMD program. These include the Liberation Tigers of Tamil Eelam (LTTE, or Tamil Tigers), Hizballāh, and the Fuerzas Armadas Revolucionarias de Colombia (FARC).

2.3.4   Education and Research

A successful WMD program would also require *human capital*—that is, technical knowledge and skills. This could come either from educating group members or recruiting specialized personnel from outside the group. In either case, the required learning would consist of both *explicit knowledge*—that which can be written down in textbooks or manuals—and, equally importantly, *tacit knowledge* derived from experience or practical instruction (Jackson 2001). In most cases, several distinct scientific and technical skills would be necessary. For example, even though Aum Shinrikyō recruited at least one scientist with a background in microbiology or molecular biology to work on its weapons, the project would probably have been more successful if Aum had also deployed a pathologist, an engineer, a meteorologist, and an aerosol physicist. Moreover, weapons work typically requires specialized engineering "tricks of the trade" that even skilled generalists are unlikely to know. This implies a significant learning curve (Gurr and Cole 2002).

Several authors argue that terrorists can now obtain explicit knowledge of CBRN from many sources, including textbooks, academic and industry publications, and the Internet. This potentially makes them more capable than their forebears (Cameron 2000; Falkenrath 1998a; Gurr and Cole 2002). Aum Shinrikyō, for example, is known to have performed an extensive literature search, including downloading Brookhaven National Laboratory's entire protein data bank, in an effort to find the chemical breakdown products of various toxins. Similarly, several publicly available poison manuals describe how to prepare CB (Stern 1999), and technical information on growing pathogens is widely available in the scientific literature. Perhaps the most obvious change is the Internet. In principle, the Web can provide valuable information that reportedly included, some years ago, the declassified patent for VX nerve agent (Gurr and Cole 2002). This, however, is an ambiguous gift since the Internet also offers significant misinformation.[39]

Terrorists also could acquire knowledge and skills through legitimate educational programs. U.S. universities alone graduate thousands of PhDs in the physical and life sciences every year, many of them foreign students. For example, Ramzī Yūsuf later applied his education at a technical college in Wales to building sophisticated bombs. Aum Shinrikyō's recruiters are also known to have targeted university graduates with scientific and technical degrees. On balance, it is probably safe to say that the barriers to acquiring explicit knowledge have been significantly eroded in recent years and that most of the remaining challenges involve tacit knowledge.

Finally, one obvious shortcut would be to recruit *former state weapons program employees*. Zanders (1999) argues that a terrorist group would be reluctant to hire scientists and technicians who did not share their ideological beliefs. On the other hand, history is replete with examples of persons who have undertaken the most nefarious operations for simple material gain, from Carlos the Jackal to the chemists that support the illegal drug trade. There has been much talk about the desperate need or mercenary bent of scientists in the weapons programs of the former Soviet Union, South Africa, Pakistan, and Iraq. Gurr and Cole (2002) cite several reasons why such scientists would prefer to work for states. However, the world does not offer many state-level jobs for weapons scientists, which may make nonstate organizations correspondingly more attractive.

2.3.5   Innovative Capacity

So far, our arguments suggest that terrorist groups with dogmatic, charismatic leaders who exercise extreme forms of social conditioning (e.g., religious cults) are among the most willing and able to pursue WMD terrorism. Yet these same groups may also be the least equipped to obtain scientific expertise. First, extremist groups draw their members disproportionately from alienated individuals. Even when these individuals have scientific backgrounds, their skills are often substandard (Falkenrath 1998b). Second, harsh conditioning and indoctrination methods tend to make even talented operatives inefficient. Something of this sort may have happened to Aum Shinrikyō, where a paranoid atmosphere based on sleep deprivation and narcotics seems to have interfered with members' ability to develop biological weapons (Rosenau 2001).[40]

2.4   Capabilities: Technical Hurdles

In addition to the foregoing general requirements, each form of CBRN poses specific and unique challenges. We address these in turn.

2.4.1   Chemical Weapons

Materials and Technology Acquisition   Chemical weapons require both precursor chemicals and processing equipment. In general, the more basic the precursor the longer and more complex the production process will be. The equipment needed to make most agents is fairly standard, although it may occasionally trigger dual-use regulations. Particularly complex chemical agents (including sarin and certain other nerve agents) often need specialized equipment capable of withstanding corrosion, high temperatures, and high pressures.

Almost any terrorist actor who possesses the requisite knowledge can obtain the precursor chemicals and equipment for simple chemical agents from normal commercial sources. Aum Shinrikyō, for example, was able to purchase multiple nerve agent ingredients, including fifty tons of phosphorus trichloride and ten tons of sodium fluoride, on the open market (Stern 1999). Precursor chemicals for more sophisticated chemical weapons are often regulated by the Chemical Weapons Convention (CWC). However, the CWC was designed with very large, battlefield-scale uses in mind. As a result, it does not cover transactions involving less than one metric ton of precursor chemicals—more than enough to mount a WMD attack (Falkenrath 1998b). Finally, terrorists could potentially steal chemical weapons agents from existing national stockpiles, including thousands of tons from the former Soviet Union.[41]

Production   The production requirements for chemical weapons depend on the type and amount of agent desired. Certain types of agents, such as hydrogen cyanide, are simple to produce. However, vesicants such as mustard and lewisite are more difficult, and most nerve agents are even more complex. Furthermore, certain production methods and high-purity products require specialized equipment (e.g., noncorrosive materials) that could draw attention to the group. Processes that yielded an impure agent could significantly limit the effectiveness of the ultimate attack.[42] Falkenrath, Newman, and Thayer (1998) assert that a smart, technically educated person with knowledge of chemistry "at the college level or less" should be able to handle at least small production runs from direct precursors within a short space of time.

For a WMD chemical attack, terrorists would also need to produce an agent in sufficient quantities for a mass casualty attack, and this amount is likely to be fairly substantial. This would not necessarily require a large facility, however, if the group was able to stockpile the agent over time (Gurr and Cole 2002). Once again, the ability to stockpile an agent for long periods would depend on its purity.

Weaponization and Delivery   Chemical agents are most effectively distributed by aerosol sprayers, volatilization on heated plates, or explosives. This simplifies dissemination and allows the use of improvised spray equipment (Falkenrath 1998a). Many chemical weapons agents also vaporize spontaneously at room temperature. These considerations make chemical agents among the easiest substances to weaponize and may well put them within the technical capabilities of many terrorist groups. Similar considerations apply to the contamination of food or water systems, although dilution effects can be a significant obstacle.

2.4.2   Biological Weapons

Materials and Technology Acquisition   The material requirements for a biological weapon include equipment such as a fermenter and, perhaps, a freeze-dryer ("lyophilizer"), a seed stock of the desired pathogen, and growth media. Some authors portray fermenters and other manufacturing equipment as specialized (Tucker and Sands 1999), while others describe it as dual-use and easily obtained (Falkenrath, Newman, and Thayer 1998). This apparent discrepancy can be explained by remembering that much depends on the type and amount of organisms desired. While standard commercial or laboratory equipment is enough for small-scale production of some agents, more specialized equipment would be needed to produce larger quantities quickly, grow exotic organisms, and/or perform advanced processing steps like microencapsulation.

Growth media are readily available from commercial sources. Similarly, seed stocks can be obtained from the natural environment, ordered from culture collections, or stolen from hospital or research laboratories. However, strains obtained in this manner are not always virulent. Additionally, U.S. culture collections have stricter controls since white supremacist Larry Wayne Harris tried to obtain plague organisms in 1995. These safeguards remain imperfect, however, and many foreign collections lack even basic controls. In any case, Aum was apparently able to obtain pathogens by setting up front companies (Claridge 1999). More advanced methods include diversion from state biological weapons programs. While this avenue implies greater risks for all parties, it could enable terrorists to obtain pathogens that have already been optimized as weapons, including organisms that have been deliberately engineered for antibiotic or vaccine resistance. Finally, terrorists could create their own pathogens from artificially synthesized DNA. Although this is still a fairly demanding experiment for academic laboratories and is probably beyond terrorists' capabilities, such techniques are bound to become more accessible over time.

Production   Growing bacteria in bulk is a fairly straightforward process, although significant skill is needed to avoid accidentally weakening the organism's virulence and infectivity factors. Methods must also be developed to store the material until it is used or processed further. Finally, containment methods must be devised to protect workers from even trace levels of pathogens.

Well-understood, relatively hardy organisms should present little trouble for a skilled microbiologist to produce in bulk (especially if agent purity is not too much of a concern, as would likely be the case in the context of terrorism). However, the expertise and equipment needed will vary according to the type of agent produced. For example, viral agents are more difficult to produce than bacteria or toxins. Falkenrath, Newman, and Thayer (1998) argue that one competent microbiologist (to produce the pathogen) and an experimental physicist or mechanical engineer (to work on aerosol delivery) could be sufficient to create a working biological weapon.[43] In contrast, Aum's biological weapons failures show that a degree in biology and unlimited finances do not guarantee that biological weapons can be successfully produced and used (Kelle and Schaper 2001).

Advanced techniques including genetic manipulation are probably beyond the capabilities—or even, given the destructiveness of natural pathogens, the desire—of most groups. However, Gurr and Cole (2002) contend that advances in biotechnology and the ongoing diffusion of knowledge could eventually allow terrorists to make more advanced agents. Finally, the amount of effort needed to achieve worker safety would depend on risk tolerance. Some organizations (even including jihadist groups that practice suicide bombing) are very aware of their members' well-being, whereas others may show little or no concern.[44] Safety would also be a security issue: given modern equipment, accidents are one of the few signals that would allow authorities to detect a terrorist production facility.

Weaponization and Delivery   In principle, "a few hundred kilograms of a properly weaponized bacterial agent, when dried and milled to a precise particle size, has the potential to wipe out the inhabitants of an entire city" (Gurr and Cole 2002).

However, such optimized weapons require a large amount of R&D. The most effective way to deliver biological agents is as an aerosolized powder or liquid.[45] Both routes require tight control of particle size and strategies to protect organisms against sunlight, oxidation, air pollution, humidity, and other environmental phenomena.[46] These R&D steps require extensive testing, which in turn increases the risk of exposure. However, this testing may be minimized or even eliminated if a group is willing to accept some uncertainty. Alternatively, terrorists could decide to use simpler delivery methods by contaminating food or water supplies or else inoculating a terrorist and sending him off to infect others.

Most observers believe that converting bulk biological agents into powder is technically demanding (Falkenrath, Newman, and Thayer 1998). The FBI's 2008 conclusion that the 2001 *B. anthracis* letters were prepared by Bruce Ivins, a government weapons scientist with access to classified information and modern lab facilities, further tends to confirm this viewpoint (Bhattacharjee and Enserink 2008). It does, however, show that the main barriers involve information and that small quantities, at least, could be made by a single technically proficient terrorist. If a dry aerosol is not attainable, Falkenrath, Newman, and Thayer (1998b) believe that terrorists could substitute the less efficient liquid form. While neither Iraqi BW scientists nor Aum Shinrikyō succeeded in weaponizing biological agents, commercial aerosol technology is constantly improving and will likely make weapons easier to build over time. Groups that decide to attack food and water supplies would also face significant obstacles. Despite popular belief, large-scale contamination of water or food supplies is surprisingly difficult (Tucker and Sands 1999).

2.4.3   Radiological Weapons

Materials and Technology Acquisition   Various radioactive isotopes can be used to make radiological weapons. These include strontium-90, cobalt-60, and cesium-137. Furthermore, these materials can be obtained from numerous civilian sources including hospital equipment, industrial plants, nuclear facilities, and geological survey equipment. Alternatively, terrorists could purchase the materials illegally. Illicit trafficking is much more widespread for radioactive isotopes than for fissile materials. Recent examples include the theft of a radioactive source in Nigeria that turned up in Western Europe, and the theft of Russian nuclear batteries (Ferguson, Kazi, and Perera 2003). Finally, Foxell (1999) argues that radiological materials could also be extracted from nuclear waste sites.

Production   This stage of weapon development involves processing highly radioactive isotopes into deliverable forms—for example, by milling metals or oxides into small particles. In principle, the shielding and containment needed for such work could greatly complicate fabrication. However, observers have yet to reach any clear consensus about how difficult this would be in practice. Instead, some authors argue that production would be relatively easy, while others are more skeptical (Ford 1998). Cordesman (2001) notes that there are "significant" disputes about how readily terrorists can "convert radioactive materials into a form that could be broadly disseminated over a wide area" and specifically notes the challenges of "grinding up" radioactive materials.

Weaponization and Delivery   Radioactive material can be dispersed using explosives or aerosol sprays, dropped from tall buildings, or used to contaminate food and water supplies. However, none of these methods is likely to produce mass casualties. Cordesman (2001) therefore concludes that it would be difficult for terrorists to spread radioisotopes "over an area larger than a single facility." Jacobs (1998), on the other hand, suggests that today's terrorist groups should be able to create effective radiological weapons.

2.4.4   Nuclear Weapons

Specialized Skills   The basic information on how to construct a nuclear bomb is readily available and a good undergraduate education in physics or nuclear engineering is widely thought to be sufficient (Frank 1967; Falkenrath, Newman, and Thayer 1998). Although even states find it difficult to manufacture sophisticated nuclear weapons, observers claim that crude devices can be built by people with a technical, but not necessarily weapons-specific, background.[47]

Materials and Technology Acquisition   A terrorist group seeking to build its own nuclear weapon would need to obtain fissile material. While estimates vary, most authors argue that a terrorist weapon would be a crude design, requiring roughly sixteen kilograms of highly enriched uranium or six kilograms of plutonium.[48] The weapon would weigh more than a ton and yield the explosive energy of between 1 and 20 kilotons of TNT (Mark et al. 1987).[49]

Practically all observers agree that terrorists lack the expertise and large industrial plants needed to make fissile material (Cordesman 2001; Falkenrath, Newman, and Thayer 1998; Kelle and Schaper 2001). This means that they must either (1) steal or purchase fissile material on the black market and build an improvised nuclear device (IND), or (2) steal or purchase an intact weapon, presumably from poorly guarded former Soviet stockpiles.[50] There have, however, been no confirmed transfers of significant amounts of fissile material from smugglers to terrorists—many of the reported sales are either law enforcement "stings" or frauds—and the situation in the former Soviet Union is ostensibly improving. Similarly, while there have been several reports of missing Russian nuclear weapons over the years, none are confirmed and most have been convincingly discredited (Sokov 2004). Additionally, Stanley Jacobs argues that ex-Soviet weapons pose little risk, since they contain Permissive Action Links (PALs), Environmental Sensing Devices (ESDs), and other features to prevent detonation by unauthorized personnel. This factor can be overstated, however, since Allison (2004) has presented convincing arguments that these safeguards can be overridden so that "the bottom line is that PALs and ESDs can temporarily delay, but cannot prevent, terrorists from using a stolen nuclear weapon." Finally, although Pakistani nuclear weapons are now thought to contain PALs, this fact provides only minor reassurance given the revelations about Pakistani nuclear scientists' links to the al-Qā'ida network and A. Q. Khān's well-organized nuclear smuggling network (Ferguson and Potter 2004).

Production   Uranium weapons can be detonated using relatively crude, "gun-type" bombs. This minimizes the need for testing and precision machining. Plutonium weapons require more advanced (implosion) designs.[51] Depending on where the fissile material comes from, producing a bomb could include safely extracting the material from its housing, machining the uranium or plutonium to the required dimensions, constructing a new weapons housing, and safely storing the completed weapon core until a bomb can be assembled. Each step implies various safety hazards, including radiation, chemical toxicity, and the danger of a conventional explosion when extracting fissile material from an existing weapon. Many writers argue that these technical requirements are just too demanding (Ford 1998; Jacobs 1998). Some authors contend, however, that a well-funded, technically adept terrorist group could overcome these challenges given significant time and effort (Schaper 2003; Ferguson and Potter 2004).

Weaponization and Delivery   Although gun and implosion weapons both require precise engineering, implosion weapons are much more difficult to build properly and would require testing. Unlike other forms of WMD, delivery of nuclear weapons would be straightforward. The completed bomb would simply be smuggled to the target area. The difficulty of this task would depend on target protection, surveillance, and related security issues.

2.4.5   State Sponsorship

Many states with a history of supporting terrorists are known or suspected to have WMD programs. Today's most prominent examples include Iran, Pakistan, North

Korea, and (until recently) Libya. Conceivably, they could extend their support to include logistical and technical assistance for terrorists seeking WMD or even a working weapon.

Scholars are divided on the likelihood of this occurring. One school of thought believes that state involvement is highly improbable, given the prospects of retribution and international opprobrium. This view is buttressed by the fact that no state has ever given another state a completed weapon. This suggests a fortiori that states would be reluctant to give substate actors control over such powerful weapons, no matter how strong their ideological affinity. However, other observers argue that states might offer terrorists assistance if their leaders felt a sense of desperation, embraced an apocalyptic millenarian ideology, or believed they could conceal their contribution. The argument is particularly strong for certain CBR agents whose origins would be extremely hard to trace from samples taken following an attack (Tucker and Sands 1999; Cordesman 2001; Stern 1999).

2.4.6   Attacks against Facilities

Attacks on existing nuclear, chemical, and other facilities offer a possible shortcut to the otherwise formidable R&D problems associated with CBRN. Furthermore, they are very much in the spirit of September 11. Nuclear power plants, in particular, are potentially vulnerable to suicide attacks using airplanes (Kelle and Schaper 2001; Behrens and Holt 2005). However, a suicide attack on a nuclear reactor or waste fuel dump would require special training so that pilots could hit the exact spot needed to liberate contamination (Ferguson and Potter 2004). Alternatively, a commando-style attack on a nuclear facility or shipment could probably be mounted with modest financial resources, although this would usually require insider cooperation.

In light of these modest requirements, many groups should be potentially capable of attacking nuclear facilities, especially in areas where these facilities are not well guarded. Several recent examples of (at least partially successful) attacks on nuclear facilities have been reported (2006; Zenko 2007). Attacks on chemical and perhaps biological facilities,[52] which are more numerous and less well protected, would presumably require similar resources.

2.5   Taking Stock: Terrorist Capabilities Today

Most of the foregoing debate is ultimately designed to address three basic questions:

• Can current terrorists inflict true (i.e., mass casualty) WMD attacks?
• Is this capability increasing?
• If terrorists' WMD capability is increasing, what is the rate of change?

Not surprisingly, the literature seldom if ever provides binary "yes" or "no" answers to these questions. Almost every author couches his or her conclusions in conditionality, and hardly anyone definitively rejects or else argues for the inevitability of WMD terrorism. Instead, opinions range from highly unlikely to extremely probable.

2.5.1   Can Current Terrorists Inflict True WMD Attacks?

Several authors claim that technical obstacles have eroded in recent years, so that WMD is now most likely within the reach of at least certain terrorist groups (Marlo 1999; Sprinzak 1998; Stern 1999). The al-Qā'ida network, which is reportedly pursuing several kinds of WMD, is by far the most commonly cited example of a group likely to "overcome the technical, organizational and logistical obstacles to WMD" (Benjamin and Simon 2005; also see Ackerman and Bale 2002). Other commentators are more sanguine about current terrorist capabilities, believing that they have been exaggerated and that technical hurdles still prevent terrorists from engaging in anything more than small- to medium-sized attacks using CBRN weapons (Cameron and Pate 2001; Pilat 1998). Finally, many commentators argue that R&D is a risky process, so that there is still a significant gap between groups' theoretical capabilities and operational reality (Cameron 2000). For example, Gurr and Cole (2002) emphasize that despite the increasing efforts to acquire CBRN "no group has ever acquired an actual 'WMD' as this term is traditionally known." Yet even the most conservative authors do not unequivocally dismiss the possibility that a group could field WMD either currently or in the near future. Substantively, most of the disagreement centers on the technical barriers to producing or delivering WMD. By contrast, most authors seem to assume that existing groups seeking CBR can readily acquire whatever raw materials and logistics they need.

This general picture is similar across the different types of WMD, although some scholars vehemently deny the idea that terrorists could acquire a *nuclear* weapon citing the difficulties of acquiring fissile material and constructing a reliable bomb (Cameron 2000; Jacobs 1998; Kamp 1998). In general, however, post–September 11 analyses have been more pessimistic, concluding that the threat of nuclear terrorism (for example, from an IND) is real (Kelle and Schaper 2001; Ferguson and Potter 2004; Allison 2004). While these studies stop short of saying that al-Qā'ida and other current groups have actually achieved this capability, they argue that the possibility cannot be ruled out (Albright, Hinderstein, and Higgins 2002).

There is also a fair amount of disagreement about terrorists' ability to acquire *radiological weapons*. While scholars agree that this possibility is far more likely than nuclear terrorism (Jacobs 1998; Ferguson and Potter 2004; Zimmerman and Loeb 2004; Ferguson, Kazi, and Perera 2003), some stress that the technical obstacles to an effective weapon are formidable (Ford 1998). Almost all knowledgeable commentators are careful to note, however, that a feasible weapon will primarily be psychological and economic, with very few physical casualties (Ferguson, Kazi, and Perera 2003; Zimmerman and Loeb 2004). In this sense, radiological weapons should be considered weapons of mass *disruption* instead of true WMD.

Finally, scholarly estimates of terrorists' *chemical* and *biological weapons* capabilities vary widely. For example, Kamp (1998) agrees with Falkenrath that "if a terrorist organization wanted to inflict mass casualties, it could easily use biological or chemical weapons which . . . are quite simple to acquire or produce." However, Zanders (1999) is more cautious, admitting that mass casualty CB weapons are feasible but emphasizing the technical difficulties and expressing doubts about terrorists' ability to achieve a high-quality weapon. Henderson (1999) is still more conservative, arguing at least for biological weapons that few terrorist groups are likely to produce agents in a form that could inflict mass casualties.

2.5.2 Are Terrorists' WMD Capabilities Increasing?

Even if terrorist groups cannot mount WMD attacks today, technological progress tends to erode technical constraints and increase terrorist capabilities over time (Hoffman 1997). Furthermore, recent history shows that terrorists can be highly innovative when necessary. For this reason, most scholars concur that "the likelihood of acts of NBC terrorism in the future is low, but it is not zero and it is rising" (Falkenrath, Newman, and Thayer 1998). Interestingly, Zanders (1999) dissents, claiming that, at least in the realm of chemical and biological weapons, terrorist capabilities are actually decreasing. He argues that increasingly visible international nonproliferation norms (and accompanying vigilance by suppliers) are making it steadily harder for terrorists to acquire equipment and raw materials from outside sources. However, this argument is probably overstated. First, it neglects the long list of unscrupulous suppliers, both state and nonstate, that have consistently flouted international restrictions on "controlled" agents and equipment. Second, current regulations were designed during the Cold War to prevent state programs from producing very large (battlefield) quantities of agent. In many cases, the amounts of dual-use materials and equipment needed to trigger surveillance are much too high to block a terrorist manufacturing program.

On balance, "analysts are now almost unanimous in concluding that it is becoming increasingly easy for terrorist groups to develop NBC weapons, yet there is a dichotomy within the literature over exactly how easy it is." This uncertainty can be traced to ambiguities in scholars' basic assumptions that need to be examined more closely (Gurr and Cole 2002).

2.5.3   What Is the Rate of Change?

If terrorists' WMD capabilities are increasing, what is the rate of change? Except for Foxell (1999), who implies that terrorist capabilities are rapidly increasing, this question is hardly addressed in the open literature.

The past decade has seen an increasing capability among many terrorist groups. Certainly, the number of terrorists who are skilled in basic tradecraft and have received military-type training does not appear to be waning, and may have received a boost from the Iraq conflict. While progress has been made in reducing the number of terrorist havens and operational cells in the West, "lawless" regions are still abundant elsewhere. At the same time, counterterrorist operations in many countries are often beset by bureaucratic inertia and an accompanying lack of imagination, dynamism, and adaptability. Finally, many terrorist groups are increasingly sophisticated. This can be seen both in their demonstrated ability to run complex transnational networks and in their willingness to innovate. The use of airplanes on September 11, shoe bombs and liquid explosives in airline plots, and cell phones in the Madrid bombings all show a willingness to try new tactics and in some cases a modest R&D capability.

At the same time, general technological advances and the rapid commercialization and diffusion of technology mean that equipment and techniques that were once a state monopoly (e.g., the ability to synthesize complex chemicals) can now be purchased off the shelf (Stern 1999; Marlo 1999). In this sense, "the terrorist organization feeds from the society that spawns it" (Zanders 1999). To some extent, this is offset by corresponding improvements in defensive technologies, although offense seems dominant at present. In general, modern society appears to be evolving in directions that make it more vulnerable to WMD terrorism. These include the "increasing density of urban areas," the "multiplicity of vulnerable targets," and Western freedoms that allow terrorists to raise funds, train, educate themselves, and procure WMD-related technologies (Campbell 2000). Finally, the normal "background noise" of modern Western society with its multiple commercial, electronic, and remote social interactions, has made it easier for terrorists to conceal their activities (Falkenrath 1998b; Stern 1999).

2.6   Conclusion

The WMD terrorism literature has reached a kind of plateau in which the same speculative, unsubstantiated interpretations are constantly recycled. To some extent this reflects a merciful lack of evidence: to date there have been few cases of (mostly ineffective) CBR terrorism and no WMD terrorism.[53] Whatever the reason, the fact remains that scholars and policymakers have reached an interpretive impasse. Unlike government bureaucrats seeking appropriations, journalists seeking readers, and an anxious public seeking reassurance, most experts have concluded that WMD terrorism is not an imminent or catastrophic threat. Indeed, they often complain that unlikely "worst-case" scenarios have led to too much money being spent on consequence management and other poorly designed measures. Yet ironically, they too have focused primarily on these low-probability, high-consequence threats, if only to minimize them. In the process, they have largely lost sight of relatively crude, low-level CR threats that pose what might be better viewed as a "high-probability, low-consequence" threat (Tucker and Sands 1999; Lia 2004 (with respect to al-Qā'ida)).[54]

Following the late Ehud Sprinzak, it is important to distinguish between (1) mass casualty attacks using conventional weapons, (2) small-scale CBR attacks, and (3) "superterrorism"—that is, "the strategic use by non-state organizations of [CBRN] to bring about a major disaster, with death tolls ranging in the tens or hundreds of thousands" (Sprinzak 2000). For now, Sprinzak's second category probably remains the most imminent threat. Such small-scale attacks would most likely take the form of a crude toxic chemical attack or a radiological "dirty-bomb" attack by an operationally sophisticated Islamist group like the terrorist cells linked to al-Qā'ida or various veteran Egyptian and Algerian terrorist organizations. Indeed, recently interdicted Islamist "toxic terror" plots in Europe show that terrorists have already planned to carry out low-level chemical attacks.[55] A second, somewhat less likely scenario would involve crude chemical attacks or minor biological contamination incidents by small, relatively isolated autonomous cells or disgruntled "lone wolves" loosely associated with the right-wing American "militia" movement. In the future, this list could expand to include certain apocalyptic millenarian religious cults, the violent fringes of the antiabortion movement, or even the most extreme and violence-prone ecoradicals.

For now, these are the "most likely" looming threats. For the immediate future, genuine WMD terrorism is likely to remain hobbled by "poor delivery mechanisms" that leave agents "primarily usable only as contaminants" (Gurr and Cole 2002). In the long run, however, large-scale CBN attacks on an American city may be inevitable. Here again, an operationally sophisticated Islamist terrorist group would be the most likely perpetrator. Other possibilities include former state bioweapons experts acting out of spite or greed, and "rogue regimes" acting out of fanaticism, desperation, or the calculation that they could conceal their involvement.

Following Powers (2001), there are three basic strategies for blocking such attacks. First, *denial* measures can be used to "retard or prevent" terrorists from acquiring CBRN. However, these are never likely to be more than partially effective given the rapidly expanding pool of impoverished weapons scientists and scientifically trained terrorists; the explosion of CBRN information and civilian "dual-use" equipment; and ongoing covert state programs and the entrepreneurial networks they breed. This is particularly true given increasing terrorist interest in CBRN and the decidedly mixed record of past efforts to stop it. Second, *defensive* steps can be taken to persuade terrorists that a WMD attack could be substantially blunted. However, these steps are technologically difficult. Furthermore, public anxiety following past attacks and media attention to the West's inadequate emergency response measures can only encourage would-be CBRN terrorists. Finally, *punitive* measures can be used to deter extremists. Even suicidal terrorists can be deterred if they value some goal, person, or object (albeit not their lives). Also, a distinction should be drawn between the actual foot soldiers who carry out the attack, whom it is difficult to deter by threat of punishment, and those who supply logistical support (e.g., financiers, scientists), who may be much more susceptible to deterrence (Roberts 2008).

However, we cannot credibly promise to destroy diffuse, transnational terrorist networks (e.g., al-Qā'ida) in the wake of a WMD attack, no matter how much we might want to. Similarly, the FBI's prolonged and expensive efforts to trace the perpetrator of the 2001 *B. anthracis* letters could persuade even vulnerable enemies that a CBRN attack is both feasible and potentially concealable. Finally, organizations with millenarian religious agendas may actually welcome the prospect of "tribulations" and a catastrophic final battle between "Good" and "Evil." This suggests that the very nonstate groups and persons that are most willing and able to carry out a WMD attack on the United States could also be the hardest to stop (Pillar 2001).

Even so, we must try. Certainly, the behavior of religious fanatics and lone operatives is difficult to predict and "we can have no confidence that we will know anything in advance," at least in particular cases (Jenkins 2000). Nevertheless, there is some room for optimism. While "technical indicators" are by themselves unlikely to to identify clandestine programs, "monitoring the groups, and then interpreting their observed actions" is a more promising approach (Gurr and Cole 2002). As Sprinzak (2000) has argued, "the vast majority of terrorist organizations can be identified well in advance . . . and the number of potential [WMD] suspects is significantly less than doomsayers seem to believe. Ample early warning signs should make effective interdiction of potential superterrorists much easier than today's prevailing rhetoric suggests."

Notes

1. Jean Paul Zanders (1999) echoes this point but adds an important clarification: While the Aum incident was the first time that nonstate actors employed an actual chemical warfare (CW) agent, it was certainly not the first time they had made use of other types of potentially lethal toxic chemicals.

2. For mentions of these contrasting post-Aum attack views, see Cameron 2000, Hoffman 2000, Leitenberg 2004, and Roberts 1997. Although the authors of these publications adopt relatively skeptical and sober approaches, each alludes to other, often unnamed persons as exaggerators. For an example of highly alarmist views concerning the imminence of WMD terrorism, see several sensationalistic books by Paul L. Williams, including Williams 2005 and 2007.

3. It is not particularly useful to define a sharp threshold number at which "casualties" become "mass casualties." However, we will understand the term in a way that includes September 11–scale casualties.

4. The best collection and analysis of definitions of terrorism is found in Schmid and Jongman 1988. Bale 2004b defines terrorism as "the use or threatened use of violence, directed against victims selected for their symbolic or representative value, as a means of instilling anxiety in, transmitting one or more messages to, and thereby manipulating the attitudes and behavior of a wider target audience or audiences." Note that this definition can be legitimately applied to both state and nonstate terrorism. However, it is not applicable to conventional military confrontations between nation-states, despite the fact that good commanders often carry out attacks in order to weaken the enemy's morale, since terrorism should not be conflated with war itself. For this reason, the term is only applicable to asymmetric conflicts.

5. The most thorough discussion and analysis of the term *WMD* is found in Carus 2006. After surveying several definitional approaches, he indicates his own preference for those that identify WMD with nuclear, biological, and chemical (NBC) weapons, although he is also willing to accept the identification of WMD with CBRN. However, he firmly rejects the inclusion of conventional high-explosive weapons under the WMD rubric (Carus 2006).

6. Congress has defined WMD broadly for criminal justice purposes to encompass such non-CBRN technologies as explosives, incendiary charges, missiles, and mines (18 U.S.C. §2332a). However, this definition is largely limited to indictments and sentencing. General discourse has been inconsistent. For example, former FBI Director Louis Freeh has used the term *WMD* to include large amounts of conventional explosives on some occasions (Freeh 1999) but not others (Freeh 2001).

7. Chemical weapons, for instance, can dissipate quickly if they are improperly aerosolized or if the weather is unfavorable.

8. For example, one can easily imagine that the same amount of agent could kill twenty people in an enclosed area or cause serious but nonmortal injuries to thousands if released outdoors.

9. These psychological effects have often been overlooked or underemphasized, which may explain why there have been so few attempts to blunt their impact with education. Reducing the psychological impact of CBRN terrorism would make such attacks less attractive in the first place, but this potential deterrent effect is hardly ever mentioned.

10. One obvious example—by reducing our vulnerability to a certain agent, we make an attack using that agent less attractive to terrorists, thus altering the characteristics of the motivational branch.

11. Gressang (2001) has also emphasized the need to explicitly analyze CBRN terrorism as a strategy for exerting an impact on target audiences.

12. Frustrated individuals, subnational groups, and governments have all pursued covert CBW programs to assassinate enemies (Bale 2006; Gould and Foll 2002).

13. The most complete catalog of past CBRN terrorist threats, hoaxes, and attacks can be found in the Monterey Terrorism Research and Education Program's WMD Terrorism database at the Monterey Institute of International Studies. The portal for this database, which requires authorization for access, can be found at http://cns.miis.edu/wmdt.

14. For perhaps the most systematic single effort to address terrorist incentives and disincentives for using CBRN, see Gurr and Cole 2002.

15. One reason for the common terrorist preference for using military-grade conventional weapons in mass casualty attacks—in addition to their proven power and effectiveness—is that "most, if not all, terrorist operations require a level of simplicity and cleverness as far from the maximum threshold of complexity as possible in order to achieve the desired outcomes" (Palfy 2003).

16. Note, however, that researchers have shown that targeted populations will get used to anything if it becomes sufficiently common, and in that sense even the fears inspired by the release of unseen chemical, biological, or radiological agents would likely become progressively less acute if terrorists regularly resorted to the use of CBR materials. See chapter 16.

17. We have already noted that terrorists could also use CBR for reasons that have nothing to do with the ambitious mass casualty attacks considered in this chapter. As noted above, most prior uses of bona fide CBR materials have involved efforts to assassinate one or more individuals (Schmid 2001) or else "tactical or discrete attacks" to achieve limited, well-defined ends (Tucker 2000a). Indeed, the Rajneesh cult deliberately used CBR materials to incapacitate rather than to kill when they spread *Salmonella typhimurium* bacteria in an effort to prevent nonmembers from voting in an upcoming local election (Tucker and Sands 1999; Carus 2000a).

18. From the days of Karl Heinzen in the mid-nineteenth century, certain radicals and observers have distinguished between terrorism as a utilitarian and thus a relatively rational act on the one hand and terrorism as an expressive act and, above all, an act of personal redemption on the other (McCormick 2003). Although these two categories are not mutually exclusive, scholars have rightly emphasized terrorism's role in serving individual and group psychological functions. See, for example, Post 1987 and Reich 1998.

19. For a detailed study of one such personal motive, self-glorification, see Borowitz 2005.

20. One such case involving the Tamil Tigers can be found in Parachini 2003. Several other cases can be found in MonTREP's WMD Terrorism database.

21. Here we are using the term *far right* merely for the sake of convenience even though fascism (and, to a lesser extent, its atypical, race-obsessed Nazi variant) was actually an outgrowth of turn-of-the-century attempts by an odd assortment of disillusioned revolutionaries and radicals to conjoin particular European intellectual currents from both the right and the left, specifically radical nationalism and non-Marxist socialism, and thereby create a new type of revolutionary nationalist movement (Weber 1964; Sternhell 1976).

22. Even so, one of their immediate objectives was to provoke state repression so as to awaken the exploited masses to the supposedly "fascist" nature of "bourgeois" pseudodemocratic states. Gurr and Cole (2002) refer to this cynical strategy as "polarizing communities." Given that CBR attacks would have invited just such an overreaction and crackdown, the evidence for terrorist interest in such attacks is surprisingly thin. For the most part, it consists

of two allegations that the Rote Armee Fraktion (RAF: Red Army Faction) was interested in CB agents. According to one story, they supposedly threatened to use stolen canisters of mustard agent against German cities. In the other, botulinum toxin was reportedly found in a makeshift laboratory at an RAF safe house in Paris. However, neither story appears to be true. For details see, respectively, Claridge (2000) and Taylor and Trevan 2000.

23. The best illustration of this is provided by the terrorist "strategy of tension" in Italy, but similar tactics were also systematically employed by neofascist terrorists in Greece, the Iberian peninsula, and parts of Latin America. For an overview, see Bale 2001.

24. The only case that we know of, which does not appear in any of the available listings of WMD terrorism incidents, was that of Eliodoro Pomar, a nuclear engineer and activist in an Italian neofascist terrorist group, the Movimento Politico Ordine Nuovo (MPON: New Order Political Movement), who hatched a plot in the early 1970s to contaminate Roman reservoirs with radioactive materials (Flamini 1981–1985). There is also another interesting case from Chile in which Eugenio Berríos, a military officer working for the Chilean secret police, reportedly manufactured sarin at a DINA "safe house" frequented by Italian neofascist terrorist Stefano delle Chiaie (Blixen 1994).

25. It is also the case that up until the 1980s few terrorist groups seem to have had sufficient technical knowledge or the type of specialized equipment required to initiate a successful WMD attack even if they wanted to.

26. Many have pointed out that religious motivations had long served as the primary inspiration for terrorism, and in that sense their recent flowering in virulent new guises is only surprising insofar as they have partially displaced secular motivations that were once thought to have signaled the decline of religiosity (Rapoport 1984). Instead, many parts of the world have seen an unanticipated resurgence of religiosity since the mid-1970s (Kepel 1994).

27. The GSPC, along with jihadist groups in Morocco, Tunisia, and Libya, is now a key component of the new al-Qāʻida fī al-Maghrib al-Islāmī (al-Qāʻida in the Islamic Maghreb) umbrella organization.

28. A few specialists have openly challenged this consensus, in part because most CBRN terrorist plots have historically been hatched by non-religious groups and in part because they see secular and religious terrorists as equally rational actors (Rapoport 1999; Dolnik 2004). While these assumptions are a useful corrective to consensus thinking, they are debatable. To the extent that violent extremist groups are absolutely convinced that they are doing God's bidding, almost any action they decide to undertake can be justified (Bale 2004a; Selengut 2003; Hoffman 1993a).

29. Pilat (2001) has objected that the depiction of religious terrorists as "unconstrained mass killers" is a "caricature." He debates the issue with Falkenrath in Pilat (1998).

30. Gressang distinguishes between religious groups that are essentially calling for political and social change, despite their overheated theological rhetoric, and those that "call for destruction as a necessary precondition for achieving [their] objectives." For his part, Juergensmeyer (1996) distinguishes between "ethnic religious nationalism" that "*politicizes* religion by employing religious identities for political ends," and "ideological religious nationalism" that "*religionizes* politics [by putting] political issues and struggles within a sacred context."

31. Aum's doctrinal motivations are described in Reader 2000 and Watanabe 1998. For a revealing insider's account of the CSA, see Noble 1998. Not surprisingly, both groups

planned and/or attempted to employ CBRN weapons against their "evil" enemies (Kaplan 2000; Leitenberg 1999; Stern 2000). Yet Aum often also carried out CB attacks for surprisingly practical reasons—for example, to eliminate external critics or former members, test delivery methods, or divert the attention of the authorities once a police crackdown seemed imminent (Schmid 2001; Marlo 1999; Zanders 1999).

32. In this context, cult groups with worldviews inspired by science fiction motifs, including the Church of Scientology and the Raëlians, may warrant special attention, particularly if they promote genetic engineering or other advanced technologies.

33. Hizballāh did carry out several mass casualty terrorist attacks against Western embassies and military bases inside Lebanon in the 1980s that could have provoked harsh retaliation. However, these attacks were made when the group was still largely a client of the Sepāh-i Pasdārān (Guardians [of the Iranian Revolution] Corps). The more thoroughly that Hizballāh is integrated into mainstream Lebanese politics, the less likely it is to carry out such attacks in the future, either inside or outside of Lebanon.

34. *Time*, December 24, 1998, transcript of interview with Usāma b. Lādin. Recent examples of jihadist support for CBRN, most notably the May 2003 *fatwā* issued by Saudi shaykh Nāsir ibn Hāmid al-Fahd and Abū Mūs‘ab al-Sūrī's 2004 and 2005 strategic analyses, can be found in Paz 2005 and Lia 2007. A useful chart summarizing specific allegations concerning al-Qā‘ida's purported acquisition of various types of CBRN, most of which have not been substantiated, can be found in McCloud, Ackerman, and Bale 2003.

35. For an excellent analysis of al-Qā‘ida's attitudes and capabilities with respect to CBRN, see Salama and Hansell 2005 and Lia 2004. For its biological and chemical activities, see Leitenberg (2005) and CNN (2002), respectively.

36. For the Order of the Solar Temple, see Hall and Schuyler (2000), Mayer and Siegler (1999), and Bédat, Bouleau, and Nicolas (2000). For the Movement for the Restoration of the Ten Commandments, see Uganda Human Rights Commission (2002) and Atuhaire (2003).

37. See the April 15, 1999, memo from Ayman al-Zawāhirī to Muhammad Atif (Cullison 2004).

38. For example, as late as 1400 very few observers could have predicted the coming substitution of highly efficient missile weapons such as composite recurve bows, which had been used for centuries by some of the world's most formidable military forces, by clumsy, primitive, and seemingly ineffective hand-held firearms. As Verton (2003) has emphasized, "terrorism ... evolves at tectonic speeds over many decades, making the process of discerning subtle changes in tactics extremely difficult, even for the trained eye. But there is a danger to this. Like seismologists who fail to detect the movements of the earth's tectonic plates and the increasing pressure those movements cause, we can be caught by surprise by a massive, life-threatening earthquake when we fail to pick up on the subterranean changes in terrorism."

39. For example, the *Poisoner's Handbook* erroneously states that ricin toxin can be mixed with dimethylsulfoxide to make a topical poison that can be absorbed through victims' skin (Garrett 2001).

40. These factors did not, however, prevent Aum from acquiring useful amounts of sarin and other chemical weapons (Rosenau 2001).

41. Programs to destroy ex-Soviet stockpiles are far behind schedule.

42. Aum Shinrikyō only used a 20 percent pure sarin solution in the Tokyo subway attack. Furthermore, it chose a decidedly inefficient method—puncturing plastic bags—to disperse the agent. This explains why an attack using one of the most toxic substances known only produced twelve fatalities.

43. The authors admit that these aerosols would be relatively inefficient. Nevertheless, they would still be deadly.

44. Iraqi technicians working on chemical and biological weapons were apparently afforded little or no protection (OTA 1993b).

45. It is more difficult to process bulk agent into a powder than a liquid. However, powders are easier to disperse since they are less likely to clog nozzles and/or subject organisms to high shear forces during spraying.

46. However, some spore forming organisms like *B. anthracis* are very robust and can survive for decades.

47. In 1987, a team of nuclear weapons designers concluded that a terrorist group, after acquiring the necessary fissile material, could assemble a nuclear weapon if it had a team of three or four specialists in the metallurgical, physical, and chemical properties of the materials (Leventhal and Alexander 1987).

48. Alternative materials (^{240}Pu, moderately enriched uranium) can also be used but require significantly greater quantities (Gurr and Cole 2002).

49. On a cautionary note, Cordesman (2001) warns that very advanced, ultraefficient designs sometimes require roughly one-third as much material as these estimates suggest.

50. Graham Allison cites numerous attempts of terrorists breaking into nuclear storage sites and poor nuclear accounting systems in Russia. He also explains how easily a terrorist could smuggle sufficient nuclear material into the United States (Allison 2001).

51. In broad terms, a "gun-type" weapon involves firing one piece of subcritical uranium into another to form a critical mass. Implosion weapons use precisely detonated high explosives to compress a plutonium core. Implosion devices are significantly more difficult to achieve.

52. Strangely, the possibility of attacking biological facilities has not previously been noticed in the open literature.

53. The cases of the attack by Dahm Y'Israel Nokeam (DIN: Avenging Israel's Blood) on a German POW camp in 1946, Aum Shinrikyō's 1995 Tokyo subway sarin release, and the so-called anthrax-letter mailings of 2001 come closest to constituting bona fide WMD terrorist attacks, although thankfully none of these fulfill all the criteria for WMD terrorism. For more on the first case, see Sprinzak and Zertal 2000.

54. As Lia (2004) justly puts it, "If al-Qaida acquires and uses some sort of nonconventional weapons, it will most probably be *an improvisational crude devise* [sic], and it will have few similarities with militarily effective chemical, biological, or nuclear weapons."

55. For a summary of one such case purportedly involving the toxin ricin, see Bale et al. 2003. In this instance, however, the cell involved never seems to have produced any ricin. An effort to employ chemical agents by Abū Mūs'āb al-Zarqāwī's network in Amman was apparently forestalled by Jordanian security forces. See "Jordan Says Major al Qaeda Plot Disrupted," CNN, April 26, 2004. For a good overview of alleged Islamist chemical plots, see Pita 2005. For a skeptical look at the alleged biological plots, see Leitenberg 2005.

3

Technologies of Evil: Chemical, Biological, Radiological, and Nuclear Weapons

Stephen M. Maurer

For most people, the image of WMD is frozen in the 1980s when the United States and the Soviet Union faced each other with thousands of hydrogen bombs. In that familiar image, WMD is ubiquitous, reliable, and massive. Absent help from hostile governments,[1] terrorist WMD would be very different. Terrorist budgets, after all, seldom amount to more than a few tens of millions of dollars—even Al Qaeda's estimated budget of $30 million per year is decidedly modest (9/11 Commission 2004).[2] Such budgets are dwarfed by the billions that state programs spent to develop first-generation nuclear, chemical, and biological WMD between the 1930s and 1960s.

These resource constraints have important implications. First, genuine (i.e., mass casualty) WMD would challenge even the largest terrorist organizations. Lacking the resources to simply duplicate earlier state programs, terrorists will need short-cuts. These include cutting corners (e.g., reduced predictability or safety); finding declassified or leaked information from state programs; or using new technologies that did not exist forty years ago. Second, it is reasonable to think that terrorists will avoid technology gambles wherever possible (chapters 1 and 2). This suggests that they will usually try to duplicate nation-state capabilities instead of leapfrog-ging or extending them. Third, the extreme cost and difficulty of nuclear weapons may make other forms of WMD comparatively more appealing. In this respect the situation resembles the late 1940s, when many states saw chemical, biological, and radiological poisons as a "poor man's atomic bomb" (Smyth 1945; Blackett 1949).[3] Fourth, genuine WMD will—assuming terrorists can achieve it at all—generate far fewer casualties than those routinely expected from a full-scale superpower exchange at the height of the Cold War. In this respect, the situation resembles the early 1960s, when modest civil defense investments and education programs could dramatically reduce expected casualties.

This chapter asks how high the barriers to terrorist WMD are at the start of the twenty-first century. Section 3.1 starts from the observation that almost all WMD technologies except nuclear weapons are based on ultrastrong poisons. It then introduces the concept of a "lethal dose" and compares different technologies (chemical, radiological, biological) along this dimension. The next three sections build on this foundation by exploring the technological challenges that terrorists would have to overcome to obtain chemical (section 3.2), radiological (section 3.3), and biological weapons (section 3.4). These sections also describe related defense, countermeasure, and cleanup technologies. Section 3.5 describes the historically preferred scenario in which poisons are delivered to victims through open-air releases. Section 3.6 examines various alternative strategies. Section 3.7 provides a brief discussion of nuclear weapons. Finally, section 3.8 presents a brief conclusion.

3.1   A Poisons Viewpoint

Most WMD technologies are based on ultrastrong poisons.[4] Mathematically, they are characterized by "dose-response functions" that say how many exposed victims are likely to die from any given exposure. It is also common to see poisons characterized by a single number, the "lethal dose–50" or "LD_{50} dose," defined as the amount of poison needed to kill 50 percent of those exposed. This figure is normally quoted in units of m/M, where m is amount of poison delivered and M is the victim's mass. We will see below that reducing complex dose-response functions to a single LD_{50} value is an oversimplification. Nevertheless, LD_{50}s provide a handy shorthand for summarizing and comparing different forms of CBRN.

Instead of using LD_{50} directly, it is often useful to ask how much poison would have to be injected into the victim's environment to deliver a given dose. This "lethal concentration–50" or "LC_{50}" can be expressed in various ways, including (molecules of agent)/(molecules of air) for vapors and mg/m^3 for dusts and aerosols (Ellison 2000). However, I will quote concentrations in (mass of agent)/(mass of air) in what follows. The LC_{50} can be calculated from LD_{50} values if the victim's weight, breathing rate, and duration of exposure are known. This chapter will follow normal practice by assuming that the victim is a 70-kilogram man who inhales 150 liters of air over a ten-minute exposure.[5]

Poisons can have several different effects. These include (1) immediate deaths, (2) long-term deaths, chiefly from excess cancers, or (3) contamination that renders areas uninhabitable for long periods. Section 3.1.1 examines LC_{50} values for victims who would die in the first hours or days following an attack. Most casualties from a chemical, biological, or toxin attack would fall into this category. Section 3.1.2 examines LC_{50} values for victims who survive the initial attack only to fall ill years or decades later. Most casualties caused by so-called dirty bombs (more accurately, radiological dispersal devices or RDDs) fit this description. Finally, section 3.1.3

looks at the ability of different poisons to persist and render areas uninhabitable for substantial periods. This discussion is most relevant to RDDs.

3.1.1   Immediate ("Prompt") Injuries

Most WMD technologies inflict the great majority of casualties within the first few hours or days following an attack. Here I summarize and compare the lethality of various chemical, biological, and radiological agents. Because most WMD strategies are based on spreading poisons in the open air, my discussion focuses on inhalation.

Chemical Weapons   Table 3.1 provides LC_{50} values for a wide range of chemical weapons.

These include weapons based on normal industrial feedstocks like chlorine (LC_{50} value of 655 ppm) and phosgene (79 ppm) as well as specially designed nerve agents like sarin (1.2 ppm) and VX (0.3 ppm) that have no civilian uses. (Interested readers can find exhaustive listings of known chemical weapons in U.S. Army 1990, Ellison 2000, and Elsayed and Salem 2006.) The range of values is substantial, with advanced chemical weapons being almost 2,500 times deadlier than common industrial feedstocks.

Biological Weapons   Because pathogens reproduce inside their victims, initial exposures can be extraordinarily low. Box 3.1 estimates LD_{50} values for ten common weapons pathogens.[6]

These figures suggest that the LC_{50} for an ideal pathogen is roughly 10^{-14} or about 100 million times more efficient than the best nerve agents. While practical weapons are unlikely to be this effective, LC_{50}s on the order of one part per trillion (ppt) are probably feasible. This still represents a millionfold improvement over the best chemical weapons and explains why state programs have worked so hard to turn these otherwise delicate and difficult-to-manufacture organisms into weapons.

Finally, it is worth noting that LD_{50} values can be seriously misleading for very low or very high exposures. For example, the LD_{50} for inhaled anthrax is very high—depending on the strain, somewhere between 2,500 and 55,000 spores. On the other hand, primate studies suggest that its LD_{10} may be as little as 100 spores and that as few as 1–3 spores are enough to infect some victims (Inglesby et al. 2002). More generally, the dose-response relationship for most pathogens is nonlinear and displays a pronounced S-shape (Peters and Hartley 2002; Williams 1966).[7] Table 3.2 documents this effect for tularemia, a traditional weapons pathogen.

Toxins   Many plants, animals, bacteria, and fungi secrete nonliving protein molecules called toxins. While some of these molecules can be made in the laboratory,

Table 3.1
Some common chemical weapons

Agent	LC_{50}	LD_{50}	Evacuation radius (initial/day/night)	State	Odor	Action
Chemical—blister						
Lewisite	17 ppm	2.1 gm/person	400 feet/0.5 miles/ 2.1 miles	Liquid	No odor when pure; geranium-like otherwise	Rapid
Mustard	23 ppm	7 gm/person	400 feet/0.5 miles/ 2.1 miles	Liquid	Garlic or horseradish	Delayed
Chlorine	655 ppm		200 feet/0.2 miles/ 0.5 miles	Gas	Bleach	Rapid
Chemical—choking						
Phosgene	79 ppm		400 feet/0.4 miles/ 1.7 miles	Gas	New-mown hay	Immediate
Chemical—nerve						
Sarin	1.2 ppm	1.7 gm/person	700 feet/1.2 miles/ 5.5 miles	Liquid	Odorless	30 seconds to 2 minutes
Soman	0.9 ppm	.35 gm/person	700 feet/1.2 miles/ 5.5 miles	Liquid	Fruity odor; impurities give odor of oil or camphor	30 seconds to 2 minutes
Tabun	2.0 ppm	1 gm/person	700 feet/1.2 miles/ 5.5 miles	Liquid	No odor; impurities give fruity or bitter-almond odor	30 seconds to 2 minutes
VX	0.3 ppm	.01 gm/person	700 feet/1.2 miles/ 5.5 miles	Liquid	No odor	30 seconds to 2 minutes

Toxin					
Botulinum	.001 ppb	N/A	Liquid or powder	No odor	12 hours–5 days (ingested); 3–6 hours (inhaled)
Ricin	2.8–3.3 ppb	N/A	Liquid or powder	No odor	18–24 hours
Staphylococcal enterotoxin B	0.02 ppb	N/A	Liquid or powder	No odor	Hours

Sources: Ellison 2000; Paddle 2006; Elsayed and Salem 2006; USAMRIID 2004

Box 3.1
An LD_{50} for pathogens?

In contrast to the situation with chemical, nuclear, radiological, and toxin weapons, the literature seldom quotes LD_{50} and LC_{50} values for pathogens. This makes it difficult to compare the lethality of biological agents against other forms of WMD. Fortunately, translating information about pathogens into a rough LD_{50} estimate is straightforward. For the noncontagious pathogens considered in this chapter, the question is equivalent to the number of organisms that must be inhaled to cause infection and death. Representative figures for both lethal and nonlethal (incapacitating) diseases can be found in USAMRIID (2004):

Agent	Number of organisms needed to establish infection	Chance that infection will lead to death
Anthrax	8,000 to 50,000 spores	High
Brucellosis	10–100 organisms	Less than 5% (untreated)
Plague	100–500 organisms	High unless treated in first 12–24 hours
Q fever	1–10 Organisms	Very low
Smallpox	1–10 Organisms	Moderate to high
Tularemia	1–50 organisms	Moderate lethality (untreated)
Venezuelan equine encephalitis	10–100 organisms	Low
Viral hemorrhagic fevers	1–10 organisms	Moderate to high

Most bacteria range vary in size from 1 to 10 μm (10^{-6} meters) in length, with anthrax (1.3 μm) and tularemia (1–2 μm) being fairly typical.* This implies that the volume of an average pathogen is roughly 10^{-18} cubic meters. Using the standard assumption that the target population is exposed to agent long enough to inhale 150 liters of air and that organisms are 1,000 times denser than air, we calculate that an idealized weapon capable of killing victims who inhaled just one pathogen would have an LC_{50} of about 7×10^{-15}. This figure is 100 million times smaller than the best nerve agents. Alibek claims that the Soviet Union was able to develop hemorrhagic fever weapon ("Variant U") that approached this single-organism ideal and Danzig suggests that smallpox virus may have a similar lethality (Alibek and Handelman 1999; Danzig 2003). However, our table suggests that most pathogens are 10^2–10^3 less efficient than this. Furthermore, real-world weapons also include significant amounts of additives, waste, and (for wet agents) water. Even so, the LC_{50} for bioweapons is probably 100,000 to one million times smaller than typical nerve agent values.

*Note: In theory, even higher LD_{50}'s can be achieved using viruses that measure as little as 10^{-8} meters in size. For most species, this advantage is offset by the fact that a large fraction of all viruses are defective and cannot propagate.

Table 3.2
Tularemia in monkeys

No. of organisms	Incubation (days)	Illness				
		None	Mild	Moderate	Severe	Fatal
10	4–10	30	40	30	0	0
100	4–7	0	50	50	5	0
1,000	2–8	0	57	57	0	3
10,000	2–7	0	3	3	13	7
100,000	3–4	0	0	0	12	8
1,000,000	2–5	0	0	0	27	18

Source: Adamovicz, Wargo, and Waag 2006

most can only be synthesized by living organisms. The vast majority of these toxins have high LC_{50} values that make them unsuitable as weapons (Dando 2001). However, a few toxins are significantly more lethal than any known chemical or pathogen weapon. Of these, the toxins secreted by *Clostridium botulinum* are by far the most lethal. At least seven distinct botulinum toxins exist in nature. The most lethal have LC_{50} values of one part per trillion (Greenbaum and Anderson 2006a; Arnon et al. 2001). Table 3.1 provides LD_{50} and LC_{50} values for several important toxins.

Advanced Bioweapons   Advances in biology and health care could potentially lead to even more effective poisons. One frequently discussed possibility would be to create weapons that insert malicious DNA into cells (USAMRIID 2004). Alternatively, weapons makers could take advantage of small molecules called bioregulators/modulators (BRMs) that act as neurotransmitters or modify neural responses.[8] Pharmaceutical companies already make small quantities of BRMs to treat arthritis and suppress cancer growth. Weapons makers who mastered bulk production could conceivably use BRMs to promote disease instead of suppressing it (USAMRIID 2004; Dando 2001; U.S. Army 1995; for further details, see Nixdorff et al. 2004).

Radiological   Radiation exposures for different isotopes depend on a variety of factors including rate of decay ("half-life"), energy released, and type of particle(s) emitted. The amount of radiation delivered is described by various related units including curies, rads, rems, sieverts, and grays. (See box 3.2 for complete definitions.)

Radiation comes in three basic forms: gamma, beta, and alpha particles. *Gamma rays* are a form of high energy X-radiation and carry no charge. Like X-rays, they

3.1.2 Long-Term Injuries

Many forms of WMD continue to cause injury long after the attack. Long-term injuries are expected to dominate RDD casualties but are typically much less important for other types of WMD.

Radiological Weapons   The general U.S. population already faces a 23 percent lifetime risk of contracting a fatal cancer. Each milligray of *gamma radiation* is believed to increase this risk by 0.008 percent. This implies that a 100 mGy exposure should generate about 40 excess fatal cancers for every 5,000 individuals exposed (AFRRI 2003). The cancers would start approximately ten years after exposure and continue appearing at a steady rate thereafter. Victims would also suffer an approximately equal number of survivable cancers.[12]

As previously noted, *alpha* and *beta emitters* are seldom dangerous unless inhaled or ingested. When this happens, lethality usually depends on how long they remain in the body before being excreted. Oxides of strontium and barium are particularly dangerous because they enter the blood rapidly and are absorbed in bone tissue. Radioactive iodine is similarly concentrated in the thyroid gland (Glasstone and Dolan 1977). Table 3.4 summarizes this information and lists some of the medical interventions that can be used to purge the body of various isotopes. It also lists the increased lifetime risk of fatal cancers from inhaled isotopes if patients are left untreated.

The implied LD_{50}s range from a few tenths of a microgram (^{252}Cf) up to roughly one-half gram for ^{137}Cs.

Chemical Weapons   Unlike RDDs, most chemical weapons casualties are prompt. Nevertheless, many traditional weapons (e.g., mustard and phosgene) commonly produce lifelong injuries, including skin burns, conjunctivitis, laryngitis, and chronic bronchitis (Harris and Paxman 2002). Blister gases (e.g., mustard, lewisite) and some nerve agents are also known to be carcinogenic (Ellison 2000).

Biological Weapons   In general, most weapons diseases have short incubation times and do not permanently injure survivors. However, a few agents—notably melioidosis ("the Vietnamese time bomb")—can be dormant for years after an exposure before causing illness (USAMRIID 2004). Other diseases leave survivors permanently disabled. For example, smallpox causes permanent scars and, in some cases, blindness (Alibek and Handelman 1999).

Toxins   Even when they are not fatal, toxins can cause permanent injury. In the case of botulinum toxin, this can include paralysis (Arnon et al. 2001).

3.1.3 Contamination

Survivors in a contaminated environment would face a trade-off between accepting increased cancer risk, abandoning the site, or cleaning it up. As we will see, the total excess cancers inflicted on individuals living in a contaminated environment would be relatively small for most reasonable scenarios. On the other hand, casualties would still be substantial compared to, say, the one-in-a-million (0.000001) risks that EPA regulates or the 0.0004 excess deaths per year at issue in some "cancer cluster" lawsuits (CBS News, 2002). To some people, this suggests that cleanup should proceed to levels mandated for everyday industrial exposures. Such arguments overlook the fact that civilian cleanup standards encode cost-benefit trade-offs for industries where prevention is both feasible and relatively inexpensive. For terrorism, on the other hand, prevention and/or cleanup will often be costly. In this case, a consistent cost-benefit analysis would normally imply looser cleanup standards than for comparable environmental or occupational exposures.

Chemical Weapons A few chemical weapons, notably mustard, can linger in soil where they remain hazardous for years. Other agents—notably choking agents (phosgene, chlorine)—are not persistent except, in some cases, for their less dangerous decomposition products (Ellison 2000). Finally, nerve agents present an intermediate case. They can linger for weeks or months in soil, porous materials, vegetation, and inside buildings or low spots that are sheltered against the wind. Contamination also depends on weather. For example, heavy rains can create lingering hazards by concentrating agent in low areas and streambeds (U.S. Army 1990).

Almost all agents can be decontaminated with bleach or sodium hydroxide.[13] Nonpersistent agents can also be dissipated by using ventilation and large quantities of water. Porous and painted materials present a special problem because they absorb agent. These may require physical stripping and removal. Military units are trained to perform decontamination within roughly twenty-four hours.[14]

Radiological Weapons Most radiological debris from an RDD would consist of loose, superficial materials. However, some contaminants, including ^{137}Cs, ^{90}Sr, and ^{60}Co, would form oxides that bind to metals. Still other radionuclides could soak several centimeters into porous materials like concrete, brick, and marble (Yassif 2004; Weiss 2005).

Loose contaminants can be vacuumed, scrubbed, and removed (AFRRI 2003). Large areas could also be deluged in water, although this would leave dilute (and possibly unacceptable) radioactivity in local lakes and streams. More advanced technologies are also available. For example, workers could use fire hoses to spray a

Table 3.4
Radionuclides: Inhalation, ingestion, and treatment

Element	Respiratory: absorption vs. deposition	Ingestion: absorption vs. excretion	Skin-wound absorption	Primary toxicity	Treatment
^{241}Am	75% absorbed, 10% retained	Usually insoluble, minimal absorption	Rapid in first few days	Skeletal deposition, marrow suppression, hepatic deposition	Chelation with DTPA or EDTA
^{137}Ce, ^{134}Ce	Complete absorption	Complete absorption	Complete absorption	Renal excretion, beta and gamma emissions	Ion exchange resins, Prussian blue
^{60}Co	High absorption, limited retention	<5% absorption	Unknown	Gamma emitter	Gastric lavage, penicillamine in severe cases
^{131}I	High absorption, limited retention	High absorption, limited retention	High absorption, limited retention	Thyroid ablation/ carcinoma	Iodine therapy
^{32}P	High absorption, limited retention	High absorption, limited retention	High absorption, limited retention	Bone, rapidly replicating cells	Lavage, aluminum hydroxide, phosphates
^{238}Pu, ^{239}Pu (metals and salts)	High absorption, limited retention	Usually insoluble, minimal absorption	Limited absorption, may form nodules	Lung, bone, liver	Chelation with DTPA or EDTA
^{238}Pu, ^{239}Pu (oxides)	Limited absorption, high retention	High absorption, limited retention	Limited absorption, may form nodules	Local effects from retention in the lung	Chelation with DTPA or EDTA
^{210}Po	Moderate absorption, moderate retention	Usually insoluble, minimal absorption	Moderate absorption	Local effects from retention in the lung	Chelation with DTPA or EDTA, pulmonary lavage

^{226}Ra	Unknown	30% absorption but 95% fecal excretion	Unknown	Skeletal deposition, marrow suppression, sarcoma	MgSO$_4$ lavage, ammonium chloride, calcium alginates
^{90}Sr	Limited retention	Moderate absorption	Unknown	Bone—follows calcium	Strontium, calcium, ammonium chloride
Tritium (^{3}H)	Minimal	Minimal	—	Panmyelocytopenia	Dilutions with controlled water intake; diuresis
Tritiated water	Complete	Complete	Complete	Panmyelocytopenia	Dilutions with controlled water intake; diuresis
^{238}U, ^{235}U: Fluorides, UO$_3$, sulfates, carbonates	High absorption, high retention	High absorption	High absorption, skin irritant	Renal, urinary excretion	Chelation with DTPA or EDTA NaHCO$_3$
^{238}U, ^{235}U: Some oxides, nitrates	Moderate absorption, high retention	Moderate absorption	Unknown	Nephrotoxic, urinary excretion	Chelation with DTPA or EDTA NaHCO$_3$
^{238}U, ^{235}U: High oxides, hydrides, carbides, salvage ash	Minimal absorption, retention based on particle size	Minimal absorption, high excretion	Unknown	Nephrotoxic Urinary excretion	Chelation with DTPA or EDTA NaHCO$_3$
Depleted uranium metal	Retention based on particle size	Minimal aborption, high excretion	Forms pseudocysts with urinary excretion, limited absorption	Nephrotoxic; deposits in bone, kidney, brain	Particulate removal when possible

Source: Armed Forces Radiobiology Research Institute 2003

sticky blue film to trap particles on surfaces so that they do not spread. After the film hardened, workers would strip it off together with the embedded radionuclides (Weiss 2005; Yassif 2004). Similarly, oxides could be removed using the same hypochlorite solutions previously developed to neutralize chemical weapons residue (AFRRI 2003). As always, porous materials would present some of the biggest challenges. Here cleanup could include removing the top five to seven centimeters of topsoil, chipping away the top millimeter of asphalt and concrete surfaces, or completely removing sidewalks and streets. For high-value historic structures, workers could also soak granite and concrete with large organic molecules called chelants that selectively bind to particular contaminants. Workers would then apply water-absorbing gels to draw the fused chelant/radioisotope molecules out of the granite. Other advanced technologies currently under development include light ablation, concrete-eating bacteria, and cryogenic blasting (Weiss 2005; Yassif 2004).

Cleanup costs depend sensitively on goals. An extreme example involves civilian nuclear power plant regulations that limit exposure for workers to five rem per year and members of the general public to 0.1 rem per year. Meeting this standard for an RDD cleanup would require extensive decontamination, including long-term evacuation, intensive washing and sandblasting, and removal of topsoil and vegetation. The total cost would reportedly be "billions of dollars" (Helfand et al. 2006; HSC 2005).

Pathogens and Toxins   Compared to other forms of WMD, pathogens pose little long-term contamination risk. There are two basic reasons for this. First, intact skin is an effective barrier against most pathogens. As a result, pathogens that settle onto surfaces pose little danger unless and until they are reaerosolized. This risk is minimal for the general public (Ellison 2000). Indeed, none of the seventy-plus victims killed by an accidental Soviet release of weapons-grade anthrax in 1979 seems to have died in this way (Ingelesby et al. 1999). Reaerosolization may, however, pose significant risks for special groups (first responders, medical personnel, laboratory workers) and activities (surgery, embalming, autopsy, centrifugation).[15]

The second reason bioweapons pose little contamination threat is that almost all pathogens (except anthrax) are fragile. As explained in section 3.1.3, most pathogens cannot survive for more than a few days in the presence of sunlight, ozone, or fluctuating temperatures (Ellison 2000).[16] While a few organisms can survive for long periods in soil, they also pose little risk unless and until they are reaerosolized. Of these, anthrax is by far the most durable and has been known to survive in soil for thirty-five years or more. However, military studies suggest decontamination is unnecessary until spores reach a density of 20 million spores per meter (Inglesby et al. 2002).[17] While plague can also survive in soil for long periods, there is no evidence that it poses a risk to humans and decontamination is not recommended (Inglesby et al. 2000).

Other weapons pathogens can survive by entering various human and animal populations. Human-to-human transmission poses a moderate risk for hemorrhagic fever and plague but is negligible for most other weapons candidates.[18] Pathogens with animal or insect hosts include plague, tularemia, typhus, Venezuelan equine encephalitis, and Western equine encephalitis. However, anthrax, brucellosis, and Q fever lack such vectors (Ellison 2001).

When required, decontamination with bleach, soap, water, and/or disinfectant gases (e.g., formaldehyde) is invariably sufficient. Indeed, 0.1 percent bleach is sufficient against all known weapons agents, including anthrax spores (USAMRIID 2004).[19] Even so, decontamination of large areas would be a major undertaking. During the 1980s, British efforts to eliminate anthrax from a World War II test site took several years and consumed 280 tons of formaldehyde (Harris and Paxman 2002). More recent U.S. efforts to decontaminate the relatively small Hart office building cost $23 million. For some pathogens, animal eradication programs would also be necessary.

3.2   Chemical Weapons

Acquiring chemical weapons would require a large investment of both capital and human resources. Consider, for example, the earliest German attacks in World War I, which took place at Ypres across a four-mile front. While operations on this scale clearly qualify as "WMD," they demanded 160 *tons* of chlorine gas or roughly 1.5 metric tons (1,500 kg) per square kilometer.[20] Manufacturing this much gas consumed a large fraction of Germany's total industrial output and—at first— exceeded Britain's capacity altogether (Harris and Paxman 2002). Since World War I, states have reduced these manufacturing challenges by inventing more efficient poisons. For instance, we have already noted that sarin is 2,500 times more lethal than chlorine. This naively implies[21] that terrorists could achieve Ypres-like results using just six kilograms per square kilometer, although this figure is almost certainly optimistic to the extent that it neglects victims' ability to shelter indoors (section 3.5). Of all subnational groups, Japan's Aum Shinrikyo cult came closest to acquiring a chemical WMD capacity. During the 1990s it used lab-scale methods to make modest (tens of kilograms) batches of sarin, VX, phosgene, and sodium cyanide. These were used for several assassinations and, most famously, the March 2005 Tokyo subway attack. The group also tried to build a facility that would have produced seventy tons of sarin in forty days. Although the project ultimately failed, Aum's experience does show that large, well-funded groups can plausibly overcome the capital and human-resource barriers to pilot-scale production. I discuss these barriers in more detail below.

3.2.1 Finding Suitable Compounds

The challenges of manufacturing and delivering large quantities of gas can be side-stepped by finding better poisons. However, this requires very substantial R&D expenditures. Only a small fraction of the 10^{40} "small molecules" that can theoretically be synthesized actually possess exceptional properties as poisons. While enlightened guesswork plays some role in finding these compounds, trial and error is indispensable. The current list of chemical agents reflects commercial- and state-sponsored testing of tens of thousands of compounds on animals (Tucker 2006; Harris and Paxman 2002).[22] As shown in table 3.1, this half-century-long research effort improved toxicity by a factor of 2,500. Agents were also improved along other dimensions, including ease of volatilization and amenability to industrial-scale production methods (Tucker 2006).

Terrorist R&D programs are unlikely to improve on these searches except to the extent that earlier state programs were hampered by requirements that terrorists can dispense with. At least two such criteria exist:

Flexibility   Military programs need weapons that can be reliably used under many different conditions, including low temperatures, high humidity, precipitation, and low wind (Tucker 2006; Roy and Pitt 2006). In principle, terrorists could forgo these benefits by waiting for the right conditions to arise. However, Al Qaeda's decision to mount attacks coinciding with U.S. millennium celebrations (9/11 Commission 2004) show that terrorists can and do place substantial value on the ability to meet specific deadlines. More importantly, many past terrorists attacks have been hurriedly mounted on an emergency basis in response to outside events.[23] Finally, waiting for ideal conditions poses its own security risks. Aum terrorists delayed a 1994 attack because they believed cold weather and rain would make their sarin less effective. This left their highly unusual, truck-mounted sprayer exposed to detection for several days (Tucker 2004).

Safety and countermeasures   Conventional militaries normally insist on using poisons that have known medical treatments. Here, the obvious argument is that terrorist fanatics may be more willing to tolerate casualties than workers in traditional chemical plants. However, it is not obvious that today's suicide bombers would similarly volunteer for a painful and squalid industrial death. More importantly, the long history of terrorist bomb-factory explosions since the 1870s suggests that accidents pose a major security weakness (Maurer 2005b). For example, bomb and gunshot accidents claimed an estimated 47 percent of all Provisional IRA members killed in Northern Ireland between 1970 and 1998 (Fay, Morrisey, and Smyth 1988), while a bomb-factory accident led to the unraveling of a major Al Qaeda plot to destroy multiple airliners over the Pacific in 1995 (9/11 Commission 2004). Aum Shinrikyo similarly abandoned its nerve gas manufacturing program after a series of accidental releases drew police attention in 1994 (Falkenrath, Newman, and Thayer 1998).

While military requirements are more stringent, then, it is hard to believe that state programs would have been orders of magnitude cheaper without them. This suggests that it is much more realistic for terrorist R&D programs to focus on replicating existing agents than to search for new and potentially better ones. Some design flexibility may, however, be possible along other dimensions. For example, terrorists could enhance a given agent's contamination potential by using thickening agents to create a honeylike consistency. Conversely, adding solvents would dramatically increase the rate at which an agent volatilized and/or penetrated skin (Ellison 2000; U.S. Army 1990).

Finally, we note in section 3.2.3 that existing agents are difficult to manufacture in bulk. Chemical weapons and precursors are also hard to purchase on the open market. Indeed, Aum Shinrikyo's decision to make sarin rather than some other agent was mainly based on a judgment that the barriers erected by U.S. "dual-use" export regulations were lowest for this agent (Sopko and Edelman 1995).[24] Terrorists could also decide to acquire ready-made but less effective off-the-shelf industrial compounds that are either known to be toxic (e.g., ammonia) or have actually served as war agents in the past (e.g., phosgene, chlorine). Aum reportedly explored this option by experimenting with sodium cyanide (widely used in gold-mining operations) in the 1990s (Sopko and Edelman 1995). (Exhaustive lists of dual-use chemicals can be found in Centers for Disease Control n.d.(b) and Ellison 2000.)

3.2.2 Designing a Delivery System

Proving that a chemical is toxic is not the same as building a delivery system and demonstrating that it will work. German experience in the 1930s shows that even well-designed chemical bombs typically destroy about one-quarter of their payload in the heat of explosion and/or drive it harmlessly into the ground. This suggests that untested devices could be extremely inefficient. Terrorists are unlikely to match the elaborate indoor test facilities that the German program used to overcome these problems (Tucker 2006).[25]

In principle, spraying is more predictable than explosions and would therefore require less testing.[26] However, simple commercial generators cannot aerosolize many war gases, including nerve agents. When aerosolization does occur, moreover, they produce relatively large droplets. The human body tends to block most of these before they can reach the lower lungs, where chemical weapons are most lethal. Homemade generators, on the other hand, are nontrivial to design and require testing. During the 1990s, Aum Shinrikyo developed a 1,000-pound, truck-mounted sprayer that used an electrically heated plate to produce nine liters per hour of sarin vapor, which was then dispersed through a fan. Although partially successful, the device malfunctioned the first time it was used and nearly killed its operator (Tucker 2006).[27]

Aum's experience suggests that terrorists may often feel a strong need to conduct tests. Indeed, Aum itself is known to have carried out tests on at least twenty-nine sheep at a remote Australian ranch. In principle, terrorists could also test their weapons by conducting small-scale attacks on the public. This, however, creates an obvious risk of detection. At least one observer correctly predicted that Aum's June 1994 attack was a "dry run" for the Tokyo subway system (Sopko and Edelman 1995).

Finally, we have already seen that chemical weapons to require attackers to transport and release very large quantities of agent. Aum Shinrikyo, for example, aimed to acquire seventy tons of sarin (Sopko and Edelman 1995). The world's most powerful helicopter can only lift about half this figure.

3.2.3   Manufacturing, Storage, and Safety

During the First World War, the resources required to produce poison gas consumed (and in Britain's case exceeded) a large fraction of the combatants' prewar industrial capacity (Tucker 2006; Harris and Paxman 2002). While these requirements are eased for individual terrorist attacks, the required production scale remains daunting. Evidence from Aum Shinrikyo corroborates this estimate. After making three laboratory-scale batches of sarin and four batches of VX, the group attempted to scale up sarin production by building a $10 million pilot-scale plant that would have produced seventy tons of sarin within forty days. However, even this figure was deemed inadequate for citywide attacks, forcing the group to focus on point targets like the Japanese parliament. The facility broke down after producing just thirty kilograms of nerve agent (Tucker 2006; Sopko and Edelman 1995).

Scaling Up   We have seen that a true chemical WMD capability demands bulk manufacturing. Industrial engineers normally distinguish between lab, pilot, and full-scale production. Laboratory methods—for example, using shaken flasks and other manual techniques—are usually sufficient to produce commercial chemicals in gram to kilogram quantities. During the 1930s, German scientists eventually adapted these methods to make up to thirty kilograms of Tabun at a time (Tucker

2006). Such quantities are already useful for operations. Aum reportedly used lab-scale methods to make the sarin used in the Tokyo subway attacks (Sopko and Edelman 1995).

Since simple nerve agents usually take several months to decay, repeated use of lab-scale methods could *theoretically* support attacks of up to several hundred kilo-grams. In practice, this number is probably illusory since each batch carries a high accident risk. Aum, for example, managed to make just three lab-scale batches of sarin and four batches of VX (Sopko and Edelman 1995). This suggests that lab-scale methods are inadequate for attacks that require more than a few tens of kilograms.

Proceeding beyond this scale requires pilot scale production. Here, batch sizes typically range from 100 to 1,000 kilograms. Aum's pilot-scale sarin plant (Tucker 2006) was in this range. The three-story facility employed about 100 members working in round-the-clock shifts. The heart of the operation consisted of five computer-controlled reactor vessels. These occupied an entire floor and were ordered through front companies (Tucker 2006). Aum also obtained sophisticated molecular simulation software to investigate possible chemical synthesis routes (Sopko and Edelman 1995).

The Aum plant reportedly cost $10 million (Tucker 2006). More generally, chemical engineers normally expect production costs to scale according to the following rule of thumb:

$$\frac{\text{Cost of pilot batch}}{\text{Cost of lab batch}} = \left(\frac{\text{Pilot process yield}}{\text{Lab process yield}}\right) \times \left(\frac{\text{Pilot quantity}}{\text{Lab quantity}}\right)^{n} \tag{3.1}$$

where n ranges between 0.3 and 1.2 for most components. For back-of-the-envelope calculations, it is conventional to set $n = 0.6$ (Grigsby 1997).

Finally, these calculations ignore technical risk. Bulk nerve agent production is difficult. Indeed, even the U.S. military proved unable to build a successful pilot-scale sarin plant in the 1950s. In the end, success only came after it recruited seven engineers who had worked on Hitler's program. Aum similarly encountered re-peated problems in its production line. Like the Americans, it tried to recruit experi-enced engineers (this time Russian) to fix the problem. Unlike the Americans, Aum was rebuffed and soon abandoned its chemical weapons program entirely (Tucker 2006).

New Technologies   The foregoing discussion is based on traditional chemical engi-neering practices. In principle, new nanotechnology methods could reduce the bar-riers to scaling up production. Scientists have long known that chemical reactions often proceed faster inside microscopic (10–300 μm) cavities. Since the late 1990s, engineers have begun exploiting this principle to design "microreactors" for making various chemicals, including weapons-related compounds like hydrogen cyanide, phosgene, and methyl isocyanate (Nguyen 2005). Commercial minireactor sales were €36 million in 2002 and are growing steadily (DeChema 2003).

The chief advantage of nanotechnology for terrorists is that it avoids the need to scale up production. Because nanofabrication depends on inherently microscopic vessels, it is normally cheaper to "number up" by building multiple copies of small-scale units than to "scale up" to larger machinery. Individual reactors currently operate at up to ten kilograms per hour or about six metric tons per month (DeChema 2003). Microreactor methods could potentially offer additional benefits, including less chance of accidents and reduced quantities of telltale raw material purchases and/or waste emissions. However, it is still not clear whether terrorists would have the technical expertise to customize reactors to make war gases that have no commercial market (Nguyen 2005).

Safety   We have already noted that manufacturing accidents pose a threat to terrorist morale and security. Because war gases are highly corrosive, leaks and accidents are common. The German program made extensive use of overpressured rooms, respirators, double-layered rubber suits, double-walled pipes, and the like. Despite this, the material's extreme toxicity meant that even minuscule leaks could and did cause illness. As a result, most workers suffered from constant, low-level poisoning and were periodically given days off to recover. Leaks within Aum Shinrikyo's plant similarly caused nosebleeds, eye irritation, muscle spasms, dim vision, and severe fatigue. While no terrorists died, at least two accidental spills escaped the plant. Neighboring residents also told police that their cows had stopped giving milk and that leaves on nearby trees had withered and died. In the end, Aum escaped detection mainly because the Japanese government was reluctant to investigate a religious organization. Such hesitancy is far less likely in the post-Aum, post-September 11 world (Tucker 2006; Sopko and Edelman 1995).

Larger accidents would be even harder to hide. World War II German weapons plants suffered fatalities at a rate of 1 percent per worker per year; nonfatal accident rates were at least ten times higher (Tucker 2006; Harris and Paxman 2002). Terrorists working in cramped surroundings with unfamiliar materials are not likely to match this safety record. Given that the symptoms of pesticide poisoning are familiar, a major accident stands an excellent chance of being detected and recognized for what it is.

Shelf Life   Because most war gases have short shelf lives, terrorists cannot simply stockpile output from a small plant to support arbitrarily large attacks. For example, sarin reportedly degrades within weeks to months (Central Intelligence Agency 1996). Tabun is only slightly more robust, losing about 5 percent of its toxicity after six months and 20 percent after three years. Although shelf life increases with purity, safety concerns make purification difficult. German experience in the 1930s shows that even large, well-funded chemical plants have difficulty pushing purity above 90 percent or so (Tucker 2006). Alternative solutions include adding stabilizer chemicals[28] or creating binary weapons that produce the weapon from more stable precursors at the time of impact. However, such measures introduce their own technological challenges. Extensive effort by Iraqi scientists in the 1990s may have extended shelf lives up to several years (Central Intelligence Agency 1996). Terrorists are unlikely to do better.

3.2.4 Countermeasures

War gases are notoriously ineffective against prepared troops. Indeed, even simple measures like masks, bleach, and soap and water can cut casualties dramatically. For countermeasures to work, however, detection must come early enough to make a difference. The simplest method is an alert population. For example, police and citizens could readily be trained to recognize the sinister quality of, say, a truck-mounted sprayer or an airplane flying below 100 meters over densely populated areas. Many war gases—including mustard, phosgene, and *impure* tabun—also have detectable odors. However, such clues are largely irrelevant in a modern setting unless target populations have been educated on what to watch for.

Absent an alert population, the obvious technological solution is to deploy cheap, ubiquitous sensors. This goal is still some way off. For now, the best sensors are military. These provide almost real-time protection (45–120 seconds)[29] but require manual operation and have large numbers of false positives from hot weather, petroleum products, pesticides, burning brush, and other sources (Ellison 2000). Civilian applications will need much more automated and reliable devices. Furthermore, military detection sensitivities are often not much smaller than LD_{50} levels. Such detectors are only effective if they can be placed upwind of the protected group—a condition that is seldom achievable in civilian life (chapter 5).

For the immediate future, the most effective way to detect an attack is to monitor symptoms in the target population. Because some individuals are unusually sensitive, detecting early cases often provides time for intervening in the great majority of cases. Detection of nerve agents is particularly straightforward. Individuals exposed to high doses display prompt, dramatic effects, while lower exposures produce the familiar (and readily diagnosable) symptoms of pesticide poisoning. In a 1994 Aum attack, doctors immediately administered blood tests that correctly diagnosed organophosphate poisoning (Tucker 2006). Clinicians in the post-Aum, post–September 11 world should have little difficulty matching this record. Other war gases are stealthier because symptoms are delayed. For example, mustard gas symptoms take between three and twenty-four hours to appear, by which time treatment may be useless (Tucker 2006). Clinicians could also have trouble diagnosing symptoms once they appeared. On the one hand, clinician notes are available for practically all chemical weapons (Centers for Disease Control n.d.(b)) and doctors tend to be relatively familiar with industrial materials like phosgene. On the other, even astute clinicians might have trouble identifying chemicals that are seldom used commercially.

3.3   Radiological Weapons

Radiological weapons (more usually *radiological dispersal devices* or *RDDs*) are weapons that spread radioactive isotopes over a wide area. In theory, some isotopes offer orders of magnitude improvements in toxicity compared to chemical weapons. These isotopes, however, are generally difficult to obtain and/or weaponize. Conversely, the RDDs that terrorists actually build are likely to be far less effective, producing few if any casualties beyond the conventional explosion used to spread contaminants.

Terrorists have so far shown little interest in RDDs compared to chemical and even biological weapons. To date, the only convincing example seems to be a demonstration device left by Chechen separatists in a Moscow park (AFRRI 2003).[30]

3.3.1   Choosing and Obtaining Suitable Isotopes

Literally dozens of commercial isotopes exist, including ^{99}Tc, ^{131}I, ^{238}Pu, ^{60}Co ^{192}Ir, ^{241}Am, ^{252}Cf, ^{235}U, depleted U, ^{67}Ga, ^{226}Ra, ^{90}Sr, ^{137}Cs, ^{3}H, ^{85}Kr, ^{232}Th, ^{14}C, ^{15}N, ^{32}P, and ^{35}S. However, many decay too slowly to pose a significant health threat or cannot be obtained in sufficient quantities to contaminate large areas (DOE/NRC Interagency Working Group on Radiological Dispersal Devices 2003; Helfand et al. 2006; Argonne National Laboratory 2005; Yassif 2004). Table 3.5 provides a list of the most likely weapons candidates. These can be further subdivided into gamma, alpha, and beta emitters according to the kinds of radiation they produce.

Gamma Emitters   Some isotopes cause damage by emitting gamma rays, a form of light that can be thought of as very high energy X-rays. These can travel for up to 150 meters in the open air before being absorbed. By far the most famous gamma emitter is cobalt-60 (^{60}Co). Cold War commentators routinely suggested that the flood of neutrons from an exploding H-bomb could be used to turn ordinary cobalt metal into radioactive ^{60}Co. Cobalt-jacketed weapons could therefore make enough radioactive material to contaminate hundreds of square miles.[31] This scenario is much less plausible for RDDs based on conventional explosives (or possibly aerosol sprays) that must obtain their radioactive payloads in advance. Section 3.1.1 has already remarked that terrorists would need roughly 9,000 kilograms of ^{60}Co to deliver a lethal dose over one square kilometer. This is five orders of magnitude larger than the one kilogram or so found in very large industrial sources. Indeed, a straightforward calculation shows that terrorists could not acquire this much ^{60}Co if they used every reactor on earth.[32] Even for advanced state programs, WMD-scale use of ^{60}Co (or, a fortiori, ^{252}Cf) is a nonstarter.

The analysis for our remaining gamma emitter, ^{137}Cs, is slightly different. Because of its thirty-year half-life, ^{137}Cs is readily produced in reactors. For this reason, very large amounts of ^{137}Cs could *theoretically* be obtained from commercial sources. In practice, however, the amount of radioactivity contained in even the largest devices is about 10 million curies—about the same as the largest ^{60}Co sources. This is far smaller than what would be needed to contaminate a square kilometer. Furthermore, large sources are rare. On the other hand, small (2,000-curie) hospital sources are much more common (Leite and Roper 1988). For this reason, ^{137}Cs is widely regarded as the leading threat among likely radiological weapons (Weiss 2005).

Alpha and Beta Emitters   As previously noted, alpha and beta particles seldom travel far. Thus they pose little danger unless ingested or inhaled. Once lodged in the body, however, their short range makes them dangerous since most of their energy tends to be deposited within a small volume of tissue.

3.3.2   Designing a Delivery System

Because gamma emitters work at a distance, weapons that contain them would have to be screened so that (at a minimum) terrorists survived long enough to manufacture and transport the weapon to an intended target. This presents a substantial technology challenge (Blackett 1949). For example, a relatively small, 2,000-curie medical source requires roughly 800 kilograms of shielding and this figure would only increase for larger weapons (Leite and Roper 1988). In principle, terrorists could reduce this burden by using just enough shielding to cast a radiation-free "shadow" in one direction. This could be done, for instance, by placing the isotope at the rear of a tractor-trailer rig behind a long, narrow piece of steel (figure 3.1).

However, this solution might not be acceptable from a security standpoint. Because gamma rays can travel up to 150 meters in the open atmosphere, a partially

Table 3.5
Candidate RDD Isotopes

Isotope	Typical uses	Half-life	Ci/g	Form	Typical radioactivity per device (Ci)	Lifetime excess cancer risk per inhaled picocurie
Gamma emitters						
^{60}Co	Gamma knife, sterilization, industrial imaging, food sterilization, fruit-fly sterilization, X-ray diagnosis, thickness gauges, seed and spice sterilization	5.3 years	1,100	Metal	0.01–1,000	3.58×10^{-11}
^{252}Cf	High-energy physics	2.6 years	540	Powder	?	2.59×10^{-5}
^{137}Cs	Gamma knife, sterilization, density and moisture gauges, thickness gauges, seed and spice sterilization	30 years	88	Soluble powder	0.003–10,000,000	1.19×10^{-11}
Alpha emitters						
^{241}Am	Smoke detectors, moisture and thickness gauges	430 years	4	Powder	0.03–22	2.81×10^{-8}
^{252}Cf	Physics research	2.6 years	4	Powder	?	2.59×10^{-5}
^{210}Po	Neutron sources	140 days	4,500	Dissolved liquid	?	1.08×10^{-8}
^{238}Pu	Weapons, power plants, pacemakers	88 years	17	Powder	?	3.36×10^{-8}
^{226}Ra	Medical needle and seed implants	1,600 years	1	Various	?	1.15×10^{-8}

Beta emitters

| ^{90}Sr | Radiothermal generators for producing electricity in remote locations | 29 years | 140 | Various | Commonly 10,000+ Ci; approximately 1,000 ex-Soviet RTGs contain 30,000–300,000 Ci | 1.05×10^{-10} |

Source: Argonne National Laboratory 2005; Davis et al. 2003; Oak Ridge National Laboratory n.d.

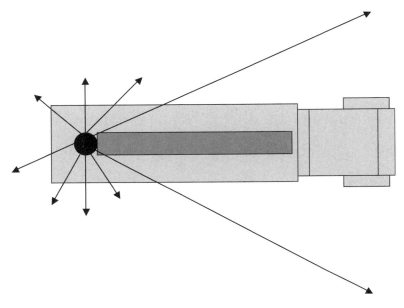

Figure 3.1
A partially shielded RDD

shielded weapon would be readily detectable by radiation monitors like those currently deployed in police cars and other locations.

As with chemical and biological weapons, bombs are a relatively inefficient way to spread radiological poisons. The U.S. Army is reported to have experimented with spraying radioactive aerosols from aircraft in the late 1940s and early 1950s. (Grover 2005). Here, terrorists' main technological challenge would involve safely milling the material into fine particles. Once this was done, dispersion could be accomplished using commercially available "dry powder generators" that force air across a fluidized bed (Colbeck 1998).

3.3.3 Manufacturing

Commentators usually assume that terrorists would purchase or steal radioisotopes from normal industrial channels. There are, however, hundreds of small research reactors and accelerators ("atom smashers") around the world that could potentially make isotopes to order.

Even after they were obtained, radioactive materials might not exist in forms that could readily be spread over a wide area. For example, cobalt, iridium, and polonium are usually solid metals that would be hard to disperse. Similarly, most strontium sources have been heat-treated ("sintered") so that they are essentially in-soluble and nondispersable. On the other hand, other materials are more tractable. For instance, americium, californium, and plutonium often exist as oxide powders, and cesium is typically stored as cesium chloride, a water-soluble powder.

Depending on the isotope, terrorists would have to mill, dissolve, or chemically alter their radioactive material to deliver an effective payload. Experience with chemical weapons suggests that even very elaborate precautions are unlikely to prevent low level worker exposure, fatal or near-fatal accidents, and/or leaks to the outside world. However, terrorists might be able to avoid this step if they designed the RDD so that the explosion processed the radioisotopes to produce oxides and nitrates over a suitable range of particle sizes (Argonne National Laboratory 2005). Alternatively, terrorists might be able to either dissolve some isotopes in water or else burn them to create a "radioactive smoke" (Zimmerman 2006).

3.3.4   Countermeasures

Radiation detectors are reliable, cheap, and increasingly ubiquitous. It is therefore reasonable to think that an RDD attack would be recognized for what it was almost immediately. Thereafter, prompt evacuation and cleanup of exposed individuals would limit further exposure. Because intact skin is impermeable to most radionu-clides, roughly 95 percent of the contamination could be eliminated by changing clothes and bathing. Failing this, prompt after-the-fact treatments could purge most isotopes from victims' bodies (chapter 12).

First responders would, as always, face special risks. However, standard issue gas masks would provide excellent protection against inhaling or swallowing contaminants. Compared to the hazards of chemical agents, moreover, caregivers would face only a moderate risk of secondary contamination from patients (AFRRI 2003).

3.4   Biological Weapons

Prior to World War II, most scientists who studied the problem concluded that pathogens were far too fragile to be used as weapons.[33] They argued that weapons diseases would not be markedly more effective than those that public health services had already brought under control; that virulence was known to fall off rapidly when organisms were stored outside the host; that organisms could not sustain virulence during fermentation, loading, and storage; and that organisms could not survive the shock of a bomb explosion (Guillemin 2005).

These sensible objections might have persisted indefinitely had it not been for the explosive growth of military R&D during World War II and the ensuing Cold War. Wartime programs succeeded in weaponizing one unusually hardy agent (anthrax) by the mid-1940s. Thereafter, massive postwar investments by the United States, United Kingdom, and USSR over a period of decades eventually succeeded in weaponizing other organisms. Despite this, the ability to inflict mass casualties remained elusive until the late 1960s when U.S. open air tests reportedly showed that pathogens released from a single aircraft could kill on a scale normally associated with atomic and even hydrogen bombs (Inglesby et al. 2002; Preston 1998).[34] Similar demonstrations were later conducted by the Soviet Union (Alibek and Handelman 1999). All of these state programs required (1) multiple, massive facilities, (2) hundreds to tens of thousands of personnel,[35] and (3). R&D budgets of (very roughly) $100 million per successfully weaponized disease.[36] Judging from the recent (early 1990s) Iraqi program, advances in biotechnology have done little to reduce these costs.[37]

The extent to which terrorists could duplicate the success of these very elaborate programs is unclear. In 1984, roughly a dozen members of the Rajneeshee cult showed that small-scale attacks are indeed possible. They used a three-person team to cultivate *Salmonella typhimurium* on a laboratory scale using ordinary glassware and growth media (Wheelis and Sugishima 2006). The Rajneeshees then used spray bottles to spread their bacterial slurry at ten restaurants in and around The Dalles, Oregon. In all, 751 people became ill, of whom 45 were eventually hospitalized. There were no fatalities (Martin 2006). Had the Rajneeshees chosen and/or been able to employ a more dangerous pathogen, their methods could plausibly have inflicted perhaps a hundred deaths.

Acquiring a genuine WMD capability would be a much larger undertaking. To date, the most credible program belongs to Aum Shinrikyo, whose scientific leader had studied genetic engineering before dropping out of Kyoto University. The group seems to have studied Q fever, anthrax, and poisonous mushrooms and may also have dispatched a team to Zaire in search of the Ebola virus. Aum is known to have mounted at least six anthrax and botulinum attacks from 1990 to 1995, all of which failed. While the reasons are obscure, the group's mistakes probably included picking low virulence strains, using low concentrations, and designing clog-prone sprayers (Wheelis and Sugishima 2006; Martin 2006; Mann and Connell 2006; USAMRIID 2004; Sopko and Edelman 1995). There is also some indication that members may have pursued the project reluctantly and/or deluded themselves with wishful thinking. The head of Aum's botulinum program reportedly admitted to colleagues that his preparations were ineffective in mice (Wheelis and Sugishima 2006).

This section examines the barriers to designing and making biological weapons. Section 3.4.1 describes how terrorists would select, obtain, and modify an organism to cause maximum damage to those exposed. Section 3.4.2 describes the additional technological hurdles needed to design suitable delivery systems. In general, these R&D challenges tend to be much more important for biological weapons than for other forms of WMD.[38] Section 3.4.3 describes the manufacturing technologies needed to support WMD-scale attacks. Finally, section 3.4.4 surveys countermeasures.

3.4.1   Choosing, Obtaining, and Enhancing a Pathogen

Many pathogens are known to have been successfully weaponized by state programs. These include anthrax, yellow fever, tularemia, brucellosis, Q fever, Venezuelan equine encephalitis, plague, smallpox, Marburg virus, Lassa fever, and monkey pox (Harris and Paxman 2002; Alibek and Handelman 1999). Knowing which technologies have worked in the past would not, however, save terrorists the hard work of duplicating state-program successes for themselves.

Choosing an Organism   The fact that a disease exists in nature does not prove that it can be made into a practical weapon. For example, some viruses (e.g., dengue) cannot be transmitted by small-particle aerosols (Borio et al. 2001). As with chemical and nuclear weapons, the best way for terrorists to minimize the chance of failure would be to choose pathogens that have been successfully weaponized by state programs in the past. Iraq's decision to pursue "classical" agents shows that even relatively large, well-funded state programs prefer to work with traditional pathogens (Dando 2001). The same reasoning applies a fortiori to clandestine groups with limited budgets.

Despite this, there are at least three reasons why a terrorist group might try to develop an agent that had not previously been weaponized. First, terrorists could decide that advancing technology and/or their own innate cleverness allowed them to improve on classical programs. The fact that Iraq pursued at least one new weapon beyond the classical list—botulinum toxin (Zilinskas 1999)—suggests that this strategy has some plausibility.[39] Whether a clandestine and presumably less well funded terrorism program would be so ambitious is less clear. Given that classical programs reportedly achieved H-bomb-scale capabilities with traditional organisms, the utility of investing in still-deadlier technologies seems doubtful.

Second, terrorists might not be able to obtain sample cultures for the pathogens they desired most. This, however, assumes that terrorists would deliberately invest in an expensive R&D program to create an inferior weapon.

Finally, most historic military programs were shaped by multiple constraints. These included focusing on agents that (1) are nonlethal, (2) do not spread from person to person, (3) cannot persist for more than a few days in the environment, (4) are deployable through reliable military methods like bombs and spraying, and (5) have satisfactory drugs and vaccines for protecting manufacturing personnel and/or friendly forces against accidental exposure (Mangold and Goldberg 1999; Alibek and Handelman 1999). This last constraint is particularly important and is believed to have roughly doubled the cost of the Soviet program (Alibek and Handelman 1999). Terrorists willing to jettison some or all of these requirements could potentially open up a range of foodborne, waterborne, and contagious disease agents that state programs have historically ignored (Zilinskas 2006).[40] Similarly, terrorists could decide to accept "friendly" casualties as the cost of working with infectious diseases, especially if they thought they could successfully hide these casualties from local authorities.

Terrorists who did decide to develop a novel weapon would pay for their decision with some combination of increased technical risk and testing costs. Consider, for example, the task facing hypothetical terrorists trying to weaponize the Marburg or Ebola viruses. Despite forty years of open research, it is still unclear whether weapons based on these diseases could cause large-scale infections and deaths.[41] On the one hand, existing guinea pig and primate data suggest that weapons ought to work. On the other, estimates based on historical outbreaks among humans are far less optimistic. In theory, this contradiction can be explained in several ways:

• Animal models are inadequate (i.e., the dose for humans is much higher than animal experiments suggest).
• The viruses do not remain respirable for long periods of time.
• Human-to-human transmission is limited.
• Virulence depends sensitively on the particular virus strain employed (Leffel and Reed 2004).

It is difficult to believe that terrorists would invest in an expensive, multiyear development effort without resolving these uncertainties. But identifying the bottlenecks and—where possible—developing work-arounds would require substantial animal testing and research. Large, well-funded state programs are prepared to make such investments. Terrorists might not be.

Obtaining the Desired Organism   Once terrorists decided on a weapon, they would still need a sample of the desired pathogen. However, isolating pathogens in the wild (Tucker 2004) and identifying suitably virulent strains is difficult, even for experts. For example, there are more than seventy different strains of *Bacillus anthracis* and hundreds of strains of botulinum. Only a few of these are sufficiently virulent to make weapons. Aum Shinrikyo reportedly picked relatively weak strains for its anthrax program and, more speculatively, may also have picked an organism that produced a relatively mild variant of the botulinum protein (Mann and Connell

2006; Mangold and Goldberg 1999). Obviously, one cannot plan on future terrorists making these same mistakes. Nevertheless, Aum's experience illustrates how insufficient animal testing can derail even well-funded and relatively expert programs. Future terrorists will have to weigh these risks against the very substantial costs and security risks associated with large-scale testing.[42]

Given these problems, it is not surprising that state weapons programs have almost always obtained their organisms from research laboratories and type collections. The FBI estimates that as many as 22,000 U.S. laboratories may hold leftover samples from outbreaks and epizootics (Guillemin 2005). Despite recent reforms, control of these materials remains highly imperfect and may be vulnerable to simple measures like the use of front companies (Falkenrath, Newman, and Thayer 1998). Furthermore, individual countries' efforts to regulate pathogens are undercut by inconsistent international standards (Tucker 2004; NRC 2006) although this problem is less pronounced for the relatively short list of traditional weapons pathogens and toxins covered by international "dual-use" export regulations (Commerce Control List 1C351).

The rise of companies that specialize in making synthetic DNA to order potentially provides a third channel for terrorists interested in obtaining pathogens. Recent experiments have already used synthetic DNA to make viruses like polio (Cello, Paul, and Wimmer 2002) and 1918 influenza (Tumpey et al. 2005). For the moment, these methods are still "very laborious and difficult" (NRC 2004). However, Gibson et al.'s (2008) successful synthesis of the relatively complex *Mycoplasma genitalium* bacterium shows that some state-of-the-art laboratories can already synthesize most if not all traditional weapons pathogens (including smallpox) if they want to. Furthermore, control of these materials remains incomplete. On the one hand, synthetic DNA—like all genetic elements associated with pathogenic organisms and toxins—is covered by "dual-use" export regulations (Commerce Control List 1C353). On the other, some companies still do not screen orders for suspicious sequences. Even where screening exists, moreover, today's technologies tend to be both over-inclusive (lumping together harmless "housekeeping genes" and genuine threats) and under-inclusive (ignoring threats beyond the relatively short list of so-called select agent pathogens). Industry initiatives to address these problems are currently underway. (IASB 2008)

Enhancing the Pathogen   Obtaining a suitable pathogen is only the beginning. Classical state programs have almost always found it necessary to modify naturally occurring pathogens to make an effective weapon. This requires alterations along many dimensions:

Infectivity   Infection primarily depends on the organism's ability to penetrate skin. Classical microbiology methods can be used to breed organisms for this characteristic. Alternatively, genetic engineering could be used to enhance organisms' ability to secrete proteinases and phospholipases that break down barriers within the skin (Zilinskas 2006).

Virulence   The ability of an organism to traverse the host's blood or lymphatic system, evade host defenses, enter target tissues, and obtain nutrients is called virulence. Virulent organisms usually secrete special proteins that interfere with the host's normal immune response. Genes for these factors could be identified and inserted. Alternatively, they could secrete enzymes to break down immunoglobulin and other antibodies (Ziliniskas 2006).

Lethality   The lethality of an organism depends on a variety of factors. These include "infectiousness" or the process of attaching to hosts; "pathogenicity," or the ability to evade the host's natural defenses and obtain nutrients; and resistance to antibiotics and vaccines. All of these factors could potentially be increased by classical microbiology or genetic engineering methods (Dando 2001; Mangold and Goldberg 1999).[43] Historical evidence suggests that concerted, state-funded efforts can increase potency by perhaps an order of magnitude.[44]

Resistance   Organisms can be modified to make treatment harder by evading standard identification, detection, and diagnostic methods (Dando 2001; Block 1999; Zilinskas 2006) or conferring resistance to current antibiotics and vaccines. This can be done by isolating drug resistant strains in the wild, using classical microbiology to breed desired traits, reengineering surface proteins so that existing drugs no longer recognize the organism, or inserting pathogen DNA into normally benign organisms (Zilinskas 2006).[45] Engineers could also modify organisms so that they continually altered themselves to evade treatment (Block 1999). However, resistance would be much less useful for attacks large enough to overwhelm public health systems by, for example, exhausting the country's vaccine and antibiotic stockpiles.

Latency   The number of casualties inflicted by a biological weapon depends sensitively on how quickly public health authorities can detect, locate, and respond to the attack. Because incubation time has substantial natural variation and depends on dose, some individuals (especially children) tend to become sick early (Walden and Kaplan 2004; Wein and Liu 2005). This means that authorities can usually infer the eventual size of the epidemic and identity of affected populations from early data and deploy resources accordingly (Walden and Kaplan 2004). This suggests that diseases can be made deadlier by reducing the latency period. Soviet scientists reportedly cut smallpox's normal seven- to ten-day latency down to one to five days, thereby compromising public health tactics based on quarantine (Alibek and Handelman 1999). Alternatively, engineers could modify an unfamiliar disease for longer latency on the theory that it would spread further before the threat was detected (Block 1999).

R&D Challenges   Terrorist programs would need skilled technicians whether they used classical nineteenth-century microbiological breeding techniques or modern genetic engineering. Since the 1970s, such skills have become increasingly common. Indeed, trade organizations estimate that about 1,500 companies currently practice some form of bioengineering (Biotechnology Industry Association 2007). Furthermore, many genetic engineering procedures can now be outsourced to companies that supply DNA to order.[46] That said, skill is not enough. All known methods for modifying organisms include a large trial-and-error component. First, and most obviously, the intended modification may not succeed. Anecdotal evidence suggests that even simple experiments seldom work the first time. Indeed, Soviet attempts to engineer vaccine-resistant strains of anthrax required "endless repetition" in the early 1970s (Alibek and Handelman 1999). Second, even successful experiments frequently exhibit a phenomenon called *pleiotropy* in which each intended modification generates unintended side effects (e.g., reduced hardiness). In the early 1980s, for example, Soviet scientists had still not created a three-vaccine resistant strain of anthrax despite a decade of effort (Alibek and Handelman 1999).[47] Historically, terrorist groups have shown relatively limited tolerance for expensive, long-shot projects.[48] While it is impossible to say just how much risk a group like Al Qaeda would be willing to tolerate, it is hard to imagine them investing a large fraction of their $25 million annual budget for a period of years to build a weapon that had, say, a 10 percent chance of success. For this reason, a rational group would almost certainly test its weapons.

But testing is complex and expensive. Terrorists would need to conduct animal-inhalation experiments using the carefully controlled, ultralow doses of interest to weapons designers. This, in turn, would require specialized aerosol generators, careful air sampling to verify pathogen concentrations, and inhalation chamber equipment. Although detailed descriptions of U.S. Army lab equipment are publicly available (Roy and Pitt 2006), reliable results would still require moderately specialized equipment and skills. The required scale of testing would also be expensive and difficult to hide. Classically, a single LD_{50} test normally consumes 60 to 100 animals, although this figure can be reduced to as few as 6 animals if experimenters are willing to accept a 30 percent uncertainty (Ecobichon 1998). Furthermore, experiments on rats or guinea pigs would also have to be validated by additional experiments on nonhuman primates. Lower animals often differ substantially from humans in absorption, metabolism, excretion, mechanisms and efficiency of repair, gut flora, and variability with which chemicals are inactivated by binding to proteins (Calabrese 1991). Similarly, species also differ in airway structure and the types and abundances of cell species that particles encounter once they reach the lungs (Crapo et al. 1987). The net impact of these differences is particularly well illustrated for tularemia strains: humans are a million times less sensitive to type B compared to type A, but there is no hint of this in rabbits and guinea pigs (Adamovicz, Wargo, and Waag 2006). Testing in cell cultures is even more uncertain. Human-subject experiments with *Coxsackie virus A* show that the dose needed to infect 50 percent of all exposed victims is twenty-eight times the dose needed to start an infection in culture (Couch et al. 1966).

An Eroding Barrier?   Continued advances in basic science can only make weapons work easier. First, better biotechnology techniques can (and almost certainly will) make existing trial-and-error methods more predictable, reducing the effects of pleiotropy. Indeed, the new field of synthetic biology has made greater predictability one of its key research goals.[49] Second, academic research may sometimes generate ideas for new and better weapons. For example, 1930s-era experiments showing that bacteria could be freeze-dried and later revived supplied essential groundwork for postwar bioweapons programs (Guillemin 2005). More recent examples include articles describing the discovery of an exceptionally virulent "Ames" strain of anthrax in the 1980s (DeArmond 2002) and contemporary experiments aimed at developing ultra-high-purity botulinum toxin as a research tool (Leitenberg 2005). Finally, basic biology research will almost certainly reveal new and unexpected mechanisms for inflicting harm. A recent experiment showing that modifying a single mousepox gene is enough to kill vaccinated mice is a particularly dramatic example (Broad 2001; Finkel 2001; Nixdorff et al. 2004).[50]

These examples suggest that some academic and commercial "experiments of concern" could pose problems for biosecurity (NRC 2004, 2006; Royal Society and Wellcome Trust 2004; Maurer, Lucas, and Terrell 2006). On the other hand, surveys of the published literature suggest that fewer than 1 percent of all experiments fit this category under even the broadest definitions (Steinbruner et al. 2007). The U.S. government's National Scientific Advisory Board for Biosecurity (NSABB) is currently working with agencies to develop standards for managing and perhaps even preventing academic experiments that pose unusual biosecurity concerns. (NSABB 2006a)

3.4.2 Designing a Delivery System

Disseminating agent in bulk is probably the single most significant technology obstacle to creating biological WMD (Falkenrath, Newman, and Thayer 1998). Here I discuss the main technologies for large-scale dissemination in the open air. Other, less conventional strategies based on spreading disease through contaminated objects, food supplies, and animal vectors are discussed in section 3.6. Strategies based on human-to-human transmission are discussed in chapter 4.

Bombs   In principle, bombs offer both simplicity and the opportunity for terrorists to escape before the attack takes place. For example, Britain's first bioweapons program used slurry-filled bombs to deliver anthrax to a target. The project was simple enough for a very small team—roughly two dozen members—to design and demonstrate a complete weapons system within two years (Harris and Paxman 2002). The bombs were reportedly effective up to 500 yards away and were tested against animals on a small Scottish island. The site remained off-limits until Britain completed a massive cleanup almost fifty years later (Guillemin 2005).

But bombs have important drawbacks. First, heat and shear forces associated with the explosion typically kill 95 to 99 percent of the pathogen payload. Weapons designers have historically tried to reduce this effect by clever bomb design, breeding strains that can survive rough handling, and filling bombs with pathogens (e.g., anthrax) that are exceptionally hardy to begin with (Moon 2006; Zilinskas 2006; Mangold and Goldberg 1999). Second, experience with chemical weapons suggests that about one-fourth of the surviving pathogens are driven harmlessly into the ground (Tucker 2006). Third, we will see below that bioweapon effectiveness falls off quickly for aerosols outside a narrow 1–5 μm size range. By some estimates, fewer than 2 percent of particles from postwar U.S. bombs were in this window. Indeed, only about 7 percent of one wartime British bomb went into aerosol at all (Guillemin 2005). Overcoming these technical problems is highly nontrivial. Despite massive efforts, the United States was unable to develop a satisfactory biological weapons bomb as late as 1953 (Moon 2006). Furthermore, even successful bombs would have relatively small blast radii. Large area coverage would therefore force terrorists to plant multiple bombs.[51]

Many of these technical problems can be overcome by filling the bomb with dried agent instead of slurry. These weapons can probably deliver about 15 percent of their payload into the air in the correct size range (Dando 2001). However, doing so negates one of the main reasons—simplicity—for using bombs in the first place.

Spray Systems: Wet Formulation   As with chemical weapons, spray devices provide a technically appealing alternative to bombs. Here, the simplest method is to spray a liquid slurry as an airborne suspension of droplets or "aerosol." However, the size of droplets must be very carefully controlled. First, droplets cannot be too large. Almost all particles larger than 10 μm[52] and 95 percent of those larger than 5 μm are filtered out by the body's natural defenses—cilia inside the nose and upper respiratory tract—before they reach the lower lungs (Glasstone and Dolan 1977). This means that bacteria distributed as 1 μm particles are hundreds of times more lethal than 10 μm droplets (Mangold and Goldberg 1999). Large particles also fall out of the atmosphere relatively quickly, depleting the aerosol as it travels downwind (Zilinskas 2006). Second, particles cannot be smaller than about 1 μm in size. There are several reasons for this. Smaller particles usually do not stick in the lungs and are quickly exhaled. Moreover, small droplets also dry out quickly, killing the organisms inside. Finally, very small droplets tend to disperse so quickly that they are diluted to ineffectiveness (Zilinskas 2006). These considerations suggest that terrorists should optimize aerosol size around a relatively narrow 1–2 μm window (Glasstone and Dolan 1977).

Most commercially available aerosol generators are poorly suited to this task. On the one hand, devices for delivering medicines produce aerosols in hopelessly small volumes (Geller 2002). On the other, large-volume applications like painting or crop spraying normally focus on depositing aerosols onto surfaces. This goal is defeated by very fine mists that rapidly blend into the air and then travel long distances before being deposited. Although these devices would produce some particles in the desired 1–5 μm range, most would not be. Finally, breaking liquids up into micron-scale particles is energy intensive. This means that commercially available, high-volume sprayers cannot be readily modified to produce the correct size range (Falkenrath, Newman, and Thayer 1998; Ackerman and Bale 2005), although some agricultural sprayers come fairly close at 20 μm (Micron Sprayers n.d.; Dunn 2003). Nevertheless, commercial aerosol technologies are constantly improving. Furthermore, a few experimental sprayers for niche applications (e.g., aircraft fire-suppression systems) generate aerosols in the required size range (Nicolaus n.d.; Combellack et al. 2004).

Even if a suitable generator were found, weapons designers would have to overcome a number of problems. First, the required droplet size (<5 μm) is comparable to the size of most bacteria (0.3–10 μm) (Heikkinen et al. 2005). This suggests that the shear forces needed to fragment bulk water into droplets will often shatter organisms instead (Roy and Pitt 2006; Zilinskas 2006; Ackerman and Bale 2005). Small-diameter bacteria like anthrax spores (1.3 μm), tularemia (1–2 μm), and viruses (typically 20 to 300 nm) would presumably be least affected (Heikkinen et al. 2005; Sobsey and Meschke 2003).

Second, wet slurries characteristically exhibit clumping effects that either clog the nozzle and/or produce particles in the wrong size range (Zilinskas 2006; Ackerman and Bale 2005).[53] Classical weapons programs overcame these problems by using additives to protect organisms and prevent clumping during spraying (Mangold and Goldberg 1999). This "formulation" is a tightly held secret and has no civilian uses or applications (DeArmond 2002). Some authors claim that it may also be possible to genetically engineer organisms so that they are easier to aerosolize (USAMRIID 2004; Block 1999).[54] In either case, formulation must be tailored to each individual organism. Developing a successful aerosol is challenging and would probably require the efforts of an aerobiologist or appropriately trained physicist, as well as expertise in bacteriology or virology, biochemistry, fermentation processes, and industrial processing. Even then, formulation design is more an art than a science and would require extensive testing (Zilinskas 2006).

Finally, most pathogens and toxins rapidly degrade in the environment. This effect is most important for vegetative bacterial cells (Roy and Pitt 2006).[55] Plague, for example, survives only minutes in the wild (Zilinskas 2006).[56] The problem is complex and depends on several mechanisms:

Light   Ultraviolet light (including sunlight) causes most pathogens and toxins to decay exponentially (Preston 1998; Dando 2001). For instance, tularemia lasts only a few minutes in sunlight and botulinum toxin degrades at a rate of 7.8 percent per minute (Dando 2001).

Humidity and temperature   Low humidity and high temperatures promote desiccation and rapidly kill the organism.

Wind speed   Winds below 5 mph are too slow to spread agent effectively. Conversely, winds above 30 mph degrade agent (Mangold and Goldberg 1999).

"Open-air effect"   Finally, a mysterious "open-air effect" boosts outdoor decay rates for many organisms. For the nonpathogen *E. coli* organism, the open-air decay rate is about 3 to 10 percent per minute on average and sometimes reaches 20 percent. The cause is unknown but is suspected to involve atmospheric oxidants including ozone, olefins, pollutants, and smog. Pressure fluctuations and air ions may also play a role. Open-air effect is known to be significant for many weapons diseases, including tularemia and brucellosis (Zilinskas 2006) and some viruses (Zilinskas 2006; Sobsey and Meschke 2003).

Most of these factors can be mitigated (at the cost of some operational flexibility) by mounting attacks at night, under conditions of high humidity and low temperatures, and when ozone levels are low. Alternatively, terrorists could use spore-forming bacteria—notably anthrax—that can survive for hours in the open air and are immune to open-air effect (Zilinskas 2006). Many—though not all—viruses are similarly hardy,[57] although they are more complicated to manufacture. Weaponeers can also search for strains that are exceptionally hardy using either classical (Mangold and Goldberg 1999) or genetic engineering methods. Soviet attempts to splice genes for making botulinum toxin into more robust (but normally harmless) organisms are a variation on this theme (Arnon et al. 2001). Genetic engineering methods could also be used to enhance pathogens' resistance to aerosolization and environmental stress (USAMRIID 2004). Finally, state programs have routinely hardened bioweapons by adding chemical stabilizers to wet agents (Mangold and Goldberg 1999). As previously noted, however, formulation design is still much more an art than a science.

No matter which R&D strategies terrorists adopt, testing would be needed to confirm that they had reached a reasonably efficient solution (Zilinskas 2006). As noted, testing with lab animals would require substantial facilities, whereas releasing test organisms into the wild poses security risks. It has been suggested that testing might not be absolutely necessary if a group was willing to tolerate "some degree of uncertainty" (Bale and Ackerman 2005).[58] However, historical experience suggests that failure rates are high enough to make this strategy prohibitive for projects that require substantial investments of time and money.

Spray Systems: Dry Powders   Modern bioweapons programs typically process wet agents further to make fine powders known as "dry formulation." Pound for pound, such weapons are far more effective than sprays. First, the technologies for releasing powders are relatively straightforward and range from mailing them in letters (e.g., Washington anthrax attacks) to pouring them from a moving car or tall building. More advanced techniques would use commercial generators that blow air across a fluidized dust bed (Colbeck 1998). Unlike wet sprayers, none of these methods impose a significant mechanical shock on organisms. Second, powder size is—once achieved—relatively stable and predictable. Here, the main challenge is developing coatings that suppress static electricity so that particles do not clump together (Zilinskas 2006; Mangold and Goldberg 1999). Finally, polymer coatings can also be used to protect (microencapsulate) the organisms against sunlight, fresh-air effect, and other environmental factors (Alibek and Handelman 1999).

Not surprisingly, the detailed recipes for making powders are classified. While expensive to develop, the formulas themselves are relatively simple. For example, the recipe for anthrax can reportedly be summarized in a single sentence: "The [Alibek] formula is simple and the formula is somewhat surprising, not quite what you'd expect. Two unrelated materials are mixed with pure powdered anthrax spores. It took a lot of research and testing to get the trick right and Alibek must have driven his research group hard and skillfully to arrive at it. 'There are many countries that would like to know how to do this,' he said" (Preston 1998). Terrorists who do not already know the secret would presumably have to experiment with such industrial processing technologies as spray-drying, milling, and microencapsulation. Even for experts, however, designing wet and dry agents is an art form. It would probably take several cycles of experimentation and testing to develop an effective weapon (Zilinskas 2006; Preston 1998).

3.4.3   Manufacturing, Storage, and Safety

As with chemical weapons, the ability to deploy laboratory (gram) scale quantities of agent would not confer a true WMD capability. Instead, terrorists would need to manufacture at least pilot (kilogram), and perhaps industrial (metric ton) scale quantities. The exact size of the manufacturing facilities would depend on several factors. First, terrorists would have to decide whether to use wet or dry agents. While dry agents offer much greater lethality, they also require additional manufacturing steps. Second, most pathogens have a relatively short shelf life. This limits the attack size that a given plant can support. Third, the extreme toxicity of biological weapons would make manufacturing accidents fairly common. Whether or not terrorist workers were willing to accept this risk, accidents would be difficult to hide in countries that operate efficient public health systems. Terrorists would therefore face a complex trade-off between capital investment (larger plants, more workers), security (larger, more detectable operations), and R&D expense (better manufacturing processes, longer shelf lives, fewer accidents).

Wet Agents   Bioweapons manufacturing begins by inserting a small sample of the desired organism into a nutrient broth ("culture") and allowing the mixture to grow in a fermenter. The fermenter is then run for a set number of hours and allowed to cool. At this point, the pathogens are separated from the broth by skimming, centrifugation, or other methods and the mudlike mass is frozen. The final step involves diluting the mass with a special solution containing preservatives, adjuvants, and other chemicals to make "formulation," a dilute, cloudy liquid suitable for spraying (Zilinskas 2006). Depending on the organism, formulation contains between 10^8 and 10^{11} organisms per milliliter (Zilinskas, personal communication).[59]

In principle, *low-technology fermenters* can consist of little more than a 55-gallon drum. Such simple fermenters usually yield about one gram of dry bacteria per liter per cycle (Shiloach and Fass 2005). During the 1970s, a U.S. neofascist group is said to have made thirty to forty kilograms of typhoid in this way (Falkenrath, Newman, and Thayer 1998; Carus 2000b). However, low-tech fermenters also have drawbacks. These include a substantial workforce, the need for significant floor space, and a nontrivial accident rate. They would also limit terrorists' ability to manufacture certain pathogens. Some agents—notably anthrax—grow readily in a wide variety of media and would be relatively straightforward to ferment (Mann and Connell 2006; DeArmond 2002). However, others pose substantial challenges. Despite concerted effort, the U.S. program was never able to produce plague in quantity although the Soviet program eventually did succeed after a massive effort involving ten institutes and thousands of scientists (Inglesby et al. 2000).

Advanced fermenters are sophisticated devices that can be programmed to maintain specific temperatures, nutrient mixes, and chemical conditions automatically. They can reportedly reach cell densities of up to 190 grams per liter, more than two orders of magnitude better than simple fermenters (Shiloach and Fass 2005). However, this performance depends on detailed, pathogen-specific recipes that require extensive trial and error to discover. Alibek reports that it took him eight months to develop efficient methods for producing brucellosis in bulk (Alibek and Handelman 1999). Success would therefore require "persistence and experimentation" (Falkenrath, Newman, and Thayer 1998). Furthermore, the industrial biotech market is small. Attempts to purchase advanced fermenters would therefore pose a significant (though perhaps acceptable) risk of detection.[60] Finally, large-scale fermentation is slow. This limits the amount of agent that can be produced at any given facility and increases the risk that organisms will evolve during the fermentation process in ways that reduce virulence and other traits.

Dry Agents   Turning wet biomass into a powder would require additional processing steps. The process begins by drying the biomass using spray- or freeze-drying equipment. For example, the United States uses Freon to freeze-dry tularemia. Next, the dried powder is milled with ball bearings or, in more recent Soviet work, strong air blasts. This reduces the average particle diameter below about 10 μm. Finally, the powder is encapsulated in a protective polymer shell (Mangold and Goldberg 1999). As with chemical weapons, bioweapons manufacturing is so dangerous that purification steps are counterproductive.[61]

Spray-drying, milling, and other material processing technologies would require significant expertise. That said, these technologies are more accessible than they used to be. Commercially available machines (*micronizers*) are already capable of producing 1–10 μm particles. Companies boast that they can be operated by "anyone . . . in their garage" (Rios 2004). Nevertheless, successful weaponization remains daunting. As previously noted, grinding technology frequently damages organisms, while spray-drying interferes with virulence (Mangold and Goldberg 1999). Controlling these effects would probably require multiple cycles of experimentation and animal testing.

Viruses and Spores   So far, our discussion has been limited to the simplest case—fermenting active ("vegetative") bacteria. Some authors report that growing bacterial *spores* (e.g., anthrax) in useful quantities is harder, "a complex task—not just hard to do, but hard to discover how" (DeArmond 2002).[62] Growing *viruses* is harder still. Because viruses require a living host, they must be grown in—and subsequently extracted from—live animals, embryonated eggs, or tissue cultures. First-generation Soviet smallpox, VEE, and Q fever weapons consumed hundreds of thousands of eggs per month. Later, the program grew viruses in cell cultures using special reactors developed for Western pharmaceutical companies. Once again, researchers had to develop elaborate recipes involving exotic growth media (e.g., green monkey kidney cells, human embryo lung cells) and detailed temperature schedules. Furthermore, growing viruses remains more art than science and some pathogens (e.g., Congo hemorrhagic fever, hemorrhagic fever with renal syndrome) still cannot be produced in volume (Borio et al. 2001). Cells grown in culture also tend to evolve over time, impairing the original organism's ability to survive outdoors and/or infect humans (Sobsey and Meschke 2003). For this reason, terrorists would have to confirm that their chosen pathogen would not be compromised by multiple passages through tissue culture in the course of breeding and manufacturing. Terrorists starting from laboratory strains might similarly have to pass them through animals or humans in order to restore their potency (Alibek and Handelman 1999).

Toxins Finally, chemical engineers have trouble synthesizing toxins larger than ten to twelve amino acids long (U.S. Army 1990). For this reason, most toxins—including all useful weapons—must be made by fermentation or special methods like infecting rats with bacteria-laced feed (Mangold and Goldberg 1999). These processes are invariably complicated. For example, *Clostridium botulinum*, the organism that makes botulinum toxin, must be grown in a special, oxygen-free liquid growth medium and then concentrated into a powder. This process is relatively sophisticated, although Aum Shinrikyo was able to purchase the required equipment (Mangold and Goldberg 1999). Still more advanced technologies would be needed to grow highly concentrated toxins in large (kilogram) quantities (Dando 2001). Postsynthesis purification would also be needed to separate the most lethal components of the toxin from raw distillate. For instance, ricin toxin can be isolated from castor bean cake and, more recently, transgenic plants. However, relatively pure versions of the toxin require advanced crystallization techniques (Greenbaum and Anderson 2006b).

Scaling Up Our analysis of open-air plumes suggests that true WMD capability would require at least one to ten kilograms of dry agent. While small in absolute terms, this would still require a thousandfold increase over the two to three grams of dry agent used in the 2001 anthrax attacks (DeArmond 2002). The required quantities of wet agent, which is orders of magnitude less dense, would likely be measured in tons.

Aum Shinrikyo's experience making slurried anthrax and botulinum toxin suggests that even laboratory-scale operations would require a substantial investment.[63] Their laboratory was staffed by a six-person team working in protective suits and measured 200 square meters. Its equipment included a glove box, incubator, centrifuge, dryer, and two 2,000-liter fermenters (Wheelis and Sugishima 2006). Furthermore, Aum was reportedly constructing a pilot-scale building at the time of the Tokyo subway attacks. This four-story production facility would have contained specialized ventilation systems and a sealed room for cultivating bacteria.

There is limited evidence that a very competent and well-funded terrorist organization could also manufacture dry agent. In 1999, the U.S. Defense Department asked three scientist-employees to create a clandestine bioterrorism laboratory. The Project BACUS team, none of whom had previously done bioweapons work, was able to purchase a fifty-liter fermenter, sophisticated milling equipment, and ancillary equipment for about $1.5 million on the open market without being detected. It then used this equipment to produce approximately one kilogram of dried bacteria—including simulated anthrax—in less than a month (Seper 2001; Miller 2001; DeArmond 2002; Inglesby et al. 2002). This quantity was already three orders of magnitude larger than the 2001 anthrax attacks. The cost of even larger facilities would presumably scale according to equation 3.1.

Storage   The shelf life for wet agents is very short, ranging from weeks to months (UNSCOM 2004). During the 1940s, the Soviet program was able to store refrigerated viruses including Q fever, smallpox, and VEE for about one year (Alibek and Handelman 1999). Toxins are even more delicate. Solutions of botulinum toxin must be protected against heat, light, and air. Even so, they are only stable for about seven days (Ellison 2000).

Not surprisingly, state programs have conducted extensive R&D to extend shelf life. One early strategy was to focus on bacteria that formed hardy spores, chiefly anthrax (Guillemin 2005). Another, more sophisticated strategy is to design dried agents (Mangold and Goldberg 1999). For example, dried plague can be stored for about a year, while dried tularemia lasts three years (Mangold and Goldberg 1999). However, this is an imperfect solution since stored agents tend to become less virulent with time (Guillemin 2005; Mangold and Goldberg 1999). A third strategy has therefore been to find unusually storable strains and/or to develop complex storage recipes. For instance, the U.S. tularemia stockpiles were reportedly stabilized by refrigerating the agent in a special mixture of skimmed milk and sucrose (Mangold and Goldberg 1999). Like most bioweapons results, the formula is presumably more art than science and would require a long and expensive series of animal experiments to replicate.

Safety Attempts to ferment, freeze-dry, and/or mill pathogens into dry powders would pose "an extreme biohazard" to persons nearby (Zilinskas 2006). Historically, most bioweapons manufacturing programs have repeatedly infected their workers. Japanese experience during World War II suggests that low-technology programs can expect casualties of about 1 percent per year (Mangold and Goldberg 1999). This would presumably increase if additional steps were added to make dry agent.

The extent to which terrorists could reduce these accident rates by adopting conventional countermeasures is debatable. Despite first-generation vaccines, U.S. Army laboratory workers who handled tularemia in the 1960s were routinely infected at a rate of 0.6 percent per person per year (Dennis et al. 2001).[64] Nor are modern facilities foolproof. In 2006, Texas A&M's state-of-the-art containment facilities released both Q fever and brucellosis, infecting four workers in all (Brainard and Fischer 2007). Terrorists are unlikely to duplicate, let alone improve on, these facilities. Nor are they likely to follow the traditional but also time-consuming and expensive military strategy of developing better vaccines. In the long run, however, they may be able to use genetic engineering to create "binary weapons." These would consist of two reagents, each of which was more or less harmless until combined. At this point, terrorists would be able to conduct kilogram-scale manufacturing without "undue risk" (Block 1999).

3.4.4   Countermeasures

The feasibility of biological weapons defense depends sensitively on (1) the availability of drugs and vaccines, and (2) the time frame available to administer them. In practice, these factors differ significantly from agent to agent (table 3.6).

Nevertheless, it remains true that vigorous countermeasures could significantly reduce casualties for most agents or, in a few cases, eliminate them entirely.

Preattack countermeasures include mass inoculation, first-responder training, stockpiling/prepositioning drugs, and (potentially) advertising campaigns to inform the public how to defend itself in an emergency. For some threats, vaccines potentially offer near-perfect protection. For example, mass inoculation with antitoxin would theoretically immunize the entire U.S. population against botulinum toxin. In this case, society's choice not to mass-vaccinate reflects an implicit judgment that the risk of an attack is too small to justify the expense of mass vaccination and/ or losing the pharmaceutical benefits of botulinum toxin (*botox*). (Arnon et al.

Table 3.6
Biological warfare agents: Vaccines, therapeutics, and incubation periods

Disease	Vaccine	Therapy	Incubation period
Anthrax	Yes	Yes	Several hours up to one week
Q fever	Yes	Yes	1–14 days
Glanders	No	Yes	1–14 days
Plague	Yes—no longer available	Yes	1–7 days
Brucellosis	No	Yes	5–60 days
Tularemia	Yes	Yes	1–14 days
Viral encephalitis	Yes	Supportive therapy only	1–6 days
Viral hemorrhagic fevers	Yes	Yes	2–21 days
Smallpox	Yes	Supportive therapy only	7–16 days
Botulism	Yes	Yes	3–6 hours
Staphylococcus enterotoxin B	No	Ventilator only	Hours
Ricin	No	Supportive therapy only	18–24 hours
T-2 mycotoxins	No	No	Minutes

Source: Davis and Schneider 2002; USAMRIID 2004; Ellison 2000

2001). The calculus is more complex in the usual case where vaccines are imperfect (tularemia) or may have side effects (smallpox).

Provided that *real-time protection* is possible, even modest countermeasures such as covering the nose and mouth with clothing can provide useful protection against inhaling pathogens and toxins (Arnon et al. 2001). Surgical masks and gas masks are still more effective (Borio et al. 2001 (hemorrhagic fever); Inglesby et al. 2000 (plague); Arnon et al. 2001 (botulinum toxin)). While current U.S. public acceptance of such measures is clearly limited, this would probably change quickly if a concrete threat emerged. More than thirty million gas masks were distributed to the British public in 1938 (Harris and Paxman 2002; U.K. Home Office [1938] 2007) and all Israeli citizens have had masks since 1991 (Barzilai 2002).

For now, the main impediment to real-time protection is insufficient warning. In principle, this could come from terrorists themselves in the same way that IRA bombers habitually warned British authorities of impending attacks or Chechen terrorists warned Russian officials that an RDD had been planted in a Moscow park. In practice, there is no reason to count on such behavior. Meanwhile, real-time

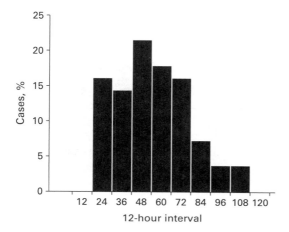

Figure 3.2
Oral botulinum poisoning: onset of symptoms. *Source*: Arnon et al. (2001)

monitoring systems for classical agents remain prohibitively expensive and feature large false positive rates (Dennis et al. 2001 (tularemia); Arnon et al. 2001 (botulinum)). Fortunately, this situation is changing. For example, better botulinum detectors are under development and the U.S. Army has already deployed one such system (Arnon et al. 2001). Improved detectors would dramatically improve the prospects for real-time response.

Finally, *after-the-fact* countermeasures tend to be most important. Practically all weapons diseases have incubation periods of days, weeks, or months, allowing substantial opportunity for intervention.[65] In principle, continuous testing offers the fastest detection times. However, this may not be politically feasible and/or cost-effective. Furthermore, many diseases lack cheap and fast diagnostic tests (Dennis et al. 2001 (tularemia); Borio et al. 2001 (hemorrhagic fever); Inglesby et al. 2000 (plague); Arnon et al. 2001 (botulinum); Inglesby et al. 2001 (anthrax)). Even without testing, however, aggressive public health surveillance of emerging outbreaks would significantly reduce casualties. For almost all diseases, there is a substantial variation in how quickly people become ill. Unless the average incubation period is very short (hours to days), detection of early casualties would allow public health authorities to identify and treat most exposed individuals with vaccines and prophylactic medicines. In practice, the efficiency of modern surveillance systems varies by disease. Where agents are already familiar and have distinctive symptoms (e.g., botulism), the U.S. Centers for Disease Control and Prevention are already reasonably efficient and would likely detect an attack promptly (Arnon et al. 2001; figure 3.2).

On the other hand, surveillance would be much less effective in cases where symptoms were unfamiliar and/or nonspecific. Examples include tularemia (Dennis et al. 2001), hemorrhagic fevers (Borio et al. 2001), and plague (Inglesby et al. 2000). In these cases, early detection would require both astute clinicians and a high index of suspicion.

3.5   WMD Attacks: Airborne Methods

Having a powerful poison is not enough. Would-be weaponeers must also find a way to spread it efficiently over broad areas. Historically, chemical, biological, and radiological weapons have almost always relied on airborne dispersal. There is widespread agreement that this is still the preferred method (Bale and Ackerman 2005; Dando 2001). Even so, the process is highly imperfect. Much of the existing literature uses a simplified model in which an initial stock of poisons is arbitrarily said to reach victims with some quoted efficiency, often assumed to be 1 percent (Arnon et al. 2001). Presumably, this conventional number can be justified by classified calculations and tests. It is nevertheless instructive to explicitly consider the physics of how aerosols disperse in air.

Plume Physics   Consider a plume of poison gas or dust that has been released from some fixed point source at a single instant. In general, the total exposure that victims receive downwind will be a complicated function of wind flows, eddies, and thermals. However, scientists have found that it is usually sufficient to ignore these details and consider average flows over time. In this approximation, an initial quantity of agent (q) released at height h above ground delivers the following concentration (c) to each downwind location:

$$\langle c(x, y, z, t)\rangle = \frac{q}{2\pi \cdot \bar{u} \cdot \sigma_y \cdot \sigma_z} \times \exp\left(\frac{-y^2}{2 \cdot \sigma_y^2}\right)$$

$$\times \left[\exp\left(\frac{-(z-h)^2}{2 \cdot \sigma_z^2}\right) + \exp\left(\frac{-(z+h)^2}{2 \cdot \sigma_z^2}\right)\right] \tag{3.2}$$

where u is the mean wind speed, x is the downwind direction measured from the release point, y is the crosswind direction, z is the vertical direction, and δ_y and δ_z are constants reflecting the tendency of particles to disperse in directions perpendicular to the wind direction as time passes (Lucas 2006). Because of dispersion, concentrations are highest along a line directly downwind of the release point and fall off with a Gaussian ("bell-curve") distribution along the y and z directions. This is reflected in the second and third terms on the right-hand side and explains the normal rule of thumb that a plume usually spreads about half as far in the crosswind direction as it does downwind (Ellison 2000). The final term shows how particles are removed ("scavenged") from the air by physical collisions with the ground (e.g., anthrax particles) and, in some cases, through chemical bonding to surfaces (e.g., many chemical weapons).[66]

The exponential terms in equation 3.2 show that plume concentrations in both the cross- and downwind directions are strongly suppressed on scales of a few kilometers. Efforts to increase the affected area by, say, doubling the amount of poison discharged cannot compete with this suppression and are therefore a relatively ineffective way to extend the plume's coverage. This explains why state programs stress spraying from mobile platforms, especially airplanes, instead.

Estimating Casualties   The concentration that victims receive at any given location is only part of the story. To estimate casualties, we also need to know the population density at that spot—70,000 people/square mile is a typical number for dense urban settings[67]—and the particular agent's dose-response curve. We have seen that most poisons display a pronounced S-shaped curve. Figure 3.3 presents a generic picture of what such a curve might look like.

It is instructive to ask what this discussion implies for attempts to increase the lethality of agents. Suppose, for example, that bioterrorists use genetic engineering to improve pathogens so that one microbe now does the work formerly done by two. This would be equivalent to doubling the dose of (unimproved) agent at each point along the plume.[68] If the dose-response relation were linear, this would also double the number of expected casualties. However, this would *not* happen for the

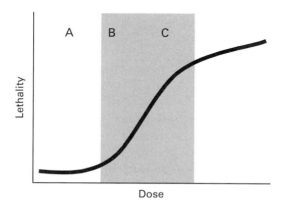

Figure 3.3
An illustrative bioweapon dose-response curve

dose-response relation sketched in figure 3.1. In this case, doubling the dose would produce hardly any additional casualties for regions A and C. Instead, most of the additional casualties would come from the relatively narrow band of doses spanned by region B. The more general point is that incremental improvements in poisons have little effect unless they are large enough to sweep significant numbers of new victims from region A into region B or C. This suggests that genetically engineering microbes to, say, double the chances that a single pathogen will produce infection is usually a poor investment.[69] More generally, simple genetic engineering modifications will often be less beneficial—and more expensive—than competing low-technology options like increasing manufacturing capacity, extending shelf life, and making delivery systems more efficient.

Beyond Simple Models   In practice, this simple physics model ignores many real-world complications. These include:

Inversion   Most weather conditions allow particles to diffuse upward, severely reducing downwind concentrations. However, atmospheric inversions place a ceiling or cap on how high particles can travel (Preston 1998).[70] Planners generally assume that terrorists would release agents under conditions that trapped particles within 100 meters of the ground (Dando 2001). This explains why aircraft releases must occur at very low altitudes. Indeed, open-air tests show that particles released more than several hundred meters above the ground cannot be detected even a few hundred meters downwind (Zilinskas 2006).[71] Turbulence also tends to move aerosols away from ground level. High winds increase turbulence and make bioweapons less effective (Zilinskas 2006).

Wind direction and speed   Chemical, biological, and radiological weapons need a wind speed fast enough to reach the target but slow enough to linger before dispersing (Tucker 2006). For example, phosgene is a relatively dense gas and can persist five minutes or more under the right conditions. On the other hand, hydrogen cyanide—the only lighter-than-air military gas—would persist less than a minute under these circumstances. High winds also increase the rate at which liquid agents disperse into the atmosphere. For discrete targets, terrorists must estimate wind direction accurately as well. Some experts believe that this may have been a contributing factor in Aum Shinrikyo's failed botulinum toxin attacks (Mangold and Goldberg 1999).

Weather   The effectiveness of spray weapons is also moderately dependent on weather. In general, gas clouds exhibit steady, even movement over flat country but tend to disperse rapidly. Conversely, clouds move slowly over broken country or brush, or in built-up areas where temperature inversions tend to contain and concentrate vapors near the ground. Other conditions accelerate dispersal. These include unstable air ("lapse conditions") and low temperatures that make many agents less volatile and promote condensation. Strangely, two agents—phosgene and lewisite—break down rapidly when relative humidity exceeds 70 percent (U.S. Army 1990).

Aerosol evolution   Chemical or bioweapons aerosols continue to evolve after release. This can improve efficiency if evaporation or turbulence from the sprayer aircraft shrinks particles into the correct size range (Levin and de Amorim 2003). However, smaller particles are also more prone to evaporation, so that pathogens may not last as long (Sobsey and Meschke 2003).

Sinks, scavenging, and degradation   Many mechanisms reduce plume concentrations over time. Once aerosols settle out of the air, they are unlikely to be disturbed enough to become respirable a second time (Dando 2001). Rain can also scavenge aerosols from the air, although this can sometimes produce other forms of contamination. Finally, many bioweapons have short survival times in aerosol. Botulinum, which is hard to concentrate and degrades quickly in the presence of oxygen, is particularly vulnerable. Experts estimate that a cloud of botulinum would extend no more than half a kilometer before being neutralized. Furthermore, only about 10 percent of the people exposed in that space would actually be killed or incapacitated (Arnon et al. 2001).

Detailed topography   Aircraft spray experiments using *Bacillus thuringiensis*, a close relative of anthrax, found that particles in the 4.3 to 7.3 μm range were reduced by a factor of 2.3 to 4.6 for people sheltering indoors. However, indoor concentrations were also slower to dissipate. As a result, indoor concentrations measured five to six hours after spraying actually exceeded outdoor ones (Levin and de Amorim 2003).

Preparedness   Effective civil defense can drastically cut WMD casualties. In World War I, for instance, respirator use by troops made chlorine and phosgene casualties relatively rare (Tucker 2006). Helfand et al. (2006) argue that "the government's ability to quickly and effectively evacuate communities or shelter populations downwind will be the single most important factor in minimizing the casualties and injuries."

Empirical Data   Collectively, plume dispersal and degradation of agent in the atmosphere mean that bioweapons fall well short of the millionfold improvements that their toxicity promises. The net result, according to the U.S. Army, is that—pound for pound—biological weapons cover about four times more surface area than chemical weapons (U.S. Army 1990). That said, very small amounts of military-grade bioweapons can potentially contaminate large areas. In the late 1960s, the United States validated its bioweapons program against animals tethered on barges near Johnston Atoll. The attack was reportedly carried out by a single jet fighter that dispersed roughly ninety kilograms of agent over a thirty-kilometer baseline that covered "thousands" of square miles of ocean (Mangold and Goldberg 1999). A 1983 U.S. government estimate based on Dugway Proving Grounds data similarly estimates that 5,000 kilograms would be needed to mount an attack along a 100 kilometer baseline for an eight meter/second wind. A four meter/second wind would require just 875 kilograms.[72]

3.6 WMD Attacks: Unconventional Methods

The physics of airborne delivery is so favorable that state weapons programs have traditionally spent little time considering alternatives. In keeping with the focus of this book, we ignore specialized uses (e.g., assassination) that are not noticeably more lethal than guns or high explosive. As the Rajneeshees showed, simple biological attacks require little more than a spray bottle (Wheelis and Sugishima 2006). The learning curve becomes steeper, however, as we consider weapons whose destructiveness significantly exceeds what can be achieved through familiar methods like high explosive.

3.6.1 Contagion

Uniquely, biological agents can pass from victim to victim. In theory, an attacker can use contagious agents to avoid the difficulty and expense of producing agents in large quantities. Effectively, the target population manufactures the poison for him. This possibility is discussed at length in chapter 4. *Animal vectors* can also be used to carry some diseases from person to person. While it is difficult to say how effective such a strategy might be, World War II programs suggest that attempts to use large animals (e.g., bats) would require an industrial-scale undertaking (Couffer 1992). State projects have historically concentrated on insects instead. Japan used fleas to spread plague in China during the 1930s, and the U.S. Army is said to have experimented with mosquitoes in the 1960s. However, neither method seems to have been particularly efficient compared to aerosols (Mangold and Goldberg 1999; Alibek and Handelman 1999).

3.6.2 Contaminated Materials

For an attacker, the single greatest weakness of delivering toxins through the atmosphere is that concentrations fall off (at least) with the square of the distance. *Contaminated food* and *water* avoid this drawback by using society's own distribution systems to deliver a lethal dose to users. On the other hand, water supplies are subject to dilution, chlorination, quality control, and recalls/alerts (Bale and Ackerman

2005; Tucker and Sands 1999). Standard chlorination is effective against most agents including tularemia (Dennis et al. 2001), hemorrhagic fever (Borio et al. 2001), and botulinum (Arnon et al. 2001). Furthermore, reservoirs are very large. For this reason, most experts think that the popular idea of poisoning a municipal reservoir would require so much toxin as to approach "science fiction" (Croddy, Perez-Armendariz, and Hart 2002).

Dilution is a much smaller obstacle for products like milk, fruit and vegetable juices, canned foods, and perhaps other food industries that use a "bow-tie" supply chain in which goods are collected and pooled in a single processing facility before being redivided for distribution (Wein and Liu 2005). In this case, poisons delivered at any point prior to pooling can reach all consumers. In their study of the California milk industry, Wein and Liu estimate that a single attack could potentially reach 100,000 consumers. Naively, ten grams of botulinum toxin would be sufficient to kill almost all of these people. More realistically, consumption would probably stop twenty-four hours after the hundredth person developed symptoms. This would prevent about two-thirds of all fatalities unless botulinum doses were so high that average onset occurred within hours or days. Pasteurization similarly destroys a large fraction of toxins and could drastically reduce casualties for an attack totaling ten grams of toxin. However, terrorists could potentially overwhelm this precaution by employing very large, kilogram-scale quantities. Wein and Liu remark that food-borne attacks are much more preventable than attacks that use aerosols or send contaminated letters through the postal system. Good physical control of storage and transfer operations is one obvious response. A nearly perfect system that tested each 55,000-gallon milk truck would add about 1¢ to each gallon of milk.

Attackers can also avoid dilution by contaminating *high-traffic areas*. In this case normal foot traffic and/or mass transit delivers victims to a stationary source of poison. During the 1960s, U.S. and Soviet biological weapons experts both conducted experiments simulating anthrax attacks on a busy subway tunnel (Moon 2006; Hart 2006). Dirty-bomb attacks could similarly be enhanced by targeting enclosed spaces and subways (Helfand et al. 2006). Finally, both the Japanese and U.S. programs are known to have experimented with contaminated products or *fomites* (Harris and Paxman 2002). Sending contaminants through the mail, as in the 2001 anthrax attacks, is the best known example of such a tactic. The U.S. attacks included five to seven letters and killed five people (Martin 2006).

3.6.3   In Situ Weapons
In the spirit of September 11, terrorists could find it easier to destroy facilities that already contain dangerous materials than to make a new weapon and deliver it to a target. These facilities could be chemical or nuclear.

In the late 1990s, EPA estimated that up to 66,000 U.S. facilities handled chemicals that posed a risk of blast damage and/or toxins to surrounding neighborhoods. Belke (2000) used data for 14,828 of these facilities to compile scenarios in which a single vessel or pipeline failure created a spill. Although the median worst-case scenario potentially caused serious injury to persons living 1.6 miles from the plant, there were also about 3,000 sites that could potentially affect people more than 3 miles away. Only about 250 facilities posed a threat to people more than 25 miles away. Most of these involved chlorine releases from 90-ton railway tank cars. The remaining cases involved anhydrous ammonia (33 scenarios), hydrogen fluoride (32), sulfur dioxide (22), chlorine dioxide (8), oleum (7), sulfur trioxide (5), hydrogen chloride (4), hydrocyanic acid (3), phosgene (2), propionitrile (2), bromine (2) and acrylonitrile (2).

The worst chemical plant disaster in history took place early in the morning on December 3, 1984, when 43 tons of methyl isocyanate were accidentally released from a holding tank in Bhopal, India, and rolled along the ground into surrounding streets. An estimated 3,000 people were killed initially and at least 15,000 have died from related illnesses since then (Eckerman 2005).

Manufacturing facilities also pose a *blast* risk. Belke (2000) found that the median U.S. plant posed a risk of serious injury up to roughly 0.4 miles away and that about 400 plants posed a risk of blast damage[73] to people living one or more miles away.[74] The explosion of a ship filled with 2,300 tons of ammonium nitrate at Texas City, Texas, in 1947 provides a useful baseline for thinking about large industrial explosions. The blast threw heavy steel debris up to 13,000 feet and broke windows up to ten miles away. The disaster killed 576 people, damaged more than a thousand buildings, and caused property damage worth $700 million in current dollars (Pandanell, n.d.; Texas State Historical Association 2006; Fire Prevention and Engineering Bureau et al. n.d.).

Finally, a facility attack could release nuclear contamination. As of 2006, there were 104 nuclear power plants and 34 research reactors operating in the United States. Each reactor core contains radioactive material inventories that are roughly comparable to the fallout expected from a ten-kiloton nuclear weapon. Many reactors also store spent fuel rods in pools of water. These pools usually contain more waste than the reactor itself. Most of this material would remain in place following an accident. However, the explosion and fire at Chernobyl ejected 3×10^8 curies of radioactive material (OECD 2002) or about 0.1 percent of the 3×10^{11} curies expected from a ground-level, ten-kiloton nuclear detonation (Glasstone and Dolan 1977). Almost two-thirds of this (60 percent) consisted of xenon, a noble gas that would have dispersed rapidly. Of the remainder, ^{137}Cs was by far the most important long-term biological hazard. Approximately 2.3×10^6 curies of this iso-

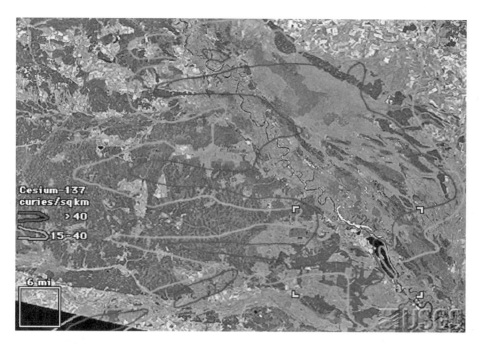

Figure 3.4
Chernobyl. *Source*: USGS Image, available at http://edcwww.cr.usgs.gov/earthshots/slow/
Chernobyl/Chernobyl1992zones

tope were produced and enough settled locally so that sites within 30 kilometers of
the facility were typically contaminated at levels exceeding 4×10^{-4} Ci/m^2. These
areas are still abandoned today. Additional, localized hot spots also formed up
to 200 miles away when rainfall washed ^{137}Cs from the air (OECD 2002; USGS
n.d.).

3.7 WMD Attacks: Nuclear Weapons

Designing and making nuclear weapons is notoriously challenging even for nation-
states. All known methods require capital investments running into the billions of
dollars, many years (often decades) of effort, and large, readily detectable industrial
signatures (Richelson 2006). This makes nuclear weapons the least likely form of
terrorist WMD. This section presents a brief review of atomic weapons and their
effects. (For further detail, see the exhaustive discussions in Glasstone and Dolan
1977, Smyth 1945, Serber [1943] 1992, and Reed and Stillman 2009.)

3.7.1   Design and Manufacturing

Nuclear bombs work by assembling a critical mass of plutonium or highly enriched uranium long enough for a nuclear fission chain reaction to start. The amount of energy released then depends on how far the chain reaction proceeds before the expanding bomb fragments are no longer dense enough to support fission (Serber [1943] 1992). This constraint is not particularly difficult for uranium bombs, which can be assembled using relatively crude methods based on firing a highly enriched uranium (HEU) projectile into an HEU target. Uranium enrichment, on the other hand, is hard. All known methods require capital investments well beyond the reach of nonstate actors.

Plutonium, in contrast, can be made relatively easily in nuclear reactors. However, plutonium bombs need to reach much higher initial densities than HEU weapons to be successful. (Serber [1943] 1992). In practice, this means using an exquisitely controlled conventional explosion to implode the material. This makes the design and fabrication of plutonium bombs much more difficult than HEU weapons. The fact that the United States test-fired a plutonium but not an HEU bomb gives some sense of the relative challenges. North Korea's failed September 2006 test similarly seems to have involved a plutonium weapon, although the resulting "fizzle" was still far more powerful than any conventional bomb. (Readers seeking an exhaustive discussion of the various technical hurdles that must be overcome to design everything from clumsy and delicate "improvised nuclear devices" to modern H-bombs should consult Reed and Stillman 2009.)

3.7.2   Blast, Flash, and Prompt Radiation

Nuclear weapons are different from other forms of WMD chiefly in their capacity to inflict physical damage from heat, air blast, and shock. Roughly 85 percent of a nuclear weapon's energy goes into these effects. Furthermore, an additional 5 percent is emitted in the form of gamma rays and other high-energy particles ("prompt radiation") that strike victims immediately and then disappear. Blast damage is caused when the expanding high-pressure region around the bomb crosses over people and structures. Because the pressurized region's energy density is inversely proportional to its volume, blast damage falls off with the cube of distance. Thermal energy and prompt radiation, on the other hand, are transmitted by photons that spread out like the surface of an expanding sphere. For this reason, radiation damage only declines with the square of distance (Glasstone and Dolan 1977).

Experience at Hiroshima (12.5 kt) provides a benchmark for the casualties expected from relatively small atomic weapons. Not surprisingly, casualties at Hiroshima were very high within 0.6 miles of ground zero, with 85 percent of those exposed dying from blast, thermal energy, and prompt radiation. Furthermore, an

Table 3.7
Nuclear weapons fatalities: Immediate effects

Yield (KT)	LD$_{50}$ range for air blast (meters)	LD$_{50}$ range for thermal burns (meters)	Range for LD$_{50}$ dose (4 Sv)-prompt nuclear radiation (meters)	Range for LD$_{50}$ dose (4 Sv)-fallout in first hour after blast (meters)
0.01	60	60	250	1,270
0.1	130	200	460	2,750
1	275	610	790	5,500
10	590	1,800	1,200	9,600

Source: Coleman et al. 2003

additional 10 percent were seriously injured. For reasons already described, however, casualties declined quickly outside this region. Thus, persons located 0.6 to 1.6 miles from ground zero suffered 27 percent fatalities and 37 percent injuries while people located 1.6 to 3.1 miles from the blast suffered only 21 percent fatalities and 25 percent injuries (Glasstone and Dolan 1977). Overall, roughly 50 percent of all deaths were caused by burns and 30 percent by prompt radiation.[75]

Table 3.7 estimates LD$_{50}$s for blast, flash, and prompt radiation for a variety of small nuclear weapons.

Significantly, these are only estimates and averages. In a real explosion, casualties would be sensitive to haze and weather, how many people were outside, whether structures are wood frame or concrete, and so on. Buildings and topography would also produce shadowing effects that significantly modified blast, radiation, and fallout effects at particular locations. While unnecessary for most policy discussion, real-world rescue and recovery efforts would need to understand these effects in detail.

3.7.3   Contamination

About 10 percent of the explosion's energy goes into creating lingering contaminants ("fallout") consisting chiefly of water and soil debris whose atomic nuclei have been rendered unstable by the explosion.[76] In all, about two ounces (57 grams) of fission products are produced for each kiloton of energy. Fallout would continue to emit medically significant amounts of radiation in the form of high-energy light (gamma rays), fast-moving electrons (beta particles), and neutrons for weeks or months (Glasstone and Dolan 1977). At one minute after a one-kiloton explosion, this represents nearly 3×10^{10} curies and dwarfs most plausible RDDs. For land explosions, 40 to 70 percent of this radiation reaches the ground locally within twenty-four hours or so. Thereafter, rates decline roughly as $t^{-1.2}$ for the next six months and more steeply thereafter. This suggests, for example, that exposures two weeks after the blast will be a thousandfold less than they were at the one-hour mark (Glasstone and Dolan 1977).

Fallout patterns vary widely depending on wind, rainfall, size of radioactive cloud, distribution of radioactivity within the mushroom head, and the size distribution of radioactive particles. However, the most serious hazard consists of visible particles ranging from particles the size of fine sand to marble-sized pieces.[77] This hazard is very different from the inhalation hazards associated with most other forms of WMD and can be dealt with by constructing dust-free shelters. The pattern of contamination is usually established within twenty-four hours (Glasstone and Dolan 1977). A typical ten-kiloton weapon would produce a footprint thirty miles long and a few miles across at its widest point. Roughly half of this area would initially be contaminated at the 100-rem level, although a narrow inner region could rise to 1,000 rem (Davis et al. 2003; Carter, May, and Perry 2007).

3.7.4   Countermeasures

Modern nuclear weapons usually include Permissive Action Links, Environmental Sensing Devices, and other technical safeguards. Reed and Stillman (2009) describe these technologies in detail. If terrorists were able to acquire and detonate a weapon, organized civil defense activities would dramatically increase the population's chances for survival. This would even be true for citizens sheltering in improvised structures (e.g., trenches covered with earth) constructed immediately *after* the attack (Goodwin 1981; Science Service Inc. 1950).

3.8   Conclusion

Small terrorist programs can produce almost any WMD technologies (except nuclear) on a small scale. However, CBR attacks that "merely" inflict casualties on a high-explosive scale—dozens or perhaps even hundreds of casualties—would likely be anticlimactic. Achieving genuine WMD will be much more difficult.

Experience with Iraq and North Korea shows that even highly motivated states find it hard to acquire the knowledge and, especially, capital needed to make *nuclear weapons*. While technology advances have eroded this barrier, change remains gradual. No policymaker should ignore the possibility that terrorists may find a shortcut—notably, obtaining weapons from a state program—or suddenly exhibit far greater technical ingenuity than past plots would indicate. That said, the barriers to acquiring genuine nuclear weapons have been and remain high.

Chemical weapons follow a similar logic. Though markedly less complex and expensive to acquire, Aum Shinrikyo's experience shows that chemical weapons still pose daunting challenges for even the largest nonstate programs. In a post-September 11 world, terrorists' ability to duplicate (let alone exceed) Aum's high-water mark is doubtful. As with nuclear weapons, technology change is eroding these barriers fairly slowly.

Most versions of *radiological weapons* would cause relatively low casualties and, to that extent, fall outside this discussion. Terrorists trying to develop a true WMD capability would need far more radioactive material than commercial sources can plausibly deliver. Given the relative maturity of current reactor- and particle accelerator methods for making radionuclides, further technology breakthroughs are unlikely. Terrorists would also need to invest substantial effort to invent a suitable delivery system. Unlike other WMD technologies, historical state program experience is limited and offers little guidance to would-be weapons makers.

For now, the most worrisome WMD threat probably involves *bioweapons* and *toxins*. Traditional large-scale fermentation requires substantial personnel and equipment, which, however, were clearly within Aum's capabilities. It is possible that somewhat smaller and less well funded groups could succeed as well. Finally, the technology barriers to bioweapons seem to be eroding faster than for other forms of WMD.

In many ways, the post–Cold War world has come full circle. In the late 1940s, most physicists believed that states would find it relatively easy to acquire (and then use) nuclear weapons. Judicious control over key technologies prevented that nightmare. While today's barriers to WMD are lower, terrorists also have far fewer resources than any state. This suggests that—as in the past—prudent technology controls can limit the rate at which WMD proliferates.

Notes

1. Readers can find a detailed history of sharing between states in Reed and Stillman (2009). Chapter 5 discusses the U.S.'s ability to trace WMD back to specific state programs. Terrorists' ability to acquire weapons by theft is addressed in chapter 17.

2. Al Qaeda's budget is fairly typical. Interested readers can find estimated budgets for many past and present terrorist organizations in Laqueur 2002. Among historic terrorist organizations, Aum Shinrikyo had by far the most resources reaching 40,000 to 60,000 members and $1 billion in assets by the mid-1990s (Sopko and Edelman 1995). These figures almost certainly provide a generous upper limit on the resources (if not necessarily the competence) available to future terrorists. Readers seeking definitive, chapter-length accounts of Aum and eleven other historic chemical and biological terrorist conspiracies should consult Tucker 2000b.

3. All major World War II combatants worked on chemical and germ weapons. There is also ambiguous evidence that Germany investigated radiological weapons (Hogg 2002). The Allies took the WMD threat seriously enough to include one million doses of botulinum antitoxin (Arnon et al. 2001) and radiation monitoring equipment in their preparations for D-Day. The United States, United Kingdom, France, and USSR also conducted massive chemical and bacterial weapons programs after the War (Harris and Paxman 2002). Finally, the United States is known to have conducted outdoor radiological weapons experiments at Utah's Dugway Proving Grounds between 1949 and 1953 (Grover 2005).

4. There are two important exceptions. Nuclear weapons kill with blast and high-energy X-rays ("prompt radiation") as well as poison ("fallout"). They are discussed separately in section 3.7. Similarly, terrorists using contagious diseases could potentially injure victims far beyond the initial attack site. Contagious bioweapons are extensively discussed in chapter 4.

5. This value is typical for victims performing office work or other light activity. A ten-minute exposure is reasonable for airborne contaminants, most of which tend to disperse quickly.

6. Strangely, the bioweapons literature seldom quotes LC_{50} values explicitly. There are, however, many good reviews of pathogens and toxins. Ellison (2000) and USAMRIID (2004) provide exhaustive data. In-depth reviews of the open literature for anthrax, glanders, plague, tularemia, Q fever, alpha viruses, orthopox viruses, viral hemorrhagic fevers, botulinum toxins, ricin, and staphylococcal and streptococcal superantigens can be found in Swearengen 2006. Readers should consult Inglesby et al. 2002 (anthrax), Dennis et al. 2001 (tularemia), Arnon et al. 2001 (botulinum), Borio et al. 2001 (hemorrhagic fever viruses), and Inglesby et al. 2000 (plague) for additional information.

7. The reasons for the S-curve are complex. First, some individuals are unusually susceptible to particular diseases. This genetic component is known to be important for both anthrax and smallpox (Griffith et al. 2001; Jahrling and Huggins 2006). Second, organisms seem to cooperate in setting up a disease state. This explains why the probability of infection rises steeply after a particular threshold is crossed. Finally, many viruses are defective and incapable of reproduction. This fraction can range from 50 percent (Semliki Forest virus) to 0.01 percent (papillomavirus), although the values for polio (0.1 to 3 percent) are more typical (Flint, Enquist, and Rancaniello 2004). This suggests that individuals who have the bad luck to inhale just a few viable organisms can be quickly infected.

8. Examples include erythropoietins, interferons, interleukins, colony-stimulating factors, stem cell growth factors, monoclonal antibodies, and tumor necrosis factor inhibitors.

9. Victims could potentially protect themselves by sheltering behind lead, steel, concrete, packed earth, or other dense materials (Goodwin, 1981).

10. Unger and Trubey (1982) provide values for a parameter Γ that allows users to calculate the health effects from any given gamma emitter. Specifically, the exposure in sieverts is equal to the quantity $A \times \Gamma \times 4.2 \times 10^{14}/T$ where A is the isotope's atomic number and T is the half-life in seconds. This figure represents the number of sieverts that a person standing one meter from one gram of the isotope would receive in a one-hour period. Note that total number of sieverts also declines with the square of the distance and/or the presence of shielding.

11. As noted, this calculation assumes exposure to a single grain of material located one meter away. A more refined analysis would take account of the fact that victims standing inside an extended cloud of aerosolized gamma ray emitters would (1) receive a large number of

small contributions from distant particles, and (2) receive disproportionate doses from particles that happened to be closer than the one-meter average. Both effects would increase LC_{50}. Given that such clouds are technologically implausible (section 3.3.1), we ignore these refinements.

12. Christine Hartman-Siantar (Lawrence Livermore National Laboratory), personal communication.

13. However, military units often use a special, highly corrosive material called DS2 to decontaminate nerve agent.

14. German Chemical Corps units demonstrated large-scale decontamination when Allied aircraft bombed several Tabun-filled freight cars in 1945. They evacuated civilians to a distance of twenty kilometers and decontaminated the area within twenty-four hours (Tucker 2006).

15. For disease-by-disease discussions, see Dennis et al. 2001 (tularemia); Borio et al. 2001 (hemorrhagic fever); Inglesby et al. 2000 (plague); Arnon et al. 2001 (botulinum); Inglesby et al. 1999 (anthrax); and Inglesby et al. 2000 (plague).

16. A few toxins are stable and can persist for extended periods (Ellison 2000). Some viruses can last for three to twelve weeks on surfaces and longer in soils (Sobsey and Meschke 2003).

17. Prior to the 2001 anthrax attacks, at least one blue ribbon panel argued that "decontamination of large urban areas or even a building following an exposure to an anthrax aerosol would be extremely difficult and is not indicated" (Inglesby et al. 1999). Following the attacks, the group softened its position to say that cleanup decisions should only be made after "full expert analysis" (Inglesby et al. 2002).

18. See, for example, Inglesby et al. 2000 (plague) and Borio et al. 2001 (hemorrhagic fever).

19. Disease-specific recommendations for decontaminating people, equipment, and areas can be found in Ellison 2000 and Dennis et al. 2001 (tularemia), Arnon et al. 2001 (botulinum), Inglesby et al. 2002 (anthrax), and Borio et al. 2001 (hemorrhagic fever). Some recommendations include bleach concentrations of up to 10 percent.

20. For purposes of calculation, I assume that the cloud was lethal up to one mile downwind, a typical number for World War I battlefields. The attack reportedly caused coughing and watery eyes up to ten miles away (Harris and Paxman 2002).

21. The six kg/km^2 figure assumes that the sarin was deposited along a line—for example, by a truck- or aircraft-mounted sprayer—and then carried downwind to create a one-kilometer-wide swath. While this is clearly sufficient to cause WMD-scale casualties for special locations like downtown Manhattan (27,000 people per square kilometer), killing millions would require the additional (and presumably unreasonable) assumption that the terrorists could go on spraying indefinitely.

22. Britain's World War I effort performed animal testing on 150,000 organic and inorganic chemicals. German nerve gas researchers similarly tested hundreds of potential compounds during the 1930s. America's World War I effort to screen 4,000 poisons was the largest military R&D program prior to the Manhattan Project (Tucker 2006; Harris and Paxman 2002). Significantly, these programs were often based on even larger R&D programs for commercial pesticides. German nerve agent breakthroughs in the 1930s and U.S./British advances in the 1950s both started with pesticide discoveries (Harris and Paxman 2002).

23. Aum Shinrikyo's rushed attacks on court officials and the Tokyo subway system both fall into this category (Tucker 2006), as do various hastily mounted attacks by 1970s-era European and Palestinian groups to recoup prestige after high-profile failures (Harclerode 2001).

24. Commerce Control List 1C350 and 1C355.

25. Declassification has reduced this barrier. Hogg (2002) reproduces a blueprint for German chemical shells.

26. The German program focused on bombs because sprayer aircraft would be exposed to ground fire. This factor is less relevant to terrorism, since fine sprays released from vehicles or buildings would be invisible. Crude spray systems would be more detectable. For example, several witnesses noticed—but did not understand—Aum's truck-mounted generator attacking a Tokyo neighborhood in June 1994 (Sopko and Edelman 1995). Aircraft spraying, which requires unusual sustained flight paths less than 100 meters above the ground would also be conspicuous.

27. An alternative and in some ways simpler strategy would be to combine agent with powders that had been premilled to the correct size range (Ellison 2000).

28. The German program reportedly improved Tabun's stability by adding chlorobenzeprene. The recipe is classified (Tucker 2006).

29. Military warning detectors can detect phosgene down to 28 ppm and sarin down to 11 ppm within forty-five seconds. They can also detect G- and V-series nerve agents down to 0.2 ppm) in less than two minutes. A more reliable card/vial system takes fifteen minutes but is more sensitive and reliable. It can detect G-agents down to 0.00009 ppm and V-series nerve gases down to 0.002 ppm. It also offers reasonable detection thresholds for mustard gas (0.03 ppm), lewisite (1 ppm), and phosgene (0.6 ppm) (Ellison 2000).

30. The literature also contains cryptic references to RDD threats by "certain deposed third-world leaders" (AFRRI 2003)

31. The 5.3-year half-life of cobalt-60 is short enough to pose a significant health hazard but long enough to outlast the two- to three-week period in which civilians could reasonably remain in fallout shelters. Not surprisingly, ^{60}Co weapons played a prominent role in various Cold War–era movies, including *Goldfinger* and *Dr. Strangelove*. Although routinely described as "dirty bombs," they should not be confused with RDDs. By definition, ^{60}Co bombs require a nuclear explosion. RDDs, on the other hand, would use a conventional explosion or (perhaps) aerosol spray generators to deliver a preexisting radioactive payload to victims.

32. Cobalt-60 is made by bombarding ordinary cobalt metal (^{57}Co) with neutrons. Nuclear weapons excepted, the best way to produce neutrons is in a reactor. However, a reactor only produces about 1,017 neutrons per second. A perfectly efficient reactor can therefore produce approximately 1,017 atoms of ^{60}Co per second or 300 kg per year. On the other hand, ^{60}Co decays with a half-life of 5.3 years. This means that a single reactor can only produce about two kilograms before the number of new atoms created per second just equals the number of decays. Assuming that every reactor in the world were used to make ^{60}Co, production would saturate at about 3,000 kilograms (Richard Firestone, Lawrence Berkeley Laboratory, personal communication).

33. Following convention, we use the term "biological weapons" to include both living organisms ("pathogens") and the nonliving protein, polypeptide, and alkaloid poisons that

they secrete ("toxins"). Although toxins are arguably a type of chemical weapon, their extreme lethality and the fact that they are usually made using fermentation techniques give them important similarities to pathogens.

34. The Johnston Atoll experiment used a jet fighter to spray agent along a line thirty-two miles long. The agent traveled for more than sixty miles before losing its infectiousness (Inglesby et al. 2002).

35. The Japanese program employed 6,000 workers, the United States program employed "several hundred" scientists and research staff, and the Soviet program employed over 50,000 people (Harris and Paxman 2002; Guillemin 2005; Martin 2006).

36. The U.S. biological weapons program spent approximately $700 million to develop defensive vaccines and offensive bioweapons between 1950 and 1970 (Harris and Paxman 2002). About half of this money was probably spent developing vaccines (Alibek and Handelman 1999). This twenty-year investment produced eight antipersonnel weapons and five anti-crop agents (Guillemin 2005; Martin 2006).

37. The Soviet program reportedly had a budget of "several hundred million" per year (Martin 2006). The much smaller Iraqi program is estimated to have spent $100 million in the late 1980s and early 1990s (Pearson 2006).

38. "In comparison to nuclear and chemical weapons (CW) programs, individuals' intellectual capabilities play a far greater role in determining the success or failure of a program than the physical resources to which they may have access" (UNSCOM 2004).

39. The Iraqis apparently believed that weapons based on botulinum toxin could defeat U.S. protective gear. Terrorists bent on attacking civilian targets would have much less reason to pursue this capability.

40. The USSR reportedly explored smallpox and plague on the theory that geographic distance would keep such weapons confined to North America (Zilinskas 2006).

41. This information may, of course, exist in the classified literature. Alibek claims that the Soviet Union successfully weaponized Marburg and Ebola, although these claims are controversial (Alibek and Handelman 1999).

42. Interestingly, Iraq never seems to have tested its anthrax and botulinum weapons (Zilinskas 2006). This may have reflected a judgment that these substances were robust and well understood. Alternatively, Iraq may have intended the weapons as deterrents, in which case an element of bluff might have been acceptable. This latter argument would not apply to terrorists.

43. British wartime work on anthrax illustrates these methods. They increased virulence by passing strains serially through thirty-six monkeys (Guillemin 2005).

44. See, for example, Harris and Paxman 2002 (UK World War II program obtained tenfold improvement in anthrax); Guillemin 2005 (U.S. program improved anthrax virulence by 300 percent); and Alibek and Handelman 1999 (1980s-era Soviet program obtained additional threefold improvement in previously weaponized anthrax).

45. Viruses, which are unaffected by antibiotics, are also advantageous along this dimension.

46. The rise of commercial "oligo" and "gene synthesis" companies has significantly reduced both the cost and skill sets required to perform sophisticated genetic engineering experiments. From the standpoint of a hypothetical terrorist, these benefits are offset by the risk that such

companies might detect—and report—suspicious orders. Informal surveys suggest that most, but not all, gene synthesis companies screen orders for potentially suspicious experiments and would inform authorities if a weapons experiment was detected (Maurer, Lucas, and Terrell 2006; Aldhouse 2005). Government and private initiatives are currently underway to improve the quality of existing screening programs and encourage more companies to practice screening.

47. A subsequent research breakthrough reportedly produced a five-vaccine resistant strain in 1989 (Alibek and Handelman 1999).

48. Bin Laden reportedly reviewed the September 11 conspiracy's chances for success at regular intervals and considered canceling it on several occasions (9/11 Commission 2004). A bioweapons attack would have a bigger payoff than the September 11 plot, but would also be correspondingly riskier and more expensive.

49. Synthetic biologists hope to develop a library of standard DNA "parts" that can be mixed and matched to create new organisms. Limiting unintended interactions—pleiotropy— is a key part of this agenda.

50. According to one Australian scientist, the experiment showed that "something we thought was hard—increasing the pathogenicity of a virus—is easy" (Finkel 2001). At the very least it offered a proof of principle. According to environmental microbiologist Ron Atlas, "If there's a lesson in this, it's that you can create a more virulent pathogen. In 99 percent of the cases you would not, but in others you can, and here's an example" (Broad 2001).

51. The objection is not fatal. Aum considered planting hundreds and perhaps thousands of spray devices inside attaché cases. The devices were apparently designed to release botulinum toxin (Wheelis and Sugishima 2006; Sopko and Edelman 1995).

52. A micron (μm) is one-millionth of a meter or about 1/5,000 inch.

53. Aum Shinrikyo's anthrax attacks reportedly failed because the group selected an avirulent, vaccine strain of anthrax (Wheelis and Sugishima 2006). Additionally, Aum's sprayers became clogged and/or produced a mist that was too large for efficient inhalation (Mangold and Goldberg 1999).

54. This would presumably be done by manipulating the natural variations in surface charge across organisms (see, e.g., Sobsey and Meschke 2003). Within naturally occurring species, some strains are known to be dramatically more viable as aerosols than others (Roy and Pitt 2006).

55. Anthrax spores can reportedly survive for hours in the wild and years when buried in soil (Zilinskas 2006).

56. The extreme difficulty of distributing plague forced the Japanese program to use fomites in the 1930s. The United States similarly tried but failed to make plague aerosols that could survive more than thirty minutes in the open air. The Russians reportedly persevered and eventually produced a plague weapon (Alibek and Handelman 1999). WHO's worst-case scenario assumes that the bacillus could remain viable for up to an hour (Inglesby et al. 2000).

57. Many viruses—and particularly negative strand viruses (Roy and Pitt 2006)—are significantly hardier than bacteria. Influenza viruses, for example, can reportedly last fifteen to thirty-six hours in aerosols (Sobsey and Meschke 2003) and roughly forty-eight hours on hard surfaces (Barry 2005). Similarly, Venezuelan equine encephalitis, a classical weapons

candidate, is said to be particularly resistant to ultraviolet ("UV") light and high temperature (Sobsey and Meschke 2003). That said, the survival rate for viruses in aerosols is complex and unpredictable. Relevant factors include virus strain and physical state (dispersed, aggregated, associated solids); temperature; whether the air contains particles or pollutants; aerosol droplet size; aerosol chemistry including pH, salts, proteins, and organic matter; and UV light. Humidity can either increase or decrease survival times, depending on the virus type. Virus survival times can also vary dramatically within the same family, genus, and even across otherwise similar strains (Sobsey and Meschke 2003).

58. Aum Shinrikyo's attacks arguably fit this mold, although these incidents could also be considered "tests."

59. Wheelis and Sugishima (2006) similarly report that a wet anthrax aerosol should contain at least 109 viable organisms per milliliter.

60. Fermenters larger than 20 liters and centrifugal separators capable of separating pathogens at rates exceeding 100 liters/hour are also subject to "dual-use" export controls (Commerce Control List 2B352b). Export controls can be surprisingly effective. During the late 1980s, the Iraqi state program sought to buy fermenters on the open market because it believed that building them internally would take too long. However, the transaction never received the appropriate export licenses. This delayed the Iraqi program even more (Pearson 2006).

61. This explains why real-world weapons are almost always less efficient than naive toxicity estimates would suggest. For example, the United States uses milled anthrax, which typically contains a large fraction of killed and damaged spores but has excellent size control, so that almost all surviving organisms fall within the required 1–5 μm size range. Conversely, the USSR used a freeze-drying process that kills very few spores but yields a highly nonuniform (1–50 μm) particle distribution (DeArmond 2002). Similar imperfections apply to toxins. The U.S. military's liquid SEB toxin is only 70 percent pure, and only 42 to 60 percent of this agent is in the desired size below 5 μm. This means that the weapon is only one-fourth (26 percent) as powerful as a naive calculation would suggest (Dando 2001).

62. These difficulties should not be exaggerated. A very small team of perhaps two dozen researchers learned how to grow and harvest anthrax between 1940 and 1942. The program reportedly grew anthrax using metal containers resembling milk churns and "harvested" spores using a vacuum cleaner–type arrangement. Bombs containing the weapon were successfully tested and ready to enter production by 1943 (Harris and Paxman 2002).

63. As previously noted, the resulting pathogens were ineffective. A more robust test program would arguably have allowed Aum to detect and fix this problem.

64. Second-generation tularemia vaccines later brought the U.S. Army's infection rate down to 0.03 percent (Dennis 2001).

65. In a few cases (e.g., melioidosis), the disease may not manifest itself for years (USAMRIID 2004).

66. This particular equation neglects gravity and assumes that every particle that collides with the ground stays there. Adding these effects is straightforward (Lucas 2006). Failure to model how particles are removed from the plume significantly overestimates concentrations at locations more than a few kilometers from the source. During the 1990s, this point was well

illustrated by the scholarly debate over whether an anthrax outbreak in Sverdlovsk came from a covert weapons plant. Messelson et al. (1994) argued that the observed casualties could have been caused by releasing just a few grams of material and were therefore consistent with a normal industrial accident. This result is typical of models that ignore collisions with the ground. Observers familiar with U.S. weapons programs disagreed, arguing that the observed casualties implied a release of up to ten kilograms (Wampler and Blanton 2001). Such estimates are typical for models that include ground collisions (Lucas 2006). Russian officials have since confirmed both that a weapons plant existed and that several kilograms were released (Guillimin 1999).

67. The estimate would also require knowledge of population density at each point within the plume. Densities would be particularly high for WMD attacks on large sporting events or built-up urban regions. For example, downtown Manhattan has a population density of approximately 70,000 people per square mile, although this would be "much higher" during the workday (Glasstone and Dolan 1977). On the other hand, much of the target population would be sheltered indoors. World War II–era planners believed that shelter effects were large enough that an optimal anthrax air raid would include 25 percent high explosive to break up structures (Harris and Paxman 2002).

68. The assumption that genetic changes are equivalent to, say, doubling the dose of a poison is reasonable for most simple modifications like increasing the amount of poison that a pathogen secretes or reducing its vulnerability to antibiotics. More complex modifications that change the synergy between organisms are harder to model.

69. Genetic engineering of contagious pathogens is potentially more rewarding but also more complex (chapter 4).

70. Urban smog provides a graphic illustration of this phenomenon.

71. Inversions are much less necessary for chemical weapons, almost all of which are significantly heavier than air.

72. Leitenberg (2005, unpublished lecture slides). Leitenberg also reports a 1986 U.S. government estimate that a submarine operating along an unspecified baseline would require 13,000 kg of dried anthrax to launch an attack on the United States. [Id.]

73. Defined as 1 psi peak overpressure.

74. For purposes of comparison, chemical explosions generate about twice as much blast as fission bombs, which spend more energy on creating heat and radiation (Glasstone and Dolan 1977). With this caveat, the discussion of blast in section 3.7 also applies to conventional explosions.

75. The two categories are not exclusive. Instead, some victims received fatal doses from both mechanisms.

76. This statement is only true for nuclear weapons that explode at ground level. The Hiroshima and Nagasaki bombs were both set to detonate at 1,670 feet above ground and produced negligible fallout (Glasstone and Dolan 1977).

77. Smaller particles linger in the atmosphere and are distributed over a large part of the earth's surface (Glasstone and Dolan 1977).

4

The New Bioweapons: Infectious and Engineered Diseases

George W. Rutherford and Stephen M. Maurer

Mid-twentieth-century state bioweapons programs were tightly focused on finding ways to deliver pathogens by aircraft and other conventional military systems. It is frequently assumed that terrorists would try to duplicate this work. However, this strategy is far from obvious. While classical state programs eventually developed technologies that could inflict WMD-scale casualties, success required decades-long, multibillion-dollar investments in learning how to disseminate organisms in the open air (Moon 2006; Hart 2006). Furthermore, attacks required facilities for manufacturing moderate (kilogram) to large (ton) quantities of agent (chapter 3). Despite declassification and general scientific and technological advances, experience with the Iraqi program suggests that these barriers still pose significant challenges even for middle-tier state programs (Pearson 2006). It is therefore reasonable to ask whether terrorists might decide to pursue different technological pathways. These alternative strategies would almost certainly use infectious and/or engineered pathogens.

The first strategy is very old. Contagious, or communicable, diseases are a subset of infectious diseases[1] in which the microbial pathogen causing the disease can be spread from person to person. At least in principle, a single infected individual can deliver contagious diseases to entire populations. This ability to self-propagate in human populations makes large manufacturing facilities unnecessary and also eliminates the very substantial R&D hurdles associated with learning how to aerosolize organisms and preserve them for extended periods in the open air. Twentieth-century weapons programs usually ignored this pathway for fear that epidemics, once started, would boomerang onto friendly populations and/or make conquered territories dangerous to occupy. However, Alibek reports that the Soviet Union believed that it could safely start epidemics in North America knowing that public health authorities would be able to contain the infection before it spread to Europe or Asia (Alibek and Handelman 1999). Terrorists might well make a similar calculation, or even decide that high numbers of "friendly" casualties were an acceptable price for destruction that could not be achieved in any other way. Pre-twentieth-century history offers numerous examples of intentional and semi-intentional use of biological weapons to inflict mass casualties.

The second strategy is much newer. Since the 1970s, genetic engineering has drastically increased researchers' ability to modify and confer new properties on microorganisms. In recent years, commentators have identified various genetic engineering projects that could potentially make it easier for terrorists to turn natural pathogens into useful weapons. Some scholars have also discussed "advanced threats" that would allow terrorists to create entirely new organisms. For each project, terrorists would have to decide whether genetic engineering's potential payoffs were worth the associated cost and risk of failure.

This chapter examines how terrorists could potentially use contagious diseases and/or genetic engineering to create WMD. Section 4.1 explores the reasons why twentieth-century state programs usually avoided contagious weapons, asks whether these constraints would similarly apply to terrorists, and introduces the three most plausible naturally occurring weapons candidates—smallpox, pneumonic plague, and hemorrhagic fevers. Section 4.2 reviews the complex biological and social factors that determine how contagious disease outbreaks spread. Section 4.3 reviews the various public health strategies that are available to counter outbreaks. Section 4.4 explains how epidemiologists use formal mathematical models to predict epidemics and examines the accuracy of such models. Section 4.5 reviews recent smallpox models. Section 4.6 looks at how genetic engineering could be used to modify existing pathogens or even create new ones, stressing the hurdles that would have to be overcome to create a predictable, useful weapon. Section 4.7 looks at the mirror-image question of how advances in biology could facilitate defense. Finally, section 4.8 presents a brief conclusion.

4.1   Do Contagious Weapons Make Sense?

Attempts to spread plague go back to at least the Scythians (400 BCE). More recent examples include deliberate attempts to spread smallpox by the Mongols (fourteenth century) and by the British in North America (eighteenth century) (Croddy, Perez-Armendariz, and Hart 2002). Strikingly, this pattern did not continue into modern times. Instead, the state weapons programs of the twentieth century focused on roughly a dozen pathogens, most of which had little or no potential for human-to-human transmission. This section examines the reasons why contagious organisms were not exploited and asks whether these constraints might be looser for terrorists. We conclude by describing the short list of naturally occurring contagious diseases that could potentially be used to make weapons.

4.1.1   Do Contagious Bioweapons Make Sense?

Military weapons are, in general, more demanding than terrorist ones. Here, we review the principal constraints on military weapons and comment on how they might be different, and in general looser, for terrorists:

Delivery methods   Military weapons must be capable of dissemination by aircraft or artillery. This usually limits the list of possible agents to organisms that can survive violent aerosolization; that can survive extended exposure to heat, ultraviolet light, and other harsh conditions in the open air; and that are capable of infecting victims through inhalation or skin contact. Terrorists can employ much simpler delivery systems that are also less stressful to the pathogen. Using infected individuals to spread contagion is technically straightforward and imposes negligible stress on pathogens.

Immediacy   Military planners need weapons that generate predictable effects on time scales that can be integrated with other weapon systems and troop movements. In practice, this means using organisms that reliably generate a high disease-to-infection ratio within a few days. Terrorists may have greater freedom to use agents that cause disease in the distant future or have unpredictable attack rates.

Targeted impact   Militaries need weapons that can be narrowly targeted onto specific regions for well-defined periods of time. This favors the use of diseases that have negligible potential for secondary transmission, that cannot survive for long periods in the natural environment, and/or that have available immunization or prophylaxis so that friendly personnel can be protected.[2] Terrorists may have greater freedom to the extent that they expect public health authorities to limit the spread of disease or are willing to accept high numbers of "friendly" casualties as an unavoidable consequence of inflicting damage.

Lethality   Military programs often prefer causing illness to death, since (1) temporary incapacity of opposing personnel is almost always sufficient, (2) nonlethal pathogens reduce political barriers to the use of biological weapons, and (3) mass illness tends to impose an enormous burden on enemy transport and medical services. Terrorists seeking a WMD capability could, by contrast, decide that they wanted to seek as many deaths as possible (chapters 1 and 2).

Mass production/storage   Military weapons must be available in large quantities to act as a deterrent, to support extended campaigns, and/or to overwhelm countermeasures by well-equipped enemy troops. For this reason, Soviet and U.S. weapons inventories were typically measured in metric tons.[3] In theory, terrorists would only need kilogram-scale quantities to mount a conventional aerosol attack on a civilian population. If terrorists used an infected human as the vector, subgram quantities would suffice.

These considerations suggest that terrorist bioweapons need not be limited to the traditional list of "select agent" pathogens that have been weaponized in the past. In particular, they open the door to contagious agents that could eliminate the need for elaborate manufacturing and delivery systems. In general, there are just three naturally occurring candidates: smallpox, pneumonic plague, and various hemorrhagic fevers

4.1.2 Candidate Agents

Smallpox is by far the most effective contagious agent. It is highly contagious and spreads through breathing or skin contact. After an incubation period lasting roughly two weeks, victims come down with fever and aches. A few days later, blisters (*vesicles*) appear, fill with pus, and then burst, causing painful itching. About 20 percent of all cases are fatal and survivors are commonly scarred for life. Although the disease has no clearly effective treatment, vaccines exist, and the World Health Organization was able to declare the disease eradicated in 1980. Today, the only known stocks are located at the U.S. Centers for Disease Control and Vector, a former weapons research facility in the Novosibirsk, Russia. However, there have been persistent reports that other nations, including North Korea (and formerly Iraq) may possess stockpiles (Croddy, Perez-Armendariz, and Hart 2002).

The second candidate pathogen, *Yersinia pestis*, the causative agent of *plague*, can be spread either through flea bites or through breathing ("pneumonic plague"). Untreated pneumonic plague is almost 100 percent fatal (Croddy, Perez-Armendariz, and Hart 2002). Unlike smallpox, plague is widely available as a reference strain in laboratories around the world. However, pneumonic plague is much less contagious and therefore less desirable as a weapon.

The third group of candidate pathogens consists of various *hemorrhagic fever viruses*, including Marburg, Ebola, and Lassa fever. Some of these have reportedly been explored as weapons agents in the past (Alibek and Handelman 1999; Croddy 2002) and there is some evidence for airborne transmission. That said, transmission is primarily through blood contact (Croddy, Perez-Armendariz, and Hart 2002), so that human-to-human transmission is mainly dangerous to medical workers, undertakers, and other narrowly defined groups. This limits the threat to the general population and makes it easier for authorities to implement simple precautions (e.g., gloves, face masks) once outbreaks are identified. Furthermore, natural outbreaks are rare and there are only a few highly specialized laboratories that handle these agents anywhere in the world. For this reason, the likelihood of a nonstate terrorist organization obtaining a propagating laboratory strain or else isolating the virus from naturally occurring cases is low.

Finally, it might also be possible for terrorists to *resurrect an extinct organism* or duplicate an otherwise tightly held organism like smallpox. In the late 1990s, scientists successfully extracted genetic material for 1918 influenza from autopsy specimens that had been embedded in paraffin and bodies buried in permafrost (Taubenberger et al. 1997). Using this material, they successfully cloned all eight fragments of the virus's genome and were able to reconstruct a virus that displayed the original strain's virulence and transmission characteristics (Taubenberger et al. 2005). It is reasonable to think that smallpox could similarly be resurrected from DNA in nineteenth-century smallpox scabs that were originally saved for use as vaccines (USA Today 2003).[4] More recently, scientists were able to reconstruct functional 1918 influenza using a manufactured DNA copy of the virus's published gene sequence (Taubenberger 2005; Tumpey et al. 2005). This was a substantial scientific undertaking, requiring highly sophisticated molecular biology and virology equipment and techniques. Furthermore, the smallpox genome is an order of magnitude larger than 1918 influenza and would be harder to synthesize.[5] That said, the 1918 influenza experiment was "not extraordinary" compared to other academic experiments and similar projects will almost certainly become easier as technology advances (Keasling 2007a).

4.2   Infectious Disease Epidemiology

Infectious disease epidemiology is the subspecialty of epidemiology that deals with the impact of microorganisms and their toxins in human populations.[6] As such, it provides the starting point for any attempt to estimate, say, the likely casualties from a contagious agent attack or the efficacy of public health countermeasures. Here, we briefly explore the many social and biological processes that determine disease transmission, morbidity, and mortality in human populations.

4.2.1   Transmission

Terrorists could initially introduce a pathogen through a variety of mechanisms including infected individuals, aerosols, fomites (objects that are inanimate like doorknobs or paper or organisms like flies that are uninfected but can spread pathogens to susceptibles), water, food, infected animals ("zoonotic diseases"), and even transfusion or implantation of infected blood or tissues. These inflict most of the casualties for classical military weapons. For contagious weapons, however, we expect most of the casualties to come from secondary transmission—that is, human-to-human transmission by the initial victims to others. Here, the main transmission mechanism is usually inhaling droplets expelled from victims' respiratory tracts.

4.3.2   Quarantine

Quarantine is the practice of limiting exposure to a potentially infectious person by limiting that person's movements; it is specifically used for persons who have been exposed to a contagious disease but have not (and may never) develop clinical disease symptoms. Like isolation, quarantine can be voluntary or mandatory. This range of interventions is often referred to as contact management.

4.3.3   Biological Controls

Biological controls include antimicrobial agents and immunizations. These can be given as therapies to people who have already been infected,[10] to keep people who have been exposed but are not yet sick from becoming infectious ("postexposure prophylaxis"), and to protect people who have not yet been exposed to infection ("preexposure prophylaxis"). All of these interventions work by stopping the pathogen from replicating in the body. Although postexposure prophylaxis has only been evaluated for a small number of pathogens, it is known to be effective for smallpox, measles, and rabies. In the case of smallpox, there are two possible immunization[11] strategies:

Ring vaccination   Authorities can form a ring of protective immunity around people known to be infected by vaccinating (1) close contacts of each known patient, and (2) the contacts of those contacts. This "ring vaccination" strategy works well where the number of infected patients is relatively small and is often used in the late stages of a smallpox elimination campaign.[12]

Mass vaccination   Ring vaccination becomes logistically difficult when smallpox has been introduced to the population through multiple carriers. At some point, it becomes easier to vaccinate the entire population. "Mass vaccination" refers to the vaccination of all susceptibles within a given county, state, nation, or other geographic area. Mass vaccination can be performed before exposure, as has been done for U.S. military and frontline health-care providers. Alternatively, it can be performed immediately after the first smallpox case(s) are identified. In the latter case, mass vaccination would include both postexposure and preexposure prophylaxis.

4.3.4   Infection Control in Hospitals

Many people infected by biological agents will seek medical care and be hospitalized. This makes infection control an especially important strategy for limiting transmission. Historically, hospitals have often been important amplifiers of various contagious diseases including smallpox, hemorrhagic fever viruses, and SARS. Hospital transmission can also cripple containment efforts by infecting badly needed health-care workers.

4.3.5 Community Responses

Various public health interventions are available at the community level to limit disease transmission. At the most basic level these interventions include information and education about simple hygiene—for example, covering coughs and washing hands. As transmission increases, public health authorities may also use additional, more intrusive measures to reduce contact between individuals. Examples of measures that can increase social distance are closing schools and day-care centers, canceling large public gatherings (e.g., concerts and sports events), asking nonessential workers to stay home, and scaling back public transportation. Many of these restrictions were successfully implemented during the 1918 influenza pandemic (Barry 2005). Other interventions used during the recent SARS outbreak, such as screening travelers for fever and distributing surgical masks, could also be considered. Yugoslavia adopted still more draconian measures to stop the spread of smallpox in 1972. These included curfews, closing mass transit systems, and imposing community quarantines that required all nonessential workers to stay home and that closed access routes into and out of affected areas (Radovanovic and Djordjevic 1979).

Community-level interventions are particularly important for diseases like smallpox that spread through the air and enter the respiratory tract. The acceptability of these methods will normally depend on several factors. These include the number of known cases, the number of people exposed, the existence of new cases that cannot be linked to previously known cases (suggesting that the outbreak is widespread), the number of generations of transmission that have already occurred, the disease's morbidity and mortality, the ease with which the organism spreads, the amount of movement in and out of the community, available response resources, and the risk of public panic.

4.3.6 Border Responses

These individual and domestic responses can be extended to include international measures. These include travel advisories, health alert notices, and caring for sick passengers. More intrusive activities potentially include screening passengers before departure and/or on arrival; quarantining travelers from areas with active outbreaks; restricting nonessential travel; and, eventually, closing international borders. The decision to take such measures would depend on factors similar to those already described.

4.3.7 The Historical Record

There is extensive experience with smallpox epidemics prior to the late 1950s. However, the most instructive example for current practice is probably a 1972 case in which a single infected individual arrived in Yugoslavia from the Middle East. The government took swift and decisive action, implementing a ring vaccination strategy that limited the outbreak to just 175 cases, including 35 deaths. Although moderately successful, this result could be misleading. First, the outbreak took place in a population that was routinely vaccinated (possessed herd immunity) and lacked widespread individual mobility. Today's U.S. population, by contrast, is highly mobile and possesses little if any herd immunity. Second, the government was forced to declare martial law within days of detecting the disease and imposed strict controls. These included quarantining up to 10,000 exposed people in requisitioned hotels, isolating entire villages, prohibiting public meetings, closing borders, and severely restricting travel. Yugoslavia also revaccinated its entire population—20 million people—within two months. Not surprisingly, these steps were intrusive and costly, and inflicted substantial harm on Yugoslavia's economy (Radovanovic and Djordjevic 1979; Barrett 2006).

More recent experiences in Africa, Europe and South America show that hemorrhagic fever outbreaks can also be chaotic and costly. When Ebola first appeared in Zaire and the Sudan in 1976, more than 600 cases were identified in rural hospitals and villages, roughly 70 percent of which were fatal. Further outbreaks followed in the Sudan in 1979, Kitwit, Zaire, in 1995, and Gabon in 1996 and 1997. The two Gabon outbreaks produced 98 cases and 66 deaths (Washington State Department of Health 2002). However, all of these outbreaks took place in remote settings in developing countries with little medical or public health infrastructure. For this reason, they may not be very predictive of what would happen in an industrialized country.

Finally, public health agencies' experiences with pneumonic plague are relatively encouraging. Despite occasional cases of bubonic plague and very rare cases of pneumonic plague in the United States,[13] there have been no mass outbreaks in modern times. That said, an intentional attack would differ in at least one crucial respect: terrorists might well be able to send multiple infected carriers against the target country simultaneously. Since local public health departments typically depend on state and national support to cope with outbreaks, an attack at multiple locations would tax and could at some point overwhelm these resources. Multiple attacks would also increase the chances that so-called superspreader diseases would grow into epidemics, a point we return to in the next section.

4.4 Contagious Disease Models

The starting point for all contagious disease models is the "mass action principle"—that is, the spread of disease in a population depends on the rate of contact between susceptible and infectious individuals (Last 1995). We have seen that this apparently simple statement encodes a variety of complex concepts, both social ("contacts") and biological ("susceptible," "infectious"). Simple mathematical models do not necessarily capture these factors well (Lloyd-Smith et al. 2007; Halloran 1998; Aparicio and Pascual 2007). Nevertheless, it is traditional—and often effective—to reduce this complexity to a single basic reproduction number, R_0. This is defined as the number of new persons who would be infected by a single infectious host in the absence of control measures (Last 1995; Dietz 1993):

$$R_0 = [\text{Susceptible contacts per unit time}] \times [\text{Transmission probability per contact}]$$

$$\times [\text{Duration of infectiousness}] \qquad (4.1)$$

If R_0 is less than 1.0, transmission will stop after a few generations. When $R_0 = 1$, one case of infection leads to exactly one new case. Such diseases are said to be "endemic" because the population can support them indefinitely without exhausting the pool of susceptibles. Finally, pathogens that possess values of R_0 greater than 1.0 grow exponentially and propagate widely throughout the population. Absent control efforts, these epidemics do not end until the pool of susceptibles is exhausted. In general, typically quoted R_0s average about 1.5 to 10 for smallpox (Aldis and Roberts 2005; Ferguson et al. 2003) and are close to 1 for pneumonic plague.

It is important to note that R_0 refers only to the susceptible portion of a population. The susceptibility of a population to an infectious agent is related to the concept of "herd immunity." Formally, herd immunity is defined as the product of (1) the fraction of a population that is susceptible to infection, and (2) the probability that a susceptible will be exposed to a pathogen. Where herd immunity is widespread, infected individuals are unlikely to encounter enough susceptibles to sustain transmission. One would expect terrorists to pick agents for which herd immunity is largely nonexistent apart from specially vaccinated populations like the military and first responders.

4.4.1 Accuracy

Mathematical models are reasonably accurate for familiar diseases like measles, where it is possible to extract R_0 empirically from public health data. Such methods would work less well for pneumonic plague and some of the less studied hemorrhagic fevers, for which empirical data are scarce or nonexistent. In this case, R_0 would have to be estimated using a combination of animal studies and analogies to known diseases. Smallpox presents an intermediate case. Although historical data exist into the 1950s, outbreaks took place at a time when American society was far less mobile than it is today. Even more importantly, disease transmission was damped by a very high herd immunity value. Since the United States stopped vaccinating its population against smallpox in 1972, today's herd immunity is probably close to zero. We will see that modern authors frequently use a wide range of R_0s when modeling smallpox, and that this accounts for much of the disagreement in their predictions.

4.4.2 Superspreaders

We have already remarked that a great deal of biology and social information is compressed in the number R_0. More sophisticated models try to improve classical techniques by identifying particularly important components of R_0 and promoting them to the status of independent variables. For example, traditional models have assumed that infected persons excrete the same number of organisms and are equally infectious. Recently, however, researchers have found that accuracy can be improved for some diseases by noticing that a small minority of infected individuals are *superspreaders*—that is, they excrete more microorganisms and infect far more susceptible individuals than the average infectious patient.[14] This phenomenon was observed in the 2003 SARS outbreak (Bassetti, Bischoff, and Sherertz 2005; McDonald et al. 2004). While SARS is an extreme case, patients suffering from smallpox and to a lesser degree pneumonic plague also display substantial variations in infectivity (Lloyd-Smith et al. 2005).

On average, superspreader models predict that a single infected carrier would cause fewer casualties than simple R_0 analyses would suggest. However, the models also predict rare, explosive outbreaks in those instances where the earliest cases happen to include multiple superspreaders (Lloyd-Smith et al. 2005). This provides another reason why terrorists might want to send multiple infected individuals into a country. The more initial contacts, the better the chances that at least one exposure will grow fast enough to cause an epidemic.

Finally, not all susceptibles are equally likely to come into contact with infected persons. In principle, these social networks can be modeled using complex computer simulations. We will encounter examples of these models in the next section.

4.5   Modeling Smallpox

Since September 11, epidemiologists have worked hard to model bioweapons attacks, estimate the number of casualties that would be inflicted, and assess public health strategies for mitigating them. Not surprisingly, most of these studies have concentrated on smallpox, with its large R_0. Here, we evaluate the state of the art by reviewing and contrasting recent models.

4.5.1 Model Types and Parameters

Mathematical models have been extensively used to simulate the effects of smallpox outbreaks and control strategies. The variables that enter into these models include:

Reproduction number The reproduction number (R_0) is usually employed as an empirical value derived from earlier experience with natural smallpox outbreaks. We have seen that it includes multiple social and biological factors and may be difficult to estimate where historical data are thin.

Population size The population where transmission will occur is usually assumed to be fixed—for instance, a city or state. In the case of an actual smallpox outbreak, however, these political boundaries would be meaningless short of total quarantine.

Background immunity This includes everyone in the population who is not susceptible. As an epidemic progresses and people recover or die, the pool of susceptibles becomes smaller unless new susceptibles enter the population.

Social mixing Modelers use various measures of social mixing. These can be either static (i.e., do not change as the epidemic progresses) or dynamic (i.e., changing over time as people try to limit exposure).

Generation time This is the amount of time that a primary case takes to infect secondary cases and is commonly denoted T_G. The longer T_G, the more easily the outbreak can be detected in its early stages.

Simple Models Simple models (for example, the so-called SIR model) divide the population into susceptible, infected, and recovered members and assume that (1) each susceptible has an equal risk of becoming infected (i.e., the spread is homogeneous), and (2) all infected individuals have a constant and equal probability of transmitting infection to susceptibles (Anderson and May 1991; Bailey 1967). These assumptions lead to chain reactions: one primary case exposes R_0 susceptibles, who then develop disease, and so on (Ferguson et al. 2003). In these models, transmission continues until the susceptible population is so depleted that R_0 falls below 1.0. Mathematically, these models are expressed by the following equation:

$$y = e^{(R_0 - 1)/T_G t}$$

where y denotes the number of infected individuals at any given time. For smallpox, T_G is typically twenty-one days, the duration between exposure and initial infectiousness in naturally occurring smallpox. R_0 typically is in the four- to ten-day range (Gani and Leach 2001; Eichner and Dietz 2004). As described above, a larger R_0 means that there are more secondary cases so that a larger proportion of the population is infected.[15] For the parameters associated with smallpox, simple models predict attack rates approaching a remarkable 100 percent in the absence of control measures.

However, these results are only as good as the assumptions we have just described. Assumption 1 is clearly an approximation since the existence of social networks means that most people's contacts are disproportionately centered on a relative handful of contacts (e.g., family members and coworkers). For this reason, it is not true that any given individual in society has an equal chance of coming into contact with any other person. Assumption 2 is similarly a poor approximation for smallpox. Instead of being constant, infectiousness steadily decreases between the early, prodromal virus-shedding phase and the final crusting over of skin lesions.

Advanced Models   Two types of modifications are usually added to make these basic models more realistic (Koopman 2003). The first simulates the biology of smallpox by introducing a noninfectious incubation period of twelve days, followed by a hyperinfectious prodromal period of two to four days and a less infectious symptomatic phase lasting about nine days until all lesions are crusted over. In this third phase, patients would most likely be hospitalized and unlikely to come into contact with more than a few medical personnel (Bregman and Henderson 2002; Dixon 1962; Eichner and Dietz 2004).

The second class of modifications tries to make the simple picture of social contact encoded in R_0 more realistic by adding parameters that reflect social and geographic variables—for example, the much greater intensity of home and work contacts compared to the average casual encounter and susceptibles' efforts to avoid exposure as an epidemic progresses (Eidelson and Lustick 2004). Ferguson, et al. (2003) list six types of sociospatial models:

Homogeneous mixing   All susceptible persons in a population are assumed to have equal probability of coming into contact with an infectious individual.

Age/social structure   Specific population subgroups (e.g., school-age children, health-care workers) are assumed to have higher probabilities of exposure.

Network structure   Social networks focus risk disproportionately on friends, family, and coworkers. In general, the smaller the network the faster the epidemic exhausts itself.

Patch models   Natural population aggregations like cities are assumed to be a proxy for high-contact probabilities. Conversely, contacts between cities are assumed to be low probability.

Individual-based models   These highly complex and computationally intensive models use algorithms to simulate the behavior of tens and even hundreds of thousands of individuals. This leads to predicted contacts between individuals that spread disease.

Deterministic and stochastic models   Deterministic models, also known as clockwork models, calculate outcomes from macrolevel data inputs. Stochastic models recognize that transmission is random and take account of individual behavior changes and changing levels of infectiousness.

4.5.2   Uncertainties

In general, the more variables a model has the more uncertain it becomes (Bailey and Duppenthaler 1980; Halloran 1998). We have already noted that some parameters can be inferred from historical observations. Even in these cases, however, parameters based on prior outbreaks may not be relevant because they were measured at a time when much of the population was vaccinated and routine control measures, such as infection control in hospitals, were less sophisticated than they are today (Dixon 1962; Fenner et al. 1988). Other parameters—especially those involving complex social contacts—cannot be extracted from historical epidemics and must instead be estimated from external sources like surveys and social science data. Finally, terrorist attacks would likely be more complex than earlier outbreaks that started with a single infected individual. For example, terrorists could start outbreaks by exposing an entire crowd to aerosols or else sending multiple infected individuals into a country. Parameter values would be particularly uncertain under these new and unfamiliar conditions. In principle, such scenarios could also introduce new dynamics that invalidated one or more of the simplifying assumptions that researchers have grown accustomed to using in natural outbreak models.

One way to estimate these uncertainties is by using sensitivity analysis—that is, calculating the range of predicted outcomes for a range of plausible inputs. The analysis of Elderd, Dukic, and Dwyer (2006) is typical. After estimating the uncertainty in their various inputs, they find it equally probable that mass vaccination would save 100,000 or 200,000 lives.

4.5.3   Control Measures

The underlying purpose of these models is to evaluate possible interventions, including

• Quarantine of exposed susceptibles and isolation of infectious symptomatic patients
• Movement restrictions, such as curfews, quarantine of cities, and closure of airports
• Ring vaccination of susceptibles who have had contact with known cases (occasionally referred to as "trace vaccination")
• Targeted vaccination of population subgroups, such as cities, workplaces, or schools
• Mass vaccination of entire populations, up to and including nations

Table 4.1
Predicted deaths, serious illness, and vaccinations from three initial smallpox cases, United States

Control strategy	Vaccinations	Serious illness*	Deaths	
			Small-pox	Vaccine
Ring strategy	4,600	93	19	0
Ring strategy plus postoutbreak vaccination of 90% of all health-care workers	164,600	101	18	1
Ring strategy plus preoutbreak vaccination of 90% of all health-care workers	9,104,600	532	18	25
Ring strategy plus preoutbreak vaccination of 90% of all health-care workers and postoutbreak vaccination of 60% of public	11,004,600	680	11	33
Ring strategy plus preoutbreak vaccination of 90% of all health-care workers and preoutbreak vaccination of 60% of public	177,004,600	9,183	2	482

* Serious illness from both smallpox and vaccination
Source: Bozette et al. 2003

• Prophylactic (that is, preexposure) vaccination of population subgroups such as health-care workers up to entire populations after an outbreak starts

Bozzette et al. (2003) provide a typical example of this approach. They present a stochastic model of how smallpox would spread through mass transit systems that includes three different R_0s (15.4 in hospitals, 3.4 in mixed settings, and 1.8 in community settings). They then ask how much benefit ring vaccination, mass vaccination, and prophylactic vaccination of health-care workers are likely to offer beyond simply isolating known cases and the susceptibles who have been in contact with them. Depending on the public health response, they conclude that an attack that started with 3 initial cases, each of which produced 5 secondary cases would ultimately inflict anywhere from 2 to 19 deaths and 93 to 9,183 serious illnesses (table 4.1).

Because Bozette et al.'s predicted outcomes differ by two orders of magnitude, their finding that preoutbreak vaccination is counterproductive seems robust despite the fact that their detailed predictions could change substantially for different input values. This shows that models are a valuable way to compare different control strategies (and combinations of control strategies) including vaccination, contact tracing, isolation, and quarantine. At the same time, sophisticated models require

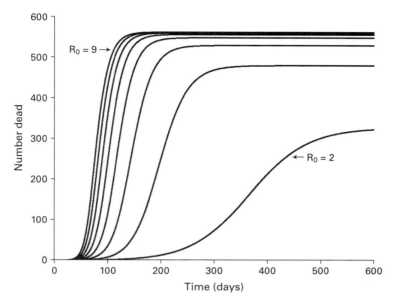

Figure 4.1
Sensitivity analysis showing how predictions of Elderd et al. (2006)'s smallpox model depend on assumed values of R_0.

substantially more parameters than simple ones. This makes their predictions just as vulnerable to uncertainties in estimated parameters, and perhaps more so.

4.5.4   Summing Up

Despite six years of concerted effort, smallpox model predictions remain very uncertain. Part of this uncertainty is well understood and can be traced to choice of input parameters, particularly R_0. As shown in figure 4.1, even advanced models tend to be uncertain by roughly a factor of two depending on how R_0 is chosen. However, there is also a deeper uncertainty. At least for now, advanced models are very sensitive to the details of how processes like social networks, smallpox biology, and community size are assumed to function. For this reason, it is still common for authors of successive models to disagree about such basic points as how best to contain an epidemic and whether control efforts would work (Cooper 2006). It remains to be seen whether future work will resolve these disagreements. In the meanwhile, systematic uncertainties associated with choice of model could be just as important as our limited knowledge of R_0, especially in an age where there is very, very little immunity in the population.

4.6   Genetically Modified Weapons

Mid-twentieth-century state programs made extensive use of classical microbiology methods to modify naturally occurring pathogens into suitable weapons. Since the early 1970s, molecular biology techniques have made such modifications easier and potentially opened the door to more ambitious projects.

4.6.1   Scenarios

Traditional genetic engineering involves transferring genetic material from one organism to another. This can be done in vivo by taking advantage of naturally occurring transfers between organisms. Alternatively, transfers can also be performed in vitro by mechanically separating DNA from its host bacteria or virus, using enzymes to cut and later reconnect the molecule, and then reinserting the modified molecule into a suitable bacterial host (Alexander 2001). Early technologies, including those used by Soviet weapons designers in the 1980s, were limited to inserting/manipulating relatively small islands of DNA ("plasmids") (Alibek and Handelman 1999). More recent technologies also allow researchers to modify the much larger collections of DNA or RNA within chromosomes and to manufacture increasingly long strands of artificial DNA and RNA in whatever sequence is desired.

Many authors have suggested strategies for making genetically engineered weapons. In its modern form, the literature begins with revelations that the former Soviet Union devoted massive resources to creating genetically engineered weapons in the 1970s and 1980s (Hart 2006). These accounts reached their definitive form in defector Ken Alibek's bestselling memoir *Biohazard* (Alibek and Handelman 1999).[16] Alibek's original claims listed six projects that he had either participated in or known about as a senior administrator for the Soviet weapons program. Additional weapons possibilities have been suggested by an influential JASONS[17] study and the U.S. National Research Council's widely cited Fink Report (NRC 2004). While not exhaustive, the combined list includes most commonly cited threats. These are, in roughly increasing order of difficulty:

1. *Manufacturing toxins*   Western drug companies routinely modify bacteria and/or create transgenic organisms to produce drug precursors and vaccine proteins (Petro, Plasse, and McNulty 2003). A priori, designing organisms to make toxins should not be significantly harder. Alibek reports that Soviet scientists modified bacteria to secrete toxins that damage myelin, the coating around nerve cells, in the mid–1970s (Alibek and Handelman 1999).

2. *Multidrug resistance*   Many antibiotic resistance genes are well known and could be inserted into pathogens. The Soviet program reputedly created an anthrax

strain that was resistant to five separate drugs (Alibek and Handelman 1999; NRC 2004).

3. *Resurrecting pathogens*   Scientists have recently demonstrated the ability to make functioning viruses from manufactured DNA (Cello, Paul, and Wimmer 2002; Tumpey et al. 2005). This potentially allows them to obtain organisms that are otherwise extinct (1918 influenza) or else only exist in a few highly guarded collections (smallpox) (NRC 2004).

4. *Safer weapons*   Manufacturing and delivery could be made safer by creating binary weapons in which plasmids from two different, separately benign organisms were combined to create a lethal pathogen hours or days before use (Block 1999).

5. *Evading diagnostics*   Organisms could potentially be engineered to evade existing diagnostic and detection methods. This could be done by changing the pathogen's surface proteins or by creating an entirely new and unfamiliar organism (NRC 2004; Block 1999). In principle, a long-latency "stealth" virus could be delivered years before it was triggered by some external or internal signal (Block 1999). Pathogens could also be engineered to present unusual clinical symptoms that would be overlooked or misdiagnosed (Petro, Plasse, and McNulty 2003).

6. *Vaccine resistance*   Organisms could potentially be engineered to evade existing vaccines. Possible methods include altering the pathogen's surface coat or conferring an AIDS-like ability to continually alter itself over time (NRC 2004; Block 1999; Petro, Plasse, and McNulty 2003).

7. *Increased transmissibility*   Organisms could be engineered in ways that facilitate transmission. This could be done, for example, by inserting the lethality of one organism (e.g., Ebola) into a much more communicable pathogen (e.g., measles) (NRC 2004; Block 1999).

8. *Altering host range*   Pathogens could be modified so that they could infect and cause disease in new species. This could include, for instance, modifying successful animal pathogens so that they became infective in humans (NRC 2004).

9. *Greater morbidity and mortality*   Alibek claims that Russian scientists made an existing pathogen (plague) still deadlier by adding DNA that allowed it to secrete myelin toxin (Alibek and Handelman 1999; NRC 2004). He has also speculated, more controversially, that Russian scientists successfully combined DNA from smallpox and Ebola to make a new organism that combined both diseases (Alibek and Handelman 1999).[18] Since Alibek, other authors have suggested that essentially new organisms could be designed to target the human cardiovascular, immune, neurological, gastrointestinal, or other systems. In principle, these agents could be optimized to cause cancers, sterilization, or debilitation (Petro, Plasse, and McNulty 2003).

10. *Easier propagation and distribution*   In principle, organisms could be engineered with respect to size, surface charge, and hardiness so that they could better survive aerosolization and exposure to the environment. Organisms could also be optimized for other delivery methods (e.g., survival in processed foods) that state programs have traditionally neglected (NRC 2004; Block 1999).

11. *Gene therapy weapons*   In principle, viruses could be designed as vectors to carry novel DNA into victims'—and in some cases their progeny's—genomes. This could be done either to cause injury or to confer immunity on a particular population (Petro, Plasse, and McNulty 2003; Block 1999).

12. *Targeted weapons*   In principle, organisms could be selectively targeted against particular groups because of genetic or cultural traits, or else made self-limiting so that they could turn themselves off after a fixed number of generations (Block 1999; Petro, Plasse, and McNulty 2003).

The question remains how difficult such projects would be. Following normal practice, we divide our discussion into two groups. We first consider "genetically modified agents" that add a small number of modifications to naturally occurring pathogens. We then discuss "advanced biological threats" that reengineer organisms so extensively that they become, in effect, de novo pathogens (Petro, Plasse, and McNulty 2003).

4.6.2   Genetically Modified Agents

In general, items 1 through 4 can be accomplished by adding, at most, a few genes to preexisting organisms. Many of these strategies have already been demonstrated by commercial and academic research. Nevertheless, significant obstacles remain.

First, the work requires significant *expertise*. Some genetic engineering technologies, notably including the ability to make familiar organisms like *Escherichia coli* drug resistant, have been widely described and (in some cases) are even available in kit form. However, extending these methods to weapons pathogens would require significant originality and skill. Even more ambitious experiments—including, for example, making artificial polio and 1918 influenza viruses—are "not extraordinary" for a well-equipped academic laboratory. They would, however, require extensive tacit knowledge. Even for academic laboratories, good technicians are indispensable (Keasling 2007a). That said, the formerly high level of expertise needed to do even simple experiments is clearly eroding. Recent advances have made genetic engineering methods simultaneously more powerful (e.g., by allowing researchers to manipulate chromosomal DNA) and more accessible (e.g., by allowing researchers to replace complex cloning experiments with artificial DNA sequences). Furthermore, basic biotechnology skills are spreading rapidly throughout the world.

Second, even talented workers often need months and sometimes years of *trial and error* to succeed. The resulting time and expense depends on how difficult it is to screen for and isolate the desired property. At one end of the scale, antibiotic resistance is relatively easy—workers simply grow organisms in the presence of antibiotics and culture those that survive.[19] Despite this, 1980s-era Soviet efforts to produce multidrug-resistant weapons diseases required years of concerted effort[20] and such projects are likely to remain challenging for even the most technically sophisticated substate groups.[21] Projects that tried to select for more complicated properties (e.g., secreting toxins; evading vaccines) would require manual experiments by trained technicians and would be broadly similar to commercial programs that reengineer bacteria to manufacture drug compounds. Such biotech ventures typically require multiyear, multimillion-dollar investments.

Third, many otherwise successful modifications would produce unintended side effects (*pleiotropy*) that compromised infectivity and other important characteristics. Because genetic engineering produces precise changes in the genome, this risk is probably smaller than for traditional microbiology-based breeding methods. Nevertheless, it remains substantial (Keasling 2007a; Tiedje et al. 1989).[22] Unless terrorists were willing to accept this risk, some form of animal testing (ideally outdoors) would be necessary. More complicated projects—for example, reengineering multiple surface proteins to avoid vaccines—would require several simultaneous gene insertions. This would geometrically increase the chance that at least one modification was pleiotropic or even fatal to the organism (Keasling 2007a).

Fourth, expressing novel traits almost always costs energy or interferes with normal metabolic pathways. This fact implies that a large percentage of organisms would be less fit (*hardy*) than the parent organism (Tiedje et al. 1989).[23] While this does not matter much for organisms that live in carefully managed environments (e.g., a production vat), weapons pathogens must routinely cope with a far harsher and more variable environment. Furthermore, complex natural environments are hard to simulate in the laboratory. This means that many problems would remain undiscovered without field testing (Tiedje et al. 1989). Experience with commercial projects suggests that overcoming these barriers would be expensive. Despite substantial resources, for instance, commercial efforts to create genetically engineered organisms for in situ remediation of contaminated sites have produced very few successful field trials (Keasling 2007a; Alexander 2001). While regulatory burdens are certainly part of this story, even programs with dozens of researchers and multimillion-dollar budgets find it hard to create bacteria that can survive in wild.[24]

Fifth, genetic modifications would need sufficient *stability* to reach victims. Even if an engineered trait reduced fitness only slightly, evolution would still work to suppress it over many generations. Because bacteria have short life spans, engineered traits could easily disappear over the weeks- to months-long time scales needed for manufacturing, storage, and incubation in victims (Tiedje et al. 1989). As with earlier microbiological techniques, stability would have to be confirmed by testing. On the other hand, researchers' ability to design stable organisms is slowly improving.[25] Stability constraints would be especially important for contagious diseases that were expected to operate through multiple generations of victims.[26]

Sixth, many weapons would require nontrivial *scientific advances*. Some of these have been (and will continue to be) supplied by normal academic research.[27] For example, there is relatively little experience with growing and manipulating most pathogens. For this reason, terrorists might have to work with *E. coli* and then hope for transfer afterward (Keasling 2007a). Similarly, a binary weapon based on combining two preexisting nonpathogenic agents to make a pathogen would have to be extremely replicable under field conditions. Substantial new R&D would be needed to reach this goal.

Finally, most of the foregoing challenges would be even harder for *contagious* organisms. For instance, it is relatively straightforward to insert toxin genes into a previously benign organism. However, it is much harder to regulate the level at which the toxin is expressed. A contagious organism would have to be carefully tuned so that the victim lived long enough to infect others (Keasling 2007a).

4.6.3   Advanced Biological Warfare Agents

More advanced weapons would require terrorists to manipulate behaviors controlled by multiple genes (items 5–8, 10), extract substantial amounts of DNA from two genomes to create a fundamentally new, third organism (items 9, 11), or program computerlike behaviors that focused pathogens on narrowly defined targets (item 12). Achieving these goals would require scientists to successfully insert dozens and perhaps hundreds of genes into organisms. Given that each inserted gene carries with it some risk of failure (e.g., pleiotropy), we would expect the overall failure rate to rise at least geometrically in the number of genes being transferred. In fact, the problem is probably harder than that since the new genes might also interact with one another and/or exhaust the number of locations where genes could be inserted without damaging the host. This latter problem would be particularly acute for viruses, which pack a long list of essential functions into very short genomes. Inserting multiple genes into these systems would almost certainly kill the organism (Keasling 2007a).

The fact that difficulties rise steeply does not make such projects impossible. For example, one recent commercial project appears to be well on its way to reengineering bacteria so that they can make precursor chemicals for the drug artemisinin. The completed organism will contain more than two dozen transferred DNA segments (Keasling 2007b). This, however, is a $43 million, three-year effort.[28] Recent R&D to create a genetically engineered AIDS vaccine by adding HIV surface antigens to a nonpathogenic virus (canary pox) are similarly reported to have cost roughly $50 million (Donald Francis, personal communication). Producing a predictably infectious engineered organism that can reliably reproduce inside a host would be similarly expensive. On the other hand, complex organisms will almost certainly become easier to make over time. Advanced synthetic biology experiments have already shown that it is possible to insert dozens of DNA fragments (genetic "parts") into organisms, and this number is steadily growing.

4.6.4 A Predictable Weapon?

Previous sections have emphasized epidemiological models' limited ability to predict casualties for smallpox and other agents that have caused outbreaks in the past. These predictions would be still harder for genetically modified weapons. In an epidemiological sense, inserting antibiotic resistance into a preexisting pathogen would probably be the simplest modification to model. This is because the engineered organism would still have the same portal of entry, tissue tropism, ID_{50}, case-fatality ratio, and incubation period. In this case, the main uncertainty would come from the lack of effective treatments. This would increase both the secondary attack rate and basic reproductive number by ensuring that victims remained infectious longer. These, however, are relatively simple effects and could be modeled semiempirically. More complicated changes—for instance, increasing an organism's virulence—would require animal testing. Even in this case, however, analogy would still be useful for engineered organisms that resembled an unusually powerful strain of the original pathogen.

The same could not be said of advanced threats that produced qualitatively new organisms by, for example, combining smallpox and Ebola within a single chimeric organism (Alibek and Handelman 1999). Such organisms would require extensive animal testing before they could be characterized. Even then, there would be substantial questions as to how reliably their effects could be predicted. For instance, pathogens that had been engineered to kill quickly might not propagate successfully if hosts did not live long enough to infect others. Similarly, some engineered pathogens might be so genetically unstable that they would rapidly mutate as they passed through a series of hosts, possibly even becoming less virulent. These uncertainties would make predictions very precarious, both for terrorists trying to invent an efficient weapon and for governments designing mitigation strategies.

4.7   Advanced Technology Defenses

The preceding section suggests that bioengineered weapons are probably beyond the reach of today's terrorists. On the other hand, it is impossible to be sure of this and, in any case, the good news may only be temporary. It is therefore prudent to ask whether modest R&D investments could improve society's defenses in the foreseeable future. Meeting the threat of existing or engineered organisms requires three general classes of technology: detectors for locating organisms in the environment, diagnostic devices for locating organisms in clinical specimens drawn from patients, and various possible countermeasures including active or passive immunization and therapeutics.

Detector technology is needed first and foremost to know when and where organisms have been released into the environment and second to understand their geographic dispersion. Much of this technology already exists (chapter 5), but would have to be improved to detect radically reengineered strains or entirely new species. Here, the principal challenges are to make existing technologies more nimble and affordable, so that detectors for previously unfamiliar strains (and even species) can be developed quickly and then manufactured and deployed fast enough to make a difference. In practice, this means extending today's very powerful and flexible laboratory technologies (e.g., PCR) so that they are affordable in much larger numbers, no longer depend on highly trained technicians, and are sufficiently robust to operate for long periods in the field. Additionally, current detection methods usually rely on clinical samples from humans and environmental samples of air, water, and soil. These capabilities could readily be extended to detect novel or genetically engineered organisms in animals besides humans. Animal sampling is already a standard public health measure for many zoonotic pathogens, including plague, rabies, and West Nile virus.

Diagnostics for detecting pathogens in clinical specimens would also be necessary. Here, the main challenge is to improve on traditional—but also slow and expensive—classical microbiology methods for growing previously unknown organisms from culture and tissue. This will require better technologies for designing, manufacturing, and deploying diagnostic kits for previously unknown pathogens fast enough to make a difference. Fortunately, this goal is very similar to the one facing detectors, so that the two technologies are likely to reinforce one another. For now, current state of the art relies on using panels of antibodies and/or gene microarrays to detect organisms that share substantial characteristics with known microbes. These methods were instrumental in detecting West Nile virus and SARS, respectively (Rota et al. 2003). Future progress will depend on extending these techniques so that scientists can detect more distantly related (or genetically modified) organisms. In scientific terms, success will probably require greatly expanded efforts to catalog the genes that cause virulence. This will allow researchers to find subtle similarities that can be used to develop signatures that even very highly modified organisms are likely to share.

Finally, *potential countermeasures* include immunizations, disinfectants, and therapeutic drugs. Current trial-and-error methods for developing *immunizing agents* still require months to years. For now, the fastest methods rely on pooling serum from a large number of patients to collect antibodies that confer passive immunity. This largely 1920s technology is still the mainstay of our treatments for toxin-producing organisms like diphtheria, tetanus, and botulism. In principle, advances in genetic engineering could deliver designer agents in a much shorter time frame. This, however, may not be possible for many years. Until then, public health strategies like the U.S. pandemic influenza doctrine (HHS 2005a) will continue to rely on traditional public health measures to delay emergence long enough so that pharmaceutical companies can develop immunizations and antiviral drugs.

Finally, new organisms would likely require *new drug treatments*. Here, the quickest response would be to test existing antibiotic and antiviral drugs to see whether they (or their chemical cousins) were effective against the new agent. These tests could likely be done using high-throughput screening techniques in culture and and/or combined with ongoing patient care. A potentially more powerful approach would be to search the new organism's genetic sequence for targets that could be attacked using novel (or, more likely, adaptations of existing) drugs. For now, however, the power of these "rational drug design" methods remains limited despite very large investments by private pharmaceutical companies. Comparatively small additional investments by homeland defense agencies are unlikely to change this picture.

4.8   Conclusions

It is reasonable to worry that terrorists, unlike state programs, would consider using naturally occurring contagious WMD agents. Of these, smallpox is by far the most dangerous. As we have seen, models predicting how many Americans would be killed in a smallpox attack remain very uncertain. The good news is that smallpox stocks are held almost as tightly as nuclear weapons. In the long run, however, terrorists may be able to resurrect smallpox from manufactured DNA. At this point, ring- and mass-vaccination programs could once again become the country's first line of defense against smallpox. Restored public health funding will be essential in supporting these efforts.

Terrorists could also pursue genetically engineered weapons. The technology for modifying not only smallpox but other, more readily available organisms is becoming increasingly available. A few modifications—for instance, drug resistant pathogens—would not be particularly difficult or expensive for modern academic or commercial laboratories. However, most would dwarf September 11's $500,000 cost and/or Al Qaeda's $30 million annual budget (9/11 Commission 2004). Terrorists would need a dramatic payoff to pursue such projects. This may not exist. Natural agents are so exquisitely evolved that engineered organisms have only limited room for improvement. Terrorists trying to acquire a traditional, military-style bioweapons capability will often find that other, less exotic methods of improving lethality—for example scaling up production facilities or designing more efficient sprayers—are more cost-effective.

The intersection between genetic engineering and contagious disease is more worrisome because it offers bigger payoffs. On the other hand, we have seen that genetic engineering projects are inherently risky and that these risks are compounded by epidemiologists' limited ability to predict how new pathogens will behave. Terrorists may have limited patience for multiyear, multimillion-dollar investments that include a significant chance of failure, particularly when the potential failure takes forms (e.g., a zero-casualties attack) that are humiliating and invite ridicule. Given that bioweapons already seem to be a fairly marginal R&D investment for terrorists, even modest public policy interventions (e.g., better screening of artificial DNA purchases and modest restrictions on "dual use" experiments) could yield important benefits.

Notes

1. The term *infectious diseases* refers to the class of diseases caused by microbial pathogens and their naturally occurring biological toxins.

2. Alibek reports that the Soviet program occasionally relaxed these requirements by, for example, weaponizing smallpox and working with agents for which no immunization existed (Alibek and Handelman 1999).

3. Alibek has claimed that the Soviet Union valued production over storage because it planned to use bioweapons early in a general war (Alibek and Handelman 1999).

4. Terrorists could not, however, culture virus from the scabs. After more than century, the virus would almost certainly be dead (USA Today 2003).

5. Influenza has about 18,000 base pairs. By comparison, Ebola has 70,000 base pairs and smallpox has 180,000 base pairs. The smallpox genome has been sequenced and is publicly available online at, for example, the University of Victoria's Viral Informatics Resource Center, http://athena.bioc.uvic.ca/poxviridae/data/NC_001611.gbk.

6. Epidemiology refers to the study of the distribution and determinants of disease and other health events in populations and the application of this knowledge to disease control and prevention (Last 1995).

7. Hosts can be humans, animals, plants, or other microorganisms. In this chapter, the word *hosts* will normally refer to humans.

8. Not all symptoms are specific. Fever is caused by the immune system and felt throughout the body. Furthermore, some infections do not cause any symptoms (i.e., disease) at all. These are said to be "asymptomatic" and can only be diagnosed through laboratory tests.

9. Human immunodeficiency virus (HIV) is a particularly notorious example.

10. Immunizations are seldom given therapeutically.

11. The term *immunization* is a general term and refers to the use of an immunizing agent (either a whole microbial organism, inactivated biological toxins, or microbial proteins) to acquire and/or enhance (boost) a host's immunological protection against a particular micro-organism or toxin. The term *vaccination* refers specifically to immunization against smallpox with *Vaccinia* virus.

12. Postexposure vaccination is practical because the immunizing agent in smallpox vaccines, *Vaccinia* virus or cowpox, has a short incubation period. Because it replicates faster than smallpox, *Vaccinia* administered shortly after exposure can stimulate a protective immune response before smallpox is widely disseminated in the body. This allows vaccination to block both clinical disease and (presumably) the viral shedding that gives rise to infectivity.

13. According to CDC statistics, ten to twenty cases of plague were reported in most years between the mid-1970s and the mid-1990s (CDC 2003).

14. Individuals probably also differ in their susceptibility, either because they possess partial biological immunity or engage in behaviors that decrease their exposure. Modeling how behaviors change as the public learns of epidemics tends to introduce even more uncertainty.

15. The R_0s used in models tend to be slightly higher than those quoted in section 4.4. This produces an intentionally extreme (and therefore conservative) case for testing public health responses.

16. Many Western biologists have expressed skepticism about Alibek's more spectacular claims (Titball 2004).

17. The JASONS are a semiofficial group of leading academic scientists who advise the U.S. Department of Defense on emerging threats and new technologies (Block 1999).

18. Petro, Plasse, and McNulty (2003) have similarly suggested that transgenic insects could be made to secrete powerful toxins.

19. The technique can also be used without genetic engineering. In this case, the antibiotic-resistant strains would be supplied by random mutations and natural selection instead of deliberate attempts at gene insertion.

20. Soviet programs quickly made anthrax resistant to a single antibiotic in the 1970s but thereafter failed to create a triply resistant tularemia strain despite ten years of "endless repetition." However, Alibek claims that breakthroughs in the mid-1980s allowed the program to create a fivefold resistant anthrax strain by 1989 (Alibek and Handelman 1999).

21. Alibek and Bailey (2004) have estimated that terrorists would need three to four years to engineer drug-resistant or more virulent pathogens.

22. One recent survey identifies a total of eight research projects to create genetically modified organisms capable of surviving and propagating in the environment. So far, only one of these has reached the field trials stage (Angulo and Gilna 2008).

23. In a few cases, unplanned changes would actually increase fitness. This, however, would be an exception to the rule (Tiedje et al. 1989).

24. Such risks would be alleviated for bacteria released into favorable environments like warm, nutrient-rich freshwater streams (Cruz-Cruz et al. 1988).

25. Perhaps the most important recent advance is the advent of techniques that allow researchers to insert DNA into the relatively stable chromosome instead of plasmids (Keasling 2007a; Panke et al. 1999).

26. Perfect stability would not be required. Even 1918 influenza became dramatically less lethal over time scales of less than a month (Barry 2005).

27. Recent examples include papers showing how viruses can be made to overcome vaccine-induced immunity (item 6), modified to attack a new target species (item 8), modified to kill infected cells more effectively or evade the immune system (item 9), and better survive airborne transmission (item 10) (Smith, Inglesby, and O'Toole 2003).

28. It is also worth noting that the engineered organism, though stable, will be sheltered within a carefully controlled industrial environment.

5

The Indispensable Technology: Detectors for Nuclear, Biological, and Chemical WMD

Simon Labov and Tom Slezak

For most of us, the enduring image of the Cold War is one of massive ICBM and bomber fleets threatening each other with mutual assured destruction. In that world, most weapons were overt, so that the ability to detect hidden WMD was secondary. People tend to forget, however, that there was a still earlier era in which detection was vital. In the decade that followed Einstein's 1939 letter warning President Franklin D. Roosevelt about the possibility of a Nazi atomic bomb, policymakers worried constantly about nuclear weapons hidden in the holds of freighters or even suitcases. Given the limits of contemporary detection systems, they were right to do so. As Robert Oppenheimer told a closed Senate hearing in 1946, the only way midcentury America could defend against a smuggled atomic bomb was to use a screwdriver to open each and every crate and suitcase entering the country (Metzger 2005).

Six decades later, the emerging threat of WMD terrorism has moved the focus squarely back to clandestine and/or unconventional delivery systems. Proposed defensive strategies invariably include five common elements: (1) deterring terrorists who might otherwise try to acquire or use WMD, (2) thwarting terrorist attempts to obtain WMD and related materials, (3) detecting and interdicting covert attacks, (4) mitigating the effects of an attack, and (5) attributing attacks to a specific perpetrator so that action can be taken to forestall future attacks. Of these, the first three strategies depend almost entirely on authorities' ability to detect hidden nuclear and biological materials, while cheap, ubiquitous sensors are an important supporting technology for the fourth. Finally, we will see that attribution also depends on detection technologies. Together, these considerations make detection technology a key part of any defense strategy.

This chapter asks how far sensor technology has come since Oppenheimer's day. Since the end of the Cold War, and particularly since September 11, there has been an aggressive push to develop and deploy improved sensors. Today, these efforts are starting to bear fruit. Section 5.1 provides an overview of the various types of nuclear, biological, and chemical sensors that are needed. Section 5.2 describes nuclear detectors, starting with basic physics and proceeding through today's applications as well as hardware still under development. Section 5.3 provides a similar account for biological sensors, and section 5.4 describes chemical sensors. Section 5.5 provides an overview of how these same detection technologies can be used to forensically attribute attacks to a specific perpetrator. Finally, section 5.6 presents a brief conclusion.

5.1   Basic Sensor Missions

Despite obvious commonalities, nuclear, chemical, and biological sensors differ in important ways. First, detection challenges vary over five orders of magnitude, ranging from hundreds of kilograms for chemical WMD to far less than a gram for contagious biological agents. This suggests that preattack detection is easier for some weapons than others. Second, existing nuclear, chemical, and biological detection technologies have very different capabilities. In the case of nuclear and chemical sensing, laboratory instruments date back more than a century and in many cases have been further developed for military use. Here, the challenge is to adapt a mature technology to make it cheaper, more portable, and less dependent on trained technicians. Modern biological sensing, on the other hand, began with PCR in the late 1980s and is still evolving. For this reason, detector R&D often involves much more basic research compared to chemical or radiation threats. Finally, modern assays have little difficulty distinguishing chemical agents from everyday materials. By comparison, bioweapons pathogens often circulate naturally in various environments and are sometimes extremely similar to related but harmless organisms. Nuclear methods fall somewhere in the middle, but tend to be similarly challenged by everyday materials.

5.1.1   Nuclear Sensors

Nuclear terrorism defense starts from the assumption that no screening technology is perfect, let alone immune to countermeasures. This point was underscored in September 2002, and again in 2003, when ABC News shipped 6.8 kg of depleted uranium from overseas through U.S. port inspection facilities without being detected.[1] More generally, the fact that single-point defenses are imperfect shows that a layered, defense-in-depth approach is needed. (Shea 2008) Figure 5.1 provides a generic illustration of nuclear detection systems currently being deployed across the United States. In addition to large fixed detectors at seaports and land crossings, the system also includes perimeter protection of selected cities and airports as well as mobile detectors mounted in patrol cars and portable units.

The idea of layered defenses demands many different kinds of sensors. These can be summarized as follows:

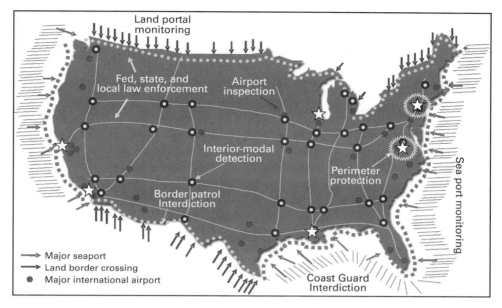

Figure 5.1
A generic detector architecture

Container inspection Very large, fixed sensors are needed to inspect ocean-borne cargo containers. The units must process containers quickly while distinguishing threats from a dizzying assortment of legitimate cargoes (e.g., bananas, leather) that have similar signatures. Moreover, follow-up inspections are labor intensive and cause expensive delays. This means that false alarms cannot exceed a few percent. Detection systems that monitor cargo containers while in transit are also under investigation. Because these detectors can accumulate data for extended periods over the course of a voyage, they can potentially provide high sensitivity. Current challenges include deciding how to distribute sensors so that they can monitor the large number of containers aboard a typical containership and finding ways to investigate an alarm in closely stacked containers that may not be accessible until the ship reaches port.

Border monitoring These large and relatively immobile sensors are needed to inspect cars and trucks for nuclear and/or radiological materials at international borders. Vehicles must be processed quickly with a minimum number of false alarms.

Nuclear material safeguards These medium-sized sensors are used to keep people from smuggling nuclear material out of controlled sites. Here, the technological problem is simplified by the fact that the target materials are known in advance.[2]

Improved sensors have been an important component of the Department of Energy's Materials Protection Control and Accounting Program (MPC&A).

Mobile search devices   A layered defense must search for materials even after they enter the United States. Possibilities include land/sea search, random checkpoints, and unannounced, semipermanent monitoring locations. These applications require detectors that can be readily transported by aircraft, vehicles, and backpacks over large geographic areas.

Portable detectors   Border guards and port inspectors need handheld units to conduct follow-up inspections. Law enforcement similarly needs such units to search packages and investigate suspicious conditions in the field. Unfortunately, the sensitivity, accuracy, and range of existing small detectors are limited.

Consequence-management sensors   Following an attack, authorities would need to screen people and objects for contamination. These tasks require detectors that are cheap, abundant, and easy to use. On the other hand, relatively high false-alarm rates may be tolerable if portable detectors are available to check results.

Ubiquitous detectors   In principle, permanent sensor networks could provide surveillance over large geographic areas. Such networks will only be practical, however, if units are cheap, require limited or nonexistent maintenance, and can operate as a network without generating too many false alarms requiring human intervention. Ubiquitous sensor networks would also provide valuable support for consequence management if an attack occurred.

In addition to these physical considerations, some detectors also face special legal and political hurdles. For example, Prosnitz (2005) has suggested that WMD detectors—particularly those that examine private citizens and their possessions—may sometimes raise search-and-seizure objections under the U.S. Constitution. Overcoming these problems could force engineers to design systems that intentionally ignore and/or discard certain types of data (Prosnitz 2005). Additionally, policymakers may decide that certain classes of detectors—notably large fixed sensors and consequence-management sensors—cannot be justified unless they can also be used to detect drugs and other nonnuclear targets. This tends to favor technologies that generate images (e.g., x-rays) over more specialized technologies that focus exclusively on, say, fissionable materials.

5.1.2   Biological Sensors

The nation's basic biodefense doctrine is set forth in Homeland Security Presidential Directive HSPD–10. While the doctrine's announced "pillars"—"Threat Awareness," "Prevention and Protection," "Surveillance and Detection," and "Response and Recovery"—are reminiscent of the nuclear arena, the emphasis is different. On the one hand, pathogens are so easy to hide that pre-attack surveillance is usually unrealistic. On the other, sensors can provide early warning that an attack has occurred. Early detection dramatically increases the odds that patients will be correctly diagnosed and treated. In the case of contagious diseases, it also materially increases public health authorities' ability to isolate infected individuals.[3]

As with the nuclear threat, biological detectors have multiple distinct applications:

Pathogen surveillance   Surveillance networks watch for pathogens before victims show symptoms. Widespread deployment requires cheap, autonomous detectors that can distinguish bioweapons pathogens from natural disease and similar-but-benign organisms in the environment. This information will often be complemented by disease surveillance networks that collect patient health information from doctors and hospitals.[4]

First responders   First responders need to know immediately whether a biological weapon is present. Current methods based on growing cultures from an initial sample are much too slow for this work. Rapid protein tests, similar to home pregnancy tests, are also available but tend to have excessive numbers of false positives.

Environmental detection   Once an attack is detected, handheld and portable detectors will be needed to supplement pathogen surveillance data so that the affected areas can be mapped. In most cases, operators will be unskilled or have only minimal training. Detectors must be affordable, able to detect pathogens at extremely low or even single-organism levels, and offer reasonable false-alarm rates.

Consequence-management surveys   Authorities must be able to determine, confirm, and announce safe zones where life can proceed as normal. Today's most sensitive pathogen diagnostic methods are all based on DNA. This means that they cannot distinguish viable pathogens from dead ones. New technologies that test for viability will be needed to fill this gap. Beyond this, different pathogens are infectious at different doses and acceptable exposure levels for humans are often controversial.[5] Authorities have yet to set standards specifying when it is safe to reoccupy an attack site—that is, "How clean is clean enough."

Medical diagnostics   Civilian doctors may not recognize weapons pathogens the first time they see them in patients. New diagnostics can fill this gap by routinely searching for these agents. Although pathogen assays exist for environmental detection, none have received FDA approval for routine use in humans and licensing requirements are strict. Moreover, simply identifying the pathogen is not enough— diagnostics will also be needed to characterize the organism (e.g., strain, virulence, drug resistance) so that authorities can design treatment regimens and public health responses. For now, the most effective method is to sequence the attack strain's genome. However, this often requires several days and faster characterization methods are needed.

Forensic diagnostics   An attack using select agents would be a federal crime if not an act of terrorism or war. Authorities will want as much information as possible about the origin of the strain, how it was grown, the presence of genetically engineered enhancements, how it was weaponized, and where and when it was produced.

Unlike the relatively static nuclear detection problem, biodetector needs are evolving and reflect a technological arms race with terrorists. While today's major threats are almost certainly limited to a dozen or so naturally occurring pathogens, genetic engineering—whether performed by natural evolution or by terrorists—is bound to produce new and increasingly unfamiliar threats over time (chapter 4). Furthermore, advances in synthesizing very long (genome-scale) strands of DNA will eventually open the door to designer threats that do not exist in nature. Future detectors may have to recognize and characterize threats that lack clear, existing templates.

5.1.3   Chemical Sensors

Most chemical weapons work in minutes, although a few can inflict injury after delays lasting up to a day. This suggests that chemical sensors must normally work within minutes:

Warning   The military has long used sensors so that soldiers can protect themselves. In principle, such systems could similarly warn the public to evacuate or take shelter. However, current false-alarm levels are still too high for civilian use. Existing detectors are also expensive and require human operators. These drawbacks limit deployment to prominent high-value targets like subways and airports.
First responders   First responders need rapid, portable detectors to detect when geographic areas, physical objects, and/or victims are contaminated. Ideally, the devices should identify specific agents so that responders can take appropriate action (e.g., announcing evacuation radii, injecting survivors with atropine).
Diagnostics   Inexpensive diagnostics are needed to triage "worried-well" victims and estimate how much agent patients have been exposed to.

Like biological weapons, the list of classic chemical agents is relatively short. Designing sensors versatile enough to detect the long list of civilian compounds will be much harder.

5.2   Nuclear Detection

Nuclear detectors have a long laboratory history. Furthermore—and unlike biological or chemical detectors—they can sometimes detect threat materials up to 100 meters away. This section reviews the basic physics behind these devices, their existing capabilities, and current R&D programs designed to improve them (Medalia 2008).

5.2.1   Detection Physics

All nuclear and radiological materials are radioactive—that is, spontaneously decay over time. This decay produces four types of readily detectable particles: gamma rays, neutrons, electrons, and alpha particles.[6] The number of particles emitted as a function of energy is called the *spectrum* and the ability of detectors to measure this relationship is called *energy resolution*. Gamma ray spectra typically show "bumps" at energies where radionuclides emit their characteristic gamma rays, and the ability of a gamma ray detector to distinguish these characteristic energies is determined in part by the detector's energy resolution. More specifically, a detector is said to have "1 percent resolution" when the number of measured gamma rays included within the range of energies at half maximum can be measured to within 1 percent of the bump's height. Resolution for many common detector materials (e.g., NaI(Tl) scintillator) is—at best—about 6 percent.[7]

Electrons and alpha particles are absorbed so readily that they do not travel far even in air. This usually makes them useless for detection. In principle, *gamma-ray spectra* provide a unique fingerprint that can be used to separate threats from common materials that contain small but detectable amounts or radioactivity like potash or kitty litter. However, real detectors are imperfect and need 1 to 2 percent energy resolution to unambiguously distinguish weapons materials (plutonium, enriched uranium) from dirty-bomb materials (e.g., medical isotopes or industrial moisture gauges) and/or benign substances (e.g., bananas). *Neutrons* provide a second possible probe. Unlike gamma rays, their spectra are not sufficiently distinct to identify specific substances. On the other hand, most everyday materials emit no neutrons at all. This makes neutrons a useful confirming signal when nuclear materials are detected.

Gamma ray and neutron spectra are degraded (or blocked entirely) when they travel through matter. For this reason, gamma ray detectors have a range of about 100 meters in the open air and a few meters for cargo. In principle, terrorists could use this fact to screen nuclear weapons or dirty bombs from detectors. This is why it is important for any detection system to include multiple sensors providing different types of information. For example, a lead box could be used to keep most gamma rays from leaving a source. However, this probably would not be enough to block neutrons unless an additional polyethylene or water shield were added. By this point, the shielding's combined weight and volume would make it vulnerable to other detectors, including truck scales or weigh-in-motion systems that work without requiring vehicles to stop.

Passive detectors measure emitted particles without disturbing the sample in any way. However, detection capabilities can usually be increased by using *active interrogation systems* that bombard samples with X-rays, gamma rays, or neutrons. *Radiography* is the oldest and simplest example of such systems. Like ordinary medical X-rays, radiographic detectors bombard targets with X rays or gamma rays and then measure how many emerge from the object. Ideally, dense objects can be detected from the shadows they cast. That said, radiographic images can be highly ambiguous when containers are filled with unknown materials in arbitrary configurations. Taking images at different energies and/or source-detector geometries alleviates but does not eliminate this problem. In principle, computer processing can turn this information into 3-D or "tomographic" images similar to medical CAT scans.

Active interrogation systems can also bombard targets with neutrons or gamma rays so that their contents briefly become radioactive. This inevitably produces a slight (if temporary) increase in the cargo's radioactivity. On the other hand, the induced signal is usually much larger and easier to detect than natural radioactivity alone. This means that sensors can use less expensive detectors, take shorter exposures, and/or detect materials that normally lack detectable radioactivity. In general, bombardment produces two signals: (1) neutrons and gamma rays are immediately produced at rates and energies characteristic of the target, and (2) emission rates change over time in ways that can be used to distinguish plutonium, say, from highly enriched uranium. Simple systems based on the former principle have existed for several decades, but can only detect fissionable materials when they are unshielded and located within a few tens of centimeters of the detector. Systems based on the latter principle typically watch for the radioactivity expected when nuclear materials decay into daughter and, after a characteristic delay, granddaughter, and great-granddaughter isotopes ("fission-chain signatures"). However, these signals are usually weak. For this reason, current systems based on this principle are usually expensive and/or yield large numbers of false alarms.[8] Further improvements will require fundamentally new signatures, a subject we return to in section 5.2.3.

5.2.2   Current Technology

Current systems can be usefully categorized by size. At the upper end of the scale, *portal monitors* are large, fixed facilities that operate around the clock to screen cargo, vehicles, and pedestrians as they pass through an entryway. Because the units are used continuously, they routinely detect radioactivity from benign shipments. This means that operators must conduct follow-up investigations to decide which alarms are genuine. For this reason, the cost of such systems is often dominated by the staffing requirements. *Mobile detection systems* and *backpacks* are significantly smaller. These vehicle- and pedestrian-mounted units are designed to conduct surveillance over large areas and are typically more affordable and have lower installation costs. However, they also tend to be less sensitive (although sometimes more discriminating) than portal monitors. Small, *handheld* devices are used for follow-up investigation when larger detectors find a threat. They are cheaper and less sensitive than larger devices. Finally, *radiation "pagers"* are pocket-sized or belt-mounted devices that warn when a source is nearby and/or measure personal exposure. They represent the ultimate in today's small, inexpensive radiation detectors.

Portal Monitors   On an average day, 360,000 vehicles, 5,100 trucks, 2,600 aircraft, and 600 vessels enter the United States at 621 U.S. border crossings. Approximately 2,400 radiation portals would be needed to screen these goods in a commercially reasonable way. The U.S. Customs and Border Protection Agency is currently in the process of deploying portals and monitors to screen vehicles and containers at a large number of locations, including international mail and express consignment courier facilities, land and rail crossings, seaports, and international airports (figure 5.2).[9]

Most ports of entry currently use nonintrusive inspection systems that combine portal monitors with 2-D gamma ray radiography systems for capturing images. While these systems are effective, more advanced instruments can significantly improve sensitivity and reduce false-alarm rates. For example, DHS is currently deploying "Advanced Spectroscopic Portals" (ASPs) that combine portal-style radiation monitoring with gamma ray spectroscopy. This latter capability provides information that currently requires secondary inspection with handheld detectors. While a recent GAO report suggests that the ASP's capabilities may be limited, this could be premature since testing has only just begun. DHS is also developing the "Cargo Advanced Automated Radiography System" (CAARS) to provide clearer and more diagnostic radiographic images. Next-generation detectors are likely to reflect various improvements, including better spectral resolution, tomographic imaging, advanced pattern recognition software, and/or systems that allow operators to transmit ambiguous images to experts for further examination.

Finally, today's portal units are expensive and very cumbersome to move. However, falling prices will eventually allow ports to deploy portal units in greater numbers. New units designed for quick deployment to arbitrary locations will similarly open up roles that are not practical today.

Mobile Detection Systems and Backpacks   Existing mobile detection systems have limited sensitivity. This restricts the rate and range at which they can detect bomb-scale quantities of nuclear material. Furthermore, most current systems (1) cannot measure the detailed gamma ray spectra needed to unambiguously identify dangerous materials, and (2) do not record the direction of incoming gamma rays. These conditions increase the number of false positives while limiting operators' ability to rapidly prosecute detections to a successful conclusion.[10] *Backpacks* have similar limitations, but are also excessively heavy and bulky. Future progress will require

(a)

(b)

(c)

Figure 5.2
Current portals and radiography systems: (*A*) radiation detection portals, Port of New York/
New Jersey; (*B*) radiation monitors, U.S./Canadian border; (*C*) mobile radiography system.

detectors that are more sensitive, have better spectral resolution, and can record the direction of incoming gamma rays.

Handhelds and Pagers *Handheld units* typically use sodium iodide gamma ray detectors whose energy resolutions ($\sim$7 percent) are only marginally sufficient to identify radionuclides. Portable germanium-based detectors ($<$1 percent energy resolution) are also available. These are more expensive, bigger, and heavier, but identify radionuclides far more accurately. The main problem with current handheld devices is that, inevitably, their detector area is limited. This limits sensitivity, range, and the ability to identify radionuclides. Furthermore, germanium-based detectors must be cooled to approximately $-280°$F. This requires liquid nitrogen or onboard electromechanical refrigeration that makes the units heavy, bulky, and expensive. Improved detector materials will be the key to overcoming these problems.

For now, *pager detectors* are the ultimate in low cost and miniaturization. Not surprisingly, their range is limited and most are not designed to identify specific radionuclides. As a result, their role is usually limited to personal protection. DHS is currently developing an "Intelligent Personal Radiation Locator" (IPRL) that will include radionuclide identification, directional information, GPS data, and real-time reporting over wireless networks (Rennie 2004). Further order-of-magnitude improvements in cost and reliability could lead to very small *ubiquitous detectors* for use in shipping containers or along sensitive perimeters (e.g., ports). Ideally, such detectors could also be deployed in large numbers to provide geographic coverage over wide areas.

5.2.3 Next-Generation Technologies

We have seen that existing systems are physically cumbersome, expensive, and seldom exploit more than a handful of the possible physics clues (e.g., energy spectra, direction, 3-D imaging) described in section 5.2.1. However, current R&D programs could fundamentally improve these capabilities. If support for these efforts continues to grow, several transformational improvements in nuclear detection capabilities are likely in the next ten years, with some prototype systems being rolled out for testing and evaluation within three years.

Key improvements are likely to include use of new signatures to improve existing detectors' discrimination against challenging nuclear materials like highly enriched uranium. New detector materials may also allow the deployment of cheaper and more sensitive sensors ranging from ubiquitous pocket-sized devices to large vehicle-mounted search systems. Lightweight, efficient systems that image gamma rays and even neutrons would provide further breakthroughs by telling operators where sources are located and providing additional clues for discriminating threats from benign materials and background radiation. Finally, all of these advances will be further leveraged through "knowledge engineering" systems that turn data and measurements into comprehensive, real-time analyses that can be used by inspectors in the field and the trained experts who support them from remote sites.

New Signatures   Most existing signatures for identifying radioactive materials were originally developed for academic laboratories blessed with abundant technical talent and expensive instrumentation. These facilities usually needed methods that offered extreme accuracy and enough flexibility to study a wide range of nuclear and nonnuclear materials.

Security applications, by contrast, favor signatures that can be implemented with primitive equipment to detect a comparatively short list of threat materials. For example, most nuclear detection systems have traditionally used signatures based on spectra (energy) and spatial (location and size of sources) information. However, research is now underway to exploit previously overlooked, temporal signatures including the arrival times of neutrons and gamma rays. By definition, all fissile materials used in nuclear weapons must be able to sustain a chain of fission reactions. These chain reactions produce neutron and gamma ray bursts that are so distinctive that even very faint signals can be used to detect fissile materials that have been shielded in ways that challenge conventional methods. Norman et al. (2004) have developed another temporal signature by noticing that neutrons bombarding fissionable materials tend to produce an excess of delayed gamma rays compared to other materials. Better still, the excess occurs over such a wide range of energies that cheap plastic scintillator systems can detect it. Norman et al. (2004) calculate that it should be possible to build portals exploiting the principle for roughly $2 million/unit.

Finally, engineers are beginning to explore a wide choice of possible new probes. These potentially include high- and low-energy neutrons, high-energy x-rays ("photofission" and "nuclear fluorescence"), and even cosmic rays. Collectively, the probes offer a wide assortment of possible signatures, including prompt and delayed gamma rays and neutrons. Many would also elicit useful spectral and directional information.

Improved Sensors: Price and Performance   Fundamental improvements in cost and sensitivity will almost certainly require better detector materials. The working goal is to find sensor materials with 2 percent energy resolution at a reasonable cost. Systems should also be light, compact, and usable by nonexperts in harsh environments. Current research tends to be focused on scintillator and semiconductor materials.

Scintillator materials emit light pulses when struck by gamma rays. Currently, most large commercial detectors use polyvinyl toluene (PVT) plastic. Although cheap (less than $1/cm^3) and rugged, the material has very poor energy resolution (~30 percent). By contrast, single-crystal NaI(Tl) scintillators provide marginal (6 to 8 percent) energy resolution but cost ten times as much. Next-generation performance will probably turn to lanthanum bromide (LaBr$_3$(Ce)) and strontium iodide (SrI$_2$(Eu)) crystals that provide 2 to 3 percent energy resolution (Shah et al. 2004; Cherepy et al. 2007). Commercial R&D programs are working hard on these crystals, although existing samples cannot yet match the size and price of NaI(Tl).[11] Meanwhile, early stage research is underway on still better candidates. For example, SrI$_2$(Eu) offers a light yield in excess of 100,000 photons/MeV (more than twice that of NaI(Tl)), as do LuI$_3$(Ce) and CaI$_2$(Eu). However the latter two crystals are currently difficult to grow even in small sizes due to fundamental phase transitions and are therefore probably not viable (Moses and Shah 2005). Other possibilities include ceramic oxide transparent ceramics (Yanagida et al. 2005; Cherepy et al. 2007; Hull et al. 2007) such as lutetium and gadolinium garnets. Although their luminescence spectra are not well matched to standard photomultiplier tubes, it may be practical to read them out using silicon photodiodes.

Unlike scintillators, *semiconductors* turn gamma rays directly into electrical signals. The current leader, high-purity germanium (HPGe), offers excellent spectral resolution (<0.5 percent) but must be cooled to an operating temperature near −280°F. This has not stopped industry from offering mechanically cooled detectors for various applications, including even handheld units (Ortec n.d.; Canberra n.d.). Not surprisingly, the units are heavy and consume large amounts of power, although R&D is currently underway to improve size, weight, battery life, and cost. Even so, room-temperature detectors would be a big improvement. For now, semiconductors made from CdZnTe ("CZT") alloy are probably closest to commercialization. R&D is still needed, however, to improve limited service lives, background noise, and small crystal size. Price, performance, and crystal size are also issues for various competing compounds including CdTe, HgI$_2$, AlSb, GeTe, and CdMnTe.

Improved Sensors: Imaging   In principle, gamma rays are detectable up to 100 meters away. However, sensors large enough to detect sources from this distance often have trouble distinguishing real signals from natural fluctuations in background radiation. Historically, this has limited some detector systems to a disappointing 10-meter range (Ziock and Goldstein 2002; Ziock and Nelson 2007). Recently, however, researchers have shown that the full 100-meter range can be restored by using imaging systems to resolve the ambiguity (Ziock et al. 2006).

DHS is currently developing a "Stand-Off Radiation Detector System" ("SORDS") prototype based on this technology. Commercial versions should deliver radically increased speed and sensitivity within several years.

Imaging with gamma rays is a real challenge. Unlike light rays, conventional lenses and mirrors cannot focus gamma rays. The traditional strategy, *narrow field collimators*, uses a slit in a thick shield. This casts a shadow so that the detector only records gamma rays arriving from certain directions. Although widely used for medical imaging, the method is wildly inefficient and cuts the gamma ray signal by a factor of 10,000. This is unacceptable for search and surveillance systems, which need to detect sources at a great distance. Heavy shielding also limits the technology's usefulness in aircraft.

Two new methods are currently being developed to eliminate these sensitivity and weight penalties. *Coded-aperture systems* let gamma rays pass through a shield with multiple holes and then use powerful computer algorithms to untangle the resulting shadows into a usable image (Fenimore 1978). Unlike traditional methods, a "coded-mask" shield only blocks about 50 percent of all gamma rays. This saves weight and increases sensitivity. A still more advanced technology, *Compton imaging*, dispenses with shields altogether by allowing incoming gamma rays to strike gas, liquid, and/or solid targets so that they produce a cascade of multiple, low-energy daughter particles. Computer processing is then used to reconstruct the original gamma ray's energy and direction from the cascade (Todd, Nightingale, and Everett 1974). Compton imagers can be lighter and more sensitive than coded-aperture systems, but are considerably more complex. However, systems have already flown on NASA satellites (Schonfelder et al. 1993) and prototypes are now being developed for field use.

5.3   Biological Detection

R&D initiatives aimed at producing civilian biodefense sensors began in the mid–1990s and accelerated dramatically after the 2001 anthrax attacks (NRC/Committee on Materials and Manufacturing Processes 2004). On the other hand, the urgency and funding of these programs seems to have declined somewhat in recent years. This probably reflects the absence of any significant bioweapons attack since 2001.

Accurate biological detection of pathogens depends on recognizing enough DNA or protein to uniquely identify the organism. Unfortunately, most current DNA methods begin by extracting genetic material from the organism and therefore killing it. This means that they cannot determine whether the organism was alive or dead at the time of sampling. The main advantage of most protein detection techniques is that they target proteins on the surface of the organism and avoid the need for an extraction step.[12] This lets researchers find out whether the organism is alive and also makes detection faster. Unfortunately, common protein techniques are usually at least 1,000 times less sensitive than typical DNA methods. Protein detection techniques based on mass spectrometry can be very precise, but are expensive and require specialized equipment.

New pathogen detection systems based on identifying unique DNA or protein regions typically pass through several R&D phases. First, the system's specific *mission* should be well defined and known in advance. Examples include environmental detection, patient diagnosis for treatment, forensic analysis, and food/water safety. At this point, researchers must define pathogen *signature(s)* from among the organism's unique DNA or protein region(s). These should be chosen in light of the mission. In practice, a single DNA or protein region can yield many different potential signatures. Depending on the mission, these signatures typically have between one and six components. Finally, researchers must develop and define *assay* procedures to exploit the signature(s). These typically include specific *detection chemistries* and instruments (*implementation platforms*). In practice, the mission will usually determine which detection chemistries and platforms are used. These choices are usually limited since most platforms can only support one or, at most, a very limited number of detection chemistries. For example, four signatures for *Bacillus anthracis* could easily run on a handheld device. However, BioWatch detectors—which require very low false-alarm rates—need several dozen signatures and this favors platforms based on multiplexed assays. Finally, applications that require more than 100 signatures usually require microarray technologies, Microarray devices can, in turn, be usefully subdivided into "planar" formats in which test molecules are attached to a motionless surface and "liquid" formats in which they are attached to tiny styrene beads that are carried along in a moving stream. Systems based on the latter format tend to have faster readouts and are more easily reprogrammed, but they are also more expensive.

Finally, operators need a clear understanding of what should be done when the assay(s) produce nonnegative results. Ideally, this should be codified in a *Concept of Operations (CONOPS)* that has been defined from the very beginning as part of the mission. Typical issues include deciding what detection levels are needed before local public health officials, the CDC, and/or the media should be notified. The CONOPS should also address broader issues about when and how authorities will decide on responses (e.g., quarantine) and how these will be implemented. Significantly, the existence of a CONOPS does not necessarily mean that authorities will follow it, as when an apparent near neighbor of *Bacillus anthracis* was detected at the Salt Lake City airport during the 2002 Winter Olympics Games. Despite four sets of confirmatory tests showing that virulent *Bacillus anthracis* was not present, reports that there might be a problem were quickly leaked to the international media (BBC 2002).

Success in these activities requires many different disciplines. These include *bioinformatics* to analyze pathogen and near-neighbor genomes and proteomes to design an initial DNA or protein signature; laboratory *bench screening* needed to weed out candidates that fail to adequately detect target organisms or else incorrectly detect nontargets; and *assay tuning* to optimize the test platform and/or combine several assays within a single procedure. *Instrument expertise* is also needed to build new platforms or modify existing ones so that they can perform the desired assays. Finally, *informatics* is used to track samples and ensure that analyses are conducted and results reported correctly.

5.3.1   Surveillance

Large-scale surveillance systems provide a strategic tripwire for determining that an attack is underway and mounting a response. Detectors that guard against aerosol attacks—presumably the most likely large-scale threat—must be able to analyze air samples around the clock.[13]

Basic Technologies   The workhorse technology for practically all current surveillance systems is *polymerase chain reaction (PCR)*.[14] PCR lets researchers target predefined DNA regions within a pathogen's genome and then uses a thermal cycling method that repeatedly doubles the number of copies in the sample until millions have been made. This technology is so powerful that it can detect DNA from a single microbe. Unfortunately, PCR has a high total cost and usually requires skilled technicians. For many current surveillance systems this means that filters must be physically transported from detectors to a central laboratory and samples prepared. Depending on the particular PCR platforms and chemistries involved, the entire process usually takes four to twelve hours. Recent years have seen concerted efforts to shorten this process. Probably the most important advance has been "real-time PCR," which tags each PCR copy with a fluorescent molecule. This lets workers indirectly observe the pathogen's presence in each thermal cycle and make rough quantitative estimates. Despite this, PCR will likely remain relatively costly, labor intensive, and slow as long as humans are involved.

Because labor is the largest single component of DNA-based surveillance system costs, there have been many attempts to find methods for conducting multiple assays (sometimes for more than one pathogen) within a single test. Current PCR platforms range from single tubes to plates containing 96, 384, and 1,536 separate wells. Depending on the method, assays may be run against a single sample or many. Current research suggests that these *multiplex methods* are usually—but not always—less sensitive than conventional singleplex tests.[15]

Because PCR detects both living and dead pathogens, R&D is currently underway to develop *viability assays* to determine when it is safe to reenter a contaminated area. These comparatively complex tests will be needed to reoccupy even modest urban targets.

Finally, researchers have begun to explore detection technologies based on *microarrays* or *chips* that place tens of thousands and even millions of spots—each containing its own unique DNA *oligonucleotide (oligo) probe* signature—on a single glass slide. When the chips are exposed to pathogen DNA, fragments bind to specific spots and are detected by optical fluorescence or electrochemical techniques. At this point, they are checked against the hit patterns expected from known pathogens. Microarrays are useful when a relatively small sample must be simultaneously compared against a large number of signatures. Their main drawback is that tests must be conducted slowly enough to give the DNA sample time to locate and bind to each probe on the array. While twelve- to sixteen-hour hybridization times are often standard, some systems reportedly take up to seventy-two hours depending on how the sample is prepared and how much target DNA it contains. When enormous quantities of target DNA are known to be present, good results can be seen in as little as two to four hours. The process can also be accelerated by using specific amplification techniques to amplify the target DNA or random amplification techniques to amplify the sample's entire inventory of DNA. Random amplification is particularly useful when there are too many DNA regions of interest to multiplex specific PCR regions successfully.

Microarrays can be used for many different purposes, including identifying organisms at the species or strain level; detecting individual gene-based mechanisms of virulence, antibiotic resistance, or other components of interest; locating regions where an unknown sample differs from a known reference; and measuring gene expression levels (Bonetta 2006). Several different microarray technologies are currently available. The least expensive, which uses mechanical pins to insert individual DNA oligos onto glass slides, can cost as little as $1 per slide in large volumes. However, these arrays are usually limited to a few tens of thousands of oligos and are prone to various mechanical problems that result in missing spots, bleeding between spots, and other problems. Other technologies place oligos on arrays using deposition techniques similar to those found in the computer chip industry. These include optical techniques based on expensive fixed masks or, more recently, digitally controlled micromirrors like those found in digital projectors and some televisions. Arrays built with fixed masks tend to use relatively short oligos (~25 nucleotides) whereas maskless techniques often include oligos 85 nucleotides or longer. Still other technologies use electrochemical deposition and even inkjet spraying to create arrays.

Current microarray systems invariably require sophisticated support instrumentation and are primarily designed for use in clinical or research laboratories. That said, the link to electronic technologies is suggestive. Some companies have already begun to insert oligos in serpentine channels sandwiched between two layers of glass. The resulting systems use microfluidic controls to perform sophisticated "lab on a chip" processes, including enzymatic reactions and extension, elution for external sequencing, or in situ sequencing of captured fragments.[16] Researchers are working hard to make gene chips sufficiently rugged, cheap, fast, and autonomous for eventual use as handheld units in the field.

Finally, current surveillance systems usually employ air filters that collect many different organisms in a single sample. Since surveillance systems process literally millions of tests each year, it is hardly surprising that random combinations of DNA extracted from different organisms sometimes mimic expected bioweapons signatures. The obvious next step is to collect and analyze additional samples. The question is what to do when these come back negative. Since live organisms cannot be cultured from most current sampling methods (e.g., dry filters), it is impossible to conduct further tests on whichever sample tested positive. In principle, authorities could do the next best thing by sampling another piece of the original filter. Because organisms tend to collect unevenly on surfaces, however, even a genuine PCR detection may not be replicable elsewhere. At this point, the meaning of an inconclusive and unreplicated positive result typically becomes a matter of judgment. For example, positive results obtained after a large number of PCR cycles should normally be viewed with suspicion. Methods that allowed authorities to conduct follow-up observations on a single sample would go a long way toward eliminating such ambiguities.

Current Systems   Traditional disease surveillance depends on public health authorities' ability to collect and analyze disease data for emerging patterns. The *BioSense* syndromic surveillance early warning program[17] embodies the latest version of this strategy. It uses powerful data mining software to spot disease trends in 911 telephone calls, pharmaceutical sales, work/school absenteeism, patient diagnoses, and other databases. Because it relies on social data, BioSense cannot identify specific biological agents and could easily be overwhelmed by "worried-well" complaints following an attack. That said, it provides an important tripwire for recognizing that an attack or natural outbreak event is underway and needs to be investigated.

Mechanical surveillance requires continuous air sampling. Systems must be sensitive, able to detect several dozen pathogens and toxins, detect threats at very low concentrations, and identify agents reliably so that false alarms are minimized. These priorities almost always come at the expense of speed and affordability. One of the first large-area detection systems to meet these requirements was the *Biological Aerosol Sentry and Information System (BASIS)*.[18] The system consists of a network of aerosol collectors backed by a central PCR laboratory. In general, response times depend on how quickly human couriers can change filters and deliver samples to a field laboratory. The system uses standard software to compare lab results against known pathogen signatures.

BASIS was designed for transient, high-visibility events.[19] In 2003, DHS extended BASIS's DNA signature technology to launch a permanent *BioWatch* program. Although the details are closely held, BioWatch is known to operate in about thirty U.S. cities. Local agencies extract samples from BASIS detectors at regular intervals and forward them to the CDC's Laboratory Response Network for analysis. The U.S. Postal Service similarly operates a PCR-based *Biohazard Detection System* network for monitoring its central mail sorting facilities (USPS 2005).

Autonomous Sensors   PCR and gene chips were born in laboratories filled with specialized equipment and labor. The challenge now is to make them more automated and autonomous. Early initiatives have involved automating individual laboratory procedures. However, more ambitious work is now underway to create systems that can conduct surveillance in the field. Ideally, these should be (1) affordable in large numbers, and (2) able to operate for long periods without support from human couriers and/or centralized laboratories. One promising example is the Autonomous Pathogen Detection System (APDS).[20] APDS units robotically collect and analyze air samples for toxins and pathogens. Furthermore, the units can operate for up to seven days without servicing. After years of testing, APDS units joined the BioWatch program in late 2007. In the meantime, DHS's Bioagent Autonomous Networked Detectors (BAND) program has focused on a still more ambitious project to develop units that can provide low-cost, continuous aerosol sampling for up to a month without human intervention. Third-generation BioWatch units are scheduled to begin early pilot testing in 2010.[21]

The Department of Defense's Portal Shield and Joint Biological Point Detection System use a different technological strategy to protect U.S. forces. These systems rely on devices called assay strips to perform protein detection. Although the strips can perform up to ten assays in thirty minutes, they require daily intervention and—unlike APDS—cannot perform confirmatory PCR tests once a threat is detected. Protein-based systems also have higher false positive rates and lower sensitivities than PCR. However, this is acceptable in a mission where troops have appropriate protective gear and false alarms pose little or no risk of litigation.

5.3.2   Warning

Military units have long used detectors to warn of attacks. These units work fairly well in high-threat environments where relatively expensive technologies and high false-alarm rates are acceptable, and where personnel theoretically possess protection gear at all times. In principle, improved versions would be ideal for airports, businesses, and other critical facilities. However, such systems must work quickly enough for citizens to take shelter or evacuate. In practice, this means that results must be delivered in approximately one minute. This is far shorter than the hours available to detect-to-treat surveillance systems like BioWatch. Furthermore, signals must be detected from aerosol burdens that are typically several thousand times larger than the expected bioweapons signature.

Most military warning detectors use "stand-off" systems based on analyzing reflected laser light for a variety of expected bioweapons signatures. These can include luminescence, turbidity, scattering, absorption, transmission, and vibration. Commercial devices are simpler and usually measure the size and shape of particles by looking at how they scatter light or fluoresce when illuminated. Current systems include the Short Range Biological Detection System (SR-BDS), which uses ultraviolet illumination to distinguish biological agents from the normal aerosol background (Fitch, Raber, and Imbro 2003).

Future R&D will be needed to achieve false-alarm rates that would be acceptable in civilian service.[22] Lawrence Livermore National Laboratory's Bioaerosol Mass Spectrometry System (BAMS) (Steele 2004) is typical of this work. Unlike earlier systems, BAMS conducts four separate measurements on particles suspended in a fast-moving stream of air. These include (1) using filters to reject particles outside the 0.5 to 10 μm range, (2) accelerating the particles in a stream of air and measuring their velocities to extract size/shape information, (3) illuminating particles with ultraviolet light and using sensors to detect the fluorescence typical of biological materials, and (4) using a mass spectrometer to extract ions from particles and their mass-to-charge ratio. Real-time pattern-recognition software compares these measurements against a database of expected pathogen signatures. Because BAMS signatures require four separate measurements, false alarms are suppressed by "orders of magnitude" compared to existing systems. At the same time, the system's ability to characterize thousands of particles per second makes it sensitive enough to detect threat organisms even when natural and man-made particle backgrounds are orders of magnitude higher (Steele 2004).

5.3.3   First Responders

First responders and Hazmat teams need to know when people, objects, and places have been contaminated. Additionally, these detectors must be fast, portable, and simple to operate. Ideally, such systems should also discriminate between dead organisms and those that remain viable and a threat. The Guardian Reader System is typical of current products. It uses assays similar to pregnancy test strips to test for anthrax and other threats (Fitch, Raber, and Imbro 2003).

5.3.4 Diagnostics

In the aftermath of an attack, doctors would need rapid, inexpensive tests to determine who among the potentially tens of thousands of "worried-well" patients had actually been exposed and needed treatment. However, current diagnostic tools like cell cultures and enzyme-linked immunosorbent assays (ELISA) are labor intensive, have relatively poor sensitivity, and typically require days to weeks to arrive at a definitive conclusion. Molecular diagnostic tests based on immunoassays are much more sensitive, but still take seven to ten days by skilled technicians at a well-equipped laboratory.

Today's most promising technologies revolve around *PCR*. The University of California Davis Medical Center is currently testing an automated system that performs PCR on dozens of nasal swabs every day during flu season. The system compares reference samples against both common respiratory viruses and biological threat agents. While further advances in miniaturization and automation are certainly desirable, the U.C. Davis prototype already demonstrates useful triage capabilities. In principle, microarray technologies offer a competing technology that can potentially test for thousands of genetic markers at a time. However, the current price—up to $400 per chip—makes them too expensive for patient diagnosis.

In the long run, knowing that an agent belongs to a particular species is not sufficient. Public health responses will be faster and more efficient if the particular strain and/or detailed information about virulence and antibiotic-resistance mechanisms are also known. Improved diagnostics will depend on developing robust sets of signatures for these mechanisms. These are likely to include a variety of signals. Researchers are currently searching for various candidates, including DNA sequences that code for antibiotic resistance and other virulence factors; special proteins secreted by virulent organisms; and certain protein byproducts (host/pathogen interaction *biomarkers*) secreted by patients who have been attacked by pathogens.

5.4 Chemical Detection

Modern laboratory analytical chemistry techniques are a mature technology for providing both qualitative identification of compounds and quantitative measurements. These methods generally include a preconcentration stage that increases the amount of material available for analysis, a separation stage to simplify the analysis of complex mixtures, and a detection stage that measures specific chemical properties (e.g., molecular weight) and/or more generic information (e.g., susceptibility to flame ionization). The resulting capabilities are extremely powerful. For example, state-of-the-art gas chromatography–mass spectrometry methods routinely separate mixtures into individual compounds and can detect 0.1 ng (0.000,000,000,1 grams) of agent in twenty to thirty minutes with essentially no false alarms.

Chemical weapons, on the other hand, pose special challenges. First, they can act on time scales of less than a minute. This means that laboratory-style separation and/or preconcentration stages are often impractical. Second, detectors must be able to distinguish agent from complex chemical backgrounds found in the environment. Failure to do this produces false alarms that undermine confidence and can even persuade users to ignore detections altogether. Finally, detectors must be robust and affordable enough to be used in the field. Current technologies are often bulky, require special consumables (e.g., pressurized gas), and/or consume large amounts of power. These issues limit the feasibility of handheld, autonomous, or widely deployed detection schemes.

Building sensors that are simultaneously fast, sensitive, robust, and affordable remains challenging (Fitch, Raber, and Imbro 2003). For now, the best sensors are military. These provide near-real-time protection (forty-five seconds to two minutes) but require manual operation and have large numbers of false positives from high temperature, petroleum products, pesticides, burning brush, and other causes (Ellison 2000). Furthermore, current real-time military sensors are most effective at detecting agents at toxic—or even near-lethal—levels. Civilian applications will require much more automated and reliable devices.

State-of-the-art civilian systems are generally designed to detect multiple traditional chemical warfare agents (e.g., nerve, blister, and blood agents) along with a variety of toxic industrial chemicals. Current products include the ChemPro 100 and RAID-M systems that use ion mobility spectrometry to detect volatile compounds. Unlike conventional gas chromatography–mass spectrometry systems, they operate quickly in periods ranging from less than five minutes down to ten seconds or so. Furthermore, they do not require sample preparation steps like preconcentration or extraction. Finally, BAE Systems' JCAD ChemSentry is one of the first commercial detection systems to use microchip fabrication technology to squeeze an array of microscopic detectors onto a single chip. Its uses surface acoustic wave (SAW) transducers to generate signals that can be compared against a library of known threats. Predictably, these devices usually offer reduced sensitivity and higher false-alarm rates compared to conventional laboratory systems.

Extensive R&D is currently underway to improve this performance. For example, DHS is currently funding programs to develop improved detectors for subways and airports and/or to support remediation of critical facilities after an attack (Fitch, Raber, and Imbro 2003). Similarly, the Defense Department is funding R&D to develop more integrated sensing systems for battlefield, facility, and individual use. This work typically cuts across multiple scientific disciplines, including advanced data analysis, networking and miniaturization. Many of the newest systems feature microscopic transducers[23] based on recent advances in conductive polymer chemiresistors (Burl et al. 2002; Gao et al. 2006), chemicapacitors (Chatzandroulis et al. 2004), as well as tiny cantilevers (Heller 2009; Loui et al. 2008) and other micromechanical sensor (MEMS) devices. MEMS devices, in particular, can be manufactured using standard semiconductor fabrication methods. This opens the door to packing large arrays of transducers onto a single chip. This should, in turn, lead to more versatile, affordable, and compact devices with greatly reduced power requirements.

5.5   Forensics

Detector technologies can also be combined with analytical methods to determine where the materials and know-how used to make WMD or WMD components came from. Here, we briefly examine some of the capabilities and limits of this rapidly developing field. (For comprehensive, book-length reviews, see Breeze, Budowle, and Schutzer 2005 and Moody, Hutcheon, and Grant 2005.)

5.5.1   Nuclear

Nuclear forensics are conventionally divided into pre- and postdetonation investigations. *Predetonation* forensics takes advantage of the fact that nuclear materials processing leaves important signatures in the form of isotope ratios, trace contaminants, and microscopic appearance. This typically makes it possible to infer how a sample of weapons-grade uranium, for example, was originally enriched (e.g., electromagnetically, by centrifuge, or by thermal diffusion), whether it has been reprocessed or used in a reactor, and whether it has been machined. Nonnuclear bomb components like high-explosives may similarly contain fingerprints in the form of synthesis byproducts, degradation compounds, and impurities. These characteristics can then be checked against samples obtained either openly or covertly from known locations. This process can usually narrow the list of nations whose facilities or technology were used to make a particular object and, in some cases, point to a unique source. Investigation of an HEU sample intercepted by Bulgarian officials in 1999 gives some idea of what is possible. While investigators were ultimately unable to determine the source from forensic clues alone, they did establish that the material had been used as fuel inside a research reactor, that this had happened in October/November 1993, that the HEU had subsequently been refined using the PUREX process, and that no U.S. reactor could have produced it (Moody, Hutcheon, and Grant 2005). As with most legal and intelligence activities, it would have been up to a prosecutor or intelligence analyst to combine these very substantial clues with other lines of evidence—for example, human espionage or communication intercepts—to complete the case against a particular point of origin.

The *postdetonation* investigation would be similar. In addition to determining the origin of the fissile material used, the investigation would need to determine the design of the weapon. Since the late 1940s, the United States has developed extensive capabilities for detecting the seismic motion, radiation, dust, gas, and other debris generated by nuclear explosions (Richelson 2006). These signatures provide powerful insights into weapons design and have been extensively validated against both theoretical models and records of historic detonations.

It is, of course, natural to ask whether terrorists could try to disguise the origin (or even point investigators to the wrong source) by deliberately adding impurities or reengineering weapons technologies to leave an altered fingerprint. This would be hard to do, however, since the fingerprints that U.S. analysts rely on are classified. Perhaps more importantly, any attempt that substantially modified nuclear weapons design or production technologies would require massive engineering and capital investments. This would largely negate the advantages of borrowing existing state technologies in the first place.

5.5.2   Biological Agents

Pathogens offer several potentially important signatures to investigators. These can loosely be divided into the DNA blueprint that describes the organism and the actual physical atoms from which it is made.

For now, *DNA analysis* of pathogens is still significantly less mature than the DNA "fingerprints" that are routinely used to prosecute human defendants in U.S. courts. The main scientific reason is that pathogen genomes are thousands to millions of times shorter than the three billion base pairs found in humans. For example, typical bacteria genomes usually contain one to five million base pairs while viruses can have as few as 7,000. This makes it much harder to find the sorts of multiple stable, inheritance-based markers that make human DNA fingerprinting possible. These problems are compounded by the fact that pathogen life spans— and hence evolution—take place on a scale of hours to days, so that a pathogen's genome will often look substantially different from the last sample known to authorities. While the rate of natural variation varies significantly from organism to organism, experience with a 2006 *E. coli* outbreak is fairly typical. In that case, investigators found that organisms isolated in patients typically differed by more than 200 genes (out of approximately 4,000), even though they presumably originated in a common ancestor (Tom Cebula, FDA, personal communication). This kind of gene plasticity is up to 1,000 times greater for RNA viruses, which constantly mutate to defeat host immune systems.

The anthrax-letter investigations of late 2001 illustrate both the strengths and limitations of these methods. Here, authorities were able to sample organisms directly from the envelopes that had been mailed to victims. Initial strain typing using then-known genetic markers quickly showed that the agent was highly similar to the so-called Ames strain.[24] However, it was hard to learn much more than this because the Ames strain had been widely shared among U.S. researchers with little or no formal record keeping. Even if this knowledge was available, moreover, it would not be surprising to find significant variations in sequences from *B. anthracis* isolates that had been grown through several generations under different conditions after having been diverted from a legitimate source. Since 2001, investigators have worked hard to gather further evidence, including full sequences of several Ames isolates. This eventually led to four mutations that the FBI was able to successfully match against cultures in a flask belonging to Army scientist Bruce Ivins. (Ivins committed suicide before the FBI could arrest him.) At the same time, Ivins's status as a U.S. government employee made it relatively easy for the FBI to find additional evidence once a match had been made. Without this evidence, the case would have been significantly more ambiguous. Strains from at least one other government lab are known to have had the same four mutations, and the odds against Ivins's sample matching by chance were still unknown as this book went to press (Bhattacharjee and Enserink 2008).

In purely scientific terms, it is reasonable to think that better understanding of pathogen genomes, coupled with improved statistical methods, will eventually improve to the point where DNA fingerprinting of pathogens is as straightforward and certain as human methods are today. For now, however, the preliminary scientific work needed to establish the mathematical/statistical foundations for determining that viral samples are related is just beginning. Just as importantly, criminal or diplomatic evidence standards are not just scientific but social. This means that they will have to be publicly validated through both the formal institutions of science—for instance, by establishing a large body of evidence in peer-reviewed journals—and other venues including public debate, education, and courtroom argument. The good news is that we know how to do this, at least in the long run. Indeed, one need only compare the current widespread acceptance of human DNA fingerprinting against the situation that prevailed at the end of the O. J. Simpson trial in 1995 (Bosco 1996).

5.5.3   Other Methods

DNA-based methods can be used on any organism descended from the attack agent. However, more tests become possible when samples of the agent itself are available. These nongenetic forensic techniques (biochemical tests, isotope measurements, or images provided by scanning electron or atomic force microscopes) often provide clues to the conditions in which pathogens were grown. In principle, these data can be used to characterize the media the pathogen was grown in. Indeed, they can trace the pathogen's water content to specific parts of the world. As in the 2001 anthrax attacks, these data can also determine what specialized preparation techniques were used to make the material (e.g., milling or encapsulation with special protective coatings) and the resemblance of these methods to, say, known U.S. and Russian manufacturing processes.

The relative importance of these methods will probably decline over time as DNA-based methods become more powerful. Even in the long run, however, they will continue to provide useful complementary information. Provided that samples of the actual attack agent can be obtained, physical methods provide important clues to how it was grown and processed. By comparison, genetic methods focus on the somewhat earlier issues of where samples of the pathogen were originally obtained, when this occurred, and whether breeding programs and/or genetic engineering methods were used to modify the strain (Breeze, Budowle, and Schutzer 2005).

Finally, it is worth remembering that a wide range of destructive and non-destructive tests are now available. Since analysts will normally be limited to trace amounts of evidence, a test program should be carefully designed from the outset. Running tests in the wrong order, for example, is likely to yield inconclusive results while consuming all of the available material (Breeze, Budowle, and Schutzer 2005).

5.5.4   Chemical

Chemical and isotopic analysis can provide important clues to the processes, facilities, and feedstocks used to make chemical weapons. However, the value of this information may often be limited for so-called toxic industrial chemicals that can be purchased in bulk from ordinary commercial sources. The situation is likely to be very different for advanced military weapons like sarin or VX. Here, processes developed by different state programs typically leave comparatively large amounts of telltale impurities. As with nuclear weapons, further refining steps and/or substantial process modifications could potentially alter these signatures. Once again, however, these subterfuges would significantly reduce the advantage of using state-developed methods in the first place.

Another important consideration for chemical forensics is understanding where and how to look for signatures after an attack has occurred. Many chemical agents (e.g., sarin) are highly reactive in the environment. This means that the agents may have to be inferred from their known degradation products. Rapid, postevent response will require a detailed understanding of which compounds to target and look for. This is especially important for chemical clues to the production process, whose concentrations will typically be extremely low compared to the agent itself.

5.6   Conclusion

Detection technologies have improved markedly since September 11 and are now entering the field in significant numbers. However, progress is still uneven. Some instrument categories (e.g., ubiquitous radiation detectors, handheld biosensors) still have substantial room for improvement. The possibility of deliberate shielding complicates the detector problem still further for nuclear detectors and may never be solved for biological agents.

Perfection, however, is not the goal. Even imperfect sensors can significantly increase the chance of detection and/or force terrorists into complicated countermeasures (e.g., massive lead shielding) that increase the risk of failure. Furthermore, efficient postattack detection can materially reduce casualties for biological weapons. Continued R&D will significantly increase the odds that terrorists will be deterred from investing in WMD or, if they do, be detected in time to stop or blunt an attack.

Notes

1. The ABC News team used depleted uranium, a byproduct of the uranium enrichment process that contains less than 0.2 percent ^{235}U and cannot be used to make nuclear weapons. This posed a much harder test than the highly enriched uranium (HEU) used in weapons, which is 150 times more radioactive. On the other hand, it remains true that HEU one of the most challenging problems for nuclear security systems since much of its radioactivity can be easily blocked with steel or lead. ABC News obtained its depleted uranium from the Natural Resources Defense Council (NRDC 2003).

2. Systems operating abroad face special challenges. Bilateral inspection agreements often limit where monitoring equipment can be placed and/or operators' ability to open weapons or containers for inspection.

3. Absent sensors, a bioweapons attack would not normally be detected until doctors diagnosed a disease that does not exist in nature (e.g., smallpox) or public health authorities noticed that a rare but naturally occurring disease (e.g., tularemia) was suddenly more prevalent. Most bioweapons pathogens can be treated successfully if they are diagnosed early. This

treatment window ranges from one to six days (e.g., anthrax) up to ten to twenty days (e.g., smallpox, plague). The corresponding window for toxins is typically shorter, ranging from minutes or hours (T4 mycotoxin) up to roughly one day (botulinum toxin).

4. See, for example, the CDC's ESSENCE II network (Lombardo, Burkom, and Pavlin 2004).

5. For many agents, the available data are limited to animal models and/or records of World War II war crimes.

6. This list does not exhaust the subatomic bestiary. So-called cosmic rays come from outer space and include an electronlike particle called the muon. In the 1960s, Alvarez et al. (1970) used muon detectors to search for hidden chambers in the Great Pyramid of Cheops. More recently, a Los Alamos team has used muons to screen cargo. They claim that their prototype device can detect a 10-centimeter uranium cube hidden in a large container in approximately one minute (Borozdin et al. 2003). Unfortunately, this may not be fast enough for a commercial system and Nature's supply of cosmic rays cannot be increased. Surveillance can also be built around exotic particles called neutrinos. These particles are so hard to detect that they require multiton sensors. On the other hand, analysis of data from Japanese neutrino detectors must take account of nuclear power plants hundreds of miles away. This capability could be useful in the Korean peninsula and other locations (Bernstein et al. 2002).

7. All resolution figures quoted in this chapter refer to spectra taken near 662 KeV.

8. This may be acceptable for detectors at nuclear materials facilities and other applications where the expected target material and geometry are known but need to be confirmed.

9. Still more units will be needed to implement various U.S. cooperative agreements with other nations, notably including the Second Line of Defense program designed to screen cargo before it leaves foreign ports.

10. Directional clues can also be used to improve the signal-to-noise ratio.

11. Lanthanum is also naturally radioactive. This may ultimately limit the sensitivity of these devices.

12. Methods that depend on detecting nonsurface proteins typically require disruptive extraction steps.

13. Surveillance systems for other threats—for example, attacks using contaminated food, water, or postal letters—would presumably have different requirements.

14. Roche, which holds key patents for PCR, offers an excellent online tutorial; see http://www.roche-hiv.com/portal/eipf/pb/hiv/Roche-HIV/pcrtutorial1.

15. Strangely, multiplex tests can sometimes be *more* accurate than singleplex results. The result is probably related to the still-incompletely understood mechanism that PCR uses to control the denaturing and reannealing of double-stranded DNA (Tom Slezak, unpublished data).

16. Interested readers should consult www.geniom.com.

17. http://www.cdc.gov/biosense/.

18. Similar systems have been developed and deployed by the Department of Defense (Fitch, Raber, and Imbro 2003).

19. Fortuitously, BASIS was being developed for use at the 2002 Winter Games at the time of the Washington anthrax attacks. Because it was the only U.S. system that could perform

wide-area pathogen monitoring, it was immediately pressed into 24/7 operation in the National Capital Region. The system has been running continuously ever since and is now a Bio-Watch lab. BASIS was also deployed, as planned, at the Winter Games, where it protected various indoor and outdoor sports arenas, urban locations, and transportation hubs.

20. http://physci.llnl.gov/recent/pdf/detecting_bioaerosols.pdf.

21. Other ambitious attempts to create autonomous PCR machines include the U.S. Postal Service's Biohazard Detection System and a commercial handheld product called the Ruggedized Advanced Pathogen Identification Device. The suitcase-sized detector can detect 100 fg of plague in about seventy-five minutes. See http://findarticles.com/p/articles/mi_qa3912/is_200310/ai_n9320164.

22. The public's willingness to put up with false alarms could, of course, increase if terrorist attacks became a reality.

23. "Transducers" are devices that turn physical inputs (here, the presence of certain chemicals) into electrical signals that can be analyzed and manipulated.

24. Despite its familiarity, the "Ames" designation is incorrect. The strain was actually isolated from a dead cow in Texas. The misattribution was caused by clerical error.

6

Securing America's Borders and Ports

Michael Nacht and Blas Pérez Henríquez

There is a tension between the need to secure America's borders and the need to move citizens, visitors, and goods expeditiously. Historically, the flow of visitors, immigrants, and merchandise into the United States has enhanced the country's cultural and economic power and accelerated global trade. Today, the rapid processing of visas, customs duties, and other regulations remains basic to U.S. competitiveness. At the same time, the threat of weapons of mass destruction (WMD) and related materials arriving at the nation's borders, seaports, and airports is too large to ignore.

Securing thousands of miles of border is a daunting task. Effective control will require radically new technologies. Learning to manage and use these technologies effectively will be even harder for border operations, which are currently fragmented among multiple U.S. federal, state, local, and tribal jurisdictions, foreign governments, and private firms. Many of these actors have incentives and interests that are only partly aligned with the security mission. Finally, border control frequently intersects with broader political and economic disputes involving immigration, privacy, civil liberties, and labor relations. In some cases, these debates attract resources that would not be available on security grounds alone. However, they can also trigger political pressures and constraints that have little or nothing to do with securing the border.

This chapter reviews the main policies, organizational strategies, and programs that have been implemented to strengthen security at U.S. ports of entry (POEs)[1] against chemical, biological, radiological, and nuclear attacks since September 11. Section 6.1 addresses the physical challenge of securing U.S. land, sea, and air POEs. Section 6.2 discusses unilateral actions taken by the U.S. government to prevent terrorists and WMD components from entering the country. Section 6.3 reviews international cooperation in this area. Section 6.4 examines the role of public-private cooperation in addressing security. Finally, section 6.5 presents a brief conclusion.

6.1   The Physical Challenge

By any measure, the physical task of border control is immense. The United States's border with Canada runs for 5,526 miles and its border with Mexico runs for 2,067 miles. The nation also has 12,380 miles of coastline, including the Great Lakes. Finally, the border includes more than 300 official POEs for land, sea, and air travel.

As of 2007, U.S. imports totaled $975 billion. This included maritime ($397 billion), air ($239 billion), and truck/rail traffic ($211 billion). Furthermore, cross-border trade is expanding much faster than the U.S. economy as a whole. This is especially true of the country's West Coast ports. In 2004 these ports handled slightly more than eighteen million TEUs in containerized cargo.[2] By 2006 the figure had jumped to just over twenty-two million TEUs (Pacific Maritime Association 2007).

6.1.1   Land Borders

Border control consists of controlling open crossings at POEs and preventing unauthorized crossings in between. Prior to September 11, government was already finding it difficult to efficiently screen and process people and goods crossing the Mexican and Canadian borders.[3] The situation between POEs was even more troubling. While all borders are somewhat porous, the situation along the U.S./Mexican border was largely uncontrolled, with thousands of undocumented workers crossing every year since the end of the last regulated workers program (i.e., the *Bracero* Program, 1942–1962). Illegal crossings along the thinly populated U.S./Canadian border were also relatively easy, although the issue attracted less attention.

The most obvious solution was to strengthen physical controls along the U.S./Canada and U.S./Mexican borders. This, however, ran counter to the goal of the North American Free Trade Agreement (NAFTA) to minimize barriers to the flow of people and goods throughout North America. International trade groups have consistently argued that it would be better to push the main line of defense outward by creating a common "North American Security Perimeter" between North America and the rest of the world. The proposal clearly raises significant trust issues, since it would necessarily make Canadian and Mexican border inspectors the main line of defense for many U.S.-bound shipments. At the same time, it would also create an opportunity to detect at least some WMD before they could reach American POEs. Implementing such an approach would require intense collaboration with multiple foreign agencies and institutions, each of which has its own priorities and operational procedures.

The Southern Border   The Mexican border contains extensive regions of extremely inhospitable and harsh terrain. To date, operational control is uneven and tends to be concentrated in heavily trafficked areas like the California/Arizona and West Texas/New Mexico corridors. The methods, routes, drop houses, and transportation networks used by drug and human traffickers provide a criminal infrastructure that terrorists could potentially use to bring WMD into the United States.

The Northern Border   Compared to the southern border, undocumented crossings along the U.S./Canadian border are rare. Nevertheless, the United States's long, thinly settled border with Canada makes it hard to detect illegal pedestrian or vehicle crossings. This problem increases in winter, when large parts of the Great Lakes area and surrounding waterways freeze over. Border control is further complicated by various social and political challenges. First, enforcement requires cooperation across multiple agencies, including the U.S. Coast Guard, the National Park Service, U.S. Immigration and Customs Enforcement, the Federal Bureau of Investigation, the Drug Enforcement Administration, state and local authorities, and, in many cases, tribal police. Second, 90 percent of Canada's population lives within one hundred miles of the U.S./Canada border. This requires POEs to screen potential terrorists from a very large background of legitimate visitors. Third, there is a long tradition of U.S./Canadian cooperation along "the World's longest undefended border." This legacy makes it relatively easy for U.S. and Canadian authorities to work together, but also creates institutional resistance to more intrusive controls. Finally, well-organized smuggling operations exist on both sides of the border. Terrorists could potentially use these groups to move people and weapons into the United States.

6.1.2   Coastal Areas and Maritime Ports

The United States has 361 ports nationwide. In 2004 roughly ten million loaded cargo containers transporting $1.5 billion worth of goods passed through these ports every day (Boske 2006). This traffic was disproportionately concentrated in a handful of POEs. As of 2004, Los Angeles, New York/Hoboken, and Long Beach handled about 40 percent of all U.S. imports that arrived by sea and the top fifty U.S. ports accounted for about 90 percent of all maritime cargo tonnage (CBO 2006). In recent years, container traffic flowing into and out of U.S. ports represented roughly 7 percent of GDP and provided jobs for over seven million U.S. workers. Since then, flows have continued to grow.

U.S. ports are owned by governments and leased to private terminal operators. Operators enjoy substantial latitude, although operations across ports tend to be similar, especially at larger facilities. Coastal areas between ports are protected by the U.S. Coast Guard in cooperation with other law enforcement agencies. In addition to Homeland Security, the Coast Guard's other principal missions include forestalling mass migrations, particularly from the Caribbean, interdicting maritime smuggling, and enforcing immigration laws against foreign sailors.

Modernization Pressures   Expanding world trade will put substantial pressures on U.S. ports to modernize in coming decades. First, modernization could potentially save the maritime industry up to $1 billion annually. Second, Mexico and Canada are building new port capacity to meet expected increases in container traffic bound for the United States. Absent modernization, U.S. ports will lose substantial business to these competitors. Third, long lines of idling trucks contribute to traffic congestion and air pollution. This has introduced additional regulatory pressure to modernize. Finally, U.S. ports have very little room to expand, particularly in New York and on the West Coast.[4] This means that U.S. ports will have to use existing land more efficiently. Today, the Los Angeles/Long Beach terminals handle 4,540 TEUs/acre/year, the highest anywhere in the United States. However, ports in nine other countries are far more productive. In order to grow, U.S. ports will have to imitate the work practices and information technology innovations found in Hong Kong (20,000 TEUs/acre/year), Felixstowe, UK (10,000), and Rotterdam (6,000) (Machalaba 2001).

Adopting these new technologies and work practices would automatically make it easier to track and monitor cargo for Homeland Security purposes. At the same time, organized labor has serious reservations about additional automation and changes to traditional work practices, especially if these changes lead to workforce reductions. These concerns are only partly offset by the prospect of higher wages for a smaller, more efficient workforce. This economic interest often translates into opposition to new security initiatives and protracted labor-management negotiations. Labor resistance tends to be significantly stronger on the West Coast, where a single union controls all terminal personnel from Seattle to San Diego, than on the East Coast, where each terminal operator faces its own collective bargaining agent.

6.1.3   Airports

The United States has 5,400 general aviation airports, including roughly 100 international airports. These represent an obvious gateway for delivering terrorists and WMD to the United States. Additionally, international airports process almost ninety million visitors annually along with large volumes of air cargo. This makes them an important target in their own right.

Airports screen customers and cargo through a combination of physical inspection and detailed monitoring of electronic records for suspicious patterns. These capabilities can potentially be enhanced by a variety of technologies, including advanced detectors for high explosives and nuclear material, biometric identifiers that unambiguously link electronic records to individuals, and improved information management systems that facilitate the real-time assembly and analysis of large data sets. However, implementing these complex technologies in a sensible way presents significant challenges.

Airport security also faces organizational challenges. Before September 11, airport security was a joint responsibility of airport operators, the more than 100 commercial airlines operating in the United States, and the Federal Aviation Administration (FAA). This highly fragmented system was further hampered by the FAA's failure to exercise coordination and oversight. In practice, airports and airlines often contracted with private security companies to screen passengers, baggage, and cargo. Overall, the system provided very little incentive for the highly competitive airline industry to invest in streamlined and effective security.

Illicit travel between official POEs is relatively small for air travel compared to water and, especially, land transportation. However, radar surveillance is incomplete and organized drug smuggling networks routinely use unauthorized aircraft to penetrate the southern border.

6.2   U.S. Government Initiatives

Since September 11 a great deal has been done to deter and defend against terrorist attacks. Much of this progress has been driven by U.S. legislation and government initiatives.

6.2.1   Legislation
Post–September 11 legislation rewrote the basic rules governing POEs. This section briefly reviews the most important changes.

Patriot Act   The Uniting and Strengthening America by Providing Appropriate Tools Required to Intercept and Obstruct Terrorism Act of 2001 (Public Law 107-56) contains several border security initiatives. First, it expanded the federal government's *surveillance, detention, and deportation powers* against suspected terrorists and broadened the criteria for denying entry into the United States. Second, it made additional *resources* available for posting more Border Patrol agents along U.S. borders, installing high-technology monitoring systems, and accelerating the adoption of machine-readable passports. Third, it authorized increased *interagency intelligence sharing*, most notably by giving U.S. consulates and immigration officers access to FBI and Department of Homeland Security (DHS) criminal records. Fourth, it tightened *visa restrictions* by mandating full enforcement of the 1996 Illegal Immigration and Immigration Reform Act (Public Law 104-0208) which had previously mandated improved monitoring of foreign students and expanded visa disclosures. The Patriot Act also enhanced enforcement by creating a Student and Exchange Visitor Program so that government agencies could share information about foreign students. Finally, the act endorsed various *technology initiatives* to improve tracking of individuals entering and exiting the United States. These included using biometric technology to confirm visitors' identities and creating tamper-resistant, machine-readable documents that rapidly connect visitors to government databases.

Several years after September 11, there is now a vigorous national debate on which features of the Patriot Act, if any, should be retained. Many universities have been especially vocal in objecting to what they see as the unnecessary restrictions on foreign students entering the United States. That said, congressional thinking continues to be dominated by security concerns and it is reasonable to think that existing restrictions will, by and large, continue.

Government Reorganization   The Homeland Security Strategy Act of 2001 mandated the largest reorganization of the federal government in over fifty years. This led to the creation of the Department of Homeland Security on March 1, 2003. The new agency included a reorganized U.S. Customs and Border Protection Service (CBP) designed to unify all law enforcement personnel and functions at the U.S. borders. CBP is responsible for overseeing operations at over 300 POEs and all the land and water in between.

EBSVERA   The Enhanced Border Security and Visa Entry Reform Act of 2001 (Public Law 107-173) was the third major statute passed in response to September 11 and was signed into law in May 2002. EBSVERA added 3,000 immigration inspectors to CBP's workforce, required universities to track and keep better information on foreign students, and heightened scrutiny of visa applications from citizens of countries deemed to be sponsors of terrorism.

Improving America's Security Act of 2007   Congress passed legislation to implement the 9/11 Commission's recommendations, including tighter screening of air and sea cargoes, in 2007. The "Improving America's Security Act of 2007" (Public Law 110-53) required foreign ports to implement radiation screening on all U.S.-

bound maritime cargo by 2012, although it also gave DHS discretion to extend the deadline indefinitely by two years at a time. In addition, it requires foreign airports to monitor all cargo carried on passenger aircraft by 2010, although this can be done using manifests without physical inspection. Finally, the legislation requires air travelers from twenty-seven countries to register online with the U.S. government as much as forty-eight hours before departure. Airlines are also required to file passenger manifests fifteen minutes after take-off so that U.S. authorities have more time to evaluate high-risk travelers. Despite this progress, Congress and the DHS continue to grapple over prioritizing resources. While "risk" is theoretically a complex function of target value, vulnerability, and likelihood of attack (chapter 7), many of these factors are hard to quantify in practice. The resulting uncertainty has encouraged the deeply political budget authorization and appropriation process to designate many "high risk" targets that almost certainly do not deserve the designation. This struggle will likely continue unless and until a new attack refocuses the nation's attention on security.

6.2.2   Implementing the Mandate

The most obvious changes since September 11 involve goals. Today, Homeland Security (expressly including WMD defense) has become CBP's "priority mission," although its "traditional missions" of interdicting illegal aliens and drugs "remain important" (CBP 2004a). As a result, POEs remain at Alert Level One, requiring inspections of individuals, cargo, and vehicles that are all dramatically higher than they were in the period before September 11. The CBP's 2007–2011 Strategic Plan (CBP 2006) similarly promises to strengthen security between POEs.

Given limited resources, these ambitious goals cannot be met unless CBP finds ways to work more efficiently. CBP's *National Border Patrol Strategy* is built around six core initiatives:

• *"Assemble the right combination of personnel, technology, and infrastructure."* CBP has placed heavy emphasis on deploying integrated, state-of-the-art sensors and acquiring and processing intelligence. It has also concentrated on teaching inspectors how to identify WMD materials, what concealment methods to look for, and how to respond to a WMD incident. These training programs range from tabletop simulations and field exercises all the way up to smuggling simulations using "live" nuclear materials at the Department of Energy's Pacific Northwest National Laboratory (CBP 2004a, 2005).
• *"Improve mobility and rapid deployment to quickly counter and interdict based on shifts in smuggling routes and tactical intelligence."* CBP has increasingly stressed the use of aircraft, boats, and "strategically placed tactical infrastructure" to cover the border (CBP 2004a).

• *"Deploy defense-in-depth that makes full use of interior checkpoints and enforcement operations to deny successful migration."*   CBP has adopted a multilayered, "defense-in-depth" approach. This means that CBP must not only protect the border, but also enforce immigration laws within the country itself. These laws have been a hot political issue in recent years—raising human rights, economic, and security concerns—and are likely to undergo additional changes over time.

• *"Coordinate and partner with other law enforcement agencies to achieve security goals."*   CBP has organized a series of interagency task forces to increase coordination and cooperation within the fragmented federal, state, local, and tribal agencies that police the border. Similarly, CBP has created Integrated Border Enforcement Teams and other liaison mechanisms for its foreign law enforcement partners. Finally, CBP works directly with the Canadian and Mexican governments to strengthen cross-border cooperation.

• *"Improve border awareness and intelligence."*   CBP has worked hard to prioritize risks using objective measures. Although well established in other fields, the methods are still relatively new in the context of homeland security (chapter 7).[5]

• *"Strengthen the CBP headquarters command structure."*   CBP has adopted a new organizational structure to acquire, act on, and share tactical intelligence quickly. The changes are also supposed to increase CBP headquarters' ability to understand and manage events as they unfold.

Inevitably, this general framework is expressed differently for land, sea, and air transport.

Land Borders   CBP has received dramatically increased personnel and other resources since September 11. For example, CBP's force on the northern border has increased from 350 to 1,000 agents supported by experimental technologies and state-of-the-art sensors. However, even these resources are not enough to search all people, vehicles, and cargo. CBP has therefore invested in a variety of information technology initiatives to supplement its physical inspections.

Passengers   There are now several programs governing the flow of passengers into the United States. The *Student and Exchange Visitor Program (SEVP)* is designed to ensure that only legitimate foreign students or exchange visitors gain entry to the United States. The program's online *Student and Exchange Visitor Information System (SEVIS)* became fully operational in August 2003. It collects, monitors, and tracks students, exchange visitors, dependents, schools, and exchange programs. CBP shares this information with various agencies including the State Department, U.S. Citizenship and Immigration Services, and U.S. Immigration and Customs Enforcement.

The DHS also launched its *U.S. Visitor and Immigrant Status Indicator Technology (US-VISIT)* system in 2003. This multibillion-dollar information technology system is designed to track the millions of foreign nationals who pass through POEs every year by recording their entries and exits from the United States, verifying their identities, and monitoring compliance with their terms of admission (GAO 2006c). Key US-VISIT capabilities include

• Collecting, maintaining, and sharing information on selected foreign nationals entering and exiting the United States.
• Identifying foreign nationals who (1) have overstayed or violated the terms of their admission; (2) may be eligible to receive, extend, or adjust their immigration status; or (3) should be apprehended or detained by law enforcement.
• Detecting fraudulent travel documents, verifying traveler identity, and determining traveler admissibility through the use of biometrics.
• Establishing new facilities and procedures for sharing information with other immigration and border agencies.
• Safeguarding the privacy of visitors.

As a complement to US-VISIT, DHS and the State Department have developed a *Biometric Visa Program* to deny U.S. entry visas to would-be terrorists and verify the identities of travelers holding legitimate visas.[6] The process begins at U.S. consulates abroad where foreign nationals applying for nonimmigrant visas are asked to provide finger print scans and a photograph. Once the prints are captured, they are transmitted electronically from the consulate's server to the State Department, where they are checked against IDENT, a DHS database that includes some five million people who may be ineligible to receive a visa. Responses typically take about thirty minutes. Later, when visa holders arrive at POEs, their fingerprints are again checked to confirm that they are the same person who applied for the visa. The program also requires visitors leaving the United States to confirm their departure by having their fingerprints checked and their visas or passports scanned. This exit data is also recorded by the system. Finally, individuals from so-called special-interest countries[7] receive additional security checks when they arrive at POEs.

Cargo   The Trade Act of 2002 (Public Law 107-210) authorized new Mandatory Advanced Electronic Cargo Information rules for air cargo entering the United States. The centerpiece of the new procedures is the Automated Manifest System, a modular software system that provides cargo inventory control and release notifications for sea, air, and rail carriers. AMS's "inbound system" expedites cargo flows by providing entry clearance before shipments arrive. The system also facilitates intermodal delivery by treating different transportation methods (e.g., rail, truck) in a uniform way. Finally, AMS reduces the number of paper documents and accelerates the processing of manifest and waybill data. The net result is that cargo moves faster, participants can track shipments more accurately, and importers have lower compliance costs.

Unlike airports, *port security* is not enforced by any government agency. Instead, it is up to each individual terminal operator to maintain adequate security through contracts with private security firms. Despite this, increased attention to security has promoted greater uniformity since September 11.

Congress federalized *aviation security* by passing the Aviation and Transportation Security Act (Public Law 107-071) in 2001. The Act created a new security entity called the Transportation Security Administration (TSA). Half of TSA's approximately $6 billion annual budget is devoted to baggage and passenger screening. Although airports still conduct access control, perimeter patrols, and law enforcement, these programs are now supervised by a TSA federal security director (FSD). However, critics argued that the new system's one-size-fits-all procedures were inefficient, particularly for small airports. In November 2004, TSA introduced a pilot program that let airports replace government screeners with contract employees. This privatized Screening Partnership Program has had only limited success in recruiting personnel who meet TSA's standards for new hires. It remains to be seen whether this program will enhance or degrade security at U.S. airports. Centralized security has also been criticized on grounds that federal supervision makes local security organizations less accountable to airport management while encouraging TSA inspectors to downplay performance problems. Recent initiatives have transferred screening to airport management while leaving audits and training within TSA. Still other measures that have been implemented or are being considered include

Prioritizing security   Best-practice airport screening is increasingly shifting from indiscriminate searches to "focused security" systems that use guards, cameras, and behavioral profiling to monitor passengers' behavior. Examples of such systems can be found in Israeli airports as well as Boston's Logan Airport. However controversial, profiling can be statistically powerful.[8] In principle, these rules could be evaded if terrorists used, for example, Western Europeans to evade profiling systems. However, Al Qaeda's ability to recruit (and trust) such people is not clear. A second difficulty is that terrorists may not know exactly what profile defenders are using. In principle, terrorists can learn something about profiles by smuggling weapons aboard aircraft in "dry runs" days or weeks before the actual attack. However, sophisticated profiling systems can largely negate this advantage by constantly making random adjustments to the criteria, so that tactics that work one day may fail the next. The techniques also face political problems because of their reliance on ethnically and politically sensitive criteria, most notably nationality and race. For this reason, efforts to make airport screening more focused frequently inherit opposition from the broader U.S. debate over profiling.

Electronic waybills In 2002, Congress required that manifests be submitted in advance for all cargo entering the United States. TSA issued rules implementing this mandate in late 2003. While the TSA's initial focus was on bombings and September 11–style hijackings, concerns that cargo planes could be used to smuggle/deliver WMD have become increasingly prominent over time. Under the current system, air cargo carriers are responsible for preparing electronic master waybills that verify cargo contents prior to arrival. While customers supply much of this information, carriers are ultimately responsible for accuracy. This legal obligation helped persuade UPS, for example, to design and implement its own voluntary radiation screening program in 2002. Reliance on private carriers has, in turn, allowed TSA to concentrate its resources in other areas, including real time computerized monitoring of waybill data for suspicious items and patterns.

6.3 International Cooperation

The United States signed Smart Border agreements with Canada and Mexico in 2001 and 2002 respectively.[9] These diplomatic agreements have resulted in several trilateral initiatives within the cooperative framework established by the North American Free Trade Agreement (NAFTA). The following are some examples of programs and investments that have been implemented to enhance security and facilitate trade.

6.3.1 Security and Prosperity Partnership

The Security and Prosperity Partnership (SPP) is a trilateral initiative negotiated by Canada, Mexico, and the United States in June 2005. The SPP is designed to promote greater cooperation and information sharing between the three countries to keep the region's borders safe yet open to trade (CBSA 2007). The SPP also works to enhance collaboration on environmental protection, food security, and public health. Current key priorities include emergency management, avian influenza, energy security, and border security/commerce facilitation. For their part, private-sector partners have now formed the North American Competitiveness Council (NACC) to participate in the SPP process by providing high-level business input to the SPP's security initiatives and to facilitate more private-public partnerships.

6.3.2 The Free and Secure Trade Program

The Free and Secure Trade (FAST) program is a Border Accord Initiative between Mexico, Canada, and the United States. The goal is to coordinate, to the maximum extent possible, processes for clearing commercial shipments at the border. The agreement stresses the development of common risk-management principles, supply chain security, industry partnerships, and advanced technology to streamline customs processing of commercial traffic.

The centerpiece of FAST is a voluntary program that gives participating carriers, drivers, importers, and (on the southern border) manufacturers expedited border processing privileges.[10] To qualify, applicants must certify that their supply chains (e.g., importers, carriers, brokers, warehouse operators, and manufacturers) conform to the security practices established by the Customs and Trade Partnership Against Terrorism (C-TPAT) program, a joint government/business initiative aimed at improving supply-chain security. In effect, this shifts some of the burden of establishing security from CBP to private partners. Since private partners are often better placed to enforce security, this can be an effective strategy. The program also releases resources so that CBP can focus on high-risk or unknown commerce.

Participation Requirements   Any truck using FAST lane processing must be a C-TPAT approved carrier, must only carry goods from C-TPAT approved importers, and must be driven by someone holding a valid FAST Commercial Driver Registration card. Additionally, containers crossing the southern border must originate with a manufacturer and be closed using special CBP high-security seals.

Registration   Importers must complete an application for C-TPAT participation with CBP. FAST importers must also possess a good C-TPAT compliance record. Finally, carriers must complete an application process that includes corporate information, a security profile, and a written Highway Carrier Agreement to participate in the program. A GAO evaluation of C-TPAT has suggested that supply-chain security could be further enhanced by improving the validation and documentation procedures followed by U.S. importers participating in the program (Caldwell 2007).

Northern Border   To qualify for FAST Highway Carrier membership in the United States and Canada, applicants must obtain separate approval from each country's FAST Processing Center. Each country performs its own independent risk assessment. To obtain U.S. approval, applicants must promise to abide by C-TPAT's required security practices and use employees who possess valid FAST commercial driver cards. CBT then performs a security review and checks for insurance through the Mellon Financial Corporation. Canadian applications are processed by Canada Border Service Agency (CBSA), Citizenship and Immigration Service for Canada (CIC), and Canada's Agence de Revenu (ARC). In both cases, successful applicants report to an enrollment center where they are interviewed, have their identification and citizenship documents reviewed, and are fingerprinted and digitally photographed. They then receive a FAST Commercial Driver Card.

FAST Cargo Release Methods   FAST is CBP's first completely paperless cargo release system. The system uses electronic data transmitters and transponders to expedite release for participating companies. FAST is currently available at nineteen crossing points.[11]

Pre-Arrival Processing System (PAPS)   Cargo outside the FAST program is screened and released by an automated Pre-Arrival Processing System (PAPS). PAPS uses barcode labels which the carrier attaches to the invoice while the truck is still outside the United States. U.S. Customs then uses the barcode to input carrier and shipment data into an Automated Commercial System (ACS) which analyses the data using the agency's Border Cargo Selectivity and Automated Targeting System software. These computer programs tell CBP officers how much inspection to conduct. If no examination is required, the CBP officer releases the truck immediately.

6.3.3   Bilateral Actions: Canada
In January 2007, Canada's Ministry of Public Safety announced that it would invest C$431.6 million over five years to reinforce smart, secure borders. The initiative includes

eManifest   This C$396 million investment will collect electronic cargo data and provide automated risk assessments for the Canada Border Services Agency ("CBSA") before shipments reach the border. Highway and rail carriers will be required to electronically submit all cargo, crew, and conveyance information in advance.

Business Resumption Plan   CBSA will devote C$24 million to joint emergency planning and harmonization with the United States. CBSA will also conduct exercises and develop protocols to minimize business disruptions following a border incident.

Partners in Protection   CBSA will spend C$11.6 million to expand its Partners in Protection (PIP) program against organized crime, smuggling, and terrorism. PIP will be closely harmonized with its American counterpart, C-TPAT.

6.3.4   Bilateral Action: Mexico
The Canadian initiatives have been matched by similar agreements with Mexico:

Megaports Agreement   The United States and Mexico signed the Megaports Agreement to prevent the smuggling of nuclear and radioactive materials in 2007. The Agreement authorizes the Department of Energy's National Nuclear Security Administration (NNSA) to work with Mexican customs officials to install radiation detectors at four seaports that collectively process almost 90 percent of Mexico's container traffic. The United States will contribute $US50 million toward the effort.[12]

SENTRI   The Secured Electronic Network Traveler Rapid Inspection Lane (SENTRI) provides a dedicated lane and expedited CBP processing for preapproved, low-risk automobile traffic. Applicants must voluntarily undergo a thorough background check against criminal, law enforcement, customs, immigration, and terrorist databases, a ten-fingerprint law enforcement check, and a personal interview with CBP (CBP 2007). They then receive a Radio Frequency Identification (RFID) card for themselves and their vehicle. All applicant data is stored in a secure CBP database in order to protect any potentially sensitive information about the individual's movements. No data are stored on the card or transmitted by RFID.[13] Membership does not exempt vehicles and passengers from screening. However, it does provide dedicated lanes that let participants cross the border faster even at peak hours. Because information about travelers is already on file, inspection times are typically reduced from thirty to forty seconds to about ten seconds on average (CBP 2007). SENTRI currently operates at eight high traffic POEs along the U.S./Mexican border.[14]

As the number of security concerns increases and the flow of people and goods across U.S. borders becomes more complex, new multilateral and bilateral agreements will almost certainly be needed to keep border processing and security capabilities current.

6.4   Public-Private Initiatives

Historically, POEs have been managed very differently depending on whether they are border crossings, maritime ports, or airports. Current public-private security initiatives reflect these divisions.

6.4.1   Land Borders

Unlike ports and airports, land POEs are invariably operated by governments. Private cooperation comes mainly through C-TPAT's efforts to manage the supply chains that lead into and out of these facilities.

6.4.2   Ports

The federal government's security responsibilities are much smaller for ports than for other POEs. Federal agencies have, however, been instrumental in encouraging port operators to introduce various initiatives and adopt more uniform practices across terminals.

Transportation Worker Identity Credential (TWIC)   Many ports have begun introducing biometric cards to monitor the flow of personnel and maritime cargo into and out of facilities and controlled areas. The Department of Homeland Security has been working with port and terminal operators to make these practices uniform. The proposed Transportation Worker Identification Card (TWIC) would be a (sometimes port-specific). ID card containing each worker's vehicle registration, driver's license, work permit, safety record, and insurance information (Ward 2001). A registry would also list this information for all truckers authorized to enter any particular port.

Radiation Portal Monitors   Ports have also begun to install portals to screen containers for radiation. As discussed in chapter 5, it is not clear that current technologies are sufficient. Indeed, current purchases may not be cost-effective and seem to have been motivated by a political need to demonstrate action at least as much as technological considerations.

Trucker Identification and Registration System   Currently, truck drivers are identified by human gate guards. This time-consuming and fallible process produces long lines and errors that could potentially jeopardize port security. Recently, individual terminal operators have extended their security perimeters so that trucks first encounter an unmanned kiosk that photographs the truck and reads its chassis number using optical character recognition. The truck driver then proceeds to a manned terminal where his or her driver's license and papers are presented. Until recently, U.S. ports seldom had reservation systems and allowed drivers to arrive unannounced. This is now beginning to change, especially at the major East and West Coast ports.

Port Personnel Biometric Smart Card Authentication System   Biometric systems like electronic fingerprint identification, facial geometry, signature recognition, and voice recognition can perform identification and authentication almost instantaneously. Every port employee and authorized trucker could potentially be issued a smart card containing the holder's unique biometric identifiers (e.g., retinal scan measurements) and the sectors of the port that he or she is authorized to visit. Each individual would then pass their card through a reader each time they entered the terminal and submit to biometric identification. In principle, RFID technology could also allow managers to track cardholders once they entered the facility.[15]

Trucker Appointment System   Some East Coast and overseas ports have introduced systems that require shippers to make electronic appointments before moving freight into or out of the port. Gate control personnel receive an electronic record before the truck arrives. The record includes driver, company, and insurance information; pickup and delivery authorization; special handling instructions; cargo-container seal numbers;[16] and a universal transaction number that can be used to track containers from origin to destination.[17]

In principle, trucks could also be authorized to proceed through the gate without stopping. Some terminals in Los Angeles/Long Beach already use a simple version of this system for so-called bobtail trucks that arrive without containers. Arrivals are scheduled in advance by fax or e-mail. When the bobtail approaches the terminal, it travels down a special lane and enters the yard after the normal identification security check but without otherwise stopping. The system is said to reduce queuing time throughout the terminal.

Some ports use an "appointment window" system in which drivers are given a specific time interval in which to enter. Truckers make these appointments over the internet. Truckers who arrive early or run late can also adjust their arrival time by cell phone. For their part, ports use automated scheduling software to stagger appointments to reduce lines, road congestion, and waiting times. Many large terminals (e.g., LA/Long Beach) also offer "pier passes" that provide access during the off-hours between 6 p.m. and 2–3 a.m. Pier passes have become very popular, and it is not unusual to see long lines of trucks waiting outside terminals for 6 p.m. to arrive.

Electronically Read Tamper Evident Seals   Smart seals equipped with GPS could potentially provide real-time evidence of tampering anywhere in the world. However, the technology remains controversial. First, serious terrorists or thieves could theoretically defeat such systems by removing an entire wall of the container and later replacing it. Second, installing such seals on the millions of containers that enter and leave U.S. ports would cost several billion dollars. Finally, the federal government, port managers, terminal operators, vendors, shippers, and other key players have yet to agree on an acceptable cost-sharing scheme.

Container Intelligence   Before September 11, painted markings were the only external form of container identification. At most terminals, human gate guards use closed circuit television to read them, although this is slowly giving way to automated optical character recognition systems. Radio Frequency Identification (RFID) tags that automatically respond to electronic interrogation signals could potentially provide a much more powerful solution. This would immediately reduce both waiting time and reduce the risk of human error. If the tags were connected to GPS, containers could also report their position anywhere in the yard. Terminals that have adopted the technology typically combine this information with video cameras so that managers can place a cursor on a particular image and immediately identify the container's contents and location. In some terminals, this has driven the UTL ("unable to locate") rate below 1 percent.

Finally, U.S. Customs authorities have introduced radiation portal monitors (RPM) at most major terminals since September 11. Trucks drive through the devices as they enter and leave the facility. The extra screening seems to have had little impact on traffic flows except in a few cases where CPT failed to train enough inspectors. More advanced devices are also being introduced to analyze container contents more accurately and detect lead shielding and other attempts to screen a radioactive weapon.

The economic impact of closing U.S. ports is very large. An independent analysis found that a four week closure of West Coast ports would produce an income loss of $4.79 billion (Anderson and Geckil 2002; see also chapter 14).

6.4.3 Airports

Airport security was federalized after September 11 to raise the quality of inspection workers and to make screening more uniform. The new Transportation Security Administration (TSA) also received a $6 billion budget to operate the system. Local airports continue to provide access control, perimeter patrols, and law enforcement under TSA's supervision.

Federalizing airport security was supposed to establish consistently high security standards regardless of airport size and function. However, some have charged that this one-size-fits-all approach is inefficient and prevents TSA officials from addressing airport-specific needs and differences (Poole and Carafano 2006). There has also been criticism that the federal government cannot adapt quickly enough to meet commercial aviation's needs. In principle, both of these problems can be addressed by reintroducing a measure of privatization into the system. Most European countries already use a performance-contracting model in which government sets high standards but lets airports decide whether to hire private companies or use their own staff (Dillingham 2001).[18] Because contracting out may be more cost-effective, the same law that federalized airport security in 2001 also established a pilot program that allowed five airports to conduct screening using qualified private firms.

Secure Flight   Secure Flight is a computerized system that checks passenger data against federal government watch lists for domestic and international flights. It also searches for suspicious patterns in data—for example, by flagging passengers who pay cash or purchase one-way tickets. It does not, however, examine records of prior trips.

The foregoing examples show that government has become increasingly reliant on public-private partnerships for new security measures and, especially, the deployment of sophisticated technologies. However, this strategy is limited by government's ability to offer incentives like reduced paperwork and quicker processing that enhance—or at least do not severely impede—private sector efficiency. Unless the United States is attacked again, commercial operators can be expected to resist measures that are expensive or threaten productivity while government will be reluctant to offer subsidies.

6.5   Conclusion

The United States is a vast country and border control will always be imperfect. Principal challenges include the extremely porous U.S.-Mexican border and inspecting the enormous flows of shipping containers without impeding the "just-in-time delivery" that is central to the modern economy. This last problem is most acute for air cargo, which remains, not surprisingly, among the most vulnerable. Furthermore, tabletop and other exercises show that agencies have yet to master various jurisdiction and communications challenges. Even so, the United States has made substantial efforts to enhance security since September 11, although there is still much to be done and the effectiveness of the existing measures is difficult to measure.

The debate over how best to protect U.S. borders is bound to continue. Only a second attack could definitively reveal the current system's weaknesses. Nevertheless, significant progress has been made. The first wave of post–September 11 border protection reforms brought drastically increased budgets and staff along with, in some cases, a new willingness to subject passengers and cargo to intrusive screening. These policies are now firmly established and are unlikely to be rolled back in any significant way. At the same time, they have reached their limits. Barring further attacks, existing budgets and/or intrusiveness have become more or less fixed and could even be reduced to pay for U.S. military operations in Southwest Asia. Interestingly, this has not stopped CBP from implementing some important second-generation reforms since 2003. These have uniformly been based on coupling new security measures to increased efficiency. Business and private citizens are happy to participate in programs like FAST, SENTRI, and C-TPAT that make entering the country faster and easier. Typically, these systems substitute trusted partners and information technology for physical inspection at the border. Given the physical impossibility of inspecting each and every person and container that enters the country, this seems like a reasonable strategy, not least because it lets CBP focus its resources on potentially high-risk people and shipments.

The question now is whether more ambitious programs are possible. In general, the easiest projects will probably be those where regulation or treaties can keep firms that upgrade security from being penalized. In a competitive economy, it is almost impossible for any single company to adopt an expensive technology like radiation screening. However, the situation is very different if government can impose uniform requirements on everyone so that no company loses business to its competitors. In this situation, businesses end up passing increased security costs on to the consumer. Given increased globalization, this will often require international cooperation among governments. As we have seen, recent experience is encouraging: U.S. trading partners clearly understand that security cooperation with the United States is good for business. Probably the hardest reforms are those that touch on organized labor. It is clear that many information technologies and work-practice changes could improve security. Unions often find such reforms ambiguous, however, because they typically *combine* higher wages *and* downsizing. Nevertheless, this trade-off will often be acceptable where the predicted downsizing is small compared to normal workforce attrition, downsized workers receive generous severance or early retirement packages, and/or failure to modernize means losing business to Canadian and Mexican ports. Where these conditions exist, government can and should take an active role in brokering appropriate deals between management and labor.

Over time, the United States has deployed multiple layers of defense at airports, border crossings, and seaports. As weaknesses in each layer have been identified—for example, unmanned border crossings—resources have been allocated to rectify the omissions and mistakes. On balance, there has been significant progress in all areas since the September 11 attacks. But weaknesses continue to be identified by Congress and watchdog groups, and it is important that these, if validated, be rectified in a timely fashion. Since government tends to move slowly, especially in the absence of new attacks, a timely response is often painfully difficult to achieve.

Notes

1. Federal law defines ports of entry as "any location in the United States or its territories that is designated as a point of entry to aliens and U.S. citizens."

2. A TEU or "twenty-foot equivalent unit" is equal to one standard cargo container. It measures $20 \times 8 \times 8.5$ feet.

3. Although the Millenium Bomb plot was successfully intercepted by alert law enforcement (9/11 Commission 2004), policymakers understood that this was largely a matter of luck.

4. Prior to the 1960s, ports were dirty and dangerous heavy industrial facilities. This depressed real estate prices and made adjoining land relatively cheap to acquire. The trend

was reinforced by high shipping costs, which encouraged heavy industry to collocate near ports. Today, ports are cleaner and more people-friendly while shipping costs have fallen dramatically. This has raised real estate values to the point where some of the nation's largest ports will run out of room to expand in the next decade.

5. The General Accountability Office (2008) has identified security vulnerabilities at unmanned and unmonitored U.S. border locations as one such priority.

6. DHS is responsible for establishing visa policy, reviewing implementation, and providing supplemental direction. The State Department has operational responsibility for managing the program.

7. "Special-interest" countries currently include Afghanistan, Algeria, Angola, Argentina, Armenia, Bahrain, Bhutan, Brazil, Congo, Cyprus, Egypt, Eritrea, Ethiopia, Georgia, India, Indonesia, Iran, Iraq, Israel, Jordan, Kazakhstan, Kenya, Kuwait, Kyrgyzstan, Lebanon, Liberia, Malaysia, Mongolia, Morocco, Myanmar, Nepal, Oman, Pakistan, Panama, Paraguay, Philippines, Qatar, Saudi Arabia, Somalia, Sri Lanka, Sudan, Syria, Tajikistan, Tunisia, Turkey, Turkmenistan, United Arab Emirates, Uruguay, Uzbekistan, Venezuela, and Yemen.

8. The computerized CAPPS system detected three of the nineteen September 11 hijackers before boarding, although then-current rules kept this information from gate screeners. U.S. visa rules similarly kept several of the plot's original personnel from entering the United States (9/11 Commission 2004).

9. For a brief review of the implementation of these accords see Meyers 2003.

10. Unlike normal carriers, inspection procedures for FAST participants do not increase during heightened alert levels.

11. Detroit was the first POE to offer FAST. Current border crossings include Alexandria Bay, New York; Brownsville, Texas; Blaine, Washington; Calexico, California; Buffalo, New York; El Paso, Texas; Champlain, New York; Laredo, Texas; Derby Line, Vermont; Nogales, Arizona; Otay Mesa, California; Houlton, Maine; Pharr, Texas; Pembina, North Dakota; Port Huron, Michigan; Portal, North Dakota; and Sweetgrass, Montana. Additional FAST sites are currently under development at Tecate, California; Calais, Maine; San Luis, Arizona; Massena, New York; Douglas, Arizona; Ogdensburg, New York; Santa Teresa, New Mexico; Sault St. Marie, Michigan; Eagle Pass, Texas; International Falls, Minnesota; Del Rio, Texas; Oroville, Washington; and Rio Grande City, Texas.

12. The Megaports program is designed to help U.S. trade partners install specialized radiation detectors at international seaports. The initiative currently includes agreements with eight nations. As of early 2008, the program had begun operational testing in three countries. The United States was also negotiating new Megaports agreements with thirteen nations.

13. Vehicles are scanned by license plate readers so that they and their occupants can be automatically checked against law enforcement databases. Physical security is implemented through a combination of electric gates, tire shredders, traffic control lights, and fixed and pneumatically operated pop-up bollards.

14. The first SENTRI site opened at Otay Mesa, California, on November 1, 1995. SENTRI Dedicated Commuter Lanes also exist in El Paso, Hidalgo, Brownsville, and Laredo, Texas; San Ysidro and Calexico, California; and Nogales, Arizona.

15. Biometric authentication systems have also been proposed for airport and airline safety (Atkinson 2001).

16. Current cargo containers are invariably sealed to prevent tampering. The massive seals can only be opened with bolt cutters.

17. Major retailers have widely adopted similar systems for warehouse operations across the United States.

18. TSA has experimented with private screening several times. In 2002, it launched a pilot program that allowed airports in San Francisco, California; Kansas City, Kansas; Rochester, New York; Jackson Hole, Wyoming; and Tupelo, Mississippi to subcontract screening to qualified private firms. Two years later, it launched a second pilot Screening Partnership Program that let airports hire contract employees instead of union members. So far, the program has had only limited success in attracting workers who meet TSA standards for new hires.

7

Setting Priorities: Assessing Threats and Identifying Cost-Effective Responses to WMD Terrorism

Thomas Edmunds and Richard Wheeler

In recent years, three facts have become increasingly clear regarding homeland security: (1) there are groups around the world that are motivated to attack the United States, (2) there remain serious vulnerabilities that, if exploited, could result in staggering consequences to population and infrastructure, and (3) there are not enough resources to fully defend all targets. This means that rational strategies must prioritize potential countermeasures according to how cost-effective they are in reducing total risk. Several approaches have been developed in the past to prioritize investments for various safety and reliability problems. However, homeland security is a much harder problem because it involves intelligent attackers instead of random failures. These attackers may be skilled and informed outsiders who can recognize and exploit weaknesses, and adapt to changing opportunities and defenses. They may even be trusted insiders. Risk analysis and operations research experts have worked hard to address these challenges since September 11.[1]

This chapter examines homeland security's unique prioritization problem using concepts and techniques from risk assessment, decision analysis, game theory, threat-based planning, and other disciplines. Conceptually, it is organized according to the subproblems that a rational risk analyst must face. Section 7.1 describes methods for characterizing an attacker's motivations, objectives, and values. Section 7.2 describes methods for assessing the likelihood of various attacks based on probability of success, consequences, and attacker motives. Section 7.3 looks at countermeasure design. Section 7.4 examines how computer models can be used to assess the effectiveness of countermeasures. Section 7.5 examines various methods for analyzing security measures in cases where attackers are assumed to be intelligent and adaptive. Section 7.6 discusses the usefulness and limitations of formal models as a tool for making real world decisions. Finally, section 7.7 presents a brief conclusion.

7.1 Motivations, Objectives, and Values of Attacker Groups

A determined, adaptive attacker can choose from many different weapons, delivery means, and targets. As a practical matter, this range of threats is so broad that comprehensive and continuous protection is unaffordable. Estimating how much the attacker values the consequences of a successful attack is an important starting point for prioritizing investments.

Consequences can be measured along many dimensions. For example, consider how an attacker might rank attack consequences according to three attributes—fatalities, cost, and symbolism. Multiattribute utility theory provides a well-established procedure for combining such attributes into a single figure of merit that can be used to unambiguously rank-order alternatives (Keeney and Raiffa 1976; Edwards, Miles, and Von Winterfeldt 2007). The process begins by designing independent, quantitative scales or "metrics" for each significant attribute. A surrogate decision maker representing the attacker is then asked to compare hypothetical alternatives that differ by two attributes. Instances in which the decision maker is indifferent to the alternatives can be used to infer the decision maker's preferences. These, in turn, can be used to assign weights to the attributes and (given enough comparisons) construct an overall multiattribute utility function. Modelers can choose many different forms for these functions. Some are simple and linear. On the other hand, more complex, nonlinear models may be appropriate when attributes are thought to interact with one another. In any case, the resulting formulas provide a single measure of the attacker's utility that neatly summarizes the desirability of a successful attack.

As we will see, complete analyses often require modelers to construct utility functions for the defender as well. Significantly, the defender's utility function may or may not mirror the attacker's. For example, the defender could seek to minimize casualties, economic damage, and symbolic impacts in the same proportions that the attacker seeks to maximize them. This corresponds to a zero-sum game and may be reasonable where the attacker's and defender's goals do mirror each other. More general analysis frameworks allow the attacker and defender to have different multiattribute utility functions. For instance, an attacker might value attacks on symbolic targets (e.g., the Statue of Liberty) highly, while the defender values human life more.

The attacker's objectives and corresponding utility function describe consequences he might seek to achieve. This, however, may not fully capture attacker behavior because it ignores the fact that some attacks are far less likely to succeed than others. For example, an improvised nuclear device (IND) detonated in a high-profile, high-density urban area would cause more casualties and economic damage than a con-

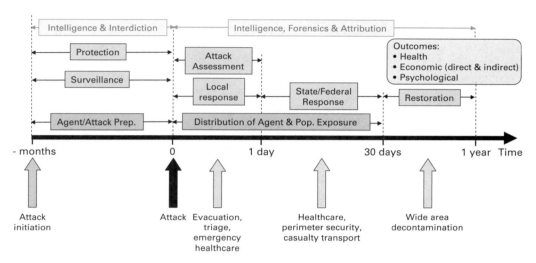

Figure 7.1
Attack scenario, preparation and response
Source: Edmunds, Wheeler, Gansemer, and Robertson (2004)

ventional explosive attack against a lower-profile target. However, it is generally thought that an IND would also be harder to acquire and deliver. The attacker would probably take this into account when deciding which weapon system to pursue and which target to attack. We turn to this subject now.

7.2 Threat Scenarios, Likelihoods, and Consequences

Attackers normally have many different strategies to choose from. These can be summarized as a set of scenarios, each of which involves a different weapon, delivery mode, or target. Figure 7.1 shows the timeline for a generic scenario and how it interacts with possible defense strategies, including intelligence and interdiction, surveillance, physical protection, and response and remediation. The scenario consequences depend on the combined outcome of the attacker's actions, weapons effects on humans and the physical environment, and the defender's preparations and response actions.

Timelines can differ considerably, depending on the scenario and especially the choice of weapon. For example, the consequences of an attack might only last several weeks for a chemical like chlorine, but years for an IND. Similarly, particular defense investments will usually have different effectiveness levels for different scenarios. In the case of nuclear weapons, for instance, the consequences of a successful

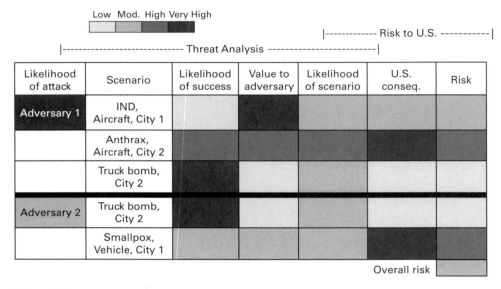

Figure 7.2
Attack scenarios, objective functions and risk

detonation are so large that detection and interdiction are critical. On the other hand, postrelease responses like minimizing exposure and initiating low-regret medical treatment (e.g., antibiotics) are much more appealing for some biological scenarios. This is especially true since detecting biological agents before release is extremely difficult (chapter 5).

We have already seen that each attack scenario offers attackers a particular utility if successful. However, a rational attacker would also want to consider the relative chance of success before deciding on a scenario. For their part, defenders need to estimate the extent to which attackers are likely to discount valuable-but-unlikely scenarios before formulating their own strategy. Figure 7.2 shows how a defense problem involving two attackers and five possible attack strategies might be analyzed. Variables are depicted using a qualitative scale[2] similar to those that are typically used to elicit opinions from experts.[3] In the example, the "likelihood of success" and "value to adversary" columns combine to produce a "likelihood of scenario" estimate summarizing the probability an adversary will execute an attack within some fixed time period, or equivalently, the frequency of attacks. This information is combined with the defender's valuation of expected consequences to arrive at an overall risk. In this example, the likelihood of attacker 1 acquiring and detonating a nuclear weapon is low but the consequences are high. In contrast, the likelihood of successfully acquiring and detonating a truck bomb is high but the consequences are limited.

In this simple example, rational attackers could be expected to pursue whichever attack scenario offers maximum expected consequences—that is, the product of likelihood of success and consequences. This analysis, however, assumes that the attacker has perfect information about several factors, including (1) the deployment of countermeasures to detect and interdict threats, (2) the effectiveness of counter-measures against each alternative attack scenario, (3) the performance of the attacker's own weapon system, and (4) the consequences of a successful attack.

Attackers will find it harder to decide on a strategy when some of these data are missing or uncertain. Consider first the limiting case in which the attacker has no information about countermeasure systems or consequences. Here, one might expect the attacker to choose randomly so that each scenario had the same likelihood. The case of substantial-but-still-imperfect information can then be thought of as a situation midway between optimizing and random behavior. To represent such a situation, we might assign a probability distribution to scenario likelihoods that is more heavily weighted to those with high expected consequences but leaves some chance that other strategies may be pursued instead. Formally, there are many possible equations that smoothly interpolate between the perfect and zero information solutions. In principle, any of these can be used to model terrorists' choice of strategies under imperfect information, although in practice some are more plausible than others. Equation 7.1 shows a particularly simple model in which the probability of terrorists pursuing a scenario depends solely on expected consequences:

$$l_i = a_g \frac{p_i v_i}{\sum_{n=1}^{N} p_n v_n} \tag{7.1}$$

where l_i = likelihood of attack scenario i
a_g = likelihood that attacker group g will attack within a fixed time period
p_i = probability of success with scenario i
v_i = consequences of scenario i if successful
N = number of scenarios

Of course, the simple example shown in figure 7.2 and discussed above is only illustrative. Real investment decisions would normally need many scenarios for the range of threats considered to yield reasonable answers. A recent Canadian effort to prioritize science and technology investments follows this basic approach by offering a "consolidated risk assessment" that explicitly identifies more than fifty scenarios involving chemical, biological, radiological, or nuclear attacks. The assessment then makes and integrates independent judgments about likelihood, technical feasibility, and impact of each scenario (Boulet 2003; Wheeler, Edmunds, and Howarth 2004; DRDC n.d.(a,b)).

This approach is based on decomposing threats into a finite number of scenarios and then finding investments that minimize the total risk from this ensemble. However, capabilities-based planning offers a potential shortcut (GAO 2007d; Caudle 2005b; Goss 2005; Davis 2002). Here, analysts start from the assumption that the uncertainty surrounding the threat at any given time is so large that it is impossible to plan specific defenses. Instead, the goal is to develop a limited set of key capabilities that are effective against entire categories of threats. For example, the Canadian study described above identifies several such "capability functions," including "surveillance and situation awareness," "communications," "detection and identification," "incident response," "public care," "site restoration," and "assessment and modeling" (Boulet 2003; Wheeler, Edmunds, and Howarth 2004; DRDC, n.d.(a,b)). It then tests these capabilities against a large sample of potential scenarios to identify gaps and, by implication, targets for investment. One limitation of this procedure is that it is hard to compare the relative importance of whichever gaps are identified. In the following sections, we show how risk managers can use more formal simulation and optimization methods to identify the highest-risk scenarios and target investment accordingly.

7.3   Attack Scenario Risk Management

The risk assessment described in section 7.2 would normally be repeated at regular intervals. Resources would then be allocated among possible short-term countermeasures (e.g., increased patrols or intelligence gathering) and long-term investments (e.g., detector research or physically hardening targets). Figure 7.3 provides a generic illustration of how scenario risk assessment and countermeasure strategies interact.

As indicated in the figure, the starting point is to develop a suite of attack scenarios that covers the full range of possible attacker objectives and capabilities. The likelihood of attack can then be estimated using the methods discussed in section 7.2, or else elicited from experts in terrorism behavior and weapons design. Significantly, studies have shown that the process of elicitation can sometimes introduce unconscious psychological biases into experts' opinions. Various methodologies and protocols have been developed to reduce this effect (Edwards, Miles, and Von Winterfeldt 2007). Finally, some authors have suggested that similar information could be obtained by establishing terrorism futures markets (Hanson 2006). This mechanism would potentially allow government to reach out beyond a narrow group of experts.[4]

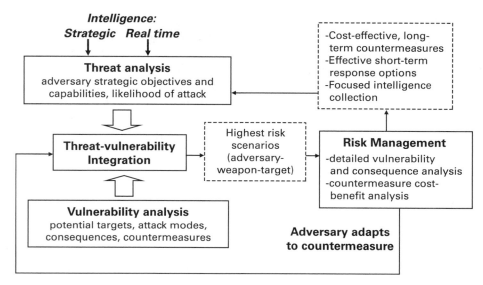

Figure 7.3
Scenario risk and assessment and management

Once scenarios and likelihoods have been estimated, the information can be integrated with data about the targets and their vulnerabilities to rank scenarios according to "risk." Algebraically, this is defined by the formula

Risk = (probability of attempt) × (probability of success)

× (consequence if successful)

In general, a comprehensive threat analysis would require analysts to consider a large number of scenarios to ensure that all risks (and especially the higher-risk scenarios) were included. Especially high risk scenarios would likely be analyzed in further detail using specially prepared models.

At this point, the value of a proposed countermeasure investment can be estimated by computing the total risk reduction that it is likely to achieve across all possible attack scenarios using an analysis similar to that shown in figure 7.2. Dividing the countermeasure's expected cost by this reduction in risk then yields a cost-benefit ratio, which provides a reasonable proxy for overall cost-effectiveness. Prioritization follows automatically by observing which countermeasure investments offer the highest cost-effectiveness ratios.[5]

Finally, we assume that the attacker can observe countermeasures and change his behavior accordingly. This, in turn, changes the cost-effectiveness ratios and implied investment priorities previously calculated. These changes will usually be inferred from analysis, expert opinion, and real-time intelligence information about threats. Emerging analytical methods can be used to revise the estimated risk profile even when the underlying data sets are extremely large (Allanach et al. 2004). As indicated in figure 7.3, these changes in the attacker's presumed behavior will then require a further round of threat specification and threat-vulnerability integration analysis. The result is an iterative loop that continues until the defender arrives at a prioritization that is stable against further changes in the attacker's behavior (Powell 2007a). Funds are then allocated to the most cost-effective countermeasures until resources are exhausted. The game-theoretic aspects of countermeasure resource allocation will be addressed further in section 7.5.3.

7.4   Computer Simulation

Computer simulations are another potentially powerful tool for estimating how possible countermeasures are likely to reduce overall risk. Once built, such models let analysts explore a wide variety of possible countermeasure architectures and also evaluate their robustness in cases where information is limited. In some cases, several different types of simulation may be needed to analyze a single scenario. This section surveys some of the most useful classes of models.

Many scenarios and countermeasures involve processes that must be repeatedly performed. Industry has developed several software packages to conduct *discrete event simulations* to analyze such problems for manufacturers (Swain 2007). These are particularly well suited to security operations like routinely screening vehicles and cargo for, say, radioactivity or chemical weapons. For example, adding a second layer of inspection increases security but adds to cost. Detailed simulation can explore the circumstances in which such trade-offs are warranted. *Queuing models* can similarly simulate processes in which members of the public individually decide when to arrive at a particular government facility seeking resources. These models are particularly useful in deciding whether current public health plans will be able to distribute antibiotics to exposed individuals quickly enough to be effective.

Finally, *phenomenological simulations* are frequently used to help evaluate risks associated with various scenarios. This broad class of models includes

• *Nuclear weapons effects*   Complex nuclear weapons codes were among the earliest computer simulations. Nuclear weapons effects based on first-principles calculations from physical laws and/or empirical data from past explosions are available in the open literature (Glasstone and Dolan 1977).

• *Atmospheric dispersion models*   Safety and security analysts use these models to track how substances like radiological, biological, or chemical agents disperse when released into the atmosphere (IMAAC 2005). The models typically start with an assumed release point, time, and amount and then calculate how the resulting plume evolves over time. This information, in turn, can be used to identify exposed populations and doses. The models can also be used to simulate the effectiveness of countermeasures when authorities' knowledge of the plume state is limited. This will likely be the case just after the release, when release characteristics must be inferred by, for example, combining readings from different detectors with recent weather data.

• *Supply-chain models* These models have been used for food-contamination threats to characterize the leading edge of exposures (i.e., determine when contaminated lots first reach consumers) and to estimate how much contaminated product will ultimately be consumed. For these scenarios, consequences are driven by the speed with which authorities can recognize the attack and respond to prevent still-unsold contaminated product from being consumed.

• *Water utility models* These models can be used to evaluate the likely consequences for attacks that inject chemical or biological agents into water supplies. In practice, useful predictions require detailed data on how populations normally consume tap water across time and space.

• *Public health warning* In many scenarios, the effectiveness of countermeasures depends on how quickly public health authorities can detect and issue warnings that a chemical, biological, or radiological agent has been released. Simulations can potentially supply this information. Obtaining data for these models can be problematic, since few (if any) public health officials have ever experienced outbreaks on scales similar to most WMD scenarios. Progress will depend on clever use of evidence from analogous cases (Inoue and Kawakami 2004).

• *Dose-response models* In the absence of chemical or biological agent sensors, the time delay between ingestion or inhalation of an agent and the presentation of symptoms to health-care officials determines when the attack is first detected. Thereafter, the interval between the onset of symptoms and normal termination of the illness in death or recovery determines the time available to treat patients. Scenario simulations must therefore include a probability distribution that specifies the range of these periods within the target population. Animal models and, in some cases, limited human exposure data are typically used for this purpose (Arnon et al. 2001; Henderson 1999; Inglesby et al. 1999).

• *Contagious disease spread* Analysts studying contagious organism attacks need clear models of how disease spreads (chapter 4). These models must be computationally efficient so that a wide range of alternative countermeasures and response plans can be analyzed. However, they must also be sufficiently complex to faithfully reproduce the social interaction patterns that drive outbreaks (Eubank et al. 2004; Meyers et al. 2003).

• *Health-care logistics*   Expected casualties depend on the rates at which health-care resources and patients arrive over time and how patients respond if treatment is administered. For each patient, outcomes can be predicted probabilistically based on known or inferred dose-response relationships and time of treatment. Simulations similar to the supply chain models discussed above are a powerful method for analyzing these problems.

7.5   Adaptive Threats

Unlike accidents, homeland security risk includes strategic behavior by a determined attacker. Adversary behavior has been modeled using a variety of techniques including game theory (Powell 2007a; Aghassi and Bertsimas 2006), probabilistic risk analysis (Beir 2006), Bayesian modeling (Pate-Cornell and Guikema 2002), and social networks (Allanach et al. 2004). However, it is difficult to validate the extent to which any of these models simulate actual attackers. This section reviews a range of models that describe how rational actors would make decisions under uncertainty. Significantly, many of these models feature adaptive attackers who can change strategies in response to a defender's actions.

7.5.1   Event Tree Models

Event tree models are often used to analyze phenomena in which sequences of chance events lead to uncertain outcomes (Clemen 2005). Event tree models for homeland security typically include a sequence of attacker choices, defender responses, and the resulting outcomes. Figure 7.4 illustrates a typical model.

In this example, scenarios evolve from left to right, probabilistic events are represented by circles, and attack outcomes are denoted by triangles. Attackers begin by choosing a weapon, transportation method, and target. These choices are *inputs* to the model and are typically elicited from experts in attacker behavior and weapon technologies. An attempt is then made to deliver the weapon to the target, which may or may not be interdicted. Interdiction, in turn, can either block the weapon entirely or cause it to detonate prematurely. The total probability associated with any given outcome is then the product of all probabilities encountered along the path that leads to it. As before, these probabilities are obtained from experts using the methods discussed in section 7.2. Similarly, the risk associated with each scenario is calculated by multiplying the associated path's probability with the consequence value assigned to its end point.[6] Finally, summing the values across all paths yields a measure of the nation's overall risk from terrorist attacks.

The probabilities and consequence estimates elicited from experts or estimated from models often have large uncertainties. These can be analyzed by assigning dis-

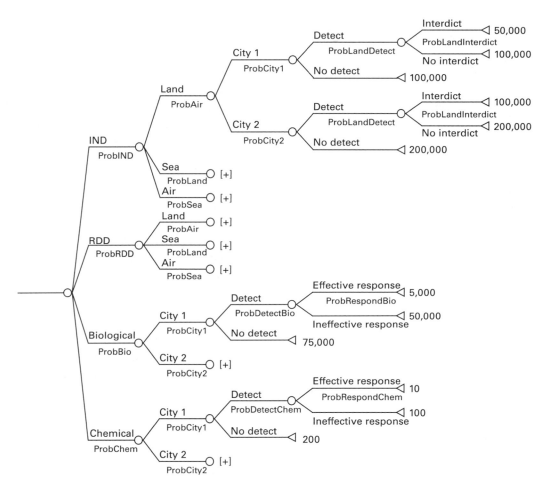

Figure 7.4
Event tree describing possible attack scenarios

tributions to each probability and consequence value used in the tree. Repeated computer simulations ("Monte Carlo simulations") are then used to calculate how the range of possible input values translates into formal uncertainties ("error bars") in the model's calculated results.

The Department of Homeland Security recently used this approach to conduct an analysis of bioterrorism threat scenarios involving twenty-eight pathogens and a seventeen-step event tree (NRC/Committee on Methodological Improvements 2007). Subsequent review by a U.S. National Academy of Sciences panel identified two areas where future analyses could be improved. First, the damages that defenders expected to suffer in a successful attack could be better analyzed by reducing stakeholder values to a suitable utility model reflecting the full range of possible consequences and their importance to the public. Second, the panel recommended extending the model to evaluate alternative risk management strategies instead of just estimating risk (NRC/Committee on Methodological Improvements 2007). This could be done by modifying the model to reflect alternative defense investments and calculating the change in risk. In general, different countermeasure architectures would then lead to increased detection and interdiction probabilities or reduced consequence values across the tree. Cost effectiveness could then be calculated and improvements prioritized as before.

The main limitation of event tree models is that attacker choices are represented probabilistically a priori and not as actors making conscious decisions on how to maximize the impact of an attack for some given set of countermeasures. Decision trees offer an alternative approach for capturing how attackers respond to changing countermeasures.

7.5.2 Decision Tree Models

Event tree models use expert opinion to establish the probability that attackers will pursue any given strategy. However, it is also possible to simulate the attacker as a rational decision maker who develops his own event tree and acts accordingly. In this decision tree approach, the attacker's actions are *outputs* of the model. Formally, this means replacing the chance nodes in figure 7.4 with decision nodes in which attackers choose whichever path promises the largest expected consequences at that point in the tree (Clemen 2005).

Decision tree methods are very useful for evaluating how an attacker is likely to change strategy in response to new security investments. Figure 7.5 shows how a "strategy switching curve" can be used to summarize this information. In this maritime security example, the horizontal axis measures the defender's ability to detect suspicious vessels at sea and the vertical axis measures its ability to board and search them. The performance of the first countermeasure system is captured by

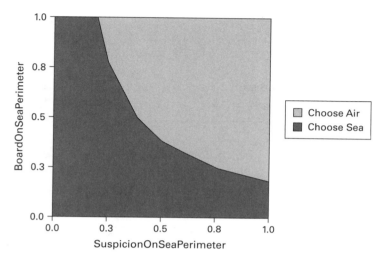

Figure 7.5
Adversary strategy switching behavior

the "Suspicion on Sea" parameter, which measures the probability that a threat vessel will be flagged as suspicious. The second countermeasure uses a fleet of ships to board suspicious vessels. This capability can be characterized in terms of a "Board on Sea" parameter.

When neither capability exists—point (0, 0) in the figure—the attacker's optimal strategy is to transport weapons by sea ("Choose Sea"). If both capabilities are nearly perfect—point (1, 1)—the attacker switches to air transport. The boundary between these two regions identifies points where the attacker switches from a maritime path to an air transport path. Finally, consider the intermediate case where the defender's SuspicionOnSeaPerimeter capability is 0.5. In this case, the defender should not invest in a BoardOnSeaPerimeter capability larger than 0.4 because this is enough to force an adaptive attacker to change his strategy to the air route. After that, further investments in either of the two maritime capabilities will be wasted, so that any remaining resources should be used to make the air pathway more secure.

Fault Tree Models Fault tree models are a variation on event and decision tree methods that were originally developed to analyze safety in nuclear reactors and other facilities featuring multiple complex subsystems (Nuclear Regulatory Commission 1975; Apostolakis and Lemon 2005). Formally, fault trees are hierarchical arrangements of AND, OR, and other Boolean logic gates that describe necessary conditions to achieve an overall goal. Figure 7.6 shows a sample tree used to

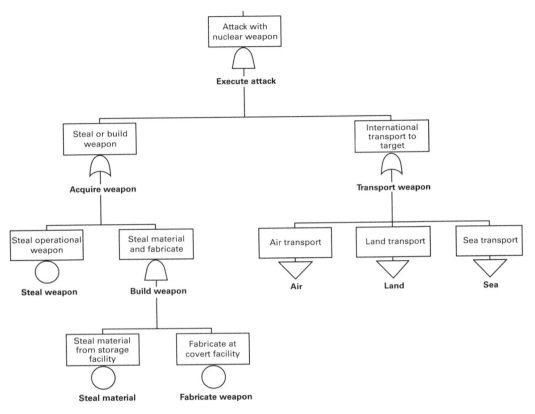

Figure 7.6
Generic fault tree analysis

evaluate nuclear attack risks. Here the top event, *Attack with nuclear weapon*, is triggered by the logical AND combination of two events: *Steal or build weapon* AND *International transport to target*. The symbol below the top-level event shows that it can only happen if *both* of these events occur. In contrast, the OR symbol beneath *Steal or build weapon* indicates that only one of the two events below must occur to reach this level. Finally, the circles at the bottom of the diagram are called "basic events." These are assumed inputs to the model that must be elicited from experts.

Fault tree models can help identify critical components where investments are likely to be unusually powerful in preventing the top-level event from occurring (Vesely et al. 1987; Vesely 2002). The main drawback of such models is that they are static: once the basic event probabilities have been established, they remain fixed. This presumes that the attacker never reacts to countermeasures. Interested readers should consult Garrick (2002) for a useful discussion of the benefits and limitations of using quantitative risk assessment (mainly fault trees) to assess terrorism risk.

7.5.3   Game Theory

As discussed above, effective countermeasure design should consider the possibility that attackers will adapt and respond to whatever measures are taken. Mathematical game theory provides a natural language for this interplay between attacker and defense strategies and has been used extensively to analyze business, warfare, ecology, and other problems (Luce and Raiffa 1957; Shubik 1982; Friedman 1986; Gibbons 1992; Thomas 2004; Reed 2006; Powell 2007a). We have already remarked that games often have zero-sum payoffs in which one player seeks to maximize some quantity (for example, casualties) that the other seeks to minimize. Alternatively, defenders and attackers can place different weights on different outcomes (e.g., symbolic attacks versus casualties) so that their respective payoff functions are no longer symmetric.

Formally, homeland security can be analyzed as a game in which two players[7] each choose from a range of possible strategies to maximize their expected payoffs. The particular strategies chosen by *both* players then determine *each* player's payoff.[8] The sequence in which players choose their strategies plays a key role in determining each game's structure and analysis. Games in which each player must choose a strategy before the other player's choice is known can be solved by finding a so-called Nash equilibrium in which no player can benefit by changing his or her strategy as long as the other players keep their original strategy (Gibbons 1992).

Consider, for example, a simple game in which a smuggler must choose a route and an inspector deploys assets to detect him. The strategies available to players are shown in table 7.1.

As often happens in real-world analyses, neither player has a clearly superior ("dominant") strategy. However, players can still maximize their expected payoff by adopting "mixed strategies" in which they randomly select a strategy according to some optimal probability distribution that can be calculated for each player. For example, the smuggler in our example can maximize his expected payoff by smuggling by air routes 34 percent of the time, land routes 43 percent of the time, and sea routes 23 percent of the time. The inspector, on the other hand, should cover these three routes 32, 24, and 44 percent of the time, respectively. If each player uses these optimal distributions, the overall probability of detection is 0.31.

Table 7.1
Smuggling game with Nash mixed-strategy solution

Smuggler strategy	Inspector strategy			
	Air	Land	Sea	Probability
Air	0.9	0.1	0.2	0.34
Land	0.1	0.8	0.4	0.43
Sea	0.2	0.1	0.7	0.23
Probability	0.32	0.24	0.44	

This simple example assumes that each player can keep his strategy choice hidden from the other. However, real homeland security problems often feature *asymmetric information* in which the defender's security measures are observable but the attacker's plans are not. Here, defenders must choose their strategy *before* the attacker, knowing that the attacker will exploit this information in its response. Formally, this type of sequential game can be analyzed as a "Stackelberg" or "bilevel" game (Bard 1998). This framework has been widely used to model smuggling networks (Woodruff 2003) and infrastructure defense (Israeli and Wood 2002; Yao et al. 2006).

7.6   Using Models for Real-World Decisions

Policy decisions regarding WMD terrorism and homeland security are routinely informed by the kinds of quantitative analyses described in this chapter. This is true across the threat spectrum. Current Department of Homeland Security examples include studies to find major gaps in the air, land, and sea pathways between U.S. ports (chapter 6); assessing different possible radiation and nuclear detection architectures (chapter 5); and (in cooperation with HHS, USDA, and DoD) using simulations to better understand the spread of contagious disease in human and animal populations (chapter 4).

These virtual testbeds allow analysts to explore policy options that could never be tested in the real world. Furthermore, the results build policymakers' intuition by identifying important illustrative cases, highlighting generic policy choices, and—through sensitivity analysis—probing the limits of their knowledge and ability to predict outcomes. This does not mean that model recommendations should automatically be translated into policy. In the end, policy making remains—appropriately—a highly democratic and politicized process. That said, giving decision makers access to the best available representations of reality can only improve the quality of their debate and, ultimately, decisions.

Despite the widespread use of models, much remains to be done. In purely technical terms, even state-of-the-art models continue to be challenged by problems that include large numbers of variables, uncertainty, and/or differences between decision makers (or at least stakeholders) over values and objectives. As a result, many interesting problems remain mathematically intractable. Even more fundamentally, methods for modeling intelligent attackers with imperfect information are still in their infancy. Finally, many existing models still limit themselves to estimating risks ("assessment") instead of analyzing solutions ("management") (NRC/Committee on Methodological Improvements 2007).

Beyond these technical issues, even well-intentioned and diligent modeling studies must be careful to frame problems in ways calculated to shed light on the specific questions that decision makers actually care about. At a minimum, the purpose for doing a risk assessment should be made clear from the outset and kept firmly in mind throughout the exercise (NRC/Committee on Methodological Improvements 2007). Finally, modelers must be careful in communicating their results to policy makers who are seldom familiar with the language of analysts or tool purveyors (NRC/Committee on Methodological Improvements 2007). Poor communication will often mean the difference between models that usefully guide real resource decisions and exercises that—though technically sound—are ultimately irrelevant.

Could these analytical tools have helped prevent the September 11 attacks? Supposing that a systematic terrorism risk assessment had been done, experts might well have overlooked scenarios in which hijacked aircraft were used to strike urban targets. In this case, analysis would not have helped. On the other hand, the idea that terrorists might try to fly hijacked airliners into cities had been prominently discussed in the 1970s (Tinnin 1977) and could well have been anticipated. Had this been done, it is reasonable to think that the assessment would have called for more antihijacking measures than simple passenger protection required. Actually implementing these measures would have usefully shifted the odds against the September 11 attacks, although no one can say whether the final outcome would have changed.

7.7   Conclusion

Formal risk analysis techniques originally developed for twentieth-century industry have provided a firm foundation for quantitative analyses of WMD terrorism. Furthermore, researchers have made significant progress in adapting these methods to include the hard case of adaptive attackers, although much remains to be done. For now, the main technical challenge consists of building models that are mathematically tractable yet sufficiently rich to analyze problems of real-world interest.

In the long run, however, these technical problems are probably less important than how society uses—and potentially misuses—these powerful tools. Certainly, it is no objection to say that the world is (and always will be) richer than any model. The value of formal models lies precisely in their power to abstract away from reality a handful of (presumably) important variables and then explore their implications using the rigorous language of mathematics. In this sense, risk analysis models are no less useful than, say, the similarly simplified models used to make economic forecasts or to analyze supernova explosions. That said, it is important to build models shrewdly and to understand not just their power but also their limits. We believe that policymakers ignore formal risk analyses at their peril. But uncritical acceptance is also unwise.

Formal risk assessment models can help decision makers clarify their assumptions, reveal unconscious biases, feed intuition, and perform automated comparisons of hundreds of different attack scenarios and countermeasures that could not otherwise be analyzed. These important advantages can potentially make homeland security investments far more efficient than they are today. Even so, these models are only tools. How useful they are is up to us.

Notes

1. The work has produced several useful review articles, including a collection of perspectives by risk analysis experts on terrorism risk published shortly after the September 11 attacks (Anderson 2002) and a later survey article discussing the use of operations research models in homeland security (Lowe 2006).

2. Decision analysts often assign numerical values to ensure that model variables are interpreted consistently and to obtain results in forms that are suitable for subsequent risk calculations.

3. The experts, in turn, must base their opinions on evidence. This potentially includes a wide range of sources including classified intelligence, interviewing terrorists, traditional scholarship, and computer models.

4. In Hanson's proposed Policy Analysis Market, traders would be allowed to purchase and sell futures based on five parameters believed to influence support for terrorism in eight Mideast nations: (1) military activity, (2) political instability, (3) economic growth, (4) U.S. military activity, and (5) U.S. financial involvement. The proposal would also allow trading on various possible consequences such as U.S. military casualties and Western civilian casualties from terrorism (Hanson 2006). Market mechanisms are potentially powerful because they can elicit information from traders who possess inside information about terrorist groups. However, even advocates of the idea admit that there would be challenges (Hanson 2006).

Chief among them is the large number of distinct markets that would have to be established to provide actionable information.

5. We assume that the proposed investments do not interact—that is, that the value of any one investment does not depend on whether others are funded. More complex combinatorial algorithms (Powell 2007b) or qualitative techniques (Cooper, Edgett, and Kleinschmidt 2001) are needed when investments interact.

6. Risk can potentially be expressed in various ways, including expected numbers of fatalities, economic damage, symbolic impact, or multiattribute utility value.

7. For the most part, our discussion follows Cold War–era game theory in which conflicts were limited to two highly visible superpower players. However, game theory also offers techniques for modeling more general situations in which there are (1) multiple players who (2) cannot perfectly observe each other's actions. For example, consider a game in which two terrorist cells each believe that it would be good to attack America even if their members are killed—but would much prefer the *other* cell's members to attack and pay with *their* lives. In this game, terrorists play against each other as well as the Americans. Typically, the result is a "mixed strategy" in which each group randomly decides whether to attack or else to wait for the other group to attack in each interval. The net result will usually be a solution in which *total* attacks on Americans are reduced relative to games where attackers are unified or can negotiate alliances with one another.

8. In some cases, resource constraints may prevent players from choosing particular strategies.

Weapons of Mass Destruction: Are Our Political Institutions Adapting?

Eugene Bardach

Just because the WMD threat is urgent, consequential, and novel does not mean that our policy institutions' responses will be immediate, effective, and creative. In some respects, these institutions are just not well suited to the task. Public-sector bureaucracies move slowly and are bound by established procedures, and the complex nature of the threat demands an unusual level of interagency, intergovernmental, and intersectoral cooperation. More importantly, the WMD problem itself is much larger than the sort of problems government must ordinarily deal with. Even if all policymakers were wise and full of understanding, and even if all implementing institutions were nimble and clever, we would still have to struggle.

Our policy institutions must do the best they can, though—indeed, better than usual. Are they measuring up? It is not possible to unambiguously answer this question. For example, if we try to evaluate efforts to prevent attacks (mostly intelligence-oriented and military approaches), we have no way of observing and quantifying attacks that did not occur. Even if estimates were somehow possible, we still cannot say what bearing our explicit efforts have on the outcome.[1]

In this chapter I take a more indirect approach. I consider not performance but adaptive capacity. I consider five elements of adaptive capacity in our institutional system, and I ask whether there is reason to think these are currently effective and cost-efficient or are moving on a reasonable trajectory in these directions. They are

- Mobilizing sufficient resources
- Expending resources wisely
- Involving the private sector
- Creating and improving institutional capacity
- Governmental learning

My conceptions of effectiveness and a "reasonable trajectory" are framed in large part by what I take to be our policy institutions' general performance in adapting to the full array of public problems. Because my sense is that our institutions generally perform in some middling way—not terribly, but certainly nowhere near a theoretical optimum—I look particularly hard for evidence that, in the WMD case, with its high stakes and severe technical challenges, our institutions might be doing *better* than they usually do.

I do not claim that these five elements of institutional capacity are the only important aspects of societal adaptation or that they derive from any widely accepted theory of process.[2] They do seem reasonably important, however. They also happen to link to phenomena such as budgeting, regulating, reorganizing, and getting bureaucracies to work collaboratively that are already familiar and reasonably well studied in political science and public management.

8.1   Counter-WMD and Counterterrorism

At the outset, let me state an assumption about the relationship between strategies aimed at terrorism in general and those aimed at WMD in particular. Often, there is so much overlap that, for many purposes, it is not worthwhile distinguishing them. For instance, most intelligence strategies against terrorism are resourced and managed generically. Even strategies aimed at particular WMD activities, such as exposing nuclear smuggling or bioweapons laboratories, are probably not very different from intelligence strategies more generally. The same applies to the interdiction of weapons and potential weapons materials, and to the hardening of potential targets.

On the other hand, the distinction between WMD and other forms of terrorism is very important for consequence management. A successful WMD attack amounts to a catastrophe. Unlike mere disasters, a catastrophe has a vast impact and significantly erodes organized response and recovery capability including communications, preexisting plans, and critical infrastructure (Quarantelli 2006). September 11 was a disaster, a huge disaster to be sure, but not a catastrophe. Hurricane Katrina, in contrast, was a catastrophe. Blowing up the White House would be a disaster for national morale, but not a catastrophe. A nuclear bomb detonated in Manhattan would be a catastrophe, with hundreds of thousands dead, and perhaps even more seriously injured (Allison 2004).

We need to think differently about catastrophe than we do about disaster. In particular, we need to think about how to write off cherished communities and places, or at least to consider doing so. Although in some quarters it is unacceptable to say so, using federal tax dollars to rebuild New Orleans to its previous state is not the obviously moral and practical thing to do. The distinction between catastrophe and disaster can also sharpen our sense of what exactly counts as WMD. A bundle of conventional explosives could count as WMD if they destroyed a tunnel that played a critical role in a regional economy.[3]

Another area in which the catastrophe/disaster distinction matters is resource allocation. For current levels of financial and organizational investment, the returns from preventing catastrophes are probably higher than mitigating them, although both investments are probably worthwhile. The organizational investment—particularly in the intelligence agencies—is particularly problematic, and I will discuss this in detail below.

8.1.1   Data and Sources

The reader must pardon another throat-clearing preliminary, this one about the data that figure in my discussion. The mobilization to counter the WMD threat is far-ranging, complex, varied, and to some degree concealed. Roughly 50,000 agencies are involved at all levels of government, ranging from the CIA and FBI at the federal level down to fire and public health departments in cities, towns, and hamlets. The strategies range from penetration of suspect Islamist groups in Germany to the installation of pathogen sensors in Chicago. The most useful sources of information about this ocean of activity are government reports and hearings (e.g., by the Government Accountability Office), reports in the quality press, writings by former government officials, and the analyses of security intellectuals in think tanks. There is only a scant academic literature assessing the nature and effectiveness of such operations, and much of this literature is based on governmental and journalistic sources in any case. I have myself done almost no original research but have relied on existing sources.

That these sources may not accurately represent the vastness and complexity of the nation's collective effort almost goes without saying. But is the admittedly imperfect representation also a biased one? I think it is, in three important respects. First, there is a tendency to report bad news rather than good, especially in the accounts of journalists and former officials. (The wary reader can offset the self-serving bias in some of these accounts to some degree). My own selection of examples may have been biased in this way as well, partly because I have become skeptical after many years of studying policymaking and implementation. To offset this bias, I tried to find examples of adaptive success. Second, the selection of data and their interpretation are almost surely skewed toward emphasizing the importance of individual competency and motivation and downplaying institutional or systemic factors. I do not at all discount the role of individuals, especially as potential antidotes to some systemic pathologies, but my goal is to rebalance the prevalent perception. The policy system's successes (troubles) coping with the WMD threat are best understood as a variant of its successes (troubles) coping with the broader problems of modern life. Third, most of the nonacademic literature does not attempt to assess trade-offs, let alone compare, even approximately, costs and benefits. If data mining violates privacy, for instance, in some quarters this is taken to be an absolute bad and the benefits of the violation are assumed to be trivial by comparison—or vice versa. I will at least try to assess how well the system balances costs and benefits.

8.2   Mobilizing Sufficient Resources

In times of crisis, it is easy for the federal government to throw money at problems. Although budgetary commitments to past and present priorities weigh strongly against change, the federal budget is large and some reallocation is possible. More important by far, though, is the ability of the federal government to engage in deficit spending, a power denied to most state and local governments. It can thus respond to new situations very rapidly, without the long and politically tortuous process of increasing taxes and fees or issuing bonds. In the six years preceding September 11, federal spending on domestic security increased from $9 billion to $16 billion. But in the year following September 11, the federal government added emergency supplemental appropriations of about $21 billion (Carafano 2007). With some blips, federal spending continued on its dramatic upward course, from $15 billion prior to September 11 to $42 billion in 2007, according to estimates by scholars from the Brookings Institution (O'Hanlon 2006).[4] State, local, and private expenditures appear to have been relatively modest.[5] Budgeted federal spending for 2008 is $44.4 billion, and the requested budget for 2009 is $48.7 billion (OMB 2008).[6]

There is, of course, the question of whether this growth is too much or too little. What forces might be causing us to over- or underspend?

8.2.1   Too Little, Too Slowly

Suppose, for the sake of discussion, that we are doing too little too slowly, an assumption supported by a broad ideological consensus among most security intellectuals. The liberal-centrist Brookings group argues that "much more needs to be done" but adds that "enormously expensive measures" are not "necessary or appropriate at this time." As of 2006, they were recommending add-ons to federal spending of $10–20 billion and private-sector additional spending at a "roughly comparable" amount. Similarly, a group of public figures and terrorist experts issued a report for the liberal Century Foundation in 2006, which claims that our post–September 11 response "undeniably has had an overseas emphasis" (meaning primarily Iraq) and proposes measures that would add an estimated $23 billion to an administration budget request of $50 billion (Beers and Clarke 2006). Philip J.

Crowley (2007), of the liberal Center for American Progress, in an overall assessment of homeland security policy in January 2007, recommends fourteen steps to improve homeland security at an estimated cost of $12 billion to $18 billion.[7] On the farther left, at least some voices are worried about underinvestment in homeland security. In its September/October 2004 issue, *Mother Jones* published an essay by Matthew Brzezinski that called the Department of Homeland Security "badly underfunded."[8] On the right, James Jay Carafano (2007), the principal homeland security analyst at the Heritage Foundation, also proposes a long list of measures and projects that seem urgent and expensive.

If we are spending too little too slowly, what might be the reasons? One possibility is that there is limited "absorptive capacity" at the level of actual implementation. If tomorrow you were to be given $100,000 by your local government, say, to make your own residential neighborhood safer, you would probably have trouble knowing exactly what to do with it. You would probably wish to establish priorities based on cost-effectiveness calculations, but you would then need to face the divisive issue of how much safer against what kind of threats. You would also need to search for and negotiate with appropriate contractors, establish government-approved accounting and documentation systems, and design safeguards against being steamrollered by local demagogues or wheedled by individuals with pet projects. As Carafano (2007) observes, the federal budget for FY 2004 actually decreased security spending relative to FY 2003, when the budget included many one-time costs, and "allowing the many agencies involved some time to absorb the large increases since September 11."

The politics of the budget process, along with its procedures, also play a role. The budget process in all large organizations, and especially in government, is conservative. It is designed to handle growth and change, but incrementally and not in leaps. For a year or two after a crisis or some other dramatic anomaly, the discourse about budgetary requests might be dominated by talk about problems and responses. But it will not be long before the discourse is drawn back to its natural state of "what you got last year" and "the increase you're asking for this year." Furthermore, increments, not problems and solutions, are the natural medium for perception as well as discussion. An increment in domestic security spending of some 200 percent from 2001 to 2007, or $15 billion to $42 billion (according to the Brookings figures above), just seems like a lot in the eyes of those officials playing the federal budget game across the agencies, the President's Office of Management and Budget (OMB), and the Congress.[9] It seems especially a lot in the absence of successful terrorist attacks on U.S. soil since September 11. For these professionals, steeped in the customs and conventions of the budgetary game, increments of 7 or 8 percent generally seem large.

Another possibility is one variant of what economists call fiscal illusion, that, at the margin, spending tax dollars is all cost and no benefit (Downs 1960).[10] It affects primarily two kinds of people in the political class: ideological conservatives, whose overweening concern for tax dollars is offered as an offset to liberals' presumed relative indifference to them; and political figures of all stripes who find it very painful to solve the problem of where, exactly, the money is to come from. It is indicative that in the published version of James Jay Carafano's Heritage Foundation lecture on "Homeland Security Spending for the Long War" (Carafano 2007), the third of his three main (bulleted) points concerned the long-term growth of entitlement spending (Social Security, Medicare, and Medicaid primarily), which he sees as a direct competitor for homeland security resources.[11] On the politically liberal side of the aisle, it is the "offensive component" of homeland security—that is, the Department of Defense and the Iraq war—that are seen as the main culprits outcompeting homeland security needs (Beers and Clarke 2006; Crowley 2007).

There may be political incentives, in most jurisdictions, to give lower priority to costly counterterrorism measures than would be optimal. Owing to several expert analyses available to the U.S. Congress, the U.S. Army Corps of Engineers, the civil engineering community, and the White House, the levee systems in New Orleans, prior to Hurricane Katrina, were known to be inadequate—the Federal Emergency Management Agency (FEMA) ranked them the number three hazard nationwide—but expensive to upgrade. From the perspective of elected officials it is often better to play the lottery and hope that such expenses can, without adverse consequences, be deferred until after they have left office. This gamble often works because the political time horizons of elected officials are usually shorter than the average expected-time-to-disaster.[12] The same logic applies to counterterrorism planning, except possibly for very salient targets such as New York City or Washington, D.C.[13]

This scanting of the long term can be somewhat offset by counterterrorism-related investments that serve other purposes as well. The "all-hazards" approach to catastrophe and disaster planning, which aims to manage generic consequences rather than the full array of differential consequences attributable to different causes (earthquake, WMD attack, chlorine gas plume), is by now the dominant approach to emergency planning, and so embodies this principle. However, as many observers have remarked, catastrophe and disaster planning are policy areas without much of a political constituency to begin with (Birkland 2006).

So far we have been explaining spending "too little too slowly" at the systemic level—budget routines, electoral incentives, absorptive capacity. But we should also look in a finer-grained way at the particular problems afflicting particular programs and projects. One problem stands out: homeland security issues are often nested in a larger set of problems that are themselves contentious and take a long time to resolve. Here are some examples:

• Improving carry-on inspections at airports following September 11 was caught up in the larger issue of privatization of government functions. The administration was reluctant to take on an extra 45,000 or so civil servants and made an ideological point about the benefits of outsourcing, and the Democrats in Congress made their own stand in opposition.

• Following a catastrophic event, the need for rapid and well-targeted communications among first responders is obvious. The Federal Communications Commission (FCC), which has been the central government actor in assigning frequencies and creating technical standards, has assimilated the emergency interoperability problem to its normal, and slow, deliberative processes. These processes have had to accommodate many parties with different interests, ranging from private-sector manufacturers to public-sector emergency-service agencies that differed among themselves on such matters as backward compatibility and the need for expensive equipment replacement programs (Mayer-Schonberger 2003).[14]

• The question of who should pay bedevils many policy choices in the domestic security area. Because in some cases so many parties benefit from security expenditures, cost-sharing arrangements are in principle logical and just, but they may be contentious when it comes to specifics. Consider, for instance, that any WMD attack—an anthrax bomb going off in Chicago, say—is likely to be aimed not merely at a physical target but at the morale and the economy of the entire nation. Preventing such an attack benefits primarily Chicagoans but also residents of Keokuk, Iowa, and Bakersfield, California. Some sort of federal subsidy is warranted in this case, but how much?[15] Such problems are particularly acute in efforts to standardize communications equipment across multiple agencies and jurisdictions.[16]

• The Cooperative Threat Reduction program, begun in 1992 as the Nunn-Lugar program, subsidizes efforts by Russia and other states of the former Soviet Union to destroy or secure thousands of "loose nukes" and other WMD. By all accounts, the program has been very successful so far but, as of November 2005, only about half the task had been completed (Public Discourse Project 2005c). Over the years it has run into a lot of trouble, some substantive, such as Russia's refusal to grant access to certain sites, but some originating in ancillary concerns, such as corruption, distaste for supplying make-work jobs to underpaid Soviet military scientists (to divert them from working for rogue states or terrorist organizations), and a suspicion that we were somehow being made fools of (Kelly 1996). Bush Administration requests for CTR and other similar counterproliferation programs typically fell 5 to 19 percent between the FY2007 and FY2008 budgets.

• At any implementation site, specific, and often unforeseen, problems may arise that delay or distort implementation. At six southern US border sites, the installation of radiation-detection portals was delayed in order to mesh with the sites' expansion activities (GAO 2006b).

This cross-hatching of policy issues, policy decisions, and policy arenas is mainly due to the sheer complexity and scope of problems and their solutions. It is also due to the nature of American government, with its traditions of federalism, separation of powers, and fragmented political parties. This system normally prevents policymakers from taking speedy, coherent, and large-scale actions, whether those actions would likely turn out as regrettable mistakes or as highly beneficial social adaptations.

8.2.2   Too Much, Too Fast

At the farther edges of the political spectrum, both right and left suspect we give too high a priority to homeland security. On the right, the big cost is in wasted dollars and, on the left, ethnic discrimination. Both sides tend to be less concerned about the loss of civil liberties and invasions of privacy.

The critique here has two primary components: there is no point paying for perfect safety, which is unachievable in any case; and, though WMD are worth worrying about, Al Qaeda and its offspring have little capacity to manage their initiation and/or delivery. And in the case of the most articulate and sophisticated of the critics, Ohio State University political science professor John Mueller, very few Islamist terrorists are on American soil anyway. But if this is the situation, why have we failed to see it? Why have we, in effect, overadapted?

Explanations differ depending on one's politics. For the libertarian right, such as the Cato Institute, the "war on terror" is yet another manifestation of the tendencies of politicians and bureaucracies to aggrandize themselves at the expense of civil society. Mueller's generally libertarian critique argues that a "terrorism industry" is responsible for the "obsessive focus on terrorism" after September 11. This is an industry pursuing "the profits of doom" and consisting of "various risk entrepreneurs and bureaucrats,...most of the media and nearly all politicians."

Some elements of the liberal left think that we are spending too little too slowly, and are happy to criticize the government for this fault. But other elements share the skepticism of the libertarian right, although their reasons are different. These skeptics on the left point to what they take to be the us-against-them-foreign policy worldview of the "neocons" in the Bush Administration.

These critiques are generally served up with a sprinkling of cynicism. But one need not be a cynic to suppose that when politicians are campaigning for election or reelection they will emphasize the issues on which they think they have a comparative advantage. In the three national elections since September 11 and up to this writing, polls have shown that the Republicans have been more trusted to protect the country from terrorism (American Enterprise Institute 2007). For example, in national polls in September 2004, President Bush was rated as better able to "handle terrorism" than John Kerry by almost a 2–1 margin (Pew Research Center for People and the Press 2004). Four years later in October 2008, a Gallup poll of the public's ratings of presidential candidates John McCain and Barack Obama still showed the greatest gap—16 percent—on their ability to handle terrorism. This was the mirror image of the two candidates' perceived ability to handle the economy (Gallup Inc. 2008). One need not be a cynic to understand why Republicans have tried to magnify their significance as warriors against terrorism after public opinion drifted away on Iraq, the privatization of Social Security, and environmental protection. As to agency officials with a homeland security mission, and vendors and technologists who might profit from selling their security services or wares, these interests are no different from those that populate any other policy sector. It would be surprising if most individuals in these lines of work did not genuinely believe in the terrorist threat and the value of persuading others to share their views.

8.2.3 Just Right?

The "too little too slowly" critique seems to me to have the better part of the argument. Mueller makes much of the fact that international terrorism "kills a few hundred people a year worldwide—not much more, usually, than the number who drown yearly in bathtubs in the United States" and that the global probability of death by terrorism, 1 in 80,000, is about the same as being killed by the impact of an asteroid or comet. But WMD attacks would be catastrophic, not merely disastrous, terrorism; and the probabilities of death would be much higher in the cities likely to be targeted (e.g., New York, Chicago, London). Also, the psychological and economic impacts of successful attacks could be immense, far worse than September 11 or Katrina. The economic losses could mount to the low trillions of dollars (Bunn 2006). Moreover, the idea that it is very difficult to create a workable and concealable nuclear device or a potent and dispersible bioagent is of small comfort if you take the long view, say twenty to thirty years. Terrorists make mistakes, they learn, they practice, they fail, they try again.[17] The roots of the problem lie in our technology, which packs more lethality into ever-shrinking and ever more accessible vessels, and in our desires for an open society. Those things will not soon change; therefore, neither will the threat.

Unfortunately, appropriate investment in our preparedness and vigilance will—should be—tied to this chronic situation as far ahead as we can see, which is not very far and, in any case, through an emotional as well as a cognitive haze. Psychologically, most people substantially underestimate the likelihood of extreme events, such as very powerful earthquakes or floods or hurricanes (Berger, Kousky, and Zeckhauser 2006). Their ability to think probabilistically is limited and in any case costly (Kunreuther and Pauly 2004). Underestimation may also avoid unpleasant realities. On the other hand, people have been telling alarmist stories about terrorists and various forms of WMD since World War II and in some cases even earlier. In retrospect, it is reasonable to think that those estimates were driven at least as much by psychology and culture as by any actual threat. We might not be able to reason with any greater clarity, whatever the direction we end up choosing.[18]

8.3 Spending the Resources Wisely

Does government spend its money wisely—that is, on the right things? No doubt governments make plenty of mistakes and waste billions. Nevertheless, some perspective is necessary. The sources of waste are diverse, and some are more forgivable than others.

Consider one of the more contentious spending programs, one often mocked from all political quarters, the State Homeland Security Grant Programs (SHSGP), which provides grant-in-aid programs to state and local government for first responders, critical infrastructure protection, mass transit systems, and port security. From FY 2001 to FY 2006, first-responder funding went from $616 million to $3.36 billion (de Rugy 2005). There is a good public-finance rationale for such a grant-in-aid program if it is allocated according to risk and the risk factors include being a target that has national significance for symbolic or economic reasons. An attack on the Golden Gate Bridge is to some degree a symbolic attack on all America; the country as a whole should contribute to protecting it and, in the event of its destruction, to mitigating the consequences and perhaps to rebuilding it. The same could be said of many other targets, including whole metropolitan areas that might come in for WMD attacks.

The divergence of allocations from risk-based principles, however, has given the program the flavor of pork (Roberts 2005). In the initial years, the allocation formula required minimum spending in each state, which meant that a sparsely populated state like Wyoming would receive $17.5 million in FY 2004. A population-based factor in the allocation formula also skewed money away from the highest-risk locales. More recently, and following much protest from the higher-risk cities and states, the allocation formula was revised to favor larger and riskier urban areas, although no extra weight is given for region of the country (GAO 2007b; Hsu and Sheridan 2007).

States pass most of the money along to localities (by law at least 80%), and here too technical rationality sometimes takes a backseat:

• $63,000 was spent on a decontamination suit in rural Washington State. The suit was immediately put into storage because the state did not have a HAZMAT team to use it (de Rugy 2005).
• $30,000 went to Lake County, Tennessee, for a defibrillator. The unit went to a local high school, which keeps it as a standby for basketball games (de Rugy 2005).
• $557,400 was allocated to North Pole, Alaska. Authorities used the money to buy rescue and communications equipment (de Rugy 2005).
• $500,000 went to Outgamie County, Wisconsin. Authorities used the money to buy chemical suits, generators, rescue saws, and a bomb-disposal vehicle, among other items (de Rugy 2005).
• Yuba City, California, bulletproofed its police station lobby and installed a ten–foot-deep barrier of steel-reinforced concrete pilings to prevent vehicles from ramming the building. Yuba City is not included on California's list of priority targets,
• The agriculture commissioner of Stanislaus County, California, bought a database. Federal authorities list the item as an intelligence gathering tool; in fact, it is used to keep track of what the county's farmers are growing and which pesticides are being used.

As often happens in federal grant programs, the logic of giving flexibility to state and local officials "who are closest to the problems" runs up against the logic of ensuring that the problems they choose to solve, and the means used to do so, reflect federal policy (Seidman and Gilmour 1986; Agranoff 1989; Oates 1972). It also runs up against the transaction costs and micromanagement needed to prevent inappropriate expenditures.

Besides classic government waste and classic pork-barrel politics (Olson 1982; Glazer and Rothenberg 2001), there is probably another element to the wide disbursement of funds in this context. This is the political reluctance to be seen as saying "Your community has too little of value to be a likely target" and/or "If you are hit, we don't care as much about your lives and well-being as we do about other people's." A journalist writing in the *New York Times Magazine* reported that officials talked about "relative worth and the right of [small-state] citizens to get the same kind of protection that they are afforded in other places in the country," as though "same" need not take account of differential likelihoods of being targeted (de Rugy 2005).

Tales of pork show up particularly often in critiques from the political right. However, by the standards of federal spending in general, or of conventional pork-barrel politics, these are small sums. If even half of all expenditures for state and local assistance were a complete waste, the loss would be only 2 to 3 percent of total spending on homeland security. Moreover, behind-the-scenes agreements by influential members of Congress, reached at the time DHS was created, have by and large kept DHS appropriations bills remarkably free of pork-flavored "earmarks." The rationale was that homeland security was too important to be subjected to all the distortions of domestic politics, although the earmarking trend has been slightly upward since 2004 (Basich 2006).

Other forms of waste are more debatable, and illustrate the difficulty of defining the concept in this area. Very large expenditures on countermeasures are often worthwhile if they actually work and the threat and risk are great. But this calculation often depends on subtle estimates such as the likelihood of a complex response system actually working in the event it has to do so; the ease with which the countermeasure can be defeated, either now or in the foreseeable future, by either (1) amateurs and semicompetents or (2) professionals and highly skilled individuals; and the rate of false alarms that occur due to imperfect detection and/or interpretation. Observers can differ greatly on such estimates. What looks like a reasonable and prudent investment to one person can look to another like a preposterous and irresponsible waste of resources. The flip side of this is that what looks like clear-sighted economizing to one person looks to another like callous indifference to life and rolling the dice with the nation's economy and morale.

A broader question is how best to allocate aggregate spending across prevention, mitigation, preparedness, response, and recovery. With regard to natural disasters, many experts tend to see higher social returns for investment in mitigation than in preparedness and response. But the political incentives favor expenditures on preparedness and response, particularly ex-post assistance and relief in the immediate aftermath of an event, with almost no attention to spending the resources in ways that mitigate future vulnerabilities (Birkland 2006). This dynamic will probably not affect mitigation investments in regard to terrorism, although other dynamics—such as electoral-cycle shortsightedness—may do so. Still, federal attentiveness to supporting local first responders does seem excessive when compared to other possible initiatives including, for example, bolstering local intelligence gathering and information sharing capabilities (Carafano and Rosenzweig 2005).

8.3.1 Crash Spending

Homeland defense, in the post–September 11 world, has amounted to a crash-spending program. As with all crash spending, moving money out the door in a generally desirable direction is more important than getting the details right. Given the urgency of responding to a threat, this is a sensible social adaptation. Some waste can, and should, be tolerated, especially because the technology of countermeasures, and of terrorist attack strategies, is in continual flux. Whether the waste has been excessive even by these relaxed standards is a legitimate question as well, however, even if it is difficult to answer.

Consider the decision by the Domestic Nuclear Detection Office (DNDO) in the DHS, in July 2006, to award contracts to three vendors to further develop and purchase $1.2 billion worth of cargo screening equipment over five years. The decision to move ahead on advanced spectroscopic portal monitor (ASP) contracts was not uncontested. Since 2003, the GAO, at least, had been questioning the ability of Customs and Border Patrol (CBP)—the responsible agency within DHS prior to the creation of DNDO in 2005—to deploy inspection portals effectively (GAO 2006a). Some months before the July 2006 contracting decision, the GAO, growing ever more skeptical of the ASP technology, asked DNDO to carry out a cost-benefit analysis. The results of the analysis, delivered in May 2006, might have convinced DNDO to move forward, but it did not convince GAO. DNDO had set a performance requirement of 95 percent reliability in identifying highly enriched uranium (HEU) when it was present, but the technical assessment showed that the prototypes, from three different manufacturers, could only detect unmasked HEU 70 to 88 percent of the time. DNDO told the GAO that they were counting on substantial improvement in the ASP technology in the future, "but they provided no additional information as to how the 95 percent performance goal will be achieved or an estimate of when the technology will attain this level" (GAO 2007c).[19]

Perhaps the most charitable interpretation of this sequence of events is that the office was realistically banking on technical improvements and that the risk of their being somewhat overly optimistic in that respect was not as bad as the risk of leaving containers unsecured until greater certainty, if not better technology, emerged. However, even if that were the case, my point about the negative impact of crash programs still holds. Being overly optimistic, even if justified, is still being something less than realistic.

8.4   Involving the Private Sector

Running intelligence and law enforcement operations are obviously public-sector responsibilities. So too are protecting public monuments, managing evacuations, and mounting military operations against terrorist training camps abroad. But the private sector has a critical role to play as well. Some 85 percent of what DHS calls "critical infrastructure" is privately owned—for example, energy generation and transmission, cyber hardware and software, financial institutions, telecommunications, chemical production and storage, and transportation facilities. A successful attack on such infrastructure could have ramifications well beyond the loss to the owners, and the owners would not necessarily take account of these when they decide how much to invest in protecting them or in restoring them to service following the attack. Regulation is probably the main governmental approach to inducing private owners to confront the possibility of these additional damages. In addition, it is the private sector that manages most of the R&D capacity in the economy. Since this capacity must be harnessed to counterterrorism objectives, and private markets often fail to internalize security risks, government needs to step in somehow.

8.4.1   Regulating

Government acts not only by spending money directly but by mandating that private parties do so as well—for example, by setting security standards for shippers or hazardous facilities and enforcing compliance. As a governmental problem-solving strategy, regulation has at least one big advantage compared to direct spending: it circumvents the constraints and the distortions and the politics of the budgetary process. In doing so, however, it runs into the constraints and the distortions and the politics of the regulatory process.

Consider first the possible distortions. The world is heterogeneous whereas regulatory standards tend to be uniform. Exceptions are always made, to be sure, but they can rarely keep up with the true variety in the world. And the more exceptions, the greater the complexity. And the greater the complexity, the greater the potential for litigation, delay, frustration, and injustice. Some objects of regulation, therefore, will be regulated too strictly and others too leniently (Bardach and Kagan [1982] 2002; Tietenberg 2006). Of the approximately 15,000 facilities in the United States that use hazardous chemicals, for instance, over 100 could endanger more than a million people if an explosion were to discharge plumes of toxic or flammable gas (or liquid) into the environment and the weather and other conditions were right (Marek 2006). But until DHS issued a regulatory rule in April 2007, security regulation of chemical plants was so lenient that the most hazardous were not controlled much more tightly than the least hazardous.[20]

Using its political influence, the chemical industry was able to fend off appropriate regulation until April 2007, aided until January 2007 by Republican control of the White House and the Congress. This fits the usual pattern of regulatory politics, in which self-conscious "concentrated interests" facing compliance costs are better able and more willing to organize in opposition than aggregations of beneficiaries who, taken one at a time, would get very small payoffs (Weimer and Vining 2005).

Politics also enters into the question of state and federal regulatory roles. Concerning "social regulation" (e.g., health, safety, environmental protection, antidiscrimination, consumer protection), the federal government is generally stricter than the states, largely because consumer groups are better represented in Washington than in state capitals. Producer groups, therefore, usually prefer state regulation, while consumer groups look to Washington and argue for federal preemption. But sometimes the situation is reversed, and chemical plant security is a case in point. New Jersey, for instance, home to 140 major chemical facilities, adopted a fairly stringent set of regulations in late 2005 and has been resisting federal preemption provisions in bills moving through the U.S. Congress. The DHS rule of April 2007 explicitly permits additional regulation by the states.

Regulating Creatively Managed creatively, regulation can be used to reward desired behavior and discourage or punish what is not desired. Under the Customs Trade Partnership Against Terrorism program (C-TPAT), Customs and Border Patrol (CBP) offers expedited and fewer inspections to shippers who voluntarily comply with CBP security guidelines and adopt a menu of "best practices" for securing their supply chains. To attract shippers into C-TPAT, CBP stresses the business value of increased protection against theft and overall improvements in supply-chain efficiency. But it stresses even more the cost-savings (for "validated partners") from a reduction in the number of random inspections, eligibility for access to FAST lanes at the Mexican and Canadian borders, consultations from CBP supply-chain specialists on regulatory issues, and other benefits under CBP control (CBP 2004b).

On paper, as a piece of regulatory program design, C-TPAT is excellent. It is results-oriented, flexible, fair-minded, and aims to minimize compliance and transaction costs while improving security. As with much regulation, however, the devil is in the details of implementation. For a period of several years, the monitoring regime in practice was too slack. The GAO issued a critical report in July 2003, noting that shippers received the benefits of reduced scrutiny simply for agreeing to participate in the program and without having their security profiles reviewed (GAO 2003b). Two years later, there was still very little monitoring of private partners' actual behavior once they had been accepted. And even validation—that is, monitoring that appropriate security systems were in place—was done haphazardly and without formal protocols (GAO 2005a).

The Achilles' heel in this otherwise well-designed government program seems to have been insufficient staffing, a common public-sector problem. CBP initially set a goal of validating all companies within three years following certification, but this proved impossible. CBP needed vastly more personnel possessing the specialized skills needed to evaluate supply-chain security. The C-TPAT budget has increased substantially in recent years, as has its staffing, and it has committed itself to validating newly certified partners within one year and revalidating existing partners every four years. But the rapid increase in membership threatens these ambitious goals (Caldwell 2007).

Government reliance on industry for self-enforcement is not the only way in which government can leverage industry effort. Government also relies on industry to come up with standards, best practices, norms, and education strategies. As noted above, DHS appears to be doing something like this. There are now fifteen sector-based planning councils made up of more or less representative owners of critical private infrastructure. Each interacts with councils of government agencies focused on the same sectors As of March 2007, all but one of these councils had submitted an infrastructure protection plan (Larence and Powner 2007).

It remains to be seen, of course, whether these plans will lead to appropriate action. The delays in developing regulations for the chemical sector, which arose primarily from the industry side, raise concerns. The DHS has also been the source of delays. It did not publish its final version of the planning framework, the National Infrastructure Protection Plan, until June 2006, and after several false starts.[21] The Century Fund's critique of progress in this area pointedly emphasized DHS's failure to stipulate outcomes and goals and to clarify industry's responsibilities (Beers and Clarke 2006). This has been a fairly common problem in government, though progress has been made in recent years at the federal level, particularly by means of management practices imposed in the course of budget reviews by the Office of Management and Budget.[22]

8.4.2   Stimulating Private-Sector R&D

The DHS in FY 2007 will spend just short of $1 billion on R&D. Spending on threats from WMD is the topmost priority, particularly radiological and nuclear threats (almost a third) (AAAS 2007). Most of these funds are spent in the private for-profit and nonprofit sectors (including several university-based "Centers of Excellence"), although substantial amounts also go for government facilities such as the National Biodefense Analysis and Countermeasures Center, which is currently under construction. The U.S. government is also in the process of spending $5.6 billion on private-sector research and vaccine production under the auspices of Project BioShield. The intention is to stockpile medicines that might be of use in the event of a bioterror attack. Many other such programs could also be mentioned in the Department of Defense, the Department of Energy, the CIA, and so on.

How effective are government's efforts to stimulate the needed R&D? Again, one must be cautious in answering this question, and the closely related question of how cost-effective such efforts are. No doubt the failures and imperfections draw more attention from the GAO and from outside critics than do the successes. That said, however, one's impressions are not, on the whole, reassuring. Project BioShield, authorized in mid–2004, has produced very little of value so far. Some of the reasons are technical: vaccines can fail in many different ways and production cycles are normally lengthy. But other reasons are institutional. Executive-branch policy-makers failed to change course even when a contract of $877 million to develop and produce 75 million doses of anthrax vaccine attracted only one serious bidder, VaxGen, a small company with a track record of no successes and one failure (an AIDS vaccine) (Lipton 2006). Moreover, the Office of the Assistant Secretary for Preparedness and Response, within the Department of Health and Human Services, along with the Food and Drug Administration, imposed unclear, contradictory, and eleventh-hour standards on VaxGen (Rhodes 2007).[23] The whole BioShield program has been criticized as lacking in strategic direction and buffeted by intense lobbying by biotech firms (Nature Biotechnology 2007; Trull, Du Laney, and Dibner 2007; Lipton 2006).

However, as the troubles with BioShield mounted, Congress did take note. Hearings were held, bills introduced, debate facilitated. In April 2007, Congress created the Biomedical Advanced Research and Development Authority (BARDA), which has been given a relatively free hand to experiment with policy design. This move is very desirable, given the numerous and subtle challenges involved in running a government program to discover and produce quantities of bioterrorism-related vaccines (chapter 15). They range from the simple design of incentives to the management of liability concerns to the protection of programs against predictable efforts (by both government and research entities) to abuse and even defraud.

We have already noted that the projected outlays of $1.2 billion by the Domestic Nuclear Detection Office for ASP cargo screening equipment look ill-advised. Most disconcerting of all, the whole Science and Technology Directorate of the DHS, which managed most of the R&D effort, was, overall, poorly managed from its inception. A congressional report in 2007 characterized the Directorate as " 'a rudderless ship without a clear way to get back on course,' criticized its lack of clear research goals, absence of detailed budget information, mystifying accounting conventions," and inability to spend prior-year appropriations (AAAS 2007). A new director, Rear Admiral Jay Cohen, who has had long experience as head of the Office of Naval Research, took office as Under Secretary for Science and Technology soon afterward and has moved quickly to reorganize the staff and refocus the effort (Magnuson 2007).

The DHS R&D effort is closely related to the department's procurement process, which has also been very troubled. There have been some bright spots, such as initially bringing in veteran Defense Department procurement specialists to establish procedures, and relying heavily on a special acquisition authority known as "other transactions" to carry out prototype and other nonstandard projects (GAO 2005a). But procurement has been widely criticized: "Hordes of critics, including former DHS executives, watchdog groups, the Government Accountability Office . . . and

Congressmen by the dozens have excoriated the department's procurement record" (Gregory 2006).[24] Not only did it fail to perform but it permitted waste on a large scale, as was evident in the aftermath of Katrina. Steven Kelman of Harvard's Kennedy School of Government, a procurement expert and former head of the Office of Federal Procurement Policy, attributed the problems primarily to lack of adequate personnel relative to the rapidly expanding workload (Gregory 2006)—a problem I noted above in conjunction with C-TPAT's implementation. The DHS, like much of the federal government, has also been losing top managers to the private sector (and to retirement) at an alarming rate (Hsu 2007).

8.5   Developing Institutional Capacity

Money is versatile, powerful, and, assuming deficit financing, relatively easy to come by. It can even be used to improve institutional capacity—for example, by buying more and better trained frontline freight inspectors, or by purchasing interoperable communications equipment, or by setting up a whole new office dedicated, say, to domestic nuclear detection. But in the final analysis, money cannot do much to improve institutional capacity, especially within government bureaucracies. The incentives and constraints that limit performance apply whether the bureaucracies are well or poorly funded. Public-sector bureaucracies normally attempt to protect their autonomy, augment their budgets, avoid conflict, deflect accountability, maintain discretionary resources, and go by the book (Wilson 1989). They generally are slow to innovate, reluctant to collaborate, and cautious about new missions that could interfere with their old missions. Sometimes there are exceptions—for instance, when there is a crisis accompanied by political expectations for bold new action, or when a new leader is installed who wants to make a reputation for him- or herself. But in general, the American tradition in public administration is to hamstring bureaucracy in the hopes of keeping it limited and nonabusive, even if doing so might also mean keeping it relatively ineffective and inefficient.

That said, the need to deal with the threat of terrorism and WMD has given rise to a universal consensus behind new and improved institutional capacity. True, there has been conflict over the details, sometimes bitter conflict, including for example, whether to create a new homeland security department. But on the desirability of capacity building per se, agreement prevails. Capacity building has appeared in four basic forms:

- Creating new organizations more or less de novo
- Reforming or reengineering existing organizations
- Reorganizing existing organizations
- Improving interorganizational cooperation

Of these four types of capacity improvement, the first is much less problematic than the others, and I will not discuss it. The other three are immensely challenging, and the landscape of public administration is probably littered with more failures than successes—and with an even greater number of specimens for which capacity improvement has not even been tried. Before turning to a discussion of these three, though, I will say a word about the meaning of "success" and "failure."

8.5.1 "Success" and "Failure"

It is, in general, hard for the public to perceive the true results of efforts at institutional capacity building, because the details of implementation are largely hidden, and those that come to light probably represent either unusual successes or unusual failures. Moreover, the appropriate standard for evaluating success or failure is ambiguous. For instance, DHS is widely criticized as being a low-performing agency (Kettl 2007). But, as is always true of policy and management, the critical question is, compared to what? In this case, it is plausible that the drastic step of reorganizing twenty-two formerly separate agencies into a single umbrella department has improved their performance relative to what it would have been otherwise? After all, there had been trends toward more voluntary cooperation, and these could have been boosted in one way or another. The answer is more likely yes than no, especially if we consider the long run.

Many critics of DHS hold it to a standard derived from a sense of what, ideally, we would like it to be able to do. That is also reasonable, especially when there is consensus on appropriate performance standards, neither impossibly high nor unjustifiably low. For instance, the failure of FEMA, and indirectly of DHS, to respond effectively to Hurricane Katrina was generally recognized as such, even by the Bush White House.[25]

One must also make allowances for trial-and-error learning. Building institutional capacity for dealing with WMD is exceedingly complex. Mistakes will be made, even very costly mistakes. How many such mistakes, and which ones, should be written off as appropriate trial-and-error learning, and how many, and which ones, debited to the poor-performance account of our institutions or our leaders? Furthermore, how much delay is optimal in sorting out legitimate disagreements over the many technical and value-laden issues that beset the process? And how much represents an indictment of "sluggish bureaucracy" or "foot-dragging, turf-protecting bureaucrats?"[26]

8.5.2 Reform/Reengineer Existing Organizations

Government agencies are notoriously difficult to reform or reengineer. Some of the main barriers are statutes that constrain managerial discretion over organizational structure and, more importantly, funding streams for identifiable programs or organizational units. Other barriers include civil service–defined job descriptions and employee tenure rules backed, in some cases, by collective bargaining agreements. In the case of our national security and law enforcement agencies, professional pride in mission and historical expertise can also stand in the way (Zegart 1999), although these can be a source of innovation and change as well.

Among all the countermeasures we can take vis-à-vis WMD, improving our intelligence capability is probably the most cost-effective. This comes about partly because the damage wrought by a successful WMD attack would be shockingly great, even if optimal response and recovery could be assumed; hence, the value of preventing it—for which intelligence is central—is very high. Second, because prevention-oriented intelligence could protect anywhere from dozens to hundreds of potential targets it amounts, in effect, to buying security at wholesale rather than retail prices. Nonetheless, upgrading our intelligence capabilities, both foreign and domestic, has proven exceedingly difficult.

UCLA political scientist Amy Zegart (2007) has estimated that 84 percent of 340 intelligence recommendations made by twelve different study groups between 1991 and 2001 about dealing with the threat of terrorism reappeared in the post–September 11 analyses by the 9/11 Commission and/or a parallel Congressional Joint Inquiry into the attacks. Her inference is that the terrorist threat was well understood but that the intelligence community (IC) failed to rise to the challenge. Zegart's explanation as to why this occurred emphasizes the fragmentation within the IC (many separate agencies with separate power bases and, within the CIA, internal "stovepipes"); career success dependent on the number of "products" produced (spies recruited, items in the President's Daily Brief, and so on) rather than on their quality; and a culture shaped by the Cold War, which, among other things, inhibited information sharing both horizontally (across agencies and stovepipes) and vertically (between collectors and analysts).[27] Of course these and related problems can, in theory, be somewhat offset by determined and creative leadership. But there is a history of presidential and congressional indifference to intelligence reform, an indifference rooted in rational political incentives to attend to more visible and less difficult issues (Zegart 2007).

The FBI, which is the closest thing we have to a domestic intelligence agency, is an even more troubling story. It has long been understood that the agency's internal incentives lead it to downplay primary prevention (before the onset of trouble) via intelligence in favor of secondary prevention (preventing recurrence) via criminal enforcement and incapacitation. Apprehending malefactors and locking them up is how FBI agents traditionally earn prestige and advancement, not disrupting terrorist networks or acts (9/11 Commission 2004; Hitz and Weiss 2004).

The country has faced a choice between creating an effective domestic intelligence and counterterrorism capacity within the FBI or setting up an entirely new agency analogous to Britain's MI5, which has as its only mission to gather intelligence and cannot bring cases against individuals. So far, we have taken the first route. Whether that choice has been effective is debated. Arguably, if we were writing on a clean slate, we would have gone the second route. But, given that the FBI exists and its supporters bitterly oppose a new agency and would probably have to compete with it for status and budget, and that this rivalry could undermine cooperation with such an agency, the choice is not so clear.[28] Much depends on how well the FBI is implementing the internal changes required to make it into an effective domestic intelligence and counterterrorism agency.

FBI Director Robert Mueller, who assumed his post a week before the World Trade Center was destroyed, seems to have aggressively pursued an agenda of what the FBI itself calls "agency transformation" (FBI 2004, 2006; *New York Jewish Times* 2006).[29] Five years after September 11, the FBI publicized a lengthy list of actions it had taken along these lines, including the creation of a National Security Branch in September 2005 and a Weapons of Mass Destruction Directorate in July 2006. During this time it also increased, among other things, its multiagency Joint Terrorism Task Forces from 35 to 101; increased the numbers of agents and police officers in these bodies from about 1,000 to 4,000; and increased its "onboard linguists" from 784 on September 11 to 1,430 and its Arabic linguists from 70 to 269 (FBI 2006).

Congressional testimony around the same time by Richard Thornburgh, U.S. Attorney General and a close observer of the FBI, praised the Bureau's transformational efforts and accomplishments. Thornburgh chairs the FBI Transformation Panel of the National Academy of Public Administration, which had been consulting with the FBI on a wide range of managerial and programmatic issues. He listed a number of improvements to the agency's general management capacity that had apparently been much needed in areas like budgeting, human resources, and strategic planning. He also pointed to two new career paths within the FBI, probably the most crucial change the bureau could undertake, for special agents in intelligence and professional information technology staff (Thornburgh 2006).[30]

As noted earlier, there is often a large gap between the formal actions of an agency, such as creating a new career track, and their real significance in implementation. Judge Richard A. Posner (2006), an incisive social observer who has studied intelligence failures, pronounces the transformation effort a failure and calls for a separate domestic security agency. Reporting on a February 2006 conference of top FBI officers from across the nation, the *New York Times* wrote: "F.B.I. culture still respects door-kicking investigators more than deskbound analysts sifting through tidbits of data." And "knowledgeable employees" said that "Muslim agents number no more than a dozen of the bureau's 12,664 agents" (Shane and Bergman 2006). The most indicative commentary comes from the May 2006 testimony of John Gannon, "a respected senior intelligence official who had spent 24 years working with the FBI in various positions" ranging from the CIA's analytic branch chief to House homeland security committee staff director, who said "'I have changed my mind [about the FBI's potential for developing a domestic intelligence capability]. I now doubt that the FBI, on its present course, can get there from here'" (Zegart 2007).

So far we have been discussing the dynamics of bureaucratic behavior as barriers to adaptation. We should not overlook the barriers to reform and reengineering created by governmentwide rules intended to prevent waste, fraud, and abuse that so often undermine many agency managers' and operatives' desires to improve performance. Air marshals anonymously take flights so as to be available in the event of a terrorist attack. But the rules are the rules: "Agents are required to check in at airport ticket counters, and in most cases display oversized credentials. Until recently, a jacket-and-tie dress code was mandated on all flights, even those filled with tourists headed for Disney World. They also were instructed to stay in designated hotels, where they had to display their marshal credentials to secure a discounted rate" (Meckler and Carey 2007).

8.5.3   Reorganizing

By any standard, there has been a lot of reorganizing. The Department of Homeland Security brought under one hierarchical roof—on paper, at least—twenty-two separate organizations. The Intelligence Community was given a controversial hierarchical superior, the Director of National Intelligence (DNI)—though the extent of that official's authority is an open question. The National Counterterrorism Center (NCTC) includes elements of the DHS, the FBI's Counterterrorism Division, the Counterterrorist Center based at the CIA, the Department of Defense, and other agencies. Customs and Border Protection (CBP) was created by merging the Customs Bureau, the Border Patrol, the Immigration and Naturalization Service (INS)'s inspectional functions, and the Agriculture and Plant Health Inspection Service (APHIS).

In the public sector, reorganizations stem from many motives, ranging from the elimination of (supposedly) costly redundancy to the political domestication of a distrusted agency. The two most visible reorganizations in the federal government's response to terrorism have been the DHS and the DNI. These have been prompted by the desire to reduce policy and operational fragmentation—that is, by a desire to increase effectiveness and efficiency. The prevailing theory has been that a common superior could improve resource allocation, planning, and operational coordination.

In addition, the lines of accountability to the White House and to Congress would become clearer and more effective. This is similar to the theory that motivated the largely successful reorganization of the military commands and the Joint Chiefs of Staff by the Goldwater-Nichols Act of 1986 (Locher 2002).[31] There are severe limitations to centralization and hierarchy, however, and it is not clear just how useful they will be in a world where situational complexity and volatility are dominant facts of life. This is one reason—among the many powerful political reasons that constrain and distort such matters (Zegart 1999)—that the reorganization of the Intelligence Community under a DNI has been very limited.

Assuming reorganization is necessary, it would be desirable for the reorganization to be implemented expeditiously and effectively. This requires leadership to mobilize needed resources and focus energy and attention. No such leadership was present at the birth of the DHS. Indeed, almost the opposite seems to have occurred (Brzezinski 2005). Knowledgeable informants have also been severely critical of DHS's failure from the first to think strategically about appropriate mission priorities (number one, for them: securing ordinary infrastructure that could be turned into weapons) or resource priorities (number one: mobilizing the business sector) (Benjamin and Simon 2005).

Why this process was so apparently sluggish and unfocused is unclear. True, President Bush had opposed the creation of a single homeland security department for several years. But once it was official, it could only make sense to move rapidly and efficiently. Instead, the president appointed Tom Ridge, a feckless leader (Benjamin and Simon 2005), as its first secretary, and then tried to install Bernard Kerik as his successor. Kerik had no federal experience, a history of sleazy practices, a reputation as a bullying leader (Blumenthal 2004), and a mixed track record of training a police force in Iraq (Bumiller 2004). The process also appears to have allowed the counterterrorism mission to degrade the capabilities of at least one important agency. The Federal Emergency Management Agency (FEMA), which had briefly flourished during the Clinton presidency, spiraled downward badly during the Bush presidency and its absorption by DHS (Brinkley 2006; Beers and Clarke 2006; Grunwald and Glasser 2005).

8.5.4   Interagency Collaboration

"Interagency collaboration" is typically a challenge for agencies, principally because agencies reflect the career and professional interests of those who work for them, and those interests are typically best served by the autonomy of their agencies against outside threats to jurisdiction, claims to expertise, and promotion ladders. The interests of legislative overseers are also typically served by the autonomy of "their" agencies, since the power of oversight committees depends on their agencies' autonomy. Rational strategic behavior aside, agencies also tend to develop a boundaries-based, tribal culture in which loyalty inward is nurtured and loyalty outward is viewed with suspicion (Bardach 1998; Wilson 1989).

The problem, of course, is that the modern world changes too rapidly for jurisdictions and habits to keep up. Reorganizations are slow, wearing, and bring mismatches of their own. Informal collaboration is often the only hope of matching problems and solutions. Nowhere is this truer than in the world of counterterrorism. And because the concerned agencies are staffed and led by large numbers of public-spirited people, the unnaturalness of collaboration, and its many pitfalls and technical challenges, may be overcome to some degree. Studies of different agencies learning to work together in various domestic contexts including high-risk families, habitat protection, and environmental enforcement show that, despite difficulties, productive collaboration does sometimes occur (Bardach 2008, 1998). In the area of disaster response, a template for multiagency and multijurisdictional cooperation has been available for over thirty years in the form of the Incident Command System. It has generally worked well and is prescribed by the DHS National Response Plan, though some scholars doubt whether it can work effectively in catastrophes or even in certain types of disasters (Rubin and Harrald 2006; Buck, Trainor, and Aguirre 2006).[32]

Collaboration problems are ubiquitous in Homeland Security. Local hospitals and clinics need to collaborate on planning for mass casualties; U.S. and foreign ports, the CBP, the Coast Guard, DNDO, shippers, customs brokers, equipment vendors, and many other parties must coordinate to manage supply-chain security; federal, state, and local agencies need to coordinate in the event of a catastrophe with significant jurisdictional spillovers; local police departments must share intelligence with one another and with the FBI (which, however, is said rarely to reciprocate); and more centralized coordination of the intelligence community had been recommended by study commissions and other observers for many years, though it was successful only in the political environment following September 11. The Food and Drug Administration and the Department of Health and Human Services' Office of the Assistant Secretary for Preparedness and Response have similarly tried to work out approval standards for BioShield products, albeit with mixed success (Rhodes 2007).

Interorganizational cooperation takes many forms. Sometimes it is institutionalized as a formal, ongoing program like the Container Security Initiative (CSI), which aims to inspect and clear containers before they are shipped from foreign shores. Others, such as the DHS's SAFECOM (charged with sorting out interoperable communications technology), involve joint policy planning but not much in the way of operational coordination. Still others, organized around emergency events, combine pre-event planning and postevent response coordination.

It is worthwhile differentiating two rather different collaborative contexts, however. One involves agencies that are sufficiently different so that competition is not a zero-sum game that potentially threatens the existence of either partner. An example would be a local police department, radiological specialists from the U.S. Department of Energy, and the state highway patrol engaged in a search for a threatened "dirty bomb." Or we might have CBP officials, port security staff, shippers' representatives, and the Coast Guard working out a plan to prevent a ship from docking until its inspection history can be validated.[33] Here agencies are merely wary and defensive of one another, each fearing, say, that collaboration might oblige them to sacrifice resources to the common effort or alter their mission priorities. While individuals—and agencies—might jockey for primacy, maneuver to offload work onto one another, and make life difficult for one another by proposing incompatible standards and protocols, nevertheless, in the end, they will work things out.

The situation is more threatening where agencies are rivals that compete head-to-head for the same spotlight or funds or other resources, such as information or informants or control over cases. Here, one agency's success just might come at the expense of the other. Almost certainly some aspect of this rivalry has been slowing down the recognized need for "the major national security institutions . . . to create a 'trusted information network.'" (Public Discourse Project 2005c). Not only are agencies on the defensive but they may be on the offensive as well. In this more threatening context, we have the examples of the Army claiming the right to fly its own aircraft in certain situations and the Air Force contesting that claim (Wilson 1989); the FBI investigating the CIA in the aftermath of the Aldrich Ames betrayal; the CIA refusing to advise the FBI of the magnitude of its losses in the Ames case or give the FBI access to its files (Mahle 2004); and the CIA and the FBI trading charges in *Time* and *Newsweek* that it was the other agency's responsibility for having lost the trail of two of the September 11 attackers in Malaysia on their way to the United States (Tenet 2007).[34]

This last set-to between agencies that ought to cooperate but historically have not also marks a less obvious set of interagency problems. In his memoir, CIA Director George Tenet (2007) provides a detailed history of how the FBI and the CIA actually cooperated willingly and competently on the Malaysian suspects over a period of many months. But agencies are composed of many units, differentiated as well as integrated, and one of the most important bases of differentiation is formal hierarchical authority. Even if senior officials have good working relationships across unit boundaries at the same hierarchical level, the goodwill may not flow very far down the hierarchy within each of the separate units. And vice versa: if line-level staff of different agencies, say, have informally developed a team approach to a shared problem, they might discover that their supervisors are not pleased. Interests, values, and situational understandings can differ greatly from one stratum of the hierarchy to another. In the case of the Malaysian suspects, the agencies' operatives were working together effectively, with the indirect blessings of the agencies' directors, but their press offices and probably other personnel too acted out old scripts.

There are no simple answers to how to get rival agencies, as opposed to merely defensive agencies, to work well together. High stakes for the public and for agency employees probably help a lot, though they are no guarantee of success. Even in wartime, the U.S. armed services have not been able to overcome rivalries in the past, even when many lives and great strategic objectives were at stake (Locher 2002). A shared culture of professionalism and intense commitment to a mission almost certainly helps. For example, the National Counterterrorism Center (NCTC) brings analysts together from different agencies to draft collective reports and also provides online intelligence syntheses to a variety of users. It is "widely considered to be one of the most successful improvements in U.S. intelligence" (Zegart 2007). Nevertheless, interagency barriers decrease its effectiveness and efficiency. Because the analysts have different security clearances, they still see different information; the information is stored on nearly thirty separate, and incompatible, networks, which require access to six different computers stored under analysts' desks ("Pizza boxes" is the wry epithet in common use). And "officials still resist sharing information with colleagues assigned from other agencies even when the rules allow it" (Zegart 2007).

Two other helpful ingredients are committed leadership and an effort to sit down and hammer out an explicit understanding about the division of labor and responsibilities (Goldsmith and Eggers 2004; Bardach 1998). Such understandings are inevitably incomplete and are likely to dissolve once the original actors depart. But given time, some progress is possible. In rare cases, a common superior can knock heads together and assert a resolution. It took decades to resolve a standoff between the fire and police departments in New York City that persisted even after their egregious failures to cooperate on September 11 (Confessore 2005).

In this connection it is worth noting the seemingly successful effort of DNI Mike McConnell and a number of other high-ranking officials in the intelligence community to create a joint-duty program. Modeled on what was done in the military by Goldwater-Nichols, it requires that senior management appointees in the IC have served one to three years outside their home agency. It also includes an educational component. The rationale is to create in the IC "a broad, enterprise-wide focus, . . . about developing leaders with the ability to integrate all of the IC's assets to accomplish [its] mission" (ODNI 2007). Although a similar program had begun in the late 1990s under George Tenet, it had run into a buzz saw of agency opposition. The current effort has powerful and extensive interagency support and already counts some 1,500 participants.[35]

8.6 Learning

In order to adapt to the WMD challenge, policymakers and implementers must contrive to learn as they go along. They must learn about the very matters discussed in this chapter so far: about the nature and magnitude of the challenge, the level of resources that need to be marshaled, how to expend them wisely, how best to stimulate and partner with the private sector, and how to build institutional capacity. Furthermore, they must create the capacity for learning per se. This means building institutions that specialize in learning and disseminating what is learned. It also means creating a culture that respects facts, analysis, and rational argument.

Political elites tend to be short on such virtues. Nevertheless, policy learning does occur, albeit slowly, unevenly, and sometimes at high cost. Homeland security seems to me to fit this general pattern. I will organize the comments that follow according to the experiential sources of learning: events, general experience with policies and institutions, "best practices," simulations, and controlled evaluations.

8.6.1 Learning from Events

The experts and commentators talk and write, but is anybody listening? No organizations, and especially no public organizations and their elected leaders, are very good at learning from events (Levinthal and March 1993; Lynn 1997). A poor federal response to Hurricane Andrew in 1992 led to a successful upgrading of FEMA during the Clinton years, but the subsequent Bush administration permitted the agency's capacity to degrade substantially. According to a team of engineering faculty based at U.C. Berkeley, the flood protection system being rebuilt in New Orleans following Hurricane Katrina "has not been significantly improved . . . Filling levees with the shells that washed out of them is like giving a Band-Aid to a patient in need of a triple bypass" (Spotswood 2006). A comprehensive analysis of the anthrax attacks and subsequent scare of October 2001 refers to "an unacceptable level of fragility in systems now properly recognized as vital to national defense" and continues, "Most of the vulnerabilities in the medical and public health systems revealed by the response remain unaddressed" (Gursky, Inglesby, and O'Toole 2003). A history of urban terror attacks in Jerusalem since the 1990s should have taught the Israelis the importance of an organized response system such as an ICS.

It seems to have had little or no effect, however, because the response to terror events even in 2002 was anarchic, with fire department vehicles blocking access roads for ambulances to the disaster scene while police were reporting these roads open (Perliger, Pedahzur, and Zalmanovitch 2005). The U.S. Army, following the trauma of Vietnam, "threw away virtually everything it had learned there, slowly and painfully, about how to wage a counterinsurgency campaign." When it went to war in Iraq in 2003, its "core document," the 1976 edition of its field manual, "did not mention counterinsurgency" (Ricks 2006). The same sorts of organizational flaws in NASA and its contractor network that caused the loss of the Space Shuttle *Columbia* in 2003 had been diagnosed following the *Challenger* disaster seventeen years earlier (Mahler 2008). In this case, external and internal pressures to launch flights seem to have impeded NASA's organizational adaption, which was then further degraded by internal politics, organizational processes, and poor risk management practices.

Such failures aside, events do provide opportunities for learning. Fortunately, these opportunities are rare. The United States and the world have never had an opportunity to learn from a successful WMD event in peacetime. The closest we have come were the 1995 nerve gas attack by a Japanese religious cult on passengers in the Tokyo subway, in which 12 commuters were killed, 54 seriously injured, and another 1,000 or so affected, and the anthrax attacks in the United States in October 2001.[36] However, learning can be based on analogous situations, such as very large scale natural disasters, and on "near-events" like jihadist organizations' attempted bombing of the World Trade Center in 1993 and failed attempts to shoot down civilian aircraft with shoulder-fired missiles.

We have had plenty of such situations. Leaving aside whether learning gets translated into organizational action, it is safe to say that important people, including elected officials, senior managers, thoughtful professionals, and many informed laypersons, have learned from these situations, often a great deal. What is learned falls into two general categories: this threat-vulnerability-damage function is worse than we thought it was; and, this prevention/preparedness/response system is less coherent/effective/responsive than we expected it to be.

Since the Progressive era, when the nation discovered the hazards of meat and patent medicines, the list of real or supposed environmental threats has only grown. This development is a function both of an increasing sense of (assumedly costless) entitlement to safety and a greater scientific understanding of the pathways along which danger travels. Periodic outbreaks of illness, deaths in mine disasters, casualties of drug side effects, lead paint, oil spills, train wrecks, black lung disease, and so on accentuate the general trend and frequently lead to new protective legislation.[37] The same pattern holds with respect to natural disasters (Birkland 2006). Since

Katrina, for instance, DHS and FEMA have been giving much more attention to all-hazards preparedness compared to the more narrowly defined terrorism threat (Skinner 2006).[38] The post–September 11 reaction sketched in section 8.1 suggests that the same can be said about terrorist events. Similarly, within weeks of the 2004 railway bombings in Madrid, Spain, the U.S. Congress appropriated an additional $100 million in railway security grants for FY 2005 (Stowsky 2006).

But if events can sometimes focus attention on inadequacies of problem recognition and/or response, they do not usually teach much about the nature of cost-effective remedies. Learning what not to do rarely implies learning what to do (Birkland 2006). An excellent case in point is the 9/11 Commission's finding that the FBI and the CIA had failed to "connect the dots" so as to see the emerging threat and preempt it. Sufficient data existed, said the commission, but it was not transmitted or, if transmitted, not acted on. Al Qaeda was more dangerous by far than we had recognized, and our capacity for prevention far worse. With regard to learning, so far so good. The commission went a step further, however, and recommended solutions to the problem, including the creation of a DNI with enough authority to reengineer the way that the disparate members of the intelligence community shared information and formed operational plans. The recommendation was, in part at least, adopted some months later. Whether this will prove to have been a wise measure remains to be seen.

Although events do not teach what to do, they do open a "policy window" (Kingdon 1995) for discussing ideas that are already current among elites who have followed the policy area for some time and have built up a store of evaluations and reasoned speculation (9/11 Commission 2004; Haveman, Shatz, and Vilchis 2005). Nearly all of the 9/11 Commission's recommendations, for instance, had been known for years. The existence of such policy elites, and their file cabinets full of proposals and arguments, increases the odds that reasonable ideas will eventually be implemented. They are far from a guarantee, however. If it is too economically or politically costly for policy-makers to act, or if there is dissension among elites on which policies should be adopted, as often happens when interagency collaboration or reform of the intelligence agencies is involved (Zegart 2007), the policy window may close with nothing being done—until perhaps there is another event that focuses attention and reopens the policy window (May 1992; Birkland 2006).

8.6.2   Direct Experience with Policies and Institutions

Congress learned from years of experience that it had to find ways to avoid turning its state and local homeland security grants into pork-barrel programs, though it has only partially succeeded. The DHS has slowly been learning how to introduce more technical rationality into the distribution formula, via risk assessment (and, to a lesser degree, the assessment of local implementation effectiveness (GAO 2007b). Given the disparate origins of the twenty-two agencies composing the DHS, it is not surprising that there have been continuous trial-and-error efforts to organize and reorganize. The largest appears to have occurred in July 2005, five months after Michael Chertoff took over from the first DHS Secretary, Tom Ridge: the major divisions of the department were dissolved and then reassembled.

As I noted above, after some early, and massive, disappointments with BioShield, Congress in April 2007 created a new implementation structure, BARDA, which seems to promise a much more flexible and creative approach.

It is through experience, and a sophisticated understanding of government institutions, that policymakers detect inadequacies and take measures to correct them. Examples such as those above could be multiplied almost indefinitely. The important questions, though, are (1) how well and how fast government actors recognize their own mistakes and begin to correct them and (2) to what extent the "solution" actually improves on the problem. And in the present context, how does learning from this sort of experience in the WMD area compare with such policy and implementation learning more generally?

Answering these questions in a systematic way is beyond the scope of this chapter. In the "Summing Up" section below, though, I attempt some speculation.

8.6.3   Best Practices

In a federal system, different jurisdictions have opportunities to learn from one another. States, Justice Louis D. Brandeis famously said, are "the laboratories of democracy," and there is some evidence that states do look to each other as sources of ideas. Federal agencies like the Environmental Protection Agency (EPA) and the Occupational Safety and Health Administration (OSHA) follow a strategy of devolving programmatic functions to the states, rendering technical assistance and then reporting regionally or nationally on "what seems to be working." Analogously, state agencies often do the same for cities and counties. The particular vehicles for disseminating ideas are varied, ranging from workshops, conferences, and professional association meetings to web sites, newsletters, and journals.

State and local governments play a central role in preparing for and responding to disasters. The seeds of the current Incident Command System were sown by the highly disorganized response to a series of forest fires in Southern California in the early 1970s. They were subsequently nourished by professional firefighting networks in California and around the country including in particular the U.S. Forest Service for state agencies that fight forest fires, and the U.S. Fire Academy for urban fire departments and volunteer fire companies (Buck, Trainor, and Aguirre 2006). The Incident Command System is often a very effective response (Bigley and Roberts

2001) and is now enshrined as the technical basis for the National Response Plan which would be invoked if (as is almost surely the case) federal government became involved following a successful WMD attack. Here, surely, is a case of the dissemination of "best practice" and societal learning to be proud of—provided the ICS actually works, which, as I remarked above, is somewhat disputed.

8.6.4 Simulations

Scores of simulations, drills, and exercises take place every year at all levels of government and in the private sector (Phillips 2006; Brzezinski 2005). The three main functions of these activities are to stimulate preparedness planning, to practice response routines in the event of an attack, and, in after-action reviews, to diagnose weak points in preparedness and execution. This last function is probably the most important when it comes to catastrophes. No matter what organizational arrangements are planned for the response phase—that is, an Incident Command System or something else—a great deal of preparatory training is required. It just won't do to have the managers from participating agencies exchanging their business cards with fires (or germs or radiation) swirling around them. Unfortunately, disaster-scale simulations are expensive and hard to organize. Hence, simulations are relatively infrequent—and catastrophe-scale simulations even less so (McConnell and Drennan 2006).

The best-known of the catastrophe-scale simulations is the congressionally mandated TOPOFF exercises (the contraction denotes participation by "top officials"), the first four of which took place between 2000 and 2007. The first enacted simultaneous events in Denver (an attack of plague bacteria); Portsmouth, New Hampshire (chemical weapons); and the Washington, D.C., area (a radiological event) (Inglesby, Grossman, and O'Toole 2001). The exercises were supposed to take place "without notice," but in fact were widely known beforehand. Realism was compromised in other important ways as well. For example, Colorado's governor was not involved in the Denver case and his role was not simulated; nor were other political figures involved. Instead, a nonpolitical Emergency Epidemic Response Committee of medical experts (EERC) was improvised to handle the crisis on its own. Furthermore, many of the unfolding elements, such as masses of patients showing up at hospitals to demand antibiotics, were entirely hypothetical. Nevertheless, TOPOFF managers "injected" them into the participants' information streams.

Despite these limitations, the first TOPOFF exercise was highly instructive, identifying problems that would otherwise have gone undiagnosed. The EERC and a larger committee of communitywide decision makers wasted endless time in conference calls, some involving fifty to a hundred persons whose roles, authorities, and even identities were unclear (Inglesby, Grossman, and O'Toole 2001). Public health professionals proved unfamiliar with the jargon and acronyms used in the emergency management community, such as the JIC, the JOC, and the DMORTs.[39] Mock antibiotics delivered to the airport ended up being unbundled by a single individual who " 'had to count individual pills and put them into plastic baggies.' Before she could even begin, there was a six-hour delay during which (hypothetical) traffic was negotiated 'in order to get the plastic baggies from Safeway' " (Inglesby, Grossman, and O'Toole 2001).[40]

Whether such learning counts for anything, of course, depends on the nature and quality of the follow-up. A 2004 simulation of a Category 3 hurricane hitting New Orleans, complete with storm surge overtopping the levees, did illuminate some lessons "later applied with successful results." Despite this, "...as a whole, the system seemed unready despite the rehearsal" (Phillips 2006). FEMA also canceled much of the follow-up work, including a projected study of how to find long-term shelter for evacuees housed at the Superdome, citing lack of funds.

Overall, however, the country has worked successfully to improve the design of simulations and systematize the process of learning from them. RAND's online Public Health Preparedness Database includes nearly forty simulations of terrorist attacks and infectious disease outbreaks. And a National Memorial Institute for the Prevention of Terrorism, funded by the DHS, hosts a Lessons Learned Information Sharing website that gives registered users access to after-action reports on various exercises (Phillips 2006).

8.6.5 Evaluations
Evaluations come on a continuum, from those that, in a methodological sense, are highly controlled to those that take advantage of what appears to be "common sense."

The Better Controlled   In a domain as vast as domestic security, there are many opportunities for controlled evaluations. Pieces of hardware such as the spectroscopic portal monitors (ASPs) mentioned above are easy to test rigorously. They are less easily tested in situ, but it is still good practice to pilot-test hardware in field situations before full-scale deployment. As the ASP case suggests, however, deployment sometimes ignores test results.

Organizational practices, such as how to conduct and make use of simulations, or how to run an effective public communications operation in times of emergency, or how to ensure that pharmaceutical stockpiles are expeditiously accessed and distributed, are harder to test. Very occasionally, managers make use of "planned variation" in which local units try novel practices in order to find out "what works" and develop best practices. An example would be having field offices of a county welfare agency try different case management procedures and compare results.[41] More common—though still a relative rarity given its potential value—is the communication across field offices of seemingly good ideas that have spontaneously emerged at one or more sites. This sort of process would be ideally suited to the FBI, say, although I do not know whether it actually occurs. To facilitate such intra-organizational learning almost certainly depends on top leadership seeing to it that field-office directors do not regard such a process as infringing on their autonomy or as a way to make invidious comparisons.

The Less Well Controlled At the opposite end of the continuum we have evaluations of the sort done by the GAO, which typically involve linking performance deficits in some federal agency (or ensemble of agencies) to commonsensically derived suppositions about one or more deficiencies in the agency's (or agencies') structure or set of practices. The GAO has paid extensive attention to agencies' counterterrorism and WMD programs.[42]

Congressional oversight committees, of course, are active in this area—sometimes too much so, because they are numerous and preparing and giving testimony can consume many hours of top executives' time.[43] For reasons of both political sensitivity and security, a fair amount of evaluating, analyzing, and reviewing is also turned over to specially appointed commissions like the National Commission on Terrorist Attacks upon the United States ("the September 11 Commission"). Finally, the United States hosts many public policy think tanks whose affiliated analysts and researchers have been scrutinizing homeland security issues since September 11 and in many cases before. Many of their products have been referenced in this chapter.

These are capabilities housed essentially outside of executive branch agencies. It would make sense to have policy-analytic and evaluation capabilities at work within the agencies as well, in analogy with the Defense Department's "policy shops" and certain domestically oriented agencies like the Department of Health and Human Services. Unfortunately, the Department of Homeland Security did not have such a policy shop until April 2007—that is, for the first four years of its existence.

8.6.6 Summing Up

Unfortunately, the social science literature on how governments, or policymaking elites, learn or fail to learn is both slim and lacking in explanatory and predictive power. Most of the literature considers the learning process through lenses appropriate for individual behavior, particularly information processing. As a result, it tends to downplay the existence and functioning of very complex processes of inter-individual and interinstitutional connectivity or lack thereof; self-interested indifference or distortion; and the uses of what might be called "pseudoinformation" in symbol manipulation. Despite this, I would like to use at least a rudimentary theoretical framework to assess whether governmental learning in the area of WMD threat management is better or worse than what we see on average. My simple framework begins with the supply and demand for "problem-solving rationality," particularly the sort of rationality that is focused on realistic problem recognition and on critical evaluation of purported solutions. In this context, "solutions" includes the whole array of social practices we call "programs" and "policies" and "institutional procedures," and so on.

First consider supply. American government is blessed with large numbers of professionals who are paid to give (or take) what they deem to be rational and disinterested policy advice. They mostly occupy staff positions in both the legislative and executive branches. In addition, many of the relevant action agencies of government are headed and/or staffed by professionals who are at least intendedly rational in their own fields of expertise—for example, fire chiefs, public health directors, and emergency management experts. Many of these individuals, and the organizational units that employ them, produce reasoned and reasonable advice. Some, indeed, are extremely talented and dedicated. Furthermore, the in-house pools of such advice are augmented by an army of contract consultants along with analysts working in think tanks. Is there reason to think that the pool of rational problem solvers is smaller or larger in the WMD domain than in other policy domains? That it is more talented and dedicated than average or less so?

On the one hand, the subject matter probably attracts individuals who are somewhat above average in problem-solving talent and dedication than government in general, much as one expects to find in the ranks of military officers. The problems are intellectually and morally challenging, and come with an aura that attaches to issues of collective fate. On the other hand, outside the intelligence community, and possibly the GAO, the relevant institutions are for the most part nothing special when considered as places to make a government career—for example, a local public health department or a state emergency services agency or a federal procurement office concerned with contracts for radiation detectors. These are not at all bad places, but neither do they radiate glory. In the think-tank and consultancy sectors, the quality of talent is high, just as it is in the WMD domain. The net result is that, when it comes to the supply of good policy-analytic thinking, the WMD domain is probably as well off as we find in other policy domains and perhaps a little better.

Turning to the demand side, policy rationality is not much wanted. The protection of private interest—commercial, financial, bureaucratic, political—greatly dominates the disinterestedly rational pursuit of the public interest. "Rent seeking" and rent protection are the order of the day. Because a proposal arguably in the public interest almost always serves someone's private interest, it will seldom be devoid of advocates. The WMD domain is probably no different than any other in these general ways. It does differ, however, in the technical difficulties that would-be rational and public-spirited policymakers face when they try to make appropriate judgments. The probabilities of attack are too uncertain, the magnitude of negative outcomes too hard to contemplate, the efficacy of counterstrategies too hard to assess. Under these conditions, it is very easy for the manipulation of symbols about mass casualties and mass destruction—or, on the other side of the political divide, allegations of ethnocentric paranoia and fondness for fascism—to drive out rational discourse. On the demand side, then, policy learning in the WMD domain is probably a bit worse than average.

Putting together our two assessments of supply-and-demand processes, then, learning in the WMD domain is probably very near the average for all policy domains. Compared to the standards we might reasonably have demanded given the individual and collective stakes, this is not a good result.

8.7   Conclusion

We have considered several adaptive mechanisms bearing on the nation's response to terrorism in general and WMD in particular: mobilizing resources, using them wisely, building institutional capacity in the public sector, utilizing the strengths of the private sector, and learning by a variety of means. Despite the pitfalls, I have occasionally judged the adaptive response by reference to some absolute standard of performance. But more commonly, I have used a relative standard based on how WMD policymaking and policy implementation stack up against similar processes in other areas of social and economic life.

The mainstream consensus among experts is that our mobilization of resources falls short, though probably not disastrously so. Such resources as we deploy are targeted about as well as government does such targeting generally. But spending and targeting money appears to be easier than building the needed institutional capacity—that is, fixing our public bureaucracies and getting them to work together—and in this regard homeland security resembles government generally. The results on this institutional front so far are very troubling, though even more disturbing is our mediocre political capacity for learning what to do and acting on such learning.

Because so much is at stake, one might have hoped for better results. Is there a reasonable prospect for improvement in the near future? Let us leave aside whether the threat environment will grow better or worse because of such events as the war in Iraq or trends such as ideological developments in the Muslim world, and consider only our capacity and motivation to cope with this environment. We can, of course, expect slow and steady incremental improvements in our capacity to mount countermeasures along the lines discussed in this chapter—for example, using risk as a basis for resource allocation, or developing more effective detection techniques, or integrating local and federal intelligence operations. Our question, though, is whether these trends can accelerate. We must therefore consider what conditions bearing on these trends might be changing, either for the worse or the better.

One clear change for the better is underway: deceleration of the large-scale organizational transitions at the federal level and their ripple effects at state and local levels. Establishing the DHS and the DNI, and efforts to reorient the FBI, are probably themselves a cause of lowered institutional capacity; and these transitions will conclude in due course within, say five to ten years.

A more debatable set of changes concerns political and policy leadership and management skill, areas less discussed in this chapter than institutional capacities and limitations but certainly of great importance. Leadership can to some degree be credited, for instance, when DNI Mike McConnell succeeds in creating a joint duty program for the intelligence community despite George Tenet's earlier failure. Similarly, FEMA flourishes when Jamie Lee Witt heads the agency, with the full support of President Bill Clinton, but it declines when President George W. Bush allows it to be demoted to just another unit within the Department of Homeland Security.

Of course, leadership need not come only from the highest-level officials. Leadership is a type of activity. It can come from anyone, in any position, who is capable of seizing an opportunity and facilitating collective action toward a worthy collective goal. It need not be overt or dramatic; it can be subtle and stealthy. But even leaders have leaders. And it would help if the leaders in official, high, and visible positions were to exercise their powers on behalf of more policy rationality and pay more attention to policy formulation and implementation in the public interest. In this regard WMD is very much like every other policy area in American government.

Notes

1. It may be, as one well-respected political scientist has argued, that the absence of terrorist attacks on U.S. soil since September 11 can be explained by the simple absence of individuals motivated to conduct them (Mueller 2006).

2. A significant omission, for instance, is recalibrating the trade-offs between security and privacy. I will simply note here that the intense and widespread debate over this matter is itself a matter for national self-congratulation, regardless of one's views on how it is turning out.

3. Some might count the explosive in this case as a weapon of "mass disruption" rather than "destruction" because it would not pose hazards to responders or the public of the same sort that nuclear, chemical, biological, or radiological weapons do.

4. Of this, the Department of Homeland Security received about $28 billion. The Brookings group has adjusted this figure to take account of an accounting change that added $17 billion in Department of Defense expenditures to the 2007 figure (O'Hanlon 2006).

5. The amount of state and local homeland security spending not reimbursed by federal grants remains poorly documented. An estimate by Bart Hobijn (2002), based on surveys of U.S. governors and mayors, projected about $2.9 billion per year in the near future. Much of this expenditure involved capital investments and was expected to decline over time. Hobijn recently estimated private expenditures for the period 2001–2005 at a modest $9.4 billion. However, he only included expenditures on security personnel and electronic protective systems (Hobijn and Sager 2007). Hobijn's estimates also do not include certain sectors, such as transportation, that incurred substantial private capital expenditures.

6. In order to compare these figures with O'Hanlon's analysis (2006), I have excluded both Department of Defense spending and the administration's 2008 request for $3.1 billion in supplemental and emergency funding. Similarly, my 2009 figure does not include the administration's $2.2 billion Bioshield request.

7. Note that it is not clear in these or in most popular discussions of domestic security expenditures what percentage of the cited amounts is one-time versus ongoing, though it appears from the context that most of it is ongoing.

8. Brzezinski himself is not necessarily identified with the *Mother Jones* left, having been a reporter for the *Wall Street Journal*.

9. This is an instance of what psychologists call a "framing effect" (Van Der Pligt 1996).

10. The term *fiscal illusion* is more commonly used in the public finance literature, however, to indicate the opposite false belief: that more spending is all benefit and no cost (Dollery and Worthington 1996).

11. As for the short term, Carafano implies that the needed funds could come from money currently spent on wasteful strategies. The Century Fund panel proposed a menu of specific cuts in the Defense Department budget. The Brookings authors say nothing about how to finance their recommendations.

12. Interestingly, a survey of city officials and state residents in California in 2003 showed that officials underestimated residents' willingness to pay higher taxes in exchange for higher security (Baldassare et al. 2003). Residents of large cities were considerably readier to pay more than were other residents.

13. For an argument that assumes the opposite incentives for elected officials, however, see Sunstein 2006.

14. In Europe, the problem is on its way to a solution because policymakers were able to build on a history of standardized frequencies linking law enforcement and emergency services across countries and to rely on the European Telecommunications Standards Institute's policy flexibility.

15. New York City pays for some intelligence agents stationed abroad, although so far the federal government has not agreed to share any of the cost.

16. Here, the case is further complicated by the fact that emergency communications are traditionally a local responsibility. A federal subsidy might induce some jurisdictions to join the

interoperable standard while others who had recently purchased new incompatible equipment might not. But does the federal government have the right to impose such a mandate? And if it does, should an accompanying subsidy take account of the costs cities may have already invested in recent upgrades?

17. Matthew Bunn (2006) offers what he calls "a plausible set of parameter values" and estimates a 29 percent probability of a nuclear terrorist attack by 2016. His parameter values appear to incorporate only a moderate level of countermeasures.

18. Some technical arguments may be raised against investment but dismissed. First, it is true that terrorists can always shift their aim from a better-protected target to a worse-protected target. But forcing terrorists to attack "second-choice" targets reduces the value of attacking in the first place. Second, any single defense can be penetrated by a clever and determined adversary. But there is value in partial defenses—"layering" or "defense in depth"—which increases the odds that one of the defenses will work and, in any case, complicates terrorist calculations and execution strategies (Flynn 2004; Schneier 2003).

19. The technical tests were also, apparently, tilted in favor of ASP by being biased against the status quo, namely, the PVT portal monitors. In addition, the DNDO violated the DHS guidelines for performing cost-benefit analyses, and seemingly relied on only eleven of at least fifty-four tests that the Department of Energy's national laboratories had performed on commercially available portal monitors since September 11 (GAO 2007c). Congress subsequently halted DNDO's purchase pending further study (Aloise 2007).

20. Note that I am referring here to security, not safety.

21. Lee Clarke (1999) has pointed to the prevalence of "fantasy planning" in the emergency preparedness field.

22. I have in mind the Program Assessment and Rating Tool (PART). See the OMB website, http://www.whitehouse.gov/omb/expectmore/index.html.

23. In December 2006, the government canceled the contract with VaxGen after the company had failed to meet a number of milestones.

24. See, for instance, House Committee on Government Reform 2006.

25. In the White House white paper of February 2006, *The Federal Response to Katrina: Lessons Learned*, President Bush is quoted as saying that "four years after . . . September the 11th, Americans have every right to expect a more effective response in a time of emergency. When the federal government fails to meet such an obligation, I, as President, am responsible for the problem, and for the solution." He also conceded that "the system, at every level of government, was not well-coordinated, and was overwhelmed in the first few days" (U.S. 2006b).

26. A different approach than using actual outcomes is to use specially constructed metrics that measure outputs or capabilities or some other corollary of actual performance. Such metrics would be useful for tracking institutional progress over time, say, on a year-to-year basis. These would be more evident to senior managers and policymakers than to members of the public, and some are already in use. See, for instance, the annual assessments made by the U.S. Office of Management and Budget of the Department of Homeland Security at http://www.whitehouse.gov/omb/expectmore/agency/024.html. Technical problems beset the design, collection, and use of relevant data—how do you measure whether an agency's "ana-

lytic capacity" has increased or an Al Qaeda agent has decided not to attempt a border crossing?—but many creative possibilities are under discussion (Caudle 2005a, 2005b; Caudle and Yim 2006).

27. She refers to the responsible factors as structure, incentives, and culture.

28. There are also some valid technical objections to splitting law enforcement from domestic intelligence (9/11 Commission 2004).

29. A year earlier the Public Discourse Project, a continuation of the September 11 Commission, published a follow-up document to their original (2004) report. They commented that the FBI's "trend line" "has been in the right direction, but far too slow" and that "the FBI's culture continues to resist Director Mueller's changes" (Public Discourse Project 2005a).

30. The GAO, in a 2004 report, said the "FBI has made significant progress in its transformation efforts since GAO last testified . . . in June 2003" but went on to note the FBI's difficulties in retaining staff with intelligence knowledge, skills, and abilities (GAO 2004a).

31. That Goldwater-Nichols has actually been successful is generally accepted by close observers, though there are dissenters. There is some concern, for instance, that it has eroded civilian control and has suppressed some of the useful criticism and perspectives that used to come from separate and rival military services (Bourne 1998). The Office of Secretary of Defense also invokes "jointness" when it advocates doctrinal changes, apparently as an ideological hammer to enforce conformity (Owens 2006).

32. Legal and political issues arising from our federal structure complicate matters (Leonard and Howitt 2006), as do issues of how state and local government can coordinate with the military in responding to an event (Lehr 2006).

33. For a much more complex case involving the Ports of Los Angeles and Long Beach, see Zegart, Hipp, and Jacobson (2006).

34. More generally on the "secret war" between the FBI and the CIA, see Riebling (2004).

35. The ODNI competed in the annual Kennedy School of Government Innovations in Government program in 2008. The program reached the finalist round, which earned them a site visit. I was the assigned site visitor and, in that capacity, interviewed many enthusiastic line-level participants and program managers. An indication of high-level support is that the ceremony surrounding the issuance of implementing instructions featured the Secretaries of Treasury, Defense, and Homeland Security; the Chairman of the Joint Chiefs of Staff; and prominent deputy secretaries from State and Energy. These agencies had also signed a so-called treaty affirming support for the program and its implementing details.

36. The Japanese were probably less ready to learn from the event than Americans would have been because they resist acknowledging terrorism. Even after the sarin gas had been identified as such, police insisted it had been accidentally produced by a gardener mixing fertilizers. Pangi (2003).

37. But this tendency is patchy and error-prone, sometimes underreacting and sometimes overreacting, although it appears that in the long run (years if not decades) learning does occur (Morrall 2003; Birkland 2006).

38. For a slightly cynical account of FEMA's oscillation between a focus on security and an all-hazards approach, see Perrow 2006.

39. "Joint Information Center," "Joint Operations Center," and "Disaster Mortuary Operational Response Teams," respectively.

40. Israel tests its disaster response system with nonsimulated alerts, such as when residents of the North were sent to shelters in 2000 because of fears that Hizbullah would attack. The state of emergency lasted only forty-eight hours, but it revealed problems in distributing food and mattresses and in confining physicians to shelters when they were needed on the outside (Merari 2003).

41. Of course, attempts should be made to control for differences among sites that may have nothing to do with the practice(s) being evaluated.

42. A GAO site search for *terrorism* or *WMD* for the period June 2006–May 2007 returned 1,170 entries, about two-thirds of them reports. The thirty to forty GAO products I have sampled in preparing this chapter have been of very high quality.

43. The *Washington Post* editorialized on December 28, 2004: "There are 79 such panels; every single senator and at least 412 of the 435 House members have some degree of responsibility for homeland security operations. By contrast, the Defense Department, with a budget 10 times that of DHS, reports to 'just' 36 committees and subcommittees...From the perspective of national security, this fragmented, dysfunctional structure is sheer lunacy. Department officials spend too much time responding to their many congressional masters; last year alone, according to the departing secretary, Tom Ridge, he and other top department officials testified 145 times before various committees and subcommittees. Moreover, such balkanized oversight is less effective rather than more so, because members of Congress suffer from parochial viewpoints influenced by their individual committee assignments and fail to develop a broad overview of homeland security priorities."

9

Responding to WMD Terrorism Threats: The Role of Insurance Markets

Dwight Jaffee and Thomas Russell

Insurance offers three important benefits that can help an economy deal with the catastrophic losses that arise from both natural disasters and manmade events: risk sharing, mitigation and price discovery. *Risk sharing* is the direct benefit of insurance, whereby those at risk from an event pay a relatively small annual premium to an insurer, which later uses its accumulated funds to reimburse those parties that suffer actual losses. Risk sharing per se, however, does not reduce the physical losses from the event. Nevertheless, most economic activities and industries could not operate without the benefits of insurance or a comparable government program. For example, in the absence of auto insurance, a family could be readily bankrupted if a family member were held liable for a large sum due to a serious auto accident. As a result, it is unclear how the automobile industry could have developed unless the risk-sharing benefits of insurance were available to eliminate this risk of personal financial disaster. We will see in section 9.1 that insurance plays as important a role in sharing the economic risks created by terrorist attacks using weapons of mass destruction as it does with the daily risks of automobile driving.

Mitigation is a second benefit of insurance, whereby insured parties take actions to reduce their expected losses in order to obtain lower premiums. The incentive to mitigate is created by *risk-based premiums*, whereby each insured party pays a premium commensurate with his or her risk. For example, when insurers charge property owners lower premiums if they protect their buildings from terrorist attacks, this gives owners an incentive to carry out this mitigation. In contrast, providing insurance *without* risk-based premiums actually deters mitigation activity, since the insured parties pay the same insurance premium and are covered for their losses whether or not they mitigate. In section 9.3.4, we discuss specific issues of mitigation as they relate to terrorist attacks.

Price discovery, meaning that insurance premiums offer a market determined quantification of an insured risk, is the third fundamental benefit of well functioning insurance markets. The accuracy of insurance premiums as a measure of risk is enhanced by the insurance industry's ability to efficiently aggregate information from a wide range of sources. The information summarized in the premiums can then be applied to resource allocation and investment decisions, of which mitigating terrorism risks is just one important case. As another example, Laster and Schmid (2005) note that the decision to produce ultralarge oil tankers was reversed when insurers indicated that they would require very large premiums to insure the tankers against environment risks.

The risk-sharing, mitigation, and price-discovery roles of insurance all rely on the fact that profit maximization within the insurance industry provides a powerful incentive to aggregate information efficiently, resulting in an accurate measure of risk that can be applied in a wide range of economic decisions. In a fundamental sense, the less transparent the risk, the more valuable insurance markets can be in providing the best available risk quantification. In this chapter, in particular, we will show that for issues of homeland security, where the risks may even be intentionally opaque, the tools and methods of insurance can have exceptional value.

Insurance benefits generally rise with the size of the possible loss, so insurance is particularly valuable for *catastrophes*, the term we use to cover both natural disasters (such as earthquakes and hurricanes) and *man-made events* (covering industrial accidents and terrorist attacks). Figure 9.1 shows the worldwide level of insured losses from each of the two categories of catastrophes as compiled by the

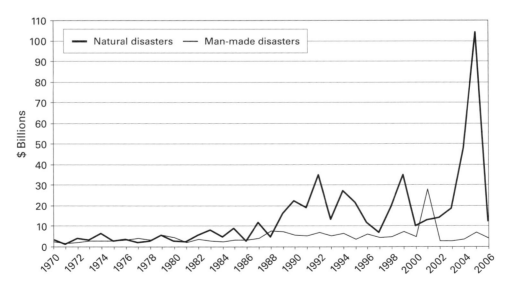

Figure 9.1
Insured losses from catastrophes, billions of dollars.

reinsurance firm Swiss Re. The September 11 attack accounts for the 2001 spike in losses from man-made losses, and Hurricane Katrina accounts for the 2005 spike in natural disaster losses. The long experience in observing and insuring natural disaster risks will provide a useful benchmark for our discussion of how insurance markets for terrorism risks might best operate.

This chapter focuses on the enormous losses that could arise from terrorist attacks using weapons of mass destruction (WMD), hereafter WMD terrorist attacks. We will see that a WMD attack could readily create $100 billion in insured losses, and some estimates exceed $700 billion, far more than even the record $100 billion loss from natural disasters in 2005. The terrorism insurance literature often refers to the risks created by WMD attacks as CBRN risks: chemical, biological, radiation, and nuclear. Table 9.1 provides a summary description of CBRN weapons compiled by the General Accountability Office (2006e). For brevity, we will refer to the full set of such attack modes as WMD risks, but we will also discuss the special issues that arise from the specific forms of CBRN attacks.[1]

While insurance is particularly valuable for catastrophic risks, catastrophic risks also raise special issues that often preclude a viable and dependable supply from private insurance providers. In fact, while the U.S. economy had functioning private insurance markets for earthquakes, hurricanes, and conventional terrorism risks just fifteen years ago, each of these private markets has since broken down as the result of a major event.[2] Given that insurance is critical to the functioning of the economy, such breakdowns in supply have always elicited a government policy intervention, ranging from attempts to reopen the private markets to the direct provision of government insurance. Whatever the specific form of government intervention, these policies have always been politically and economically contentious.

This chapter analyzes the issues that arise in providing insurance against WMD terrorist attacks and evaluates alternative solutions for the United States. The chapter is organized as follows. Section 9.1 summarizes the basic principles of insurance and the benefits it provides in the context of WMD terrorist attacks. It also surveys the reasons why so few private insurance markets currently operate to provide coverage against catastrophic risks, including WMD terrorist attacks. Section 9.2 describes the range of governmental solutions that have been tried or are currently proposed for insuring terrorism risks. Section 9.3 analyses the issues and recommends strategies for providing viable WMD terrorism insurance for individuals and firms. Section 9.4 provides a brief conclusion.

9.1 Basic Insurance Principles

We begin by reviewing the basic economics of insurance as it relates to WMD terrorism.

Table 9.1
Description of CBRN weapons

	Weapon description	Examples of agents
Nuclear	A nuclear explosion would have immediate blast effects that would destroy buildings. The explosion also would produce high-energy radiation and extreme heat, and form a cloud from which highly lethal radioactive material would fall. The overall effect would depend on the size of the weapon and how high above the ground the detonation occurred.	The explosion of the weapon, a bomb or missile, would be generated through nuclear fission of uranium or plutonium or nuclear fusion of hydrogen atoms.
Biological	Biological attacks can involve two basic types of biological agents: contagious and noncontagious. With most biological agents, an attack may not be recognized immediately because the symptoms may be attributable to several causes or because the disease the agent causes has an incubation period.	Many different agents such as smallpox or anthrax, each with its own characteristics, could be used for biological attacks.
Chemical	Chemical attacks entail the dispersal of chemical vapors, aerosols, liquids, or solids and affect individuals through inhalation or exposure to eyes and skin. Chemical weapons act very quickly to kill or harm humans, often within a few seconds.	Many different agents such as sarin and hydrogen cyanide, each with its own characteristics, could be used for chemical attacks.
Radiological	A "dirty bomb" uses conventional explosives to disperse radioactive material across the immediate area, which could vary in size depending on the amount of explosive. The primary short-term exposure hazard to humans would be inhalation of radioactive material suspended in the dust and smoke from the explosion.	Different radioactive agents, including americium, cesium, and plutonium, could be used to create a dirty bomb.

Source: Government Accountability Office 2006e

9.1.1   Demand for Insurance

Consider an individual facing a choice between a sure loss of $100 or a risky loss of the same expected value, say a 1 percent chance of losing $10,000 ($100 = .01 × $10,000). Most individuals are *risk averse*: they would opt to pay the sure cost of $100 in order to avoid the small chance of losing the larger $10,000. Using this definition, it is easily proven that risk averse individuals should always fully insure their risks, as long as the insurance premium is *actuarially fair*, meaning that the premium equals the expected value of the loss (Arrow 1965).

Of course, insurance companies have operating costs and expect to earn a profit, so quoted insurance premiums generally include a *loading*, which is the amount by which quoted premiums exceed the actuarially fair amount. When insurance premiums include a loading, the optimal behavior is for parties to insure only a part of the full risk; in the preceding example, for instance, an insured party might accept a deductible amount of $1,000 relative to the full $10,000 risk.[3] The perception of actuarially unfair premiums may also arise if the insured parties believe that the likelihood of the loss and/or the size of the loss are smaller than the actuarial values being used by insurers to set their premiums. Although we would theoretically expect firms to be less risk averse than individuals, in practice we observe firms purchasing insurance in much the same manner as individuals.[4]

9.1.2   The Costs of the September 11 Attack

Terrorist attacks inflict losses on various insurance lines, including property and casualty, workers compensation, and life insurance. Part A of table 9.2 shows how the total insured losses from the September 11 attacks of $35.9 billion were distributed across the various lines of insurance. Property and casualty coverage includes property damage, business interruption, liability, and related risks. Workers compensation insurance covers workers injured on the job and is required in all states. Life insurance, of course, provides compensation upon a death.

The total costs of the September 11 attacks also include uninsured losses, indirect economic costs, and even unquantifiable effects such as pain and suffering or the dread of a future event. Part B of table 9.2 shows the support that the various forms of federal disaster assistance provided after the September 11 attack. The largest transfer was provided under the Federal Victims Compensation Act, which paid nearly $7 billion to the families of September 11 victims, in return for which the families relinquished any right to sue those considered to be responsible. The total sum for all federal assistance was $30.5 billion in then current dollars, about equal to the total insured losses measured in Part A in 2006 prices. Finally, in Part C of table 9.2, the estimates from Hartwig (2006) indicate that the economic losses in New York City alone exceeded $90 billion and that the total economic costs associated with September 11 approach $200 billion.

Table 9.2
Estimated costs of the attack on September 11, 2001

A. Insured Losses*

Insurance category	Cost, $billion, 2006 prices	Percent of total insured losses
Property damage	$11.9	33.1%
Business interruption	$11.2	31.1%
Liability, aviation, misc.	$8.6	24.0%
Workers' Compensation	$2.0	5.6%
Life insurance	$1.1	3.1%
Event cancellation	$1.1	3.1%
Total insured losses	*$35.9*	*100.0%*

B. Federal Disaster Assistance**

Assistance category	$billion	Percent of total assistance
Federal Victims Compensation Act	$7.0	23.0%
New York City infrastructure	$5.6	18.4%
Revitalization of Manhattan economy	$5.5	18.0%
Grants to U.S. airlines for losses sustained	$5.0	16.4%
Housing assistance, facility rebuilding, etc.	$4.8	15.7%
Initial response, search and rescue, debris removal	$2.6	8.5%
Total federal assistance	*$30.5*	*100.0%*

C. Total Economic Costs*

Geographic area	$billions	Percent of U.S. total
New York City alone	$90	45.0%
Total U.S.	*$200*	*100.0%*

Sources: * Hartwig 2006; ** Congressional Budget Office 2007

9.1.3   The Structure of Insurance Markets

In insurance markets, policy holders contract directly with *primary insurers* who normally write the policies and settle claims. The largest U.S. property and casualty insurers by revenue are American International Group, Berkshire Hathaway, State Farm, and Allstate. Primary insurers may hold the risks they underwrite, or they may transfer the risks to counterparties, primarily reinsurance firms and capital market investors.

Reinsurers are insurance firms that accept and diversify risks from primary insurers for a fee. Most of the world's largest reinsurers reside outside the United States, including Swiss Re and Munich Re. For most insurance lines, an active reinsurance market exists on a continuing basis. In fact, approximately two-thirds of the $35.9 billion in insured losses from the September 11 attack were paid by reinsurance firms (Insurance Information Institute 2007b). However, just as the primary insurers exited the terrorism risk line immediately following the September 11 attack, so did the reinsurers. Indeed, the reinsurers' exit proximately caused the overall market failure so that any solution will have to reactivate the reinsurance market or provide a substitute for it (American Academy of Actuaries 2006).

Capital market investors represent a second set of counterparties to whom primary insurers can transfer those risks that they choose not to hold themselves. *Insurance linked securitization* (ILS) is the primary mechanism though which both primary insurers and reinsurers transfer their catastrophe line risks to capital market investors. We provide more details on ILS in section 9.3.3. To date, however, ILS has not succeeded in offsetting the main supply-side problems that face the provision of terrorism insurance (Doherty et al. 2005).

9.1.4   The Supply of Catastrophe Insurance

Despite continuing strong demand, the private supply of most lines of catastrophe coverage has recently broken down. We now survey the two primary explanations for this failure in the supply of catastrophe insurance, namely large losses and limited information.

Large Losses Could Bankrupt Insurers and Reinsurers   Catastrophic risks are created by low-probability, high-consequence, events. Table 9.3 shows the insured losses for property damage alone from the world's five largest natural disasters and terrorist attacks.

Hurricane Katrina, with over $41 billion in insured property damage, is currently the world's single most costly event. According to Zanetti, Schwartz, and Lindemuth (2007), when business interruption losses are included, the insured losses from Katrina reach $66 billion, and the total damage created by Katrina is estimated

Table 9.3
The most costly natural disasters and terrorist acts, by insured property, in billions of 2006 dollars

Natural disasters		Terrorist acts	
Hurricane Katrina August 2005	$41.9	World Trade Center September 2001	$11.9
Hurricane Andrew August 1992	$22.3	NatWest Tower bomb London, April 1992	$1.0
Northridge earthquake January 1994	$17.0	IRA car bomb Manchester, UK, June 1996	$0.8
Hurricane Wilma October 2005	$10.6	World Trade Center Garage, February 1992	$0.8
Hurricane Charley August 2004	$8.0	Financial District bomb London, April 1992	$0.7

Source: Insurance Information Institute n.d., 2007a

to be $144 billion. In this chapter, we use the experience of how insurance markets responded to these large natural disasters to project how insurance markets and the government might and should respond to WMD terrorist threats.

Among the terrorist acts shown in table 9.3, only the losses from the World Trade Center attack of September 11 are of the same order of magnitude as the largest natural disasters. Otherwise, not one of the terrorist acts created insured property damage above $1 billion. In catastrophe insurance markets, events with insured losses at or below $1 billion do not create a major concern. This is one reason why the World Trade Center garage attack in February 1992 did not focus insurance industry attention on the possibility of much larger future losses from terrorist attacks. Today, of course, there is full recognition that a WMD terrorist attack is possible, and, as we will see later, the damages could readily exceed $100 billion.

The potentially large losses from catastrophic events create serious supply problems for the insurance industry for two related reasons. The main problem is that the annual premiums obtained by catastrophe risk insurers necessarily represent only a small fraction of the indemnification payment that will become due if and when the dire event occurs.[5] For example, when insuring a 1 in 100 year event, the annual actuarially fair premium would equal just 1 percent of the total loss. While insurance companies can accumulate reserves to cover even the worst outcome in principle, a variety of tax, accounting, and profit issues make it uneconomic for them to do so (Jaffee and Russell 1997).

As of year-end 2007, all property and casualty insurers held $518 billion in capital to cover losses, of which it is estimated that 38 percent or $197 billion could have been transferred to pay terrorism losses (Hartwig 2006). Of course, a specific terrorism event will normally affect only a small number of firms, and their capital will be only a small part of the industry aggregate. Furthermore, reinsurers face the same issues as the primary insurers: The American Academy of Actuaries (2006) estimates that reinsurers currently maintain at most $9 billion in reserves to back-stop all terrorism risks, while CBO (2007) indicates that no more than $1.6 billion is available to cover WMD terrorism risks. Clearly, these sums are highly inadequate if the reinsurance industry is to cover $100 billion plus terrorism events.

The bottom line is that the losses that could be created from a large conventional terrorism act, let alone a WMD terrorism attack, could readily bankrupt any insurer or reinsurer that happened to retain a significant amount of that particular risk. We thus conclude, consistent with GAO (2006e), that most insurance managers are unwilling to offer catastrophe coverage because they perceive that taking on such risks exposes their firms to a serious chance of bankruptcy. The obvious desire to avoid bankruptcy is reinforced for multiline insurance firms that earn a significant share of their profits from noncatastrophe insurance activities such as auto insurance. The managers of such firms reasonably conclude that it would be imprudent to offer catastrophe insurance if this creates a risk of bankruptcy for their otherwise safe and profitable firms.

There may also be a principal-agent conflict between the managers of insurance firms and their shareholders. The shareholders may be enthusiastic for the high returns, albeit high risks, available from insuring catastrophes, because limited liability restricts their maximum loss. Managers, in contrast, may feel that the bankruptcy of their firm would put their entire career in jeopardy, along with reducing the value of any shares and options they hold in their firms. The following quote from Edward Liddy, president of Allstate Insurance, in the *Wall Street Journal*, September 6, 2005, illustrates this concern: "The insurance industry is designed for those things that happen with great frequency and don't cost that much money when they do. It's the infrequent thing that costs a large amount of money to the country when it occurs—I think that's the role of the federal government."[6]

Finally, insurers may also avoid catastrophe risks because they fear that rating agencies may downgrade their firms (GAO 2006e).

The Difficulty of Ascertaining Actuarially Fair Premiums   For catastrophe lines, where by definition events occur rarely, the historical data normally used for premium setting are necessarily limited. This is especially true for WMD terrorist risks for which, fortunately, no historical data are available. Of course, insurers can still set premiums using the evidence from comparable events, or from models of the risks. However, managers still know that they might underestimate the risk and therefore include an "ambiguity" component in their premiums.[7] As a result, consumers may protest that the premiums are too high.

All states also have insurance commissioners, who command various degrees of control over the allowed levels of insurance premiums. In the case of catastrophe insurance lines, it is not uncommon for consumers and the regulators who represent them to feel that the premiums charged exceed the level justified by the actuarial risk and the need for a fair profit. Where they have the power, the regulators may place a ceiling on the allowed premiums. And even where the regulators allow the higher premiums, customers may feel their insurer is "gouging," and take all of their insurance business to another firm. In either case, insurance firm managers often conclude that the best business decision is for their firm simply not to offer catastrophe coverage.

9.1.5   Insurable and Uninsurable Risks

Most insurance providers have long excluded the risks created by acts of war, as well as most chemical, biological, radiation, and nuclear (CBRN) risks, from their policies (GAO 2006e). These risks are considered to be uninsurable because they represent the extreme form of the circumstances under which the private market supply of catastrophe insurance breaks down, namely large size and sparse data for premium setting. On the other hand, going back no more than fifteen years, coverage was readily available for earthquake, hurricane, and conventional terrorist risks. But since then, the supply of coverage from the private market broke down for each of these major catastrophe lines following, respectively, the Andrew Hurricane of 1992, the Northridge earthquake of 1994, and the September 11, 2001, terrorist attack.[8] In each case, coverage for the respective risks was readily available the day before the event, and almost no new coverage was available the day after; furthermore, for all three lines, the coverage that is available today is primarily the result of government intervention. The lessons from all three examples are very similar; in keeping with the focus of this chapter, the next section concentrates on the availability of WMD terrorism insurance following September 11.

9.2   Insuring Losses from Terrorist and WMD Terrorist Attacks

Prior to September 11, coverage for conventional terrorism attacks was readily available from property and casualty, workers compensation, and life insurance firms; acts of war and WMD events, however, were commonly excluded from standard property and casualty policies. Most insurers simply did not consider the possible losses from conventional terrorist attacks to be a significant cost element (Laster and Schmidt 2005). A further factor that motivated terrorism coverage on commercial structures—office buildings, shopping centers, factories and warehouses, and so on—was that most lenders required that "all risks" coverage be maintained on the mortgaged structures, and it was customary to include conventional terrorism as part of an "all-risks" policy. For workers compensation insurance, a further factor motivating supply was that all states required (and still require) that firms maintain workers compensation coverage and that this coverage even include WMD terrorist risks (GAO 2006e). State laws also generally required the inclusion of terrorism risks in insurance policies.

On the day following the September 11 attack, most major insurers announced they would no longer offer terrorism coverage on any new property and casualty policies. The insurers also announced that they wanted to exclude terrorism risks from workers compensation. However, this would have required changing the state laws and has not occurred to date. No concerted efforts were made to exclude terrorism risks from life insurance policies, in part because most life insurers maintained geographically diversified books of business, and in part because such an exclusion would have also required changes in state laws (GAO 2006e).

The exit of insurers from terrorism coverage on September 12 created a panicked reaction in the construction and mortgage markets, where participants feared that most new activity would end if terrorism insurance were not available.[9] This created an immediate call to the federal government to provide coverage, one way or another. Interestingly, it took more than fourteen months to enact federal legislation. In the intervening period, commercial mortgage lending and construction slowed down, but so did economic activity in many sectors of the economy.[10] The somber predictions of major economic disaster never transpired, which is one reason Congress was able to take its time in settling on a response. Another helpful factor was that the existing policies, most of which had one-year duration, all stayed in force until they expired (on average six months later). A third factor was that some insurers allowed policy holders to renew, but at much lower coverage limits, and mortgage lenders accepted this as a temporary expedient in anticipation of a forthcoming federal plan. Finally, some states, including New York and California, required insurers to continue offering terrorism coverage.

9.2.1 The Terrorism Risk Insurance Act of 2002 and Its Extensions

The promised federal response finally occurred in the form of the Terrorism Risk Insurance Act (TRIA) of 2002, which became law on November 26, 2002. TRIA had a sunset expiration planned for year-end 2005. However, congress passed an extension, the Terrorism Risk Insurance Extension Act 2005 (TRIEA), two weeks before TRIA expired. TRIEA has the same basic concept but changed some of TRIA's parameters. Although TRIEA was also viewed as a temporary (two year) arrangement, Congress passed a further extension, the Terrorism Risk Insurance Program Reauthorization Act (TRIPRA), in 2007. This extended government presence in the industry through 2014.

While the details of government support have evolved from TRIA to TRIEA to TRIPRA, the program's essential features have remained the same. Here we describe the current TRIPRA scheme, although we refer to the combined legislation as TRIA for brevity. (A fuller discussion of these terms with detailed references to the legislation can be found in Russell and Thomas 2008.)

• *Definition of terrorism*   An act of terrorism is any violent act causing damage to the United States or to a U.S. flag vessel or air carrier as certified by the Secretary of the Treasury. TRIPRA removed the requirement in prior legislation that the act be committed on behalf of foreign interests. Acts of domestic and foreign terrorism are now treated on an equal footing.

• *Insurer obligations*   Insurers[11] are required to "make available property and casualty insurance coverage for insured losses that does not differ materially from the terms, amounts, and other coverage limitations applicable to losses arising from events other than acts of terrorism" (TRIA §103.C.1.b). This clause was interpreted as requiring insurers to continue offering terrorism coverage as was standard before September 11. The "make available" clause generally did *not* apply to WMD terrorism coverage, since that coverage was rarely offered prior to September 11. However, TRIA's benefits (see below) would apply equally well to an insurer who chose to offer WMD terrorism coverage.

• *Government reinsurance*   TRIA provides insurers with government reinsurance, whereby a part of certain terrorism losses would be reimbursed by the U.S. Treasury. As of 2007, the key features were as follows: (1) Losses must exceed a $100 million "trigger" before TRIA coverage is activated.[12] (2) Each insurer has a deductible limit equal to 20 percent of its total property and casualty insurance premiums earned in 2006. The deductibles for the largest insurers now exceed $1 billion (CBO 2007). (3) For amounts above an insurer's deductible, the government will reimburse the insurer for 85 percent of its terrorism losses. (4) The liability of the U.S. government and insurers combined is capped at $100 billion. It is presumed that Congress would take further action were losses above the cap to occur. (5) Insurers pay no premiums or fees for their government-provided reinsurance. This feature limits the incentive of insurers to quote risk-based premiums, which in turn limits the mitigation benefits that can be expected from TRIA. (6) The government must recover 133 percent of any TRIA payments it makes up to $27.5 billion, which is called the *industry retention* level, by imposing a surcharge on all applicable property and casualty policies. For government payments that exceed the $27.5 billion threshold, the Secretary of the Treasury has the right to impose continuing surcharges until all government payments are recovered.

The U.S. insurance industry has generally and strongly supported TRIA and its extensions, which is perhaps surprising for two reasons: (1) the industry quickly exited terrorism insurance after the September 11 attack, and (2) as a result of TRIA's deductible formula, the industry is exposed to significant losses for events up to the September 11 scale (Dixon et al. 2007; CBO 2007).

One possible explanation for the industry's support is that it has sufficient resources to cover conventional terrorism losses up to September 11 levels; after all, all of the insurance claims from September 11 were paid. Indeed, given that the reinsurance benefits under TRIA apply equally well to conventional and WMD terrorism risks, insurers might also be willing to offer WMD terrorism coverage, even though TRIA does not require them to do so. In fact, very little WMD terrorism coverage has become available under TRIE and TRIEA (GAO 2006e).[13] GAO (2006d) references two special factors, beyond large size and hard-to-compute costs, that might persuade insurers not to offer WMD terrorist coverage: (1) that the insurers already have substantial WMD exposure from state laws that require such coverage in Workers' Compensation policies, and (2) the possibility that the full extent of WMD losses might not be determined until years after the event.

Ibragimov, Jaffee, and Walden (2008) offer an alternative explanation for the industry's endorsement of TRIA, namely that each insurer is prepared to offer terrorism coverage as long as it is knows that all other insurers will do the same. (This is exactly the form of TRIA's "make available" clause for conventional terrorism risks). The fact that TRIA's "make available" clause does not apply to WMD terrorism then explains why insurers may not be willing to offer WMD terrorism coverage.[14]

9.2.2   WMD Terrorism Insurance

Even though TRIA does not require insurers to make WMD terrorism coverage available, the question still arises as to why insurers would not voluntarily offer this coverage, given that TRIA provides free Treasury reinsurance for WMD losses on the same terms as conventional terrorism losses. To answer this, we return to the question of why certain risks are deemed "uninsurable." Earlier, we pointed out that the two main issues for the provision of all forms of catastrophe risks by private insurers are (1) the potentially large size of the risks, and (2) the difficulty of quantifying the actuarial costs. We first focus on the potentially enormous losses that could be created by a WMD terrorist attack, based on four separate analyses of the potential losses.

Table 9.4
Potential losses from WMD attacks, $ billions

	Property damage	Workers compensation	Total losses
Sarin gas attack (1,000 kg ground dispersal)	21	7	28
Dirty bomb (15,000 curies of Cesium-137)	62	0.2	62
Anthrax attack (1 kg anthrax slurry)	35	26	61
Anthrax attack (10 kg anthrax slurry)	112	59	171
Anthrax attack (75 kg anthrax slurry)	266	74	340
Sabotage attack on nuclear power plant	202	15	217
Nuclear bomb (1 kt)	140	100	240
Nuclear bomb (5 kt)	250	200	450

Source: Risk Management Systems (2005)

Estimates from Risk Management Solutions Inc.   Table 9.4 provides estimates of potential insured losses from specific CBRN attacks by Risk Management Solutions Inc. (RMS), a firm that specializes in estimating expected losses from catastrophic events for the insurance industry.

The RMS estimates range from a $25 billion sarin gas attack to a $450 billion tactical nuclear bomb. Property damage represents the larger part of all total losses, although workers compensation losses are also significant in almost all cases. It should also be recognized that the RMS results exclude two other sources of losses. First, the RMS estimates exclude insured losses on business interruption and life insurance risks. Second, the estimates exclude any "multiplier" costs that would arise from economic disruptions across the full economy (chapter 14). Earlier, we noted that the economic losses created by September 11 far exceeded insured losses; similarly, the economic losses of the London subway bombing in July 2005 are put at $4 to $6 billion, even though insured losses were minimal (RMS 2005).

Estimates from the American Academy of Actuaries   Table 9.5 provides an alternative set of projections from a study by the American Academy of Actuaries (2006) of insured losses from possible CBRN incidents.

In New York City, a large CBRN event could cost as much as $778 billion, with insured losses for commercial property at $158 billion and for workers compensation at $483 billion. In comparison, we earlier noted that the total industry capital currently available to cover terrorism losses is about $185 billion. In addition to New York, three other cities were included in the analysis: Washington, D.C., San

Table 9.5
Insured loss projections from WMD terrorist attacks, $ billions

Type of coverage	New York	Washington	San Francisco	Des Moines
Group life	$82.0	$22.5	$21.5	$3.4
General liability	$14.4	$2.9	$3.2	$0.4
Workers comp	$483.7	$126.7	$87.5	$31.4
Residential property	$38.7	$12.7	$22.6	$2.6
Commercial property	$158.3	$31.5	$35.5	$4.1
Auto	$1.0	$0.6	$0.8	$0.4
Total	$778.1	$196.8	$171.2	$42.3

Source: American Academy of Actuaries, Response to President's Working Group

Table 9.6
Allocation of insured losses by insurance lines from anthrax attacks, $ billions

	Indoor attack	Outdoor attack
Property	$1.1	$100.4
Workers' compensation	$6.1	$43.5
Group life	$0.3	$2.5
Individual life	$0.2	$2.1
Accidental death/dismemberment	$0.2	$1.5
Health	$0.0	$22.4
Total	$8.0	$172.3

Source: Rand (2005b)

Francisco, California, and Des Moines, Iowa. Clearly a CBRN attack could cause insured losses on an unprecedented scale.

Anthrax Release Estimates from the RAND Corporation   The RAND Corporation in conjunction with RMS has carried out an extensive analysis of the possible losses that would be inflicted by anthrax attacks (Carroll et al. 2005).[15] The RAND study evaluates two different anthrax attack scenarios, one within a single large building, the other an outdoor release that is widely disbursed. Table 9.6 summarizes the study's major quantitative results. For the indoor anthrax attack, the estimated total insured losses are about $8 billion, including over $6 billion of workers compensation claims and over $1 billion of property damage claims (primarily the estimated costs of decontaminating the building, including the possibility that the building and its content would need to be replaced). The total insured losses from an outdoor anthrax attack are estimated to be over $172 billion, more than twenty-five times as large as the indoor attack. Here the largest component, over $100 billion, is property damage, reflecting the large number of buildings affected and the large costs of decontaminating them. The next component, $43 billion, is workers compensation claims.

The RAND study also evaluates who would be responsible for paying these claims under the 2002 TRIA act. For the indoor anthrax attack, the firm(s) insuring the building would pay all the claims, since it is expected that their losses would be less than their TRIA deductibles. In other words, given the relatively small total insured losses of $8 billion, there would be no payments from the U.S. Treasury.[16] As noted earlier, the insured losses would have to exceed the September 11 scale for any significant U.S. taxpayer liability to accrue under TRIEA.

Interestingly, individual insurers are not expected to reach their company-specific deductibles for the outdoor anthrax attack either, assuming that the affected buildings were relatively small and insured by a diverse set of firms. As a result, the insurers would pay all claims from their own resources. Thus, even though the losses created by the outdoor anthrax attack are twenty-five times as great as the indoor attack, U.S. taxpayers still have no liability because losses are dispersed across many insurers.

The Nuclear Threat: Lessons from Nuclear Reactor Accidents   A nuclear terrorist attack could be expected to take one of three basic forms: (1) the dispersal of radioactive material sprayed from an airplane or through a conventional chemical explosion—a so-called dirty bomb; (2) an attack on a nuclear reactor, also with the goal of dispersing radioactive material; and (3) the detonation of a nuclear bomb.

No such attack has occurred to date, and therefore no data are available to measure its effects. However, approximately 443 nuclear reactors exist worldwide, including 104 in the United States. These reactors all face the risk of an uncontrolled nuclear chain reaction, leading to a core meltdown, and quite possibly to extensive radioactive emissions. Such a failure did, in fact, occur at Chernobyl's Reactor no. 4 in 1986. The effects of a core meltdown and radioactive emissions from a nuclear reactor could reasonably parallel the effects of terrorist attacks (1) and (2) above. Nuclear reactors, fortunately, provide no parallel to a terrorist nuclear bomb attack, since nuclear reactors are incapable of creating a nuclear explosion. A nuclear bomb attack is also widely considered to be technically the most difficult, and therefore the least likely. In any case, in this section we analyze the available evidence on the effects of radioactive release from a nuclear reactor and how insurance markets and governments have responded to this risk.

In 1982, Sandia National Laboratories prepared a study of the effects of a core meltdown and radioactive release at one of the two Indian Point nuclear power plants north of New York City on the Hudson River. The study estimated 50,000 near-term deaths from acute radiation and 14,000 long-term deaths from cancer. A much more recent study, Lyman 2004 estimates 44,000 near-term deaths and as many as 518,000 long-term cancer deaths within fifty miles of the plant. The latter study simulates 140,000 different weather combinations and then employs a Value At Risk (VaR) methodology, with the above results based on the 95th percentile among the worst outcomes. The varying results can be traced to the use of different input parameters, a newer computer simulation, and population growth since 1982.

Heal and Kunreuther (2007) provide some rough estimates that translate the losses from a nuclear reactor meltdown into dollar amounts. They project business losses in the $50 to $100 billion range, and as much as $300 billion dollars in human death costs. This total is within the range of the estimates provided in tables 9.4 and 9.5.

Even as the first U.S. nuclear reactor was planned, private insurers anticipated the enormous meltdown costs and refused to offer coverage. Doomsday meltdown scenarios were easy to put forward, and of course it was impossible to counter these with a historical record of safe performance. In addition, anytime the word *nuclear* is used, special alarm bells sound.[17] As a result, private firms were unwilling to construct or manage nuclear reactors, since they feared that, in the absence of insurance, the losses created by an accident could lead to bankruptcies.

The specific solution that was developed to insure nuclear reactor risks is also useful in analyzing the more general problem of insuring CBRN terrorism risks. The key step for nuclear reactors was the 1957 Price Anderson Act (hereafter PA Act), which limited the liability of the nuclear reactor industry. Further discussion can be found in Heal and Kunreuther 2007. Like TRIA, the PA Act was viewed as a temporary measure, providing what was thought would be enough time (ten years) to enable the private insurance markets to assess and price this risk. In actuality, the Act was renewed repeatedly. The most recent extension in 2005 extends the Act through 2025.

The original 1957 PA Act placed a $560 million ceiling on the potential liability of nuclear power plant operators. Below that limit, the private insurance industry was to insure $60 million, with the federal government insuring the next $500 million. The role of the federal government as direct insurer was phased out in 1977. Under the current Act, private insurers are required to provide $300 million in insurance and the nuclear power industry itself provides further coverage up to a total of $10 billion. No liability claims can be brought against nuclear reactor operators above this $10 billion limit, although in the event of a major accident Congress could decide to offer additional indemnification, perhaps in a manner similar to the Federal Victims Compensation Act following the September 11 attack.

It is intriguing that despite cries of uninsurability, private capital now provides $10 billion of insurance to the nuclear reactor industry. The first $300 million of this is provided by an insurance pool, American Nuclear Insurers (ANI), half of which is reinsured with Lloyds. The remainder is provided through a contract administered by ANI, in which the operators of nuclear plants guarantee payments of $100.6 million per reactor per accident payable in annual assessments of $15 million (inflation adjusted) per operator per year for ten years. In effect, the nuclear reactor industry has been required to create a mutual insurance pool in which each operator is obligated to contribute funds if and when a loss occurs.[18]

By arranging for ex post assessments, this scheme overcomes the need to hold large amounts of capital ex ante, one of the major impediments to writing catastrophe insurance (Jaffee and Russell 1997). To be sure, as Heal and Kunreuther (2007) point out, $10 billion in coverage is well short of the estimated $100 billion plus in losses that would be caused by a reactor meltdown in a populous state. Nevertheless, an examination of the PA Act establishes a point sufficiently important that we might consider it a general principle of catastrophe insurance: *No matter how large the aggregate loss, private capital can be induced to flow into any line of insurance so long as the price is right and individual company losses can be limited.*

Heal and Kunreuther (2007) also suggest that the U.S. government would likely intervene if losses exceeded the $10 billion coverage limit. The annual actuarial cost to the government of extending this additional coverage represents an implicit subsidy from U.S. taxpayers to the nuclear reactor industry.[19] Heyes and Heyes (2000) estimate that the annual subsidy per nuclear reactor is about $2.3 million, or an aggregate annual subsidy (for 104 reactors) of $239 million. It is also worth noting that the PA Act does not try to apply risk-based pricing, and thus provides no incentive for operators to invest in mitigating nuclear reactor risks. To be sure, the U.S. Nuclear Regulatory Commission (NRC) sets standards and monitors U.S. reactors for safe operation, so that additional financial incentive might be irrelevant. Heal and Kunreuther, however, suggest that the NRC inspections are inadequate and that price incentives through risk-based insurance would be valuable. More generally, Heal and Kunreuther conclude that more of the nuclear reactor risk "could surely be met through the private sector." Nevertheless, Geoffrey Rothwell (2002), a longtime observer of the PA Act, has observed that—despite its failings— no better alternatives were readily available.

9.2.3   Estimating the Likelihood of a WMD Terrorist Attack

The insurance industry cites imprecision in the estimated likelihood of a WMD attack as a second reason why these risks are uninsurable. For example, former Senate Majority Leader William Frist suggested in 2005 that a biological attack in the next ten years was all but certain.[20] On the other hand, there are experts who point out that such extreme estimates have little scientific underpinning. For example, Mueller (2007) points out:

Even with the September 11 attacks included in the count, however, the number of Americans killed by international terrorism over the period [1975–2003] is not a great deal more than the number killed by lightning—or by accident-causing deer or by severe allergic reactions to peanuts over the same period. In almost all years the total number of people worldwide who die at the hands of international terrorists is not much more than the number who drown in bathtubs in the United States—some 300–400.

The absence of objective analysis is of particular concern given human beings' well known tendency to overestimate the probability of easily imagined events. As Tversky and Kahneman (1973) have noted, decision makers are frequently subject to an "availability bias," which causes them to link ease of imagining with a higher judged probability, even when there is no actual correlation. (See also Sunstein 2003.) For example, the effects of a terrorist nuclear bomb attack are readily imagined based on film footage of actual nuclear bombs. To overcome this availability bias, data that quantify the objective likelihood of such attacks must be obtained and analyzed. Such data would measure both the desire of terrorists to obtain such weapons and their ability to do so.[21] Similarly with respect to bioterrorism, Leitenberg (2004, 2005) has noted that an analysis of bioterrorist risks must evaluate the actual ability of terrorists to mass deliver a toxic agent.[22]

Clearly, as economists, we do not possess the expertise to sort through these various viewpoints. But, then, neither do private insurance companies. This means that the risk is not amenable to precise probability calculation and becomes "ambiguous" in the sense of Ellsberg 1961. It is well known that insurers are "ambiguity averse" (Hogarth and Kunreuther 1989; Kunreuther, Hogarth, and Meszaros 1993), preferring to insure risks with known actuarial probabilities compared to risks where it is difficult to determine the likelihoods.[23] When we add to this the fact that insurance executives may also suffer from availability bias and overestimate the likelihood of attack, insurers' claim that CBRN risks are uninsurable becomes more understandable.

9.2.4   Uninsurability Revisited

These facts make the insurers' case for excluding WMD risk appear plausible, but, at a deeper level, it is far from clear what principle of profit-driven insurance makes this particularly ambiguous and large risk uninsurable. After all, private insurers currently underwrite conventional terrorism risk, and although the federal government does backstop the largest losses, a private insurer such as AIG still has exposure to terrorist loss in excess of $3 billion.

It is particularly puzzling why any individual insurer would cite aggregate maximum loss as an argument for not taking at least some part of the risk. Profit driven insurance companies are free to limit their total exposure on any one class of risk to any amount they wish. In addition (up to state regulatory constraints) they are free to raise the quoted premium to any level that they feel compensates them for any ambiguity in the underlying probability. This suggests that private insurers should be willing to underwrite at least some amount of WMD terrorism risk. To be sure, the total supply available from the private sector may still fall short of total demand, but the standard reaction of private insurers has been to exclude all WMD terrorism risk, not just to limit the insured amount. We have already noted that the pattern of complete withdrawal from the catastrophe lines of insurance following a large loss is well established and is certainly not unique to WMD coverage.

9.3   Policy Options for Creating Viable WMD Terrorism Insurance in the United States

The discussion so far has documented the important value that derives from making insurance available to cover the losses that could be created by either conventional or WMD terrorist attacks. It has also shown that the U.S. property and casualty insurance industry is firmly set against providing coverage for even conventional terrorism risks in the absence of government support, not withstanding the view of the current authors and other commentators that terrorism risks should be insurable by the private U.S. industry.

Given that TRIPRA has extended government presence in this industry through 2014, it seems reasonable to ask what the most effective form of this intervention might be. We focus in particular on the most effective means for the government to support a private market for insuring WMD terrorist risks, a coverage that is basically unavailable today. Our discussion begins with the evidence showing that, given a choice, private insurance markets are generally preferable to government programs. We then consider two specific concerns with government programs, namely that they may crowd out private market activity and that they provide limited mitigation benefits. We also consider the potential for funding private markets for terrorism insurance with financial market capital. Finally, we describe and evaluate a variety of alternative strategies that government could use to support private terrorism insurance markets.

9.3.1   Private vs. Government Insurance Markets

The risk-sharing benefits of insurance intrinsically require a social undertaking if not by private groups then with the government. Thus, when private insurance markets fail, individuals and firms are quick to petition the government to fix the failure, even if this means that the government becomes the insurer. But there are also long-standing objections from economists who point out that government insurance is likely to be less efficiently provided than comparable private coverage (Priest 1996). We now review some key aspects of this debate in the context of WMD terrorism insurance.

In broad outline, insurance markets must provide contract design, premium setting, policy sales and marketing, claims adjustment, and reinsurance. We can look to existing government insurance programs to evaluate how well the government succeeds in carrying out these various functions. The specific government programs we consider are the California Earthquake Authority, the Florida Hurricane Fund, the Federal Housing Administration mortgage loan program, the National Flood Insurance program, and finally TRIA.

Contract Design   The government generally performs poorly when it designs insurance contracts. For example, the California Earthquake Authority (CEA) was created to provide coverage for homeowners after many insurers withdrew their coverage in the aftermath of the Northridge earthquake.[24] Prior to Northridge, about 36 percent of California homeowners elected the optional earthquake coverage that must be offered in the state. Now, after more than 10 years under the CEA plan, about 12 percent of California homeowners maintain earthquake insurance with the CEA (Zanjani 2006). Homeowners commonly cite high deductible limits and other limitations as reasons for passing up CEA policies. To be sure, other factors are also at work here, including the common perception that the premiums are too high, but all of them point to overall contract design and marketing failures by CEA.

Premium Setting   Most government insurance plans are required to set "actuarially determined" premiums, with the intent that premiums should be risk-based so that the plans should at least break even over time. This is true, for example, of the California Earthquake Authority (CEA), the National Flood Insurance program (NFI), and the FHA mortgage insurance plan. The terrorism risk plan, TRIA, is actually an exception in that reinsurance is provided free of charge. Nevertheless, the CEA, NFI, and FHA programs have all failed to reach the goal of actuarial- and risk-based premiums. The problem is that political reality inevitably intrudes, creating pressure both to subsidize premiums and to eliminate any risk-based variations. As an example of subsidized premiums, the National Flood Insurance program recently required a congressional appropriation in excess of $20 billion as a result of its Katrina losses, an amount about equal to the premiums (net of operating expenses) collected by the program in the approximately fifty years of its prior existence. We have already pointed out that the TRIA program, which provides terrorism reinsurance at no cost, also fails to create risk-based premiums.

Policy Sales and Marketing   Government insurance plans can perform acceptably well in policy sales and marketing, but only because they outsource this function to private market agents. This is necessarily the case for the TRIA and Florida Hurricane reinsurance plans, where the retail insurance policies are sold by the market's primary insurers. But it is also true for the California Earthquake Authority, National Flood program, and FHA mortgage plan where the government is the primary insurer: in each case, policies are sold by authorized private market agents, who then transfer the risk to the government plan.

Claims Adjustment   The situation here is the same as policy sales, namely that most government plans outsource this function to private market insurers.

Reinsurance   Reinsurance might be considered the least intrusive of government insurance activities, since the programs become active only when claims are filed, which should be an infrequent event. And indeed, no claims have been registered under TRIA. The Florida Hurricane Fund, however, has been less fortunate: as shown in table 9.3, Florida has suffered three of the most costly natural disasters in U.S. history since 2004: Hurricanes Katrina, Wilma, and Charley. These disasters wiped out the fund's reserves, forcing Florida to use public money to cover the losses. Once again, a government plan has ended up subsidizing insurance costs, especially in the most disaster-prone coastal areas.

9.3.2   Will Government Terrorism Insurance Crowd Out Private Markets?

The TRIA legislation provides free reinsurance with respect to both conventional and WMD terrorism risks. This has raised concern that TRIA will crowd out any attempts to create a viable and independent private market for terrorism insurance. In fact, the 2002 TRIA legislation anticipated this issue and was explicitly designed to be temporary:

The United States Government should provide temporary financial compensation to insured parties, contributing to the stabilization of the United States economy in a time of national crisis, while the financial services industry develops the systems, mechanisms, products, and programs necessary to create a viable financial services market for private terrorism risk insurance (§101.a.6).

However, when the 2002 Act reached its sunset date in December 2005, it was extended for two years by TRIEA, and has now been extended for a further seven years. Given that it is no longer viewed as a temporary program, it seems appropriate to evaluate the concern that TRIA and similar reinsurance legislation will continue to crowd out private activity, thus making a return to a private system of terrorism insurance impossible.

To demonstrate a claim of crowding out, it must be shown that the private market would have operated in the absence of the government action, and that the private market fails when the government program is present. With respect to the former factor, it seems clear that private industry was simply unwilling to provide terrorism coverage from the September 11 attack continuing through the passage of TRIA in November 2002. Moreover, as just indicated, TRIA was explicitly cast as a temporary measure, with the clear goal of stimulating the private market's recovery. For this reason, there is no basis for a charge of crowding out during this period. TRIEA, which extended TRIA in December 2005, raised more serious concerns. Here too, however, careful studies by the U.S. Treasury, General Accountability Office, and Congressional Budget Office all supported a general conclusion that the private market for terrorism was still not viable, and that the TRIA extension was in the public interest.

The extension of the legislation through 2014, however, amounts to a de facto recognition that, at least for the foreseeable future, there is no hope for a sustainable, purely private, terrorism insurance industry. This raises the question of how much of this market failure is due to TRIA itself. Here, the most worrisome aspect for crowding out is that the government reinsurance is provided gratis. There is no way, of course, that private reinsurance markets can compete with a free government program, and in this sense the government program is creating a self-fulfilling basis for its own existence—a hallmark of crowding out. On the other hand, TRIA's deductible and coinsurance requirements still force private industry to hold a substantial part of the first-loss components of the overall terrorism risk. For this reason, crowding out has at least been avoided in the lower tier of terrorism risk. It is very important, however, that this private market activity be sustained in future government programs.

9.3.3 Capital Market Resources to Fund Catastrophe Insurance

After the failures of the Florida hurricane insurance market in 1992 and the California earthquake insurance market in 1994, it became evident that financial markets could potentially revive private catastrophe insurance markets by providing a direct and dependable source of capital for both primary insurers and reinsurers. Indeed, since one of the primary purposes of reinsurance is to provide capital to direct insurers, it is even possible that capital from financial markets could replace rein-surance firms—who had proven unreliable partners exactly when they were most needed—completely. It was also hoped that the financial markets would prove a deep source of capital, since even catastrophic losses of $100 billion should be man-ageable when compared to a stock market in which daily losses of a trillion dollars are not uncommon. Finally, it was noted that catastrophe risks are not correlated with the macroeconomic and financial risks that dominate investor portfolios and that financial market investors would see this as a particularly valuable feature.

Markets have responded to these arguments by developing *insurance linked securities*, with *catastrophe bonds* the most active example for catastrophe risks. The concept is modeled on securitization as first developed in the U.S. mortgage markets, and has now expanded to cover business and consumer loans as well as a wide range of corporate risks. The first step is to transfer risks to a special purpose vehicle (SPV). The SPV in turn transfers risks to financial market investors like hedge funds. These investors earn an annual fee for bearing the risk (comparable to the premium paid to a reinsurance firm), but must indemnify the issuer for the losses created if and when the catastrophic event occurs. (There are, of course, many details, but this is the main idea. Interested readers should consult Guy Carpenter & Co., and MMC Securities 2007, as well as Helfenstein and Holzheu 2006 for fur-ther discussion.)

Figure 9.2 shows the expansion in the catastrophe bond market since 1997. While growth has been steady, the about $8.5 billion in outstanding bonds through year-

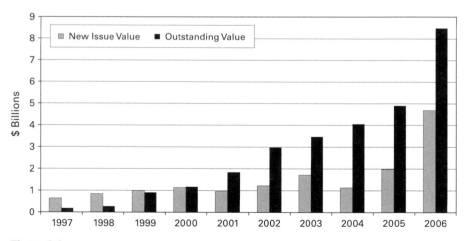

Figure 9.2
Catastrophe bonds: New issues and outstanding

end 2006 represented only about six percent of the corresponding volume of traditional reinsurance. The main reason is that, based on the relatively low level of natural disaster losses after the early 1990s (compare figure 9.1 prior to Katrina), reinsurers have steadily returned to the market with competitive coverage offers.

Figure 9.2 also shows that new issues of catastrophe bonds expanded rapidly in 2005 and 2006, as insurers used the financial markets to replace exiting reinsurers as a source of capital. This new capital, however, came at a price. Figure 9.3 shows that the cost of this capital, measured as the interest rate paid relative to LIBOR,[25] rose dramatically in 2005 for wind related risks. This suggests that the reinsurance industry remains a fickle source of catastrophe risk capital: when times are good, reinsurers are active; but when major disasters strike, they withdraw, leaving the financial market as the principal, albeit costly, capital source for the primary insurers.

Of all the insurance-linked securities and catastrophe bonds measured in figures 9.2 and 9.3, only one is directly related to terrorism and a second set covers mortality risk of which terrorism is one possible source (the rest only cover natural disaster risks). The direct terrorism bond was called Golden Goal Finance and covered cancellation risk for the 2006 FIFA World Cup football tournament from terrorism and

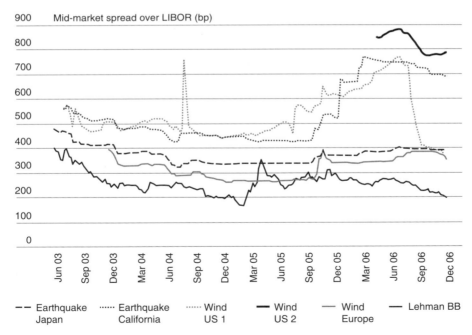

Figure 9.3
Catastrophe bond yields relative to LIBOR

some lesser hazards. The second set is a series of three bonds issued by Swiss Re (Vita Capital I, II, and III), which cover excess mortality risk from pandemics along with terrorism and natural catastrophes. No securitizations issued so far have covered terrorism risks to U.S. property.

Thus, despite fifteen years of quite positive experience with funding natural disaster risks, capital market investors remain wary of investing in conventional, not to mention WMD, terrorism risks. The primary issue seems to be informational, i.e., that capital market investors feel even less secure than primary insurers and reinsurers in evaluating the expected losses from the various conventional and WMD terrorism risks. Additionally, investors may expect terrorism attacks to have greater negative effects than natural disasters on the stock market and macroeconomy, so that terrorism risks offer investors smaller diversification benefits compared to natural disaster risks.[26] There is, furthermore, limited demand by the insurers and reinsurers to transfer conventional terrorism risks, and essentially no demand to transfer WMD terrorism risk (since almost no coverage is being offered in the primary markets in the first place). The demand to transfer conventional terrorism risks could, however, rise as more coverage is provided by the primary insurers and as TRIA deductibles and coinsurance rise over time. And were new legislation to require insurers to "make available" WMD terrorism coverage, then the demand to transfer WMD risks would also rise, perhaps dramatically.

9.3.4 Government Terrorism Insurance and Mitigation Activity

We noted at the outset of this chapter that mitigation incentives were a primary benefit of insurance, assuming that the insurance is provided on the basis of risk-based premiums. We now focus on how providing insurance for WMD terrorist risks affects the incentives for private parties to mitigate the likely losses from such attacks. For a variety of reasons, the picture is mixed.

Risk-Based Premiums   Insurers set the premiums charged to policyholders based on their expected losses, including the cost of reinsurance. Reinsurance under TRIPRA, however, offers no incentive for risk-based pricing, since the government's coverage is provided without charge on all risks. Private insurers and reinsurers, on the other hand, do use risk-based pricing to the extent that their expected losses differ across properties and coverage. Risk-based pricing provides an incentive for policy holders to mitigate their risks, although their ability to do so may be limited (see the next items).

Building Size and Location   Large trophy buildings in the centers of major cities are likely to be the favored terrorism targets, but it is clearly not possible to change the size or location of existing structures.[27] New construction will respond to the incentive to create a less tempting target, but given the extended durability of existing structures, it will take decades to achieve a pervasive effect. The CBO (2007) also points out that moving business activity out of central city locations will eliminate the benefits of agglomeration, which was a common reason for forming cities in the first place. In other words, moving activity to smaller buildings away from the center city has its own costs.

Mitigation Actions   Beyond size and location, all structure owners can take actions to reduce the likelihood of a terrorist attack or else to reduce losses if an attack occurs. For example, checking the bags of all who enter a building, and similar precautions, may reduce the likelihood of a successful bomb attack. Similarly, better air circulation and purification systems may reduce the effects of various biological, chemical, and radiation attacks. To the extent that insurers use risk-based insurance premiums, landlords would have an incentive to carry out such mitigation. However, no amount of private mitigation may be able to provide protection against extreme WMD attacks like a nuclear bomb. Both Carroll et al. (2005) and CBO (2007) also comment that the cost of carrying out terrorism risk mitigation often exceeds the likely savings from lower premiums.

The Social and Private Benefits of Mitigation   Risk-based insurance premiums give landlords a private incentive to mitigate. However, this private benefit can exceed the social benefit. The problem is that terrorists are strategic, and will redirect their attacks to the least protected structures. Thus, while landlord A may act to reduce the losses from an attack on her building, her actions may raise the likelihood of an attack on the building of landlord B. Of course, this will raise the incentive of landlord B to mitigate, and so on throughout the city. Because landlord A does not internalize the costs imposed on landlord B, this leads to too much mitigation from society's standpoint. In practice, of course, other factors—notably the free reinsurance provided by the TRIA program—limit incentives to mitigate. For this reason, it is not clear whether the current overall system creates too much or too little mitigation.[28]

Liability as an Alternative to Insurance as an Incentive to Mitigate   A recent study by Lakdawalla and Talley (2006) discusses landlord liability as a mechanism for encouraging mitigation that is separate and distinct from risk-based premiums.[29] The basic idea is simple enough: if negligent landlords expect to be held liable for losses that their tenants suffer in an attack, then they will invest in an an appropriate level of deterrence. However, the resulting system of awards turns out to be counterintuitive, often prescribing damages payments from seemingly unlikely defendants to equally unlikely plaintiffs. For example, an individual walking past a building suffering a terrorist attack might be required to pay damages to the landlord if the volume of nearby street traffic helped make the building a target. The authors therefore conclude that the tort system is an unlikely mechanism for implementing mitigation incentives and end by endorsing insurance, perhaps coupled with direct compensation to victims, as a more effective mechanism.

The impact of the tort system can be seen in two cases we discussed earlier, the nuclear reactor industry and the development of ultralarge oil tankers. In the former case, the perceived liability was so large that the industry was unwilling to build and operate reactors until government passed legislation creating an insurance pool and capping overall liability. In the latter case the insurance premiums required to cover possible environmental claims exceeded the benefits of larger tankers, which were then cancelled.

9.3.5 Alternative Strategies for Government Intervention

We now consider some alternative policies for stimulating the provision of private WMD terrorism insurance in the United States. We start with a discussion of the permanent renewal of a TRIA-based policy, in which the government continues to provide reinsurance for the top tiers of the terrorism risks, but with a proposed expansion of the "make available" requirement to include WMD terrorism risks. Although this is the most likely form for congressional action, at the end of this section we also survey alternative policy options that have been proposed and appear worthy of continuing consideration.

Extend TRIA and Expand the "Make Available" Clause to WMD Terrorism   The most immediate strategy for creating a viable supply WMD terrorist coverage in the United States is to rewrite TRIPRA so that the "make available" clause applies to conventional and WMD terrorism risks alike. This solution, however, is strongly resisted by the insurance industry. For example, the Aon Corporation made the following key points as part of a lengthy contribution to the U.S. Treasury and President's Working Group on Terrorism Insurance:

• WMD losses present "a potential for insured loss exposure in excess of the TRIA annual aggregate reinsurance capacity of $100 billion."
• WMD losses threaten to expand "deductible and coinsurance exposures."
• The (re)insurance industry views WMD event exposure as a "company killer" (Aon Group 2006).

Because Aon's viewpoint is so typical, it is worth examining in more detail. In the first place it is difficult to see why the addition of WMD risks poses a risk of exposure beyond the $100 billion cap. Under current TRIPRA provisions, the maximum for a private insurer's losses is equal to the company's deductible plus 15 percent of its aggregate losses up to $100 billion. This is true whether the loss is due to a conventional or a WMD terrorist attack, so adding WMD coverage cannot increase insured losses above the $100 billion limit.

On the second point, Aon is right to note that the addition of WMD liability would raise the probability of loss, and hence the company's expected loss, below the $100 billion cap. On the other hand, insurers would presumably charge additional premiums to cover the expected additional risk. This means that net expected profits could be higher when WMD coverage is provided.

In any case, it would not be difficult to craft legislation to address industry's specific concerns. For example, new legislation could recognize two forms of terrorist attack, conventional and WMD. If the attack was certified to have used WMD, then it could be assigned lower deductible and coinsurance requirements than for a conventional attack. Such changes would moderate the industry's maximum loss from a WMD terrorist event, and allow a satisfactory apportionment of risk between the public and private sectors.[30]

Since 2001, the financial situation of insurers has improved markedly, their protests to the contrary, so that requiring them to cover WMD risk with a $100 billion cap ($65 billion after taking the deductibility of losses for tax purposes) would be a far less burdensome task today than it was when TRIA was enacted. Indeed, private workers compensation insurers already provide WMD terrorism coverage and are supported by the TRIEA backstop. We turn now to the special issues raised by this line of insurance.

The Special Problem of Workers' Compensation The workers' compensation line of insurance raises special issues with regard to WMD attacks. The problems are unrelated to insurance principles, but instead reflect the special history of workers' compensation insurance in the United States (Moss 2002). In the early twentieth century, the number and intensity of work stoppages in response to on-the-job injuries were becoming ruinous for management and workers alike. This led to a compromise solution in which workers gave up the right to sue employers for job-related injury, while employers accepted a duty to purchase workers compensation insurance without any exclusions.

The absence of exclusions for workers' compensation has forced private insurers to provide WMD terrorism coverage, notwithstanding their claims that such risks are "uninsurable." As table 9.5 shows, the exposure to this line is significant: workers' compensation losses in an attack on New York City could amount to $483 of the total projected $778 billion loss, and in all four cities workers' compensation would account for more than 50 percent of the total loss. Conventional and WMD terrorist attacks would also distribute losses quite differently between personal lines (such as workers' compensation and life insurance) on the one hand and business and property damage on the other. For example, as shown in table 9.2, less than 9 percent of the total losses from the conventional September 11 attack were related to the personal lines. WMD attacks, in contrast, would be expected to create exceptionally large losses for the personal lines including life insurance and workers' compensation.

The size of workers' compensation WMD exposure is not small. If a company in the District of Columbia (where the death benefit is worth approximately $1.8 million) were to lose 300 employees as a result of a terrorist attack, the total claim would reach $500 million (NCCI 2006). However, not all of this falls on the private sector. In four states and two territories,[31] workers' compensation insurance is provided by a state-run monopoly, and in thirteen other states a not-for-profit state enterprise competes with the private sector.[32] Still the private sector's exposure is significant. In California, for example, the share of the risk taken by private insurers rose rapidly between 2005 and 2006 (from 58 to 69 percent) and the state is actively campaigning to expand the private market even further.

Since private insurers voluntarily accept their exposure to WMD risk in the workers' compensation line, extending future TRIA legislation to expand the "make available" requirement would appear feasible.

Government Pricing of Terrorism Insurance   An important criticism of the TRIA legislation is that the terrorism reinsurance is provided without charge.[33] A common response is that pricing terrorism risk is a difficult task for private insurers and well beyond the ability of the government. Priest's (1996) analysis, however, suggests a more realistic answer, namely that government insurance invariably becomes subsidized insurance. Nevertheless, it behooves proponents of risk-based pricing of government insurance to provide a reasonable mechanism.

Lewis and Murdoch (1996) and Cummins, Lewis, and Phillips (1999) offer a solution in which the government would auction a fixed amount of reinsurance contracts to private market insurers and reinsurers. The contracts would obligate the government to indemnify the insured party for any losses created by the insured event. The experience gained in designing catastrophe bonds (section 9.3.3), would provide a practical template for such contracts. The proposed auction would identify the proper market price for the reinsurance coverage, and would also ensure that the contract was awarded to the entities for which it had the greatest value, that is, the highest bidders. The program would also be self-financing in the sense that the premiums determined in the auction should equal the expected losses. Of course, the actual losses in any year could exceed the expected losses, but good fortune should be equally likely and the government should break even over time. Finally, the mechanics for such government auctions could be readily developed by following, for example, the methods already used to auction Treasury bills and bonds.[34]

Lender (Not Insurer) of Last Resort   TRIA and related proposals that provide a government backstop for terrorism insurance basically enlist the government as the *insurer of last resort*. However, the fundamental market failure that requires government intervention occurs in the *financial*, not the *insurance* markets. That is, the primary concern of insurers is how they can access sufficient capital to pay for catastrophic losses if and when they occur. Obtaining access to capital is fundamentally a financial problem: indeed, we have seen under TRIA that industry proceeds rapidly and efficiently with the work of an insurer—that is, designing contracts and underwriting policies—as soon as it is confident of a capital backstop. This suggests that government could quite possibly backstop terrorism insurance markets by acting as the lender, instead of the insurer, of last resort.

Acting as the lender of last resort, of course, has been the core activity of central banks for hundreds of years. Central banks adopted this method to stop bank runs and thereby protect the stability of the commercial banking system. The need for central banks to provide liquidity to the financial system is long established, although it should be recognized that it reflects a financial market failure; otherwise, a bank in need of liquidity would just sell some of its assets to the "market," and there would be no need for the government/central bank to intervene.

In this sense, problems caused by a liquidity crisis in the banking system and catastrophe insurance disruptions have a common source, namely a lack of ready capital. Of course, there are differences. A solvent bank facing a bank run has a balance sheet with sound, pledgeable, assets such as bonds and loans. The existence of these assets allows the central bank to act as the lender of last resort without putting itself at any serious financial risk. An insurer, however, having paid out its reserves after a catastrophe, has no such accumulated assets to discount. This difference, however, is one of degree and not kind. Just as certain events create a flight to quality among potential providers of liquidity to banks, so do certain events create a liquidity crises for catastrophe insurers. Though made in the context of banking, the following recent statement by a former chairman of the Federal Reserve System applies equally to catastrophe insurance:

Policy practitioners operating under a risk-management paradigm may, at times, be led to undertake actions intended to provide insurance against especially adverse outcomes.... When confronted with uncertainty, especially Knightian uncertainty, human beings invariably attempt to disengage from medium to long-term commitments in favor of safety and liquidity.... The immediate response on the part of the central bank to such financial implosions must be to inject large quantities of liquidity (Greenspan 2004).

The lender of last resort scheme discussed here has many details requiring further attention, but it is of some interest that a scheme with many of these features has recently been instituted by the state of Florida. (Interested readers should consult Jaffee and Russell 2007b.)

9.3.6   Global Responses to the WMD Problem

Terrorism is a global problem and some form of government support for terrorism insurance exists in many countries. Prior to September 11, countries such as the United Kingdom, Israel, South Africa, and Spain had already experienced terrorism attacks, and in these countries, government programs were already in place to support private markets. The attack on September 11 caused many other countries—for example, France, Germany, and Australia—to put in place their own government programs. (Interested readers can find a review of these programs in Guy Carpenter & Co 2007.) WMD risk is handled in different ways in different countries. Here is a brief list:

United Kingdom   In the United Kingdom, the government-supported terrorism reinsurance pool, Pool Re, makes no distinction between conventional and WMD risk (a nuclear exclusion was deleted in 2002). The UK also has a sizable private market in which WMD risk is typically excluded.

France   In France the government terrorism insurance scheme GAREAT excluded nuclear attacks until 2006. Today, WMD risk is treated no differently from conventional terrorism.

Germany   In Germany WMD risk is excluded from the government terrorism scheme Extremus.

Australia   In Australia the government run reinsurance pool ARPC includes chemical and biological loss but excludes nuclear.

As this list shows, experience with WMD risk varies from country to country, but as the UK and French examples show, several public programs currently include WMD risk.

9.4   Conclusion

Although experts disagree on how close terrorists are to having a WMD capability, there is no disagreement on how avidly such weapons are sought. And if they were available, there is little doubt that they would be used. For this reason, the continued exclusion of WMD risks from property insurance contracts under TRIPRA is a matter of significant concern. It is not credible to argue, as many insurers do, that WMD risk is "uninsurable" when, as we have seen, providers of workers compensation routinely provide this insurance. The workers compensation insurers must find the government backstop sufficiently reassuring to continue to offer this coverage.

The problem is property casualty insurance. Even though, as we have seen, the total after-tax loss to the property insurance industry under TRIEA cannot exceed $65 billion, and even though total reserves exceed $500 billion, the industry continues to claim that adding WMD risk would threaten it with bankruptcy. But as we have seen, this argument can always be addressed by adding special provisions that reduce the industry's burden. Requiring insurers to add WMD risk would seem by far the simplest fix.

Going forward, the TRIA arrangement has been renewed for another seven years despite the fact that insurance companies have had ample time to recover from September 11 and the likelihood that free reinsurance will only induce further dependence on government largesse. Congress's failure to include CBRN events in the "make available" requirement, however, means that special attention must be paid to the WMD issue, particularly as it relates to workers compensation. Removing the loss cap could force private workers compensation insurers to abandon the line. This, in turn, would force government to intervene so that the burden still fell on the public sector. Including WMD risks in future government schemes can avoid this result.

In concluding, we propose a simple rule the government could adopt as a guide to providing efficient and effective terrorism insurance: *When intervening in terrorism insurance markets, government plans should mimic as closely as possible what operative private markets would have done.* Following this rule would encourage the designers to resist government subsidies and to endorse risk-based premiums.

Notes

1. Technically, a CBRN attack need not be massive; for example, in 1984 members of the Rajneeshsee cult poisoned a few salad bars in Oregon. However, the focus of this chapter—and most of the CBRN insurance literature—is on massive attacks. It has also been suggested that a nuclear attack is of a different kind compared with the other CBRN modes; we address special issues associated with nuclear attacks in what follows.

2. The events were Hurricane Andrew in 1992, the Northridge earthquake of 1994, and the September 11, 2001, terrorist attack. The private market for flood insurance in the United States broke down after disastrous floods along the Mississippi River in 1927 and a federal program has provided most U.S. flood insurance since then.

3. Arrow (1965) shows that deductibles, in which insured parties are indemnified only for losses above some limit, represent the optimal form for partial insurance. Deductible policies are preferable to coinsurance policies, in which the insured party is indemnified for a fixed percentage of all losses, because they allow full recovery above the deductible limit. This is the same range of losses in which insurance provides the greatest benefit.

4. The incentive for a firm to purchase insurance is reduced, and may vanish, when the firm is owned by a large number of individual investors, each of whom owns an infinitesimal share of the firm and holds a diversified portfolio of such securities (Smith 2005). In practice, concern with the costs of bankruptcy, the incentives of managers (as opposed to those of shareholders), and tax effects combine to cause most firms to purchase insurance against a wide range of risks (Jaffee and Russell 2006).

5. A related problem is that catastrophe losses tend to be geographically concentrated and to have a simultaneous impact on several insurance lines. This makes it difficult for insurers to maintain a diversified risk portfolio (GAO 2006e). Furthermore, the large fixed costs of entry into a catastrophe line—to create underwriting skills, marketing ability, and claim resolution facilities—make it uneconomic for an insurer to maintain a diversified portfolio by taking on just a small amount of risk in each catastrophe market.

6. However, Warren Buffett, whose firm Berkshire Hathaway now owns a range of insurance and reinsurance firms, has taken a different tack. Buffett's firm has at least twice put its sizeable capital at risk to take on catastrophe risks, once taking on earthquake risk after the Northridge earthquake and more recently, in 2006, taking on hurricane risk the year after Katrina. In both cases, Berkshire Hathaway prospered because the insured events did not occur.

7. There is a well developed literature on "ambiguity aversion" which shows that, in practice, individuals shy away from taking gambles when the true odds of the events are hard to determine. See Ellsberg (1961) for the behavioral evidence and Hogarth and Kunreuther (1989) for an application to insurance markets.

8. The private market for flood insurance in the United States broke down even earlier; most U.S. flood risks have been covered by the federal National Flood Insurance (NFI) program since 1968. The NFI program faced a $20 billion deficit following Hurricane Katrina. Flood insurance is similarly a government responsibility in most other developed countries, although it appears that England has maintained a unique public/private partnership for insuring floods (Jaffee 2006).

9. Anecdotes also circulated concerning policy terminations or enormous premium increases on policy renewal. For example, it was reported that prior to September 11, O'Hare airport in Chicago paid a $125,000 annual premium for $750 million of terrorism coverage. When it renewed after September 11, it was required to pay $6.9 million for just $150 million of coverage (Zanetti, Schwartz, and Lindemuth 2007). Other entities, including NFL football teams, could not obtain any coverage at all. Tenants in landmark buildings also found reason to move into less likely targets as their leases ran out. Abadie and Dermisi (2006), for example document how vacancy rates in three Chicago trophy buildings, including the Sears Tower, rose relative to other Chicago office buildings.

10. The value of U.S. nonresidential construction did fall by about $100 billion (at annual rates) or about 6 percent from 2001-Q2 to 2002-Q3. Nonresidential construction activity,

however, had fully recovered by 2002-Q4 while residential construction activity rose steadily throughout the period. GNP also rose steadily over this period, albeit at a relatively slow rate.

11. TRIA relates only to specific lines, including most commercial property and casualty insurance and workers compensation. It does not relate to health, life, malpractice, commercial auto insurance, or various other lines.

12. The $100 million TRIEA trigger avoids a strategic gambit in which an operating company could create its own "captive" insurer to obtain low-cost TRIA indemnification if the firm were attacked. The $100 million loss trigger is meant to preclude indemnification if an attack were to occur against just one such firm.

13. Losses due to fire following a WMD attack would be covered by fire insurance policies in certain states.

14. In the 2007 renewal of TRIA, the question of how best to deal with WMD risks was left for further study. The pros and cons of permanent government intervention in this industry have been extensively debated (Dixon et al. 2007; Doherty et al. 2005; and Jaffee and Russell 2006).

15. In fact, anthrax has been publicly released at least twice, once in 1979 in the Soviet city of Sverdlovsk and again in the 2001 U.S. mailings.

16. The RAND study assumes that all of the buildings are fully insured against an anthrax attack. In fact, the U.S. Treasury (2005) reports that only about three percent of buildings actually have CBRN coverage. This reinforces the RAND study's conclusion that no U.S. taxpayer funds would have been spent to pay TRIA claims from such an event.

17. In his economics Nobel Prize acceptance speech, Schelling (2005) explains the nonuse of nuclear weapons after World War II in part by the concern that the word *nuclear* brings to strategic war analysis. Also note that private insurers had no problem providing Union Carbide with insurance to cover its fertilizer manufacturing plants in India, even though the 1984 Bhopal gas tragedy caused approximately 3,800 deaths and several thousand other permanent and partial disabilities. The final settlement for the disaster totaled $470 million, of which private insurers paid $200 million.

18. The result actually recreates an old form of insurance called an "assessable reciprocal mutual."

19. Interestingly, the Nuclear Energy Institute published a fact sheet titled "Price-Anderson Act Provides Effective Nuclear Insurance at No Cost to the Public" in June 2006. The "No-Cost" statement presumably refers to Tiers 1 and 2 that, indeed, are funded by the industry. The article, however, makes no reference to the Tier 3 exemption from any claims above the $10 billion limit. These will be paid by the "public" either by the individuals directly affected or through government payments funded by U.S. taxpayers.

20. William Frist is quoted as saying that "an inevitable bio-terror attack" would come "at some time in the next ten years." Views like this persuaded the United States to spend more than $33 billion on bioterrorism countermeasures between 2002 and 2006 (Agence France Presse 2005).

21. Osama bin Laden's desire for such a device has been noted frequently. See, for example, the testimony of Jamal Ahmad al-Fadl, a native of Sudan and ex-bin Laden associate, in the trial of the earlier World Trade Center bombing (*United States of America v. Usama bin*

Laden, et al., 2001). On the other hand, it is clear that even committed nation states such as Iran and North Korea face significant, though as Langewiesche (2007) notes not insurmountable, obstacles in developing and delivering the weapons.

22. For example, the Aum Shinrikyo Tokyo subway gas attack achieved very little, although it was four years in the planning with a generous budget and virtually no monitoring by the Japanese police.

23. It is also sometimes suggested that terrorists are strategic in their choice of targets and that this complicates the process of computing event probabilities (Willis et al. 2005). However, if we can decipher the specific strategy employed by terrorists, then this should actually facilitate the determination of event probabilities. Or, if we cannot decipher the specific strategy, then the distribution of actual events should be observationally equivalent to the types of stochastic processes that Mother Nature employs in creating natural disasters.

24. See Zanjani 2006 for a recent analysis of the California Earthquake Authority.

25. LIBOR stands for The London Interbank Offered Rate. This interest rate is commonly used as the standard against which other interest rates are measured.

26. In technical terms, natural disasters might be considered "zero beta" or "low beta" risks, since they tend to be uncorrelated with other factors that influence stock prices. According to the capital asset pricing model, investors should be willing to pay premium prices to obtain securities with low or zero betas. This argument would not, however, apply to terrorism risks to the extent that they are considered more likely to affect the stock market and macroeconomy.

27. The owners of trophy buildings in city centers will face higher premiums for their terrorism insurance, and may also be forced to accept lower rents, in order to keep their tenants from choosing safer locations in buildings that are smaller and/or further removed from the city center.

28. Kunreuther and Heal 2003 discuss a case in which the benefits of mitigation require simultaneous group action, so that if one party fails to carry out his share, the group as a whole has less incentive to mitigate.

29. An even more direct mechanism would be to hold the terrorists liable, but the paper assumes this is not possible.

30. Such an arrangement was part of the House version of TRIPRA (HR 2761) but was dropped from the final legislation.

31. North Dakota, Ohio, Puerto Rico, the U.S. Virgin Islands, Washington, and Wyoming.

32. Arizona, California, Colorado, Idaho, Maryland, Michigan, Minnesota, Montana, New York, Oklahoma, Oregon, Pennsylvania, and Utah.

33. This could only happen in the United States, since comparable plans in European countries all charge a fee. There is an explanation: gratis government reinsurance could be interpreted as an export subsidy, which European Union rules prohibit.

34. A scheme in this general form was proposed in the U.S. House of Representative as H.R. 846, the Homeowners Insurance Availability Act of 2005, but did not pass.

10

The Fire Next Time: Managing Large Urban Fires

Stephen M. Maurer, Jason C. Christopher, and Michael Thompson

Nuclear terrorism is the latest chapter in a defense problem that dates back to the late 1940s. Indeed, we have come full circle. Civil defense was largely abandoned after the Soviet threat grew to include thousands of thermonuclear weapons in the 1960s. By contrast, the current threat envisages one or, at most, a few atomic weapons.[1] In this sense, the situation resembles the late 1940s, when the Soviet threat was not very different from the massive air attacks that various combatants had managed, sometimes reasonably successfully, in World War II.

While the fireball and blast effects from an atomic weapon would kill tens of thousands immediately, experience at Hiroshima and Nagasaki suggests that many others would survive only to die in the ensuing fire. The atomic bomb dropped on Hiroshima killed 70,000 to 80,000.[2] Of these, more than 20,000 were probably killed by fire after the blast (see figure 10.1). The bomb also destroyed 4.7 sq. miles around ground zero. Of these, however, the initial blast only destroyed about 3.14 sq. miles. The remaining 1.56 sq. miles, 33 percent, was largely or entirely destroyed by fire and could in principle have been saved (USSBS 1946a; figure 10.1). World War II experience with conventional bombing is also instructive. Once started, uncontrolled fires could spread to much larger areas—and potentially kill more people—than atomic bombs. Examples include Dresden (25,000 to 35,000 killed, 5.8 sq. miles destroyed), Hamburg (45,000 killed, 4.0 sq. miles), and Tokyo (83,000 killed, 15.8 sq. miles).[3] Not surprisingly, combatants believed that uncontrolled fires were "more powerful than any and all munitions" (Friedrich 2006).

U.S. analysts who studied Hiroshima shortly after the war concluded that it was "unlikely that any public fire department in the world, even without damage to equipment or casualties to personnel, could have prevented development of a conflagration in Hiroshima, or combated it with success at more than a few locations along its perimeter. The total fire damage would not have been much different"

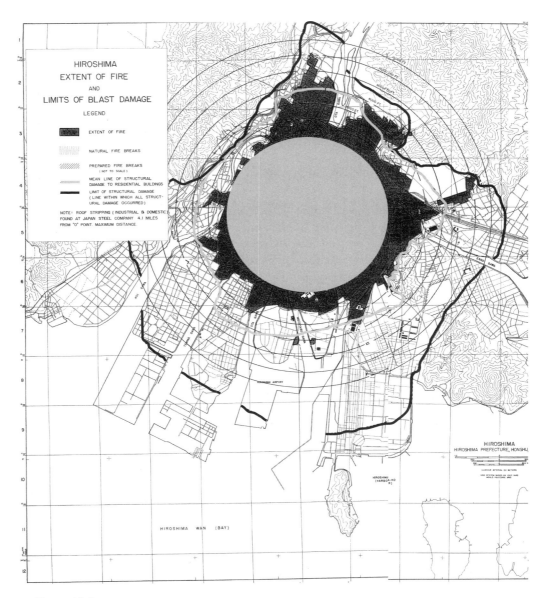

Figure 10.1
Fire and blast damage at Hiroshima. The inner circle shows the area that was destroyed by the fireball and blast. This area would have suffered near-total destruction even without the subsequent fire. The dark region around the circle shows areas affected by the subsequent fire. The total area occupied by the circle and dark surrounding region is roughly 4.7 sq. miles. The gray ring around the fire area shows the mean line of structural damage to residential buildings. No structural damage occurred beyond the black line. *Source*: USSBS, 1946a.

(USSBS 1946a). But that was more than sixty years ago. It is worth asking whether we could do better today.

This chapter describes methods for fighting large urban fires and the prospects for implementing them. Section 10.1 begins by describing the main characteristics of large urban fires using historical experience from Germany and Japan. Section 10.2 examines the methods that were developed to fight these fires. Section 10.3 looks at how recent advances in understanding and predicting fires could potentially extend firefighters' capabilities. Section 10.4 explores the high-technology tools that would be needed to make this vision a reality. Section 10.5 examines the organizational challenges of implementing this vision. Finally, section 10.6 offers a brief conclusion.

10.1 Large Urban Fires

Large urban fires are a complex phenomenon and only partly understood. This section reviews what is known about large fires in general and fires set by atomic weapons in particular.

10.1.1 Conventional Incendiary Bombing: From Ignition to Firestorm

Conventional World War II bombing raids produced three types of fire. The first, following the initial raid, consisted of several thousand small, *localized fires* within the space of a few square miles. Unless stopped, these quickly merged into fewer but more intense *mass fires*. In World War II, the transition from localized to mass fires typically took fifteen to thirty minutes.[4]

There are two basic types of mass fires: conflagrations and firestorms. In a *conflagration*, fires spread relatively slowly and are driven by ambient wind, topography, and conducted heat. For present purposes, conflagrations have two important characteristics. First, despite extensive property destruction, conflagrations have surprisingly low casualties. In 1666, London burned for four days and 32,000 homes were destroyed, but only eight lives were lost (Brode and Small 1986). The San Francisco Fire of 1906 similarly burned for three days over an area of five square miles, leaving 100,000 homeless. Despite this, only 452 deaths were recorded, although the true figure was probably several times larger (Fradkin 2005).[5] Second, slow-moving fires can in principle be managed. We return to this subject in section 10.2.

Firestorms are different. Here, localized fires or conflagrations develop a coherent structure in which a central column of rising air draws wind from all directions like the updraft in a chimney. This stokes the fire, increases the updraft still further, and produces a runaway reaction (Eden 2004; Postol 1986). At this point, the firestorm becomes self-sustaining until everything that can burn has been destroyed. Because of the inrushing wind, firestorms tend to be stationary and self-limiting

(Glasstone and Dolan 1977).[6] The transition from initial ignition to firestorm took just twenty-three minutes in Hamburg (Middlebrook 1980) and about ninety minutes in Dresden (Taylor 2004). Thereafter, it took roughly two to two and a half hours for the Hamburg fire to peak (Middlebrook 1980). The Dresden fire similarly seems to have peaked several hours after the original strike (Taylor 2004). The Hamburg storm started to subside about three hours after it had started and disappeared entirely within five to six hours (Middlebrook 1980).[7]

Despite massive bombing, most German and Japanese fires never became firestorms (Taylor 2004; Hoyt 2000) and the precise conditions needed for the transition are only partly known. There is, however, widespread agreement that the requirements include (1) at least eight pounds of fuel per square foot of fire area, (2) a wind of less than eight miles an hour, (3) localized fires covering at least one-half square mile, (4) delivery of munitions within an unusually short period of time, and (5) simultaneous fires in at least half the area's structures (Glasstone and Dolan 1977; Postol 1986).[8] Even then, however, firestorms are not inevitable. Hamburg's storm, for example, seems to have required unusual weather conditions including a long period of hot (80°F) daytime weather, unusually warm nights, 30 percent humidity, and a stalled low-pressure zone in close proximity to high pressure over the city (Beck 1986; Middlebrook 1980). More generally, whether a transition occurs is widely thought to depend sensitively on a large number of factors including climate, rain, snow, visibility, temperature, atmospheric inversions, cloud cover, fuel type, fuel distribution, and time since last precipitation (Eden 2004).

World War II firefighters were almost entirely helpless against firestorms and could do little more than let them burn themselves out. This is still true today (Eden 2004). Firestorms are also far more lethal than conflagrations. In the latter, people have historically had an excellent chance of walking out. Most Hamburg residents who survived either fled as the firestorm was just beginning or hid in public bunkers with specially constructed smoke- and gastight doors. However, simple basement shelters were not enough (Middlebrook 1980). Not a single survivor emerged from the central regions of Hamburg's firestorm (Taylor 2004).

10.1.2   Atomic Bombs and Fire

Though highly suggestive, World War II conventional bombing attacks differed from an atomic strike in several important respects. First, planners had many hundreds of bombers at their disposal and could therefore target multiple regions at once. These targets were deliberately designed—not always successfully—to promote the firestorm transition and complicate defense. By contrast, fires from a nuclear weapon would be limited to a radius of a mile or so and, within that perimeter, concentrated in the half mile closest to ground zero. These conditions are only slightly more favorable than the minimal firestorm requirements cited in section 10.1.1. Second, nuclear blast damage is much more severe near ground zero than for conventional bombs. This may make firestorms less likely, since collapsed frame buildings do not burn as readily as damaged ones, while other fuel sources will often be blanketed in fire-resistant masonry rubble (Glasstone and Dolan 1977). Finally, nuclear weapons introduce at least two fundamentally new effects—an initial flash and a massive ensuing shockwave—not found in conventional explosions. There is some evidence that the flash would be unusually efficient at starting fires but also that the shockwave would blow out some fires before they became established. The extent to which these effects cancel one another remains controversial, at least in the open literature, although many Cold War analysts seem to have concluded that flash effects would dominate (Eden 2004).[9]

Hiroshima   The Hiroshima bomb was dropped in a flat area containing many buildings. Radiant energy ("flash") from the explosion caused many materials (e.g., dark curtains, paper, and dry rotted wood) to catch fire up to two-thirds of a mile from ground zero. Damage from the ensuing blast wave—for example, broken gas lines, short circuits, and the like—was probably effective in setting secondary fires up to a mile or so away (Glasstone and Dolan 1977).

These localized fires merged into a mass fire "showing many characteristics usually associated with firestorms" after about twenty minutes. These included winds that blew toward the city center from all directions and peaked at thirty to forty miles per hour roughly two to three hours after the explosion. Fire damage also followed the typical firestorm pattern: limited fires outside the initially ignited area and complete destruction of almost everything that could burn within (USSBS 1946a; Glasstone and Dolan 1977).

Nagasaki   The Nagasaki bomb was dropped well away from the city center and fell in a long narrow valley which probably did not contain sufficient fuel to sustain a firestorm. Despite this, the fire became "well established" about two hours after the explosion. Although "no definite firestorm occurred," winds increased to thirty-five miles per hour and remained above normal for another seven hours (USSBS 1946a; Glasstone and Dolan 1977).

Classified Simulations   The U.S. Department of Defense studied the fire problem intermittently until the end of the Cold War, and this work has now been largely declassified. In general, the studies led to a renewed appreciation that "superfires" could inflict two to four times as many casualties as blast and cause damage up to twenty-five times farther away (Eden 2004; Postol 1986). Furthermore, some investigators developed new computer models that supposedly made the transition to firestorms far more predictable—and much less dependent on detailed local conditions (e.g., weather)—than World War II experience suggested. However, these assertions remain intensely controversial, with many scholars holding to the older orthodoxy that the transition to firestorms was basically unpredictable (Eden 2004). Perhaps more importantly, the studies almost always invoked Cold War scenarios in which ignition was optimized by detonating warheads twenty to fifty times larger than the Hiroshima explosion at high altitude (Eden 2004). For this reason, their relevance to terrorist use of Hiroshima-scale weapons at ground level is limited.[10] (Interested readers should consult Postol 1986 and Brode and Small 1986 for open-literature examples of this work.)

10.2   Classical Firefighting Solutions

Despite significant destruction and loss of life, experience with disasters and World War II bombing raids shows that large urban fires can sometimes be resisted. Firefighting techniques were massively documented by the postwar U.S. Strategic Bombing Survey for both Germany (USSBS 1947a) and Japan (USSBS 1947e).

10.2.1   Fighting Large Urban Fires

Tactics for fighting large urban fires include numerous methods that modern firefighters seldom, if ever, learn or practice. Many also require extensive knowledge and cooperation by civilians. These methods include

Underground shelters   The firebombing and burning of cities in Germany sent the urban population underground. However, this strategy was not sustainable for long periods. First, professionals often had little chance of putting out thousands of small localized fires in the first half hour following an attack. It was therefore very important for civilians to emerge from their shelters in time to extinguish localized fires before they could grow into mass fires (Taylor 2004). Second, mass fires and especially firestorms eventually filled underground shelters with superheated and/or poisonous gases. The U.S. Strategic Bombing Survey estimated that 60 to 70 percent of all German civilian fatalities came from CO_2 poisoning and that another 5 to 15 percent died from burns and inhaling superheated gas (USSBS 1947a; Postol 1986). Atomic bomb survivors might well be forced to seek shelter belowground. This, however, would be futile unless they understood the dangers of sheltering too long.

Water corridors   German firefighters found that the most effective way to rescue trapped civilians was to pump water high into the air to create tunnels of water so that survivors could evacuate the city. The water was usually drawn from local rivers and pumped through special hoses that created water spouts every fifty feet or so (Friedrich 2006). The corridors were only effective, however, to the extent that people understood the method and were prepared to use it.

Firebreaks   German firefighters sometimes created firebreaks that remained effective up to windspeeds of fifty miles an hour (Friedrich 2006). However, success required shrewd placement and "a strong phalanx of workers" who could establish the breaks quickly. Untrained teams could be counterproductive. During the San Francisco Fire of 1906, firefighters "dynamited buildings already on fire and simply made an avenue for the spread of the conflagration instead of creating an obstacle to its advance" (Fradkin 2004).

Civil defense   German and Japanese authorities tried to teach their populations how to shelter underground and avoid the dangers this entailed, evacuate a burning city, and fight small fires until professional firefighters arrived. This sensible advice was repeated in 1950s-era U.S. civil defense programs (Science Service Inc. 1950). In principle, today's Community Emergency Response Team (CERT) program could be expanded to teach similar civil defense skills for use against a wide variety of natural and manmade threats.

Outside help   Following attacks, the number of emergency workers in a medium-sized German city typically swelled from about one thousand first responders to almost ten thousand (Friedrich 2006). The workers were drawn from surrounding communities and included firefighters, medical workers, infrastructure repair specialists, decontamination personnel, production engineers, and other specialized workers. However, even though help arrived quickly—firefighters from surrounding towns began arriving in Dresden thirty minutes after the attack—it was almost always too late to prevent local fires from merging into a conflagration or firestorm.

Postwar analysis suggests that these methods saved many civilian lives and that this was true even in cities that experienced firestorms. Perhaps the most spectacular success came after the firebombing of Brunswick, in which "only" 560 people or 0.28 percent of the population died (Friedrich 2006). On the other hand, these successes were not achieved easily. Tasks like setting up water corridors were complex and almost certain to fail if not practiced ahead of time. Similarly, civilians had to know and practice what was expected of them.

10.2.2   Contamination and Bomb Damage

The firefighting organizations that responded to an atomic bomb would be crippled in multiple ways. Significant challenges would include

First-responder casualties   At Hiroshima, 70 percent of firefighting equipment was crushed in the collapse of firehouses and 80 percent of firefighters were unable to respond (Glasstone and Dolan 1977; USSBS 1946a).[11] Casualty rates this high would greatly impair or obliterate central command and coordination in the first hours after an attack. Thereafter, resources and organization would be supplied from the outside.

Firefighting infrastructure   Water pressure fell to zero at Hiroshima. While pumping stations were largely unaffected, approximately 70,000 aboveground pipe connections in buildings and dwellings failed. Belowground pipes and mains were similarly damaged by collapsing buildings and fires near ground zero (USBSS 1946a; Glasstone and Dolan 1977). British, German, and Japanese civil defense partly compensated for falling water pressure by pumping water from streams and rivers. This, however, was a substantial effort and often required advanced preparation (USSBS 1947a, 1947e, 1947f). Nevertheless, it is reasonable to think that at least some U.S. fire departments could match this capability. For example, San Francisco used fireboats to pump water from the bay into an auxiliary water system after the Loma Prieta earthquake (1989).

Electromagnetic pulse   Nuclear weapons emit a powerful electromagnetic pulse (EMP) at the moment of detonation. The pulse would probably destroy most electronic devices within two miles of ground zero and affect others up to eight miles away. Computers and other semiconductor-based devices are especially vulnerable (Glasstone and Dolan 1977). While militaries routinely shield devices against high levels of EMP, this protection is expensive. For civilian purposes, it would probably be sufficient to adopt a lesser standard that allowed devices to survive outside the kilometer or so blast radius in which reinforced concrete firehouses are likely to collapse in any case (USSBS 1946a). Even without hardening, electronic infrastructure would begin to flow back into the attack site as help arrived from other communities.

Mobility   Vehicle traffic at Hiroshima and Nagasaki was immediately snarled by debris, flame, and/or downed bridges. For example, one fire company that survived the Nagasaki bomb found that it could not penetrate closer than 1.25 miles to ground zero. Despite this, many areas at Hiroshima and Nagasaki remained accessible. World War II responders relied on runners, motorcyclists, and bicyclists to operate in areas that would otherwise have been inaccessible. Contemporary planners should carefully consider similar low-technology strategies (Glasstone and Dolan 1977).

Radioactivity   First responders in many locations would have to conduct firefighting and rescue operations wearing hot, bulky hazmat suits. Even then, they would have to undergo periodic decontamination and keep careful track of how much radiation they received. These measures would clearly degrade efficiency, especially if responders had not conducted realistic exercises beforehand. That said, such problems are potentially manageable. Military units routinely practice working in radioactive environments.

10.3   Twenty-First-Century Firefighting Solutions?

Professional firefighters will almost certainly be overwhelmed in the critical first hours when localized fires transition to a conflagration or, possibly, a firestorm. In this situation, high technology would be far less valuable than civilian self-help in extinguishing fires. High technology would be similarly helpless once a firestorm started except, possibly, at the edges. Conflagrations, however, are another matter. Here, local firefighters would have time to organize and outside responders (at least on a state basis) would have time to intervene. Could high technology improve matters?

Conflagrations are highly dynamic and change abruptly on time scales from hours to days. Yet these changes can, in principle, be predicted from the laws of physics. In theory, this should allow future firefighters to identify, prioritize, and suppress emerging threats before they become unmanageably large. Success would, however, require a continual cycle in which firefighters:

· Acquire and update very *detailed knowledge* of the fire
· Invent and update *multiple alternative plans* to fight it
· Use *computer simulations* to predict the fire's future course under each plan and select the best one
· *Communicate* and *implement the preferred plan* before it becomes obsolete

In many ways, this problem is not very different from the familiar military challenge of "getting inside the other side's decision cycle"—that is, updating and implementing plans faster than an opposing army can react. For this strategy to work, however, fire managers would have to complete their decision cycles within, at most, an hour or so. Given the complexity of the problem and the number of responders and assets deployed, this would require large investments in automation and computer processing. The twenty-first-century dream of high-technology firefighting is, at bottom, an information technology problem. This section looks at emerging technologies that would allow decision makers to predict the future course of large fires and model different options for containing them. Specific technologies and organizations for acting on this information are discussed in sections 10.4 and 10.5.

10.3.1   Computational Fire Modeling

Decision makers are only as good as their ability to predict what the fire will do next. This is the province of computational fire modeling. In principle, fire modeling is analogous to predicting other complex processes like weather or hurricanes. However, it has many more variables and these often interact in highly nonlinear ways. Traditional fire models try to calculate this physics in explicit detail.[12] But even the largest contemporary supercomputers have trouble running these models fast enough to be useful. More recently, researchers have begun exploring truncated models based on a reduced set of variables. The hope is that reasonably predictive models can be built despite these simplifications.

Physics-Based Models   Researchers at Los Alamos and Lawrence Livermore National Laboratories have worked since the mid–1990s to develop detailed physics models that can predict the behavior of large fires in real time (Heller 2002). Their goal is to develop models that can predict fire behavior for firefighters on scene, and to eventually extend these models to include large urban fires. However, current prototype models are so complicated and contain so many interacting variables that they require supercomputers.[13]

For now, state of the art is represented by Los Alamos/Lawrence Livermore's Higrad-Firetec model. Its variables include fuel type, density, 3-D structure, and locations; humidity; air temperature; air pressure; precipitation; fire and smoke locations; terrain; roads, schools, fire stations, electrical transmission lines, fire hydrants, and other landmarks; and regional weather patterns. The program also contains extensive subroutines for calculating combustion chemistry, convection, smoke obscuration, smoke dispersion, and numerous other processes. The computer calculates these quantities separately for millions of one-meter cells every thousandth of a second. So far, the results are encouraging: Higrad-Firetec has already produced reasonably accurate simulations of various historical fires including the Oakland Hills (1991) and Corral Canyon (1996) conflagrations (Heller 2002).

Truncated Models   Even Higrad-Firetec is not a pure physics model—for example, some fire-propagation physics has been simplified to reduce computation loads (Mandel et al. 2007). However, much more aggressive simplification is possible. Mandel et al. have built a simple prototype model that successfully predicts fire temperature at one location. Unlike traditional fire simulation, the program uses a subroutine called DDDAS (Dynamic Data-Driven Assimilation System) that compares recent predictions against events on the ground and then continuously changes the model to make it more accurate.

Prospects   Researchers readily admit that their models are not yet up to the task of managing a large urban fire in real time. On the other hand, the work has advanced reasonably well. For now, the main impediment to progress seems to be limited funding. However, Moore's law and steady increases in processing power practically guarantee that the problem will be solved within a few decades. At that point, commanders' ability to manage fires will be limited solely by their ability to translate model predictions into action on the ground.

10.4   Advanced Firefighting Technologies

Popular depictions of firefighters celebrate individual heroism. However, organization and technology also matter and this is especially true for large fires. Firefighting is most effective when groups of individuals are organized to work as teams instead of stand-alone participants. Militaries have understood this principle since ancient times and have evolved sophisticated command and communication structures to get the most from people and assets. In modern militaries, information technology is responsible for much of this leverage. As we will see, similar products have become increasingly available to firefighters since the late 1990s.

Collectively, these new tools promise to make classical methods more effective and turn strategies based on computational fire models from dreams into reality.

10.4.1   New Technologies

At the most generic level, information technologies collect data and turn it into commands. We examine each of these functions separately.

Data Collection   The fire models discussed in section 10.3 have a voracious appetite for real-time data. Paradoxically, truncated models that depend on error correction may require even more. In principle, technologies exist for this. Aircraft can take multispectrum images, drop hardened sensors in the fire's path, and radio back data in continuous telemetry streams. U.S. military Predator aircraft are already being deployed for this purpose. They use special heat-measuring sensors to generate digital images that can be relayed anywhere in the world by satellite within five to ten minutes (Pasztor, Rundle, and Karp 2007). Modern military responders similarly take weather, plume-line, and other data for a thirty-block radius around fire scenes. By comparison, civilian firefighters are still generally limited to what they can see with their eyes.[14]

Command and Control   Until recently, fire departments were typically limited to four radio channels, three of which were used for dispatch. This left only one voice channel to control actual firefighting operations and no data links. Furthermore, firefighters wearing gloves or bulky safety equipment often found the equipment hard to use. These problems were compounded if the firefighter was wearing a mask and had to shout or pull the mask away from his or her face to be heard. Finally, equipment tended to be unreliable because of blind spots, garbled messages, and outright failures from heat, rough handling, and battery problems.[15]

Improved radios began entering service in the late 1990s. Today, state-of-the-art radios often feature twelve operations channels and can be expanded up to thirty-two. Similarly, breathing masks now come with a built-in speaker. This lets firefighters communicate without shouting or removing their masks. However, systems still do not transmit data. In principle, advanced information technology can be used to locate, track, and direct firefighters inside burning buildings; compare this information against digital floorplans; report firefighters' heart rates, temperature, and other biometric data; track and optimize the use of people and assets across large geographic areas; and detect and limit the amount of time that workers are exposed to radiation. However, collecting, transmitting, and processing this data is bound to be costly. Local fire departments have yet to make this investment.

10.4.2   Barriers to the Acquisition and Use of IT

Information technology would materially improve local fire departments' ability to fight everyday fires and could be critical in a large urban fire. That said, it faces numerous obstacles.

Training and Doctrine   Purchasing hardware is not enough. To get full value, local departments must also develop creative tactics for using technology and teaching it to members. This takes time and tends to make information technology less attractive than more familiar investments.

Limited Resources   First-responder budgets are notoriously tight. In 2003, for example, several Bay Area departments slashed their budgets by millions of dollars and closed engine companies.[16] In principle, advanced technologies can make these limited budgets go further. However, most fire departments prefer to invest in trained human beings. This is only partly motivated by a desire to protect existing jobs. Fire departments typically believe that trained people are more important, versatile, and useful than machines. This is often a defensible judgment, particularly for departments that discount the risk of very large fires where advanced technology is most valuable.

Federalism   Most local fire departments are small. This balkanization implies that no single department can capture the full benefit of investing in the capabilities needed to fight very large (multiple jurisdiction) fires. In principle, this could be remedied by cooperation across agencies. However, coordination is hampered by the fact that different departments acquire technology at different times. This can lead to situations in which early technology adopters are stranded by changing standards and thereafter lack the money to retool.[17] Coordination across departments is further complicated by political struggles for control and honest differences over the amount of WMD risk. Finally, local departments know that the federal government frequently subsidizes homeland security investments and/or provides resources for fighting large fires. This federal spending tends to crowd out local investment in assets that the federal government may later supply gratis.

Grant Support   Despite recent reforms, many federal grants are misallocated—that is, distributed according to population instead of perceived terrorism risk. Furthermore, grants seldom pay for the full life-cycle cost of equipment since local departments must usually pay for upkeep, upgrades, maintenance, and other expenses.[18] Finally, federal grant procedures are often arcane. Departments that lack professional grant-writing staff may not know that money is available and/or submit unnecessarily flawed proposals.

Technology Issues   Information technology poses a particularly difficult innovation problem for various reasons. These include

Misunderstood needs   Customers seldom know what information technology can do, while technologists seldom understand user needs. Software engineers who lack firefighting experience will often be seen (sometimes correctly) as intruders trying to sell a product that is unnecessary or even irrelevant. Many firefighters believe that simple is better, that even "ruggedized" information technology is fragile, and that "gadgets" are not necessary for people who know how to do the job properly. These concerns may often be valid in an environment where products are dropped, burned, get wet and smoky, and/or are used by people who are not used to information technology or have been made clumsy by gloves and protective gear.

Compatibility issues   Incremental investments are often impractical. Information technology frequently comes in the form of networks or systems that must be purchased wholesale. Furthermore, existing equipment may be incompatible with new purchases or else require expensive upgrades.

Classification   Some information technology is classified. Despite their importance to civil defense, civilian fire departments may not have access to the most capable technologies.

Cultural Resistance   Firefighters often resist new techniques and equipment. For example, hardly any firefighters used air packs when they were first introduced in the 1970s. Instead, it took twenty years before studies persuaded most departments that the technology really did save lives.[19] Information technologies that reduce humans' role in decision making also face an additional hurdle. First responders are culturally predisposed to trust humans, not machines.[20]

Cultural resistance can be overstated. Once senior firefighters are convinced that a system is needed, rank-and-file opinion generally follows. Furthermore, fire departments are paramilitary organizations with well-defined chains of command. If workers are told to use specific new equipment, they will do so. This, however, requires strong leadership and/or strong outside political pressure. Politicians may be reluctant to spend this political capital.

10.5   Organizational Challenges

So far we have assumed that firefighters belong to a single, monolithic organization. In fact, the personnel and equipment needed to fight large fires comes from dozens of individual fire departments. In the 1970s, a series of disastrous Southern California fires uncovered multiple problems including organizational differences among agencies, lack of accountability, and the absence of any well-defined command structure. California responded by developing a new Incident Command System (ICS) that was later adopted throughout the country.

ICS provides a unified command structure for all events. Small events are handled by one or, at most, a few commanders. As the incident grows, more agencies are included within the same organizational structure, command post, and incident plan. Since these agencies also use ICS, coordination problems are minimized. Additional commanders can also be added when tasks become too large for any single person to manage (SFFD 1995). For now, the main drawback of ICS is that it seldom extends beyond firefighters and police to include the emergency medical services, hospital, and public health personnel who would respond to a WMD attack. Since the mid–1990s, the federal government's Metropolitan Medical Response System (MMRS) program has worked to broaden the ICS model. MMRS focuses on training, preparing, linking, and coordinating this broader community, particularly in the first forty-eight hours of an emergency.

The 1991 Oakland and Berkeley Hills fires also revealed shortcomings in how agencies respond to large events that span city or county borders. These included incompatible radios, nonstandard fire hydrants, and other problems. California has since created a Standardized Emergency Management System (SEMS) initiative to develop and enforce common practices across jurisdictions. In principle, local departments that refuse to participate cannot receive state disaster preparedness funding.

Finally, a state that finds itself overwhelmed can request assistance from sister states and the federal government through the Emergency Management Assistance Compact (EMAC). In many cases, this may not be a practical option for fast-moving urban fires. Nevertheless, the Compact could easily come into play where disasters occur in small states or near a border.

10.5.1 Prospects

Despite initiatives like ICS, many responder agencies think of each other as rivals and seldom share information except for the very largest events. Even then, federal, state, and local agencies arriving at major incidents typically insist on using their own separate communication systems. Information technology solutions will not provide full value unless and until these fragmented systems are unified.

10.6 Conclusion

Firefighting is a potentially powerful policy lever for reducing the human and physical casualties that would otherwise be inflicted by a terrorist nuclear bomb. World War II experience shows that classical techniques like setting up water corridors and using civilians to fight fires until professional firefighters arrive can be very effective. These capabilities could be greatly improved by civil defense programs that told citizens how to protect themselves and their communities. Emerging technologies are also important. Computational fire modeling, in particular, could dramatically improve firefighters' ability to anticipate and manage conflagrations.

Advanced information technology can potentially make all of these strategies significantly more effective, particularly in the middle and late stages of a conflagration. In this sense, fighting large urban fires has become an information technology problem. To be effective, however, the new technologies must be taught, trained, and planned for. Preparing for large urban fires will inevitably draw resources away from other activities. Depending on the perceived WMD risk, this may not be warranted. There is also a deeper problem: even if such steps are warranted, politicians may feel that preparedness exercises—for example, asking firefighters to practice the construction of water corridors—will upset the public. This is especially true of civil defense campaigns designed to communicate with the public directly.

Notes

1. Atomic bombs range in yield from 0.1 to a maximum of 500 kilotons of TNT. Hydrogen bombs theoretically have unlimited yields and are typically measured in the millions of tons (Mt). Hydrogen bombs are so complicated that there is essentially no chance of a terrorist group acquiring one except by gift or theft (Malik 1985).

2. Casualties at Nagasaki were far smaller: 35,000 killed and 1.8 sq. miles destroyed. The lower figures are attributable to local topography around ground zero and the fact that a firestorm (section 10.2) failed to emerge. Interested readers should consult the definitive accounts in USBSS 1946a and Glasstone and Dolan 1977 for details.

3. The German experience has been well documented in Friedrich 2006, Taylor 2004, and Middlebrook 1980. Hoyt 2000 similarly provides an exhaustive catalog of the firebombing campaign against Japanese cities.

4. For example, the Tokyo fire emerged as a continuous inferno within fourteen minutes (Hoyt 2000) and the Hamburg fire became a square mile conflagration within twenty minutes (Taylor 2004). The initial Dresden fires similarly merged into a conflagration within half an hour (Taylor 2004).

5. Interested readers can find extended discussions of historic civilian and wartime fires in Postol 1986 and Brode and Small 1986.

6. This statement is only an approximation. Firestorms are so hot that radiant heat can ignite fuel hundreds of feet *outside* the fire. At Hamburg, however, this effect probably extended the initial firestorm area by no more than a few hundred yards in every direction (Beck 1986; Middlebrook 1980). The Hamburg firestorm was also spread by rapidly changing wind directions that continually injected new flames from unexpected directions (Beck 1986). However, this phenomenon was probably caused by bombs that exploded after the fire was already burning (Middlebrook 1980). This effect would not be present in fires caused by a single nuclear bomb.

7. Our discussion has followed traditional fire science practice by dividing mass fires into "conflagrations" and "firestorms." Since the 1960s, however, some researchers studying nuclear fire have advocated a new definition that divides large fires into "mass fires" that burn large areas simultaneously and "line fires" where the total area on fire at any one time is comparatively limited. This new distinction reflects the (still-controversial) claim that the self-organizing firestorm principle can give rise to both stationary Hamburg-type fires and—in the presence of high natural winds—moving fires as well (Eden 2004). Following this usage, our term "conflagration" would be called a "line fire." Suffice to say, the moral is the same: in the new language, nuclear strikes that evolve into "line fires" are potentially manageable, those that evolve into "mass fires" are not.

8. High-rise buildings discourage fire formation because fuel is dispersed vertically and the structures act as baffles. However, they also pose the greatest threat of loss of life and could divert first-responder resources to a handful of locations.

9. It is instructive to consider a flash-ignited firestorm that subsequently fails to spread. In this idealized case, the area ultimately burned depends entirely on the radius at which the flash energy per unit area falls below the threshold needed to start a storm. Interestingly, the Hiroshima fire was limited to regions within about 1.1 miles where the flash exceeded 10 cal/cm^2. Postwar scholars usually employed slightly higher thresholds up to 20 cal/cm^2, probably reflecting an implicit judgment that the slightly slower flash expected from very large Cold War warheads would provide a less effective ignition source.

10. For reasons explained in chapter 3, scientists expect flash (and therefore fire) to be much less important for small weapons. Similarly, World War II experience suggests that localized fires need to cover at least 0.5 sq. miles before a firestorm transition can occur. These conditions were easily satisfied by the large, 300-kiloton to 1-megaton airbursts invoked by Cold War fire researchers (Eden 2004). However, this would not be true of the far smaller, 10–15 kiloton bombs considered in most terrorism scenarios.

11. Many surviving personnel would also be diverted to rescue work and not available to fight the fire. In Hamburg, the storm spread so rapidly that firefighters were forced to concentrate on rescuing victims (Beck 1986). Furthermore, those first responders who did penetrate the firestorm area were often trapped and killed when hurricane-force winds collapsed buildings onto their escape routes (Postol 1986).

12. For the long history of classified nuclear fire simulations through the end of the Cold War, see Eden 2004.

13. Supercomputers typically perform hundreds of billions of operations per second compared to a typical PC's 100 million or so operations. The Los Alamos/Lawrence Livermore researchers used a computer called BlueGene/L. It can perform 360 trillion operations per second (Heller 2002).

14. San Francisco Fire Chief Robert Navarro, personal communication.

15. "Those things were awful. No one could ever hear you, the repeaters never worked to transmit your message, and they felt like they weighed about ten pounds" (George Bruce, personal communication).

16. William Storti, T/Lieutenant, San Francisco Fire Department, personal communication.

17. Larry Garde, Chief Engineer, Telecommunications and Information Services, San Francisco Fire Department, personal communication.

18. Asking grant recipients to share the cost of hardware may, of course, be desirable to the extent that it discourages the acquisition of costly or inefficient equipment.

19. The fact that most fire departments continue to use red fire engines even though yellow trucks have fewer accidents, fewer lawsuits, and lower insurance premiums shows that the process is far from perfect.

20. Battalion Chiefs John Murphy and Paul Chin, personal communication.

11

Public Health Preparedness for Chemical, Biological, Radiological, and Nuclear Weapons

Lois M. Davis and Jeanne S. Ringel

The U.S. public health and health-care delivery systems are important components of our nation's preparedness against terrorism and other public health threats (Trust for America's Health 2006). The September 11, 2001, terrorist attacks and the anthrax attacks later that year renewed government, public health, and medical personnel's awareness of chemical, biological, and, to a lesser extent, radiological and nuclear threats. It also underscored the importance of ensuring the nation's overall preparedness and ability to respond to terrorism and other public health emergencies. Toward this end, the federal government has invested more than $5 billion (Nelson et al. 2007) in public health preparedness at the state and local levels since 2001. With an investment of this magnitude questions naturally arise as to what return has been received. Is the nation prepared to effectively respond to the next public health emergency? This is a challenging question to answer for a number of reasons. First and foremost, there is no clear, consensus definition of what public health preparedness is and thus no specific goal against which to gauge progress. In addition, because the investment is relatively recent, there is very little literature evaluating the effectiveness of these federally funded programs. The effect of preparedness activities on the public health system more generally also complicates the question. Some states have leveraged preparedness resources to improve day-to-day public health activities (Staiti, Katz, and Hoadley 2003). However, others have cut state budgets in response to the federal increases, thereby shifting funding away from more traditional public health activities like tuberculosis prevention and control. Finally, the federal contribution to state and local public health preparedness has declined more than 20 percent over the past several years, raising concerns that much of the post-2001 progress will not be sustained (NACCHO 2007).

This chapter presents a broad overview of the nation's public health response system, recent efforts to improve preparedness, and options for moving forward. Section 11.1 reviews federal efforts to define WMD threats and priorities. Section 11.2 looks at the current national response framework for a coordinated response in four functional areas. Section 11.3 looks at the issues in implementing this framework at the state and local levels, with a focus on coordination issues. Section 11.4 assesses the current state of public health preparedness. Finally, section 11.5 presents some brief conclusions.

11.1   Characterizing and Prioritizing WMD Threats

From a planning perspective, there is considerable overlap between public health emergency preparedness for natural disasters and for WMD. While WMD do require some unique preparation and response activities, they also share many public health functions with natural threats like pandemic influenza or hurricanes. Public health agencies are increasingly adopting an all-hazards planning approach that is flexible enough to accommodate different types of emergencies. That is, they have focused resources on improving preparedness to conduct activities or purchase equipment (e.g., interoperable communications) that can be used for both WMD response and other public health emergencies like pandemic influenza or hurricanes.

Public health planning is also complicated by uncertainty about the type and scale of the anticipated attack: "Future terrorist attacks could vary in many different ways, such as the agents or weapons employed, the size of an attack, the kind of release, the location (rural area or a city), and whether it occurs inside a building or outdoors" (Davis et al. 2003). Perhaps the most important dimension is advance warning. Advance warning is common for many natural disasters (e.g., hurricanes, West Nile virus) and would also be realistic for some WMD based on contagious agents (e.g., smallpox). In such cases, public health officials will often have time to put surveillance systems and other public health measures in place as the disease spreads over time.[1] The situation is different for other forms of WMD like noncontagious biological, chemical, and radiological agents. In these cases, attacks may only be detected after victims have been exposed. This makes advance preparation key to ensuring U.S. preparedness.

Understanding the similarities and differences between different threats is the first step in informed planning and prioritizing scarce resources. The Centers for Disease Control and Prevention (CDC) has prepared an important framework for understanding terrorist-related public health threats. In the case of bioterrorism, the CDC categorizes agents along four separate dimensions: (1) the anticipated number of illnesses and deaths; (2) the ability to reach large populations based on the difficulty of mass producing and distributing the agent, the agent's stability, and the potential for person-to-person transmission; (3) public perception and the potential for fear and civil disruption; and (4) special public health preparedness needs like stockpile requirements, enhanced surveillance, or diagnostic tools for responding to an attack. These dimensions have, in turn, been used to assess priorities. For example, Category A agents like anthrax, botulism, tularemia, smallpox, plague, and viral hemorrhagic fevers (e.g., Ebola) rank high across all four dimensions (Khan 2003; CDC n.d.(d)). Category B bioterrorism agents rank comparatively lower across the four dimensions but still require substantial preparedness investments. Examples include brucellosis, food-safety threats, and ricin toxin. Finally, Category C bioterrorism agents do not currently present a high bioterrorism risk. These include emerging pathogens that could be engineered for mass dissemination like Hanta and Nipah viruses (CDC n.d (a)).

The CDC similarly lists various chemical weapons categories, including biotoxins, blister agents/vesicants, blood agents, caustics (acids), choking/lung/pulmonary agents, incapacitating agents, long-acting anticoagulants, metals, nerve agents, organic solvents, riot control agents/tear gas, toxic alcohols, and vomiting agents (CDC n.d.(e)). Unlike the CDC's lists of biological agents, however, the list of chemical agents is not prioritized. The CDC similarly lists various radioactive isotopes that might be used to make weapons and provides information for the public and professionals on how to cope with them (CDC n.d (c)). The CDC stops short of prioritizing these threats or assessing their importance relative to chemical or biological agents.

11.2 National Response Framework

The National Response Plan (NRP) outlines a "single, comprehensive approach to domestic incident management to prevent, prepare for, respond to, and recover from terrorist attacks, major disasters, and other emergencies" (DHS 2006). The NRP takes a functional approach by grouping the required planning, support, resources, program implementation, and emergency service capabilities into Emergency Support Functions (ESFs). One basic tenet of the NRP is that incidents should be handled at the lowest jurisdictional level possible. This means that all responses are local in the first instance and that the federal government's role is to supplement state and local resources if and when they are overwhelmed and at the request of state governors. DHS can also declare an "Incident of National Significance" (INS) in consultation with the White House and other agencies whenever "[there is] an actual or potential high-impact event that requires robust coordination of the federal response in order to save lives and minimize damage, and [to] provide the basis for long-term community and economic recovery" (DHS 2006).

Once a potential or actual INS is declared, federal medical assistance to state and local levels is coordinated under ESF-8. This assistance is subdivided into four functional areas: (1) assessment of public health and medical needs (including behavioral health), (2) public health surveillance, (3) medical-care personnel, and (4) medical equipment and supplies. These areas, in turn, embrace a wide range of specific activities including, but not limited to, increasing medical-care surge capacity, implementing a quarantine, deploying medical countermeasures and medical supplies from the Strategic National Stockpile (SNS), evacuating hospital patients, and identifying victims and providing mortuary services. Other activities (e.g., planning, coordination within and across agencies, and communication) cut across these core functional areas and support them. We discuss each functional area separately in what follows.

11.2.1 Functional Area 1: Assessment of Public Health/Medical Needs

Federal response depends on assessing the event's impact and identifying state and local needs. Institutionally, the federal government starts this process by deploying an Emergency Response Team, Advance Element (ERT-A). Team members usually include a Federal Emergency Management Agency (FEMA) representative, a state representative, and various specialists. Depending on the emergency, these can include hazardous materials (hazmat), medical, mass-care, and/or infrastructure experts. Within this team, the medical specialist has the primary responsibility for assessing medical infrastructure (hospitals, clinics, and pharmacies), environmental health, sanitation, special needs populations, emergency medical services, and patient evacuation needs and capabilities. In general, the ERT-A works closely with state and local authorities to facilitate their requests for assistance.

While the ERT-A focuses on damage to infrastructure, state and local public health authorities are responsible for assessing health needs. This information is used to help identify, prioritize, and target relief efforts where the need is greatest. However, the work can still take several days and new technologies are currently being developed to collect these data faster. For example, a North Carolina team of state and local public health officials has developed a powerful new rapid needs assessment system that takes advantage of handheld computers, geographic information system (GIS) mapping software, and Global Positioning System (GPS) technologies. When Hurricane Charley hit North Carolina in 2004, the team was able to collect 210 surveys from 30 block groups, analyze the data, and prepare a complete report overnight (NACCHO 2007).

The demand for hospital care will surge following any large-scale disaster. This makes it critical for public health authorities to be able to identify available hospital beds and staff at the local level. Information technology systems for monitoring available beds would allow public health and medical-care providers to better manage the influx of patients and demand for medical supplies. Denver Health's Hospital Available Beds for Emergencies and Disasters (HAvBed) system provides a typical example of this technology. It combines data from existing systems (e.g., databases that support hospital divert status) to provide real-time information about availability (Philips and Knebel 2007).

Once resource needs are identified, local authorities can decide whether they need state assistance and states can request help from the federal government. If a state anticipates that its resources may be exceeded in an emergency, a governor can request assistance from the federal government and/or other states through mutual aid and assistance agreements (DHS 2008). In many circumstances, this process works well. However, Hurricane Katrina provides an example of how the scope of a disaster can become so large—and damage or destroy so many local resources (e.g., infrastructure)—that the public health system has great difficulty assessing medical needs in a timely way.[2] In situations where states may be overwhelmed due to the catastrophic nature of a disaster or public health emergency, the federal government may want to be proactive in reaching out to states and helping them to develop a formal assistance request.

11.2.2 Functional Area 2: Public Health Surveillance

Public health surveillance has been described as the "ongoing, systematic collection, analysis, and interpretation of health-related data essential to the planning, implementation, and evaluation of public health practice, closely integrated with the timely dissemination of these data to those responsible for prevention and control" (Thacker and Berkelman 1988). Surveillance is a primary function of public health in both in its day-to-day and emergency response roles.

Surveillance would play a critical role in determining that a biological attack has occurred, identifying the agent, evaluating the likelihood of transmission, and identifying exposed populations (Bullock 2002). Because biological agents can be released in an aerosol form, it could take days or even weeks to detect an attack. Given that time is of the essence in treating these illnesses and mitigating transmission, improved surveillance systems could potentially save many lives.

Traditional public health surveillance consists of both passive and active systems. *Passive surveillance systems* depend on physicians and hospitals to identify and voluntarily report cases. The National Notifiable Disease Surveillance System (NNDSS) is an example of such a system and is built around a state-developed list of notifiable diseases.[3] Physicians who diagnose these diseases must report the information to state authorities, who, in turn, are required to compile the information and share it with the CDC. However, in many cases, the reporting process is still paper-based. This means that it can take a long time for information to pass from the local level to the state and/or the CDC. In addition, reporting obligations are seldom enforced so that underreporting is thought to be a problem. It is estimated that passive surveillance systems only capture 5 to 60 percent (Campos-Outcault, England, and Porter 1991; Marier 1977) of reportable-disease cases. This delays response actions and results in some cases that could have been prevented (CDC 1992).

These concerns limit the usefulness of passive systems like NNDSS for detecting biological attacks quickly. That said, initiatives are currently underway to improve these systems. Several steps focus on improving identification and diagnosis by physicians and labs. For example, the CDC is taking steps to educate physicians by publishing detailed case definitions for likely biological agents and posting webcasts, slide presentations, and other physician training materials on its website (CDC n.d.(d)). The CDC is also taking steps to enhance laboratory capacity for identifying agents and confirming physician diagnoses. The *Laboratory Response Network* (LRN) is a nationwide network of local, state, and federal public health, food testing, veterinary diagnostic, and environmental testing laboratories that provides the laboratory infrastructure for responding to biological and chemical terrorism and/or other public health emergencies (CDC 2007b). The CDC also supports training and new equipment to build member laboratories' capacity and speed.[4]

In addition, the CDC is working to make reporting more timely. Its *National Electronic Disease Surveillance System* (NEDSS) uses information technology to transfer surveillance data securely over the Internet. However, the system has yet to be implemented in all states. The CDC is also working to improve the capacity of public health departments to receive and analyze disease reports. The CDC (2003a) recommends that public health departments maintain a single, well-publicized phone number for receiving urgent case reports around the clock and that a trained public health official respond to all calls within thirty minutes. However, a recent study of nineteen local health departments found that just half (53 percent) had the recommended single phone number and that the mean response time was fifty-five minutes (Dausey, Lurie, and Diamond 2005).[5]

Unlike passive systems, *active surveillance systems* require public health personnel to (a) actively pursue information about new cases from physicians, hospitals, and laboratories, and (b) follow up known cases. They also require a cadre of trained epidemiologists to compile and analyze these data. In recent years, the focus has been on developing new methods like *syndromic surveillance*, which aims to speed detection by analyzing symptoms data before physicians have arrived at a diagnosis. Data sources are usually electronic and come from emergency rooms, physicians' offices, over-the-counter pharmaceutical sales, and absenteeism reports. These sources are analyzed at frequent intervals and used to identify disease clusters for aggressive, targeted investigations (CDC 2004d; Stoto, Schonlau, and Mariano 2004).

The federal government has made a substantial investment in syndromic surveillance at the national, state, and local levels. At the national level, its *BioSense program* generates near-real-time surveillance data from Veterans Administration and Defense Department health-care facilities, private and public hospitals, state and regional surveillance systems, and national laboratories (CDC 2007a). The data are then analyzed using sophisticated statistical methods. Access to these results is provided over a secure web page limited to the CDC, state and local public health authorities, and participating health-care organizations (CDC 2004d; Loonsk 2004). Because syndromic surveillance methods are still relatively new, they have yet to be fully evaluated. However, there is growing skepticism about the value of syndromic surveillance for detecting biological attacks. One survey found that the effectiveness of syndromic surveillance is limited by the inherent trade-offs between sensitivity, timeliness, and false positives (Stoto, Schonlau, and Mariano 2004). New York City's health department, which implemented syndromic surveillance in the early 1990s, similarly found that many signals turned out to be nothing and that investigating them wasted valuable resources (McKenna 2007).

Other forms of surveillance rely on *environmental monitoring systems* to detect biological or chemical attacks. DHS's *BioWatch program* uses pathogen detectors to collect airborne particles onto filters. These filters are periodically retrieved and analyzed in laboratories. Some have questioned whether the BioWatch program is a reasonable and effective response to bioterrorism. The primary concern is that the system is best suited to detecting large-scale releases (Shea and Lister 2003). The Central Intelligence Agency (2003) has suggested that this threat may be less important than small-scale attacks that the system might not detect.

There are a wide range of surveillance systems in place at the national, state, and local levels (Stoto 2003). One problem with this patchwork of systems is that it can be difficult to synthesize information from multiple sources to get a clear picture of what is happening, both within a state and at the national level. Improvements in information technology and efforts to make reporting formats more consistent have helped, but critical gaps remain.

11.2.3 Functional Area 3: Medical Personnel

Since 2001, the federal government has invested in improving the public health and health-care workforce's ability to respond to terrorism. Major initiatives include funding academic Centers for Public Health Preparedness, cooperative agreements with states to enhance preparedness, and efforts to develop and build systems to coordinate medical volunteers. One major stumbling block has been the absence of a clear definition of what a "prepared workforce" is. Moreover, it is not clear who is included in the public health workforce. In current usage, the term includes "all those responsible for providing the essential services of public health regardless of the organization in which they work" (HHS 1994). This definition is very broad and includes many occupations and nongovernment workers. These include dentists, physicians, nurses, social workers, educators, biostatisticians, and epidemiologists. For example, a nurse in a private hospital that works to prevent nosocomial infections (i.e., diseases that originate in a hospital) would be included. By this measure, there are probably half a million public health workers in the United States, although the vast majority (86 percent) are employed by public health agencies at the federal, state, and local levels (HHS 2000).

While public health's presence in emergency or disaster response is not new, there has been a renewed emphasis on the need for better integration of emergency preparedness and public health since September 11. The emergency preparedness mission has changed the mix of personnel and skills that public health agencies need. This includes a new emphasis on hiring people with emergency management or military backgrounds with expertise in incident management. Integrating these new hires with more traditional public health staff has created predictable tensions. The new hires worry that public health's traditional emphasis on careful analysis could impede action in an emergency. For their part, traditional public health staff worry about the "militarization" of public health, arguing that the traditional focus on providing care for the public and understanding community needs remains valuable and could be overlooked.

Federal, state, and local authorities have also developed significant training programs to help ensure that the public health workforce is prepared to respond to a large-scale emergency. That said, it is still too soon to say how effective these programs have been. One widely discussed idea has been to develop emergency preparedness core competencies for public health departments. These competencies would, in turn, provide a yardstick for evaluating the effectiveness of training. In the meantime, the CDC has developed multiple initiatives to deliver training. First, the CDC's Centers for Public Health Preparedness program funds colleges and universities to develop, deliver, and evaluate preparedness education programs for public health workers, health-care providers, students, and others (CDC n.d.(d)). Topics include the use of incident command systems, personal protective equipment, worker safety, and various tabletop exercises. Although a number of centers have been funded and various program activities undertaken, no systematic evaluation of this overall model has yet been conducted. Second, the CDC has joined forces with the National Association of County and City Health Officials (NACCHO) to fund eight Advanced Practice Centers (APCs). The program's goal is to identify and develop demonstration programs and practices that can be shared with other health departments.[6] Third, the CDC disseminates emergency preparedness training resources directly through its website.[7] Training materials are provided for different scenarios (e.g., bioterrorism, chemical, and radiation emergencies), including such topics as treating mass casualties, administering mass prophylaxis, and decontamination procedures. The program is addressed to a wide range of audiences including first responders, physicians and hospitals, and public health personnel. However, its effectiveness as a vehicle for distributing training materials has yet to be systematically evaluated.

Absenteeism is also expected to be a problem. Surveys indicate that one-fourth to one-third of the health-care workforce may not show up for work during a biological, chemical, or radiological attack because of fears for their personal and/or their family's safety. The problem is particularly acute for attacks involving contagious pathogens (Qureshi et al. 2005). Various strategies have been implemented to encourage workers to respond in an emergency. First, at least one state has used its CDC grant money to provide standby pay of $200 per month for public health nurses who obtain training and commit to participate in an emergency. Second, some communities have promised to give families of public health and medical personnel higher priority for drugs and vaccines if an attack occurs. Third, many jurisdictions have tried to enhance workers' personal safety by purchasing training and personal protective equipment.

Finally, the day-to-day public health and medical workforce is not large enough to treat mass casualties. As such, supplemental personnel would be needed to carry out an effective medical response. These personnel will be more effective if several issues are addressed ahead of time. For instance, medical personnel coming from other states are generally not licensed to provide medical care at the attack site. Allowing these personnel to treat victims could create legal liability for volunteers and the organizations that host them. Efforts are currently underway to promote agreements in which states would recognize each other's medical licenses in the event of a large-scale disaster. Even then, however, there would still be no quick way to verify out-of-state credentials and skill levels. This could force volunteers to sit idle until their credentials were verified. This was a problem in the response to Hurricane Katrina. Although many health-care professionals volunteered, public health authorities lacked systems to coordinate volunteers and match their skills to identified needs. The absence of an agreed-on method for verifying health-care workers' credentials and skills was particularly problematic (Ringel et al. 2007). Congress has since moved to fill this gap by instructing the Health Resources and Services Administration (HRSA) to create an Emergency System for Advance Registration of Health Professions Volunteers (ESAR-VHP). The goal of the program is to assist states in developing standardized preregistration systems for medical volunteers (HRSA n.d.). Despite progress, the system has yet to be fully implemented.

Still other federal, state, and local program levels are designed to facilitate relief across state lines if mass casualties occur. For example, the federally coordinated

National Disaster Medical System (NDMS) is designed to route medical personnel, supplies, and equipment to affected areas. The heart of the system consists of rapid response Disaster Medical Assistance Teams (DMATs) that deploy with enough supplies to maintain operations for seventy-two hours.[8] Once activated, DMAT members become federal employees; this automatically means that their licenses and certifications are recognized by all states and protects them from malpractice claims (HHS 2007). However, the DMAT system encountered some problems during the response to Hurricane Katrina. In Houston, for example, available personnel were overwhelmed by the volume of evacuees (approximately 68,000) who arrived at the triage center in a short period of time. One interviewee reported that DMAT teams were requested but were never sent or did not arrive in time (Ringel et al. 2007).

The Emergency Mutual Assistance Compact (EMAC) provides another mechanism that states can use to request medical assistance following major disasters. It provides formal structures for requesting and receiving aid and speeds the process by resolving many key issues—for example, liability and reimbursement for equipment and personnel—in advance (EMAC n.d.). HHS's Medical Reserve Corps (MRC) similarly helps communities recruit, train, and credential medical volunteers to meet surge demand in an emergency. Volunteers include physicians, nurses, pharmacists, and various nonmedical personnel who provide administrative and logistical support skills. The MRC currently includes more than 120,000 volunteers and is organized into 689 units (MRC n.d.).

11.2.4 Functional Area 4: Medical Equipment and Supplies

An effective response depends on medical equipment, supplies, and pharmaceuticals. The CDC-administered Strategic National Stockpile (SNS) is the country's primary mechanism for distributing medical equipment, supplies, and pharmaceuticals in an emergency. SNS can deliver "Push Packages" to any state within twelve hours. Because the Push Packages are designed to arrive when needs are still being assessed, they contain a broad range of medical assets that might be needed. Thereafter, more targeted pharmaceuticals and/or supplies can be deployed from SNS's vendor-managed inventories (i.e., caches stored in the vendors' warehouses) within twenty-four to thirty-six hours (CDC n.d.(e)).[9] On arrival, state and local officials would immediately take control of SNS materials and assume responsibility for distributing them.

Many states and local governments also maintain their own medical materiel caches. These stockpiles are paid for from a variety of sources, including the CDC, DHS, HRSA, and state and local tax dollars. The caches provide a hedge in case SNS is overwhelmed by a nationwide event (e.g., pandemic influenza) and can also be used to fill the twelve-hour gap before Push Packages arrive. However, the existence of multiple stockpiles raises coordination issues in terms of which populations are covered and which materials are stockpiled. This problem is further aggravated by differences in how stockpile programs (and grant authorities) define geographic coverage, likely threats, and deployment time frames (ASTHO 2005). Better planning and coordination are needed to eliminate the resulting duplication and gaps between stockpiles.

11.3   Implementing the National Response Plan at the State and Local Levels

ESF-8 is limited to specifying how federal agencies would support the response to an Incident of National Significance, facilitating coordination, and providing guidance for the development of detailed supplemental plans and procedures at the federal, state, and local levels. It does not, however, impose a specific state and local response strategy (DHS 2006). Because public health is a state function under the Constitution, there is substantial variation in how states organize their public health systems. This means there is no "one-size-fits-all" model for how a public health and medical-care emergency response should be carried out. CDC guidance to states explicitly recognizes this fact, noting that states differ in many ways (e.g., size, public health system organization, risks) and "addresses important areas of preparedness and response that can be tailored to the needs of the individual jurisdiction" (CDC 2001). This section briefly introduces the key players who would be involved in a response, recent efforts to coordinate their planning and response activities, and how they would conduct risk communication to the public before, during, and after an event.[10] Finally, we turn to coordination problems that tend to impede key players' planning and preparedness activities.

11.3.1   Key Players

Many players are involved at the state and local levels in implementing the National Response Plan's four functional areas. These include state and local public health departments, hospitals and health-care providers, hospital associations, pharmacies, law enforcement, fire departments, National Guard, emergency management agencies, emergency medical services, Red Cross, and mental health and social service providers. Of these, public health departments, hospitals, and health-care providers tend to be the key players in implementing the health and medical response at the local level.

Public Health Departments   State public health systems vary along several dimensions. Some states have a freestanding agency; others house public health within a larger department of health and human services. In some states, the system is centralized, with a state agency exercising direct control over local health departments staffed by state employees. Elsewhere, the system is more decentralized and local health departments exercise greater control over public health policy and service delivery (Wasserman et al. 2006). Finally, there are states that fall in between these two extremes. Public health departments also differ in the services they provide. Some health departments provide direct medical care through public hospitals and clinics; others limit themselves to ensuring that health-care services are available and facilitating connections between providers and patients. Given these differences, response strategies will clearly differ from community to community. Some public health departments have the personnel to provide emergency medical-care services, whereas others must rely on hospitals and other private health-care workers to provide services. While variation in how the public health system is structured in different states is not inherently bad—indeed, it provides useful room for experiment—it does complicate the process of delineating public health departments' roles in responding to an emergency.

Emergency response is most effective when all organizations understand their roles and responsibilities. During Hurricane Katrina, roles and responsibilities were often unclear. For example, some special needs shelters were inadequately staffed because it was not clear which agency was responsible for providing medical personnel (Ringel et al. 2007). Response organizations can avoid these problems by discussing the allocation of tasks as an explicit part of the planning process. Coordination is often complicated, however, by the wide range of organizations involved: "The U.S. 'public health system' is not a single entity, but rather a loosely affiliated network of more than 3,000 federal, state, and local public health agencies, often working closely with private sector voluntary and professional health associations" (Trust for America's Health 2006).

Hospitals and Health-Care Providers   According to the American Hospital Association's 2005 annual hospital survey, there are 5,756 registered hospitals in the United States including 4,936 community hospitals (American Hospital Association n.d.). Other health-care providers include clinicians, insurance plans, group purchasers of health-care services, and independent physicians and networks. These can be public, private/for-profit, or private/not-for-profit organizations. Not surprisingly, communication, collaboration, and planning among these various entities are limited (IOM 2003).

11.3.2   Planning Prior to an Event

Prior to September 11, many state and local public health departments lacked plans for responding to terrorist events.[11] The Public Health Security and Bioterrorism Preparedness and Response Act of 2002 was designed to close this gap by authorizing additional funds for federal bioterrorism preparedness programs and grants to states. The CDC and HRSA are responsible for distributing these grants to the states (and ultimately localities) through cooperative agreements. CDC cooperative agreements focus on state and local preparedness planning (including SNS stockpile deployment), surveillance, epidemiology, and laboratory resources; information technology (including the Health Alert Network (HAN)); threat communication; and education and workforce training (Trust for America's Health 2006). Funds are apportioned between state and local jurisdictions based on "consensus, approval or concurrence between state and local public health officials for the proposed use of these funds" (CDC 2004b).

The CDC and HRSA cooperative agreements also establish goals and benchmarks for measuring public health preparedness, although meeting the specified critical benchmarks does not necessarily demonstrate adequate preparation. Since 2005, critical benchmarks for public health agencies included developing "scalable plans" for local, statewide, and regional responses to bioterrorism, catastrophic infectious disease, and other public health emergencies; maintaining a 24/7 system for activating emergency responses; conducting exercises to test all plans on an annual basis; reviewing and assessing changes needed to comply with the National Incident Management System (NIMS); conducting vulnerability assessments; updating and refining state, city, and regional response plans to correct deficiencies uncovered during exercises or actual events; and expanding communication capabilities (CDC 2004a).

The HRSA cooperative agreements were similarly intended to support hospital preparedness (Trust for America's Health 2006). Priority areas included administration, surge capacity, emergency medical services, links to public health departments, education and training, and preparedness exercises. The HRSA funds were distributed according to a population-based formula that required states to distribute at least 80 percent of all funds to hospitals, emergency medical systems, and other health-care entities (Trust for America's Health 2006). The CDC and HRSA also created a set of crosscutting benchmarks to encourage their grantees to cooperate with one another (Trust for America's Health 2006). These included requiring recipients to specify how public health departments and the hospital/health-care system would be integrated into NIMS-compliant incident management systems, as well as training staff to respond in a coordinated, nonoverlapping manner.

Other entities have also developed planning requirements. For example, the Joint Commission on the Accreditation of Healthcare Organizations (JCAHO) now requires health-care organizations to prepare emergency plans that address mitigation, preparedness, response, and recovery; perform hazard vulnerability assessments; conduct drills for a wide range of contingencies; and develop procedures that address emergency care, evacuation, and decontamination. While JCAHO

(2005) requires members to adopt an "all-hazards" command structure, no specific system (e.g., ICS) is required. JCAHO (2005) has also developed a planning guide for the many small rural and suburban communities that have found themselves struggling to meet post–September 11 mandates. The guide provides strategies and planning tools that health-care providers, public health leaders, elected or appointed officials, and others can use to establish an effective community-based management planning process.

Finally, JCAHO (2006) has published a report detailing the health-care community's responsibility for planning, building, and setting up "surge hospitals" as temporary stopgap facilities in an emergency. Drawing on Hurricane Katrina, the report describes what surge hospitals are, what planning is needed to support them, how they can be set up, and who should take responsibility for them. Local, state, and federal authorities can use this information to prepare detailed plans. JCAHO is also drafting a set of minimum standards to govern safety and care standards in these settings.

11.3.3   Incident Management

A large-scale bioterrorism attack would involve multiple federal, state, local, and tribal governments, private-sector companies, and nongovernmental organizations (e.g., the American Red Cross), each of which has its own characteristic disciplines, command structures, communication systems, and emergency management protocols. Response organizations have long recognized the need for a unified, nationwide emergency management system that could coordinate these disparate elements.

By the mid-1980s, fire, police, paramedics, and other first responders had developed a common Incident Command System (ICS). However, most hospitals and public health agencies used their own incident command and management systems, and many personnel had less training on ICS than their emergency-responder counterparts. In 1987, the Hospital Council of Northern California moved to bridge this gap by creating an ICS-like Hospital Emergency Incident Command System (HEICS). HEICS defines a common management structure, responsibilities, reporting channels, and standard nomenclature to help hospitals communicate with other emergency responders. Although adoption remains voluntary, HEICS has been widely adopted across the western United States (San Mateo County Health Services 1998).

September 11 accelerated efforts to improve coordination between hospitals, health agencies, first responders, and other response organizations. In 2003, the White House directed the Secretary of Homeland Security to develop a National Incident Management System (NIMS) (U.S. Government 2003a). NIMS provides a nationwide template and unified approach for incident management, standardized command and management structures, and a framework for cooperation in preparedness, mutual aid, and resource management (FEMA n.d.). In 2005, experience with Hurricane Katrina and fears of pandemic influenza brought renewed attention to the gap between hospitals and other first responders. The National Bioterrorism Hospital Preparedness Program (NBHPP) explicitly requires participating hospitals and health-care systems to adopt NIMS and train health personnel in ICS (HHS 2005c).

11.3.4 Risk Communications with the Public

Public behavior is a key part of preparedness. Preemergency risk communication seeks to educate employers and the general public about a threat and how to mitigate losses and take protective actions (Davis et al. 2003). Here, the goal is to change people's behavior. Successful public health campaigns (e.g., seat belts, smoking, disaster preparedness) raise awareness, offer straightforward guidance, and are periodically reinforced over time (NRC 1989). They also recognize that people differ in the amount of information they want, the degree to which they feel they can exercise control over exposure and/or remediation, and their tolerance for risk. This means that multiple messages must be devised to reach and persuade different populations and groups.

Emergency risk communication, on the other hand, provides warnings and guidance immediately before and during a specific emergency. This needs to be an interactive process. Successful communication should not only satisfy the public that they have been adequately informed within the limits of available knowledge, but also improve officials' available information (NRC 1989). Because risk communication is tightly linked to risk management, improved risk communication often means modifying previous risk analyses to reflect the public's concerns.

Although much energy has been devoted to developing and disseminating risk messages, much less research has been done to gain a systematic understanding of how and why risk communication succeeds. Common problems include (1) establishing credibility, (2) creating understandable and informative messages, (3) preparing messages in an emergency, (4) capturing the intended audience's attention, and (5) providing sufficient information to draw satisfactory conclusions (NRC 1989). Poorly crafted, inadequately prepared, or conflicting messages can quickly erode trust that authorities need in order to provide leadership. Finally, communications must use language and concepts that their target audience readily understands. Failed risk communication can make it hard for the public to prioritize and/or decide what to do in an emergency (NRC 1989).

The 2001 anthrax attacks revealed important weaknesses in how public health messages about bioterrorism and other public health emergencies are communicated to the public. Stein et al. (2004) interviewed federal employees who had potentially been exposed to anthrax to find out why they did/did not follow the government's advice to take prophylactic antibiotics. Employees who decided against prophylaxis usually followed the advice of private physicians, whereas those who complied had usually consulted multiple sources. The study highlighted the need for better integration between the public and private health-care systems and the importance of equipping private physicians for their role in helping their patients decide what to do during a crisis.

A second study of postal workers (and Capitol Hill staff) exposed to the 2001 anthrax attacks found that some minorities felt that they had been excluded from communication and planning. The finding confirmed the importance of developing individualized messages for different segments of the population (Blanchard et al. 2005). Since then, there have been several successful examples of targeted communication campaigns during more recent outbreaks. For example, during the SARS outbreak in 2003, the New York City health department worked with universities and high-tech companies to reach their Asian employees and others who traveled frequently to Asia (Stoto et al. 2005). In California, a mosquito control district similarly developed special pamphlets, posters, and other communication materials in multiple languages to communicate the risk of West Nile virus (Stoto et al. 2005). That said, many jurisdictions are still poorly equipped to communicate in multiple languages and lack established relationships with key community leaders and groups. This is particularly true for ethnic-minority and low-income communities, who may have a more guarded attitude toward government, including public health agencies. For instance, Stoto et al. (2005) found that language and cultural barriers continued to hamper the California Public Health Department's efforts to communicate with Asian Americans during the SARS outbreak. Finally, many health departments have found themselves overwhelmed by the sheer number of calls that they receive during outbreaks. This can divert capacity that would otherwise be used to communicate with "hard-to-reach" populations, including ethnic minorities, migrant workers, and homeless people.

Post-anthrax experiences with disease outbreaks and other nonterrorist emergencies have also uncovered examples of inadequate communication plans and poor coordination when local and state health departments, hospitals, and local officials communicate to the public. For example, Stoto et al. (2005) found that New York City health department officials had trouble communicating what they felt was a clear scientific case for using pesticides to control the West Nile virus. Despite their best efforts, public concerns over increased pesticide risk continued to rise over time. State and local health officials also had trouble speaking with one voice, reaching out to minority and affected communities, and addressing the worried well. While

Louisiana officials found that local media tended to embrace their message, national coverage was more sensational (Stoto et al. 2005). Similarly, Colorado health officials noted that state and local press releases often reported different numbers of West Nile cases, largely because some organizations reported "cases under investigation" instead of "confirmed cases." This encouraged the media to distrust both sources of information.[12] At least some of these difficulties may have been caused by the media's failure to understand the public health system and the science behind contagious outbreaks. HHS has since developed a reference guide that reporters can read to educate themselves about terrorism and/or public health emergencies (HHS 2005b).

11.3.5 Coordination

Local public health departments must be able to work seamlessly with each other and with a variety of other actors, including hospitals and/or hospital councils; medical providers; the CDC and other federal agencies; emergency medical services, fire, law enforcement, and other first responders; emergency management; and interagency disaster planning groups and task forces.[13] Furthermore, these organizations must work together on many different issues. Some of the most important ones are illustrated in figure 11.1.

Coordination is further complicated by the fact that—unlike law enforcement, fire, and other emergency responders—public health agencies seldom have com-

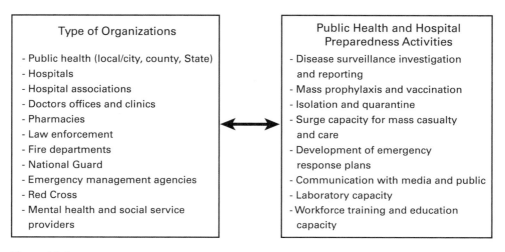

Figure 11.1
Typical preparedness activities and organizations involved

mand and control authority over the resources they need. Instead, they must rely on a host of other individuals and organizations like health-care providers, emergency responders, and other public health agencies (e.g., in bordering jurisdictions and other levels of government) to mount an effective response (Stoto et al. 2005).

Previous studies have found that public health authorities and hospitals face especially high coordination barriers. These include differences in funding; differences in organizational mission, culture, and priorities; overlapping roles that can lead to turf battles; incompatible information management systems; and differences in leaders' commitment to success (GAO 1992; Edwards and Stern 1998; Martinson 1999; Lasker et al. 1997). Differences in mission and culture run especially deep for collaborations between public and private entities like health departments and for-profit hospitals. For example, while many for-profit hospitals include community service in their missions, hospital CEOs differ widely in how they see their role in public health preparedness and the extent to which they encourage personnel to participate in preparedness (Davis et al. 2006a) "Because of its history, structure, and particularly the highly competitive market in health services that has evolved since the collapse of health-care reform efforts in the early 1990s, the health-care delivery system often does not interact effectively with other components of the public health system" (IOM 2002).

There are also deep disconnects between public health and medicine. Focus-group interviews have shown that public health professionals see medicine as an arm of public health, whereas medical professionals view public health as a subspecialty of medicine (Lasker et al. 1997). Focus-group participants were also unable to articulate or agree on a precise definition of their relationship and few could describe how the activities of the other discipline are relevant to what they did. This may be because members of the two fields have had little or no experience working with each other's discipline (Davis et al. 2006a). The situation is aggravated by the ongoing restructuring of health-care, including the replacement of individual practitioners with corporations, the changing role of government, and the severe fiscal constraints imposed by managed care, government downsizing, and privatization.

Although federal bioterrorism funding is specifically aimed at encouraging collaboration, health departments and hospitals still do not fully understand each other's roles or the benefits of coordination (Davis et al. 2006a). Preparedness exercises continue to show that public health departments are often unaware of hospitals' response plans. Conversely, hospitals often fail to include local health departments in their exercises. The fact that states and localities manage CDC and HRSA cooperative-agreement funds differently only adds to the problem.

Public health agencies, general hospitals, and emergency responders also differ in the priority they place on preparing for different types of WMD (Davis et al.

2006a). This reflects differences in organizational mission. A 2003 survey found that local health departments tend to focus on biological events; hospitals, EMS agencies, and local emergency management offices tend to prepare for chemical events (albeit with biological events a close second); and law enforcement and fire departments tend to focus on conventional explosives and then chemical incidents. To the extent that these perceptions translate into different investment patterns, coordination becomes even more complicated.

Law enforcement and other first responders would have multiple responsibilities in a public health emergency. These could include enforcing quarantines, managing crowds, or participating in joint investigations with public health departments (Davis et al. 2006b). Many observers have criticized the lack of integration between the public health and medical communities (Hamburg 2001). In a 2003 survey, Davis et al. (2006b) found that only a quarter of all law enforcement agencies and a third of all fire departments reported having participated in joint preparedness activities with local health departments since September 11. On the other hand, a significant number of local health departments reported working with law enforcement and fire departments during the same period. This inconsistency suggests a disconnect between how emergency responders and public health assess progress in integrating their preparedness activities and that improvements are still needed. Davis et al. (2006a) have also conducted a series of case studies to examine integration between public health agencies and hospitals. Because JCAHO has emphasized disaster preparedness for many years, hospitals tend to have a longer history of establishing preparedness and coordination relationships with first responders. By contrast, first responders have seldom seen public health departments as important partners, much less leaders, until recently (Davis et al. 2006a).

11.4   Taking Stock

So far, we have treated preparedness as a series of individual problems and reviewed the various programs that have been launched to address them. What we would really like, however, is a global assessment of the nation's ability to respond to a WMD attack. This section briefly reviews the overall state of the public health system and the prospects for improving it. We then review the sometimes controversial attempts to assess preparedness as a whole.

11.4.1   Public Health Infrastructure

The U.S. public health system had deteriorated significantly in the years before September 11 (IOM 2003). Deficiencies included outdated and vulnerable technologies, a poorly prepared workforce, antiquated laboratories, lack of real-time surveillance and epidemiological systems, ineffective and fragmented communication networks, incomplete emergency preparedness and response capabilities, and a lack of essential public health services in some communities (IOM 2002). According to the Public Health Foundation, fixing these public health deficiencies would cost more than $10 billion (Trust for America's Health 2006).

The heart of the problem is funding. Today, approximately 70 percent of America's public health spending comes from state and local sources, and the federal government supplies the rest (Trust for America's Health 2006). Given the financial situation in many states, progress almost certainly depends on significant federal investment. In 2000, Congress passed the Public Health Threats and Emergencies Act (Public Law 106-505) to address the nation's decaying public health infrastructure. The act included grants to state and local governments that emphasized building capacity to identify, detect, monitor, and respond to public health threats including bioterrorism. This focus on providing resources for preparedness planning, exercises, and equipment has sharpened since September 11. We have already seen how the Public Health Security and Bioterrorism Preparedness and Response Act (Public Law 107-188) channeled CDC- and HRSA-administered grants to state and local health departments, hospitals, and other health-care agencies. In all, the federal government has allocated more than $5 billion[14] to improve U.S. preparedness for bioterrorism since September 11 (Nelson et al. 2007).

There is little doubt that these resources have improved federal, state, and local preparedness. At the same time, the response to Hurricane Katrina shows that much remains to be done. Moreover—and despite statutory "nonsupplantation" provisions—some states have made offsetting cuts in their support for local public health programs. In these cases, the net effect has been to promote bioterrorism preparedness at the expense of traditional public health functions like tuberculosis prevention (Katz, Staiti, and McKenzie 2006). State and local health departments have also expressed concern about the stability of federal bioterrorism funding. CDC and HRSA spending declined by roughly 3 percent ($40 million) between 2003 and 2005 (Katz, Staiti, and McKenzie 2006).[15]

Bioterrorism funding since September 11 has helped many local health departments hire staff and fund specific training and planning activities. This has made it possible for many health departments to become more involved in preparedness. However, there is still room for improvement. In a series of case studies, Davis et al. (2006a) found that a number of participants believed there should be more flexibility in how cooperative-agreement money is spent, who can receive it, and when funds can be spent on coordination with private partners. Respondents also complained that federal and state delays in processing proposals often led to situations in which local health departments only received grants late in the fiscal year. This led to some projects being rushed and money being spent less effectively than it otherwise would have been (Davis et al. 2006a).

11.4.2 Assessing Public Health Preparedness

Given these large investment, how prepared is the United States? On average, there has clearly been progress. A 2003 nationwide survey found that many general acute-care hospitals took significant steps after September 11 to update mutual-aid agreements and response plans for chemical, biological, and radiological attacks. Furthermore, roughly 70 percent of hospitals and 42 percent of local public health departments had conducted risk assessments. On the other hand, this progress has been uneven. In general, local public health departments that see their jurisdictions as likely terrorist targets have been much more willing to update their WMD response plans and invest in preparedness than other jurisdictions. Hospitals that perceive a high terrorism threat have been similarly more likely to buy detection and decontamination equipment (Davis et al. 2006b). A recent assessment of states' public health preparedness for disasters and public health emergencies reflects these mixed results:

• Although all states have a basic plan to respond to bioterrorism, planning for chemical and radiological threats has lagged behind.
• Plans tend to be limited to the public health sector, are not well coordinated with emergency responders, and seldom include the private sector and surrounding communities.
• Plans are not consistently tested and exercised and there are few procedures for incorporating lessons learned.
• Despite dramatic improvements in laboratory capabilities, shortages of reagents remain.
• While a number of states have joined the CDC's National Electronic Disease Surveillance System, public health information technology is still outdated.
• Median state spending for public health is only $31 per person per year, and an additional $2.6 billion would be needed to equalize spending across the states.
• Only fifteen states and two cities have received the highest preparedness rating for distributing and administering SNS medications.
• Although Congress appropriated $5 billion for pandemic influenza preparedness, the U.S. vaccine industry remains fragile, with only limited incentives to pursue R&D for new vaccines.
• Shortages of doctors, nurses, facilities, beds, medical supplies, and equipment mean that the United States has very limited surge capacity.
• Government risk communication strategies are outdated and do not sufficiently include the public in planning (Trust for America's Health 2006).

This assessment is admittedly controversial and more precise statements are hard to come by. Standardized measurements of organizational and community readiness would help. Since September 11, the CDC and HRSA have repeatedly worked to establish preparedness metrics. Despite some incremental improvements, however, existing measurements still depend on unverified/self-reported information, focus on process versus outcomes, and suffer from other problems (Trust for America's Health 2006). Other federal, state, and nongovernmental attempts to create objective performance metrics have been similarly controversial. Observers argue that they usually include "ambiguous and uncertain preparedness goals, a lack of agreement about what the measures should aim at and how they should be interpreted, and a weak system of accountability for producing results" (Nelson et al. 2006).

Ultimately, progress is impossible without some basic consensus on what constitutes a well-prepared community. RAND recently convened a panel of experts who proposed a list of sixteen elements grouped into three categories: (1) a preplanned and coordinated rapid-response capability; (2) an expert and fully staffed workforce; and (3) accountability and quality improvement (Nelson et al. 2007).[16] This list—or something like it—represents an essential first step in developing the metrics needed to judge preparedness and identify areas that need improvement.

11.5 Conclusion

However important, public health preparedness is just one aspect of the United States' overall preparedness effort. Although we have focused on public health departments and hospitals, many aspects of public health preparedness (e.g., SNS distribution, quarantine plans) need support from law enforcement, emergency medical services, and other actors outside the public health system. This wider group will bring their own funding sources, missions, organizational characteristics, and priorities to the planning table. It is not enough for health organizations to coordinate with one another. They must also build relationships outside the health-care field.

Federal investments since September 11 have increased the country's ability to respond to public health emergencies. For example, the influx of bioterrorism funding for expanded laboratory, surveillance, planning, and communication capabilities has served to improve public health preparedness generally. However, the absence of standardized metrics makes it hard to know where we stand and what remains to be done. More consistent public health emergency preparedness concepts and doctrines are clearly needed. Accountability also requires a much clearer definition of federal, state, and local actors' respective responsibilities (Lurie, Wasserman, and Nelson 2006).

Despite substantial investments in public health infrastructure development and preparedness, it is not clear how much preparedness has actually improved. There is anecdotal evidence that some localities and states cut traditional public health funding as federal funding became available. In addition, many local public health departments have commented on the resulting shift in emphasis away from traditional public health functions and toward bioterrorism. The key issue that localities and states currently face is how to sustain these investments in public health preparedness as federal funding is reduced.

Finally, recent progress remains tentative without a long-term strategy for sustaining the system. Money is scarce, and federal, state, and local governments continue to quarrel over who should pay for public health. This disagreement is particularly debilitating for challenges (e.g., rebuilding the public health workforce) that cannot be addressed within a year or two. The increasing importance of individual practitioners and private sector health-care providers has, if anything, made the problem more complicated. Progress will depend on communities' willingness to bring all the relevant stakeholders together to prepare and plan for a wide range of potential public health threats.

Notes

1. Many natural disease outbreaks (e.g., West Nile virus) similarly evolve over periods of months or years (Stoto et al. 2005).

2. Indeed, public health staff were themselves among the storm's displaced victims.

3. Because the list is compiled at the state level, a few diseases are notifiable in some states but not others. The Council of State and Territorial Epidemiologists (CSTE) offers a recommended list, but its suggestions are not binding.

4. For more information on the LRN, see http://www.bt.cdc.gov/lrn/.

5. Response times also showed substantial variation, ranging from 0.5 to 2,470 minutes.

6. The programs are archived at http://www.naccho.org/topics/emergency/APC.cfm and http://www.naccho.org/toolbox/program.cfm?id=9.

7. http://www.bt.cdc.gov/training/#new. Additional training programs are archived and available through the NACCHO website: http://www.naccho.org/topics/emergency/APC.cfm. The APC Toolbox (http://www.naccho.org/toolbox/program.cfm?id=9) also contains useful resources, including exercises, drills, protocols, and planning guidance developed by APCs.

8. DMATs consists of professional and paraprofessional medical personnel brought together to serve as rapid-response teams that can be deployed to disaster sites. For additional information on the NDMS, see http://www.oep-ndms.dhhs.gov/index.html.

9. For additional information about the Strategic National Stockpile see http://www.bt.cdc.gov/stockpile/.

10. Planning, coordination, and risk communication with the public support the core functional areas described above.

11. A nationwide survey conducted just prior to the September 11 terrorist attacks found that only about one-third of local public health departments and hospitals had plans in place for responding to a moderate-sized biological attack. Shortly after September 11, the corresponding figures for moderately sized chemical attacks were 27 percent for local health departments and slightly over 50 percent for hospitals (Davis and Blanchard 2002).

12. The media has also been frustrated by public health department confidentiality regulations that limit its ability to interview victims.

13. The private sector also plays a role in public health planning. Possible tasks include educating employees, using company communication networks to provide information to employees, customers, and tenants; distributing vaccines; surveillance reporting; and providing supply chain and logistics expertise to move government personnel and supplies to the scene of the emergency.

14. In addition to the CDC's Public Health Preparedness and Response for Bioterrorism and HRSA's Bioterrorism Hospital Preparedness cooperative agreements, this estimate includes a variety of federal bioterrorism programs.

15. The drop has also been geographically uneven, with the CDC's Cities Readiness Initiative redirecting resources to cities thought to be high-risk terrorism targets (Katz, Staiti, and McKenzie 2006).

16. The panel defined public health preparedness as "the capability of the public health and health-care systems, communities, and individuals, to prevent, protect against, quickly respond to, and recover from health emergencies, particularly those whose scale, timing, or unpredictability threatens to overwhelm routine capabilities. Preparedness involves a coordinated and continuous process of planning and implementation that relies on measuring performance and taking corrective action" (Nelson et al. 2007).

12

Recovering from Nuclear and Radiological Attacks

Christine Hartmann Siantar, Tammy P. Taylor, and C. Norman Coleman

Modern nuclear preparedness programs are based on more than fifty years of trying to protect civilians against nuclear attacks. This history is both a blessing and a curse. On the positive side, much is known about the effects of nuclear weapons. We can draw significant benefit from Cold War research in radiation effects and counter-measures. On the negative side, there is a danger that preparedness for one (or even a few) terrorist nuclear weapons will be confused with the nuclear Armageddon threatened in the Cold War. Preparedness in the context of "mutually assured destruction" (i.e., the enormous nuclear stockpiles that still exist in the United States and former Soviet Union) entailed the nearly impossible task of mounting a significant medical or environmental response to hundreds of very large (megaton-scale) hydrogen-bomb explosions. By comparison, a terrorist attack would be a relatively isolated event involving one or at most a few atomic (kiloton-scale) weapons. This scenario is far more manageable than the nuclear nightmares of the 1960s.

This chapter reviews the science and technology behind nuclear preparedness and response. Section 12.1 briefly reviews modern civil defense and the physical characteristics of nuclear weapons and radiation dispersal devices ("dirty bombs" or RDDs). Section 12.2 explores the biological effects of radiation. Section 12.3 examines current and projected technologies for managing and treating radiation victims. Section 12.4 describes what is known about radioactive contamination in the environment and current plans to address it. Section 12.5 examines current environmental decontamination technologies. Section 12.6 identifies some R&D priorities for the future. Finally, section 12.7 presents a brief conclusion.

12.1 Civil Defense, Nuclear Weapons, and RDDs

Modern thinking about WMD terrorism grows out of the long history of civil defense and nuclear weapons research. This section provides a brief review. (Interested readers should consult chapter 3 and Glasstone and Dolan 1977 for further details.)

12.1.1   Civil Defense History

Over the past century, the United States has addressed preparedness issues under the general heading of civil defense. This distinctively twentieth-century idea was principally shaped by anticipated or actual military actions against civilian populations. For example, in World War I, Germany used strategic aerial attacks on towns and cities to undermine the ability and willingness of France, Belgium, and England to wage war (Garrison 2006). During World War II, the German blitzkrieg and Allied bombings of Dresden and Tokyo offered terrifying examples of civilian targeting. All of these actions led countries to believe that protecting civilian populations was essential for overall national defense. In the United States, the first civil defense office was created by President Franklin D. Roosevelt seven months before the Japanese attacked Pearl Harbor (Homeland Security National Preparedness Task Force 2006).

The atomic bombings of Hiroshima and Nagasaki demonstrated a new kind of weapon that could inflict potentially devastating impacts on civilian populations and the environment. Predictably, this led to expanded U.S. civil defense efforts. In the late 1940s, few Americans understood the difficulty of defending against nuclear bombs. During this time the government sponsored numerous studies aimed at developing a nuclear civil defense strategy. This work led President Harry Truman to establish civil defense planning within the National Security Resource Board in 1949. The issue became even more pressing after the Soviets tested their first atomic bomb later that year. Congress responded with the Civil Defense Act of 1950, which created the Federal Civil Defense Administration (FCDA) as an umbrella agency for guiding the planning, organization, and operations for each state's separate civil defense programs. FCDA also provided states with matching funds for supplies and equipment. FCDA lasted until 1958. Since then, its responsibilities have passed through twelve successive federal civil defense agencies, including most recently the Federal Emergency Management Agency (FEMA). The current Department of Homeland Security combines FEMA with twenty-one other agencies and is responsible for preventing and responding to terrorist attacks as well as natural disasters (Homeland Security National Preparedness Task Force 2006). The Department of Health and Human Services' Office of the Assistant Secretary for Preparedness and Response is similarly responsible for medical responses to a terrorist attack (ASPR n.d.).

Civil defense efforts peaked in the 1960s at roughly $150 million per year (Garrison 2006) or about $1 billion in current dollars. This level provides a rough upper bound on what a robust modern civil defense effort would cost.

12.1.2   Physical Effects of Nuclear Weapons and RDDs

Nuclear weapons are qualitatively different from earlier bombs in both their extreme explosive energy and their ability to generate and deliver significant doses of ionizing radiation and radioactive materials over a wide area. This latter capability has both short- and long-term effects that can potentially inflict mass casualties. By comparison, radiological dispersal devices (RDDs) would be far smaller events in terms of both explosive energy and radiation.[1]

Blast and Heat   The blast and heat from an RDD would be, at most, equivalent to that of a large conventional explosion. A nuclear explosion would, of course, be much larger. Approximately 50 percent of the weapon's energy would be delivered to the target as shock or bomb blast. This would cause multiple injuries including fractures, lacerations, ruptured ear drums and viscera, and lung hemorrhage and edema. An additional 35 percent of the weapon's energy would be delivered as heat and light. These would cause thermal injury, including flash burns, flame burns, flash blindness (due to temporary depletion of photopigment from retinal receptors), and retinal burns.

Radiation   The final 15 percent of a nuclear explosion goes into creating radioactive materials that pose a lasting health threat, although the total amount of contamination is highly sensitive to environmental conditions (e.g., weather) during and shortly after the explosion (Walker and Cerveny 1989; NCRP 2001; Dainiak 2002; Mettler and Upton 1995). Contamination effects would become steadily more important over time. These would normally drive cleanup costs and the decision to reinhabit affected areas. We have already remarked that most practical RDDs generate far less radiation than a nuclear explosion. In general, response and recovery technologies that work for nuclear weapons will a fortiori work against RDDs.[2]

12.1.3   Modern Civil Defense Planning

Modern U.S. civil defense planning envisages three general phases following a nuclear or RDD attack (ORP n.d., 2007). Figure 12.1 describes how the threat and protective measures would evolve over time.

Conceptually, the response can be divided into three distinct phases:

• *The early ("emergency") phase*   This phase begins with the attack and emphasizes immediate decisions for protecting the public at a time when actual radiation measurements are limited or nonexistent. In the case of an RDD, first responders would need appropriate detectors to recognize that a radiation threat existed and establish an initial perimeter around the threat. Thereafter, responders wearing appropriate protective equipment would begin to (1) determine the extent, intensity, and type of radioactivity, (2) decontaminate and treat the injured, and (3) rescue, evacuate, and/or help survivors find shelter. These activities would continue into the intermediate phase.

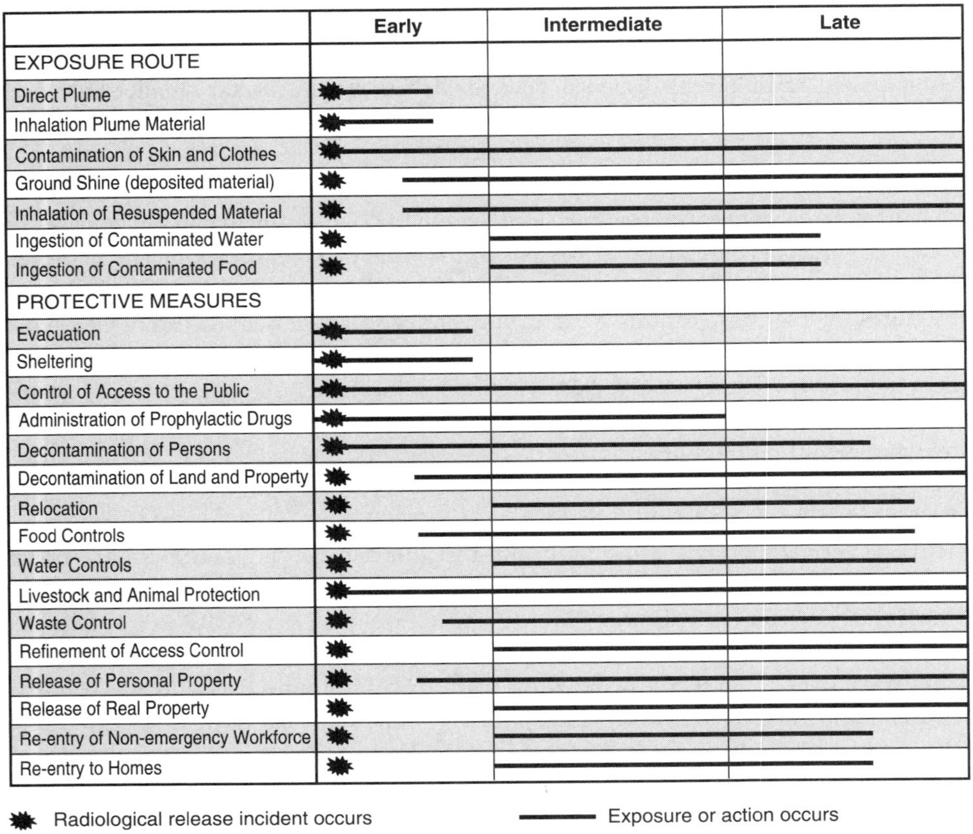

	Early	Intermediate	Late
EXPOSURE ROUTE			
Direct Plume	✹—		
Inhalation Plume Material	✹—		
Contamination of Skin and Clothes	✹————————————		
Ground Shine (deposited material)	✹ —		
Inhalation of Resuspended Material	✹ ——————————		
Ingestion of Contaminated Water	✹	———————	
Ingestion of Contaminated Food	✹	———————	
PROTECTIVE MEASURES			
Evacuation	✹—		
Sheltering	✹—		
Control of Access to the Public	✹————————————————————————		
Administration of Prophylactic Drugs	✹—		
Decontamination of Persons	✹————————————————————————		
Decontamination of Land and Property	✹ —		
Relocation	✹	————————————————	
Food Controls	✹ ——————		
Water Controls	✹	————————————————	
Livestock and Animal Protection	✹—		
Waste Control	✹ —		
Refinement of Access Control	✹	———————	
Release of Personal Property	✹ ——————		
Release of Real Property	✹	———————	
Re-entry of Non-emergency Workforce	✹	———————————	
Re-entry to Homes	✹	———————————	

✹ Radiological release incident occurs   ——— Exposure or action occurs

Figure 12.1
Nuclear response: Exposure routes and protective measures *vs.* time. *Source*: Protective Action Guidelines 1992.

• *The intermediate phase*   This phase begins when the radioactive source has been brought under control and releases have stopped.[3] This would usually take place within a few hours but could take longer if the initial event was not accompanied by an explosion, so that the attack's time and location(s) were initially uncertain. At this point, authorities will usually possess significant information about victims' exposures and the presence, type, and amount of radiation in the environment. Measures to protect the population could include evacuation and the establishment of exclusion zones; preliminary decontamination and removal of radioactive debris from the attack site; and/or restrictions on the use of contaminated food or water. Responders would also work to reestablish critical infrastructure, services, and

Table 12.1
Response worker guidelines

Total effective date equivalent (TEDE) guideline	Activity	Condition
5 rems	All occupational exposures	All reasonably achievable actions have been taken to minimize dose.
10 rems*	Protecting valuable property necessary for public welfare (e.g., a power plant).	Exceeding 5 rems unavoidable and all appropriate actions taken to reduce dose. Monitoring available to project or measure dose.
25 rems**	Lifesaving or protection of large populations	Exceeding 5 rems unavoidable and all appropriate actions taken to reduce dose. Monitoring available to project or measure dose.

*For potential doses >10 rems, special medical monitoring programs should be employed, and exposure should be tracked in terms of the unit of absorbed dose (rad) rather than TEDE (rem).
**In the case of a very large incident such as an IND, incident commanders may need to consider raising the properly and lifesaving response worker guidelines in order to prevent further loss of life and massive spread of destruction.

products for people living in the region. This could include operating some systems under special engineering and administrative controls designed to keep workers' radiation exposure to acceptable levels. Tables 12.1 and 12.2 summarize the guidelines that local officials would use to make these decisions.[4]
• *The late phase*   This period covers long-term recovery and cleanup actions and would probably include extensive decontamination and debris removal. It would typically last months or even years. The ultimate goal would be to reduce radiation to "acceptable levels" that allowed unrestricted, long-term use of the site. Local authorities would normally set these levels in consultation with federal government experts.

12.2   Biomedical Effects of Radiation

Most heat and blast injuries would occur in the immediate aftermath of an attack. Thereafter, the recovery process would be dominated almost entirely by radiation

Table 12.2
Protective actions for radiation exposure

Phase	Protective action	Protective action guide	Reference
Early	Limit emergency worker exposure	5 rem (or greater under exceptional circumstances[1])	EPA PAG Manual
	Sheltering of public	1 to 5 rems projected dose[2]	EPA PAG Manual
	Evacuation of public	1 to 5 rems projected dose[3]	EPA PAG Manual
	Administration of prophylactic drugs	For potassium iodide, FDA Guidance dose values[4,5]	FDA Guidance[6]
Intermediate	Limit worker exposure	5 rem/yr	See Appendix 1
	Relocation of general public	2 rems, projected dose first year. Subsequent years: 500 mrem/yr projected dose	EPA PAG Manual
	Food interdiction	500 mrem/yr projected dose	FDA Guidance[7]
	Drinking water interdiction	500 mrem/yr projected dose	EPA guidance in development
Late	Final cleanup actions	Late phase PAG optimized for conditions at the site	—

1. In cases when radiation control options are not available or, due to the magnitude of the incident, are not sufficient, doses above 5 rems may be unavoidable. For further discussion see PAG Manual at Appendix 1.

2. Should normally begin at 1 rem; however, sheltering may begin at lower levels if advantageous.

3. Should normally begin at 1 rem.

4. Provides protection from radioactive iodine only.

5. For other information on medical prophylactics and treatment see http://www.fda.gov/cder/drugprepare/default.htm or http://www.bt.cdc.gov/radiation/index/asp or http://www.orau.gov/reacts.

6. "Potassium Iodide as a Thyroid Blocking Agent in Radiation Emergencies," December 2001, Center Drug Evaluation and Research, FDA, HHS (http://www.fda.gov/cder/guidance/5386fnl.htm).

7. "Accidental Radioactive Contamination of Human Food and Animal Feeds: Recommendations for State and Local Agencies," August 13, 1998, Office of Health and Industry Programs, Center for Devices and Radiological Health, FDA, HHS (http://www.fda.gov/cdhr/dmqrp/84.html).

Source: EPA/Office of Radiation Programs 1992

injuries. A great deal is known about the biomedical effects of radiation from detailed studies of Hiroshima and Nagasaki victims, industrial and military accidents, and cancer treatment. That said, a ground-level detonation would cause a very different spectrum of injuries from the atomic bombings that ended World War II.

Radioisotopes emit both charged and uncharged particles. *Charged particles* (e.g., electrons, positrons, and alpha particles) deposit dose locally, causing skin burns and internal organ damage. Organ damage, in turn, depends on contaminant chemistry and human physiology. For example, bone tends to absorb disproportionate amounts of radioactive strontium while the thyroid takes up iodine. *Uncharged particles* (neutrons and high-energy photons) penetrate and exit the body far more readily. For internal contamination, this means that uncharged particles usually deposit relatively little radiation before leaving the body. However, they often make it possible to diagnose the presence of radioisotopes inside the body.[5] Uncharged particles are also the prime source of radiation absorbed from sources in the environment.

The amount of radiation that individuals receive is known as the radiation absorbed dose, or simply *dose*. Dose measures the accumulated total amount of ionizing radiation energy absorbed per unit mass of tissue. In practice, dose can be delivered through both external and internal exposure. External exposure typically results from a passing radioactive cloud, smoke, or dust; a lump of radioactive material (a "radiological exposure device"); or exposure to contaminants lying on the ground. Internal contamination occurs when unprotected individuals ingest, inhale, or are wounded by radioactive material. These doses depend on how much material is deposited; how it enters the body; its chemical form, its radioactive decay half-life and the type of radiation it emits; and how quickly the body eliminates it. The metabolic path taken by a radioactive isotope is the same as that taken by nonradioactive isotopes of the same element within the body. However, the type of radiation delivered and resulting dose distribution depend on the specific radionuclide. For example, ^{131}I and ^{125}I have similar distributions in the body but very different dose distributions.

An organism's biological response to ionizing radiation starts at the moment of exposure and continues through the appearance of clinical symptoms. Initial damage, which takes place within a few seconds, involves DNA strand breaks and oxidative damage to cellular molecules. This is followed by cell-level changes in gene expression, protein modification, and signal transduction. These changes take place within minutes and can produce cell death and/or genomic instability hours or weeks later. Cell death in rapidly dividing tissues (e.g., skin, blood/lymphatic, and

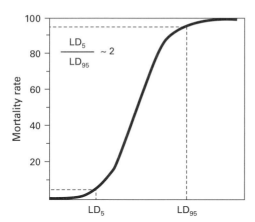

Figure 12.2
The risk of death vs. time: early (noncancer) effects. *Source*: Anno, 2003.

gastrointestinal tract) leads to acute radiation syndromes that occur over periods ranging from days to more than a month. However, cell death in slowly dividing tissues may not produce disease symptoms for months or years. Finally, the effects of genomic instability are lifelong and show up as excess cancers and birth defects. Mutagenic or teratogenic effects are also expected, although these have not been seen to date (Otake 1998; Otake, Yoshimaru, and Schull 1987; NRC 1990). Early effects follow a sigmoidal curve, as shown in figure 12.2.

Absent medical intervention, 50 percent of the adults exposed to 4.1 grays (Gy)[6] of gamma radiation will die within a few weeks. This is known as the "lethal dose" or LD_{50} (Anno et al. 2003). For many effects (e.g., cancers) the probability of delayed injury is linear in exposure, although this remains controversial for low doses. However, some birth defects are known to follow a more complex, linear-quadratic relation. Examples are shown in figure 12.3.

The effects of ionizing radiation also depend on how long the exposure lasts. For chronic exposure, in which the radiation dose is spread out over a long period of time, injury can be mitigated by the body's natural radiation damage repair mechanisms. This means that, dose for dose, chronic effects are much less significant than they would be for an acute exposure. Chronic exposures typically involve internal contamination from inhaled or ingested long-lived radioisotopes like ^{137}Cs, ^{131}I, or ^{90}Sr. These isotopes would be among the most worrisome fallout components from a nuclear explosion, although external contamination would remain the main concern. Terrorists might also be able to obtain them for use in an RDD.

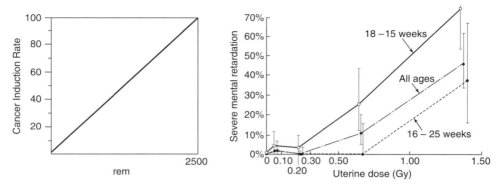

Figure 12.3
Risk of death vs. late effects (cancers and mental retardation). (*A*) cancer incidence vs. absorbed dose; (*B*) mental retardation vs. dose absorbed in utero. *Source*: Otake, Yoshimaru, and Schull 1987 and Otake 1998.

12.2.1   Acute Radiation Injury

Acute radiation injury, in which victims receive whole- or significant partial-body irradiation greater than approximately one Gy within short period of time, typically produce early effects including nausea, vomiting, hair loss, fatigue, slow wound healing, and other, possibly fatal medical complications. Fast-dividing cells, including spermatocytes as well as skin, bone marrow, and intestinal crypt cells, are the most sensitive to such injury. Acute exposures are typical of the initial ("prompt") radiation from a nuclear explosion and of the fast-decaying isotopes contained in fallout in the first hours after the blast.

In addition to skin burns, the three main acute radiation clinical syndromes are denoted hematopoietic, gastrointestinal, and cerebrovascular. The *hematopoietic* syndrome includes lymphopenia (immune suppression), granulocytopenia (infection), or thrombocytopenia (bleeding) and occurs at relatively low doses. *Gastrointestinal* symptoms occur at moderate doses and include headache, nausea, vomiting, or diarrhea. Finally, *cerebrovascular* signs and symptoms occur at high doses. They include headache, impaired thinking, disorientation, impaired coordination of limbs and torso (ataxia), seizures, prostration, and hypotension. Some signs and symptoms are similar across a wide range of radiation doses while others (e.g., cerebrovascular symptoms) only appear at high whole-body doses.

Figure 12.4 illustrates the time profile and severity of various clinical signs and symptoms for different dose ranges. Depending on the absorbed dose to critical organs, symptoms appear within hours to weeks and follow a predictable clinical course. Each syndrome can be divided into four phases. The first, prodromal phase,

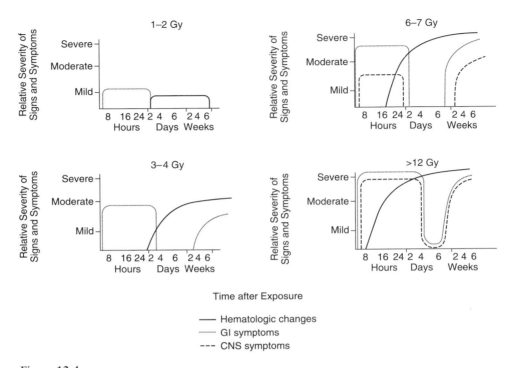

Figure 12.4
Time-to-manifestation for hematologic, gastrointestinal, and central nervous system symptoms vs. whole-body dose. *Source*: Waselenko, 2004.

usually occurs in the first forty-eight hours but may develop up to six days after exposure. The second, latent phase is usually a short period characterized by improvement of symptoms and apparent recovery. This effect is transient, however, lasting for several days to several weeks. At this point, the patient enters the third, manifest illness stage, which may last for weeks or months. This stage is characterized by intense immunosuppression and is the hardest to treat. The final stage is either recovery or death. Recovery is normally complete, although chronic radiation injury and long-term effects can sometimes occur. For very high exposures, all four stages are compressed into a period of hours and lead to early death. Table 12.3 summarizes the effects of acute exposure for various total doses (Waselenko et al. 2004).

12.2.2   Long-Term Radiation Injury

If the radiation-injury victim survives the acute (hematopoietic and gastrointestinal) phases of radiation sickness, potentially chronic organ injuries can still occur. Total-

Table 12.3
Phases of radiation injury

Dose range, Gy	Prodrome	Manifestation of illness	Prognosis (without therapy)
0.5–1.0	Mild	Slight decrease in blood cell counts	Almost certain survival
1.0–2.0	Mild to moderate	Early signs of bone marrow damage	Highly probable survival (>90% of victims)
2.0–3.5	Moderate	Moderate to severe bone marrow damage	Probable survival
3.5–5.5	Severe	Severe bone marrow damage; slight GI damage	Death within 3.5–6 wk (50% of victims)
5.5–7.5	Severe	Pancytopenia and moderate GI damage	Death probable within 2–3 wk
7.5–10.0	Severe	Marked GI and bone marrow damage, hypotension	Death probable within 1–2.5 wk
10.0–20.0	Severe	Severe GI damage, pneumonitis, altered mental status, cognitive dysfunction	Death certain within 5–12 d
20.0–30.0	Severe	Cerebrovascular collapse, fever, shock	Death certain within 2–5 d

* Modified from Walker R. I., Cerveny R. J., eds. (21). GI = gastrointestinal.
Source: Waselenko (2004); adapted from Walker (1989)

body radiation is frequently used in therapeutic bone marrow transplants for cancer therapy and provides important information about the types of injuries expected in the months or years following exposure. Delayed symptoms include cataracts, respiratory failure, chronic kidney failure, and developmental abnormalities (Waselenko et al. 2004; Moulder et al. 2002; Moulder 2004; Belkacemi et al. 1998; Clark 1993; Miralbell et al. 1996; Cohen 2000; Leiper 1995; Boulad, Sands, and Sklar 1998). The seriousness of these injuries means that it is important for authorities to identify, track, and provide follow-up treatment for individuals who have been exposed to relatively high doses of radiation.

Carcinogenesis and Heritable Effects   The main long-term effect of ionizing radiation exposure is increased cancers. Data from atomic-bomb survivors and other irradiated populations shows that the relationship between cancers and absorbed dose varies with the type of cancer. In general, excess deaths from nonleukemia cancers are linear with exposure, while leukemia data are more compatible with a linear-quadratic relationship. Based on the available evidence, the U.S. National Academy of Science's BEIR V committee has estimated that the population-weighted average lifetime excess risk of death from cancer following an acute absorbed radiation dose to all body organs of 0.1 Gy is 0.8 percent (NRC 1990).[7] By way of comparison, cancer currently accounts for 23.1 percent of all U.S. deaths (ACS 2007).

Victims exposed in utero can also suffer mental retardation. Japanese atomic-bomb survivors exposed at a gestational age of eight to fifteen weeks[8] suffered severe mental retardation at a rate of roughly 4 percent per 0.1 Gy (gamma ray dose equivalent). Although less risk occurred for exposures at other gestational ages, limited available data suggest that there may be no threshold below which exposures are "safe," at least when the brain is in its most sensitive stage of development (Otake 1998).

Finally, heritable effects (increased genetic mutations) have been demonstrated in animals and are presumably also present in humans. Heritable effects of radiation (effects on the genes and chromosomes of reproductive cells) are well characterized in the mouse. Extrapolating this data suggests that at least 1 Gy of low dose-rate, gamma ray or electron/positron radiation is required to double the mutation rate in humans. Heritable effects of radiation have not been seen in the children of atomic-bomb survivors—the largest group of irradiated humans who have been followed in any systematic way. However, extrapolations from animal data taken at low mean doses (less than 0.5 Gy) suggest that the predicted effect is too small to be seen given the group's limited sample size (NRC 1990).

12.3   Medical-Response Technologies

Medical responses to radiation can be conveniently divided into three categories:

Evaluation   This critical first step determines whether victims will be treated or released. Medical responses to even comparatively small RDD attacks would be complicated by the fact that radiation injury is initially invisible for almost all levels of exposure while public fears are substantial. Historic experience with an accidental release in Goiania, Brazil suggests that responders would have to process more than 1,000 uninjured ("worried-well") patients for every individual who sustained physical radiation injury (IAEA 1988). Medical resources would be stretched even further if a nuclear weapon was used. In either case, early and accurate evaluation is the key to focusing scarce resources for maximum effectiveness.

Surface decontamination and decorporation   Initial treatments would focus on removing radioisotopes carried on victims' persons (decontamination) or inside their bodies (decorporation). Most radioisotopes take days or weeks to deposit their full dose in a contaminated victim. Timely decontamination can therefore eliminate a large fraction of radiation that victims would otherwise receive. This is a powerful technique for limiting injury and simplifying subsequent treatment.

Mitigation and treatment   Follow-up treatments consist of mitigating radiation injury before symptoms appear and timely, aggressive treatment thereafter. With proper care, patients can survive radiation exposures of approximately 3–8 Gy and possibly even higher.[9]

All of this calls for an orderly and preplanned medical response (Philips and Knebel 2007). Generic approaches can be found in algorithm-based medical responses and detailed playbooks by the Office of Preparedness and Emergency Operations (Coleman et al. 2007). The following sections review state-of-the-art medical treatments and current initiatives to expand and improve them.

12.3.1   Evaluation and Assessment

Evaluation and assessment require four basic classes of tools:

Radioisotope contamination detectors and radioisotope dose-assessment tools These detectors range from simple Geiger-Mueller-type equipment to tools for inferring exposure from body fluids and (potentially) computational tools for estimating the total dose received ("committed dose") from measurements taken after patients have reached a caregiver.

Biomedically based dose-assessment tools   In many cases, the level of radioactive contamination measured on patients may not reflect the actual dose received. This is particularly likely where distant external radiation sources like ground shine (i.e., radiation deposited in the environment), atmospheric fallout, and environmental radioactive contamination are significant. In this case, biological assays will normally be needed to assess patient exposure. The accuracy and threshold(s) required of these tools will vary depending on the type of triage/assessment being performed and whether other injuries are present.

"You're OK" markers   "Worried-well" patients will likely number in the thousands for almost any nuclear or substantial RDD attack. Reliable discriminators for identifying patients who do not need further immediate care will be needed to conserve scarce dose-assessment and medical-treatment resources.

Tags for future tracking   Long-term radiation injuries can be treated more effectively if they are detected early. This may require monitoring thousands of exposed individuals for decades. An efficient system should tag individuals and record their location at the time of exposure.

Within these classes, no single tool is likely to be best for every occasion. For example, some tools must be simple enough for use by paramedics in the field, while others can be used by doctors in well-equipped hospitals. Similarly, the number of patients to be examined—and the average patient's needs—will usually change over time. This section reviews existing technologies and current research to improve them.

Measuring Radioisotope Contamination   Detecting contamination is the critical first step in designing treatment (Taylor et al. 2003; AFRRI 2003). The *Geiger-Mueller* counter is the most common device for detecting beta- and gamma-emitting radioisotopes. Unfortunately, high radiation levels can saturate Geiger counters so that readouts appear low and may even fall to zero. Geiger counters are also less accurate in extreme heat and humidity. Finally, they have only a limited ability to detect ingested beta- or gamma-emitting radioisotopes and cannot detect pure alpha-emitting or low-energy beta-emitting radioisotopes inside the body at all (Taylor et al. 2003). *Ionization chambers* have similar limitations to Geiger counters, except that they remain accurate at significantly higher dose rates.

Surface sampling can also be used to detect the presence of weakly penetrating alpha or beta radiation. Samples are typically obtained by wiping textured "swipes" (e.g., filter paper) across the surface to be tested. The method only works for "transferable" isotopes that have not bonded to the surface. Nose swabs can also be used to test potentially contaminated patients. In the field, dried paper or swabs are usually delivered to a *scintillation counter* for analysis. This procedure is sufficient to identify alpha radiation from plutonium or polonium sources or weak beta radiation from tritium contamination. More sensitive measurements require *proportional counters*. Although proportional counters are the most common laboratory device for measuring alpha radiation, they are still not widely available in the field. However, the Department of Energy's Radiological Assistance Program (RAP) has begun to deploy mobile proportional counters for field use (DOE n.d.(b); NNSA n.d.; Taylor et al. 2003).

More accurate estimates of internal radiation dose require caregivers to collect patients' effluents over an extended period. Careful measurements of excreted radiation can then be used to estimate the total internal body burden (Taylor et al. 2003). Depending on the radioisotope's physical and chemical properties, the excretion process can sometimes take place so slowly that samples must be taken over a period of months.

Estimating Absorbed Dose from Radioisotope Contamination   Once contamination has been measured, the question becomes "How much radiation has the patient absorbed?" For the past several decades, the International Commission on Radiation Protection (ICRP) has worked with various university and national laboratory workers to develop consensus *occupational health models* that let clinicians infer absorbed dose when the environmental exposure is known. These models now exist for many radioisotopes.[10] However, these models are very context-dependent and must be used with care. For example, respiratory uptake is known to depend sensitively on particle size and aerosol chemistry and could differ markedly from ICRP models. Finally, medical treatment (wound cleanup, administration of chelating agents, and so on) can also alter the behavior of the radioisotopes in the body.

Despite these shortcomings, emergency responders will usually find a simple instruction set or "playbook" such as the "Radiation Event Medical Management" or "REMM" (HHS n.d.) sufficient for identifying patients who should be further evaluated for decorporation treatment. Once these patients are identified, more sophisticated models can be used to refine dose assessments for both short- and long-term management.

Biomedically Based Dose Assessment   In many cases, caregivers may not know how much radiation patients were exposed to. In this case biomedically based dose assessment must be used. The Armed Forces Radiobiology Research Institute's Radiation Emergency Assistance Center/Training Site and other groups have developed software that caregivers can use to infer received dose from patient symptoms (Sine et al. 2001).[11] The International Atomic Energy Agency has similarly developed guidelines for recording clinical signs and symptoms of radiation injury (IAEA 2005). Finally, the Medical Treatment Protocols group has developed a quantitative system that caregivers can use to assess the severity of clinical symptoms according to a numerical grading scheme (Fliedner, Friesecke, and Beyrer 2001; HHS n.d.).

Currently, the three most useful biological/clinical signatures for calculating the exposure dose are time to onset of vomiting, lymphocyte depletion kinetics, and the presence of chromosome dicentrics (Waselenko et al. 2004). The simplest diagnostic is onset of vomiting. More than 90 percent of patients who receive 6 Gy or more will begin to vomit within an hour. On the other hand, the average time to onset for victims in the 1–3 Gy range is more than two hours and 50 percent of these patients never vomit at all. Unfortunately, there is still considerable variability between patients (figure 12.5a; Goans and Waselenko 2004). This limits the usefulness of this otherwise simple diagnostic. A potentially more accurate method relies on *absolute lymphocyte counts* obtained by examining multiple blood samples over time. In the first twelve hours following an exposure, counts only fall below normal ranges for patients who have received 9 Gy or more of radiation. However, patients who receive 5 (3) Gy exposures only develop detectably low counts in twenty-four (twenty-eight) hours. Thereafter, lymphocyte numbers continue to decline faster in patients who have received large doses. Like vomiting, however, the method is

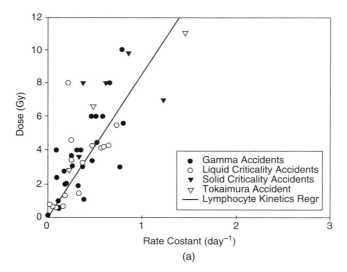

(a)

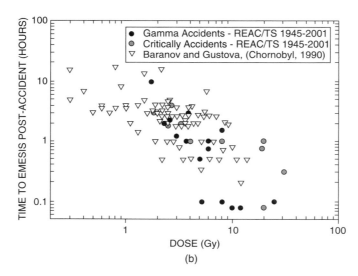

(b)

Figure 12.5
Variability in dose-response relations. Dose vs. (A) lymphocyte kinetics and (B) time-to-vomiting. Data based on gamma-ray, criticality, and Chernobyl accidents. *Source*: Goans and Waselenko, 2004.

uncertain. Figure 12.5b presents accident-victim data showing the considerable variability in lymphocyte depletion between patients (Goans and Waselenko 2004).

Currently, the most accurate dose-assessment methods depend on chromosome-aberration cytogenetic bioassays, and especially the lymphocyte-dicentrics assay introduced by Bender and Gooch (1966). Although normal chromosomes have a single center (centromere), dicentric chromosomes have two. This damaged DNA is produced almost exclusively by radiation. Furthermore, the number of dicentrics per lymphocyte increases with dose. For example, technicians expect to see about four dicentrics per fifty cells for 1 Gy, but fifty-one dicentrics per fifty cells at 5 Gy.[12] Nevertheless, the method has important limitations. First, large samples are needed in order to acquire statistically meaningful results at low doses, although rapid assays based on just fifty cells can still provide useful initial estimates (Alexander et al. forthcoming). Second, caregivers must wait at least 24 hours after exposure to draw blood samples that reflect a whole-body dose. Finally, the analysis takes forty-eight to seventy-two hours to perform. This suggests that the method has little value for first responders, although refined dose estimates can be useful for long-term care.

"You're OK" Markers   For now, there are no good initial screening methods for discriminating exposed victims from the so-called worried well. This is particularly true when the victims themselves carry no measurable contamination or may have been exposed to an external source. New approaches based on biomarkers and physical signatures are currently being developed to solve this problem.

Tracking Victims   Most of today's extensive data on the effects of ionizing radiation comes from tracking studies of Hiroshima and Nagasaki survivors (NRC 1990). More recent tracking programs, notably including Chernobyl, have added still more data. In most cases, the main limitation has been estimating how much radiation individual victims received. Better dose information will be the key to improving tracking studies for better long-term care and, eventually, scientific understanding.

Advanced Technologies   Contamination detectors and tracking tools are mature technologies. For this reason, significant improvements are unlikely to happen soon. For now, the main technological opportunities relate to dose assessment and "you're OK" markers. Here, R&D has centered on developing new biological and physical markers than can serve as cheap and reliable postexposure dosimeters. *Biomarkers* have been the subject of intensive research for many decades (Blakely et al. 2001; Mendelsohn, Mohr, and Peeters 1998; Gledhill and Mauro 1991) and include a variety of chemical and biological properties. Typical examples include nucleic acids, proteins, and small molecule metabolites. Biomarkers can be used to track physical damage (cell lysis, oxidation byproducts, or DNA breakage), biochemical changes (presence of new metabolites or changes in levels of key gene products), and/or changed tissue composition. These, in turn, have been used or proposed for various purposes, including diagnosing exposure to biological and chemical agents, evaluating susceptibility to disease, designing patient-specific therapies, measuring organ system function, and predicting recovery from injury or disease (Waselenko et al. 2004; Moulder 2004).

Efforts to develop effective biomarkers for radiation exposure have been revolutionized by several recent advances. These include an increasingly sophisticated understanding of early biochemical responses to radiation exposure at both the cell and tissue level (Woloschak and Paunesku 1997; Fornace et al. 1999), technologies that permit genome-scale analysis of cellular transcriptional and proteomic profiles (Fornace et al. 1999; Tusher, Tibshirani, and Chu 2001; Chee et al. 1996; Lockhart et al. 1996; Lipshutz et al. 1999; Jain 2002; Kukar et al. 2002; Issaq et al. 2003), improved ability to detect and quantify biomolecular signatures, bioinformatics methods for analyzing large biological data sets (Krieg et al. 2004; Dudoit et al. 2002; Werner 2001; Peterson 2002, 2003), a more explicit understanding of how early DNA damage occurs, detailed knowledge of radiation damage products and the cellular pathways that lead to radiation injury (Thompson and Schild 2001; Burma and Chen 2004; Fernet and Hall 2004; Kurz, and Lees-Miller 2004; Meek 2004), and increasingly systematic proteomic/genomic/metabolomic profiling of what healthy human tissues and serum should look like (Tirumalai et al. 2003). Finally, while most research and technology development has so far centered on genomics and proteomics, other potential molecular classes could prove useful as indicators of radiation dose. Examples include small molecule metabolites, lipids, and glycosylated biomolecules (Alexander et al. forthcoming).

The challenge is to exploit this knowledge to find markers that reliably track radiation exposure. For now, this technology is in its infancy. Most existing work comes from academic institutions and government laboratories; industry has devoted relatively little effort to the problem and commercial assays do not exist. Conceptually, the first step will be to identify candidate markers for radiation damage. Follow-on research will then be needed to understand how well the candidates track total dose, discriminate between different types of radiation and/or different exposure patterns over time, and can be used to infer clinical or biologically relevant effects within the body. R&D will also be needed to distinguish pathological conditions from the normal expression range of candidate markers in healthy people, patients with preexisting conditions, and other confounding factors including age, gender, and genetic background. Finally, researchers will have to compare the value of single markers against methods that rely on multiple signatures (Alexander et al. forthcoming).

Biomarkers are not the only new technology able to estimate how much radiation patients have been exposed to. Several techniques estimate exposure by looking for physical and chemical changes in tissue and/or materials that people commonly carry. Examples include luminescence, nuclear track analysis, electron paramagnetic resonance, breath analysis, and ultrasound. The oldest method, *luminescence*, relies on the fact that heating can reverse radiation damage to a wide variety of natural and manufactured materials and that these objects often give off visible light in the process. Initial methods based on prompt phosphors and photoluminescence were limited to relatively small numbers of materials. However, improved heating control led to the development of thermoluminescence (TL) methods that can reliably reconstruct past radiation exposure for a large number of so-called wide-gap insulators, notably including quartz and feldspar (Aitken 1985). Although originally developed for archaeological dating, current methods are also capable of detecting the very low dose ranges relevant to medicine. Quartz, in particular, is ubiquitous in soil, building materials, and fiber-optic cable. Table salt can similarly serve as a radiation dosimeter (RERF 1983; Khan and Delincée 1995; Espinosa et al. 2004; Kaibao et al. 1986; Fleischer 2002).

Optically stimulated luminescence (OSL) uses visible or infrared light instead of heat to stimulate luminescence. For example, irradiated tooth enamel releases a broadband visible light signal when stimulated with infrared photons and a near-ultraviolet signal when stimulated with green light. Current instruments should be sufficient to detect 15 Gy exposures in nondeproteinated (i.e., whole-tooth) enamel with a signal-to-noise ratio of three. Straightforward improvements (e.g., optimizing the wavelengths used to stimulate and detect fluorescence, better tooth-to-detector geometries) should improve detection to approximately 0.25–0.5 Gy (Godfrey-Smith and Pass 1997). In principle, a portable OSL dosimetry instrument based on these principles could be used to evaluate survivors and would be no more dangerous than shining a strong light into someone's mouth (Huntley, Godfrey-Smith, and Thewalt 1985; Godfrey-Smith and Pass 1997). Similar methods could also be used to measure the effects of gamma, alpha, and beta radiation on various materials that victims commonly carry on their persons. Potential radiation markers include diamonds and other semiprecious stones; semiconductors in cell phones, personal digital assistants, and car keys; and quartz in watches and watch faces.

Alpha particles from uranium, plutonium, and nuclear weapons also leave microscopic tracks in glass and many plastics, including those used in watch crystals and eyeglass lenses. These *nuclear tracks* can be detected after etching with a strong base solution. Unfortunately, this data cannot be calibrated well enough to estimate exposures for specific individuals. The technique can, however, be used to map how much radiation different geographic areas have received (Phillips et al. 2006).

Electron paramagnetic resonance (EPR)[13] detects radiofrequency emission when the unpaired electrons generated by radiation exposure are placed in a high magnetic field. The main advantage of EPR is that it extends the list of potential detectors to include a wide variety of organic and inorganic materials. This includes the inorganic hydroxyapatite component of tooth enamel and bone that, alone among living tissues, is able to retain evidence of absorbed radiation long enough to support human risk assessment. In principle, this could be used to make in vivo measurements on teeth (Miyake et al. 2000; Swartz 2004b). So far, however, the technology has only been demonstrated in lab animals while human volunteers have suffered microwave burns (Swartz 2004a, 2004b; Ikeya and Ishi 1989). Nevertheless, further development based on smaller magnetic fields could provide a practical in vivo dose assessment of teeth and bones. The goal, as always, is to develop a portable instrument that can rapidly assess clinically relevant exposures in the field (Yamanaka, Ikeya, and Hara 1993).

Medical injuries from a nuclear or RDD detonation will often involve combined injury from both burns and radiation. High-frequency *ultrasound devices* have already been developed to image burns. Two pilot studies indicate that both pulse-echo ultrasound and standard B-scan ultrasonic imaging can also detect burns from high-level radiation exposure. This could potentially help hospitals distinguish radiation victims from the worried well (Goans and Cantrell 1978; JIWG 2005; Alexander et al. forthcoming). However, significant work will be needed before the technique is ready for widespread use.

Finally, gamma ray exposure creates large numbers of free radicals that can be detected in human breath. Several studies suggest that *breath analysis* is a potentially powerful tool for rapidly separating patients needing treatment from the worried well (Kharitonov and Barnes 2001; Arterbery et al. 1994; Mueller et al. 1998; Von Basum et al. 2003). Unfortunately, the same gases can also be produced by medical conditions that have nothing to do with radiation exposure. It is also not clear whether the method can be used to estimate radiation dose.

12.3.2   Mitigation

Medical intervention is conventionally divided into (1) prophylaxis, administered before exposure, (2) mitigation, administered before symptoms develop, and (3) treatment. However, prophylaxis is largely irrelevant to civilian defense.[14] Accordingly, this section focuses on mitigation steps. Treatment options are discussed in section 12.3.3.

Most current mitigation technologies are based on limiting the radiation dose that victims receive and, with it, the risk of future medical problems. Treatments that decontaminate victims' bodies are very powerful. Indeed, such simple steps as removing the outer garments and brushing off exposed surfaces can remove most contamination. Additional steps include gently washing exposed skin with soap and water[15] and bagging contaminated clothing and personal effects and placing them outside or otherwise away from people.

At this point, caregivers must turn to decorporation—that is, removing isotopes that may have already entered victims' bodies. Depending on the circumstances, this may be indicated either before a firm diagnosis ("empiric therapy") or after a urine sample has been screened. REMM guidelines for decorporation are relatively isotope-specific. Nevertheless, treatment options share several generic features. First, caregivers can give patients *diluting agents* to flush ingested poisons from the body before they can be absorbed. Gastric lavage and emetics should be administered promptly to empty the stomach completely. Purgatives, laxatives, and enemas can similarly be used to reduce residence time in the colon.

Second, caregivers can administer *blocking agents* to prevent the body from absorbing radioisotopes. For example, ion exchange resins can be used to limit gastrointestinal uptake of certain ingested or inhaled radioisotopes. Provided that they are administered quickly, stable iodide compounds can similarly block uptake of radioactive iodine by the thyroid (see figure 12.6). This is especially important for

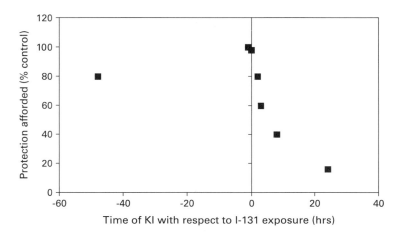

Figure 12.6
Percent thyroid protection from ^{131}I after a single 130 mg dosage of KI. *Source*: Zanzonico and Becker, 2000; Blum and Eisenbud, 1967; Sternthal et al., 1980; Ramsden et al., 1967.

children and adolescents, whose thyroids incorporate iodine much more actively than adults.

Various treatments exist for removing agents that have already been absorbed into the body. These therapies are more effective when they are administered promptly. The basic principle is to use chemicals that bind tightly with radioisotopes to form water-soluble molecules that can be excreted as urine. For nonmetals, so-called *mobilizing agents* are used. These include alginates like ferric ferrocyanide (Prussian blue) for accelerating excretion of ^{137}Cs and propylthiouracil and methimazole for removing radioiodine from the thyroid. *Chelation agents* are similarly used for radioactive metals. Calcium edetate (EDTA), an approved treatment for lead poisoning, can also be used to remove many heavy-metal isotopes. It must, however, be used with extreme caution when kidney disease is present. An investigational drug, diethylene triamine pentaacetic acid (DTPA), promises to be more effective in removing many of the heavy-metal, multivalent radioisotopes, including plutonium, polonium, and other transuranics. Because it forms more stable complexes than EDTA, radioisotopes are less likely to escape before excretion. Similarly, dimercaprol forms stable chelates that can be used to remove radioactive isotopes of mercury, lead, arsenic, gold, bismuth, chromium, and nickel. Finally, penicillamine is known to form chelates with copper, iron, mercury, lead, gold, and possibly other heavy metals. (Interested readers can find further details in *Medical Management of Radiation Casualties Handbook* (AFRRI 2003) and "Radiation Event Medical Management" (HHS n.d.).)

Increasingly, mitigation means more than just decontamination and decorporation. Various drugs are currently being investigated to mitigate radiation damage to the body. These include pentoxifylline, angiotensin-converting enzyme inhibitors, and angiotensin II (AII) receptor antagonists. All of these drugs act by reducing the spread of radiation damage or symptoms. Although their respective mechanisms of action are still undetermined, pentoxifylline is known to target fibrosis. AII antagonists may similarly act to ameliorate kidney and possibly lung injury (Moulder 2004; Coleman et al. 2004).

12.3.2   Treatment

At present, there are no FDA-approved agents for treating acute radiation syndrome. However, hematological cytokines are used in cancer care and might be approved for mitigation or treatment under an Emergency Use Authorization from the FDA or through an Investigational New Drug protocol (Waselenko et al. 2004; Alexander et al. forthcoming; Coleman et al. 2003). Additionally, various drugs are available to facilitate recovery after radiation damage has occurred. These include hematopoietic cytokines, which have been used to treat cancer patients undergoing radiation therapy as well as accident victims suffering from hematopoietic system syndrome (Coleman et al. 2004). Other possible treatments include granulocyte and granulocyte-macrophage colony-stimulating factors, mucosa-stimulating growth factors such as keratinocyte growth factor, and platelet-stimulating drugs.

Besides exploring these drugs, researchers are currently investigating cell-based therapies for restoring damaged bone marrow, skin, or gastrointestinal tract tissues. Investigators are also evaluating the long-term use of relatively nontoxic agents including soy isoflavones and vitamin analogs. Genistein, a soy isoflavone, is already known to promote survival in mice when administered both before and after exposure (Coleman et al. 2004; Landauer, Srinivasan, and Seed 2003).

12.4 Radioactive Contamination in the Biosphere

Survivors' health can also be improved by minimizing radioisotope contamination in the environment. Nuclear weapons detonated at or near the surface of the earth generate large amounts of radioactive debris. Of these, ^{137}Cs, ^{131}I, and ^{90}Sr are by far the most important isotopes. In the case of an RDD, the dominant contaminant would be whichever isotope(s) the terrorists managed to obtain and disperse. Researchers have focused for many years on understanding the air, land, and water routes by which contaminants migrate and, eventually, enter the food chain or otherwise reach victims (SCOPE 1993).

12.4.1 Air Pathways

Airborne transport is important for nuclear weapons and other violent events that inject radionuclides high into the atmosphere. For example, the Chernobyl accident demonstrated that large (>10 μm) particles can be transported more than 100 kilometers away. The ultimate destination of these contaminants is determined by various factors, including the location and manner of release, regional weather systems, and the chemical and physical form of the isotopes and any particles they may be attached to. By comparison, RDDs inject comparatively little contamination into the upper atmosphere. Instead, radionuclides stay in the atmosphere for relatively short periods and fall to earth locally. Unlike nuclear weapons, the resulting fallout patterns are usually shaped by low-level winds and local topography (e.g., urban canyon effects), although limited effects can occur farther downwind.

Radioactive particles and gases ultimately reach the ground through gravity and turbulence (so-called dry deposition) or precipitation (wet deposition). Precipitation is a particularly powerful mechanism for focusing fallout into local "hot spots." Deposited material can also reenter the atmosphere a second time (resuspension), allowing contamination to spread to new areas over time and/or creating an inhalation hazard long after the original event. Similarly, contaminated water can sometimes be blown back onto land as seaspray (SCOPE 1993).

These processes are still not understood in sufficient detail to predict contamination patterns from an accidental release or intentional attack. Deposition is known to be highly variable over space and time. Better prediction will require detailed, quantitative understanding of many key processes. These include the physical and chemical properties of radioisotopes generated in a nuclear or RDD fireball; the subsequent evolution of gas and aerosol contaminants during atmospheric transport; the interaction of radioactive aerosols with cloud droplets; the effects of rain, snow, and other forms of wet deposition; the effects of weather, convection, frontal systems, and complex terrain in accelerating deposition; and so-called occult deposition through ground-level cloud, fog, and mist. Our understanding of resuspension processes that inject contaminants back into the atmosphere from terrestrial and marine reservoirs is similarly rudimentary (SCOPE 1993). Current estimated resuspension rates were developed decades ago. Detailed experiments with surrogate contaminants are needed to improve them.

12.4.2   Land Pathways

Radioisotope transport on land depends primarily on soil geology, vegetation types, and water movement. While some radioisotopes reach the soil immediately, other contaminants are intercepted by foliage, depending on multiple factors including plant-tissue type, roughness, and surface area. At this point, small amounts of contaminants enter the plant and migrate to its roots. Thereafter, groundwater, grazing animals, and cultivation continually cycle contaminants throughout the topmost layers of soil. Groundwater can also be taken up by plants and eventually animals. These processes are very complex and depend on various factors, including plant and animal metabolism, grazing, harvesting, and excretion. This can potentially lead to reentry into drinking water and food, producing new contamination hazards long after the original event.

Traditional attempts to trace these pathways have usually assumed that potassium is a good chemical surrogate for radioactive cesium and that calcium as a good surrogate for radioactive strontium (SCOPE 1993). More recently, the Chernobyl accident has prompted extensive research on the long-term movement of real contaminants along terrestrial pathways. These include such worrisome isotopes as cesium (^{137}Cs), strontium (^{90}Sr), cerium (^{144}Ce), and ruthenium (^{106}Ru). The degree to which individual species bind to rock at any given concentration in groundwater turns out to be important. Species that bind strongly tend to remain in the top layer of soil where they can become candidates for colloid transport or resuspension in the atmosphere. For example, soil concentrations of ^{137}Cs did not measurably decline during the first seven years after the accident (Kashparov et al. 2000). By contrast, ^{90}Sr dissolved in groundwater much more readily and migrated into the underlying soil (Lujaniene et al. 1998; Andersson and Roed 1999). Experience in decontaminating U.S. nuclear weapons facilities has similarly contributed to our understanding of how radioisotopes interact with various soil substrates (Committee on the Remediation of Buried and Tank Wastes 2000).

Radionuclides also enter plant life through surfaces (e.g., leaves or bark) and root uptake. The amount of contamination absorbed depends strongly on local conditions. In the area around Chernobyl, roots absorbed 200 times more ^{90}Sr than foliage did. In this case, uptake was greatly accelerated by strontium's ability to dissolve in water. Contaminated plants can also release radionuclides through death, decay, and forest fires. Fires in contaminated areas near Chernobyl routinely raise the amounts of airborne contaminants by several orders of magnitude, although this effect is temporary (Kashparov et al. 2000). The destination of these contaminants depends sensitively on winds and other postfire conditions (Andersson 1999).

Despite these advances, much remains to be learned. More understanding is needed of how readily plants and animals take up different radioisotopes; the behavior of radioisotopes in organically rich soils, particularly with respect to processes that operate over long periods of time; the physical migration of contaminated particles;[16] the rate at which different isotopes leach from fallout particles; the role of microorganisms in modifying and transporting contaminants; the impact of agriculture on migration; and the role of resuspension and other processes that can create new hazards long after the original event. Similarly, despite steady improvements, numerical models of how radioisotopes pass through the food chain still need further validation—for example, by testing young animals. Finally, our knowledge remains notably uneven. Researchers know much more about how the main nuclear weapons contaminants behave compared to isotopes like ^{110}Ag that might be released by an RDD. Similarly, our knowledge of how radioisotopes behave is much more complete for agricultural systems than for forests and other natural and seminatural ecosystems.

12.4.3 Water Pathways

Ice and water (e.g., rivers, lakes, estuaries, shelf seas, deep oceans, ice sheets, glaciers, groundwater, and ground ice) cover a large fraction of the earth's surface and provide major pathways for contamination. Transfer depends on multiple factors, including whether the contaminant is solid or dissolved; chemical interactions between the solid and liquid phases; and processing by living things. Water chemistry is particularly crucial in determining which radioisotopes dissolve and what compounds they form. Results will typically be different depending on whether the water is aerobic or anaerobic, saline or fresh, and (for freshwater) alkaline or acid. The ratio of solids to dissolved contaminants also varies depending on the size and chemical composition of sediment and bedrock grains and whether these surfaces have been modified by inorganic (e.g., oxyhydroxide) or organic deposits. The net effect of these very complex processes is to transport, mix, dilute, and sometimes even concentrate dissolved contaminants. Contaminants that enter the water as solid particles can also settle out at very different rates depending on the type of contaminant and how they initially entered the water (SCOPE 1993).

Much remains to be learned. Radioisotope migration in water is known to depend sensitively on thin film layers floating on the surface, microorganisms, and certain solid/liquid suspensions called colloids. Research is particularly urgent for freshwater pathways, especially lakes, which are known to be vulnerable to pollution. Collaborative international efforts to study known hot zones (e.g., Chernobyl and several polar sea locations) will go some distance toward filling these gaps.

12.4.4   Urban Environments

The distribution pattern of fallout in urban areas depends on weather (i.e., wet or dry), the nature of the surfaces it falls on, and the physical and chemical properties of the isotopes themselves. This initial pattern is modified by subsequent washoff, usually in the form of precipitation on outdoor surfaces and deliberate cleaning within structures. The net result is that contamination tends to become highly variable over time with relatively clean locations in some areas (e.g., impervious surfaces) and hot spots in others (e.g., soil, drainage areas). Detailed simulations of urban cleanup strategies suggest that digging up gardens and defoliating trees are among the most cost-effective ways to eliminate contaminants (SCOPE 1993).

The processes by which urban materials absorb and retain radioisotopes are still incompletely understood. Improved decontamination methods depend on filling this gap. Stable isotopes (e.g., tritium) are a particularly promising way to simulate fallout contaminants and improve existing contamination and cleanup models (SCOPE 1993).

12.5   Remediation Technologies

Current methods reflect more than sixty years of practical and laboratory experience in removing radionuclides from contaminated equipment, structures, and geographic regions. This section discusses what we know about the decontamination problem, current state of the art, and directions for future research.

12.5.1   Knowledge Base

Decontamination refers to the process of removing radioisotopes from objects, structures, and geographic areas to limit health risks to the general public, reduce the danger of airborne resuspension, permit access to contaminated sites, and facilitate waste disposal. Most of what we know about decontamination comes from U.S. nuclear weapons testing in the 1940s and 1950s, U.S. nuclear weapons accidents in the 1960s, experience at Chernobyl, and controlled laboratory testing.

Nuclear Test Data   Operation CROSSROADS (1946) showed that contamination from a weapon detonated approximately 500 feet above the ocean created relatively little fallout, so that exposed ships were relatively easy to decontaminate. By contrast, detonating an identical weapon underwater made some ships unsafe to board and others accessible only for short periods of time. The underwater explosion also contaminated the ocean itself, forcing support vessels away from the test area. These results prompted further experiments to see how ships and buildings could be decontaminated following a shallow-water explosion. In Operation CASTLE (1954), panels of various building materials were exposed at different orientations to the explosion and their contamination measured. Various cleanup methods were then tried, including low-pressure washing, water scrubbing, pressure washing, detergent washing, and hot rinsing. In general, rough surfaces were the most easily contaminated and the most resistant to cleanup. For example, fire-hose washing reduced contamination on asphalt and gravel roofing material by just 41 percent compared to 93 percent for high-pressure washing and hot-rinsing methods on sheet metal. Contamination also depended sensitively on the material's orientation, with horizontal surfaces retaining 5 to 300 times as much radioactivity as sloped surfaces (Becker et al. 2002).

Systematic experiments on typical urban materials began with Operation PLUMBBOB (1954)'s series of tests in the Nevada desert. The PLUMBBOB tests found that simple decontamination technologies such as vacuuming, pressure washing, detergent washing, and steaming were highly efficient. The data also imply that decontamination would be relatively straightforward for nonporous or painted building materials exposed to an RDD.[17] Unfortunately, the PLUMBBOB studies failed to measure certain quantities (recovery of material, mass balance versus concentration) that are needed for computer modeling and prediction. They have never been replicated.

Accidents   Several accidents provide practical experience with decontamination and recovery in RDD-like situations. In January 1966 two hydrogen bombs hit the ground after a midair collision near Palomares, Spain, dispersing plutonium over a wide area. The United States mounted a substantial effort to rehabilitate the site by removing and replacing contaminated soil and plants. The removed material was stored as low-level radioactive waste. Today, the land is used for commercial agriculture. A bomber crash near Thule, Greenland, in January 1968 similarly produced RDD-like contamination of snow and ice. This, too, was collected and disposed of (Becker et al. 2002).

Probably the most informative RDD-like accident involved a range safety officer's decision to destroy a live, nuclear-tipped missile that failed during liftoff in 1962. The high-explosive charge spread plutonium across the missile's erector base, shelter building, and launchpad. The U.S. military painted the structures to fix contamination in place and continued to use them safely thereafter. Most of the structures were later demolished during decommissioning. However, the launchpad was scabbled (rough-cut) to a depth of seven millimeters and the debris vacuumed for removal.

Not surprisingly, the Chernobyl accident provided a proving ground for testing various decontamination technologies. Roed and Andersson (1996) studied methods for decontaminating sandstone walls. Some of the walls had been exposed to small particles of uranium fuel that contained various fission products. Others had been exposed to rainwater containing ^{137}Cs. Four methods were tested: soaking the surfaces with an ammonium nitrate solution for thirty minutes and then removing it; applying a clay (montmorillonite) paste to the surface and then peeling or vacuuming it off after it dried; hosing the surface with high-pressure (150 bar) water; and wet sandblasting. Of these, sandblasting appeared to be the most effective. See table 12.4.

Andersson and Roed (1999) later developed an urban-area cleanup guide based on their studies of decontamination at Chernobyl. The guide contains detailed information about numerous urban surfaces including asphalt, concrete, roofing materials, walls, trees, lawns, and cultivated areas. Table 12.5 summarizes how effectively

Table 12.4
Decontamination technology: Removing fallout from sandstone walls near Chernobyl

Technology	Wall 1 (dry-deposited ^{137}Cs)	Wall 2 (wet-deposited ^{137}Cs)
Cation exchange	67%	21%
Clay treatment	10%	Not tried
High-pressure hosing	28%	32%
Wet sandblasting	95%	83%

Source: Adapted from Roed and Andersson 1996

different techniques can reduce victims' exposure to wet- and dry-deposited ^{134}Cs. Significantly, decontamination must take place within a few days of the original release to be fully effective.

Laboratory Studies   Real, Persin, and Camarasa-Claret (2002) conducted laboratory tests of clay tiles and concrete slabs that had been dry deposited with ^{134}Cs and ^{85}Sr aerosols and subsequently exposed to simulated urban pollution (calcium sulfate, organic matter) and rainfall. They found that rainfall reduced ^{134}Cs contamination by 5 to 6 percent for both materials. However, ^{85}Sr was reduced by 12 percent for concrete and 29 percent for tile. Soaking for twenty-four hours in highly concentrated ammonium chloride and oxalate solutions removed 70 and 90 percent of ^{134}Cs from tile and concrete, respectively. By comparison, ammonium chloride only removed 40 percent of the ^{85}Sr from concrete and 50 percent from tile. Oxalate was ineffective in removing ^{85}Sr.

Commercial Experience   In addition to the foregoing, significant decontamination experience has been accumulated for commercial nuclear power facilities and the cleanup of the U.S. nuclear weapons facilities. (Readers seeking further information should consult NRC 2000.)

12.5.2   State of the Art

The decontamination problem—and our capacity to meet it—depends sensitively on the extent of damage. In the worst-case scenario of a nuclear attack on an urban center, radiation levels will decay slowly. This may preclude decontamination of the most heavily damaged areas for between twelve and thirty months. Thereafter, the speed of decontamination programs may be limited by the need to manage worker exposure and/or a shortage of qualified workers. Deciding when to commit

Table 12.5
Dose-rate reductions in urban areas following decontamination

Decontamination technology	Immediate dose-rate reduction (dry-deposited ^{137}Cs)	Immediate dose-rate reduction (wet-deposited ^{137}Cs)
Wall hosing	1–6%	1–6%
Roof hosing	7–14%	4–11%
Vacuum sweeping	7–14%	14–27%
Road hosing	7–14%	14–27%

Source: Adapted from Andersson and Roed 1999

workers to individual decontamination tasks will require sophisticated cost-benefit calculations.

Once recovery operations begin, heavy equipment will have to clear areas that suffered heavy destruction. The resulting waste is likely to include rubble, concrete, asphalt, and other building materials, along with significant amounts of earth and plant material scraped from the topmost layers of the soil. Workers would likely pack this waste into improvised containment vessels (e.g., railcars) for burial at a remote location that receives minimal precipitation. This landfill would have to be carefully lined and monitored for leaks.

There is no consensus strategy for rapid, large-scale remediation of buildings that are contaminated but otherwise largely intact. However, EPA would probably try to evaluate various technologies that have been demonstrated on a smaller scale by the nuclear power industry and/or decommissioning activities at U.S. weapons sites. These tests would have to take place quickly, since the task of restoring highly contaminated areas would become steadily more difficult over time. Decontamination options would depend on the depth to which contamination had penetrated and the types of stones found in masonry buildings. (Interested readers can find a review of these materials in Becker et al. 2002.) Structures that could not be efficiently decontaminated would almost certainly be demolished and the rubble disposed of alongside buildings destroyed in the blast.

Decontamination becomes steadily more cost-effective away from ground zero and will often be practical where visible damage is small or sites have special cultural or economic value. In general, there are two types of contamination. *Removable contamination* is similar to dust that settles on a table, and can be wiped away relatively easily. This will be a significant issue for restoring the interiors of homes or buildings exposed to fallout. *Fixed contamination*, on the other hand, is tightly bound to substrates through diffusion and chemical interaction. This latter category presents most of the challenges associated with decontamination. Given today's technologies, demolition and disposal may often be the most cost-effective way to decontaminate facilities.

Policymakers would have a long list of decontamination technologies to choose from. Choice of method would normally depend on the problem being considered:

• *Contaminated buildings* Options would include temporary abandonment, demolishing and replacing the structure, or decontaminating to levels consistent with public health. In general, the simplest and least costly technology is soap-and-water wash-down, which costs pennies per gallon and does not require special protective equipment beyond that normally required to protect workers visiting a contaminated site. More aggressive decontamination methods, such as strippable coatings or light-fixative aerosol fogging, can cost $50–$100 per gallon as well as requiring specialized training and protective gear. Finally, very aggressive decontamination methods include acid wash-down followed by a neutralizer rinse. These methods can cost $100–$1,000 per gallon and require specialized equipment (e.g., fume hoods) as well as very intensive training and protective gear. In general, these technologies also pose safety hazards and require more planning (Carlsen 2004).

• *Pathways, stairs, parking lots, streets, and other large paved areas consisting of asphalt, concrete, granite, marble, slate, sandstone, gravel, etc.*   Options would include washing with water or chemically enhanced solutions; chipping (scabbling) of contaminated upper layers followed by resurfacing with asphalt or concrete; or demolition and removal. Isotopes that are not promptly removed will normally migrate deeper into the material, particularly when rain or snow is present. At this point, washing and chipping solutions may become prohibitively expensive compared to demolition and removal (Becker et al. 2002).

• *Grassy areas, medians, parks, and locations with exposed ground or vegetation* Removal and burial of contaminated material and replacement by clean fill is normally the most cost-effective method.

• *Contaminated transportation infrastructure (e.g., bridges, subways)*   Public transportation systems combine very high decontamination and replacement costs with relatively predictable, short daily exposures to members of the traveling public. Policymakers could well decide that it made sense to revise acceptable dose rates upward once nondestructive technologies encountered diminishing returns.

• *Automobiles*   Many of the nondestructive techniques summarized in table 12.4 could potentially be applied to automobiles.

12.5.3   Doing Better

Existing decontamination technologies were developed primarily for decommissioning U.S. weapons facilities and the commercial nuclear power industry. For this reason, methods are significantly biased toward dilution and/or destructive removal of existing infrastructure. Developing new technologies will be challenging. First, there is the problem of scale. RDD or nuclear weapons explosions can potentially contaminate very large areas, generate many different possible radioisotopes or mixtures of isotopes, and deliver contaminants in a wide range of chemical and physical (aerosol, solid, and dissolved) forms. Second, our knowledge is bound to be imperfect. Successful technologies must therefore be sufficiently flexible to bridge current uncertainties about contaminants' physical and chemical properties, the mechanisms by which they are deposited on surfaces, and the absence of experimental data for many urban materials. These uncertainties are particularly great for the extreme conditions near ground zero. Finally, the technologies must work when responders have only imperfect knowledge of the problems they face. Real-world disasters will almost certainly be different from academic projections, let alone training exercises. They are also likely to be dynamic, with contaminants dispersing—sometimes because of responders' own actions—and changing their physical-chemical properties over time.

So far, relatively little effort has been invested in developing new decontamination technologies. As we have seen, it is very unlikely that any one "breakthrough" technology will be appropriate for every radionuclide, substrate, and contamination problem. This suggests that individual emerging technologies from industry, academia, and national laboratories need to be coordinated with one another to avoid duplication and fill existing gaps. One reasonable first step would be to create a nationally recognized independent test center to evaluate products, determine their capabilities (including decontamination efficiency), and delineate the conditions, contaminants, and substrates for which they are suitable. Over time, gaps in both technology and basic science would become apparent. This would allow policymakers to prioritize R&D around modifications to existing/emerging technologies and/or basic science initiatives needed to fill the remaining knowledge gaps (Taylor et al. 2003).

Continual assessment of emerging technologies will also help prioritize the relatively short list of technologies that can be commercialized and stockpiled at strategic locations around the United States. In general, versatile technologies that address multiple needs will be more valuable than those that do not. Technologies that have significant non–civil defense applications will also be desirable to the extent that private demand makes commercial production more attractive (Taylor et al. 2003).

12.6   Putting Science to Work

The work described in previous sections, though far from complete, provides a powerful fund of basic knowledge for (1) diagnosing and treating radiation exposure in the direct victims of an attack, and (2) anticipating, managing, and preventing additional exposures from radionuclides released into the environment. The question now is whether society should take the next step of turning this knowledge into technology and capabilities. On paper, at least, this seems a sensible investment. Current simulations routinely predict that, depending on the size of the nuclear blast, weather, and other conditions, tens of thousands of the victims could receive exposures of between 3 and 5 Gy from fallout. While these doses are normally fatal, aggressive treatment could make them survivable for the great majority of patients. These odds could be greatly improved by disseminating information so that people could protect themselves in the first hours after an attack. Such steps could keep victims' doses well within the survivable region. Even assuming that the chances of a nuclear attack in the next decade are on the order of a few percent—a figure far smaller than the 50-50 probability routinely estimated by respected scholars like Allison (2004)—the expected number of lives saved still measures in the many thousands. Adopting a fairly typical federal-agency assumption of $4–6 million per life (Kaiser 2003) suggests that research and preparedness activities totaling in the hundreds of millions of dollars would be reasonable. This is not very different from current funding projections. Priorities would include:

Civil defense   Providing information about self-decontamination and sheltering, including a list of emergency supplies to have on hand, would be helpful. While communication is a challenge, possible methods include the Internet, mailings, and local information sessions. However, it would be important to assess the impact of these various approaches (including compliance rates) so that time and resources are spent wisely.

Improved planning and modeling tools   Technology advances over the past fifty years could put powerful modeling and decision support tools in the hands of planners and first responders. These include real-time programs for modeling blast damage, radiation, and fallout plumes (Nasstrom et al. 2005). Detailed modeling could similarly provide much more insight into the timing and range of injuries expected to appear after a ground-level urban detonation.

Better diagnostic and treatment technologies   Experience from radiation accidents and cancer treatment provide important knowledge that could be used to improve diagnostic and treatment technologies. Laboratory assessment is essential and more facilities for conducting hematology assays, radiobioassays to measure internal contamination, and cytogenetic biodosimetry are needed. A rapid screening tool for distinguishing those who do need immediate medical intervention would also save enormous time, resources, and personnel while reassuring the "worried well." Further investment is also necessary to develop medical countermeasures for managing acute radiation syndrome. Given the similarity between radiation injury and tissue injury in general, most of the radiation countermeasures could also be used in the treatment of cancer, inflammation, and perhaps age-related illnesses.

Remediation technology   Remediation and cleanup technologies following an attack are comparatively less urgent because there would be weeks to months for on-the-job learning. That said, advance investment in some technologies—notably products and procedures for immobilizing radionuclides in the immediate aftermath of an attack—could produce large savings in total cleanup costs. Beyond this, the central discussion of how (and how much) to clean up should not be left until an attack actually occurs. Response will be much more effective if society has considered and even reached some agreement about these issues in advance. The "Protective Action Guides" (ORP n.d.) have made significant progress in building this consensus among federal agencies.

Sixty years of basic research have opened up a wide range of technological strategies that could significantly reduce casualties from an RDD or nuclear attack. The required investments are not trivial, but neither are they overwhelming. Ultimately, the decision to spend this money is a political one that should be based on science and technology that are currently available or in development. Nevertheless, it is important for politicians to realize that relatively modest but wise investments could plausibly have a major impact on preparedness.

12.7   Conclusions

Recovery from nuclear and radiological weapons attacks is dominated by the problems of real or potential human exposure to ionizing radiation, either directly from the original weapon or through fallout. Human exposure, in turn, involves multiple impacts ranging from life-threatening acute radiation sickness in the short term to long-term cancer, retardation, and (possibly) gene-pool impacts. Medical intervention aims to identify, assess, track, mitigate, and treat exposed victims. Environmental remediation complements these efforts by limiting radiation exposure, particularly over the long term.

Current-generation assessment methods rely on clinical signs and symptoms, supplemented by time- and resource-intensive technologies like hematology assays, tissue bioassays, and cytogenetics. Over the next five to ten years advances in genomics and molecular marker science, coupled with clever micro- and nanotechnology should deliver much cheaper identification and assessment tools. Promising research also exists that would let responders estimate victims' exposure from tooth enamel, diamonds, and/or other materials. Finally, treatment technologies have received a significant boost from oncology and hematology experience and new approaches are under development. As with assessment tools, research and FDA approval is limited by the absence of peacetime patients on whom new treatments can be tested. The FDA has introduced several innovations to address these problems, including a new "Animal Rule" that allows licensing based on animal tests where human studies are not feasible or ethical (Gronvall et al. 2008).

Today's investments in civil defense and decontamination are still very small relative to what is already known and could be done. Further technological improvements will require a deeper understanding of contamination pathways and chemistry. Environmental technologies similarly need to be tested, commercialized, and strategically stockpiled. All else being equal, technologies that are versatile or have significant dual-use civilian functions will be more attractive than those that do not.

Overall, the greatest challenge for nuclear and radiological recovery is perception. Current U.S. policy still heavily favors detection and prevention over response and recovery. However, this strategy is much more doubtful than it was in an era when deterrence could be achieved by political means. At the same time, the payoffs from investing in response and recovery are much greater than they used to be. The resurgence of Hiroshima and Nagasaki suggest that recovery from one or at most a few detonations is a realistic and attainable goal. Although many lives would surely be lost in a nuclear attack, many lives could also be saved with proper preparation and investments. In the post–September 11 world, it is important to take a modern look at recovery. Timely social and technological investments can significantly reduce loss of life and property from a nuclear or radiological attack.

Notes

1. The relative dangers posed by explosion and radiation would depend on the RDD's construction. At one end of the scale, an RDD could be designed to distribute radiation without any explosion at all. In this case, attacks would be covert and might not be noticed for some time. At the other end of the scale, RDD designers could combine small amounts of radioactive material with large quantities of explosive. At the limit, such weapons would be physically indistinguishable from a large truck bomb.

2. This is particularly true of medical technologies designed to treat acute radiation syndrome. The converse, of course, is not true: technologies that are effective against RDDs are not necessarily useful against nuclear weapons. For example, treatments that block radionuclides from entering the body and/or remove them from patients are typically more useful against RDDs than nuclear weapons.

3. In the case of an RDD, the explosion's radioactive plume would typically disperse in an hour.

4. Interested readers should consult the "Protective Action Guides" (ORP n.d.) for further details. Significantly, these guidelines are *not* meant to establish binding regulations. Decisions on allowable exposure would be made by local officials drawing on expert advice.

5. This is the basic principle of diagnostic nuclear medicine.

6. A unit of radiation exposure. See chapter 3.

7. Gamma ray equivalent dose. The lifetime risk also varies considerably with age at the time of exposure (NRC 1990).

8. Gestational age measures the fetus's age from the mother's last period.

9. Some drugs (e.g., hematopoietic cytokines) can be used for both mitigation and treatment. Mitigation will often be needed at lower radiation doses when patients have also suffered burns or other nonradiation injuries.

10. The International Commission on Radiation Protection has published extensive data on doses to members of the public (ICRP 1989–1996), workers (ICRP 1988, 1997), and related topics (ICRP 1980, 1986, 1994a, 1994b, 1996).

11. AFRRI's Biological Assessment Tool software is available online at www.afrri.usuhs.mil/.

12. Readers should note that each cell has multiple chromosomes.

13. Also referred to as electron spin resonance or ESR.

14. Prophylactics would be useful to the extent that they could be administered before fallout reached victims or to protect first responders. Examples of prophylactic pharmaceuticals include amifostine and tempol. These drugs scavenge the free radicals that would otherwise be released during the initial phases of radiation injury and can protect a broad range of cellular and tissue systems within the body. They are only effective when administered before exposure (Coleman et al. 2003).

15. Hair should be washed without shampoo or conditioner.

16. These effects are particularly important near the release, where contamination tends to take the form of particles.

17. The PLUMBBOB experiments also measured how contaminants migrate over time.

13

Remediation Following Chemical and Biological Attacks

Ellen Raber, Tina Carlsen, and Robert Kirvel

A terrorist attack involving chemical or biological warfare agents would require decision makers to make timely and informed choices about whether and how to respond. Following the confirmation of a release (chapter 5) and the completion of immediate first-response operations to limit casualties and property damage, recovery would require a broad range of actions. Remediation technologies are only part of the solution. A terrorist attack on public facilities would also require careful judgments that take into consideration both health-protective technologies and consensus-based cleanup goals (Raber et al. 2001, 2004). In general, our discussion focuses on cleaning up public facilities following a terrorist attack because such remediation represents an urgent problem of national importance. Cleaning up private facilities is less well studied but is presumably analogous. Even in the public sector, some aspects of the cleanup problem have important political implications that are still not resolved.

Section 13.1 presents a brief account of the Tokyo chemical weapons (1995) and American *B. anthracis* (2001) attacks and explains how these events have reshaped expert thinking about remediation. Section 13.2 describes how modern consensus concepts describing response and recovery actions have replaced earlier usages that were often inconsistent, ambiguous, and contradictory. Section 13.3 introduces a decision framework for managing the aftermath of an attack and addresses the related issues of cleanup or clearance goals (i.e., How clean is clean enough?). Section 13.4 reviews existing technologies for meeting clearance goals in indoor and semi-enclosed settings. It also describes new technologies that may soon be available and research on wide-area decontamination of an entire city. Section 13.5 describes what is known about clearance goals for chemical and biological warfare agents. Finally, section 13.6 provides a brief conclusion.

13.1   Recent History

Current response and remediation thinking has been shaped by the Tokyo chemical weapons (1995) and Washington, D.C., *B. anthracis* (2001) attacks. This section briefly reviews the history of the two attacks and how responses to the incidents have influenced subsequent thinking.

13.1.1   The Tokyo Attacks

In 1995, terrorists used sarin nerve gas to attack the Tokyo subway system. The attack killed twelve people and affected approximately 5,000 others (Nagao et al. 1997). As usual for chemical attacks, symptoms ranging from distress to death occurred within seconds.[1]

13.1.2   The 2001 *B. anthracis* Attacks

Shortly after the September 11 attacks, cases of inhalational anthrax began to appear in Florida, Washington, D.C., and New York.[2] Suspected or confirmed *B. anthracis* contamination was reported in at least seven U.S. states.[3] Unlike the Tokyo attacks, symptoms were slow to develop, as is typical for biological agents. Because medical interventions are most effective when implemented promptly, authorities mounted a massive effort to identify, treat, and track approximately 10,000 potentially exposed individuals. Even so, five deaths occurred among those receiving postsymptomatic treatment (GAO 2003c; EPA 2002). Expensive programs were also mounted to decontaminate and refurbish contaminated facilities. The efforts to remediate sites contaminated by *B. anthracis* spores were unprecedented. The three most important lessons from the cleanup experiences were that (1) fumigation is usually necessary for indoor releases involving significant amounts of *B. anthracis* spores, (2) remediation (including fumigation) is complex, time consuming, and costly, and (3) preparedness and planning are critical to improving the quality and timeliness of future cleanups. The combined medical and decontamination response resulted in total costs approaching $1 billion.

The attacks underlined the importance of interagency coordination at the national level and the need for establishing clearance goals that had never before been codified. The Comprehensive Environmental Restoration, Compensation, and Liability Act (CERCLA) gives the Environmental Protection Agency (EPA) oversight authority for environmental cleanup, particularly for outdoor contamination. However, the *B. anthracis* cleanups at various locations were handled quite differently, depending on who owned a particular facility. The Federal Bureau of Investigation (FBI), Centers for Disease Control and Prevention (CDC), and state and local public health departments all played major response roles.

In the private sector, cleanup efforts were largely decided by economics. For example, NBC and ABC both hired hazardous waste contractors to perform surface cleanups at their New York offices. The sampling and cleanup at ABC took about three weeks and reportedly cost several hundred thousand dollars. NBC similarly resumed normal business after about one month of *B. anthracis* cleanup. By contrast, tenants of the privately owned Florida office park moved out, leaving the landlord with decontamination responsibilities that he could not afford. Political and bureaucratic issues also delayed cleanup. In July 2005, the owner of the building assigned MARCOR Remediation to finish the cleanup begun by another contractor. The Palm Beach County Health Department lifted the quarantine order on February 12, 2007.

Public-sector cleanup was largely driven by politics. For example, the EPA was immediately called in to manage cleanup at the Hart Senate Building. Here, no expense was spared to decontaminate and characterize the facility as quickly as possible. In the end, cleanup took about three months and the remediation of office buildings on Capitol Hill cost about $28 million. Cleanup at the Department of State Annex–32 cost $27.4 million, and combined cleanup costs at the Trenton and Brentwood postal facilities totaled about $200 million.

13.1.3   Remediation Planning

Lines of authority are considerably clearer today than they were seven years ago. For example, the National Response Framework identifies the EPA as the lead agency responsible for remediation and cleanup. In some cases, however, the roles and responsibilities of other agencies are still unclear. In particular, the interface between local public health agencies and CDC remains complicated, and most jurisdictions have yet to define their response and recovery roles.

Since 2001, researchers around the country have worked on many different fronts to bring technical insight and operational consistency to the cleanup challenges posed by chemical and biological attacks.[4] In particular, researchers at Lawrence Livermore National Laboratory (LLNL) and other national laboratories have worked hard to develop methods for quickly and cost-effectively reopening public facilities, such as airports and subways, following an attack. A general remediation plan has been delivered to the Washington Metropolitan Area Transit Authority, and a biological remediation plan for San Francisco International Airport (LLNL 2007) was later approved by the EPA and the Department of Homeland Security (DHS). A plan is also being written for remediation following a chemical agent attack at Los Angeles International Airport. The San Francisco and Los Angeles documents are intended to serve as templates for other critical transportation infrastructure. Preparedness workshops have been held to foster awareness and

Response and Recovery Activities					
(Crisis Management)		**(Consequence Management)**			
Notification	**First Response**	**Remediation/Cleanup**			**Restoration (Recovery)**
		Characterization	**Decontamination**	**Clearance**	
Receive and assess information

Identify suspect release sites

Relay key information and potential risks to appropriate agencies | HAZMAT and emergency actions

Forensic investigation

Public health actions

Screening sampling

Determination of agent type, concentration, and viability

Risk communication | Detailed characterization of agent

Characterization of affected site

Site containment

Continue risk communication

Characterization environmental sampling and analysis

Initial risk assessment

Clearance goals | Worker health and safety

Source reduction

Decontamination strategy

Remediation Action Plan

Site preparation

Waste disposal

Decontamination of sites, items, or both

Verification of decontamination parameters | Clearance sampling and analysis

Clearance decision | Renovation

Reoccupation decision

Long-term environmental and public health monitoring |

Figure 13.1
Response and recovery phases to a chemical or biological event.

planning at several East Coast airports, more workshops are planned for other parts of the country, and a biological remediation plan is being developed for Grand Central Terminal in New York City.

13.2   Overview: Basic Concepts

In the past, inconsistent terminology has often led to confusion. Figure 13.1 presents modern consensus definitions of the main response and recovery phases following a terrorist incident, along with the principal activities associated with each phase.[5]

In general, actions following a terrorist attack can be divided into six principal phases (LLNL 2007). The phases are:

• *Notification* Response begins when an Emergency Operations Center (EOC) identifies an incident or obtains knowledge of a threat. The main task is to gather and share information with appropriate response agencies.

• *First-response phase* An Incident Command team of law enforcement and emergency personnel is activated. Depending on the event, members are likely to include security, medical, and hazardous materials (hazmat) experts. The main tasks include controlling the contaminated area and crime scene; rescuing, evacuating, quarantining if necessary, and otherwise managing victims; eliminating conditions (e.g., fire or explosion) that pose immediate threats to human health; and minimizing the spread of contamination. The phase continues as long as emergency personnel are present and ends when conditions immediately dangerous to human health are brought under control and law enforcement (usually the FBI) returns control of the site to response and recovery personnel.

• *Characterization* The chemical or biological agent is reliably identified, the location and extent of contamination are characterized, and the agent's identity is confirmed with standard analytical techniques. Samples can include surface wipes and swabs, large-volume air filters, vacuum samples, water, and vegetation. The agent's environmental characteristics (e.g., survivability on surfaces) and potential threat to humans and the environment are examined.

• *Decontamination* Detailed decontamination plans are prepared and implemented. For some nonpersistent chemical or biological agents, natural attenuation may be adequate. If so, authorities can simply wait for a predetermined period and then reopen the site. Surface decontamination and medical interventions may also be sufficient in cases where the agent is not persistent or contamination is limited. Cases involving extensive indoor contamination by persistent agents such as *B. anthracis* require more elaborate methods. Here, decontamination usually begins with *source reduction*—that is, removing items and precleaning surfaces to reduce the amount of contaminant. Source reduction is followed by *site preparation*, including sealing openings to prevent leaks, setting up fumigation equipment, and pretesting reagents and delivery systems. Decontamination ends when the treatment chemicals have been removed or neutralized and all related decontamination activities, including waste disposal, are complete. *Outdoor wide-area decontamination* is challenging, particularly for persistent biological agents. To date, there has been relatively little testing to evaluate the impact of cleanup methods on the environment and their interaction with hydrogeological conditions such as soil porosity or permeability.

• *Clearance phase* Authorities determine whether it is safe to reoccupy a facility or area and resume normal activities. Experts review and evaluate key data including characterization and clearance sample results, records of the decontamination process, quality assurance/quality control (QA/QC) results, biological culture tests (in some cases), and other information. All data are compared against clearance goals to judge the effectiveness of decontamination and to determine whether or not to reoccupy the facility. The final decision is made by local, state, or federal public health officials and/or government agencies, depending on jurisdiction. The decision on clearance is passed on to the facility owner, who typically determines when or whether to reopen in conjunction with local public health officials. In the case of outdoor public areas, public health officials will likely make the decision to reopen a given area.

• *Restoration phase*   The site is prepared for reoccupancy. Actions include renovating areas that have undergone fumigation as well as the potential for longer-term monitoring.

13.3   Decision Framework

The problem of decontaminating and cleaning up chemical and biological warfare agents in the public sector is not only agent-specific but also site-specific. In terms of agent specificity, an important consideration is the persistence of a given agent. For example, most biological agents degrade naturally in the environment with time and exposure to ultraviolet light or moisture and humidity. Others, notably *B. anthracis* spores, are highly persistent. The chemical agents, VX and sulfur mustard, also tend to be persistent. In terms of site specificity, three general scenarios span the range of possible sites and responses. First, decontamination can take place in an open setting, such as an outdoor location in a city. Here, many environmental variables must be considered, and dilution or natural attenuation may be appropriate depending on the type of agent. Simply waiting is also sometimes sufficient. Second, decontamination can take place indoors—for example, in an airport terminal. Here, decontamination of ventilation systems is usually a high priority and public-perception issues are important. Finally, decontamination can take place in a semienclosed setting, such as a subway system. This hybrid situation combines aspects of the outdoor and indoor scenarios. To date, most planning has focused on the indoor and semienclosed scenarios.

An appropriate decision framework must define procedures for evaluating the hazard posed by the agent in air, on surfaces, or in water; assessing the exposure potential to people; and deciding on the need for remediation (e.g., decontamination) if warranted. Quantitative risk assessment and other qualitative considerations, including stakeholder concerns, are all necessary inputs to this process. Finally, the framework must lead to a cleanup or clearance goal that defines the amount of contamination—usually expressed numerically—that provides acceptable protection to human health and the environment following a cleanup operation.[6]

Figure 13.2 presents a simplified, risk-informed decision flowchart for decontamination-phase activities involving a biological warfare agent.[7] The process begins after a site has been thoroughly characterized. Work then proceeds with de-

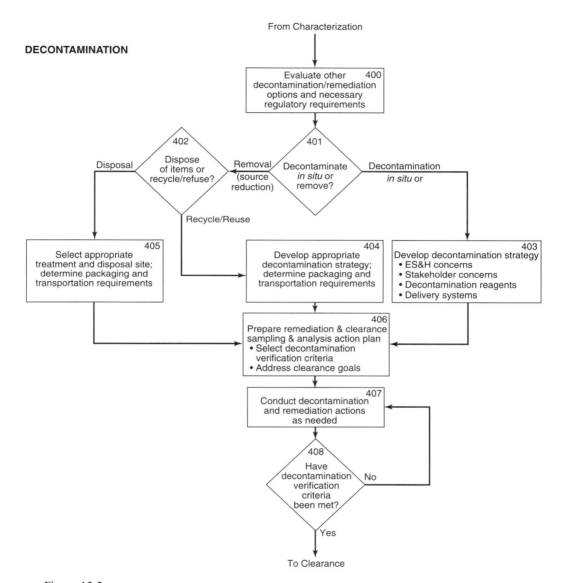

Figure 13.2
Decision process for the decontamination phase of response to an attack involving a biological warfare agent.

cision makers developing an overall strategy addressing the key issues of whether or not to decontaminate and, if so, how (items 400–404). A long list of factors must be considered.[8] A group of experts then develops a detailed decontamination strategy and writes it down in the form of a Remediation Action Plan or RAP (item 406). The RAP spells out an overall plan for decontaminating the site and its contents. Because the decontamination strategy can directly affect subsequent clearance sampling strategies, a clearance plan is usually also created at this time.

The RAP generally addresses a long list of topics, including how the agent has been contained at the site; how the agent and site have been characterized; how remediation workers will be decontaminated after working at the site; clearance goals to be met following decontamination; how the site must be prepared before decontamination starts; what items will be removed from the site (source reduction) or disposed of; a precise description of how the site will be decontaminated; whether any essential items will be decontaminated offsite; how the results of decontamination will be verified, including what clearance sampling and analysis will be done; and specific criteria for reaching a final clearance decision (i.e., declaring the site acceptable for reoccupancy).

Health and safety requirements must also be addressed (item 403) for all response and recovery workers, such as emergency medical personnel, police, firefighters, and short- and long-term remediation workers. The requirements are summarized in a Health and Safety Plan (HASP) that identifies site hazards and appropriate controls to protect employee health and safety. The HASP is a living document and can be revised as necessary to reflect changes in site conditions or operations over time.

Before decontamination begins, the site and its contents need to be prepared for cleanup. *Site preparation* can involve many different tasks, including assembling decontamination unit(s) for workers; testing the contaminated site for leaks; constructing internal waste-processing units; installing and testing systems to generate treatment chemical(s); installing and testing chemical-, temperature-, and humidity-monitoring systems; installing and testing air-scrubbing systems; and subdividing spaces with temporary walls, if needed, to create smaller units. Site preparation for fumigation tends to be particularly expensive, complex, and time consuming and must be carefully planned and documented. Decisions must also be made about source reduction—that is, permanently removing materials from the site. Decontamination produces its own additional waste, including wastewater from rinsing personal protective equipment, employee shower water, and scrubbers. Finding disposal or treatment facilities that will accept treated or untreated waste is a major issue.

Once the EPA approves a particular decontamination method, the site is prepared and decontaminated according to the RAP. Decontamination is carefully monitored and evaluated to ensure that it has been done correctly. In some situations, state and local regulations may also affect the selection and use of particular decontamination strategies. The clearance phase begins after all decontamination activities have been completed and verified.

13.3.1 Selecting Appropriate Decontamination Technologies

Successful remediation requires careful risk evaluation and communicating timely and consistent information to the public. Failure to do so can seriously compromise human health (NRC/Committee on Standards and Policies 2005). Decontamination plans must also clearly reflect input from public and regulatory stakeholders. At the same time, decontamination is ultimately a cost-benefit issue (Fitch, Raber, and Imbro 2003). Appropriate decontamination method(s) must balance the cost of remediation against meeting specified clearance goals. Where natural attenuation is not sufficient, decontamination requirements for civilian sites tend to be extremely demanding. The ideal decontamination method would be effective against all chemical and biological agents; noncorrosive, nonhazardous, and biodegradable with environmentally acceptable residues; and effective in a period of hours rather than days. Formulations should also make maximum contact by adhering to walls and ceilings, be inexpensive and widely available, have long shelf lives (at least a year), and be easy to deploy and apply using various methods (e.g., hand spraying or application by a portable machine) with minimal training.

For biological agents, it is important to know whether the organism is alive (viable) or dead. Current sampling methods typically rely on the polymerase chain reaction (PCR) to identify organisms from their DNA. The methods are fast but cannot distinguish between living and dead organisms. Determining viability usually means growing the bacteria samples in culture at a certified Laboratory Response Network (LRN) laboratory. The final determination regarding viability can take up to seventy-two hours depending on the organism. More rapid methods that combine PCR and culture methods are currently being developed and could be available within a few years.

Unregistered sterilants and pesticides need an EPA crisis exemption before they can be used for biological decontamination in the United States.[9] A state or federal agency must submit a written request describing the antimicrobial product(s) to be used; how, when, and where they will be used; data demonstrating efficacy of the product(s) for the intended purpose; and how human health and safety will be protected. The EPA issued several such exemptions for antimicrobial pesticides following the *B. anthracis* attacks in 2001. It is currently exploring ways to precertify products and streamline or possibly eliminate the potentially lengthy crisis exemption process. These requirements do not apply to chemical decontamination and no crisis exemptions would be needed.

13.4   Decontamination Technologies

Table 13.1 summarizes various commercial products that are currently available to decontaminate chemical and biological warfare agents. Many decontamination technologies were available by the late 1990s and have been discussed in detail by Barrett et al. (1999). Here, we focus on some of the most common technologies along with more recent systems that have been tested experimentally.[10] In general, decontamination technologies can be functionally divided into three categories:

• *Surface decontamination*   Targeted decontamination of exposed surfaces, localized hot spots, large-area walls, floors, and ceilings; and outdoor soil and concrete/asphalt areas
• *Volumetric decontamination*   Treating large volumes of air with decontamination reagents in the gas or vapor phase, including related delivery and air-handling systems
• *High-value decontamination*   Technologies for decontaminating sensitive electronic equipment and other valuable items

Each of the three categories typically requires different kinds of sampling and, sometimes, preparation (e.g., equipment and mechanical setup). We discuss them in turn.

13.4.1   Decontaminating Exposed Surfaces
A variety of products have been developed to decontaminate surfaces. These include the following:

Liquid chlorine dioxide is a strong oxidant produced by mixing products containing sodium chlorite or stabilized chlorine dioxide with another reactive chemical, often an acid. Commercial sterilants produced by mixing chlorine dioxide with water have been used with pets, farm animals, and bottling, food-processing, and food-storage plants since the 1960s. Chlorine dioxide is effective on exposed surfaces against mustard, VX, and biological agents. It was widely used following the 2001 *B. anthracis* attacks.
High-test calcium hypochlorite (HTH) mixed with water has a long history for disinfecting swimming pools. HTH is effective against both chemical and biological agents on surfaces. However, it is highly corrosive, forms a toxic vapor, attacks skin, and must be rinsed off after application.
Sodium hypochlorite and similar oxidants are effective against a broad range of chemical and biological agents, including *B. anthracis,* and are often mixed with water. Ordinary household bleach typically contains about 5 percent sodium hypochlorite in water. For surface cleanup of chemical and biological agents, the bleach is usually diluted by adding 1 part bleach to 9 parts water. Japanese authorities used

Table 13.1
Summary of selected decontamination technologies listed alphabetically by type of application

Biological warfare agents	Chemical warfare agents
Aqueous-based for exposed surfaces	*For surfaces and hotspots*
All-Clear	All-Clear
CASCAD Foam	Binary ionization technology (BIT)
Chlorine dioxide (ClO$_2$) liquid	CASCAD Foam
Household bleach (5% sodium hypochlorite in water)*	L-Gel
	Sandia Decon Foam DF-200
HTH (5% calcium hypochlorite)	Chlorine dioxide (ClO$_2$) liquid
Hydrogen peroxide	Decon Green
L-Gel	GDS 2000
Peroxyacetic acid	Household bleach (5% sodium
Peroxyacetic acid/hydrogen peroxide sterilant	hypochlorite in water)
Sandia Decon Foam DF-200	HTH (5% calcium hypochlorite)*
Virkon S™	Supertopical bleach (93% calcium hypochlorite and 7% sodium hydroxide)
Gases and vapors	*For volumetric spaces*
Chlorine dioxide (ClO$_2$) gas*	Ammonia gas
Ethylene oxide	Ammonia gas and steam
Glutaraldehyde	Chlorine dioxide (ClO$_2$) gas
Modified vaporous hydrogen peroxide (mVHP®)	Forced or hot-air ventilation
	Modified vaporous hydrogen peroxide (mVHP®)
Paraformaldehyde	Natural attenuation (room-temperature or
Steam	hot-air ventilation)
Vaporous hydrogen peroxide*	Nitrogen tetroxide
	Ozone
	Perchloryl fluoride
	Steam
For sensitive equipment and items	*For sensitive equipment and items*
Ethylene oxide,	Chlorine dioxide (ClO$_2$)
Methyl bromide	Modified vaporous hydrogen peroxide (mVHP®)
Paraformaldehyde	Solvent bath (ultrasonic solvent wash and dry)

* Current standards

sodium hypochlorite to decontaminate sarin residues following the Tokyo subway attack. Bleach solutions are corrosive and toxic, but they are also inexpensive and widely available.

Hydrogen peroxide has long been used as a sterilant and is marketed under a variety of commercial names. Three to 25 percent solutions are known to be effective against biological agents at 20°C. The pharmaceutical industry routinely uses commercial preparations based on liquid peroxyacetic acid/hydrogen peroxide to sterilize clean rooms and biological containment facilities.

L-Gel is an amorphous silica gel (Raber and McGuire 2002) that uses both oxidation and hydrolysis to decontaminate chemical and biological agents. Field tests have shown L-Gel to be more effective against VX, soman, and sulfur mustard than calcium hypochlorite for various materials including acrylic-painted metal, polyurethane-coated oak flooring, and indoor-outdoor carpet. The product's consistency is similar to room-temperature Jell-O. Stirring liquefies the gel so that it can be applied to walls and ceilings. L-Gel does not present an inhalation hazard, causes minimal collateral damage, and is relatively inexpensive. Rinsing is optional after use; in the absence of rinsing, any dried residue may need to be vacuumed from indoor areas and discarded. L-Gel is currently being developed as a commercial product but could be immediately obtained from LLNL in an emergency.

Decon Foam (DF–200) from Sandia National Laboratories is a rapid-response product (Tadros and Tucker 2003) that requires relatively little supporting equipment or water. It is effective against both chemical and biological warfare agents. Its ingredients are similar to those found in hair conditioner and toothpaste and pose little danger to health, environment, or property. The binary system requires mixing, and workers must wait six to ten hours for the foam to collapse. Decon Foam was used for anthrax decontamination in selected areas of various congressional office buildings and in the ABC News and New York City post office buildings and is currently being evaluated by the U.S. Army and the Marine Corps. Spray and fog versions are also being developed.

Virkon S, which was initially produced in the United Kingdom, is a powder that dissolves in water. It has been used in Europe to disinfect anthrax-exposed cattle and hospital equipment and surfaces exposed to biological agents. Tests have shown that it is effective against bacteria, viruses, spores, and fungi. Disney Cruise Line and Holland America both use Virkon S to clean and disinfect their ships.

Binary Ionization Technology (BIT) is a patented spray process that has been tested against biological agents but has received only limited testing against chemical agents. The disinfecting mist is delivered as charged droplets and then dissociates into water and oxygen. It does not damage treatment surfaces and requires no cleanup.

All-Clear is a mixture of biocides, surfactants, wetting agents, enzyme, and buffer powder that can be used as a decontamination foam for both chemical and biological agents. It has a long shelf life, can be quickly deployed, is commercially available, and is nontoxic and noncorrosive. All-Clear is effective against G agents and VX, and tests against mustard are pending. However, the EPA has not yet approved All-Clear for use against biological agents.

CASCAD is a user-friendly, water-based, biodegradable, nontoxic product useful for vehicle and equipment decontamination. Unlike some other oxidants, it is only minimally corrosive and does not attack paints or rubber materials.

Decon Green is a relatively nontoxic material that includes baking soda, 35 percent hydrogen peroxide, a surfactant (wetting agent), and other materials. Decon Green has been successfully tested against VX, soman, and mustard.

GDS 2000 is a commercial, nonaqueous solution with demonstrated effectiveness against chemical agents. It can be used over a broad temperature range from subzero to 50°C and provides superior decontamination of painted and polymeric materials compared to water-based solutions. However, indoor uses require posttreatment washing and the product cannot be shipped or stored in concentrated form.

13.4.2 Decontaminating Interior "Volumetric" Spaces

Volumetric decontamination includes technologies used to treat rooms, enclosed atria, ventilation systems, and the interior spaces of buildings. The simplest method is ventilation—that is, diluting contaminants with outside or heated air. In many cases, ventilation is an effective and inexpensive method for large-scale chemical decontamination. Ventilation works best for spaces that border on hard surfaces, are contaminated with nonpersistent and especially gaseous chemicals (e.g., sarin), and are relatively lightly contaminated.

Ventilation is not always enough, particularly when biological agents are involved. Several technologies have been developed to decontaminate entire buildings and hard-to-reach spaces (e.g., ventilation ducts):

Chlorine dioxide gas is an EPA-registered sterilant. In 2001, it received crisis exemptions and was used to clean up *B. anthracis* spores at the Hart Senate Office Building along with mail and packages at several postal facilities. It offers good penetration and can in principle be used to decontaminate large spaces. However, logistics become very complex for large applications. Much of a building's contents can be left in place, which limits the amount of waste that needs to be disposed of. Waste disposal is an important element in total remediation costs.

Vaporous hydrogen peroxide is a promising decontaminant for buildings. STERIS provides a commercial version (vaporous hydrogen peroxide technology or VHP®)

that can be used to decontaminate large spaces. VHP® is already an EPA-registered sterilant, is known to be effective against biological agents, and was used to decontaminate *B. anthracis* spores in 2001. It can also be used to decontaminate many different chemical agents including VX, soman, and mustard. The decomposition products (water and oxygen) of VHP® leave no residue and present minimal corrosion risk. However, the method requires multiple, widely spaced hydrogen peroxide generators for large spaces and/or where large amounts of concrete are present.[11] Furthermore, hydrogen peroxide vapor is usually near the saturation point in air, making humidity control necessary. STERIS is currently working with Edgewood Chemical and Biological Center to develop an improved *modified vaporous hydrogen peroxide process* (mVHP®) that vaporizes a liquid peroxide mixture and blends it with small quantities of ammonia. This is a particularly promising technology for heavily contaminated spaces and persistent agents (LLNL 2007).

Paraformaldehyde is becoming known as a highly effective decontamination option against biological agents, but it is not effective against chemical agents. It is compatible with most materials, offers good penetration, and minimizes waste disposal costs because many building contents can be left in place. Its main disadvantage is that it is difficult to neutralize on a large scale, making it most useful for small structures. It also leaves residues that must be washed away.

13.4.3   Decontaminating High-Value Items

Attempts to decontaminate high-value objects such as airport baggage-screening equipment or the U.S. Capitol's artwork can potentially do more harm than good. For biological contaminants, three fumigants—ethylene oxide, methyl bromide, and paraformaldehyde—are available to decontaminate items that can be moved to off-site treatment facilities. The methods are suitable for artwork, computers, personal items, and luggage. Sterilizing radiation can also be used for certain applications. Small items contaminated with chemical agents can similarly be removed to sites offering commercially available industrial cleaning systems (e.g., degreasing equipment) or solvent baths. In either case, cleaning agents must be carefully chosen so that they do not react with the materials being cleaned.

Decontamination is more difficult when equipment is so large or sensitive that it must be cleaned in place. Water-based solutions can be used to clean equipment housings, but—like most cleaning agents—such solutions cannot be used inside machinery because of corrosion, residue, and/or chemical reaction concerns. Fortunately, several promising candidates are in the early stages of development and testing. In the meantime, facility managers should plan on replacing essential equipment following an attack.

13.4.4   Emerging Decontamination Technologies

Most commercially available products have major drawbacks, and no single approach can serve all decontamination needs. Technologies for reliably penetrating inaccessible areas (e.g., ductwork) and reagents that leave no residue, are nontoxic, avoid collateral damage, and have acceptable cost are a high priority. At least three U.S. national laboratories (Sandia, LLNL, and Los Alamos) are currently developing and testing environmentally acceptable decontamination systems that can be deployed using a variety of methods. The EPA has also been developing and evaluating decontamination technology. However, in contrast to the development and testing of decontamination technology for the military, funding for civilian-sector decontamination technologies has been limited. Civilian-sector issues are quite different from military requirements, and additional funding would likely lead to more environmentally acceptable methods that could potentially be applied on an urban scale with limited impacts to human health and the environment.

So far, we have focused on cleaning up individual sites and facilities. Cleaning up an entire city ("a wide-area urban event") after a chemical or biological attack would be far more difficult. Challenges include (1) the lack of any simple scheme for prioritizing the hundreds of facilities and areas that would need to be cleaned, (2) the lack of technologies for large-scale sampling, (3) the lack of decontamination methods suitable for large-scale outdoor settings, and (4) the need to resume operations quickly for economic, social, and national security reasons. DHS/DOD's *Interagency–Biological Restoration Demonstration* (IBRD) program is designed to fill some of these gaps. Although built around a hypothetical aerosolized pathogen attack on Seattle, the program's overall goal is to develop a template and decision protocol that provides a coordinated approach for cleaning up an entire city. Experts will identify technologies for better, cheaper, safer, and faster decontamination as well as methods to evaluate success. Research will focus on developing the following:

• Environmentally acceptable technologies for decontaminating large outdoor areas and surfaces
• Technologies for decontaminating sensitive equipment and other high-value items
• Improved technologies and methods for decontaminating interior spaces
• Technologies for decontaminating large volumes of waste to the point where it can be safely disposed of in landfills or otherwise treated
• Methods that might reduce inhalation hazards, particularly for spores[12]
• Improved methods for sampling and characterizing surface and airborne hazards
• Improved risk assessment methods for establishing outdoor clearance guidelines

The IBRD program is expected to recommend specific technologies by mid-2010.

13.5   Establishing Clearance Goals

A clearance goal answers the question "How clean is clean enough?" and is fundamental to almost every aspect of the remediation process. The answer to what a
clearance goal should be plays an important role in determining what detection
levels and sampling techniques are adequate. Other considerations include how
many samples must be collected for characterization and to validate decontamination, where samples need to be collected, which decontamination agents are chosen,
how the final clearance decision is made, and many other issues (Carlsen, Mac-
Queen, and Krauter 2001).

13.5.1   Biological Warfare Agents

Determining how many organisms constitute an infectious dose is a science issue.
However, establishing what decision makers and stakeholders are willing to accept
in terms of risks is a social issue. Successful remediation requires stakeholder inputs,
and past experience—for example, comparing the relatively modest NBC and ABC
office-building cleanups against those on Capitol Hill—suggests that public perceptions often determine cleanup requirements. However economics and inconvenience
can persuade stakeholders to accept higher risks (chapter 16).[13] Current policies reflect a mix of scientific, social (public perception), bureaucratic (i.e., regulatory and
legal), and practical (cost and time) considerations.

A complete risk assessment should always consider natural attenuation—simply
waiting—as an option. Natural attenuation can be an adequate strategy for
eliminating many biological warfare agents that exist as vegetative cells or are
nonpersistent—that is, do not live for more than a few hours outside a host. In
such cases, remediation might not be required at all, or else required in only a
limited way (e.g., reoccupation following relatively limited sampling). Instead,
microbiology experts and public health officials would specify when sites could be
reentered. In recent years, the EPA has begun to accept strategies that combine natural attenuation with long-term environmental monitoring for various sites where
soil and groundwater have been contaminated by organic chemicals and/or radioactive tritium. The approach has not yet been applied to biological warfare agent contamination. Moreover, natural attenuation is not an option for spore-forming
organisms, notably *B. anthracis*. This is especially true for indoor releases where research shows that spores can remain viable for long periods (Sneath 1962; Block
2001; Pepper and Gentry 2002).

For many biological agents, authorities would have to consider other remediation
options, such as decontamination. Before selecting a decontamination technique,

however, it is necessary to define the overall clearance goal for determining whether remediation is successful. Unfortunately, the published literature does not provide established cleanup levels for biological agents. Decision makers must therefore rely on other precedents. For instance, the 2001 U.S. anthrax cleanups defined successful decontamination as no growth of *B. anthracis* spores on all clearance samples (GAO 2003c). A National Academy of Sciences committee has likewise found that there is no scientific basis for establishing a level of residual *B. anthracis* contamination that can safely be left behind (NRC/Committee on Standards and Policies for Decontaminating Public Facilities 2005).

The problem is not limited to *B anthracis*. Whereas dose-response information is available to a limited extent for certain biological agents (see table 13.2), information on the relationship between dose and response is not by itself sufficient to make confident judgments about infectivity and virulence.[14]

Certifying that a building can be "safely" reoccupied is a complex process. In part, the decision depends on technical issues, such as sampling procedures, decontamination technologies, and quantitative risk assessment methods. However, the National Academy of Sciences committee was careful to point out that the decision also depends on the perceptions of stakeholders, users, and the public: "An official declaration that a building is safe for reoccupation is meaningless if the occupants and other stakeholders do not *perceive* it as safe.... Conversely, the expert appraisal of a building as not yet safe for occupation may be out of step with the ideas of building owners and users who are eager to reoccupy a structure." The committee recommended the development of a uniform, nationwide scientific and technical approach to making future safety decisions (NRC/Committee on Standards and Policies for Decontaminating Public Facilities 2005).

At present, insufficient information is available on which to base "safe" numbers for residual biological warfare agents after decontaminating a public facility. The overwhelming consensus among experts is that the cleanup goal for indoor *B. anthracis* contamination will remain *no growth on any clearance sample* for the foreseeable future.[15] Our knowledge gaps are even greater for outdoor environments. Risk-analysis methods still cannot establish an acceptable level of *B. anthracis* contamination outdoors due to the lack of available experimental data. Difficulties include large uncertainties between laboratory experiments and historical human exposures and uncertainty in the degree to which weaponized anthrax can be reaerosolized and inhaled. In addition, natural background levels of *B. anthracis* can be found in many areas of the United States, which suggests sufficient health protection may not require cleanup levels defined as "no growth" from surface samples.

Table 13.2
Dose-response (published data or inferred) and cleanup guidelines for microbes

Agent type and name	Is dose-response information available?[a]	Dose-response source in the literature	Is a specific cleanup guideline available?
Bacteria			
Salmonella	Yes	Fazil 1996; Holcomb et al. 1999; Havelaar and Garssen 2000	None identified but *Salmonella* is on the list of agents for which the EPA is developing the Ground-Water Disinfection (GWD) Rule.[b]
Shigella	Yes	Crockett et al. 1996	None identified but *Shigella* is on the list of agents for which the EPA is developing the Ground-Water Disinfection (GWD) Rule.[b]
Enteropathic *E. coli*	Yes	Haas et al. 1999	Water guideline: Heterotrophic plate count ≤ 500 CFU/ml.
E. coli O157:H7	Yes in animals	Haas et al. 2000	MCL violation if more than 5% of samples are total coliform-positive in one month.
Vibrio cholerae	Yes	Haas et al. 1999	None found in reviewed literature.
Campylobacter	Yes	Medema et al. 1996	None found but *Campylobacter* is on the list of agents for which the EPA is developing the Ground-Water Disinfection (GWD) Rule.[b]
Listeria	Yes in animals	Haas 1999	None found in reviewed literature.
Bacillus anthracis	Yes in animals	Haas 2002	No growth on any clearance sample.[a]
Francisella tularensis	Yes in animals	Oyston, Sjostad, and Titball 2004	None found in reviewed literature.

Table 13.2
(continued)

Agent type and name	Is dose-response information available?[a]	Dose-response source in the literature	Is a specific cleanup guideline available?
Viruses			
Adenovirus	Yes	Haas, Rose, and Gerba 1999	Drinking water maximum contaminant levels (MCLs) are only specified for viruses considered to be "enteric." Recommendation is for 99.99% removal or inactivation of enteric viruses. Adenovirus, Coxsackie virus, and echoviruses are on the Contaminant Candidate List, but MCLs are not yet established by the EPA.[b]
Echoviruses	Yes	Haas, Rose, and Gerba 1999	
Coxsackie virus	Yes	Haas, Rose, and Gerba 1999	
Ebola	Yes, in animals	Johnson et al. 1995	None found in reviewed literature.
Lassa virus	Yes, in animals	Stephenson, Larson, and Dominik 1984	None found in reviewed literature.
Variola major	Yes	Wehrle et al. 1970	None found in reviewed literature.
Protozoans			
Giardia lambia (cysts)	Yes	Rose, Haas, and Regli 1991	Yes in water. The standard is 99.9% removal or inactivation
Cryptosporidium (oocysts)	Yes	Haas et al. 1996; Messner et al. 2001; Teunis, Chappell, and Okhuysen 2002	Yes in water. The standard is 99% removal as of 1/1/2002 for systems serving > 10,000, and 99% removal as of 1/14/2005 for systems serving < 10,000.

[a] Adapted from NRC/Committee on Standards and Policies 2005
[b] Macler and Regli 1993

Table 13.3
Airborne (inhalational, ocular), 8-hour, Acute Exposure Guideline Level 1 (AEGL-1) values for selected chemical agents

Chemical warfare agent or toxic industrial compound	8-hr exposure AEGL-1 values (mild to no effects) in mg/m^3
Tabun (GA)	0.0010[a]
Sarin (GB)	0.0010[a]
Soman (GD)	0.00050[a]
VX	0.000071[a]
Sulfur mustard (H, HD)	0.0080[a]
Hydrogen cyanide	1.1[b]

[a] NRC 2003
[b] NRC/Committee on Toxicology 2002

13.5.2   Chemical Agents

In contrast to the situation for biological warfare agents, several agencies have developed toxicological parameters for chemical agents and toxic industrial compounds (TICs), and authoritative guidelines are now available from more than a dozen sources.[16] Such guidelines can be assessed to help set acceptable short- and long-term exposure levels for workers and members of the public who come into contact with chemical weapons (tabun, sarin, soman, cyclosarin, VX, sulfur mustard) or the main TIC vapors of concern (hydrogen cyanide, cyanogen chloride, and phosgene).

The CDC, National Research Council Committee on Toxicology, and numerous investigators familiar with the manufacture, battlefield use, and legacy of chemical weapons agents agree that the most likely exposure routes are inhalation of vapor or aerosol and direct vapor eye (ocular) contact. Some suggested exposure guidelines for inhalation and ocular contact are listed in table 13.3. The 8-hour exposure AEGL-1 values shown in this table are the airborne concentration (expressed as milligrams per cubic meter) of a substance above which it is predicted that the general population, including susceptible individuals, could experience notable discomfort, irritation, or certain asymptomatic, nonsensory effects. The effects for a one-time exposure of eight hours or less are not disabling and are transient and reversible when exposure ends. As is apparent from the table, more quantitative cleanup values and monitoring levels exist for chemical than for biological agents.

Chemical agents can also contaminate soil or other types of sediment in which they could become a problem (to water supplies, for example). Health-based environmental screening levels (HBESLs), calculated using EPA chronic risk assessment methods, are available for soil contamination. The levels shown in table 13.4 are

Table 13.4
Health-based environmental screening levels for chemical warfare agents in residential and industrial soil

Chemical warfare agent	HBESL for residential soil (mg/kg)	HBESL for industrial soil (mg/kg)
Tabun (GA)	3.1	82
Sarin (GB)	1.6	41
Soman (GD)	0.31	8.2
VX	0.047	1.2
Mustard (HD)	0.55	14
Lewisite (arsenic fraction)	7.8	7.8

Source: Adapted from Raber et al. 2004

low-level concentrations of individual chemical agents in residential and industrial soil, which, if not exceeded, are unlikely to present a human health hazard for specific exposure scenarios (U.S. Army/Center for Health Promotion and Preventive Medicine 1999). Table 13.4 values were derived from the U.S. EPA Region III Risk-Based Concentration (RBC) model (EPA 1996) and are appropriate for use where cumulative effects (e.g., multiple exposures to one chemical or an exposure to more than one chemical) are not anticipated.

Depending on ambient temperature, moisture, airflow, and other parameters, many chemical agent and TIC vapors would dissipate rapidly. This is especially true of the G-series nerve agents (tabun, sarin, soman, and cyclosarin) and the three TICs of concern (hydrogen cyanide, phosgene, and cyanogen chloride). Depending on the circumstances, natural attenuation may often be an option for these chemical agents and TICs.

Dissipation is less likely for a few agents, such as VX and thickened sulfur mustard. These materials can readily penetrate porous materials (e.g., concrete, plastics), particularly when delivered in the form of liquid aerosol droplets. Thereafter, they can slowly reemerge to create a long-term contamination hazard. Table 13.5 lists reference doses (RfDs) that estimate how much agent the human population, including sensitive subpopulations, can safely ingest without appreciable risk over periods ranging from seven years to a human lifetime.

13.6   Conclusions

The past seven years have seen unprecedented planning and research devoted to the problem of remediating sites contaminated by chemical and biological warfare

Table 13.5
Ingestion guidelines for chemical warfare agents and toxic industrial compounds of concern

Agent type and name	Reference dose (RfD or RfD$_{est}$) (mg/kg/day) Ingestion: estimate of daily exposure level for the general population when the chronic exposure duration is from 7 years to a lifetime
Nerve agents	
Tabun (GA)	4×10^{-5}[a]
Sarin (GB)	2×10^{-5}[a]
Soman (GD) and cyclosarin (GF)	4×10^{-6}[a]
VX	6×10^{-7}[a]
Blister agents	
Sulfur mustard (H and HD)	7×10^{-6}[a]
Choking agents	
Phosgene (CG)	Not available[b]
Blood agents	
Hydrogen cyanide (AC)	0.02[c]
Cyanogen chloride (CK)	0.03 and 0.05[d]

[a] Opressko et al. 2001. The values for nerve and sulfur mustard agents are RfD estimates (RfD$_{est}$) by the National Research Council Committee on Toxicology and have not been reviewed by the EPA's Integrated Risk Information System (http://www.epa.gpv/iris/). The value for GF is also an estimate and has not been reviewed by IRIS.
[b] Not available through USEPA Integrated Risk Information System (http://www.epa.gov/iris/subst). The phosgene RfD was still under discussion when this book went to press.
[c] USEPA Integrated Risk Information System (IRIS); available online (www.epa.gov/iris).
[d] Opresko et al. 1998. The value of 0.03 mg/kg-day for cyanogen chloride is an estimate (RfD$_{est}$) and has not been reviewed by IRIS (USEPA Region 9, 2004). The RfD of 0.05 mg/kg/day for cyanogen chloride can be found online (http://www.epa.gov/region09/waste/sfund/prg/index.html).

agents. Nevertheless, much remains to be done. Outstanding tasks include faster response methods, more efficient environmental sampling and characterization techniques, faster laboratory analysis methods to confirm decontamination, more cost-effective cleanup and decontamination techniques, new methods for decontaminating sensitive equipment and wide-area outdoor sites, and above all, new decontamination approaches that minimize the health risk to exposed populations.

Beyond these technical issues, successful remediation and decontamination programs must also address stakeholder concerns. Careful strategies should expressly consider how the site will be used; how contaminants are likely to be transported and how they could reach exposed populations (e.g., inhalation, skin contact); potential economic damage to land, water, and equipment with and without remediation; the cost and availability of various remediation options; the impact of delay on social and economic welfare; the danger that remediation will generate waste and secondary contamination that may make things worse instead of better; and the public's confidence in remediation methods, including clearance goals and verification sampling. In the end, technical expertise and public perception must interact. Certainly, public perception and stakeholder issues will influence cleanup requirements. However, it is equally true that economics and inconvenience will influence stakeholders to accept higher risks.[17]

Notes

1. We know of no published estimates for costs associated with response to the Tokyo attack.

2. Anthrax disease can occur in inhalational, gastrointestinal, and cutaneous forms. Inhalational anthrax is rare in nature but common following exposure to weaponized *B. anthracis* spores.

3. Although many people and the press used the expression "anthrax attacks" to describe what happened, such language is not strictly correct. The clinical term *anthrax* refers to the disease caused by the spore-forming bacterium *Bacillus anthracis*, which is often abbreviated *B. anthracis*.

4. DHS's Directorate of Science and Technology has formed various partnerships with the national laboratories and others to coordinate and share knowledge and capabilities.

5. The concepts were developed through interagency cooperation between experts from the DHS, EPA, the national laboratories, and other agencies. Although originally developed in the context of biological attacks, the chart identifies activities associated with either a chemical or biological attack.

6. Civilian clearance goals are more challenging than military ones. For the military, the primary concern centers on battlefield issues rather than protecting the health of individuals and the affected population is, in any case, young and healthy. Civilian clearance focuses on protecting the public, which includes members who are immunocompromised, pregnant women, elderly, and infants.

7. Interested readers can find details in Raber et al. (2002).

8. Agent-specific factors include the pathogen's identity, formulation, and key characteristics (e.g., species and subspecies, environmental persistence, and ability to aerosolize); mode of delivery and the nature and extent of spread; results of environmental sampling including location and quantities detected; epidemiological evidence of disease in humans; and potential health risks. Site-specific factors include the nature of the site (an entire facility or only one area; rural or urban environment; outdoor or indoor location); the toxicities of decontamination chemical(s); public perception, including acceptance of the decontamination process;

environmental concerns, including potential byproducts, air emissions, and residues; the availability of test data showing that the selected decontamination process is effective; conditions required for effective decontamination including relative humidity, temperature, and fumigant concentration and duration; the duration and cost of decontamination; and potential collateral damage from decontamination.

9. All new formulations sold as biocides must be approved by the EPA under the Federal Insecticide, Fungicide, and Rodenticide Act (FIFRA). FIFRA authorizes state or federal agencies (including the EPA) to issue crisis exemptions that temporarily permit the use of unregistered products.

10. Many other products exist whose claims have yet to be substantiated by experiment.

11. Concrete degrades rapidly at high concentrations of VHP®.

12. In one intriguing project, researchers plan to evaluate the extent to which soil particles either naturally bind to *B. anthracis* spores or can be induced to do so. Successful coagulation would reduce or eliminate the chance that spores would be reaerosolized to become an inhalation hazard.

13. The question of which risks are tolerable is complex. Familiarity is clearly important. For example, the public routinely accepts hospital and swimming-pool disinfectant methods even though they do not guarantee zero risk.

14. The conclusion is necessary for several reasons. First, there are usually large differences among the numbers of organisms inhaled by different people. Second, particularly susceptible people (e.g., immunocompromised individuals) may be susceptible to even one organism. Finally, some diseases are transmissible from person to person. In this case, even an asymptomatic person could potentially infect a large population.

15. In practice, statisticians and laboratory analysis experts will also have to specify the number, type, placement, and handling of samples that need to be taken before *no growth* can be declared.

16. Leading references include CDC 2003b, 2004; NRC 1999, 2001, 2003; NRC/Committee on Toxicology 2002; ACGIH 2003; EPA 1991, 1996, 2005; EPA/Office of Emergency and Remedial Response 1996; NIOSH/OSHA 2006.

17. This work was carried out under the auspices of the U.S. Department of Energy by Lawrence Livermore National Laboratory under Contract DE-AC52–07NA27344.

14

Estimating the Economic Impacts of WMD Attacks

Peter Gordon, Bumsoo Lee, James E. Moore II, Qisheng Pan, JiYoung Park, and Harry W. Richardson

American antiterrorism policy needs risk assessment (chapter 7) to deploy U.S. scientific and technical assets more efficiently. But while the costs of various countermeasures are usually known, their benefits hinge on the losses that could be prevented. Improved analysis will require a better understanding of the short-term economic impacts of various real and hypothetical events. Can these losses be estimated? Here we review the growing social science and policy analysis literature that attempts to apply and extend existing economic analysis tools to terrorist attacks. Although the results of these studies are not detailed forecasts, they do provide first-order estimates of possible losses and provide a basis for comparing likely losses from different attacks.

Section 14.1 discusses attempts to model the nationwide impact of terrorist attacks, most notably including attacks that lead to prolonged shutdowns of the U.S. border. These are aggregate models for the entire American economy. Section 14.2 shows how spatial models can be used to trace losses at both the local level (e.g., greater Los Angeles) and across the fifty states (e.g., attacks on major seaports, theme parks). These models highlight localized effects that tend to be obscured by aggregate analyses, especially when local effects cancel each other out. They also provide a potentially compelling framework that local constituencies can use to decide when they should be politically willing to support national-level terror prevention programs. Section 14.3 addresses alternative approaches for making models more realistic. It focuses on efforts to capture the "resiliency" of real-world economies—that is, their ability to adapt, adjust, and mitigate problems as they emerge. Section 14.4 reviews attempts to use other, mostly noneconomic disciplines to explore how cities would likely respond to attack and the policy prescriptions that these analyses imply. Finally, section 14.5 presents a brief conclusion.

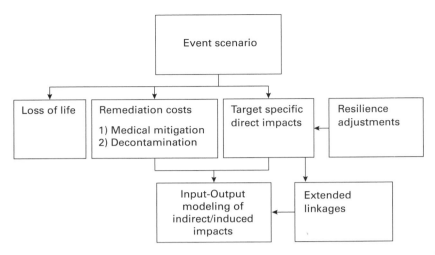

Figure 14.1
Analytical framework for case studies using input-output analysis

14.1   National Models and Impacts

There are several straightforward methods that can be used to assess the aggregate, nationwide impact of a terrorist attack. For example, the Department of Commerce's Bureau of Economic Analysis (BEA) and the private Minnesota Implan Group (MIG) both offer user-friendly and up-to-date input-output models of the U.S. economy. These can be adapted to assess the cost of hypothetical terrorist attacks.

Our general conceptual approach is summarized in figure 14.1. The starting point is to postulate attack scenarios: This provides the initial conditions for our model. Developing plausible scenarios in enough detail to support modeling turns out to be the main challenge in our work. We use past events as well as simulations from workers in other fields to characterize such important variables as expected loss of life, likely duration of business interruptions, and the remediation costs associated with different attacks (Lee et al. 2008; Lee, Gordon, and Moore 2007). The accuracy of any input-output model depends on obtaining plausible estimates for these exogenous (direct) effects. Once these direct effects are specified, we use input-output modeling to estimate the various indirect (endogenous) effects that would likely flow from them.

14.1.1   Discrete Impacts

Proceeding in this way, we have analyzed the economic impacts of various localized, one-time attacks on U.S. targets. These include an agroterrorist attack on romaine lettuce farming, an attack on a major U.S. airport terminal, an attack on a major U.S. urban center, and an attack on a major league sports stadium. Table 14.1 summarizes the results of our estimates.

The losses range from $77 million (the romaine lettuce attack) to $422 billion (the air terminal attack) (Lee, Gordon, and Moore 2007). The large losses from the latter come from reduced postattack passenger air travel, modeled on actual air travel losses in the two-year period after September 11.[1] This is the only one of our four models that predicts an economic impact beyond the first year. This result agrees with an earlier study by Gordon et al., which found similarly large loss estimates associated with a shutdown of U.S. airports, primarily for the same reason: Long-term reductions in air travel demand similar to those observed following the nation-wide airport shutdown on September 11 (Gordon et al. 2007). We assumed that this drop in demand would be repeated by a shutdown following a successful surface-to-air missile ("MANPADS") attack on a commercial airliner. Given this result, countermeasures may be cost-effective for attack probabilities as low as 30 percent.

14.1.2   Border Closing

We have also conducted a related but much more ambitious study to investigate the national economic impacts of restricting or even closing the nation's borders. In the maximum impact case, there is no travel or trade except for piped energy like oil and natural gas. These extreme measures may be realistic for an international epidemic, which could either be manmade (e.g., smallpox) or natural (e.g., avian influenza). We conducted our simulations for 2001, the year for which we have the most data, using USIO, a forty-seven-sector aggregation of the national IMPLAN model. Demand-side and supply-side versions were used.[2] Our most optimistic scenario showed that a one-year border shutdown would reduce U.S. output by $1.68 trillion. Since our models are linear, shorter closings would generate proportionately smaller impacts.[3]

These disruptions are severe, well beyond anything that the U.S. economy has ever experienced in any one year. Given the size of our extrapolation, these estimates are subject to many caveats. Nevertheless, the size of our projected economic losses is striking and comparable to the dollar value of the 383,000 mean estimated fatalities predicted for the pandemic itself (Murray et al. 2006).

These losses can be disaggregated into several distinct components. First, the effects of terminating international air traffic in both directions create a $215 billion

Table 14.1
Economic impacts of four hypothetical terrorism scenarios

($ thousands)	Direct	Indirect	Induced	Total
Stadium scenario				
a. Low-impact scenario				
Loss of lives				−57,240,000
Remediation expenditures (+)	290,505	216,267	423,056	929,827
Reduced household spending (−)	−286,158	−186,561	−303,210	−775,929
Reduced demand for sports attendance (−)	−1,635,638	−433,480	−2,797,730	−4,866,848
Substitutions (+)	817,818	820,591	919,293	2,557,702
Business interruption costs (−)				−538,875
Total				−61,952,949
b. High-impact scenario				
Loss of lives				−57,240,000
Remediation expenditures (+)	290,505	216,267	423,056	929,827
Reduced household spending (−)	−286,158	−186,561	−303,210	−775,929
Reduced demand for sports attendance (−)	−5,452,126	−1,444,933	−9,325,763	−16,222,822
Substitutions (+)	2,726,063	2,735,306	3,064,312	8,525,680
Business interruption costs (−)				−538,875
Total				−73,308,923
Urban-center scenario				
Loss of lives				−2,160,000
Remediation expenditures (+)	133,932	93,803	183,611	411,346
Reduced household spending (−)	−131,929	−86,011	−139,791	−357,731
Business interruption costs				−3,850,951
Total				−5,957,336

Table 14.1
(continued)

($ thousands)	Direct	Indirect	Induced	Total
Airport scenario				
Loss of lives				−1,080,000
Remediation expenditures (+)	151,920	105,887	207,274	465,081
Reduced household spending (−)	−149,647	−97,563	−158,564	−405,774
Reduced air travel (−)	−152,334,000	−114,422,000	−153,699,000	−420,455,000
Total				−421,475,693
Romaine lettuce scenario				
Loss of lives				−54,000
Remediation expenditures (+)	2,112	1,463	2,840	6,415
Reduced household spending (−)	−2,080	−1,356	−2,204	−5,641
Reduced exports of Romaine lettuce (−)	−10,266	−3,862	−9,667	−23,795
Total				−77,021

loss in the *transportation industry* including ancillary sectors like hotels, meals, shopping, and the like.[4] This estimate includes mitigation in the form of an assumed 25 percent increase in telecommunications purchases by grounded U.S.-based business travelers. Alternatively, it is possible to assume more extensive mitigation in which 65 percent of U.S.-based international outbound trips are for pleasure and are replaced by domestic trips. This reduces net losses to about $96 billion.

Second, we estimated the separate impacts of export and import closures on *commodity trading*, including the extreme case in which only oil and gas imports are allowed to continue. In the interests of conservatism we also assumed that U.S. exporters and importers would mitigate by selling to each other once the borders were closed. We did this by analyzing trade flows at the six-digit NAICS level.[5] This scenario is very optimistic since it ignores specializations beyond the six-digit NAICS level and also neglects transactions costs. Nevertheless, it does make the impacts from our modeling assumption of fixed technological coefficients less severe. Even with this mitigation, however, trade reduction still costs the economy more than $1.5 trillion.

Third, we estimated the losses expected from shutting off *legal immigration* for one year. There are approximately one million legal immigrants each year, and their job sectors are known. Applying Borjas's (2003) labor supply elasticity of 0.3, and boosting wages correspondingly, we used a Leontief price model to calculate higher prices in all forty-seven USIO economic sectors. Household final demand was then reduced in light of these higher prices. This resulted in a $10 billion loss.

Fourth, we explored the effects of stopping *illegal immigration*. Because the annual number of illegal immigrants is unknown, we explored low (406,000), middle (628,000), and high rate (850,000) scenarios. A similar range of assumptions was used to explore the distribution of illegal immigrants across U.S. industry. Using the same approach previously applied to legal immigrants, we found annual losses ranging from $1.3 billion to almost $2.8 billion.

Finally, we also considered results from the loss of *cross-border shopping*. Incoming crossings (not by air) at all ports of entry are reported online by the Bureau of Transportation Statistics at http://www.transtats.bts.gov/Fields.asp?Table_ID=1358. There were 302 million crossings in 2005. We assumed that each shopping visit included $100 in retail expenditures and that about 60 percent of all crossings were by foreign-based shoppers entering the United States (Soares, n.d.). This led to an impact of almost $29 billion. On the plausible assumption that U.S.-based shoppers would substitute domestic purchases for shopping abroad, we arrived at a mitigated net loss of slightly less than $10 billion.

The foregoing conclusions ignore state-by-state impacts. Better estimates will require spatially disaggregated models.

14.2   Spatial Models

Assessing local impacts requires subnational models that combine spatial and economic detail. Our group uses the Southern California Planning Model (SCPM) to investigate impacts over scales embraced by the Greater Los Angeles metropolitan area's 3,000+ traffic analysis zones. The SCPM integrates an input-output model, a model of the region's highway network, and a spatial allocation model. We have also studied impacts across states by using the National Interstate Economic Model (NIEMO). NIEMO is a multiregional input-output model that estimates impacts for the fifty states and the District of Columbia. NIEMO is currently available in both demand- and supply-side versions. We frequently use both models, often in a single study. For example, when we model port closures, demand side models allow us to model losses when foreign markets for U.S. goods are abruptly cut off. Conversely, supply-side models tell us what happens when American industry can no longer sell to foreign markets.

In addition to spatial data, all of our models separately track forty-seven different industrial sectors. We refer to these as the "USC Sectors" in what follows.[6]

14.2.1   SCPM Applications: Studying the LA Metropolitan Area

Leamer and Thornberg (2006) point out that the resiliency of the U.S. economy makes it difficult for highly localized shocks to trigger a recession: the economy did not slow down, for example, after September 11. They also argue that it would be difficult to mount a successful attack of sufficient magnitude to close the Ports of Long Beach and Los Angeles. While we agree with this general assessment, we believe that a few scenarios are large and feasible enough to justify studying the secondary costs that a successful attack could inflict. We have used SCPM to explore the Los Angeles metropolitan area's expected economic losses from various attack scenarios. These include radiological and/or high explosive attacks on Los Angeles' twin ports and a radiological attack on downtown LA.

Attacks on the Twin Ports of Los Angeles–Long Beach   We used SCPM to study an attack on the twin ports of Los Angeles and Long Beach using radiological bombs with and without the concurrent destruction of freeway access bridges leading into the ports. Our loss estimates cover a wide range, depending on whether the ports are shut down by very small bombs (15 days) or whether the access bridges are also destroyed (120 days). In the minimum case, the direct, indirect and induced[7] losses only total $138.5 million, with two-thirds of the impact confined to the LA region. In the 120–day case, estimated damages rise to more than $34 billion, with two-thirds of the impact being felt outside the region.

As before, these estimates can be disaggregated into several components. We start with explicit and imputed *transportation costs*. Because SCPM features a highway network with finite (congestible) carrying capacity, our model allows us to estimate traffic flows and allocate indirect and induced losses that flow from greater delays across LA's traffic analysis zones (TAZs, census tract–like spatial units). We find two kinds of impacts that largely offset each other. When ports are closed there are many fewer freight trips and this reduces traffic. However, the loss of critical bridges also increases congestion on the remaining highways. The net impact can be positive or negative. We have explored alternative scenarios assuming $35 per hour for freight travel costs and a plausible value-of-time estimate for passenger travel of between $6.50 and $13.00 per hour. For the case of the 120–day disruption and assuming a baseline travel cost of $7.9 billion, gains from the reduced number of trips keeps net losses below 1 percent. Assuming higher travel-time values yields baselines of $18.8 to $37.5 billion. In these scenarios, passenger travel cost impacts range from very small net improvements to losses of about 2 percent.

We have also attempted to measure the effects of a radiological bomb on *household disruption*, *business losses*, and *real estate values*. According to our best estimate, these would total $4 billion. Blast damage would be minor, with deaths and serious injuries limited to a range of perhaps 50 meters. Physical infrastructure damage would similarly be negligible, except at ground zero. All remaining economic losses would be attributable to evacuation from areas contaminated by the bomb's radiological plume. Conversations with government officials suggest that the outer evacuation zone would be defined by the need to limit occupants' entire accumulated exposure from the incident to one rem. There are standard formulas for converting releases of radiation to plume areas and shapes, subject to wind direction and other climatic conditions. We assumed that the radiation plume would occupy a long narrow ellipse four kilometers long and more than 200 meters wide with an inner and more contaminated zone about 200 meters across (0.03 km^2). In the ports case, the wind usually comes from the southwest, so the plume would not affect Los Angeles International Airport or other strategic locations except for the ports themselves.[8] We assumed a one-week evacuation in the Outer Zone. This may be conservative because some firms and households may only trickle back with a lag after being given permission to return. Because the health effects are long-term, the decision to allow a return may be determined as much by normative and political choices as scientific knowledge.

The economic impacts in this scenario depend sensitively on the assumed radiation plume, including such variables as the amount of explosive used, the mass of radioactive particles released, wind direction and weather, and downwind population and business densities. Losses also depend on policymakers' reactions, for example whether they decide to order an evacuation and if so when they allow people to come back. Given these uncertainties, we only report our estimate of *maximum* economic impacts under reasonable assumptions. We assume that 377,442 of 401,147 persons living in the 30 TAZs as of the 2000 census would be evacuated. This leads to a total estimated output loss of over $4.1 billion. Two-thirds of the losses take place within Los Angeles County, but almost one-quarter would leak outside the five-county metropolitan region.

Declining property values would contribute only a small part (about $167 million) of the loss. This is based on our assumption that the first year after the attack would witness a 25 percent drop in both residential property values and retail trade.[9] We also assume a 10 percent fall in other business activities and that these businesses leave the region. If businesses relocate elsewhere within the region, net effects would be minimal apart from redistributing geographic trade patterns.

As for *travel behavior*, we assume that authorities will permit citizens to drive through the plume area (with suitable advice about the use of windows, air conditioning, and regular car washes).[10] Despite this, the average length of personal trips would increase as plume area residents were forced to shop and access services outside their neighborhoods. Although there are fewer total trips, the remaining trips are longer and produce more congestion. We estimate the imputed value of the resulting lost time at $1.63 billion.[11]

An Attack on Terminal Island   Terminal Island accounts for about 55 percent of the ports' trade and could in principle be isolated by taking down three highway bridges and a single rail bridge.[12] We assumed simultaneous conventional bomb attacks large enough to destroy all four bridges. We then estimated the potential economic losses associated with isolating Terminal Island. The major problem was estimating how long the island would remain closed. Our shortest assumption was three to four months based on a scenario in which one or more of the destroyed bridges was replaced with relatively high-capacity friction pile bridges. However, these low clearance structures would interfere with shipping lanes. The other "book-end" was two years to permit the total rebuilding of the bridges in their original form. Although physically realistic, this choice is likely to be driven more by institutional pressures than physical constraints.

We estimate that a one year closure would have an economic cost of $45 billion, with roughly two-thirds outside the region and one-third within. Because our model is linear, this estimate can easily be adjusted for longer or shorter closures yielding bookend impacts ranging from $15 to $90 billion. Even though other estimates of how long it would take to reopen Terminal Island are somewhat speculative, it is clear that a successful attack would be costly and that substantial investments to defend the facility are justified. If an attack did occur, substantial cost savings could similarly be derived from efforts to accelerate the reopening date.

We also investigated the geographic distribution of impacts. About 65 percent of both output and job impacts were experienced outside the region. Of the intraregional impacts, 68 percent occur within Los Angeles County, although the impacts in the other counties and especially in Orange County (parts of which are relatively close to the ports) were substantial. Not surprisingly, within Los Angeles County, about one-half of the impacts occurred in the two port cities and these fall overwhelmingly in Los Angeles rather than Long Beach.[13]

According to our model, highway travel time costs would only increase by about 0.04 percent or $58 million per year. As in our radiological bomb scenario, reductions in freight traffic largely offset the cost of longer personal trips. Here, however, delays from increased congestion on freeways and arterial roads largely stem from the fact that cars can no longer use the Vincent Thomas Bridge as a convenient link from cities in the Los Angeles Harbor area to Long Beach. This value is lower than the $90 million delay cost associated with our 120-day radiological bomb scenario because disruptions to LA's transportation infrastructure are more localized.

It is important to note that the foregoing delay costs do not include bridge repairs. Current estimates from the California Department of Transportation suggest that replacing the Oakland Bay Bridge's eastern span will eventually cost more than $6 billion. This span carries 275,000 passenger-car equivalents per day, approximating the Vincent Thomas Bridge. The other bridges serving Terminal Island are smaller and would be cheaper to replace. This suggests, very roughly, that all four bridges could be replaced for $12 billion. These costs would rise if construction was accelerated, although it is difficult to tell by how much. We have seen that the benefits of accelerated construction are easy to estimate and would total $3.75 billion per month.

The foregoing discussion suggests that government planning to protect, reconstruct, or rapidly erect temporary replacements for these bridges should be a clear priority. This result resembles earlier work by us that helped convince policymakers that accelerated repairs to freeway bridges following the Northridge Earthquake were amply justified on economic efficiency grounds.

An Attack on the Los Angeles Central Business District   We also studied a radiological bomb attack on a prominent downtown Los Angeles office building (Pan et al. 2007). Although there are several large office buildings in LA's core Central Business District (CBD), choice of target (especially with a radiological bomb) does not significantly affect our conclusions.[14] We estimate that a radiological bomb attack on downtown Los Angeles might cause economic losses totaling $6 billion. This impact is much smaller than a comparable attack on more CBD-oriented metropolitan areas like New York, Chicago, or San Francisco. It would also be much less damaging than an attack on the city's ports. Measured by dollars of trade, Los Angeles hosts America's largest port complex. By comparison, its financial and office sector is comparatively minor.

These economic facts suggest that pressures to reopen quickly would be much greater following a port attack than an attack downtown. An additional factor would be the authorities' much greater ability to control how workers and/or the military reentered the ports. This could include a variety of preventive measures potentially including asking workers to wear film badges, protective clothing and other equipment. In the downtown case, control over the general public would be much more limited. This would probably imply a more cautious schedule for resuming activities, particularly in the inner plume zone.

14.2.2 NIEMO Applications: Studying Nationwide Impacts

Attacks on Any of Three Major U.S. Seaports We used our interstate model NIEMO to estimate industry and state-level impacts from the short-term closure of three major U.S. seaports—Los Angeles/Long Beach, New York/Newark, and Houston (Park et al. 2007).[15] We estimated that a one-month closure of the Los Angeles/Long Beach port complex would cost the U.S. economy approximately $21 billion. Closing the New York–New Jersey and Houston ports would inflict losses of $14.4 billion and $8.4 billion, respectively. In general, the indirect economic losses felt in other states would depend on the size of each state's economy and its distance from the attack.

Attacks on Theme Parks We also applied NIEMO to trace the interregional economic effects of attacks on major theme parks (eleven individual parks plus two geographical clusters) located across eight states.[16] In some of our scenarios, we assumed that an attack on one theme park would be perceived as an attack on all ("spillovers"). However, we also examined a more conservative assumption in which an attack on one park did not affect attendance at others. Finally, we investigated the very probable scenario that even a major terrorist attack would not eliminate American vacations, but only shift them from theme parks to other destinations. We modeled this scenario by substituting visits to national parks for theme parks.

Based on these assumptions, we found that a theme park attack with spillovers would cause business interruption losses of between $19 billion and $23 billion plus up to $12 billion of additional airline revenue losses. Without spillovers, the impacts range from just $500 million to $11.3 billion. These numbers are comparable to the costs of September 11. Allowing tourists to substitute other destinations produces only partial mitigation because of people who decide to stay home, increase their savings, and/or postpone vacation decisions. There are also offsets. Despite having important national parks, Florida and California are net losers while states such as Arizona, Utah, and Wyoming gain overall.

These results certainly justify more expenditures on prevention. The problem is spillover scenarios. Small parks may not be able to afford prevention, particularly when most of the benefits flow to larger rivals. Methods for overcoming this problem potentially include government subsidies and/or coinsurance schemes among theme park owners.

Hurricane Katrina and the Ports of New Orleans   While we have used NIEMO to study various hypothetical terrorist attacks, it is important to check the model against actual events. Natural disasters provide this opportunity. However, applying NIEMO to the effects of Hurricane Katrina presented difficult challenges. We approached the problem by extrapolating monthly data for historic export and import trends. Comparing actual post-Katrina port performance against these extrapolations then let us estimate direct import and export losses by product sectors. Inserting these losses into our model led to the following key findings:

• *Resilience*   Seaborne exports to foreign countries from the Customs District slowly recovered. However, exports to other parts of the United States took much longer to recover. Imports from other U.S. ports were less affected than imports from abroad.
• *Ripple effects*   The interruption in foreign trade triggered additional losses throughout the U.S. economy. The estimated size of these multipliers were slightly larger for analyses based on the demand-side (2.2–2.4) compared to the supply side (1.8–1.9).
• *Distribution effects*   Several states gained from the disruption, producing a positive sum for the nation as a whole. Nearly three-quarters of all export losses were located in Louisiana. Apart from Louisiana, the biggest indirect impacts were felt in Texas and California.[17]

An FMD attack on the United States   We also applied NIEMO to estimate the state-by-state and sector-by-sector economic impacts of a hypothetical bioterrorist attack using foot-and-mouth disease (FMD) pathogens. FMD is a highly contagious viral disease that affects cloven-hoofed animals such as cattle, swine, sheep, goats, and deer. It can be transmitted not only by direct contact but also by air and even inanimate objects like animal byproducts, water, and straw. In theory, terrorists can easily disseminate the FMD virus by introducing a single piece of contaminated meat or sausage to a farm or feedlot.

The assumptions that drive our model are summarized in table 14.2. We assumed an attack on feedlots in California. The state's expenditures on decontamination, quarantine, and indemnification activities enter the model as increased final demands for industrial sectors such as veterinary services and environmental and other technological consulting services. However, the net effect to the overall California economy is negative and leads to reduced household spending. We model this using known expenditure patterns by households in the $35,000–$50,000 income bracket. Federal reimbursement for state-level decontamination, quarantine, and indemnification activities shifts some of this loss to taxpayers nationwide, reducing household consumption across the United States.

Table 14.2

Foot-and-mouth disease: Direct impacts

	Scenario 1	Scenario 2	Scenario 3	Scenario 4
Changes in meat demand				
Foreign exports of red meat	−65%	−80%	−65%	−80%
Domestic demand for red meat			−10%	−10%
Domestic demand for poultry			+10%	+10%
Response costs				
Compensation costs	−$1,171.126 millions × 1.05 reduction in overall household expenditure			
Cleaning and decontamination costs	−$118.829 millions × 1.05 reduction in overall household expenditure +$118.829 millions in environment consulting and waste and disposal services in California			
Quarantine costs	−$286.9 millions × 1.05 reduction in overall household expenditure +$286.9 millions in veterinary services in California			

Notes: The lower bound for the decrease in foreign exports (65%) is drawn from the 2001 FMD case in the United Kingdom, while the upper bound (80%) is based on the 2003 BSE case in the United States. The decrease in domestic demand for red meats and the increase in poultry demand are based on the results of a CGE study by Devadoss et al. 2006. Response costs are funded by tax dollars, which reduce household consumption; the cost of administering the tax adds at least 5% to the total. In the interests of conservatism, we ignore the efficiency losses associated with taxation.

We also model the social costs that are incurred in transferring purchasing power from taxpayers to government. These broadly consist of the administrative cost of collecting taxes, compliance costs for taxpayers, and deadweight losses. In the interests of conservatism we did not consider the deadweight loss associated with additional taxation. After looking at the relevant economic literature, we decided to reduce household consumption (final demand) by $1.05 for each dollar that the government spent on FMD mitigation. We also estimated direct losses in final demand for red meat and associated substitution effects from 2001 IMPLAN data for each of our four scenarios. These industries correspond to two of the forty-seven product sectors in our model. Finally, we calculated direct impacts by state and used them as inputs to the demand-side version of NIEMO.[18]

Depending on scenario, the model yielded indirect economic impacts ranging from just under $23 billion to just over $34 billion. Domestic and international demand reductions were overwhelmingly the largest source of these losses. Although the scenario outbreak was presumed to occur in California, reduced demand hit all major farm states hard.

14.3   Other Macroeconomic Impact Models

Existing economic impact models are short-term. Long-term effects would allow society to restructure the economy to provide work-arounds for lost or damaged assets. These effects have never been adequately modeled. But even in the short term, existing models do not simulate the market's ability to adjust. The heart of economics, after all, is the ability of markets to reallocate production and consumption to accommodate new facts of life.

Rose (2006) explores various concepts of resilience and adopts a working definition of "*economic resilience* as the ability of a system to maintain function (e.g., continue producing) when shocked....A more general definition that incorporates dynamic considerations, including stability, is the ability and speed at which a system recovers from a severe shock to achieve a desired state." He then subdivides resilience into two main categories:

• *Inherent*   Inherent resilience refers to individual firms' and markets' normal ability to deal with crises (e.g., by substituting other inputs for those curtailed by an external shock, or reallocating resources in response to changing prices).
• *Adaptive*   Adaptive resilience refers to peoples' ability to overcome crises through ingenuity or extra effort (e.g., by increasing input substitution possibilities in individual businesses, or strengthening markets by providing information to match suppliers with customers).

Rose also suggests that computable general equilibrium (CGE) models can be used to model of this phenomenon: "In terms of actual measurement of resilience, input-output (I-O) models of disaster impacts capture only quantity interdependence, often referred to as indirect or multiplier effects. Computable general equilibrium (CGE) models and macroeconometric models capture both price and quantity interaction through the explicit inclusion of market forces." Rose, Oladosi, and Lao (2007) used this approach to simulate a major water outage in Los Angeles county. Business interruption costs of a two-week event were found to be $20.7 billion but only $2.3 billion once a variety of rescheduling options are included. The resilience opportunities are, however, the authors' rough estimates and they concede that further study is needed.

We take a different approach, studying how measured input-output coefficients change in real economies following a major disaster. One of the sharpest limitations associated with conventional input-output models is that they assume fixed coefficients. This means that they cannot be used to study input substitution—that is, technology choice. Standard input-output models combine observed final demand with fixed coefficient matrices to estimate total value added. Our FlexNIEMO model takes a fundamentally different approach. It assumes that the value added and final demand are fixed and then uses maximum likelihood methods to estimate how much the coefficients change following a shock. Since final demand is not really fixed, our results only set an upper bound on resiliency. Nevertheless, our analysis of Louisiana Customs District data from 2003 to 2005 suggests that substantial input substitution may well have occurred following Katrina. For now, this research is still in its early stages. The inferred coefficient changes will become much more useful when they have been checked for realism against evidence of what is technically feasible.

Finally, Stinson (2007) analyzed resilience by analyzing several widely used macroeconometric models in which the consumption function includes a consumer sentiment variable. He then looked at how various terrorist attacks had depressed the well-known Michigan Consumer Sentiment Index in the past. This enabled him to conduct various macroeconomic simulations. For example, if future attacks were large enough to depress the consumer sentiment index one standard deviation below previous experience, Stinson found that U.S. GDP would fall by $200 billion over four years. Similarly, a two-standard deviation drop would depress GDP by $400 billion over five years.

14.4   Microeconomic Impact Studies and Other Approaches

The formal analysis of terrorist attacks is still a relatively new field and many approaches have yet to be investigated. This section reviews several leading efforts to extend existing academic disciplines into this new field.

14.4.1   Hedonic Land Studies

Real estate economists have pioneered the application of hedonic land-value studies[19] to explore how real property's various attributes affect market value. Redfearn (2005) has extended this approach to test the market's perception of post–September 11 risk for single-family homes surrounding Los Angeles's most plausible targets—its twin seaports, its downtown, and its international airport. He found no evidence that homebuyers had reduced their bids because of proximity to these possible terrorist targets.[20]

Interestingly, this result may not hold for commercial real estate markets. Abadie and Dermisi examined Chicago office vacancy data and found that properties in the vicinity of landmark buildings experienced significantly higher vacancy rates than other nearby office buildings (Abadie and Dermisi 2007). Similarly, Drennan (2007) studied the relocation decisions of large firms displaced by September 11. He found that almost half decided to stay in downtown Manhattan and that nearly 30 percent relocated to midtown. Only 1 percent left the metropolitan region. Drennan emphasized the importance of New York's agglomeration opportunities (positive spillovers resulting from proximity) for these enterprises. Many of these may now be network-based (and thus less dependent on proximity) but the fact that almost 80 percent of the relocators chose to stay in the high-rent areas of Manhattan is revealing.

14.4.2   Experimental Economics

The new field of experimental economics, which relies on laboratory experiments involving human participants, offers promising new analysis tools. Schuler (2007) reports on an experiment in which "buyers" and "sellers" in a simulated electricity market were faced with a limited number of buy and sell choices. The market was cleared each day by computer to update prices and quantities, allowing experimenters to evaluate the efficiency gains of various pricing options. Not surprisingly, allowing actors to make real-time price adjustments increased the system's performance and reliability. Operators of electrical systems under terrorist threat can learn much from these and similar experiments.

14.4.3   Engineering Systems Approaches

Lave et al. (2005) apply an engineering systems approach to power system vulnerability that focuses on "infrastructure failure interactions"—for example, when power failures cause traffic lights to fail, which then impedes emergency response. Some practical technological options (e.g., installing long-life batteries at each traffic stoplight) have obvious dual-use advantages in reducing vulnerability to both terrorist attack and extreme weather blackouts.

14.4.4   Cost-Benefit Analysis

In a more recent paper, Lave, Apt, and Morgan (2007) apply formal cost-benefit analysis to compare the improved reliability offered by various backup systems against costs. Eleven policies that would augment both reliability and resiliency (improved operator transmissions and communications, multiple transmission lines, physical barriers at key substations, and so on) are tested. Once again, the value of backup systems is multiplied by the fact that they offer four benefits (improved protection against ordinary mechanical failure, natural hazards, human error, and terrorist threats). In most cases, the crucial step is to recognize interactions when they exist.

14.4.5   Scenario Analysis

Scenario analysis has been pioneered and applied by researchers at RAND (Meade and Molander 2006). The method depends on assembling experts to examine various "what-if" questions; the experts also interact via a "strategic planning" exercise in order to suggest realistic policy choices and responses. The resulting studies emphasize how unexpected effects are not always captured by economic approaches based on extrapolating events at the margin.

14.4.6   Urban Planning Methods

Finally, urban planning techniques hold great promise for future research. Many countries are fortifying their major cities and public buildings to prevent attacks by vehicle bombs and weapons of mass destruction. However, some observers are concerned about erecting ever more barriers, bollards, armed guards, and gatehouses around buildings and public spaces. Do hard, physical barriers around buildings and public spaces make us safer, and if so at what cost? Of course, fortifying our cities may increase rather than reduce our fear, and the enhanced fear may reinforce the demand for protection. But it is not clear that the substantial resources expended make us any safer and the consequent reduction in access detracts from the value of urban life and its built-up environment. As pointed out by Coaffee (2003) and Glaeser and Shapiro (2002), security concerns explained why we originally lived in cities. In practice, however, defense requires so many resources that we end up protecting only parts of our cities. Of course, there are merits in reducing terrorists' access to target buildings because the effects of an explosion decay rapidly with distance so that buffers (e.g., concrete bollards) can reduce the risks from vehicle bombs (Little 2007). However, there is also considerable damage to the quality of urban life: we may end up with mass agoraphobia and what Little calls "architectural taxidermy."

The private sector tends to protect office buildings, shopping malls (against both crime and terrorism), and residential developments by limiting access while the public sector concentrates its attention on a limited number of public buildings. The inevitable consequences are increased social segregation and reduced mobility. The urban transportation sector illustrates these problems. In New York, London and Madrid (though not Los Angeles and Houston), trip makers frequently use public transport to minimize door-to-door travel times. Security measures that increase trip times and transit fares raise these costs significantly. Conversely, measures that reduce congestion can actually improve security. One rationale for the London Congestion Charging Scheme (LCCS) introduced in 2003 and the LCCS extension, which followed in 2007, is that introducing surveillance cameras to the Boroughs of Westminster, Kensington and Chelsea would deter terrorism. This is another example of the "dual-function" approach: policy instruments that reduce congestion cost can also improve security.

14.5   Conclusion

For the first time since the War of 1812, defending targets on U.S. soil has become a national priority. The number of potential domestic targets for terrorists is nearly infinite and resources for homeland defense are annually allocated on a very large scale. This has prompted DHS and others to ask policy analysts to adapt their toolkit to this new problem. This chapter has surveyed recent contributions from a number of social scientists who have taken up the challenge.

Nearly all politics are local and economic assessments are more interesting when the "who pays" and "who benefits" questions are addressed. This makes detailed economic impact studies an important corrective to earmarks and pork-barrel politics. Investigating key scenarios also helps bound the set of policy steps that public authorities should consider. Resources for mitigation, protection, and response are scarce; the set of projects to which they might be committed is large; and, as we have seen, the expected cost of defending the wrong structures can be expensive.

The best approach may be more fundamental. Historically, security implied compact cities, such as the medieval walled cities—for example, York, Avila, or Carcassonne. However, changes in technology suggest that the preferred urban form of the future will likely be much more widely dispersed. Urban targets are attractive because of their spatial concentration. Conversely, urban decentralization not only reduces the damage but makes targets easier to protect (Frey and Leuchinger 2007; Glaeser and Shapiro 2002). In the Digital Age, there may no longer be any great benefit to having government buildings centrally located. The same is true of private facilities; a centrally located sports stadium poses much higher risks than one on the periphery.[21]

Interestingly, most city and regional planners now advocate compact "livable city" plans that are thought to offer environmental and sustainability benefits. In our view, it is time to rethink this conclusion from a counterterrorism perspective. Decentralization increases resilience, regardless of whether we are talking about the electrical system (Lave, Apt, and Morgan 2007), protecting buildings against vehicle bombs (Little 2007), or the ability of firms to relocate to other centers within the same metropolitan area if one location is attacked. Indeed, much of the resilience following September 11 flowed from the rapid relocation of economic activities to other sites in midtown Manhattan, suburban New Jersey, and other locations.[22]

Notes

1. These losses are based on the differences between actual monthly post-event air-travel volumes and those projected by extrapolating from past trends.

2. The demand-side version of the model includes multipliers that track the repercussions following from reduced demands, in this case reduced export demands. The supply-side version of the model includes multipliers that track the repercussions following from constraints on inputs, in this case reduced availability of imports.

3. In the interests of a conservatism, we reported only Type I multiplier results. Type I multipliers exclude the repercussions associated with reduced labor use and therefore reduced consumption by households. Multiplier results would be approximately 50 percent greater if Type II results were computed. Type II multipliers include the further multiplier effects associated with changes in labor demand and resulting changes in consumption. Given the limited mitigations that we were able to include, we prefer the more conservative results. Dividing the low-range estimated gross output loss by an aggregate multiplier of approximately 1.77 (from our results), we get an overall GDP loss of approximately $1 trillion or approximately 12 percent of 2001 GDP.

4. We divided international travel into four types of trips: U.S.-based (inbound and outbound) and international-based (inbound and outbound). We assumed that each round trip costs $1,000 in airfare and that two-thirds were purchased from U.S. carriers. We also estimated ground expenditures for each type of trip.

5. An alternative mitigation approach would be to assume that buyers run down inventories, effectively deferring transactions until the borders reopen.

6. The USC system categories are designed to reconcile data from several major industrial classification systems including SIC, SCTG, NAICS, HS, and others.

7. Induced losses include the effects of changes in household income and spending.

8. EPA guidelines suggest that the critical early phase of exposure would last about four days (Rosoff and Von Winterfeldt 2007). The duration of intermediate and later phases is variable and subjective, and could range from weeks to years.

9. For the most part, shopping and services consumption would shift outside the plume area. As a result, we expect input-output effects to be modest.

10. A more extreme measure would be to close entry and exit roads and especially freeways.

11. The figure is based on a personal trip imputed cost of $13 per hour and a freight trip cost of $35 per "passenger car equivalent," which assumes that one truck is the equivalent of 2.25 cars.

12. The Terminal Island docks are accessed by three major highway bridges: the Vincent Thomas Bridge, the Gerald Desmond Bridge, and the Commodore Schuyler F. Heim Lift Bridge. A rail bridge (Badger Bridge) runs parallel to the Heim Bridge and handles 21 percent of Terminal Island's trade. The bridges are all high enough to permit ship traffic in the waters between the coast and Terminal Island. The Desmond Bridge, for example, rises 250 feet above the water, although some experts think that it is still too low for problem-free movement.

13. This is true partly because Los Angeles' large size captures a high share of the indirect and induced losses and partly because most of the Terminal Island facilities are owned by Los Angeles rather than Long Beach.

14. President George W. Bush has said that Los Angeles' tallest office building, sometimes called the Library Tower but more precisely the U.S. Bank building, was a potential target on September 11.

15. We used demand-side NIEMO to study the effects of export losses but refrained from using supply-side NIEMO to estimate import losses. This was done to avoid counting some impacted firms twice.

16. We identified the theme parks by state but intentionally refrained from using smaller geographic units in order to avoid identifying individual facilities.

17. Our analysis should be considered provisional because it combines results from both the supply- and demand-side versions of NIEMO. Conceivably, this may have produced some double-counting of losses. If a business fails for demand-side reasons (e.g., inability to obtain raw materials), for example, it cannot be destroyed a second time for supply-side reasons (e.g., inability to ship finished products to foreign markets). In principle, our approach could generate such results.

18. We believe that demand-side impacts would dominate supply-side impacts originating in shortages of livestock due to animal slaughter.

19. These are statistical estimates of how location, neighborhood, and building attributes contribute to total property value.

20. This result is in marked contrast to a similar study by Smith and Hallstrom (2005) of how Florida home buyers viewed hurricane risk. They found that markets in Lee County, Florida, received a loud wakeup call following Hurricane Andrew even though no properties were damaged. The analysts found that property values fell by 19 percent in response to the event.

21. See Blomberg and Sheppard 2007 for a dissenting view.

22. Drennan (2007) points out that one-half of the offices displaced by September 11 found alternative space in downtown Manhattan itself. This suggests that, contrary to Glaeser and Shapiro, the advantages of agglomeration still outweigh high rents and the anticipated risk of terrorism. That said, the destruction that occurred on September 11 was geographically confined. Decentralization incentives will be much more powerful if and when terrorists demonstrate a convincing WMD capability.

15

Squeezing Value from Homeland Security Research: Designing Better R&D Incentives

Stephen M. Maurer

Earlier chapters have identified multiple instances in which new technologies and products could materially reduce the risk of a terrorist WMD attack, mitigate casualties, or accelerate recovery. Examples of such potentially transformative technologies include new vaccines and other countermeasures against bioweapons, advanced methods for detecting nuclear, chemical, and biological weapons (chapter 5), techniques for removing radionuclides following a dirty-bomb attack, and better diagnostics for estimating radiation exposure in patients (chapter 12).

Years after September 11, the track record is not encouraging. In 2004, Congress launched a ten-year initiative called "Project Bioshield" (Public Law 108-276). The centerpiece was a $5.6 billion fund for purchasing new vaccines and other countermeasures if and when they were developed.[1] However, the program has produced few products and is widely considered a failure (Matheny et al. 2007). Given that civilian drugs cost about $800 million on average, inadequate budgets cannot be the whole story. As a result, Congress seems to have concluded that better incentive design could rescue the program (Lieberman 2004). This led to extensive debate of various ad hoc suggestions, including transferable patent rights and prizes between 2004 and 2006. In the end, however, none of these suggestions was adopted. Instead, the 2006 Pandemic and All-Hazards Preparedness Act (Public Law 109-417) (Bioshield II) passed the incentive-design problem on to a new agency called the Biomedical Advanced Research and Development Authority or BARDA. BARDA has broad discretion to design incentives and an initial budget of more than $1 billion.[2] How should it (and, by extension, other federal agencies) go about designing rational, evidence-based incentives?

Since the early 1990s, economists have developed a rich literature for designing innovation incentives. This chapter uses these ideas to present a coherent framework for addressing homeland security's many R&D challenges. Section 15.1 begins by describing the basic incentive mechanisms normally used to promote innovation and discusses their generic strengths and weaknesses. This discussion is limited to the relatively simple situation in which a single, one-shot breakthrough is needed. Section 15.2 generalizes this discussion to include multipart innovation, in which success requires successive steps along a development "pipeline" (e.g., drugs and vaccines) or simultaneous advances in several quasi-independent technologies (e.g., weapons systems). Section 15.3 uses this framework to analyze four grand-challenge R&D problems, including Bioshield. Finally, section 15.4 presents a brief conclusion.

15.1   Strategy: Basic Incentive Mechanisms

Policymakers have very few levers for influencing innovation.[3] In what follows, I will normally assume that their ability to supply good science ideas, genius, and luck are limited. However, this is not the whole story. Incentives and institutions also matter. Assuming that a goal is technologically possible, how should R&D be organized to yield the best possible chance of success?

This chapter argues that incentives should be selected like any other tool. Engineers are seldom sentimental about choosing between, say, steel fasteners or brass. It all depends on the job. I argue here that politicians should similarly set aside their ideological biases when choosing between, say, patents and government contracts. Instead, the sole criterion should be selecting whatever method is most likely to succeed for the particular R&D challenge at hand. This chapter presents a logic- and evidence-based framework for making this choice. Section 15.1.1 lists the main social challenges that R&D projects face. Section 15.1.2 introduces specific incentives (e.g., patents, prizes, grants, contract research) and describes their generic strengths and weaknesses in overcoming each challenge.

15.1.1   Defining the Problem: Goals and Challenges

Clear thinking requires explicit goals. This chapter assumes that homeland security has a much longer list of needed technologies than budgets to develop them. In what follows, I will usually assume that government wants to acquire innovations at the lowest possible cost. However, one can easily imagine different goals (e.g., spare-no-expense, crash development). In general, new goals will change our judgment of which incentive system is best for a particular project.

I have already said that projects face both social and scientific challenges. Clearly, no amount of clever incentive design can overcome the latter. However, social challenges can and do differ from project to project. Following the economics literature, I will focus on the following generic challenges:

Efficient procurement   New products should be developed at the lowest possible cost, particularly when this can be done without substantially delaying discovery or increasing the risk of failure. High R&D costs limit the number of technologies that can be developed.

Efficient access   Once a product is invented, we want it to be affordable. This is true whether the consumer is the federal government or a private party trying to improve its own security. In either case, high prices will limit use and/or absorb funds that could otherwise be spent on other security measures.

Agency problem (sponsors)   Researchers often worry that the sponsor will fail to pay promised rewards. Sponsors may have to offer a larger reward to cover such skepticism.

Agency problems (researchers)   Researchers may shirk, avoid, or overstate the value of their work. In each case, sponsors end up paying more for the same amount of effort.

Eliciting information   Many R&D problems make use of information scattered across the globe. This information can either be scientific (e.g., ideas for a new drug, knowledge of a critical gene sequence) or social (e.g., whether the U.S. government would use a proposed product if it existed).

Financing   Researchers often lack the internal funds and/or access to outside capital needed to fund their work. In such cases, research cannot proceed unless sponsors provide up-front resources.

Political feasibility   Different institutions face different political obstacles. Regardless of economic merit, politicians may sometimes choose incentive systems because they hide costs, obscure responsibility for failure, or sound "entrepreneurial."

15.1.2   The Innovation Toolbox: Comparing R&D Incentives

This section reviews the surprisingly short list of incentives that have been developed to elicit innovation and comments on each one's strengths and weaknesses. My discussion is deliberately generic. No matter how well implemented, we will see that each incentive has certain inescapable strengths and weaknesses. What are they?

Patents   Patents and related forms of intellectual property give inventors the legal right to prevent would-be competitors from copying their inventions. Like any other power to exclude, this creates a monopoly—that is, the power to charge more for the patented invention than the (economic) cost of production. This monopoly profit may sometimes be justified if it allows manufacturers to recoup their R&D costs.[4] Compared to our list of social challenges, this scheme has various strengths and weaknesses:

Efficient access   Because patents (by design) lead to high prices, consumers inevitably buy less of the patented good and/or reduce expenditures on other goods, including security. When the market contains just one customer (the government), this effect is partly offset by buying power on the consumer's side so that prices are set by haggling. Nevertheless, the government would get much better prices if the invention were in the public domain so that multiple companies could compete to make it at the lowest price.

Eliciting information   Intellectual property rewards researchers who are willing to disclose their knowledge and ideas in a public document (the patent application). For this reason, patents are a powerful mechanism for eliciting information that is privately held and/or scattered across the globe. This information may be scientific (i.e., the existence of a particular protein) or social (whether consumers want a new product).

Agency problems (sponsors)   An advantage of patents, at least in principle, is that the "sponsors" (including government) cannot manufacture drugs for themselves. This means that patentee/manufacturers can usually recover their reward. On the other hand, patent owners must sometimes enforce their patent rights against competing drug manufacturers in court. The prospect of costly litigation may deter R&D investment.

Agency problems (researchers)   Patents face minimal agency problems on the researcher side because researchers must deliver and sell an actual product to receive their reward.

Efficient procurement   The level of effort invested by researchers depends on the breadth and duration of their expected patent monopoly. [5] This is set by legislation. When Congress sets large rewards, companies racing for a reward may invest in "crash" or duplicative programs to increase their chances of being the first to invent and, hence, to patent.

Financing   Researchers receive nothing under the patent system until they deliver and sell an actual product to consumers. Until then, R&D must be financed by internal funds, outside borrowing, and equity. Historically, high-technology companies (e.g., computing, drugs)[6] have found outside financing almost impossible to acquire. This means that R&D is limited to internal funds and leads to a kind of rationing in which only the most profitable projects are pursued.

Political feasibility   Patents pay for innovation by imposing a de facto monopoly tax on each unit sold. However, many consumers do not understand that such a tax exists and/or cannot estimate its size. This means that patents are politically favored. Many politicians are also ideologically inclined to associate patents with free market virtues.[7]

Patents are an effective way to promote discovery. However, they have two important drawbacks. First, the patent monopoly makes knowledge more expensive. This means that consumers will ordinarily use patented inventions less and/or cut other security expenditures to pay for them. Second, patent rewards only work where a consumer market exists and is large enough to cover R&D costs. The problem in many homeland security contexts—say, bioweapons vaccines—is that private-sector demand is virtually nonexistent. On the other hand, this would not matter if industry expected government purchases to fill the gap. At a deeper level, therefore, the failure of patent incentives reflects corporate skepticism that government is willing to pay prices for new products that are high enough to cover industry's R&D investment.

Boosted Demand   Perhaps the simplest way for government to overcome investor skepticism and restore patent incentives is to announce an immediate and permanent increase in what it is willing to pay. Such "boosted-demand" schemes share the generic strengths and weaknesses of conventional patents along most dimensions. This includes efficient pricing, agency problems on the researcher side, eliciting information, and internal financing. The principal differences are

Agency problems (sponsors)   The main weakness of boosted-demand schemes is that commercial drugmakers know that government may later decide (1) to reduce previously announced budgets, or (2) use its buying power ("monopsony") to drive hard bargains that do not cover drugmakers' R&D costs. Drugmakers will normally demand a premium to cover these risks.

Political feasibility   Boosted demand requires large, immediate spending increases. This makes it more visible—and less politically feasible—than schemes based on future payments.

Boosted demand will clearly work if the boost is large enough. Indeed, British government statements that it would be interested in purchasing an effective meningitis vaccine led to three such products in the late 1990s (Kremer and Glennerster 2004). Such successes do not, however, imply that boosted demand is efficient, since other mechanisms may be able to elicit development at lower cost. In the United States, Bioshield I legislation relied almost exclusively on boosted demand to promote innovation. However, strong industry skepticism undercut this incentive so that almost no R&D occurred (Lieberman 2004).

Prizes   We have seen that researchers in boosted-demand schemes normally demand a premium to cover the risk that sponsors will fail to pay a good price if and when the innovation is delivered. One obvious fix is to make the promised reward legally enforceable—that is, a prize.[8]

Governments have offered innovation prizes since ancient times (Scotchmer 2004). In recent years, policymakers have increasingly discussed prizes as a reward for drug development. For example, the Gates Foundation has explored an "Advanced Purchase Commitments" scheme in which sponsors would promise to pay a fixed price for, say, the first ten million doses of a new antimalaria drug (AdvancedMarkets Working Group 2002). Other, less ambitious schemes involve offering "tournament" or "best-entry prizes" to whichever researcher(s) achieve the best results within some predefined period. Best-entry prizes are already widely used to solve chemical engineering problems (Boswell 2003).

Prizes are similar to patents along several dimensions, including ability to elicit information and financing. However, they are significantly different in most other respects:

Efficient access   Probably the biggest advantage of prizes over patents is that there is no patent monopoly. Instead, sponsors pay researchers for their invention out of general revenues. Thereafter, any company can compete to sell the invention to consumers. This drives down prices and encourages maximal use by government and consumers.

Efficient procurement   Prize systems require sponsors to set the amount of the researcher's reward. A surprising number of commentators and policymakers recommend simply asking industry how much reward it needs.[9] However, this gives industry an obvious incentive to lie in the usual situation where sponsors lack detailed knowledge of R&D costs. Absent this information, sponsors will almost always set prizes too low or too high to elicit the desired level of effort. In the former case, innovation will stall; in the latter, government will overpay. I explore some practical methods for estimating reward size in section 15.3.1.

Agency problems (sponsors)   Many prizes depend on clear rules (e.g., the "fastest airplane," "first person to fly across the Atlantic") that can be readily enforced in court.[10] Sometimes, however, a prize's greatest strength may be its capacity to elicit unanticipated solutions to existing problems or to solve problems that the sponsor was unaware of. Here, it may be impossible to word the prize sufficiently clearly to avoid agency problems. That said, sponsors may still be able to adopt commitment strategies that limit their ability to renege. For example, sweepstakes frequently promise that "all prizes will be awarded." Absent evidence that the sponsor favors one contestant over another, such promises provide a powerful assurance that the best research will be rewarded. Alternatively, sponsors can promise to pay prizes according to a preannounced algorithm. Finally, prizes can also be designed to include marketlike tests of value. In eighteenth-century France, for instance, sponsors rewarded inventors with sliding-scale prizes based on how many factories adopted their machinery (Foray and Hilaire-Perez 2005). Similar schemes could be used for homeland security technologies that must be purchased by a large class of users.

The foregoing discussion suggests a trade-off between enforceability and flexibility: making rewards more mechanical also makes them clumsier, so that more innovations end up being overrewarded. Prize designers will normally adopt whichever trade-off offers the best ratio of benefits to cost.

Agency problems (researchers)   Like patents, prizes for finished products entail minimal agency problems because researchers must deliver a product to earn their reward. That said, tournament/best-effort prizes may encourage researchers to overstate the value of their work and/or distort their R&D in directions that favor early, visible results.

Eliciting information   Like patents, prizes are a powerful method for eliciting new ideas. However the amount and kind of information depends on the prize. "Targeted" prizes specify a particular problem and, in some cases, generalized approaches for solving it. By contrast, "blue-sky" prizes give contestants broad freedom to choose solutions and even problems, with rewards going to whichever contestant produces the most valuable research. We have already seen that targeted prizes tend to have clearer rules and therefore create fewer agency problems on the sponsor side. Targeted prizes may not be feasible, however, where sponsors have only limited information about how best to proceed.

Political feasibility   Prize payments tend to be more visible than patent revenues and are, to that extent, politically disfavored. Despite this, recent prizes by DARPA and NASA show that this mechanism is politically feasible (DARPA n.d.; NASA n.d.).

Prizes exhibit some of the best features of patents, notably their ability to elicit widely scattered information and control agency problems on the researcher side. For this reason, policymakers frequently consider prizes in cases where normal patent incentives have failed to deliver a product. The main drawback of these schemes is that sponsors seldom possess accurate knowledge of research costs. This means that sponsors will often set prizes (1) too low, so that no inventions occur, or (2) too high, so that sponsors pay too much for the desired level of effort.

Contract Research   The most obvious way to obtain R&D is to purchase it. Government success stories like the Polaris and Apollo programs show that contract research can be extremely effective. Compared to prizes, contract research presents relatively little danger of overpayment. However, this advantage may be offset by greater agency problems on the researcher side:

Efficient procurement   Like prizes, sponsors pay for contract research directly. Unlike prizes, however, sponsors face little risk of over- or underpaying researchers. Instead, they can invite companies to compete for the right to perform the contract either informally (by comparing advertised prices) or formally (through sealed bids). In either case, sponsors can be reasonably sure that the winning vendor will charge less than its nearest competitor's R&D costs. This provides a powerful constraint on procurement costs.

Agency problems (sponsors)   Research contracts tend to be relatively clear and can be enforced in court. This reduces sponsors' incentives to renege. Knowing this, researchers will not normally include a premium to cover the risk of nonpayment. Frequent progress payments can reduce sponsors' incentives to renege still further.

Agency problems (researchers)   The main weakness of contract research is that it gives researchers opportunities to cheat. Possible tactics include inflating charges for work performed and overstating results in order to keep revenues flowing past the point when projects should be terminated. The significance of these agency problems depends on sponsors' ability to monitor and punish cheating. All else being equal, contracts that involve standard labor operations (e.g., drawing blood and performing lab tests at regular intervals) will have fewer problems than those that require discretion or creativity (e.g., inventing a "better" drug). Sponsors with substantial purchasing power also have more power to control agency problems. If researchers believe that repeat transactions are likely to be large and significant, they will work hard to keep the sponsor's business.

Eliciting information   Sponsors normally decide what R&D to purchase without seeking input from vendors. In this case, contract research does little or nothing to elicit information. However, it is possible to build hybrid systems that evade this limitation. For example, the Pentagon frequently invites vendors to submit competing proposals. The system resembles a prize, since the Pentagon normally allows winners to build the proposed product at above-normal rates of return (Rogerson 1994; Maurer and Scotchmer 2004). The net result is that sponsors surrender some cost containment in exchange for more creativity.

Financing   Sponsors typically reimburse contractors at frequent, regular intervals. This minimizes the need for outside financing compared to prizes or patents.

Given that most homeland security technologies lack plausible civilian markets, direct government payments are often necessary. This means that procurement strategy frequently comes down to a choice between prizes and contract research. As always, there is no general solution to this problem. Instead, policymakers must compare the likely overpayments associated with prizes against the inefficiencies associated with contract research. I will analyze one such problem in section 15.3.1.

Grants   Grants typically pay for work in advance. Like patents and prizes, grants are an effective method for assembling widely scattered information:

Efficient procurement   Grant proposals provide little cost containment beyond an implicit assurance that promised research results will generate sufficient benefits to cover the cost of any sums invested. Since grants reward the best idea, no effort is made to find the lowest cost researcher. If ideas are scarce, that may be an acceptable trade-off.

Agency problems (sponsors)   Researchers usually receive funds before they begin work, obviating agency problems on the sponsor side. Grants paid over multiyear periods are more uncertain.

Agency problems (researchers)   Researchers who fail to perform know that they will be less likely to receive grants in the future. Simple models suggest that the power of this mechanism to control agency problems is weaker than patents but stronger than contracts. Moreover, agency problems grow as sponsors' grant spending increases (Maurer and Scotchmer 2004). Empirically, grants seem to do a reasonably good job of controlling agency problems on the researcher side even in areas (e.g., basic science) where monitoring is nearly impossible.

Eliciting information   Because grants are awarded competitively, researchers have a short-term incentive to suppress results that are likely to help rivals. In the long run, researchers must prove to grant agencies that their work has yielded benefits. This provides a powerful reason to publish on time scales comparable to the grant cycle.

Financing   Even more than contracts, grants do a good job of providing up-front financing. This is particularly important for academic and other small researchers who lack internal funds.

Transferable Intellectual Property Rights   Transferable intellectual property rights, sometimes called "TIPRs" or "wild card patents," allow companies that develop a new homeland security technology to claim extended rights on an unrelated patent of their choice (Kremer and Glennerster 2004) (A weaker version of this proposal would give them "priority review vouchers" providing for accelerated FDA review of any drug they select. (Ridley, Grabowski, and Moe 2006)). The strengths and weaknesses of the scheme are similar to those of patents, with some significant exceptions:

Efficient procurement   TIPRs concentrate homeland security costs on the small and essentially random group of consumers who happen to use a particular product. This poses substantial fairness issues. Furthermore, TIPRs are most effective when they extend preexisting "blockbuster" patents. Since most companies do not own blockbusters, this suggests that TIPRs would have to be transferable. But transferable rights also have problems. First, companies would almost always use TIPRs to extend blockbusters—that is, the patents that would benefit consumers most if they were allowed to expire. This would aggravate efficient access problems for the overall economy. Second, firms that participate in the trades would demand a share of the reward. This means that only part of the incentive would be available to elicit new R&D.

Agency problems (researchers)   Conventional patents do not generate rewards unless and until consumers actually buy the patented invention. This provides a useful test of whether the invention is valuable in the first place. TIPRs break this link, since the extended product is different from the invention being rewarded. Instead, sponsors and other experts would have to decide whether the new invention was worth rewarding. Patents would no longer provide a market test of value.

Political feasibility   The hidden tax imposed by patents is less visible than an explicit payment and is therefore politically attractive. It is difficult to see why Congress would consider such an awkward mechanism solely on economic grounds.

Wild card patent schemes have been repeatedly suggested as a mechanism for funding neglected-disease research (Kremer and Glennerster 2004) and were seriously considered—although ultimately rejected—in the debate leading up to the Bioshield II legislation in 2006.

Hybrid Incentives   So far we have assumed that the policymakers would use the foregoing tools separately. However, politicians often try to combine patents with other methods such as prizes or contracts. Examples include prizes that allow winners to claim intellectual property and cooperative research and development agreements ("CRADAs") in which governments lend goods, services, and sometimes cash to proprietary development programs.

Policymakers should view such models with skepticism. I have repeatedly stressed that prizes, unlike patents, do not fix an artificially high price on knowledge. Naively, combining prizes with patent rights seems to offer the worst of both worlds. Nevertheless, it is possible to imagine several relatively narrow scenarios in which hybrid schemes might offer an improvement:

Unusually expensive R&D projects   Hybrids may make sense in the somewhat special case where the patent reward is too small to cover the researcher's expected R&D costs. In this case, the government supplies the missing reward and the researcher—who cannot recover its R&D expenses without the patent reward—provides some assurance that it is not just collecting government R&D support (Maurer and Scotchmer 2004).

Escaping political constraints Government may be politically constrained from paying the full cost of R&D even when that would be the right thing to. In this case having the invention at a high price, though clearly inefficient, is still better than having no invention at all.

Imperfect capital markets I have remarked that firms that lack access to external financing may not be able to invest in R&D even where facially adequate patent rewards exist. In these circumstances, limited government support may fill the gap caused by weak capital markets (Cabral et al. 2006).

High prices aside, all of these schemes face a serious danger. Companies asking for government support have an obvious incentive to plead poverty. Furthermore, we will see in section 15.3.1 that it is often very hard for government to confirm how much profit a company "needs" to start an R&D program. In this environment, government subsidies can easily replace ("crowd out") private funds that the company would otherwise have spent on R&D. In the worst-case scenario, tax dollars simply replace private capital without any net increase in society's research effort.

15.2   Strategy: Multipart Innovation

So far, our discussion has assumed that innovation is a single, one-shot process. This section examines how incentive strategies change when policymakers must provide incentives for more than one development task. For example, many products require *serial innovation*—that is, successful completion of several independent R&D project steps in a particular order. Here, the main choice is between *end-to-end (E2E)* strategies that establish a single reward for the entire R&D process and *pay-as-you-go (PaYG)* solutions that offer a separate reward for each development substep. Similarly, some products require *parallel innovation*, in which researchers conduct multiple projects simultaneously. *DARPA-style technology programs* are particularly well suited to these problems.

15.2.1   Serial Innovation: End-to-End Solutions

End-to-end systems mimic the patent system by offering a single reward that elicits development *as if* the process involved just one task. As we will see, the incentives described in section 15.1.2 can change significantly when they are embedded in an E2E framework. Furthermore, real-world E2E schemes cannot choose from the full menu of possible incentives. For example, no sponsor is likely to pay drug researchers hundreds of millions of dollars and then wait fifteen years for something to happen. This automatically takes grants, contract research, and other mechanisms that involve up-front payments off the table.[11] Depending on the innovation problem, the fact that these tools are missing from the toolbox described in section 15.1.2 may not matter. On the other hand, I argue in section 15.3.1 that contract research is a potentially powerful method for keeping late-stage drug testing affordable. E2E schemes pay a significant (if arguably nonfatal) price for giving up this incentive.

Flexibility and Learning   By definition, E2E sponsors set incentives at the outset and cannot adjust them afterward. This does not matter in the case where early-stage R&D does not teach sponsors and researchers anything about the prospects for completing later stages successfully. Instead, Park (2006) has shown that sponsors' *expected* costs for this scenario are the same in both E2E and PaYG schemes. Because E2E rewards are paid out less often than PaYG awards, however, individual payments will inevitably be larger. This difference should not matter for sponsors (e.g., the federal government) that have unlimited access to financing. The difference could matter politically, however, if very large E2E awards achieved a salience that equivalent (but individually smaller) PaYG payouts did not.

The situation is more complicated where early-stage results provide information about the chances for late-stage success. Consider first the case where both sponsors and researchers learn over time. Under an E2E system, sponsors can do nothing with this information: having announced the researchers' reward at the outset, sponsors are helpless to change it. Under PaYG, however, sponsors can use the new information to fine-tune rewards so that they just barely induce researchers to go on to the next step. Each fine-tuning reduces the overpayment that sponsors would otherwise make under an E2E system. For this reason, sponsors pay less under PaYG than they would in E2E (Park 2006).

The case is very different where researchers learn from early-stage R&D but sponsors do not.[12] Because sponsors learn nothing, they cannot use the added flexibility of PaYG to fine-tune their reward. Researchers, on the other hand, may drop out of a PaYG system if the new information shows that late-stage rewards are too small. Here, E2E has an advantage. Although the reward was originally intended to cover the combined costs of both early- and late-stage research, the researcher's early-stage R&D costs are "sunk"—that is, spent and unrecoverable. Knowing this, a rational researcher will ignore past expenditures and ask instead whether additional expenditures are likely to return a profit. Given that E2E rewards are large, this will often be true. This suggests that sponsors who do not learn from experience receive more value under E2E than they would in a PaYG system (Park 2006). While I will neglect these effects in what follows,[13] real-world programs should consider them before proceeding.

Setting the Reward   In the simplest model, researchers should respond to any reward that is large enough to cover their expected R&D costs plus some small profit. This means that sponsors' ability to set E2E rewards depends on their knowledge of researcher costs. By far the best option would be to obtain this information from researchers themselves—for example, by advertising contracts for competitive bidding. Unfortunately, E2E and contract research are usually incompatible.[14] This means that sponsors must try to estimate these costs for themselves.

Because sponsors' estimates are necessarily uncertain, they should normally be thought of as a range instead of a single number. It is instructive to ask how sponsors would use this range to arrive at a reward. Probably the most natural solution is for sponsors to offer a prize equal to the high end of the range, since this ensures that R&D will actually go forward. If they do this, however, they will typically overpay by 50 percent of the estimated range.[15] Alternatively, sponsors can offer smaller prizes in return for accepting some risk that R&D might stall. This, however, means that sponsors will purchase less R&D effort in expectation. Finally, sponsors may sometimes be able to finesse their ignorance by offering a low reward at the outset and steadily adjusting it upward over time.[16] However, this must be done slowly because companies will simply defer research if they expect prizes to grow faster than their internal rate of return (Kremer and Glennerster 2004). Overpayment turns out to be the principal argument against E2E solutions to the Bioshield problem (section 15.3.1).

In fact, the foregoing discussion is oversimplified. In many cases, rewards will have to be significantly larger than costs to elicit R&D. This can happen for at least three reasons.

Nonpayment risk   By definition, E2E rewards are only paid once contestants have sunk their R&D costs and find themselves in a vulnerable bargaining position. This increases incentives for sponsors to renege. Knowing this dynamic, rational researchers may refuse to invest at all absent (1) legal and practical assurances that the sponsor will fulfill its commitment, and (2) an additional premium to cover any remaining risk of default. This need for clearly enforceable commitments exposes a trade-off, however, since sponsors would ideally prefer some flexibility to change reward size if innovations turn out to be less valuable than they hoped. In practice, real world E2E schemes will almost always sacrifice some combination of clarity and flexibility, making them consistently less cost-effective than theory suggests.

Availability of outside financing   Companies that lack access to outside financing must ration internal funds. This means that they will only invest in the most profitable projects. This dynamic is particularly important in the pharmaceutical industry, where outside lenders find it very difficult to confirm borrowers' assertions that particular R&D ideas are likely to pay off.[17] Section 15.3.1 will discuss how this increases the uncertainty—and hence the cost—of E2E incentives in the Bioshield context.

Political feasibility   Despite these limitations, there are often powerful political reasons to choose E2E systems over PaYG. First, expenditures will normally be easier to hide if taxpayers find promises to pay money in the future less objectionable than current expenditures. Second, E2E systems relieve government officials of having to decide which scientists, scientific approaches, or scientific opportunities should be funded. This increases their ability to escape blame in the event of failure. Finally, some politicians may find E2E systems ideologically congenial because they require less government involvement and/or can be readily structured in ways that include patents.

15.2.2   Pay-as-You-Go Solutions

E2E schemes mimic the patent system by pretending that serial development is a single, monolithic process. If sponsors choose, however, they can drop this assumption and specify a different incentive for each individual step in the development chain. Unlike E2E, PaYG schemes force sponsors to make repeated judgments about which research projects to invest in, much as a private company would. In practice, this means that governments and their advisors must be able to manage and outsource research directly, instead of leaving these decisions to commercial experts. Surprisingly, there is ample precedent for such strategies. For example, most vaccines have historically been developed by nonprofit researchers (e.g., the Pasteur Institute) or military labs (e.g., USAMRIID) and even today, government agencies frequently fund preclinical programs or possess specialized equipment and expertise that private firms lack (OTA 1993a; Spivey et al. 2002). The question, then, is less whether government R&D is feasible—clearly, it is—but whether it is efficient.

PaYG's main advantage is that it replaces the firms that would normally compete for an E2E prize with an in-house government management team. This has the effect of cutting out the intermediaries who would otherwise collect overpayments under an E2E system. Unlike E2E sponsors, PaYG managers do not have to estimate researcher costs; instead, they can simply put the work up for bid and pay for whatever costs are actually incurred. For this strategy to make sense, however, government innovation teams must (1) have access to markets for outsourced R&D services, (2) be able to administer outsourcing contracts as efficiently as a private firm, and (3) make innovation investments as cleverly as their private-sector counterparts. I now examine these issues in turn.

Availability of Outsourcing Services   The existence of outsourcing services will normally differ from industry to industry. It is worth noting, however, that outsourcing is readily available for two crucial homeland security technologies—vaccines and drug development.

Administering Outsourced Contracts   Competitive bidding is a powerful method for obtaining contract services at the lowest possible price. Once the contract is signed, however, sponsors must still keep researchers from claiming payment for fictitious work or else slanting results to prolong R&D programs that ought to be terminated. Companies that purchase outsourcing services routinely hire large audit staffs to limit these sources of waste. Predictably, auditing works much better for routinized, well-defined tasks than for research that requires creativity and discretion. This suggests that the savings from PaYG will normally vary from industry to industry. Sponsors can also use the promise of future business as a deterrent to waste. Suppliers are much less willing to underperform on current contracts when their "preferred vendor status" is at stake (Maurer 2005a).

Are Government Managers Efficient?   Provided that Congress offers competitive salaries, there is no obvious reason why government cannot hire program managers from the ranks of respected private sector scientists. For this reason, any doubts about government managers centers less on their technical competence than the incentives they face. In the private sector, efficiency is driven by profit-maximizing shareholders who ruthlessly detect and defund failed research. In the public sector, manager competence is an empirical question whose answer will normally change from program to program. I return to this issue in section 15.3.1. PaYG incentives may also limit the information available to managers in other ways. Unlike prizes and other E2E incentives, PaYG rewards provide relatively little incentive for industry to reveal information held by its employees and/or academic scientist-consultants. This may be a significant drawback for innovation problems (e.g., drug discovery) where information tends to be widely scattered and/or proprietary.

15.2.3 Parallel Innovation

The Pentagon's Defense Advanced Research Projects Agency (DARPA) has acquired a near-mythic reputation for innovative and successful R&D. It is not surprising, therefore, that commentators and policymakers frequently urge "DARPA-like" solutions to Bioshield and other homeland security R&D problems. These arguments are almost always based on a perception that normal peer-reviewed grants are indecisive and risk averse and that a new agency might be bolder (Cooke-Deegan 1996; Smith, Inglesby, and O'Toole 2003). This could well be true on the theory that practically all organizations senesce and that the best way to instill boldness is to start over. That, however, is not really an argument for DARPA models per se. After all, one could equally well create newer and presumably bolder agencies to administer conventional grants and contract research. Is there anything fundamentally distinct about the DARPA model beyond its catchy name?

A close review of DARPA suggests that its successes (e.g., Polaris missile submarines, early computers) are overwhelmingly clustered in "systems technologies" that require multiple independent advances to be successful (Waldrop 2001; DARPA n.d.). Such problems face special coordination problems, since researchers working on one subproblem usually have no way of telling whether workers on other subproblems are likely to succeed. Yet without this knowledge, they (and the sponsor) may decide that it is too risky to do any work at all. In what follows, I describe how the DARPA model generates signals that allow researchers (and DARPA itself) to judge the overall probability of success despite limited knowledge and expertise.

Consider, for concreteness, a computer project that needs three separate breakthroughs (CPUs, software, and tape drives) to be successful. Because researchers value their own time, no one will accept a DARPA grant if they expect their project, say CPUs, to fail. Conversely, the fact that respected researchers have accepted DARPA grants to develop, say, software and tape drives provides a powerful signal to would-be CPU developers that they are not wasting their time. This signaling function works even though CPU developers may know nothing at all about software and tape-drives. The system also produces valuable information for sponsors: if nobody is willing to develop, say, tape drives, the sponsor needs to add some replacement technology to its overall technology portfolio.

The question remains whether DARPA models offer advantages to homeland security. The problem here is that, unlike Pentagon weapons, very few homeland security technologies can be divided into multiple parallel subproblems.[18] Without this feature, there is no particular reason to think that the DARPA "brand" is any more useful than agencies modeled on, say, NSF or NIH. Congress's disappointing experience in creating a Homeland Security Research Projects Agency (HSRPA) in 2002 and a Biomedical Advanced Research and Development Authority (BARDA) in 2006 seems to confirm this assessment (Matheny et al. 2007).

15.3 Four Challenges

I have already emphasized that no single best R&D "solution" exists. Instead, policymakers must tailor R&D institutions to the particular social challenges they face. These challenges will normally differ from problem to problem and even for different stages of the same problem. This section begins the task of designing logic- and evidence-based strategies for attacking four of homeland security's most pressing technology challenges.

15.3.1 The Bioshield Problem

The "Bioshield problem"—developing new vaccines and drugs against weapons pathogens—has received far more attention than any other homeland security R&D challenge. The good news is that Congress has given BARDA broad discretion to design novel incentives, including grants, contract research, prizes, and unspecified "other transactions."[19] But how should the federal government use this freedom? As usual, I assume that funds are limited and that policymakers prefer whichever incentive(s) elicit the most inventive effort per dollar spent.

Far more than any other homeland security technology, drug innovation is massively sequential, requiring roughly a dozen separate and distinct steps between idea and working product. I therefore focus on the basic question of whether it is more cost-effective for agencies to offer multiple, relatively small incentives at various points along the drug development pipeline (pay-as-you-go or PaYG) or else offer a single, large reward for finished products (end-to-end or E2E). My analysis begins by briefly describing what a PaYG strategy would look like and some possible sources of inefficiency. I then compare the overpayments expected under an E2E system. A final section compares the two and asks whether government innovation teams are inherently less efficient than their private-sector counterparts.

Designing Pay-as-You-Go Incentives. Drug discovery consists of a "pipeline" of roughly one dozen separate and distinct R&D steps. Interestingly, the pharmaceutical industry often uses PaYG incentives—including intellectual property rights, contract research, and even prizes—to purchase R&D at various points along the development pipeline. For example, large drug companies typically outsource about 30 percent of their R&D budgets (Pollack 2002) and spend an additional 10 percent on drugs "licensed in" from other companies (DiMasi, Hansen, and Grabowski 2003). Indeed, some "Virtual Pharmas" outsource all R&D functions except for portfolio management, study design, and interactions with regulators (Graff 2004; Norris 2003). Investors' willingness to fund such ventures represents a market judgment that PaYG strategies are at least approximately competitive with traditional in-house development.

The question remains what a PaYG drug development strategy would look like. In broad outline, several generalizations are possible:

Information The need to collect widely scattered ideas and information declines steadily as drugs progress through the pipeline. In principle, there are roughly 10^{40} "small molecules" that might be useful as drugs (Landers 2004). This number makes it overwhelmingly likely that most new drugs have never been synthesized—let alone investigated—before. Because researchers are forced to break new ground, existing stores of human knowledge are increasingly irrelevant once a lead compound has been identified.

Agency problems   Early-stage researchers need to be creative, and must therefore be given substantial discretion. This, however, makes it hard for sponsors to monitor and evaluate what researchers are doing. The resulting agency problems explain why biotech companies usually wait to purchase ideas until *after* they have been turned into specific compounds that they can test for themselves (Garth and Stolberg 2000). By comparison, late-stage human trials are relatively standard exercises that are easily monitored and require little discretion. This implies that agency problems steadily decrease as compounds progress through the drug discovery pipeline.

Cost   R&D becomes steadily more expensive as drugs progress through the pipeline. Three-quarters of all R&D expenditures occur after drugs enter the preclinical stage (DiMasi, Hansen, and Grabowski 2003; Global Alliance 2001).

This picture has important consequences for incentive design. In the early phases where information and agency problems dominate, we have seen that grants and prizes are appropriate tools. After testing begins, the problem shifts to cost containment. Competitively bid contracts are a potentially powerful lever in this environment. Table 15.1 presents a more detailed look at the incentives that PaYG designers might choose at each step of the pipeline.

Is Pay-as-You-Go Efficient?   PaYG depends on efficient outsourcing. Naively, one might think that government could outsource R&D just as efficiently as large pharmaceutical companies do. However, we have already noted that contract research breeds *agency problems* that encourage researchers to shirk or prolong work. Commercial pharmaceutical firms use large liaison staffs and the prospect of repeat business to discourage such practices. Because Bioshield's budget is many times smaller than the average Big Pharma company's, government managers will have less control over vendor cheating. In principle, we can estimate the size of this effect. For example, press accounts suggest that providers of chemistry R&D services have historically earned profit margins of 15 to 20 percent. Assuming a 10 percent return to capital, this suggests that researcher cheating earns supernormal profits of at most 5 to 10 percent. In the late 1990s, Big Pharma used aggressive cost-control programs to cut this figure in half (Hume and Schmitt 2001). This suggests that Bioshield's reduced purchasing power would make outsourced research, at most, about 5 percent more expensive than corresponding purchases by Big Pharma. Furthermore, Bioshield might be able to outsource some activities *more* efficiently than Big Pharma. Asian firms can reportedly manufacture many of the intermediate chemicals used to make drugs for 5 percent less than U.S. and European companies. Despite this, drugmakers seldom outsource manufacturing to Asia for fear that their patented compounds would be pirated (Winder 2003). Government managers, on the other hand, could potentially take advantage of these savings by developing Bioshield drugs outside the patent system.[20]

End-to-End Incentives   We have seen that sponsors' ability to control E2E overpayments depends on their ability to estimate R&D costs. For now, the estimate by DiMasi, Hansen, and Grabowski (2003) reflects the state of the art. They find that new drugs that reached the market in 1997 cost $802 million on average, taking account of failed projects ("dry holes"). This figure is, however, highly uncertain; indeed, DiMasi and colleagues admit that the actual number could be as low as $684 million and as high as $936 million (95 percent confidence limit). This range implies an uncertainty of ± 16 percent. In fact, sponsors' knowledge of R&D costs is even more uncertain because they must extrapolate from DiMasi, Hansen, and Grabowski's 1997 estimate to drugs that will only appear fifteen to twenty years from now. As DiMasi and colleagues point out, R&D costs are known to have fluctuated wildly in the past. A more recent paper by Berndt et al. (2005) confirms this impression. They try to estimate how much reward would be needed to provide adequate R&D incentives for a malaria vaccine. While no uncertainties are quoted, their result appears accurate to within (perhaps) ± 20 percent.[21] Finally, even this estimate might be conservative since there are at least three reasons why an efficient prize might not equal average per-drug R&D costs:

Internal financing   There is good evidence that pharmaceutical companies lack access to outside capital. This forces them to ration their internal funds so that only the most lucrative projects are funded. Commentator estimates of the market reward needed to elicit commercial R&D typically range from $200 to $500 million (Maurer 2005a). This suggests an implied uncertainty of 40 percent.

Patent incentives   The foregoing estimates document R&D costs for companies racing to develop rich-nation drugs. However, these depend on patent law—if Congress decided to make patents broader (narrower), companies would spend more (less) per program. Given that homeland security budgets are tight, policymakers would much prefer to know the minimum feasible ("bare-bones") cost of R&D. In principle, this can be done by preparing a pro forma budget based on (1) the market price of each required R&D step, and (2) adjustments for the cost of failed projects and interest rates. To date, the best-known example of such an estimate comes from the Global Alliance for TB Drug Development. It argues that a bare-bones drug discovery program should cost between $115 and $240 million.

Table 15.1
Drug discovery pipeline and possible PaYG incentives.

Discovery phase	Main social challenges	Time/cost/proba-bility of success	Preferred institutions
1. Basic research			
Effective R&D requires detailed knowledge of disease organisms and how they interact with the human body.	Agency problems on the researcher side; eliciting information.	N/A	Grants
2. Target identification and validation			
Basic understanding of how diseases work yields ideas for manipulating and interfering with them. Researchers use these ideas to find proteins ("targets") that control metabolic functions within the human body.	Agency problems on the researcher side; eliciting information.	1–2 years Moderate 30%–50%	Best-entry prizes. Open source.
3. Lead compound discovery			
There are currently four broad strategies for finding "lead compounds":			
High throughput chemistry			
Large drugmakers hire staff chemists to create "libraries" containing tens of thousands of chemicals. They then use robots to screen the libraries against promising targets. Automated screening reportedly costs a few dollars per sample or about $1 million per search.	High throughput chemistry has minimal agency problems. First, it is a largely robotic process that can be easily monitored by sponsors. Second, researchers also have little or no a priori knowledge of whether they will find leads. The risks are scientific, not social.	~1 year $100,000–$1 million 60%–65%	Contract research. Best-entry prizes.

Combinatorial chemistry

Experiments blend a handful of building-block molecules to create hundreds of thousands or millions of compounds at once. Lead compounds are identified if and when one of these compounds binds to the target protein. Tens of thousands of dollars.	Agency problems on the researcher side. Because experiments are individually designed, they depend on researchers' motivation and judgment.	~1 year 100s of thousands of dollars?	Grants. Best entry prizes.

Computational chemistry

Chemists are increasingly able to build computer models of molecules that do not currently exist. This potentially allows them to suggest drug candidates that ought to be synthesized.	Agency problems on the researcher side. Computer models demand significant creativity from researchers.	~1 year 10s of thousands of dollars?	Grants. Best entry prizes.

Bioprospecting

In some cases, lead compounds may already be known from anecdotes, folklore, serendipitous research, or prior R&D.	Eliciting widely scattered knowledge from around the world.	N/A	Prizes. Open source?

4. Lead compound optimization

Once a lead compound has been discovered, chemists modify it to find potentially workable drugs.	Modest agency problems on the researcher side.	1+ years Millions to 10s of millions of dollars. 55%	"Big science" grants. Contract R&D.

5. Preclinical R&D

Preclinical trials use tests on tissue cultures and animals to determine the risk that a compound poses to humans and the environment. They also document how effectiveness and/or toxicity vary with dose.	Cost containment. Agency problems on the researcher side.	$2.5–$5.0 million 3–6 months 50%–60%	Contract R&D.

Table 15.1
(continued)

Discovery phase	Main social challenges	Time/cost/probability of success	Preferred institutions
6. Process development Chemical engineers must turn laboratory-scale, experimental compounds into working drugs. This involves designing safe, economical, and regulatory-compliant methods for producing drugs in bulk; enhancing stability; and modifying formulas to enter the bloodstream more predictably.	Cost-containment. Eliciting information	$50 million Up to 4 years ?	Contract R&D. Best entry prizes.
7. Phase I trials Phase I clinical trials are used to determine safe doses and identify side effects. They are typically performed on twenty to eighty healthy volunteers.	Cost containment. Agency problems on the researcher side.	$15 million 21.6 months 71%	Contract R&D; use of competitive bidding and repeat contracts to enforce low prices; in-house management of all FDA contacts.
8. Phase II trials Phase II trials are designed to obtain data on short-term safety as well as limited information about efficacy. Tests typically involve 100 to 300 patients suffering from the targeted disease.	Cost containment. Agency problems on the researcher side.	23.5 million 2.1 years 0.44	Contract R&D; use of competitive bidding and repeat contracts to enforce low prices; in-house management of all FDA contacts.

9. Phase III trials	Phase III trials are designed to gather precise information on effectiveness for specific indications, search for rare and unknown side effects, optimize delivery methods and doses, and provide evidence for product labels. Trials typically include several hundred to several thousand subjects and are far more expensive than other research.	Cost containment. Agency problems on the researcher side.	$125 million 2.5 years 68.5%	Contract R&D; use of competitive bidding and repeat contracts to enforce low prices; in-house management of all FDA contacts.
10. FDA approvals	FDA approval is based on a written New Drug Application (NDA) containing summaries, individual study reports, and tabulated data on up to 50,000 patients. The process culminates in a hearing at which the FDA can grant, reject, or defer the application pending further information. Large drugmakers typically invest several human-years in preparing for hearings, although smaller companies make do with less.	Cost containment. Agency problems on the researcher side.	$3 million 6–8 months 95%	Contract R&D; in-house management of all FDA contacts.
11. Manufacturing	Manufacturing costs are roughly comparable to R&D expenditures for most commercial drugs. Manufacturing issues are particularly pressing for vaccines and biopharmaceuticals, which must be made using the same techniques that will be employed in full-scale production. This means that sponsors must often invest in full-scale facilities before test outcomes are known.	Cost containment. Agency problems on the manufacturer side.	N/A	Contract production; use of competitive bidding and repeat contracts to enforce low prices.

Source: Maurer 2005a

Atypical firms   The foregoing estimates refer to an average firm. Sponsors, on the other hand, may be quite happy if only one qualified firm responds to their incentives. Sponsors should tailor their incentives to firms that have exceptionally low costs or are unusually optimistic (Farlow 2004). Unfortunately, these characteristics are even harder to estimate than average cost data.

This discussion suggests that the cost penalty for E2E is very large compared to PaYG. In principle, future scholarship could reduce this penalty by delivering improved R&D cost estimates.[22] That said, academics have worked hard to refine drug cost estimates since the 1970s. At least in the short term, further dramatic improvements seem unlikely.

Are Government Teams Inherently Less Efficient?   Naively, PaYG strategies seem much more efficient than the 20 to 30 percent overpayments conservatively associated with E2E. This, however, assumes that government drug discovery teams are about as efficient as private ones. Is this really true?

Neglected-disease research offers a potentially powerful test. Today, there are roughly one dozen nonprofit drug discovery teams working on cures. Preliminary data suggest that they have managed their drug portfolios just as effectively as private-sector teams would (Moran et al. 2005). The field is still young, however, and these results will be much more convincing if and when the teams actually deliver new drugs to market. In the meantime, anecdotal evidence suggests that institutions like the U.S. Army's Medical Research Institute of Infectious Diseases or the Pasteur Institute have been remarkably successful in the past.[23] Detailed econometric studies of these programs would go some distance toward establishing the relative efficiency of government and private-sector programs.

It is also useful to ask what theory has to say. Since nonprofit drug discovery teams usually include highly respected alumni of commercial programs, ability is not the issue. Instead, any inefficiency should be traceable to the fact that nonprofit teams have different incentives. In principle, a cleverly designed program can eliminate these differences by tying nonprofit incentives to (presumably efficient) private ones. One powerful way to do this would be for Congress to challenge private-sector drug companies to loan star employees (or even entire development teams) to the Bioshield program for a fixed period of time, say five years. The idea has precedent: during the Second World War, Washington borrowed thousands of "dollar-a-year-men" from industry to administer the war effort. Similarly today, Big Pharma could hardly refuse a public appeal from Congress. At the same time, companies would immediately understand that lending employees to Bioshield would give financial markets important insights into the quality of their R&D

staffs. This would provide a powerful incentive for companies to send their best researchers to Washington. Furthermore, the employees themselves would realize that their Washington duty was only temporary and that it was important to keep their former (and future) private sector employer happy. This would keep their incentives quasi-private throughout their government tour.

Choosing a Strategy   In the end, the choice between PaYG and E2E will always contain an element of uncertainty. Nevertheless, it is important to choose. Both PaYG and E2E programs have significant economies of scale—that is, large programs are inherently more efficient than small ones.[24] This provides a powerful reason to fund one or the other, but not both.

15.3.2   Ubiquitous Chemical and Bioweapons Detectors

During the Cold War, the U.S. government mounted gamma ray detectors on telephone poles near every major city so that an atomic explosion could be confirmed within minutes (Sagan 1993). Gamma rays, however, can be readily detected and converted into electrical signals. Pathogen threats are much harder. First, detection depends on DNA and other signatures that are largely unknown. Second, converting these signatures into a useful signal normally requires elaborate "wet lab" techniques that are slow, expensive, and require repeated human intervention (chapter 5). The challenge is to automate these methods for use in in cheap, autonomous units that can be deployed like smoke detectors.

Signatures   Effective bioweapons detectors need a list of distinctive "signatures" (e.g., genes that code for toxicity) to distinguish pathogenic organisms from their harmless cousins. This information can be obtained by conducting experiments, gathering existing knowledge held by widely scattered individual researchers, and reviewing the scientific literature. It is reasonable to think that these gaps will eventually be filled by normal, grant-funded academic science. So far, however, university researchers have paid relatively little attention to the problem.[25] One obvious way to accelerate research would be to offer targeted grants to academic scientists willing to do this work. Industry could also play a role to the extent that research requires large-scale experiments that cannot be comfortably performed within a university or national lab. Conventional contract research would work well in this context.[26]

Developing autonomous detectors   Autonomous detection is a hard technological problem that will almost certainly require unusual, outside-the-box ideas.[27] This implies that (1) researchers will need considerable discretion so that sponsors must worry about agency problems, and (2) the ability to elicit widely scattered ideas is important. These observations suggest that sponsors should consider using grants or prizes. While these methods tend to overreward inventors, the cost of building prototypes is likely to be relatively small in a program aimed at making tens of thousands of units. For this reason, even large overpayments at the prototype stage should not matter. In principle, a hybrid system that combined patents with government-funded grants or contracts might also make sense if detector technology had substantial civilian applications. This, however, would mean passing R&D costs on to purchasers—surely a disadvantage for a technology designed to be ubiquitous.

15.3.3 Radiation Diagnostics

Physicians responding to a nuclear or radiological attack would need cheap diagnostic kits to separate exposed victims from large numbers of "worried-well" citizens. Here, the main R&D challenges would be to discover "biomarkers" (e.g., messenger RNA, gene expression, cell-damage indicators) for radiation exposure; evaluate the best ones; and package them in cheap disposable kits:

Finding candidates In principle, there are two ways to find biomarkers. First, researchers can mount an exhaustive search of possible candidates by some combination of literature surveys and (where no literature exists) animal testing. These activities would not be noticeably different from other forms of basic research and could presumably be supported by grants. Second, clever biologists—particularly in the former Soviet Union—may already have ingenious ideas for candidates that ought to be investigated. Prizes are a sensible tool for eliciting this information.[28]

Evaluating biomarkers Candidate biomarkers must be thoroughly tested for consistency across populations and genders, feasible sampling methods (mouth swab, hair follicles, and so on), false positive and negative rates, and various other factors. This information almost certainly does not exist anywhere on earth. Furthermore, it is likely to be ethically available from just one source: measurements on cancer patients undergoing radiation treatment. In this environment, techniques (prizes, patents) designed to elicit widely scattered information are not particularly useful. Conversely, contract research and ordinary grant-supported science should work relatively well.

Manufacturing biomarker kits It is widely assumed that biomarker kits would be similar to today's home pregnancy tests. If so, commercialization would require negligible ingenuity, whereas competitively bid manufacturing contracts would be a powerful way to contain costs.

15.3.4   Cargo-Screening Technologies

The U.S. government has sought unambiguous, cost-effective methods for detecting nuclear weapons materials inside cargo containers for decades. As described in chapter 5, recent work at the Lawrence Livermore National Laboratory (LLNL) suggests that a prototype detector is within reach (Norman et al. 2004). At this point, the sole remaining innovation tasks are to (1) commercialize the prototype design so that it is sufficiently robust and user-friendly for everyday industrial use, and (2) manufacture it in volume. Many firms are capable of this work (Scales, Kim, and Carpio 2005). In these circumstances, it would be sensible for government to issue detailed specifications of what it wanted built and advertise competitively bid contracts to manufacture a fixed number of units. Alternatively, government could announce a prize where two or more companies could compete on quality. This may be desirable if the quality of any one program's design is unpredictable. Like all prizes, this method would carry a significant risk of overpayment compared to a competitively bid contract. Hybrids of these two approaches, in which companies could not recover their commercialization costs without selling units over and above those found in the R&D contract, might be an attractive solution to this trade-off.

15.4   Conclusion

Homeland security depends sensitively on developing new technologies, yet the results from even well-funded programs like Bioshield and BARDA have so far been disappointing. While this could theoretically be fixed by throwing more money at the problem, radically increased budgets are politically unlikely. This leaves better incentive design. While Congress's debates have been inconclusive, modern innovation economics provides a natural framework for moving forward. Doing better will require a hard, unsentimental look at cost containment, but this is eminently feasible. If Pfizer can manage an annual R&D budget of $7 billion, the federal government should be able to squeeze comparable value from Bioshield's far smaller, $500 million-per-year program.

Notes

1. Bioshield I created a new body within the Department of Homeland Security called the Homeland Security Advanced Research Projects Agency or HSARPA to administer the fund. However, HSARPA could only use one method—procurement contracts—to foster R&D. Furthermore, all contracts had to specify that vendors would deliver a fixed number of units; that delivery would take place within eight years; and that at least 90 percent of all payments would be made after delivery began (§319F–2(c)(7)(C)(ii)). The rate at which HSARPA could

write contracts was also limited. For example, the agency could commit no more than $890 million in the first year and no more than $3.4 billion in the first five years of the program (§510(a)).

2. Bioshield II authorizes BARDA to promote countermeasure technologies and related "strategic initiatives" by awarding "contracts, grants, and cooperative agreements," and entering into "other transactions, such as prize payments" (§§319L(c)(4)(B)(iv) and (D)). The act also gives BARDA special authority to pay exceptionally high salaries to attract highly trained program managers and consultants (§§319L(c)(7)(A)(i), C(i)). Finally, the act amends Bioshield I so that HSARPA can promise "milestone" payments totaling up to 50 percent of the total contract before delivery, as long as individual payments are less than 5 percent (§319L(c)(5)(D)).

3. This section, and the chapter as a whole, owes a large debt to chapters 2 and 8 of Suzanne Scotchmer's *Innovation and Incentives* (2004). Readers who seek a more rigorous presentation should consult that book.

4. In a competitive market, manufacturers will accept any price that promises a profit over their expected costs in the future. On the other hand, they will *not* insist on recovering R&D and other "sunk costs" that have already been spent. Knowing this, manufacturers will not invest in R&D in the first place when they expect markets to be competitive. The patent system, which gives inventors a temporary monopoly, is one way of fixing this problem.

5. For competitive markets, a profit-maximizing company will continue to invest in research as long as the expected reward exceeds the expected investment. The "expected reward" is defined as (total reward) × (probability of success).

6. Historically, computer companies found it very difficult to obtain outside financing. The rise of venture capital funds starting the 1950s has only partly alleviated this problem (Maurer 2006). Large pharmaceutical houses continue to fund almost all research from internal sources (OTA 1993a).

7. Patents have not always been viewed so favorably. U.S. courts showed a marked antipathy to patents in the 1880s, 1930s, and—to a lesser extent—the 1960s. French politicians showed a similar preference for prizes over patents in the late eighteenth and early nineteenth centuries (Scotchmer 2004).

8. Prizes have become very popular in recent years and there is now a large literature on when and how policymakers should offer them. Technical discussions of prize economics can be found in Maurer and Scotchmer 2004, Scotchmer 2004, and Cabral et al. 2006. For a semipopular treatment, see NRC/Committee on Design 2007.

9. Thus, for example, Senator Joseph Lieberman (2004): "[Private drugmakers] will not say what package of incentives would be sufficient to persuade them to take up biodefense work.... If the incentives in BioShield or BioShield II are not sufficient, we need to know what incentives are sufficient.... And only industry can give us a clear answer to these questions. We cannot have a dialogue on these urgent questions without the government listening and industry speaking." Not surprisingly, industry has not been shy about telling government that it needs more money—for example, in a recent article by two biotech executives urging policymakers to "reach out" by, among other things, "increas[ing] contract margins" (Gilmore and Lambert 2005). Indeed, it is hard to imagine why companies would say anything else.

10. *Himfar v. United States* (1966) (the United States could not renege on a unilateral promise to purchase domestic manganese ore at predetermined prices). In many cases, prizes are more enforceable than patent rights.

11. Of course, sponsors could control agency problems by entering long-term contracts that provide for progress payments contingent on researchers' performance. According to my definitions, however, such contracts would no longer be an E2E reward. Repeated, continually updated rewards are the hallmark of PaYG systems.

12. This scenario is plausible for drug discovery, where information asymmetries between researchers and outside organizations tend to be substantial.

13. Because Park's models are polar cases, real-world sponsors and researchers would fall somewhere in the middle. Although the analysis is highly model-dependent, this suggests that the differences between E2E and PaYG will normally be small (Park 2006).

14. E2E would require sponsors to make a single, lump-sum payment for all work performed at the end of the project. However, such payments become increasingly unrealistic for projects like drug discovery that cost millions of dollars and may take a dozen years to complete. The reason has to do with agency problems: Researchers know that sponsors will have a strong incentive to renege (or at least demand a better price) once the work is done. E2E prizes face a similar problem but usually mitigate it by making payment contingent on objective performance standards ("first new smallpox vaccine") that can be enforced in court. Contract researchers have no such standard: They expect to be paid even if the work fails to generate a product. This makes it easy for government to demand ex post price reductions by arguing that the work was done badly

15. I assume that probabilities are symmetrically distributed within the quoted range.

16. In the case of drug research, sponsors could easily wait ten to twenty years before rewards were large enough to elicit R&D. If R&D costs rise in the interim, development may never begin at all.

17. The fact that large drugmakers fund almost all of their R&D investments from internal cash flows suggests that investors find it hard to monitor company research and therefore demand a premium to cover the risk of being misled (OTA 1993). On the other hand, the fact that venture capital firms routinely invest in biotech companies suggests that these risks are manageable.

18. The Bioshield II legislation mentions three possible candidates—rapid diagnostics, broad-spectrum antimicrobials, and vaccine manufacturing technologies (Public Law 109-417 §319L(c)(4)(D)).

19. The legislation also relaxes earlier constraints on HSARPA's ability to make predelivery "milestone payments."

20. Whether Congress would allow programs to take advantage of the low prices offered by foreign companies, let alone companies with a history of patent infringement, is another matter. U.S. policymakers might also worry that Asian companies would use contracts to make bioweapons vaccines as a way to learn Western manufacturing standards. This would create long-term competition for U.S. drug manufacturers.

21. Berndt et al. (2005) argue that a rational drug company should normally set its R&D budget equal to its expected revenues less marketing costs. Since drug revenues are known,

this means that R&D budgets can be inferred by estimating how much money is spent on marketing. While Berndt et al. admit that published estimates range from 15 to 36 percent, they reject these figures without explanation in favor of a much smaller, 10 percent figure. This leads to a relatively large R&D estimate of $2.56 billion. They then adjust their estimated reward upward a second time (to $3 billion) based on an assertion that "a malaria vaccine may be more difficult to develop than the typical new chemical entity." Both adjustments are, of course, conservative to the extent that they provide safety margins against underestimating the true R&D cost. Suffice to say, an unadjusted calculation would have produced a much smaller estimate.

22. Policymakers may eventually be able to refine their estimates by considering such project-specific factors as disease type; availability of animal models; availability of experience with closely related compounds; how well basic science understands the disease; and whether the desired product is a drug or vaccine. For now, however, such adjustments fall outside the current state of the art.

23. USAMRIID developed a long list of vaccines against weapons diseases from the 1960s through the 1980s. Examples include vaccines against Argentine hemorrhagic fever, Venezuelan equine encephalitis, Rift Valley fever, tularemia, infant botulism, and other diseases (Covert 2000). Detailed records of USAMRIID's spending can be found in the agency's annual reports. Other examples of successful nonprofit programs include the March of Dimes (Salk and Sabin polio vaccines) (Smith 1990) and the Pasteur Institute (rabies, BCG vaccine, yellow fever, polio, hepatitis B, shigellosis) (Pasteur Institute n.d.). Some critics have argued that the U.S. Army program was relatively inefficient during the 1990s. The reason seems to be policymakers' decision to replace in-house R&D with a "privatization" scheme in which development was placed in the hands of outside contractors (Senate Armed Services Committee 2000). This created significant (and predictable) incentives for the outside vendor to shirk work not found in the earlier, in-house program.

24. We have seen that PaYG programs use the prospect of repeat business to extract value from researchers. This tactic is most effective for large, well-funded programs. Similarly, many commentators argue that companies do not trust federal agencies to pay E2E rewards when the time comes (see, e.g., Gilmore and Lambert 2005). This implies that E2E prizes would need substantial risk premiums to be effective. Corporate skepticism would be much less of a problem for large programs that made frequent payouts.

25. Tom Slezak, personal communication.

26. There is also the subsidiary problem of publishing academic discoveries in forms that industry can use. Academic databases frequently suffer from incompleteness, unsophisticated software, limited attention to user needs, and other weaknesses that limit their value to industry (Maurer, Firestone, and Scriver 2000). Academic-industrial database collaborations are a natural way to overcome these difficulties (Maurer 2003).

27. Multiple, well-funded R&D programs have attempted to build autonomous pathogen detectors for over a decade (Walter 1999). The fact that no clear winner has emerged suggests that this is not a situation where sponsors already know the correct engineering approach and are simply asking researchers to fill in details.

28. In principle, patent incentives should already have elicited this information. The fact that they have not done so suggests that would-be inventors are skeptical of the government's willingness to purchase patented diagnostic kits even if they existed.

16

Fear Itself: Predicting and Managing Public Response to a WMD Attack

Stephen M. Maurer and Michael O'Hare

Washington policymakers routinely treat the period from the aftermath of a large WMD attack to the resumption of normal government and economic life as a kind of terra incognita where logic and evidence have nothing to say. Paradoxically, this does not stop them from confidently predicting widespread, irrational rioting and panic. As Herman Kahn (1962) noted half a century ago, this simultaneously vague-but-dark image of the "unthinkable" is profoundly dangerous because it relieves citizens and leaders of their obligation to think about what they would do in an emergency. Certainly, Kahn would not be surprised to hear DHS boast that it is "strongly focused" on "prevention"—and that anyone who asks the agency to spend more time on postattack scenarios (e.g., planning for mass casualties) has no "grasp of reality" (Jordan 2006).

There is no doubt that the aftermath of a large WMD attack would be exceptionally difficult to manage well, and challenge American society in ways not seen since World War II (405,000 killed, equivalent to 891,000 today), the 1918 influenza pandemic (675,000 killed, equivalent to 1.9 million today), or even the Civil War (560,000 killed, equivalent to 5.4 million today). It does not, however, follow that scholarship is helpless to provide evidence or insight. Certainly, we can learn much from the collapse of Axis societies at the end of World War II; the bombings of Dresden, Tokyo, and Hiroshima; the Spanish influenza pandemic of 1918; and Europe's vast nineteenth-century cholera outbreaks. Indeed, some of these catastrophes were more challenging in their time than any likely WMD attack: unlike, say, the destruction of Dresden, attacked U.S. cities would still be embedded within a much larger and still functioning society.

Of course, a WMD attack would clearly present unknowns and surprises. Most evidently, it would provoke fears of "invisible" contamination that social psychologists are only beginning to understand. This chapter reviews what is known about the public's likely response to WMD terrorism and how government can influence it for the better. Section 16.2 reviews the various physical impacts that different forms of WMD inflict on targets. Section 16.3 asks how the public would react to these impacts and what psychological stresses would flow from them. Section 16.4 asks how preattack leadership can increase the country's resilience to an attack. Section 16.5 asks how postattack leadership can make public responses more effective. Section 16.6 looks at the special challenges of long-term remediation and recovery. Finally, section 16.7 presents a brief conclusion.

16.1   Physical Impact

Twentieth-century history offers a depressing wealth of evidence on how WMD affects civilian populations. These traumatic "natural experiments" include large-scale chemical weapons use against thousands of civilians in Ethiopia (1935), Bari, Italy (1943) (Harris and Paxman 2002), Bhopal, India (1984) (Eckerman 2005), and Iraq (1988) (Tucker 2006); large-scale radioactive contamination of civilians at Chernobyl (1986); pandemic influenza (1918) (Barry 2005; Garrett 2007); massive conventional firebombing in Europe (Beck 1986; Friedrich 2006) and Japan (1943–1945) (Hoyt 2000); and the atomic bombings of Hiroshima and Nagasaki (1945) (Hersey 2001; Hoyt 2000; USSBS 1946a, 1947b). In general, effects would depend strongly on which kind of WMD was used.[1] Atomic weapons are the most powerful form of CBRN along most relevant axes, including casualties, physical destruction, and long-term contamination. By comparison, chemical and biological weapons would usually produce fewer—though still potentially extensive—casualties and would cause little or no physical destruction or (anthrax excepted) long-term contamination. Finally, radiological weapons would cause minimal casualties or damage apart from long-term contamination and would claim relatively few lives even along this dimension (chapter 3).

Despite local devastation, the scale of destruction would be modest on a national scale. Katrina flooded an area of New Orleans measuring 144 square miles and including 110,000 of the city's 180,000 buildings (Delahanty 2006). This zone of physical destruction is much larger than anything plausibly achievable by terrorist WMD up to and including kiloton-scale nuclear weapons.

16.1.1   Casualties
Very large numbers of *dead and wounded* are a defining feature of WMD. For most WMD, casualties would be relatively localized both in space and time. We discuss these first. Casualties from contagious diseases would accrue more slowly and are discussed separately below.

Classical CBRN   The approximately 15-kiloton explosion at Hiroshima provides a useful benchmark for the 10-kiloton terrorist bomb invoked by most scenarios.

Within the innermost kilometer people died almost instantaneously, well-built structures were destroyed, and houses were flattened. Between one and two kilometers from ground zero, many people were killed and almost all were seriously injured, while houses were destroyed and fires broke out everywhere. Finally, people were injured and houses were half-damaged up to four kilometers from the explosion (USSBS 1946a). All told, the explosion killed 100,000 victims or roughly 40 percent of the city's population. An additional, comparable number suffered serious injuries and many more were trapped beneath collapsed buildings. These casualties presented a horrific scene. Refugees who walked out of Hiroshima's city center in the first hours after the attack saw bodies everywhere, often lying side by side with the injured and sick. Most survivors also displayed horrifying injuries, including contusions, burns, and uncontrolled vomiting (Hersey 2001).

In theory, very large scale chemical or biological attacks could inflict comparable casualties, although these would often be delayed by twenty-four hours or so. In practice, imperfect delivery systems and victims' ability to shelter inside buildings would probably limit losses to subnuclear levels. A radiological weapon would inflict no immediate casualties at all except for the conventional explosion used to spread its radioactive payload.

For most forms of CBRN, apparently healthy survivors would suffer *delayed illnesses and deaths* for several weeks. Simulations suggest that the number of delayed radiation deaths from a nuclear weapon would be comparable to deaths from the original explosion (Helfand 2006). Delayed casualties would also be substantial for a biological agent or toxin (e.g., botulinum) attack, with survivors showing no symptoms for the first twenty-four hours and dying in the days or weeks afterward. Some chemical weapons (e.g., mustard) can also inflict delayed casualties, although death usually occurs within twenty-four hours. In addition to this short-term delay, nuclear, radiological, and some chemical weapons would also impose a *long-term cancer and disease burden* beginning roughly ten years after the attack.

Finally, victims would sustain *secondary injuries* from their own response to the attack. Examples would likely include traffic accidents and road rage (Hyams, Murphy, and Wessely 2002; Becker 2004), exposure (particularly in a winter attack), disease, civil disorder, and the like. These would increase responders' workloads (Becker 2004) but would also become increasingly preventable as time passed. Ironically, government efforts to help citizens defend themselves would also produce casualties, as when Israeli civilians mistakenly injected themselves with nerve gas antidotes and used gas masks incorrectly during Iraqi SCUD missile attacks in 1991 (Hall et al. 2003; Pastel 2001).

Contagious Disease   Apart from nuclear weapons, only contagious disease (e.g., smallpox 1918 influenza) has a demonstrated history of inflicting Hiroshima-scale casualties. During the 1918 epidemic, the United States suffered roughly 675,000 excess deaths (equivalent to 1.9 million today), with mortality reaching 30 percent in some areas (Barry 2005). Compared to other forms of WMD, casualties would accumulate gradually. Experience with natural epidemics suggests that there would be an initial, explosive growth phase in the first one to two weeks, followed by a slow decline to background levels one to two months later (see figure 16.1). This would potentially give policymakers more time to block, reduce, or delay transmission[2] (Barry 2005). Contagious diseases would also differ from other forms of WMD because of their ability to spread beyond the initial attack site. This would limit policymakers' ability to target national resources on a single hard-hit region, although they would still be able to focus doctors, nurses, and supplies on whichever regions were suffering most at any given time.

Historic epidemics have often generated so many casualties that the sick and dying could no longer be removed from peoples' homes. This led to further deaths from infection and inadequate care. It also forced survivors into intimate contact with corpses—frequently of loved ones—for days and even weeks. While the health hazard from unburied corpses is usually minor (Scanlon, McMahon, and Van Haastert 2007), the implications for morale and long-term psychological damage are another matter. During the 1918 influenza pandemic, mass graves, bodies stranded at home, and family members forced to bury their own dead provided powerful symbols of the country's inability to function (Barry 2005; Schoch-Spana 2000). Relieving this situation would absorb resources that could otherwise be spent on survivors' physical welfare, particularly if authorities were forced to observe normal funeral practices (e.g., allowing access to the deceased, avoiding cremation or mass graves) (Alexander and Klein 2003) and identification/records protocols (Scanlon, McMahon, and Van Haastert 2007).

Despite these horrific casualties, damage to the overall society would be remarkably superficial. Modern estimates suggest that a twenty-first-century pandemic influenza that killed hundreds of thousands or even millions would cost the U.S. economy roughly 1 to 2 percent of GDP. Studies of the 1918 pandemic have similarly found that most of the effects were short-term (Garrett 2007).[3] Hard-hit areas would remain embedded within a functioning, and indeed wealthy society.

16.1.2   Impact on First Responders and Caregivers

Large-scale WMD would kill first responders and generate an enormous caseload for those who survived. The Hiroshima bomb killed or injured 90 percent of the city's doctors and nurses and essentially destroyed all hospitals closer than 5,000 feet to the explosion (USBSS 1947b). When the bomb fell, Hiroshima's largest hospital had 600 beds—most, as in today's U.S. hospitals, already filled. Within twelve

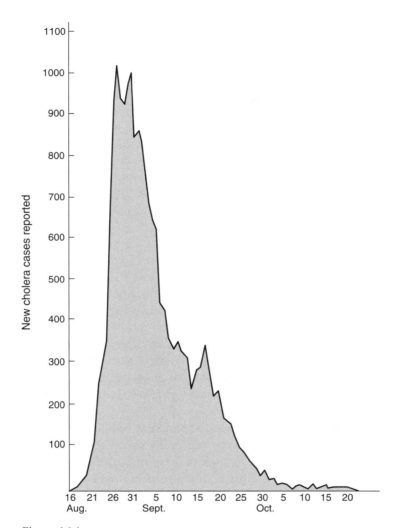

Figure 16.1
Hamburg cholera cases, 1892. *Source*: Evans, 1987.

hours, it had received 10,000 patients. Against this, the hospital could provide just six doctors and ten nurses—about 7 percent of normal personnel. The hospital had also sustained substantial physical damage including collapsed ceilings, damaged instruments, and broken drug bottles. At this point, normal care became physically impossible. Instead, doctors and nurses were reduced to simple tasks like binding up cuts so that patients did not bleed to death and applying compresses to burns.[4] Patients (and, eventually, hundreds of corpses) lay in halls, stairs, building grounds, and open spaces for blocks around. Medicines were quickly exhausted and the place stank with vomit and dirt. While doctors seem to have done what was physically possible (Hersey 2001), the U.S. Strategic Bombing Survey concluded that there was "no organized medical care" for the first three days (USSBS 1947b). At least in principle, casualties from very large releases of chemical, biological, or toxin weapons could similarly overwhelm local responders and caregivers. HHS estimates that a 1918-like influenza pandemic would generate two patients for every mechanical ventilator and four to five patients for every bed (Schoch-Spana et al. 2007).

Caregivers would face special stresses. These would include overwork, lack of sleep, and inability to contact loved ones (Hersey 2001). Inability to save patients—in 1918, death rates in some emergency hospitals exceeded 25 percent *per day* (Barry 2005)—would also take a heavy emotional toll. Finally, caregivers would face substantial personal risks, including secondary contamination from CBRN agents in victims' clothes, skin, and even (for radioactive particles and germs) inside patients' bodies. Precautions (e.g., face masks, "moonsuits") would add to workloads and afford imperfect protection. In general, caregivers could expect to suffer much higher casualties than the general population.[5]

As at Hiroshima, outside police, doctors, nurses, and medical supplies would begin arriving within twenty-four hours. However, staff levels would remain grossly understrength and unpredictable for weeks.[6] It took the staff of Hiroshima's largest hospital six days to clear the facility of dead bodies and debris and another six months to resume anything resembling normal operations (Hersey 2001).

16.1.3   Damaged Infrastructure

Atomic weapons are uniquely destructive. At Hiroshima, 62,000 out of 92,000 buildings were damaged beyond repair, with regions near the center smashed flat.[7] Despite debris, however, most streets remained passable on foot and survivors were able to walk out of the city (Hersey 2001). Other forms of WMD would be minimally destructive by comparison. However, similar economic impacts could be inflicted by contaminating large areas with fallout (e.g., from an atomic bomb or damaged nuclear plant) or anthrax. These would presumably resemble the thirty-kilometer-wide exclusion zone surrounding Chernobyl (Chernobyl Forum 2005)[8] and the (since remediated) exclusion zone around the United Kingdom's Gruinard Island weapons testing facility (Harris and Paxman 2002). By contrast, the contamination from most radiological weapons would be only slightly larger than that associated with current "cancer cluster" sites like Fallon, Nevada. In this case, the decision to reoccupy the site would be as much political as scientific.

16.1.4   Supplies and Electricity

Many survivors would lose possessions including automobiles, clothing, housing, food, and money. Loss of electricity would similarly destroy perishable food stocks within in a few days. Thereafter, essential services, including medical care, would depend on batteries, generators, and firelight. In Hiroshima, it took three months to restore water and power (Hersey 2001).[9] Shortages would produce social responses ranging from congregating in lines to looting to flight. These would inevitably add to responders' workloads and could potentially spread disease and/or contamination (Reissman et al. 2006).

16.1.5   Government Infrastructure

Government—by definition—conducts its business over distances that are large compared to a human being's physical ability to see and be heard. This requires elaborate machinery for collecting and processing data, reaching decisions, and preparing and transmitting orders. Historic epidemics have repeatedly stressed these channels[10] and it is likely that a large WMD attack would, at least briefly, overload them entirely. The fragility of modern *communication* and *information processing* hardware would probably make this situation worse. Recent large disasters (e.g., September 11, Katrina) have almost always featured significant communication failures.[11] Finally, government infrastructure would be further stressed by the *death, incapacity, or absence of senior leadership*. This would not matter much in the immediate aftermath of an attack, when communication failures would make command impossible in any case. Nor would it matter in the long term, once leaders were replaced.[12] There would, however, almost certainly be some loss of efficiency in the first weeks and months following an attack.

The inevitable, albeit temporary, retreat of government would also leave a vacuum. During the 1918 influenza epidemic, individuals responded with behaviors ranging from voluntarism and self-help to vigilantism, including "shotgun quarantines" of some towns in the Far West and Alaska (Barry 2005).

16.1.6   Communications

Nuclear weapons would destroy *mass media* and *personal communications* for several miles around the attack site. For example, about 80 percent of Hiroshima's telephone system was damaged and no service was restored for nine days (USBSS 1946a). However, mass media from surrounding areas would remain operational, providing service throughout the affected area (Carter, May, and Perry 2007). Non-nuclear attacks could similarly cripple communications if casualties were high enough.[13] This, in turn, would make much of the *financial system*, including credit cards and check clearing, unavailable. Delivering emergency funds to victims was a refractory problem for FEMA in New Orleans.

Initially, survivors would depend on battery- and hand-cranked AM radios for news and official information. If necessary, these could be supplemented by air-dropped radios and emergency transmitters supplied by U.S. Army and Navy psychological warfare units (CBS News 2003). As in many cities devastated by World War II, the financial system could also revert to older systems like barter, rationing, and scrip. This would only be possible, however, as long as survivors depended on government goods and services. A renewed private sector would require at least minimal financial instruments.

16.2   Short-Term Psychological and Social Impacts

As already noted, twentieth-century history provides depressingly abundant evidence on how civilian populations respond to WMD. This has been supplemented in recent years by the experience of smaller casualties from September 11, the Madrid train bombings, and other terrorist attacks. For convenience, we distinguish between members of the public who are injured or witness traumatic events at close hand ("survivors"); members of the public who experience the attack solely through media accounts and word of mouth ("citizens"); and first responders, caregivers, and government elites.

16.2.1   Survivors

There are extensive accounts of what it is like for members of a modern society to experience an atomic bomb, large urban fire, or pandemic disease outbreak. This provides extensive evidence of how people are likely to behave during and after an attack.

Panic   Panic is an intense fear reaction in which social cohesion breaks down in favor of individual, self-serving efforts to flee or seek safety (Alexander and Klein 2003) or, more technically, "an acute fear reaction marked by loss of self-control which is followed by nonsocial and nonrational flight" (Perry and Lindell 2003; also see Pastel 2001). Civil defense planners of the 1930s and again in the 1950s routinely expected mass panic (Bailer 1980; Pastel 2001), and these expectations were further reinforced by nuclear-holocaust novels and disaster movies from the 1950s forward.[14]

This expectation is almost certainly wrong. To the contrary, there is overwhelming agreement among scholars that panic is rare even in catastrophes (Schoch-Spana et al. 2007; Engel et al. 2007; Fischhoff et al. 2003; Perry and Lindell 2003; Alexander and Klein 2003; Glass and Schoch-Spana 2002; Durodie and Wessely 2002; Pastel 2001). Far more typically, social cohesion and emotional attachment to others increases, so that ordinary people work together and even risk their lives for strangers (Speckhard 2007; Hall et al. 2003). This is well illustrated by September 11, the Madrid and London train bombings, and Russian terrorist attacks, where crowds and passersby have invariably been calm and orderly and helped to evacuate the wounded (Speckhard 2007). The same behavior was also evident on a much larger scale during the European and Japanese air wars (Friedrich 2006; Hoyt 2000; Hersey 2001). While there were certainly instances of individual panic, "any evidence of widespread disorder or rioting seems totally lacking" (Beck 1986; also see Pastel 2001).

None of this is to say that people are not afraid, only that they manage to retain self-control despite acute fear (Perry and Lindell 2003). Panic does indeed happen when fear rises to unmanageable levels. However, this threshold seems to require overwhelmingly terrifying events like combat, imminent fear of death, or being trapped inside burning structures (Speckhard 2007; Perry and Lindell 2003; Durodie and Wessely 2002; Pastel 2001). Even in these situations, moreover, panic often fails to materialize (Perry and Lindell 2003). In principle, this high threshold could be reduced if members of the public lost faith in each other and/or their leaders, so that individuals could rationally decide that collective action was impossible. Once again, however, panic is not inevitable. In the New Orleans floods, for example, survivors remained astonishingly patient and compliant despite clear evidence of government incompetence (Thevenot and Russell 2005).[15]

Shock, Anxiety, Depression   Immediately following an attack, most survivors would be stunned and numbed, operating in a dissociative state as if watching from outside themselves (Friedrich 2006; Thompson 1986). However, the instinct to act constructively would still be strong in most of the population.[16] Historically, most people rescued in disasters have been saved by family members, friends, co-workers, neighbors, and strangers, often before professional responders have even arrived on the scene (Schoch-Spana et al. 2007; Perry and Lindell 2003; Glass and Schoch-Spana 2002). This includes very large and horrific disasters like Hiroshima, where survivors helped each other evacuate, rescued buried victims, and tended the wounded (Hersey 2001).[17] The instinct to help would also prompt adjoining communities to converge on the scene (Perry and Lindell 2003), as happened at both Hiroshima (Hersey 2001) and New York following the September 11 attacks (Glass and Schoch-Spana 2002).

Once the immediate danger was past, survivors would be anxious, depressed, fearful, horrified, and disgusted. In roughly three-quarters of the population, the dominant reaction would be apathy, docility, indecisiveness, lack of emotion, mild stupor, and psychosomatic symptoms. The remainder would include groups that focused on constructive (but often marginal) activities as a coping mechanism and groups that behaved inappropriately, including a small minority whose "psychopathic ways" were formerly constrained by social pressures. Once the cause of the disaster was seen to pass, roughly 90 percent of the population would show a return to awareness and recall. They would, however, remain highly dependent, emotional, and vulnerable for some time (Thompson 1986). This mass anxiety would often produce constructive action. Indeed, witnesses of the European air war remembered that the hundreds of thousands of homeless and injured people who wandered Berlin complained less than they normally did and gave "an incredibly disciplined impression" (Friedrich 2006).

The intense emotion of survival would also produce a state of high autonomic arousal. This would leave victims with a diminished ability to control their emotions and subject to mood swings, make them markedly more gullible and vulnerable to snap decisions, encourage the formation of small unstable groups, and promote the spread of rumors (Thompson 1986). Some of the more debilitating and nonconstructive emotions would include anger, depression, scapegoating, and paranoia, particularly in cases where victims felt that their legitimate needs had not been met (Alexander and Klein 2003). Given this background, simple tasks like standing in line could produce stress and even violence (Reissman et al. 2006). First responders would also be targets, even when they were clearly doing everything possible to help.[18]

Uniquely among WMD agents, a *contagious disease* epidemic would provide days and weeks for government advice and private reflection. Popular behavior in this context is likely to be extremely rational.[19] Once the epidemic hit, fear and horror would be less intense—but far more prolonged—than with other forms of WMD. Survivors of historic epidemics typically report experiencing a constant, sickening "fear and nervousness" for weeks on end (Evans 1987). For many, this would be aggravated by forced intimacy with sick patients and corpses. Efforts to prevent contagion would also take a psychological toll. Survivors of past epidemics uniformly recall being cut off from normal human contact as social life ceased, cafés emptied, streets were deserted, and people stopped kissing, shaking hands, or even facing one another (Evans 1987; Barry 2005; Schoch-Spana 2000). Materially, the economy would also slow to a crawl for the month or so that the epidemic lasted. In 1918, many large businesses saw absenteeism reach 40 to 60 percent, while farms and small businesses stopped operating entirely (Barry 2005).

Finally, survivors might have to cope with *follow-on WMD attacks* (Carter, May, and Perry 2007). Many disasters produce a kind of operant conditioning in which survivors of an earthquake, say, are much more afraid during aftershocks than during the original quake. This can include very modest stimuli—for example, when passing airplanes caused many Hiroshima survivors to repeatedly panic and hide (Thompson 1986). Despite this, limited contemporary evidence suggests that civilian populations would be resilient. For instance, Israelis facing SCUD missiles (Durodie and Wessely 2002) and suicide bombers (Speckhard 2007) quickly become habituated, making rational adjustments to avoid the threat where possible but otherwise carrying on life. Similar reactions also occurred on a much larger scale during the European and Japanese air wars. That said, the increasingly catastrophic raids[20] clearly traumatized survivors, made them apathetic, and reduced productivity. The attacks also bred resentment between different regions of the country, distrust of government, and exaggerated rumors of losses.[21] Despite this, support for the regime was not significantly eroded[22] (Friedrich 2006; Beck 1986; Hoyt 2000; USSBS 1947c, 1947d).

Flight, Hoarding, and Looting   Mass flight has both rational and emotional components. After the Hiroshima explosion, 100,000 people fled the city and many briefly became refugees across Japan.[23] In large measure, this was a rational response to the situation. After the bomb exploded, it was immediately obvious that the city center could no longer provide food or shelter and survivors acted on this information. Unfortunately, rationality is useless without information. Today's average American knows very little about how to protect himself from WMD and, in particular, the importance of sheltering in place (Wray and Jupka 2004; Becker 2004).[24] Emotion would almost certainly fill this vacuum. Just as many Hiroshima survivors fled the city to rejoin family (Hersey 2001), modern surveys show that many Americans would similarly do "whatever they had to" to reunite family (Henderson et al. 2004). However, the desire to reunite family can also discourage flight. Two-thirds of all Americans say that they would stay in their communities during a smallpox epidemic (Fischhoff et al. 2003).

There would also be hoarding. Contemporary surveys show that many U.S. citizens would hoard supplies following a bioweapons attack even if existing household stocks were adequate (Glik et al. 2004).

Finally, desperate people loot, and this may be entirely rational. During World War II, Germans who were bombed were measurably more likely to engage in hoarding, black-market activity, riots and demonstrations, looting, crime, and delinquency (USSBS 1947c). Strategic bombing similarly made Japanese more obsessed with finding solutions as individuals instead of trusting each other and acting cohesively (USSBS 1947d). Nevertheless, the danger of looting—like panic—seems overstated.[25] Civility, mutual aid (Glass and Schoch-Spana 2002), and obedience to authority (Perry and Lindell 2003) usually increase while crime falls during disasters (Perry and Lindell 2003).

Voluntarism   Voluntarism can be a powerful force for filling personnel gaps when normal staff are overwhelmed, potentially including such critical categories as firefighting, caregiving, and first response (Friedrich 2006; Hersey 2001; Barry 2005).[26] That said, volunteers have a tendency to wilt in the face of prolonged, gruesome, arduous, or frightening duties. During the 1918 influenza epidemic, many volunteers quit after a single shift while the supply of new volunteers quickly dried up. On the other hand, volunteers with professional training—including student and retired nurses and doctors—usually kept working until they themselves were infected (Barry 2005). This suggests that preemergency training and/or indoctrination can usefully increase volunteer resources.

Resistance to Authority   Most CBRN attacks would be over by the time that government restored its command and control capabilities. In this case, compulsory measures would be limited to restoring order, restricting access to contaminated areas, enforcing mass burials, and limiting the movements of contaminated individuals. Here, compulsion is likely to be limited and, in any event, aligned with community's predispositions.[27]

The situation would be very different for contagious weapons. In this case, government would have both the power and the scientific justification to impose quarantines and similar measures on reluctant populations.[28] Historically, however, such measures have often been costly and sometimes counterproductive. First, they are economically damaging. Quarantines almost always damage retail shopping (Schoch-Spana 2000), stifle internal trade, and cut exports and imports nearly to zero. In the nineteenth century, the resulting unemployment and price increases often spilled over into violence (Evans 1987). Second, measures that conflict with community norms are bound to cause pain and resentment. Historic flashpoints have included attempts to close churches, separate patients (especially children) from family members and force novel burial practices onto communities (Evans 1987; Schoch-Spana 2000; Glass and Schoch-Spana 2002).[29] Third, the public may decide that authorities are misguided. For instance, patients and their families have often seen crowded and understaffed emergency hospitals as a death sentence (Leavitt 2003; Barry 2005). Fourth, communities may decide that sacrifices are being unfairly distributed. For example, Milwaukee (1894) experienced widespread rioting after the government tried to force immigrants into emergency hospitals while isolating middle-class patients in their homes (Leavitt 2003).[30] In some cases, perceptions of unfairness can even shade into conspiracy theories. Early nineteenth-century rumors that the government—backed variously by outside doctors, Jews, and aristocrats—was trying to murder the peasants seem grimly quaint now (Evans 1987). However, African-American rumors that AIDS is a CIA conspiracy (Assim 2005) show that similar theories still exist at the margin and could potentially reemerge in a crisis. This would be particularly true if the burden of the attack fell disproportionately—as it usually would—on some regions and communities but not others (Thompson 1986).

Resistance would take many forms. These could include refusing to take recommended treatments (Reissman et al. 2006; Lemyre 2005),[31] refusing to don masks (Schoch-Spana 2000), fleeing from anticipated quarantines (Evans 1987), fleeing from police, and hiding sick children who might otherwise be taken away (Barry 2005).[32] More violent methods could include threatening officials at gunpoint (Evans 1987) and assassinating public health officers (Barbera et al. 2001; Evans 1987).[33] At its most extreme, resistance could become organized and community-wide. In the nineteenth century, extended riots[34] often neutralized government's ability to enforce quarantines for weeks at a time. Prominent examples included Quebec (1885), Muncie, Indiana (1893) (Barbera, et al. 2001), Milwaukee (1894) (Leavitt 2003), and Central Europe (1832) (Evans 1987). Resistance would also feed on deeper resentments. For example, riots in Milwaukee (1892) were stoked by tensions between poor immigrants and the city's nativist middle class (Leavitt 2003).[35] Modern surveys showing that 72 percent of Americans believe that wealthy citizens would be vaccinated first during an outbreak and that 22 percent believe that African Americans would experience discrimination suggest similar fault lines today (Eisenman et al. 2004). Nor is it hard to believe that illegal aliens—already fearful of detection and deportation—would hide illness, remain untreated, and resist public health officers' "contact tracing" efforts to locate exposed individuals (Eisenman et al. 2004).

Somatic Diseases and the Worried Well   Since CBRN agents are normally invisible, people often do not know whether they have been exposed. Stress and intense anxiety are normal in this situation—and would often produce a racing heart, shortness of breath, flushing, nausea, diarrhea, and other symptoms similar to the (usually nonspecific) effects of CBRN (Hall et al. 2003; Hyams, Murphy, and Wessely 2002).[36] This explains why the number of survivors exhibiting symptoms almost always dwarfs the number exposed. Predictably, the effect is smallest when the attack's outer edges are well defined in space and time. Following the Tokyo subway attacks, 4,500 people sought medical attention compared to 1,000 exposed. By comparison, surveys indicate that over 100,000 people considered themselves "high risk" following the Washington anthrax attacks (Reissman et al. 2006) and up to 125,000 people asked to be screened for radiation injury compared to the 250 who were actually exposed after scavengers in Goiania, Brazil, cut open a discarded medical radiation source in 1987 (Alexander and Klein 2003; Hyams, Murphy, and Wessely 2002; Becker 2004).

Actual WMD attacks could also give rise to imagined ones. Stressful times often produce psychogenic illnesses similar to hysteria.[37] Imaginary poison gas attacks are particularly common and have been reported from many societies, including the United States (1944), Palestine (1989), Soviet Georgia (1989), and Tokyo (1995). Episodes are especially likely when people believe that they are being victimized by powerful enemies (Bartholemew and Wessely 2002; Speckhard 2007). Outbreaks usually begin when members of a small, cohesive group are exposed to a benign agent like smoke. The contagion then spreads verbally or through media exposure to other members of the group, after which it jumps to other groups with real or imagined links to the first one (Speckhard 2007; Engel et al. 2007). Outbreaks are particularly common when the threat has some plausible basis in reality. When Iraq fired SCUDs at Israel, approximately 40 percent of those closest to the scene reported breathing problems even though no gas warheads were used (Bartholomew and Wessely 2002).

Screening patients for worried-well and psychogenic illnesses would drain person-nel and complicate public health systems' ability to detect follow-on attacks. Even when the symptoms lacked any physical basis, failure to take patient complaints seriously would invite accusations that government was uncaring, incompetent, or malevolent while encouraging citizens to be noncooperative and aggressive (Speck-hard 2007; Alexander and Klein 2003).

16.2.2 The General Public

Except for a fast-spreading contagious disease, most of the country would not be directly affected by a WMD attack. Citizens would, however, be subjected to trau-matic images coupled with the fear of follow-on attacks.

Morale People frequently react to news of an attack by looking for ceremonial gestures and opportunities to become involved even if their contributions are more psychological than physical (Shepperd 2001). In addition to its direct material bene-fit, giving community groups and individuals a positive and active role in recovery is thought to (1) boost morale (Perry and Lindell 2003), (2) reduce dread by giving the public a sense of control, and (3) mitigate mental health impacts (Glass and Schoch-Spana 2002).

Terrorists would almost certainly exploit low morale by trying to persuade the public that it was better to make concessions than to continue suffering. This strategy has a certain plausibility given Americans' low tolerance for casualties since World War II. At the same time, limited wars like Vietnam and Iraq are a poor analogy for WMD attacks on the United States. This is particularly true if terrorist leaders could not compel their followers to stop fighting, so that WMD attacks would continue with or without a "peace agreement." To be credible, terrorist leaders would have to show that either (1) they could prevent group members from splintering into "rejectionist" cells, or (2) they controlled WMD so tightly that no rejectionist could acquire it. Absent one of these (unlikely) conditions, peace would be impossible and the struggle would continue on the early twentieth-century pattern of "total war." Public support for such a policy would probably be robust. We have already seen how even horrific bombing failed to stop citizens from supporting their respective governments in World War II.[38]

Mental Health   It is normal for the public to feel stress following a major terrorist attack. Surveys conducted after September 11 suggest that 90 percent of all Americans felt upset, had difficulty concentrating, had trouble falling or staying asleep, and/or suffered from other stress-related symptoms (Salerno and Nagy 2002). These symptoms can be severe. Surveys conducted in cities hit by major terrorist attacks find that citizens report symptoms consistent with PTSD two to three times more than usual. Examples include Oklahoma City (8 percent) (Sprang 1999), Israelis facing suicide bomb attacks (10 percent) (Bleich, Gelkopf, and Solomon 2007), and New York following the September 11 attacks (7.5 percent) (Salerno and Nagy 2002). These emotional reactions fall off with time, geographic distance, and social distance (Speckhard 2007; MacCoun 2005)[39] and return to baseline values for most people within a month. A substantial minority, however, continue to suffer. This explains why many measures of distress (e.g., emergency room visits, drug and alcohol abuse, work absenteeism) remain high after the first month (MacCoun 2005) and are still detectable one year later (Alexander and Klein 2003). PTSD symptoms are particularly durable. People who report such symptoms immediately after an attack are still likely to have them eighteen months later (Salerno and Nagy 2002).

Stigmatization   CBRN attacks would generate widespread suspicion that people and goods from the affected region were contaminated. During the Hamburg cholera epidemic of 1892, surrounding regions closed their borders, punished and deported refugees, and destroyed goods with disinfectant. River and maritime traffic also stopped, devastating the city's trade-based economy, while rail traffic fell 24 percent and stopped covering its costs (Evans 1987). While these responses had some physical basis, psychological effects ("stigmatization") were probably dominant.[40] More recently, the widespread stigmatization of people and products after scavengers accidentally released radiation in Goiania, Brazil, had no physical basis at all. Despite this, consumers in the rest of the country stopped purchasing the province's agricultural products, airline pilots and hotels refused to do business with Goianian citizens, and crowds stoned Goianians' automobiles (Becker 2004).

16.2.3   Elites

Elites would face substantial challenges in retaining public trust, coordinating with each other, and reaching rational decisions among themselves.

Communicating with the Public   Trust in government usually rises significantly in the early phases of a crisis (Perry and Lindell 2003) but erodes afterward. On the one hand, people believe "with intense emotion" that government has an obligation to provide accurate and complete information (Wray and Jupka 2004; Reissman et al. 2006; Henderson et al. 2004; Fischhoff 2006). On the other, they know that leaders are often tempted to minimize some risks to avoid panic, exaggerate others for effect (Fischhoff 2006), and exercise "spin control" to suppress facts that might lead to blame (Glass and Schoch-Spana 2002), all of which makes them deeply suspicious of government information (Henderson et al. 2004). This volatile combination of intense emotion and suspicion suggests that citizens could lose trust quickly following a WMD attack.[41] Once lost, government credibility would be very hard to restore. Historically, governments have lost credibility in various ways:

Deliberate misrepresentations   Leaders rarely lie to citizens, if only because the temporary advantages of manipulation are seldom worth the ensuing, semipermanent loss of trust and control.[42] Notable exceptions include Japanese officials' attempts to suppress news of the Tokaimura fuel reprocessing accident and Russian leaders' efforts to downplay the Chernobyl and Kursk disasters (Alexander and Klein 2003).[43]

Optimistic predictions   During both the Hamburg (1892) and 1918 influenza epidemics, a combination of incomplete records, rapidly changing facts, and wishful thinking encouraged leaders to make optimistic predictions that later turned out to be false (Evans 1987; Barry 2005). Early assurances that the 2001 anthrax outbreaks had been traced to natural sources are similarly said to have undermined public confidence (Lemyre et al. 2005). Unfortunately, it is hard to see what officials could have done differently. Given that most outbreaks do not lead to epidemics (or bioterrorism) government optimism is often warranted.

Clarity vs. nuance   Science seldom deals in certainties and no health official can promise that CBRN is perfectly harmless. However, the public craves clarity and tends to see nuanced statements as equivocation (Hyams, Murphy, and Wessely 2002). People are also less likely to comply with vague statements (Perry and Lindell 2003). Finally, vagueness adds to mental health burdens. Although reassuring in the short run, vague reassurances tend to become steadily less effective over time except as reminders that people ought to be afraid (Durodie and Wessely 2002).

Changing and conflicting messages   Scientific evidence is almost certain to change over the course of an outbreak (Stein et al. 2004). Furthermore, U.S. federalism routinely splinters "official" advice across dozens of entities that often have honest disagreements.[44] These inconsistencies can easily be seen as evidence of incompetence or inequitable treatment (Gursky, Inglesby, and O'Toole 2003). During the Washington anthrax attacks, for instance, state and local governments frequently offered different recommendations about who should receive antibiotics and/or be vaccinated (Hall et al. 2003), while elected officials criticized and sometimes overruled their own health departments (Gursky, Inglesby, and O'Toole 2003). These disagreements were amplified by the media (Gursky, Inglesby, and O'Toole 2003) and compared against dissenting viewpoints from outside the government. Indeed, minority views often received disproportionate attention because of the media's tendency to treat equal time as a proxy for balanced reporting (Hyams, Murphy, and Wessely 2002).

Poor coordination   The Washington anthrax attacks show that government efforts to speak with a single voice are inevitably imperfect. Although the CDC was widely recognized as the lead agency, many local officials insisted on presenting what they called a "competition of ideas" (Chess, Calia, and O'Neill 2004). Additionally, state health officials ordered local officials not to use CDC recommendations unless and until the state approved them. This process often took days, leaving communication crippled in the interim (Chess, Calia, and O'Neill 2004).

Given these challenges, authorities should expect to lose at least some credibility over the course of an emergency. This damage will normally be limited, however, as long as respected third parties are available to review and endorse government messages. Early government efforts to co-opt the press can be dangerously counterproductive in this regard. During the 1918 influenza epidemic, government officials persuaded most newspapers to downplay the epidemic in the interests of national morale. This, however, produced a widening gap between what people read and what they could see for themselves. In the end, the press lost so much credibility that government could no longer turn to it for validation (Barry 2005).

Targeting Relevant Audiences   Most people get their information from television and, to a lesser extent, the Internet and newspapers (Glik et al. 2004). Despite this, government cannot limit communication to these channels. First, many people who rely on television also distrust it. This situation can quickly become demoralizing unless alternative communication channels are available to confirm television's message (Henderson et al. 2004).[45] Similarly, many demographic groups (e.g., ethnic minorities, rural populations, non-English speakers) tend to ignore or mistrust mass media. Distrust is particularly strong among African Americans and Native Americans (Henderson et al. 2004).[46] Reaching these individuals requires multilingual materials and culturally relevant messages delivered through respected, community-based organizations and authority figures (Schoch-Spana et al. 2007; Glass and Schoch-Spana 2002). Second, mass media is a one-way communication mechanism. This means that authorities usually have no way of knowing when their message is being ignored or misunderstood. Finally, mass media do not let the public ask questions and challenge statements. This makes it easy for listeners to conclude that information has been managed or withheld (Henderson et al. 2004). Empirical studies show that direct personal contact (e.g., through workshops and town meetings) is very important in persuading people to trust and act on health information (Glass and Schoch-Spana 2002).

These limitations suggest that alternative, nonmedia channels are important. Examples include communicating through tribal governments (Henderson et al. 2004), mass mailings, community meetings, social organizations, local employers, and suburban newspapers (Chess, Calia, and O'Neill 2004). Although generally more labor intensive, two-way channels (e.g., town meetings, briefing union representatives) are a particularly powerful way for authorities to build trust and/or convince audiences to change their behaviors.

Coordination   Approximately 50,000 federal, state, local, and tribal entities are currently responsible for homeland security (Markle Foundation 2002). While the effective number of players would be much smaller following a WMD attack, coordination remains a significant problem. Even when agencies want to cooperate, the mechanics can be overwhelming. City, county, and state officials found it extremely hard to share information and recommendations during the 2001 anthrax attacks (Gursky, Inglesby, and O'Toole 2003).

Elite Panic   We have seen that the myth of public panic and disorder—particularly among the poor and minorities—is deeply ingrained in American culture. Elites share this misconception. Indeed, they often reinforce it by participating in exercises that emphasize rioting, looting, and vigilantism (Glass and Schoch-Spana 2002).

Some scholars have suggested that this myth of public disorder provoked a very real "elite panic" during Hurricane Katrina. This was expressed through hasty, disproportionate promises to shoot looters and through armed intervention by soldiers and police (Tierney 2006). At a minimum, these initiatives diverted responders and resources away from activities that would have been more useful and less alarming. In principle, a visibly panicked leadership could also undermine public confidence in their leaders' honesty and competence (MacCoun 2005). At this point, elites' exaggerated fear of public panic could become a self-fulfilling prophecy.

16.2.4 First Responders and Caregivers

Responders and caregivers have a long record of staying at their post in the face of horrendous challenges. For example, doctors and nurses overwhelmingly continued working at Hiroshima (Hersey 2001), during the 1918 influenza epidemic (Barry 2005), and during the Hamburg (1892) cholera outbreak (Evans 1987). Historically, the main source of defections has been the innate human desire to rejoin (and if necessary protect and care for) children and other family members (Hersey 2001; Evans 1987; Barry 2005).[47] Modern surveys confirm that these traditional concerns remain central today (Becker 2004). Subsidiary factors have traditionally included fears for personal safety (Schoch-Spana 2000), fears of stigmatization (Reissman et al. 2006), and a reluctance to abandon one's usual patients to care for strangers. More recently, first responders have also expressed fears that terrorists will target them for follow-up attacks (Becker 2004).

16.3 Long-Term Psychological and Social Impacts

As the months passed, remediation would increasingly focus on managing survivors' long-term health risks and deciding when and how the public should reenter contaminated sites. These costs could vary by several orders of magnitude (chapters 12 and 13) depending on the public's view of "acceptable risk." This section reviews what is known about the public perceptions of CBRN and how these fears are likely to evolve in a postattack world.

16.3.1 Reoccupying Contaminated Sites

Policymakers (and even some scholars) routinely claim that the costs of decontaminating and reoccupying facilities would be inflated by the public's exaggerated estimates of CBRN risk.[48] Indeed, the claim is sometimes made that a "dirty bomb" that killed *zero* victims might nevertheless paralyze economic life. This is far from obvious. Seventy years ago, politicians, citizens, and policymakers similarly believed that modern air forces would panic citizens into a "knockout blow" that no nation could survive (Bailer 1980). This clearly did not happen. Nevertheless, it remains possible that invisible contaminants—which produce unique psychological responses compared to other threats (Speckhard 2007; Perry and Lindell 2003)—might promote more lasting and disabling fears.

The decision to reenter a contaminated site would ultimately turn on individual judgments about estimated risk, and how large a risk was acceptable. In principle, such judgments are highly complex and depend on hundreds of potentially relevant facts. In practice, however, social psychologists have found that the public typically turns to "mental models" based on radically truncated ("heuristic") sets of facts. Since the 1970s, scholars have explored these models by documenting unconscious patterns in how people answer risk surveys. The resulting literature offers important insights into how the public judges CBRN risk and how these opinions would likely evolve following an attack.

Estimating Risk   Individuals deciding whether to reenter a contaminated site would first have to decide how large the risk was. Public risk-of-death estimates are known to be skewed in at least three ways. First, actuarial estimates show that the largest commonly discussed risks are roughly a million times larger than the smallest ones. However, surveys show that people's subjective estimates seldom vary by more than a thousand. This compressed scale overvalues small risks at the expense of large ones (Slovic, Fischhoff, and Lichtenstein 2004b) and systematically boosts estimates for carcinogens (including CBRN) compared to other risks.

Second, people overrate the risks of easily imagined events. This *imaginability* variable, in turn, depends on a variety of factors including the existence of recent well-publicized disasters, public discussion, and especially movies, books, and other cultural content (Slovic, Fischhoff, and Lichtenstein 2004b). In the case of CBRN, imaginability is powerfully reinforced by ideas of unseen contamination that date back centuries in Western culture. These ideas have been further developed by a genre of end-of-the-world novels that were already publicizing visions of plague and atomic warfare before World War I (Weart 1989; Wald 2007; Kraus, Malmfors, and Slovic 2004). Stories involving WMD proliferated in the 1930s[49] and were updated in the 1950s to include nuclear and germ weapon holocausts.[50] Since then, the WMD genre has remained strong while branching into parallel, supporting narratives about nuclear power, pesticides, genetically modified foods, and worldwide pandemics.[51] This has made WMD terrorism threats vividly imaginable to Western audiences regardless of actual evidence.

Finally, the public similarly exaggerates risks associated with *memorable* events that generate dramatic images (Slovic, 2004a). At least in prospect, CBR fits this category. On the other hand, CBR's invisibility and the absence of dramatic explosions or wreckage are not naturally dramatic. For this reason, images of an actual attack might well decrease memorability over time.

Accepting Risk Survey data show that the public is less willing to tolerate some risks than others. Here, the main predictors are *familiarity* and *dread*.[52] As figure 16.2 shows, the public is markedly less tolerant of "unfamiliar risks," a category that has been defined to include involuntary, delayed, unknown, uncontrollable, or new risks. The public is also significantly less tolerant of "dread risks," that is, risks that are certain to be fatal (often for large numbers of people) if things go wrong (Fischhoff et al. 2004). The power of these variables is clearly visible in modern attitudes toward radiation. As figure 16.3 indicates, civilian nuclear power is widely feared because the risk is involuntary, uncontrollable, likely to be catastrophic, fatal, and new. On the other hand, medical X-rays are seen as voluntary, controllable, and familiar. This explains why, despite multiple similarities to civilian nuclear power, the public hardly ever fears X-rays. Today's image of CBRN is even more unfamiliar and produces more dread than civilian nuclear power. Following an attack, however, the decision to enter contaminated areas would usually be voluntary, controllable, familiar, and (at low levels) nonfatal. It is tempting to think that attitudes toward CBRN would start to resemble current attitudes toward medical X-rays at least as much as those toward civilian nuclear power.

Finally, risk estimates are not the whole story—uncertainty also matters. Survey evidence shows that people do not like to think about small but nonzero risks. Today, they reduce this *dissonance* by insisting that risk estimates are far more certain than they actually are, pretending that small risks are actually zero (Slovic, Fischhoff, and Lichtenstein 2004b), avoiding discussions of the problem, and/or rationalizing risks that cannot be changed (Slovic, Fischhoff, and Lichtenstein 2004a). The situation would be very different, however, following a WMD attack. At this point, CBRN could no longer be ignored or prevented. Instead, people would presumably try to convince themselves that the now-unavoidable risk was harmless. Similar thought processes have already been documented to explain the modern public's indifference to such (comparatively) unavoidable radiation risks as household radon, medical radiation, and worldwide nuclear weapons arsenals (Slovic 2004b).

Current attitudes toward radiation would not, of course, change overnight. However, it is reasonable to think that dissonance would be strong enough to change opinions relatively quickly, most likely within a period of weeks or months. Interestingly, something similar seems to have happened in Goiania, Brazil, after scavengers accidentally released radiation from discarded medical equipment in 1987.

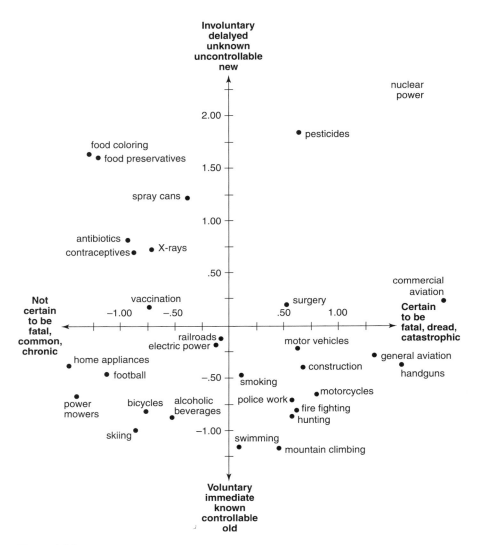

Figure 16.2
Public willingness to tolerate risk. Survey data shows that public willingness to tolerate risk is markedly lower for activities that are rated high along the dread (x-axis) and/or familiarity (y-axis) axes. *Source*: Fischhoff et al., 2004.

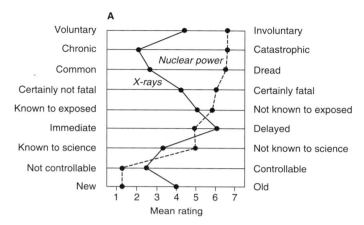

Figure 16.3
How dread and unknown risk shape attitudes toward different forms of radiation. *Source*: Fischhoff et al., 2004.

As previously noted, the initial radiation release caused massive anxiety and stigmatization. One month later, however, Goianians began criticizing the press for exaggerating and feeding panic. At this point, the local press started to write articles emphasizing how life had returned to normal, and this new editorial slant diminished public fear still further. Attitudes outside the affected region—where dissonance was presumably less powerful—changed more slowly but made a similar adjustment after several months. For example, market prices for Goianian exports fell sharply after the accident but then returned to normal thirty to forty-five days later (Leite and Roper 1988; Slovic 2004b).[53]

Finally, the decision to reenter contaminated facilities would also depend on social forces. Most obviously, authorities (possibly backed by public opinion) could urge workers to reopen facilities for the good of the economy. Civilian office workers would presumably be the least responsive to these pressures since—unlike doctors or police—they would feel little or no preexisting professional obligation to take such risks. On the other hand, the desire to return to normal and earn a living would be powerful inducements to rationalize and reevaluate contamination risks. Blue-collar workers' response would be more complex. At least potentially, union leaders could play a constructive role as trusted third parties able to assess and validate government recommendations. Unionization would also facilitate measures (e.g., film badges) that made CBRN threats seem less invisible and more controllable than they otherwise might be.

16.3.2   Long-Term Mental Health Issues

Long-term psychological consequences would be disproportionately concentrated among people who had witnessed death, handled the dead, seen large-scale property destruction, or lost neighbors, friends, and relatives (Perry and Lindell 2003). Because they produce explosions and violence, nuclear weapons would be a uniquely powerful generator of such images. Evidence from the London blitz suggests that 43 percent of survivors showed some evidence of psychiatric illness despite excellent mental health planning and precautions (Thompson 1986). Similarly, roughly one-third of those present in the World Trade Center collapse (Hyams, Murphy, and Wessely 2002) and Oklahoma City bombings (Alexander and Klein 2003) suffered PTSD.[54]

Most nonnuclear forms of CBRN would affect fewer victims and generate fewer images graphic enough to cause PTSD. Instead trauma would depend on how survivors interpreted their memories in light of their belief systems. The most debilitating condition—frequently reported at Chernobyl—would probably consist of repeated, obsessive fast-forwarding to thoughts and images of expected suffering. Other symptoms would likely be similar to hysteria, somaticization, sociogenic illness, "worried-well" anxiety, and other syndromes that operate through victims' beliefs (Speckhard 2007).

Regardless of form, large CBRN attacks would also induce numerous non-PTSD conditions, including acute stress, depression, pathological grief, substance abuse, panic disorders and other phobias, and survivor's guilt (Engel et al. 2007; Alexander and Klein 2003; Perry and Lindell 2003; Hersey 2001; Thompson 1986). Many of these conditions would be further exacerbated by the knowledge that the attack was intentional and the lack of any rational relationship between perpetrators and victims (Perry and Lindell 2003). Most disorders would become apparent within weeks or months, although sufferers would often delay seeking help. Other conditions like smoking and substance abuse could take longer to develop (Engel et al. 2007).

16.3.3   Cultural Legacy

A very large WMD attack would leave a permanent mark on American life and culture. Some of these syndromes—for example, a national stereotype of resilience to attack (Durodie and Wessely 2002)—could reflect useful learning and a shared memory for the population to draw on in future crises. However, other cultural impacts would be negative. Among survivors, fears of contamination would temporarily depress birth rates much as they did following Chernobyl, the U.S. bombing of chemical plants in Serbia, and the Tokyo sarin attacks (Hyams, Murphy, and Wessely 2002). In the longer run, Russian history suggests how national trauma could potentially lead to a culture of drug and alcohol abuse; the coarsening and brutalization of public life; a massive psychological burden on survivors and their children; an obsessive national preoccupation with past tragedies; and even a kind of morbid pride in the national capacity for suffering (Merridale 2000). While WMD attacks are not likely to reach this level of trauma,[55] milder forms of these disorders should probably be expected.

16.4 Preattack Leadership and Policy Levers

Society's resilience to large WMD attacks can be significantly improved by investing in specialized training and assets, conducting public education, and preparing emergency personnel to be psychologically resilient in a new and traumatic environment.

16.4.1 The Public

For most types of WMD, outside support and direction will be minimal in the first few hours following an attack. Teaching people how to protect themselves is a powerful lever for limiting damage and casualties during this period.

Education There are at least four reasons to educate citizens in advance of an attack. First, rational decisions require data. We have already seen that very few citizens know much about WMD agents or how to avoid them. However, Israeli experience shows that even simple lessons (e.g., how to bioseal rooms) can dramatically improve peoples' ability to defend themselves (Speckhard 2007). Second, education gives people time to think about how they would react in an emergency. Preattack plans will normally be more effective than those invented on the spot.[56] Third, government credibility may fall precipitously following an attack. This will not matter so much if citizens have internalized the main lessons (e.g., "shelter in place") already. Finally, surveys show that many (though not most) Americans associate WMD with helplessness, confusion, futility, and especially a "pervasive sense of fatalism." This could produce dangerous inaction in an emergency (Henderson et al. 2004).

These arguments all suggest the need for government information campaigns telling people how to avoid, treat, and survive WMD in an emergency (Henderson et al. 2004; Carter, May, and Perry 2007). Unfortunately, such campaigns would also inspire citizen dread, cause stress from anticipated suffering, and prepare communities to absorb damage (LaPorte 2007). This is very different from politicians' customary strategy of using dissonant images to get voters' attention but then promising to intervene *before* anything bad happens.[57] Furthermore, we have already seen that public discussion boosts imaginability. Paradoxically, efforts to educate the public about WMD could end by amplifying dread (Slovic 2004a).

Reducing Dread and Building Confidence   In its most ambitious form, an education campaign could reduce dread by challenging the twin myths that (1) radioactivity, contagion, and chemical weapons are invariably fatal, and (2) the public would panic or otherwise behave incompetently in an emergency. Social psychologists provide some grounds for optimism. They argue that current mental models of contamination depend on a handful of fundamental misconceptions ("knowledge gaps") that could, in principle, be corrected. These include scientifically doubtful beliefs that contact with even a single atom of carcinogen will probably cause cancer; that contamination is unbounded and permanent; and that this permanence implies that risk reduction can never be too expensive (Slovic 2004b).[58] That said, the history of industry public relations offensives that set out to challenge long-established cultural narratives about, say, civilian nuclear power or carcinogens, is not encouraging. The basic problem is that changing people's minds starts by making them uncertain and, to that extent, induces dissonance. People resist this by overvaluing existing opinions, resisting new evidence, and practicing denial (Kasperson et al. 2004).

At least potentially, attacking the myth of panic might be easier. Drills and practice events could not only prepare people to act but also show them that they can reach higher than they believed possible. Exercises could similarly train leaders to improvise by "discover[ing] their own propensities in the face of very unusual situations and increase[ing] their skills at working with novel combinations of institutional and community leaders" (LaPorte 2007).

Developing a Consensus Response   Inviting the public to join in preattack planning would promote acceptance and make citizens complicit in their own protection. Potentially important planning areas include

Quarantine and decontamination procedures   Quarantine and decontamination include multiple contentious procedures like asking people to strip naked and/or to surrender contaminated car keys and mobile phones. Asking the public to help design decontamination responses would increase the legitimacy of these steps while ensuring that authorities paid appropriate attention to, say, backup methods for contacting and reuniting families (Speckhard 2007). More generally, it seems natural for authorities to enlist labor and religious leaders' help in designing epidemic control measures (Glass and Schoch-Spana 2002), particularly where these depend on widespread voluntary compliance. Community-level involvement would be particularly useful in reducing the practical, cultural, religious, and psychological costs of coping with large numbers of corpses (Schoch-Spana et al. 2007).

Emergency hospitals   History suggests that basic care following a WMD attack—binding wounds, treating burns, cooling fevers—is far more important than advanced medicine. Reducing this observation to clear guidelines would give caregivers valuable information while reinforcing public confidence in emergency hospitals (Schoch-Spana et al. 2007). At the same time, minimum standards would have to be achievable. Abandoning previously announced standards in an emergency would be deeply counterproductive.

Remediation standards Deciding how much contamination is acceptable involves cost-benefit judgments that are entirely distinct from, say, peacetime nuclear power regulations. Indeed, citizens might well decide that they were willing to trade a small increase in lifetime cancer risk for the ability to return home and resume work. Reducing these trade-offs to formal cleanup standards would cap remediation costs and, potentially, limit the attractiveness of CBR terrorism in the first place. Unfortunately, some activists resist new cleanup standards on the ground that regulators might be encouraged to revisit power-plant regulations as well (Palmer 2005). Similarly, bureaucrats trying to calm the public after an attack might seize on power-plant standards for their symbolic value even if the results were prohibitively costly (Fischhoff 2005).

Identifying and credentialing volunteers Volunteers were routinely turned away during the 2001 anthrax attacks because there was no way to train or credential them (Casani, Matuszak, and Benjamin 2003). However, a large attack would almost certainly force radical departures from normal credentialing, union practices, and minimum professional skills.[59] Advance planning would allow authorities to identify, recruit, and indoctrinate volunteers who could serve in an emergency[60] and establish procedures for credentialing additional volunteers after an attack.

Leaders will often be reluctant to involve the public, since any meaningful partnership cedes power and entails discussions that could lead to controversy and deadlock on what were previously obscure and apolitical issues. At the same time, public involvement frequently surfaces new information and ideas (Schoch-Spana et al. 2007), legitimizes planning, and builds important habits of cooperation. These would be valuable assets in an emergency.

16.4.2 First Responders and Caregivers

A large WMD attack would create far more casualties than first responders, caregivers, and public health officials could treat. Suitable planning can help ensure that these services degrade gracefully without catastrophic collapse.

Concrete Steps Scholars have suggested various investments that would increase the system's resilience to stress. These include

Training Responding to a WMD attack would require a suite of specialized skills (working in biohazard suits, decontamination procedures) that are seldom, if ever, needed in peacetime. Despite exercises, most first responders report that they are inadequately trained to use these tools.[61] Learning these skills on the fly would impose unnecessary stresses and encourage mistakes.[62] For example, responders using biohazard suits for the first time often experience overheating, fatigue, hyperventilation, and even panic. Unnecessary use can also persuade the public that the situation is more dangerous than it actually is (Alexander and Klein 2003).

Expanding public health   Recent budget cuts have eroded public health agencies' capacity to detect outbreaks and conduct trace-and-contain operations against contagious diseases (Speckhard 2007). Similarly, current mental health staffs are almost certainly too small to triage worried-well survivors (Engel et al. 2007; Speckhard 2007) and identify patients who need long-term counseling (Alexander and Klein 2003). Expanded public health budgets would go a long way toward meeting these needs.

Surge capacity   Certain assets (e.g., specialized laboratory equipment and training) are hard to expand quickly in an emergency. In such cases, it may be important to purchase key assets in advance; cross-train workers on skills that will likely be scarce in an emergency; and develop plans for accommodating foreseeable labor shortages and casualties (Reissman et al. 2006; Casani, Matuszak, and Benjamin 2003).

High-risk groups   It is reasonable to think that various groups—including older people, children, mothers of young children, and immunosuppressed patients—could be unusually vulnerable to long-term physical and/or mental injury in a WMD attack. Furthermore, these high-risk groups may be different depending on the type and scale of attack. More needs to be done to identify these groups and specify the conditions under which specifically targeted interventions are likely to be cost-effective.

Communications   Strained communications during a WMD attack are inevitable, but the breaking point can be postponed. Mayer-Shonberger (2003) presents a detailed survey of the incompatible telecommunications and data standards that prevent emergency response agencies from communicating with one another and early U.S. and European initiatives to solve it. Congress authorized $1 billion in new grants to help first responders purchase compatible ("interoperable") equipment in 2005 (NTIA n.d.).

Exercises   Most WMD attacks would require coordinated, simultaneous responses from multiple jurisdictions and agencies. These problems would be especially acute for contagious disease outbreaks that covered large geographic regions. For example, quarantine authority would probably be relinquished to state and then federal authorities as the contagion spread across county, state, and international borders. However, few local or state agencies have specific guidelines on when to establish quarantines (Barbera et al. 2001) and boundaries and responsibilities would seldom be clear in a fast-moving epidemic (Barbera et al. 2001). Control centers, liaisons, and response teams can be counterproductive in an emergency if they have not been carefully thought out and practiced in advance (Speckhard 2007).

Psychological Factors   Human organizations can be remarkably resilient in the face of trauma. Indeed, elite military units are expected to absorb 40 to 60 percent killed and wounded before becoming ineffective (U.S. Army 1994).[63] These conditions are unlikely to be encountered in any plausible WMD attack apart from an atomic explosion. Elite military units, however, are highly self-selected, professional, trained, disciplined, and indoctrinated. The challenge for policy is to confer at least a measure of this resiliency on ordinary paramilitary (police, fire) and civilian (hospital, public health) organizations. This can potentially be done in several ways:

Training and professionalism   In addition to its direct benefit, training shows workers that they can trust themselves and their colleagues, provides shared experiences that reinforce professionalism and discipline, and allows responders to internalize behaviors until they become automatic. These lessons almost always reduce the psychological impact of an emergency and make workers more resilient to collapse (Alexander and Klein 2003).[64] Other measures to reinforce professionalism—for example, finding ways to honor brave health-care workers—may also be useful (Speckhard 2007). Finally, realistic training about radiation would go some distance toward establishing a basis of informed consent that would allow government to send first responders into a city hit by a nuclear weapon (Carter, May, and Perry 2007).

Psychological support services   U.S. Army experience shows that prompt treatment can return 50 to 70 percent of battle-fatigue casualties to combat within three days and most of the remainder to useful duty within a few weeks. By contrast, casualties who leave the combat zone seldom return to duty and often sustain long-term psychological injuries (U.S. Army 1994). In principle, similar on-scene support programs could be used to stiffen first responders' resolve and reduce their chances of long-term trauma.

Protecting family members   We have seen that first responders work better when they know that family members are safe. Giving family members preferential medical treatment and priority access to scarce drugs is a powerful (if potentially controversial) method for keeping responders on the job.

Engaging first responders and their representatives   The extent to which responders will be asked to take unusual risks and/or suffer casualties should be discussed with workers and union representatives in advance. Agreement will almost always stiffen responders as long as authorities do not try to renege after an attack.

16.5   Postattack Leadership and Policy Levers

Government command and control will reemerge within twenty-four hours for almost all CBRN attacks. Thereafter, the success of remediation and recovery operations will turn on leaders' ability to enlist public trust and cooperation.

16.5.1   Reuniting Survivors

The urge to reunite family is so basic that it cannot realistically be blocked. Authorities can, however, facilitate and channel it. Moving survivors to safety and reuniting them with family members quickly provides a natural biochemical antidote to panic and depression. If this cannot be accomplished physically, government should provide virtual links like telephone and e-mail (Speckhard 2007; Alexander and Klein 2003). The natural impulse to reunite could also be harnessed by teaching people how to protect and care for each other. In the case of a contagious bioweapons attack, for instance, explaining methods for home-based treatment, supportive care, nutrition, sanitation, and infection control could help reduce workloads for first responders and hospitals (Glass and Schoch-Spana 2002).

16.5.2   Communication

Early restoration of communications and, especially, responsible mass media would be an important goal in its own right. Perhaps the most obvious benefit would be the increased morale and efficiency generated by survivors' realization that things were returning to normal. Similarly, many disaster survivors are obsessively devoted to news reports and even treat them as a kind of therapy for making sense of what has happened (Thompson 1986). News organizations, on the other hand, would inevitably turn to government for much of their content. Government's ability to supply this information will be critical to recovery.

Effective communication builds trust in public health officials, increases voluntary compliance, suppresses rumors and anxiety, and enlists community support (Barbera et al. 2001). Since the 1970s, social psychologists have learned a great deal about risk communication. In general, persuasiveness increases with the number of messages, the number and reputation of sources, clarity, and trust. Messages are also more powerful when they are dramatic and lend themselves to positive symbolic associations. Communication tends to be fragile, however, since messages lose credibility quickly when they are disputed. Furthermore, not all messages have the same weight—for example, it is almost always easier to scare people than to unscare them (Kasperson, et al. 2004). Government information programs should be carefully designed to exploit these principles:

Volume   Government messages are usually delivered through mass media. If the media's voracious appetite for information is not met, the press will become frustrated and fill the vacuum from other sources (Hyams, Murphy, and Wessely 2002; Durodie and Wessely 2002). Similarly, most survivors can be expected to take some form of action. If government fails to recommend actions, people will invent their own strategies based on whatever information they have. These strategies will often be needlessly inefficient and/or counterproductive (Perry and Lindell 2003).

Consistency   Government should have a clear media message at all times (Hall et al. 2003) and suppress inadvertent contradictions and mistakes as soon as possible (Chess, Calia, and O'Neill 2004). Acknowledging that the speaker "does not yet know but the following steps are being taken to find out" will often be safer than reversing misstatements later on (Hall et al. 2003).

Honesty   We have already noted that two-way communication is a good way to show the public that they are not being manipulated (Fischhoff 2006). Credibility can also be bolstered by offering credible scientific authority and timely and accurate information that explains the rationales for difficult decisions (Hall, et al. 2003). Finally, government should deal fairly and openly with unproven assertions and new hypotheses (Hyams, Murphy, and Wessely 2002).

Symbolism   This aspect of communication is obviously much more art than science. That said, symbolic leadership would be a powerful lever for ensuring that the attack did not widen preexisting class, political, and regional fault lines. One way to do this would be to organize a visibly bipartisan response to the crisis similar to the one that followed September 11. However, images of shared suffering could also be important. Britain's wartime decision to emphasize two bombs that fell on Buckingham Palace was useful not least because it helped to defuse the very real resentments caused by German targeting of London's East End (Thompson 1986).

The Internet   The Internet would present special issues (1) because of its emphasis on interactive, two-way communication compared to other media, and (2) the absence of any substantial historical disaster experience that government leaders could turn to. Its strengths would include helping citizens get civil defense and other information tailored to their needs; supporting first responders; providing online rendezvous points where survivors could quickly leave messages for family and friends; and helping citizens question (and therefore ultimately come to trust) government messages. The Internet's main weakness, of course, would be its tendency to breed and amplify rumors. This too might be an improvement, however, to the extent that the inevitable postdisaster rumor mill was displaced from essentially invisible oral conversations into online text that the government could monitor and respond to in real time.

Designing and prototyping messages   Successful communication means finding out what facts people consider critical and then concisely delivering this information in ways that fit the intended audience's natural thought patterns (Fischhoff 2006). Surveys show that survivors would be most interested in the current status of the attack, possible protective actions, and detailed medical information about exposure and treatment (Henderson et al. 2004; Glik et al. 2004). By contrast, more general information about epidemiology or science would be much less interesting (Glik et al. 2004). Finally, even the best communicators cannot accurately predict when a message will be understood, particularly for novel subjects. For this reason, prototype messages should be tested on focus groups in advance, preferably before the attack occurs (Fischhoff 2006; MacCoun 2005). The CDC has already funded such prototyping (Vanderford 2004), although it is hard to know whether authorities would actually use these messages in an emergency.

All of this is easier said than done. There are obvious tensions between accuracy and timeliness, clarity and good science, and multiple sources and a common message. However, these conflicts can often be minimized by dividing topics among multiple nonoverlapping speakers—for example, by assigning a public figure for political messages and a technical expert for practical advice (Henderson et al. 2004; MacCoun 2005; Hall et al. 2003). Government can also demonstrate sincerity by transmitting its messages through trusted and independent third parties. TV weathercasters are particularly suited to this role, since survey data shows that they are widely seen as apolitical and unbiased (Becker 2004; Henderson et al. 2004).[65]

Messages should also be prepared in special formats that target narrowly defined, high-priority groups (Glik et al. 2004). In such cases, the best communication channels will often use social networks instead of formal mass media. Since these channels tend to be labor intensive, government may have to triage its audiences (Chess, Calia, and O'Neill 2004) by deciding which groups see themselves as high risk and/or are most likely to spread resistance and anger if they are ignored.[66] Minority groups will often receive a high priority since they tend to distrust government messages and are less reachable through conventional, mass media channels (Wray and Jupka 2004).

16.5.3 Compulsion

The myth of widespread panic biases leaders toward using compulsion even when scientific rationales are weak. For this reason, it would be useful to teach elites that panic is a rare phenomenon that can almost always be avoided.[67] Even when compulsion is scientifically justified, moreover, attempts to quarantine large areas and/or low-risk groups will often generate resistance. Regardless of their theoretical utility, therefore, actual quarantines may be so imperfect that they are not worth doing (Hall et al. 2003). Less intrusive alternatives will often include helping families care for their sick, mandatory vaccination and/or face masks, voluntary curfews, restrictions on assembly and mass transit, and telling people how to avoid disease (Barbera et al. 2001).

When quarantines are necessary, authorities can use various strategies to minimize resistance. First, they can design quarantines that segregate people according to preexisting social groups instead of creating arbitrary clusters of strangers (Glass and Schoch-Spana 2002). Second, they should take steps to mitigate foreseeable economic dislocations and stigma. These include making relief payments to unemployed workers and (as in the Brazilian radiation leak case) certifying that individuals have been examined and are free from contamination (Becker 2004). Third, authorities should avoid using the emergency for partisan advantage (MacCoun 2005). Indeed, they may often decide that it is sensible to consult with political opponents and other groups that lack formal legal authority.[68] Finally, future quarantines will almost certainly be tested in court and/or subjected to judicial supervision for adequacy and fairness (Barbera et al. 2001). While these proceedings have an obvious tendency to amplify conflict, they also provide a potential mechanism for demonstrating that government responses are rational and fair.

16.6   Remediation and Recovery

Remediation and recovery will demand much more work than government workers can provide. Progress will be faster if government can find ways to empower public voluntarism and creativity.

16.6.1   Demonstration
The most persuasive speech is action, and authorities' credibility will largely depend on their ability to show reasonable progress relative to challenges (Fischhoff et al. 2003). Historically, the removal of bodies has been a powerful and heartening signal that conditions are returning to normal. Confidence would also be reinforced by successful efforts to reestablish order and control (e.g., by restoring utilities),[69] organize survivors into purposeful activities, and tell people how to get government help (Alexander and Klein 2003; Barry 2005).

16.6.2   Organizing Adaptive Work
Control is bound to shift to the local level in the immediate aftermath of an attack. The larger question is whether some of it should stay there. Local social organizations will often be better placed to distribute food and medical care than outside

specialists (Barry 2005). Social organizations also have clear advantages in enlisting volunteers and encouraging community compliance (Leavitt 2003).

More generally, the public frequently shows resourcefulness, mutual aid, cooperation, and collective action in emergencies (Glass and Schoch-Spana 2002; Alexander and Klein 2003). Effective leadership needs to enlist and coordinate these instincts. Three months after the atomic bombing, Hiroshima's population began spontaneously returning to the city's outskirts. The government channeled the public's obvious desire to rebuild by paying people to clear streets, gather scrap, and erect shanties to live in (Hersey 2001).[70]

Community participation is particularly important for *adaptive* work that no one knows how to do (Heifetz 1994). Such work is common in situations where limited resources make familiar solutions impossible. In the weeks and months following an attack, citizens would have to function without family members, parents, police, or traffic lights; neighbors would have to learn how to share privately owned generators and organize collective child care; low-level government workers (e.g., school bus drivers) would be responsible for deciding how important assets could best serve the community; and government administrators would have to cope with the loss of "essential" people and assets. Grassroots improvisation and innovation are far more likely to solve these problems than central direction. As Schoch-Spana et al. (2007) have argued, elites should expect and promote society's talent for devising self-organized solutions and optimizing the use of communally held resources.

16.6.3 Managing Long-Term Health and Psychological Impacts

A large WMD attack would generate costly long-term health issues, including chronic injury and disease, reproductive uncertainties, mental health problems, and increased psychogenic symptoms (Wessely, Hyams, and Bartholomew 2002). Detailed health surveillance would be needed to track these problems, design responses, and avoid accusations of insensitivity and incompetence. Failure to do this would lead to accusations of cover-up, ill-advised treatments, a confused public, and protracted scientific and legal disputes (Hyams, Murphy, and Wessely 2002). To some extent, educating the public so that it can make its own informed judgments about reentering a particular area could be a partial solution (Carter, May, and Perry 2007). That said, the government would almost certainly have to set at least some minimum standards. This would be particularly necessary in the post-attack climate since—as we have already argued—psychological factors could persuade many people to underestimate the health risks associated with reoccupying their communities and workplaces.

Long-term mental health issues would become increasingly important—and expensive—as the disaster receded into history. While it is reasonable to think that early intervention could go a long way toward reducing this burden, the precise nature of these interventions is still not clear. Today, Western governments almost always take aggressive steps to see that terrorism victims are identified and treated. However, recent work suggests that intrusive psychological debriefing immediately after a trauma seldom helps and is sometimes harmful (Speckhard 2007). Moreover, such aggressive interventions would not be feasible following a mass casualty attack in any case. The problem, for now, is that there is no scholarly agreement on what an effective, low-cost, and high-volume mental health response would look like. Focused research is urgently needed on this issue.

In the meantime, mental health injuries are too important (and potentially preventable) to ignore even if the answers must sometimes be cobbled together from historical analogy and educated guesswork. Probably the most sensible strategy for mitigating mental health impacts would be to adopt the 1940s-era consensus that civil defense should build enough organizational capacity to mount a massive "wave of social help, hot tea and sympathy to snatch people out of their introversion and to link them up again with the outside world" (Thompson 1986). This advice intersects with more recent work emphasizing the therapeutic value of simply putting survivors together so that they can see that apparently strange behaviors (e.g., obsessive fear, engaging in pointless, after-the-fact avoidance strategies) are common and nothing to be ashamed of (Speckhard 2007). Shared experiences in meeting and then overcoming the disaster would also be therapeutic. Interestingly, Russian survivors of wartime trauma almost always deny that they suffer from PTSD. While they are clearly traumatized in other ways, the shared hardship of rebuilding postwar Russia seems to have been beneficial (Merridale 2000).

Finally, an attack would produce at least some positive outcomes. These could include a more united community, new personal strengths, more closely bonded relationships, constructive revision of life priorities, closer family ties, and greater ability to express emotions (Alexander and Klein 2003). National leaders could potentially nurture these positive outcomes through symbolic, FDR-style communications and actions.

16.7 Conclusion

There is overwhelming historical and psychological evidence that the public meets attacks with calm and resilience. Modest public policy interventions can potentially reinforce this resilience by (1) teaching individuals how to protect themselves during the inevitable interval when government command and control fail, (2) correcting inaccurate, culturally inspired beliefs that CBRN is so lethal that fatalism and passivity are the only appropriate response, and (3) reaching out to nongovernment elites (union representatives, social organizations, journalists) through consultation, education, exercises, and the like.

Almost all of these steps would be inexpensive and easy to implement. For example, it would be trivial—and very valuable—to send every U.S. household a pamphlet explaining the main forms of WMD and how to defend against them.[71] The real obstacle is that such messages would be extremely dissonant, not least because they admitted that government cannot protect its citizens in the first hours after a large WMD attack. That said, responsible leaders have a duty to start the conversation. This, in turn, will require U.S. elites to overcome their traditional (and faintly contemptuous) belief that the American public would panic in an emergency. Academics can and should take a leading role in correcting this demonstrably false—and very dangerous—illusion.

Notes

1. Interested readers should consult Davis et al. 2003 for detailed descriptions of the effects expected from attacks using hydrogen cyanide, sarin nerve gas, a radiological bomb, an atomic bomb, anthrax, and smallpox.

2. Delay is important. Because of evolution, pathogens often become markedly less infective and/or lethal over time (Barry 2005).

3. As in most large epidemics, 1918 influenza casualties actually increased wages by reducing the supply of labor. There is some evidence that children born during the epidemic sustained in utero injuries that reduced their earning power later in life (Garrett 2007).

4. Historical experience with natural pandemics is similar. In the case of 1918 influenza, casualties quickly exhausted the available supply of hospital beds, laboratory facilities, ambulances, hospital supplies (e.g., drugs, linens, gowns), nurses, doctors, pharmacists, morticians, and gravediggers. At the height of the Philadelphia outbreak, one agency reported that 2,758 out of 2,955 calls for nurses (93 percent) went unfilled. Hospital hallways, barracks, gymnasiums, armories, parish halls, and tents were all pressed into service (Barry 2005; Schoch-Spana 2000). As at Hiroshima, basic nursing care—rest, hydration, cooling fevers—saved many more lives than advanced treatments (Barry 2005).

5. Doctors and nurses were disproportionate victims of 1918 influenza (Barry 2005). Almost ninety years later, health-care workers similarly accounted for half of all Toronto SARS victims (Schoch-Spana et al. 2007). The problem is complicated by lack of decontamination training and equipment. During the 1995 Tokyo subway attacks, 135 ambulance workers and 110 medical staff were exposed to sarin on victims' clothes. Thirty-three of them required hospitalization (Tucker 2006).

6. At the end of the third day, Hiroshima's main hospital still had only eight doctors to care for 10,000 patients (Hersey 2001)

7. Surveys from Nagasaki show that light frame homes collapsed at distances up to 1.4 miles from ground zero (Glasstone and Dolan 1977).

8. Readers interested in a graphic and well-researched, albeit fictional, account of the exclusion zone should consult Cruz-Smith (2006).

9. Power outside the "devastated areas" of the city was also lost, but was restored the following day (USSBS 1946a).

10. Late nineteenth-century European cholera outbreaks and the 1918 influenza pandemic were both marked by breakdowns in authorities' ability to obtain accurate information, determine whether the number of cases was increasing, or find out which interventions were effective (Evans 1987; Barry 2005; Schoch-Spana 2000). Reduced ability to collect, process, and act on data has been a hallmark of natural contagious disease outbreaks since ancient times. Records from Asia Minor complain that deaths from a sixth-century plague were so numerous that the authorities could no longer record them (Keys 1999). Coincidence or not, the Dark (i.e., unrecorded) Ages followed immediately afterward. Government command and control took many centuries to recover. As late as the Battle of Hastings (1066), commanders assembled soldiers into lines just 1,250 yards across because more extended operations could not be controlled from horseback. Extended military operations on the ancient pattern did not reemerge until the fourteenth century (Hittle 1944).

11. During the New Orleans floods, local, state, and federal agencies were sometimes reduced to making judgments based on CNN coverage (Tierney 2006).

12. This "decapitation" scenario mattered a great deal in the Cold War, when deterrence depended (at least theoretically) on a unified command and the decision of a single national leader. In the long term, however, hardly anyone is indispensable. Stalin's attempt to decapitate the Polish state by murdering more than 20,000 officers, officials, engineers, doctors, lawyers, professors, and journalists failed to stop the Poles from forming an underground government and fielding large conventional armies throughout World War II (Folly 2004).

13. Telephone service was routinely rationed during the 1918 influenza pandemic (Barry 2005; Garrett 2007).

14. The genre's most imaginative, influential, and prolific exponent was a novelist named Philip Wylie—a famous misanthrope who once wrote an extended indictment of motherhood (Wylie [1942] 1955). Predictably, practically all Wylie novels (e.g., Wylie 1957) feature extended scenes of panic and chaos. Interestingly, at least some of Wylie's contemporaries saw things differently. George Stewart's plague novel, *Earth Abides*, shows much more awareness of the historical evidence. There, the narrator remarks that civilization "had gone down gallantly. Many people were reported as escaping from the cities but those remaining had suffered ... no disgraceful panic. Civilization had retreated, but it had carried its wounded along, and had faced the foe. Doctors and nurses had stayed at their posts, and thousands more had enlisted as helpers. Whole areas of cities had been designated as hospital zones and points of concentration. All ordinary business had ceased, but food was still handled on an emergency basis. Even with a third of the population dead, telephone service along with water, light, and power still remained in most cities. In order to avoid intolerable conditions which might lead to a total breakdown of morale, the authorities were enforcing strict regulations for immediate mass burials" (Stewart [1949] 1989). Today's popular (and also elite) stereotypes of mass panic would look very different if Stewart had dominated the genre instead of Wylie.

15. The myth of panic can also become self-fulfilling. While most people think that they themselves would behave well in a radiological or smallpox attack, they expect almost everyone else to panic (Fischhoff et al. 2003).

16. A relatively small fraction of victims would suffer a state of shock marked by docility, disoriented thinking, and (sometimes) a reduced awareness of their surroundings. This state is particularly common in disasters that occur suddenly, happen without warning, and/or involve widespread destruction, traumatic injuries, and death. The syndrome usually dissipates within a few hours with little (if any) treatment and has no known long-term impact on mental health (Perry and Lindell 2003).

17. Interestingly, survivors may sometimes take action even though official authority has forbidden it. During World War II, German civilians ignored official warnings after the raid on Leipzig by emerging from their cellars to extinguish fires. This action may have saved them from the fate that befell Dresden, most of whose citizens lingered in cellars and eventually died there (Taylor 2004).

18. Efforts to triage survivors by refusing to treat those who were going to die anyway produced rage at Hiroshima (Hersey 2001). During the Tokyo subway attacks, lack of proactive public communications coupled with media images of suffering similarly led to fear of commuting, absenteeism, mistrust of public authorities, insomnia, depression, anxiety, and uncertainty about long-term health (Lemyre et al. 2005).

19. During Hamburg's last major cholera outbreak (1892) middle-class citizens debated Robert Koch's recent discovery that the disease was spread by microbes and decided that it was reasonably safe to stay in the city so long as they took precautions (Evans 1987).

20. The Allied raids killed 305,000 Germans, wounded another 780,000, and left 7.5 million homeless (USSBS 1945). The firebombing of Japan claimed 300,000 lives (Hoyt 2000).

21. It also bred enormous pressure for retaliation. In the short run, promises of revenge helped to support morale by providing a "narcotic" that kept people going. However, this was followed by disappointment and depression when the V-1 raids against England failed to change anything (Friedrich 2006). The German experience suggests that perceived inability to "hit back" at terrorists would create significant problems for U.S. leaders. As with the V-1 campaign—or the 1942 Doolittle Raider strike on Japan—this would generate significant pressure for projects that had doubtful military value.

22. Isolated raids early in the war produced widespread sleeplessness and anxiety, particularly among those who had not experienced them firsthand. When bombing became widespread in 1940, however, citizens met it cheerfully, pitching in to clean up and vowing to outlast the British. This feeling slowly eroded with the growing realization that the war was lost (Friedrich 2006). When British raids on Hamburg killed an estimated 60,000–100,000 Germans in 1943, Hitler briefly speculated that further, similar raids might knock Germany out of the war (USSBS 1945). In fact, this did not happen. Although feelings of "deep dejectedness" and "helplessness" overtook much of the population, solidarity and loyalty to the regime remained almost entirely unaffected. By 1944, continuing stress had produced a situation in which most Germans lived in a perpetual state of apathy and fatigue, punctuated only by the weeklong periods of pain and despondency that followed actual raids. Hysterical collapse and absenteeism became increasingly common late in the war (Friedrich 2006). The bottom line was that workers continued to work but with significant lost productivity due to apathy (USSBS 1947c).

23. The German and Japanese governments also organized massive evacuations to limit their citizens' exposure to future air raids. Roughly 7 percent of all Germans and one-quarter of all urban Japanese—8.5 million people—were evacuated during the war (USSBS 1947c, 1947d). Evacuations following contagious disease attacks would probably be much smaller since refugees would face hostility and organized opposition from surrounding regions. Even so, about 6 percent of Hamburg's citizens managed to flee the city during a cholera outbreak in 1892 (Evans 1987). In 1994, 600,000 individuals similarly fled Surat, India, following an outbreak of pneumonic plague (Ramalingaswami 2001).

24. For example, survey data shows that only 38 percent of Americans plan to stay at home after a contagious bioweapons attack (Nicogossian et al. 2007). Failure to stay at home during an epidemic increases the risk of becoming sick and, once ill, spreading the infection to others.

25. This was particularly evident in the the wildly overheated press reports that followed Hurricane Katrina (Thevenot and Russell 2005).

26. Voluntarism can also change public behaviors and, through them, slow the spread of contagious disease. Shortly after World War II, New York authorities stopped a smallpox outbreak by persuading 6.4 million of the city's 7.5 million citizens to stand in long lines to receive vaccinations. Approximately two million New Yorkers had already been vaccinated when the emergency began (Leavitt 2003).

27. Attempts to enforce mass graves and abbreviated funeral practices would be a possible exception and flashpoint.

28. In addition to quarantine, other possible measures would include closing borders, isolating victims in their homes or emergency hospitals, travel restrictions, mandatory vaccination, targeted distribution of medicines and vaccines (Eisenman 2004), enforced wearing of gauze masks, ordinances against spitting, suspending movie houses and theaters, closing schools and churches, stopping funerals, curtailing retail hours (Schoch-Spana 2000), barrier environments and mandatory decontamination facilities, and the forcible destruction of personal clothing and property (Alexander and Klein 2003).

29. More recently, decontamination practices following the Tokyo subway attack provoked widespread criticism for their apparent disregard of survivors' dignity and personal privacy (Alexander and Klein 2003).

30. That there was a scientifically plausible reason for the policy—immigrants, after all, lived in crowded tenements and the rich did not—is neither here nor there (Leavitt 2003).

31. During the 2001 anthrax attacks, for example, only 44 percent of high-risk individuals actually completed the recommended course of antibiotics (Reissman et al. 2006; Lemyre et al. 2005).

32. The urge to keep families united is extremely strong. During the European air war, many parents similarly resisted having their children evacuated to the countryside (Beck 1986). According to the U.S. Strategic Bombing Survey, "The evacuation program, in general, produced widespread dissatisfaction and confusion. Of all parts of this program, the evacuation of children, particularly if they were sent long distances from their families, had the most adverse effect on morale" (USSBS 1947c).

33. Public health officials were, for example, assassinated in both the Muncie, Indiana, small-pox outbreak (1893) (Barbera et al. 2001) and cholera epidemics in Central Europe (1832) (Evans 1987).

34. Modern readers should not be misled by the term *riot*. Unlike, say, the riots of the 1960s, nineteenth-century "riots" were broadly based, organized assertions of community values against outside intervention. The Milwaukee immigrant women who gathered each day for months to beat any health department official who dared to enter their neighborhood (Leavitt 2003) presented an entirely different—and potentially much deeper—challenge to government than, say, the transient rage of the Rodney King riots.

35. Early nineteenth-century riots in Central Europe were similarly linked to the revolutionary atmosphere of those years (Evans 1987).

36. Victims in Goiania even displayed blisters, burns, and/or reddened skin reminiscent of radiation exposure (Becker 2004; Pastel 2001).

37. Psychogenic illness and clinical hysteria have identical symptoms. These include nervous excitation, loss or alteration of bodily functions, nausea and vomiting, headache, dizziness, weakness, fainting, and hallucinations (Engel et al. 2007; Bartholomew and Wessely 2002; Pastel 2001).

38. World War II conventional bombing did make German and Japanese civilians more willing to criticize their leaders for failing to protect them, and this reaction was also seen at Hiroshima (USSBS 1947c, 1947d).

39. Though less important than physical distance, television watching can significantly increase stress by allowing viewers to constantly replay and personalize the experience. Television also helps viewers to imagine themselves as victims of future attacks (Speckhard 2007).

40. The physical case for quarantine in Hamburg (1892) was debatable even at the time. The fact that gravediggers had trouble getting subsequent employment suggests a strong psychological component (Evans 1987).

41. This is particularly true since communities that have seen their sense of well-being undermined already have a strong tendency to react to official reassurance with anger and disbelief (Hyams, Murphy, and Wessely 2002).

42. The trade is not, however, unthinkable. After the Chernobyl accident, Soviet leaders reportedly promised citizens that they would return to their homes shortly because they feared that evacuation would take too long if people tried to take household goods with them. Whether or not this calculation was correct, it provides a plausible example of a case where dishonesty might have been justified.

43. During World War II, the Japanese and to a lesser extent the German governments tried to conceal military defeat from their respective populations. Allied strategic bombing's principal effect on morale seems to have come from demonstrating in an unmistakable way that the war was lost (USSSB 1947c, 1947d). Japanese propaganda in particular never recovered from this blow to credibility (USSSB 1947d).

44. Surveys show that survivors of a radiological attack would contact, among others, fire and police chiefs, sheriff's departments, emergency management and civil defense officials, military/national guard units, and county health departments (Becker 2004).

45. Informal channels are particularly important when government tries to change public risk perceptions by, say, persuading people that CBRN are potentially survivable. Peoples' assessment of risk is known to be influenced by social networks roughly as much as by mass media. Furthermore, social networks are often composed of like-thinking individuals who reassure each other that there is no need to change the group's existing beliefs. Campaigns limited to mass media have little chance of engaging this resistance (Kasperson et al. 2004; Durodie and Wessely 2002).

46. Ironically, Spanish speakers often believe that English language news is less emotionally tinged and therefore more trustworthy. They do, however, worry about missing vital communications (Henderson et al. 2004).

47. For WMD (unlike most natural disasters) this instinct would be powerfully augmented by caregiver guilt over receiving special protective equipment not available to loved ones (Thompson 1986).

48. Some forms of CBRN are unlikely to produce public anxiety. Following a (nonanthrax) biological attack, measured levels of pathogen quickly fall to "no-detect" levels and the public would presumably accept this. Here we focus on the much harder problem of public attitudes toward sites that retain measurable (though often minuscule) contamination.

49. Fears of germ and chemical warfare were ubiquitous in the 1930s, beginning with Aldous Huxley's prediction in *Brave New World* that the next war would be fought with anthrax bombs. Contemporary surveys suggest that 20 percent of the listeners fooled by Orson Welles's famous *War of the Worlds* hoax thought they were hearing garbled accounts of a German gas attack (Bartholomew and Wessely 2002).

50. Leading authors included Philip Wylie and Nevil Shute. Although less apocalyptic, Ian Fleming repeatedly extended the WMD idea to include terrorism. Strikingly, James Bond's adventures in *Moonraker*, *Goldfinger*, and *Thunderball* all involve substate actors that manage to acquire nuclear weapons. The villains in *Goldfinger* also possess nerve gas and have optimized their bomb as a radiological weapon (Fleming [1959] 2002).

51. Beginning in the 1970s, public anxiety over invisible hazards expanded into various subdebates around nuclear power, pesticides, genetically modified food, electric power, and cell phones (Hyams, Murphy, and Wessely 2002). Later, during the 1990s, bioweapon fears received an additional boost with the emergence of journalistic "outbreak narratives" focusing on how tropical diseases could potentially infect developed nations (Wald 2007). This new genre was immediately influential: Bill Clinton became profoundly interested in biological warfare after reading Richard Preston's bestselling *The Cobra Event* in 1998. Clinton was reportedly so alarmed that he asked U.S. intelligence officials to assess the book (Mangold and Goldberg 1999).

52. There is also some evidence of a third variable, *disaster potential*—that is, the number of people potentially exposed to a single incident (Slovic, Fischhoff, and Lichtenstein 2004b).

53. Commentators often ask why terrorists have not mounted small-scale CBR attacks, and particularly radiological "dirty bombs," already. The answer may be that terrorists understand that such attacks are far more spectacular in prospect than they would be in hindsight. High-profile terrorist organizations need to convince their followers and the world that they are on an upward trajectory. Attacks that leave their intended audience with a sense of anticlimax or even derision are counterproductive.

54. Western culture may be particularly susceptible to PTSD. Fewer than 3 percent of Tokyo subway victims showed symptoms of PTSD five years after the attack (Lemyre et al. 2005) and most Russian combat veterans similarly deny suffering from the condition (Merridale 2000). This does not, of course, mean that survivors do not suffer from guilt, nightmares, obsessive thoughts, and the like—only that they do not rise to the level of clinical PTSD (Merridale 2000).

55. Russia's case is clearly unique. More than fifty million Russians died from violence, famine, and epidemic disease between 1914 and 1953. Furthermore, half of these deaths occurred between 1941 and 1945. The resulting social trauma was further aggravated by totalitarianism and imposed silence (Merridale 2000).

56. Strong emotions discourage people from considering alternatives, make reaching a decision seem artificially urgent, and encourage premature closure (Hall et al. 2003). Angry people are also more likely to scapegoat others and show unreasonable optimism about their ability to solve problems (Fischhoff 2005).

57. Politicians are rewarded for shouting down leaders who introduce dissonant discussions. Ronald Reagan was ridiculed in the 1980s for suggesting that "with enough shovels" U.S. citizens could survive a nuclear war (Scheer 1983), just as, more recently, DHS was criticized for urging citizens to stock up on duct tape.

58. Glass and Schoch-Spana (2002) similarly argue that government education could increase the public's sense of control—a well-established element of dread—by "demystifying the world of microbes" and explaining how people could protect themselves against a biological weapons attack.

59. During the 1918 influenza pandemic, state authorities allowed dentists to treat people, graduated medical students early, and routinely accepted help from out-of-state volunteer doctors and nurses. However, labor practices continued to limit the number of nonactive nurses and doctors who could volunteer (Barry 2005; Schoch-Spana 2000).

60. Simple promises to serve in an emergency might not suffice. Only 1,045 out of 100,000 doctors who had joined the U.S. government's volunteer registry answered the call in 1918 (Barry 2005).

61. For example, only 24 percent of private physicians believe that they are personally prepared to respond to bioterrorism (Stein et al. 2004).

62. Responders in one recent NATO exercise turned away victims because they did not know how to decontaminate them. In an actual attack, such incompetence would have discredited the government while allowing contamination to spread (Speckhard 2007).

63. This may be optimistic if losses are concentrated in a short period of time. In 1944, an elite British aircrew reached the breaking point after 20.6 percent of the force was lost over a two-day period (Cave-Brown 1978). Such cohesion is still extraordinary.

64. The U.S. Army (1994) estimates that unusually tough training and esprit de corps can reduce battle fatigue by a factor of ten. Most combat units typically sustain one battle-fatigue casualty for every one or two soldiers wounded. By comparison, elite Ranger and Airborne units have historically suffered roughly one battle-fatigue casualty for every ten wounded.

65. News anchors by contrast are seen as contaminated with bias and sensationalism (Henderson et al. 2004).

66. During the 2001 anthrax scares, postal workers at the Monmouth facility near Washington, D.C., quickly decided that they were prime targets and demanded the same facility assessments, nasal swabs, and prophylactic medicines that they saw on television (Chess, Calia, and O'Neill 2004).

67. Public exercises would go some distance toward demonstrating the ability of large groups to behave in a collectively reasonable way.

68. Historic examples include efforts by Social Democrats to convince their followers to observe government health decrees during Germany's nineteenth-century cholera outbreaks (Evans 1987), enlisting priests to pick up bodies and conduct ceremonies over mass graves during the 1918 influenza outbreak (Barry 2005), and meeting with union leaders during the 2001 anthrax outbreak (Chess, Calia, and O'Neill 2004). The downside, of course, is that these groups can disagree with the government's position. In recent years, hundreds of hospitals and unions have refused government requests to vaccinate workers against smallpox (Hall et al. 2003).

69. During World War II, damage to utilities (especially transportation) was an especially powerful factor in breeding defeatism among Japanese civilians (USSBS 1946b).

70. The U.S. Strategic Bombing Survey reports that 137,000 citizens had returned to Hiroshima by November 1, 1945, compared to a preattack (August 6) population of 245,000 (USSBS 1946a). Allowing for deaths, practically all survivors must have returned by this point. Interestingly, the survey took a decidedly gloomier view of civilian initiative than Hersey did. The survey criticized the population for leaving Hiroshima "literally deserted" after the bombing, although it also admitted that this was "in many respects fortunate" since surrounding areas were better able to care for victims. The survey also reported that citizens were still showing "poor recuperative powers" when it visited the city three months later. At that time, "The first street car was beginning operation, people wandered aimlessly about the ruins, and only a few shacks had been built as evidence of reoccupation of the city. No system for collection of night soil or garbage had been instituted. Leaking water pipes were seen all over the city with no evidence of any attention. It was reported that following the bombing several days were required for disposal of the dead and then they were simply piled into heaps and burned without attempts at identification or enumeration. . . . All in all, there appeared to be no organization and no initiative."

According to the survey, programs to collect garbage and night soil and increase the supply of safe water were only undertaken after the Occupation "through the initiative of the Military Government." Conditions at Nagasaki were likewise said to be "very primitive" three months after the bombing although "a semblance of medical care and sanitary procedures had been reestablished." This progress was also attributed to the Occupation government, which was said to have "directed and forced" the "entire program" onto the Japanese (USSBS 1947b).

71. For historic examples of such civil defense manuals, see Science Service (1950) (atomic weapons) and UK Home Office (1937, 2007) (chemical weapons bombs).

17

Preventing WMD Terrorism

Deborah Yarsike Ball, Lucy M. Hair, Thomas McVey, and Michael Nacht

Preventing WMD terrorism will require the international community to work together to stop the spread of WMD expertise and technology, secure existing weapons and materials, and detect and intercept illicit trafficking. In particular, it will require a renewed focus on keeping powerful state-developed technologies from falling into terrorists' hands. While there is no known example of states providing WMD to terrorists, it is equally true that states with active covert WMD programs are disproportionately likely to support terrorism. And, all five countries designated by the U.S. State Department as sponsors of terrorism—Iran, North Korea, Syria, Sudan, and Cuba—are "known or suspected to have programs for the development of nuclear, biological, or chemical weapons" (State Department 2007; Perl 2004). Many of these same countries are also known to have received WMD technology from the A. Q. Khan network.[1] Whether or not Pakistan was aware of Khan's actions, the case shows how the mere existence of nuclear-armed states tends to promote further proliferation (Koch 2004). Russia, with its huge arsenal of nuclear weapons and materials, unevenly secured facilities, and widespread corruption similarly creates a significant risk that terrorists could steal or divert WMD for their own ends.[2]

U.S. antiterrorism policy must utilize all elements of national power, including diplomacy, intelligence, military action, law enforcement, economic policy, foreign aid, and homeland defense (9/11 Commission 2004). Preventing WMD terrorism will require the international community to stop the spread of WMD expertise and technology; secure existing weapons and materials; and detect and intercept illicit trafficking. This chapter reviews the problem, describes what has already been accomplished, and suggests future initiatives. Section 17.1 summarizes what is known about terrorists' ability to make or obtain WMD and identifies chokepoints where prevention strategy can make a difference. Section 17.2 reviews the various international treaties, norms, and programs that have already been implemented to stop the spread of WMD. Section 17.3 asks how future policy initiatives could make existing safeguards even stronger. Many of these opportunities involve helping states that are willing to follow best practices and international norms but cannot because of weak government or limited resources. Section 17.4 presents a brief conclusion.

17.1   Nature of the WMD Terrorist Threat

Preventing WMD use, with its potentially devastating consequences, has become a major focus of U.S. foreign policy (WMDC 2006). Indeed, the Bush administration's decision to invade Iraq was largely driven by a desire to keep the fruits of that country's WMD programs (later found to be inactive) away from terrorists. The 2003 *National Strategy for Combating Terrorism* concludes that modern technology and advanced communications have significantly increased terrorist organizations' ability to acquire and use WMD since the early 1990s (U.S. Government 2003b). While this is probably true, it is hard to be more precise about the risk. On the one hand, information about terrorists' ability to produce their own WMD is extremely limited. On the other, terrorists' ability to divert, purchase, or steal WMD depends on the security of state stockpiles. This information is almost always carefully protected.[3]

Some generalizations are still possible. Nearly all experts agree that nuclear weapons would be the most destructive form of WMD, but are also the hardest to acquire. By comparison, only the most advanced biological weapons could potentially cause comparable loss of life. These may, however, be easier to develop. Finally, chemical weapons are far less powerful than either nuclear or biological weapons. Furthermore, the chemical industry has worked with federal and state governments for many years to develop emergency response procedures for toxic chemical releases and/or pesticide poisonings. This suggests that the United States is much better prepared for a chemical attack compared to biological or nuclear threats (NRC/Committee on Science and Technology 2002; Cheremisinoff 1995; EPA 2006b). This is fortunate, since chemical weapons are also much more readily available than other forms of WMD and to that extent more likely to be used.

Arms control measures do not have to be flawless to be effective. There are numerous wrong paths in WMD development, and each repeated failure or dead end increases the risks of delay, exposure, or abandonment. The more obstacles or failure modes that exist, the more likely the WMD terrorist is to fail—or, better yet, decide against investing in R&D in the first place. Measures that add to these obstacles and failure modes, for example by making it harder for terrorists to obtain controlled materials and/or recruit specialists, can significantly increase these odds.

This section examines these technical hurdles in detail and explores their implications for policy. We also summarize the principal barriers in boxes that readers can refer back to as necessary.

17.1.1 Nuclear and Radiological Weapons

Nuclear and radiological threats can be divided into four broad categories: (1) detonation of a ready-made nuclear weapon such as that used on Hiroshima and Nagasaki; (2) detonation of an improvised nuclear device (IND) crudely fabricated from stolen or diverted special nuclear material (SNM);[4] (3) sabotage of nuclear power or reprocessing plants or other facilities that contain highly radioactive materials; or (4) detonation of a radiological dispersion device (RDD) or "dirty bomb" that uses conventional explosives to spread nonfissile radioactive material (NRC/Committee on Science and Technology 2002; Ferguson and Potter 2004). Of these, only the first two categories would produce a nuclear explosion. The damage expected from sabotaging a nuclear power or reprocessing plant, though significantly smaller, would also be enormous. The 1986 Chernobyl nuclear reactor accident forced roughly 350,000 people from their homes and twenty years later they have yet to return. The incidence of cancer among these survivors is also likely to be several times greater than normal (Chernobyl Forum 2005) and long-lived radioactive material will be scattered over the countryside in both airborne and fixed forms for centuries.[5] By comparison, an RDD would cause relatively little damage or contamination. While there is no known example of an RDD attack, a package containing cesium–137 was discovered in Moscow's Izmailovsky Park in 1995 (AFRRI 2003).[6]

Obtaining the material, expertise, and/or equipment to make a nuclear weapon from scratch would be much more difficult than carrying out a chemical or biological attack. Here, the main barrier is making plutonium and/or enriched uranium. On the one hand, plutonium does not exist in nature and must be produced in nuclear reactors. On the other, natural uranium must be enriched before it can be used in a bomb. Both activities require scientific expertise and large-scale facilities that terrorists almost certainly lack (CNS 2005). For this reason, many experts believe that nuclear terrorism is much less likely than a chemical or biological attack (Ferguson and Potter 2004). However, these barriers would be far lower if terrorists were able to obtain plutonium or enriched uranium since "the basic technical information needed to construct a workable nuclear device is readily available in the open literature" (Ferguson and Potter 2004). The technical challenges would be even lower if terrorists managed to steal a completed weapon, although in most cases they would still have to overcome security interlocks designed to prevent unauthorized use.

Fortunately, nuclear weapons and to a lesser extent fissionable materials are typically protected by high security. Nevertheless, terrorists could potentially overcome these safeguards in several ways. One strategy would be to use financial and/or ideological appeals to suborn *current* and *former insiders* working at a nuclear facility (Ball and Gerber 2005). The insiders could, in turn, use their access to steal needed materials and/or contribute their technical know-how to building a weapon. These vulnerabilities are compounded by the fact that many Russian facilities lack the audit and control systems needed to detect diversion by insiders (NRC/U.S. and Russian Committees 2005). Furthermore, insiders in many countries may be vulnerable to recruitment. For instance, a 2003 survey of 600 Russian scientists suggests that younger scientists have adapted to institutional changes since the fall of the Soviet Union better than older ones, but also tend to be less socially responsible (Gerber and Ball forthcoming). This might make them vulnerable to financial recruitment by terrorists. Similarly, press accounts report that jihadist sympathizers in Pakistan's military and domestic intelligence agencies are vulnerable to terrorists' ideological appeals and could become a source of "nuclear material, equipment or scientific know-how" (Moreau and Hirsh 2007).

A second possibility would be for *outsiders* to storm a facility and take material and/or weapons by force. This may be difficult, however, since outsiders typically lack detailed knowledge of security vulnerabilities and/or where to go once they gain access. In this case, the most promising strategy will normally be a combined strategy based on *insider-outsider collusion*. On the one hand, this would make insider recruitment easier by allowing terrorists to recruit low level employees who would not otherwise be useful. On the other, it could markedly improve the chances of an attack by providing information about security vulnerabilities such as when employees change shifts, how often workers check weapons and materials, and/or identifying times when guards sleep or get drunk.

Given the difficulty of making enriched uranium or plutonium from scratch, nuclear security is only as good as the nuclear weapons states' ability to physically control their arsenals and weapons material stockpiles. It follows that policy should focus on bolstering this control. This can be done by helping states to fill gaps in existing physical systems (e.g., security fencing, guards, and material tracking systems), reducing arsenals and plutonium/uranium stockpiles, and ameliorating conditions (e.g., corruption, low pay, ideological discontent) that might encourage insiders to collaborate with terrorists. The Cooperative Threat Reduction (CTR) program was created by Congress in 1991 to focus on these issues in Russia and other states of the former Soviet Union (section 17.2.2).[7] Many observers believe that the program could be usefully extended, albeit with suitable modifications, to Pakistan and other nuclear weapons states in the developing world.

17.1.2   Biological Weapons

In principle, biological weapons can yield near-nuclear and even nuclear-scale casualties. However, the range of potential impacts is very broad and is potentially mitigated by terrorists' lack of sophistication and/or society's ability to develop defensive vaccines and treatments. Despite recurring fears, actual historical development and use of biological weapons has been limited (Kellman 2006; Tucker 2000b). However, experience with the Rajneeshees in Oregon, Aum Shinrikyo in Japan, and the 2001 U.S. anthrax letters does show that significant, if limited terrorist attacks are already feasible. Furthermore, revelations regarding the former Soviet, Iraqi, and South African biological weapons programs show that more ambitious technologies are possible and plausibly available to substate actors (Guillemin 2005).

Terrorists trying to obtain biological weapons would face very different challenges compared to a nuclear program. Basic materials (e.g., pathogen samples, reagents) are usually far less tightly guarded than uranium or plutonium and/or are frequently available from natural sources. Moreover, biological weapons programs are hard to distinguish from legitimate biology research and can frequently take advantage of commercially available goods and services. Finally, weapons manufacturing facilities are far less expensive, easier to hide, and require much less specialized equipment than nuclear ones. Collectively, these observations imply that information and know-how—not physical assets or materials—constitutes the main barrier to acquiring biological weapons (box 17.1).

In principle, terrorists can acquire this information in several ways. Most obviously, they could try to develop a biological weapon from scratch. For sophisticated

Box 17.1
Resources required for a successful bioweapons program

- Specialists in multiple disciplines (*see text*)
- Means of obtaining virulent strain of pathogen
  By isolation from nature
  By theft
  By deception
- A laboratory/production facility
- Production equipment
- Ancillary supplies and matériel
- Explicit expertise in pathogen production and weaponization
- Implicit or tacit expertise in pathogen production and weaponization
- A suitable delivery method and equipment
- Ability to work in secrecy

mass-casualty weapons this would require assembling *multiple specialists* into a core team including (1) a bacteriologist or virologist to obtain and work with the pathogen, (2) a veterinary science or animal husbandry expert to conduct animal experiments, (3) a laboratory safety and construction expert to create an improvised R&D facility, (4) a biochemical engineer to develop processes for making pathogens in bulk, and (5) an aerobiology and aerosol science expert to design efficient distribution systems. Beyond this core team, additional specialists including (6) a mechanical engineer to design sprayers and other delivery systems, and (7) a doctor or nurse to monitor workers' health and administer prophylactics or drugs would also be useful. While these disciplines are fairly common, some—particularly aerosol science and biochemical process engineering—are unusual and could significantly complicate recruiting. Technical experts would also have very different backgrounds and motives compared to typical terrorist "foot soldiers." This would further complicate terrorists' efforts to recruit and retain experts. Finally, terrorist leaders would have limited technical knowledge. This would interfere with their ability to manage the program, set realistic goals and schedules, or detect fraud.

Even then, no team could realistically hope to know everything it needed to. Terrorists would have to conduct research to fill these gaps. This would be relatively straightforward to the extent that it involved *explicit knowledge* that is already codified and publicly available in, for example, literature or patents. Al-Qaeda seems to have devoted at least modest effort to collecting publications on pathogens and biological warfare (Leitenberg 2004). Gaps involving *tacit knowledge*—that is, "the unarticulated personally held knowledge that one acquires through a practical hands-on process, either through 'learning by doing' or 'learning by example'" would be much harder to fill (Vogel 2006).[8] Tacit knowledge is particularly important for technically ambitious projects and seems to have played a large role in Aum's failure to develop a working biological weapon (Vogel 2006). For this reason, future terrorists are likely to make tacit knowledge a high priority. According to a U.S. "red-team" exercise that simulated a covert biological weapons laboratory (Project BACUS), much of this knowledge could probably be acquired within eighteen months. Al-Qaeda is similarly reported to have recruited a PhD biologist and paid him to perform various tasks. These included visiting a British BL-3 facility's pathogen collection, trying to obtain anthrax vaccine, and attending various European pathogen conferences (Leitenberg 2004).[9] Significantly, efforts to obtain tacit knowledge would often force terrorist researchers to reach out to former colleagues for advice, equipment, and material. This can pose substantial security risks. For example, UK intelligence personnel first learned of South Africa's apartheid-era biological weapons program after members tried to obtain information from British biodefense employees (Gould and Hay 2006; Mangold and Goldberg 1999).

Given these difficulties, terrorists could decide that it was easier to recruit current or former insiders who had worked for state weapons programs. As with nuclear weapons, these insiders could potentially contribute (1) specific physical materials (e.g., samples of weapons-grade anthrax or even smallpox), (2) explicit classified recipes for making bioweapons, or (3) tacit expertise useful in developing and manufacturing biological agents and/or building systems to deliver them. Compared to nuclear weapons, however, the value of these shortcuts would probably be limited. First, state biological weapons programs have historically been much smaller than nuclear ones. This means that alumni would be harder to locate and recruit. Second, biological weapons—unlike nuclear ones—are not dominated by a handful of material and information bottlenecks. For this reason, terrorists would probably have to recruit a different insider for each of the various technical steps needed to achieve a working weapon.

Even with insiders' help, terrorists would probably still need a relatively complete, well-funded R&D team. Furthermore, experience with state programs shows that such a program could fail in multiple ways (box 17.2). This suggests that policy should focus on making it harder for terrorists to overcome technical problems by obtaining specialized advice and equipment from government insiders or commercial sources. This is particularly important since R&D only has to succeed once. Once terrorists develop a working recipe, follow-on attacks will require much less effort, investment, lead time, and risk.

Biological weapons laboratories and production facilities are relatively small and can often be readily masked by commercial or academic cover stories. This means

Box 17.2
Bioterrorism failure modes

• Detection of procurement of equipment and matériel (e.g., Larry Wayne Harris, a U.S. survivalist, was discovered attempting to obtain pathogen cultures from the ATCC by deception)

• Detection at R&D or production stages (e.g., R.I.S.E., a domestic terrorist group in the United States, was discovered trying to acquire and cultivate pathogens)

• Inability to recruit suitable specialists/detection during acquisition of specialized knowledge.

• Execution of attack with nonvirulent pathogens (e.g., Aum Shinrikyo's attack on the Japanese parliament)

• Failure of effective dispersion during terrorist attack (e.g., Aum Shinrikyo)

• Abandonment of the program by technical specialists

• Abandonment of the program by leaders of the terrorist group that biological weapons operations will normally have the fewest physical signatures of any form of WMD. Significantly, law enforcement and export control officials failed to notice when the DoD's BACUS group used commercial purchases to construct a simulated biological weapons factory (Miller, Engelberg, and Broad 2002).

17.1.3   Chemical Weapons

Chemical weapons include both traditional war gases (e.g., mustard, sarin) and the toxic industrial chemicals (TICs) that are an unavoidable byproduct of modern life. Provided they are efficiently disseminated, traditional chemical weapons could potentially kill hundreds or thousands of victims. These numbers are markedly smaller than nuclear (and some biological) scenarios, but still qualify as WMD. The recent use of chlorine tanks by terrorist groups in Iraq shows that TICs (e.g., chlorine and ammonia) also pose a potential threat. Although TICs are orders of magnitude less lethal than traditional war gases, they are much more widely available and can be purchased in sufficiently large quantities to inflict similar death tolls (HHS 2006).

The knowledge, training, and methods for making even sophisticated chemical weapons and TICs are widespread in industrialized nations (box 17.3). For this reason, terrorist R&D could be built around a relatively small team of chemists and/or chemical engineers. Beyond this minimum requirement, additional specialties in pharmaceuticals, agriculture, aerosolization, and ordnance could be useful. The core team could also fill its knowledge gaps from such readily available sources as journals, academic institutions, commercial vendors, and informal contacts with colleagues. Most of this R&D would probably focus on developing new production

Box 17.3
Resources required for a successful chemical weapons program

- Suitable specialists
  Explicit expertise in chemical weapons production and weaponization
  Implicit expertise in chemical weapons production and weaponization
- Means of obtaining the desired chemical weapons
  By production
  By purchase
  By theft
- A laboratory/production facility
  Production equipment
  Ancillary supplies and matériel
- A suitable delivery method and equipment
- Ability to conduct work in secrecy

recipes, scaling up laboratory methods to pilot-scale production, and designing delivery systems.

During the mid-1990s, Aum used lab-scale methods to repeatedly make gram- and even kilogram-scale batches of Sarin (Bellamy 2002; Smithson and Levy 2000).[10] Furthermore, Aum completed and tried to commission a much larger, pilot-scale plant that would have made batches in the hundreds-of-kilogram range. While this project was ultimately abandoned because of inexperience, incompetence, or perhaps impatience, Aum's example could potentially inspire future terrorists to do better (Tucker 2000a, 2006; Lifton 1999; Kaplan and Marshall 1996). A competent terrorist R&D team could reasonably hope to start laboratory-scale production within several months, or possibly even weeks if the basic materials are available. This would quickly generate the gram quantities needed for assassination. Furthermore, repeated use of lab-scale methods could potentially accumulate ten kilograms or so of agent within several months to a year. This is potentially enough to inflict mass casualties. Still larger quantities would remain impractical, however, unless the team was able to design, test, and build a pilot-scale plant. This would probably take several years. In addition to a core R&D team, such a project would also require substantial numbers of construction personnel and manual workers.

As with biological weapons, terrorists could also turn to commercial sources to fill gaps in their knowledge or competence. This is straightforward for TICs, which can be purchased or stolen from commercial sources in any moderately industrialized nation. Obtaining production equipment and precursor chemicals for chemical weapons would be somewhat more complicated. Like Aum, terrorists would probably purchase these materials through front companies. The similarities between nerve agent and agricultural pesticides would facilitate such deceptions (Tucker 2006). Alternatively, terrorists could target markets where regulation is ineffective. Societies in chaos (e.g., Iraq) or undergoing rapid economic expansion (e.g., China and India) would be especially vulnerable to theft or covert purchases. Finally, terrorists might be able to obtain help from individual state weapons program insiders or even organized trafficking networks on the A. Q. Khan model. These sources would be particularly useful for problems that lack close civilian analogues, notably including the formidable problems associated with manufacturing nerve agents in bulk.

Pilot-scale manufacturing operations would require a building-sized facility and specialized chemical processing equipment. These would be much larger and harder to disguise than a comparable biological weapons plant and would most likely require an elaborate cover story. Alternatively, terrorists might try to disguise the facility in much the same way that Aum hid its Kamikuishiki facility behind a large religious shrine. Finally, terrorists would have to design an effective delivery system.

Possible methods include vaporizing the material on hot metal plates, adapting agricultural sprayers, and using explosives to spread the agent. Though reasonably straightforward, primitive versions of these technologies are often highly inefficient. Despite extensive effort, Aum was never able to build a reliable and effective system.

On balance, a terrorist chemical weapons program would require a competent R&D team, moderately large and specialized production facilities, and repeated interactions with commercial vendors. While significantly nontrivial,[11] the relevant technologies are already widely available in most cases. As with biological weapons, measures aimed at denying "dual-use" equipment and know-how to terrorists who have reached a dead end could be important. Here, the challenge will be to detect terrorist conspiracies against the background of normal industry transactions. Policy solutions will usually rely on bolstering government regulation and empowering those closest to the scene—chiefly colleagues and commercial vendors—to notice and report suspicious patterns.

17.2   Current Nonproliferation Treaties, Agreements, and Programs

The current international response to WMD terrorism includes a complex web of legally binding treaties, conventions, and political statements of intent. These are complemented by increasingly sophisticated interdiction efforts and ongoing programs to help states reduce access to materials, technology, and expertise.

17.2.1   International WMD Treaties

Attempts to outlaw weapons of mass destruction date back to the first Hague Peace Conference in 1899 and the 1925 Geneva Protocol that prohibited the battlefield use of asphyxiating, poisonous, or other gases and bacteriological methods of warfare. In January 1946, the UN General Assembly called for the elimination of atomic weapons and other major weapons capable of inflicting mass destruction (WMDC 2006). Since then, three major international WMD Treaties have entered into force: the Treaty on Non-Proliferation of Nuclear Weapons (IAEA 1970), the Convention on the Prohibition of the Development, Production and Stockpiling of Bacteriological (Biological) and Toxin Weapons and on their Destruction (UN, n.d.(b)), and the Convention on the Prohibition of the Development, Production, Stockpiling and Use of Chemical Weapon and on their Destruction (UN, n.d.(a)). Collectively, these treaties establish strong global norms against the development, production, stockpiling, and use of WMD. These norms, in turn, support deterrence by providing political and legal benchmarks for holding states accountable.

Nuclear Non-Proliferation Treaty   (NPT) seeks to prevent the spread of nuclear weapons in exchange for the nuclear powers' commitment to promote the peaceful uses of nuclear energy and pursue eventual nuclear disarmament. The NPT recognizes five Nuclear Weapons States (United States, Russia, United Kingdom, France, and China) and designates all other member states as Non-Nuclear Weapons States. This distinction is sometimes seen as "discriminatory" because it subjects the Non-Nuclear Weapons States to significantly more stringent verification and monitoring obligations than Nuclear Weapons States. India, Pakistan and Israel, with their known or suspected nuclear programs, are not parties to the NPT and are not treated as Nuclear Weapons States for purposes of the NPT. North Korea, a former party to the treaty, formally withdrew in January 2003. The International Atomic Energy Agency (IAEA) has also found that Iran is in violation of the NPT. Despite this, Iran had not formally withdrawn from the treaty as this book goes to press.

The NPT verification regime is implemented by an international expert body (the International Atomic Energy Agency (IAEA). The IAEA is responsible for verifying that member states have declared all peaceful uses of nuclear energy and are not engaged in covert nuclear weapons programs. IAEA implements this verification regime through bilateral agreements with states that allow it to inspect declared nuclear facilities. In its original form, this regime had significant loopholes that Iraq's nuclear program exploited in the 1980s. In 1997, members adopted an Additional Protocol that broadened the IAEA's authority to conduct inspections (ACA 2006). The additional protocol is intended to extend the IAEA's safeguards from a system designed to track previously declared materials and activities to one capable of gathering a comprehensive picture of a state's nuclear activities, including any exports and imports of nuclear materials. The protocol also gives the IAEA the right to check for clandestine facilities by conducting "challenge inspections" at any facility, whether or not previously declared. However, the new powers only apply to states that have signed and ratified the protocol. The verification regime can also be hampered by access restrictions in the IAEA's bilateral agreements with particular states and the agency's own limited budget.

It is often difficult to determine that a state's nuclear program is peaceful while respecting national sovereignty and proprietary/commercial information. This sometimes undercuts the Non-Nuclear Weapons States' willingness to support intrusive monitoring and verification. Enforcing meaningful compliance has also proven difficult. The 2005 NPT Review Conference produced widespread recognition that the compliance regime was imperfect and resulted in a Special Committee on Verification to study possible reforms. So far, however, discussions have mainly focused on technical issues at the expense of larger, overarching political obstacles.

Additionally, findings of noncompliance must be agreed by the IAEA Board of Governors and then forwarded to United Nations Security Council for action. In recent years, it has become apparent that this highly political process can easily deadlock.

Over time, several weaknesses have become apparent in the NPT. Nonparties (India, Pakistan, Israel) have developed nuclear weapons with impunity. Furthermore, North Korea, a party to the treaty, withdrew shortly after its nuclear capability was discovered. The IAEA also found that another party, Iran, was in violation of the treaty. Iran has endured sanctions while continuing to expand its ostensibly peaceful uranium enrichment capabilities (Panofsky 2007).

Biological Weapons Convention (BWC)   The BWC was the first multilateral treaty to ban the acquisition and retention of an entire category of weapons. International efforts to add a verification regime to the BWC in 1990 enjoyed initial U.S. support. However, the initiative later failed after the U.S. concluded that the proposed monitoring and compliance mechanisms would be ineffective. Key factors in the U.S. decision included the difficulty in determining whether or not an activity is legitimate rather than weapons-related, the rapid pace of technological development, and limits on access designed to protect proprietary information. The United States and other members do, however, continue formal information exchanges as part of a "confidence building" strategy designed to build trust that members are, in fact, complying with the treaty (Borrie 2006; Chyba 2006). Despite these efforts, the BWC is known to have been violated by the former Soviet Union, Iraq, Libya, and apartheid-era South Africa (Guillemin 2005).

Even without a formal verification regime, the BWC has established an important norm against biological weapons. At a minimum, this has forced covert programs to operate in extreme secrecy, thereby complicating attempts by government agencies (usually the military) to detect waste and corruption. This was almost certainly a contributing factor in the relative ineffectiveness of both the 1974–1978 Iraqi program and the apartheid-era South African program. Nevertheless, the absence of verification and compliance regimes has made some suspicious of its effectiveness, especially with respect to Russian bioweapons capabilities (Rissanen 2003).

Chemical Weapons Convention (CWC)   The CWC largely supersedes the 1925 Geneva Protocol and bans the development, production, stockpiling, transfer and use of chemical weapons. It also establishes global norms by requiring States Parties to declare any chemical weapons–related activities, secure and destroy any existing stockpiles, and inactivate and eliminate all chemical weapons production facilities. Like the NPT, the CWC establishes an institution (the Organization for the Prohibition of Chemical Weapons or OPCW) to oversee and conduct verification. Because most toxic chemicals and weapons precursors have legitimate peaceful applications (OPCW 2007), the CWC verification regime focuses on intended use rather than any specific chemical structure. This has the added benefit of flexibility, since it automatically extends coverage to new weapons compounds if and when they are discovered. The CWC also lists various chemicals that can either be used as chemical weapons themselves or are used in the manufacture of chemical weapons in three categories (called schedules) along with an additional group call "unscheduled discrete organic chemicals." The verification regime authorizes monitoring whenever commercial activities involving any of these substances—including production, processing, consumption, export, and import—exceed specified threshholds (UN, n.d.(a)).

The CWC has materially reduced U.S. and ex–Soviet stocks of chemical weapons. As of March 2007, the U.S. had destroyed 40 percent of its chemical weapons stockpile (CMA 2006), while the former Soviet Union had destroyed approximately 18 percent (Litovkin 2007). The CWC also had a positive impact by promoting U.S. legislation to prevent chemical and biological weapons transfers to Iran in 1992 and again in 2000. When these laws were later invoked against Chinese companies and individuals, the Chinese government responded constructively by passing various new regulations. These included "Measures on Export Control of Certain Chemicals and Related Equipment and Technologies" and an accompanying "Related Equipment and Technologies Export Control List." That said, the current CWC regime still reflects significant compromises and gaps. These may or may not be addressed in the future (Tucker 2007).

A core challenge to the CWC is that the same chemicals that can be used to make weapons are widely available in agriculture and research. This makes compliance verification extremely difficult. In addition, many CWC member states have yet to submit documents and/or enact implementation legislation called for by the Treaty (Tucker 2001).

Despite the successes of the NPT, CWC, and BWC, these treaties present only a partial solution. While the treaties establish global norms, they lack legal jurisdiction over nonsignatory states as well as nonstate actors. Additionally, international law is still grappling with how to respond to countries that have violated treaties and subsequently withdrawn (for example, North Korea).[12] Over the past twenty years, the international community has worked hard to fill the remaining gaps with agreements and programs that focus on making weapons and weapons materials more secure and/or improving verification (Perkovich et al. 2005). Sections 17.2.2 through 17.2.6 describe many of these efforts.

17.2.2   Cooperative Threat Reduction Programs

The U.S. Congress created the Cooperative Threat Reduction (CTR) Program in 1991 to help the states of the former Soviet Union prevent the transfer or theft of nuclear weapons, related materials, and/or expertise to other nation-states or terrorists. Most of these programs have focused on eliminating existing weapons systems, improving site security, upgrading tracking and accounting procedures, and increasing controls over insiders' access to material and weapons.

DoD Cooperative Threat Reduction Program   This Department of Defense program works primarily with the Russian Ministry of Defense and was initially focused on enhancing the safety, security, control, and accounting of nuclear weapons. As of January 2005 it had assisted in the elimination of almost 600 Russian intercontinental ballistic missiles and thirty nuclear powered ballistic missile submarines (GAO 2005c). Since then, the program has expanded to include Biological Weapons Proliferation Prevention and Chemical Weapons Elimination programs. By 2005, CTR had spent more than $800 million funding numerous projects including construction of the Shchuch'ye chemical weapons destruction facility, demilitarization of former chemical weapons production facilities in Volgograd and Novocheboksarsk, projects to improve the security of pathogen collections inside former biological weapons facilities at Obolensk (SRCAM) and Kolt'sovo (Vektor), and various joint programs to find civilian employment for biological weapons researchers and their institutions (GAO 2005c).

Material Protection, Control, and Accounting (MPC&A)   The U.S. Department of Energy's Material Protection, Control and Accounting (MPC&A) program began working with Russia's civilian Ministry of Atomic Energy in 1993. However, it soon expanded to include nuclear weapons sites and materials operated by the Russian Federation's Ministry of Defense. Since then, the United States has spent nearly $1 billion to protect these assets against both insider and outsider threats. This work has included (1) physical protection improvements such as fences, alarms, video surveillance systems, metal doors, and guard force training; (2) material control systems, including nonreplicable seals to protect nuclear material containers against tampering or theft; and (3) computerized material accounting systems to track nuclear material inventories by quantity, type, and location (CNS 2003). In recent years, the program has also worked on projects to turn weapons-grade nuclear materials into low enriched uranium and other forms that cannot be readily used to make weapons (DOE, n.d.(a)).

Second Line of Defense (SLD) The programs described so far concentrate on securing material in place. In 1998, the SLD program was created to establish a second line of defense by strengthening the capability of governments to detect and deter illicit trafficking in nuclear and other radioactive materials by sea and across borders. The program began by working with Russian customs authorities and has since expanded to include more than twenty-three countries. The program provides interdiction training, monitoring equipment, and communications at various international borders throughout Russia, Greece, Central Asia, Eastern Europe, the Caucasuses, the Baltic, and the Mediterranean (DOE, n.d.(a)). The *Megaports Initiative*, which began in late 2002, similarly provides radiation detection equipment for key international seaports in order to screen cargo containers for nuclear and radioactive materials. This strategy effectively extends the U.S. security perimeter so that containers are inspected before ships arrive at a U.S. port. The program complements the Department of Homeland Security's *Container Security Initiative* (CSI), which has developed minimum standards for screening cargo and high-risk containers at all ports that ship significant volumes to the United States.

Eliminating Weapons-Grade Nuclear Material Various agreements have been designed to secure and/or dispose of ex–Cold War stocks of fissionable material so that they do fall into the hands of terrorists or rogue nations. The principal programs include

Global Threat Reduction Initiative (GTRI) This DOE program focuses on removing and/or securing high-risk nuclear and radiological materials and equipment internationally.[13] GTRI will make weapons grade highly enriched uranium (HEU) less available by helping countries convert existing research reactors and medical isotope manufacturing facilities from HEU to low enriched uranium (LEU). The program also works to repatriate spent U.S. nuclear fuel from foreign research reactors and recover high-risk radiological sources from around the world. Parts of the program also help to secure and dispose of domestic U.S. radiological materials. In general, however, it has not been easy to extend the CTR program beyond the former Soviet Union. Pakistan, in particular, has resisted intrusive monitoring of its nuclear weapons facilities in general and U.S. involvement in particular.

Plutonium Power Reactor Agreement (PPRA) This U.S.-Russian project is working to close fourteen plutonium production reactors in the U.S. and thirteen in Russia. The agreement provides for reciprocal monitoring visits to each country's closed reactors. Some of the Russian reactors provided heat and power to tens of thousands of people in Siberia. The United States agreed to help replace these facilities with fossil fuel plants under its Elimination of Weapons Grade Plutonium Production program (DoE, n.d.).

Highly Enriched Uranium (HEU) Purchase Agreement   The United States signed this agreement with Russia in 1993 to downblend 500 metric tons of HEU (90 percent U-235)[14] from dismantled Russian nuclear weapons into low enriched uranium (LEU; less than 5 percent U-235). The project will take more than twenty years to complete. The resulting LEU will be sold commercially to American nuclear power plants at no cost to the United States or Russia. The first shipment of LEU arrived in the United States in 1995. Today, approximately thirty metric tons are converted and processed each year. Additionally, special monitoring visits are conducted each year to provide transparency and confidence in Russian HEU declarations and to ensure that the HEU is being converted to LEU (DOE, n.d.(a)). Although the monitoring does not verify the HEU's source with high certainty, it does confirm that the total amount of HEU is being reduced (Bunn 2003).

U.S.-Russia Plutonium Disposition Agreement   In 2000, the United States and Russia each agreed to destroy at least 34 metric tons of plutonium. The United States plans to fulfill its commitment by burning 25.5 metric tons as mixed oxide (MOX) fuel and immobilizing the rest in glass blocks. For its part, Russia intends to burn all 34 metric tons as MOX. However, implementation has been slow because of various issues relating to technology, liability, and monitoring and inspections.

Keeping Scientists Gainfully Employed   The collapse of the Soviet Union cut Russian funding for scientific research by 75 percent between 1991 and 1994 and these levels remained low throughout the 1990s. This led to a disastrous drop in Russian scientists' status, living standards, and prospects (Ball and Gerber 2005). The resulting proliferation threat prompted the international community—including both government and private organizations—to create a series of programs aimed at keeping former WMD scientists gainfully employed while redirecting their work from military to civilian R&D. Collectively, these programs have employed tens of thousands of scientists and, in the process, helped to educate them in Western scientific norms while integrating them into the international scientific community so that they can compete for contracts. As a result, there are now hundreds of collaborative efforts between Russian scientists and Western universities, companies, and governments. Survey evidence suggests that these nonproliferation assistance programs have significantly reduced Russian scientists' willingness to work in countries like Iran, North Korea, and Syria, and promoted a shift in attitudes away from the hierarchically administered, noncompetitive Soviet system. An added advantage is that these programs have given scientists a stake in emerging institutions that deemphasize military research in favor of civilian applications (Ball and Gerber 2005). At the same time, changes in the *average* scientist's attitudes are only part of the problem and it is much harder to know how effective these programs have been in reaching *every* scientist who might be tempted to sell information to terrorists. Furthermore, the United States first began implementing CTR in an era when the Russian Federation was weak and possessed only limited economic resources. Since then, rising oil prices have transformed Russia's economic and political strength. This will almost certainly dampen Congress's enthusiasm for funding future CTR initiatives in Russia, although extensions to countries outside Russia could well be viewed more favorably.

Some of the larger programs include

International Science and Technology Center (ISTC)   Thirty-seven countries are currently members of this international organization, including Russia, the United States, Canada, the European Union, Japan, Norway, and the Republic of Korea[15] (ISTC 2007). Since its founding in 1992, ISTC has disbursed more than $600 million to support research projects by more than 50,000 scientists in the Commonwealth of Independent States. In order to receive ISTC funding, research teams must include former weapons scientists. ISTC provides funds so that these scientists can travel to foreign conferences, upgrade their telecommunications and computer facilities, attend seminars on management, entrepreneurship, and grant writing, and apply for patents. In addition, the ISTC acts as a clearinghouse for connecting applicants to private firms interested in developing and marketing their research.

Global Initiatives for Proliferation Prevention (GIPP)   This DOE program includes the *Initiatives for Proliferation Prevention* (IPP) and the *Nuclear Cities Initiative* (NCI). Since 1994, IPP has helped more than 14,000 former weapons scientists in Russia, Kazakhstan, Ukraine, Armenia, and Georgia develop proposals for long-term applied research projects with U.S. industry (DOE, n.d.(a); Weiner 2002). NCI focused on reducing the size of Russia's ten closed nuclear cities by helping scientists to develop business plans, find investors, and promote startup businesses to obtain civilian work (Bunn 2002). NCI stopped operating in 2006. Since then, GIPP has expanded to include Libya and other countries beyond the former Soviet Union.

International Association for the Promotion of Cooperation with Scientists from the Commonwealth of Independent States and the Former Soviet Union (INTAS)   The European Commission established INTAS in 1993 to promote collaborations between European industry and Russian researchers in the physical, life, and earth sciences, chemistry, aerospace and engineering, mathematics, economics, and the social sciences. The European Commission stopped funding new INTAS projects in 2007 (INTAS n.d.).

CTR has gone a long way since the early 1990s toward helping the states of the former Soviet Union reduce their WMD stockpiles and meet international best practice standards for securing what remains. As a result, the risk that terrorists could exploit ex-Soviet stockpiles and personnel to obtain WMD has been significantly reduced. Although there is still much work to be done, CTR has been a good investment in increasing nuclear security. Many of these programs have also expanded over time to address new or additional vulnerabilities.

17.2.3 Counterterrorism Agreements

Modern efforts to keep WMD out of the hands of terrorists began with the CTR programs but were broadened following September 11 to include various programs by the Group of Eight (G8) nations.[16] In 2002, the Group's Canada meeting established the *G8 Global Partnership* as a high-level of political commitment "to prevent terrorists or those that harbor them from acquiring or developing nuclear, chemical, radiological, and biological weapons; missiles; and related materials, equipment and technology." In support of these goals, members promised to contribute $20 billion to the Global Partnership by 2013. The funds are intended to establish cooperative programs to aid states in fulfilling their commitments to:

• Strengthen and fully implement multilateral treaties and other international instruments
• Develop effective measures to account for and secure the production, use, storage, and domestic and international transport of controlled materials
• Develop appropriate effective physical protection measures
• Implement effective border controls, law enforcement programs, and international cooperation to detect, deter, and interdict cases of illicit trafficking
• Maintain effective national export and transshipment controls over items on multilateral export control lists
• Strengthen efforts to manage, reduce, dispose of, or eliminate stocks of fissile, chemical, and biological materials for defense purposes (Group of Eight 2003)

Like previous U.S.-Russian programs, the Global Partnership's efforts are largely focused on securing, consolidating, and reducing nuclear and chemical weapons and materials in the former Soviet Union. Within this framework, efforts to destroy chemical weapons, dismantle decommissioned nuclear submarines, find employment for former weapons scientists, and dispose of fissile material have received the highest priority. Many existing nonproliferation and CTR programs were also included under the G8 Global Partnership umbrella. Since 2002, the G8 donor countries have gradually expanded these programs to include similar activities in Libya and Iraq. The G8 has also reaffirmed its commitment to counterterrorism at each subsequent meeting. Instead of starting new programs in 2005 and 2006, however, the G8 shifted its focus to supporting United Nations counterterrorism initiatives and programs (Group of Eight 2005, 2006). That said, the G8 members' political commitment to the Global Partnership remains in place even though financial follow-through by some members has been slower than expected.

In 2003, the United States built on these initiatives by announcing a formal National Strategy on Combating Terrorism to "deny WMD to rogue states and terrorist allies who seek to use them" (U.S. Government 2003b). In its original form, this document focused on implementing better controls for weapons technologies and materials. Since 2006, the strategy has been expanded to include various institutional and motivational factors including (1) promoting democracy as a long–term antidote to terrorism and (2) building institutions and structures to combat terrorism, including stronger international accountability standards and improved cooperation among domestic agencies (U.S. Government 2006c).

In April 2005, the UN General Assembly unanimously adopted the first counterterrorism convention since September 11. The International Convention for the Suppression of Acts of Nuclear Terrorism builds on twelve earlier international terrorism conventions and protocols by providing a legal basis for international cooperation in the investigation, prosecution, and extradition of those who commit terrorist acts involving radioactive material or nuclear weapons (UN 2005).

Despite these initiatives, difficulties persist in implementing these agreements, particularly with respect to information sharing. In part, this reflects the nearly universal reluctance of governments (especially in non-Western countries) to share information bearing on national security. Counterterrorism agreements, however, face the special problem that—despite conventional terrorism in the former Soviet Union and elsewhere—WMD terrorism is primarily seen as a U.S. concern.

17.2.4   International Export Control Guidelines

The forty-five-member Nuclear Suppliers Group (NSG) was established in 1974 to control exports of nuclear technology and materials. It focuses on developing export control guidelines to prevent sensitive materials, equipment, and technology from being diverted from peaceful uses to unmonitored nuclear fuel processing and/or nuclear weapons projects. Participating governments are responsible for implementing NSG Guidelines according to their own national laws and practices (NSG n.d.).

In 1985, chemical weapons use in the Iran-Iraq War prompted creation of a second, fifteen-member "Australia Group" to control exports of chemical and biological weapons technologies. Since then, membership has expanded to thirty-nine members plus the European Union. Like the NSG, the Australia Group seeks to harmonize national export licensing measures to prevent the spread of chemical and biological weapons materials and know-how (Australia Group 2007). Australia Group restrictions seem to have been instrumental in blocking Iraq from acquiring large (5,000-liter) fermenters and other equipment that could have been used to freeze-dry bacteria.[17]

17.2.5   Physical Protection Standards

Establishing legally binding commitments for the physical protection of national, international, and cross-border transfers of nuclear material has been difficult. While international standards, guidelines and technical assistance often exist, governments are reluctant to share security information about potential vulnerabilities and detailed protection measures. This makes it hard to confirm that adequate security mechanisms are in place.

Best practices standards for physical protection have existed since *IAEA Information Circular 225* (1977) (Bunn 2007). Modern efforts start with the Convention on the Physical Protection of Nuclear Material (CPPNM), which entered into force in 1987. The CPPNM requires members to establish physical security over material that is imported, exported, or in transit across national borders; share information to facilitate the recovery and protection of stolen material; criminalize acts that use nuclear materials to harm the public; and prosecute or extradite those accused of such acts. However, the CPPNM only applies to nuclear materials being transported across national borders for peaceful purposes and leaves domestic security to individual states.

The UN Security Council moved to close these gaps by passing Resolution 1540 in 2004 (UN 2004). It calls on states to take domestic responsibility for establishing "appropriate" and "effective" protection measures for all nuclear, chemical, and biological materials and their means of delivery. This includes (1) implementing accounting and physical protection governing production, use, storage, and transportation, and (2) establishing export and transshipment controls. The UN also established a committee to interpret and aid states in implementing UNSCR1540. The committee began work by asking member states to submit national reports on their respective physical protection programs. However, implementation has been slowed by resistance to internationally mandated requirements in some countries and lack of resources in others. Furthermore, there are no formal measures for ensuring that countries comply with whatever international standards are eventually established.

In 2005, eighty-nine countries agreed to an Amended CPPNM that would require states (1) to physically protect domestic civilian nuclear facilities and materials, and (2) to enhance cooperation in locating and recovering stolen or smuggled nuclear materials. However, the amendment stops short of establishing uniform physical protection standards so that states will still have discretion to set standards based on their own individual threat assessments. The treaty is not yet in force.

Finally, the United States, Russia, and the G8 launched a Global Initiative to Combat Nuclear Terrorism in July 2006 which calls on "like-minded nations" and the IAEA to work together to "enhance the effectiveness of national systems for accounting, control, physical protection of nuclear materials and radioactive substances, and the security of civilian nuclear facilities, and, where necessary, to establish such systems." As of October 2006, sixty-two nations had joined this nonbinding partnership (U.S. Government 2006a) and were working to develop improved physical protection and accounting procedures for domestic nuclear materials. The United States has made it clear that it considers the Initiative a test of members' willingness to implement earlier promises under the International Convention for the Suppression of Acts of Nuclear Terrorism, the CPPNM, and UNSCR1540. That said, the Global Initiative, like UNSCR 1540, does not establish funding or verification mechanisms. For this reason, its practical impact will probably be limited (Nikitin 2006).

17.2.6 Interdiction and Enforcement

Not surprisingly, U.S. policy following September 11 included a renewed readiness to enforce international norms against WMD aggressively with methods up to and including armed interdiction. By far the most important example so far has been the U.S. interception of a North Korean ship carrying SCUD missiles destined for Libya in December 2002. The operation seems to have played a significant role in Libya's subsequent decision to renounce its WMD programs (Jentleson and Whytock 2005).

The United States further extended and formalized this program in 2003 by launching a Proliferation Security Initiative (PSI) to promote worldwide cooperation to prevent and interdict shipments of WMD and related materials by land, sea or air. Unlike previous treaties, agreements and U.S. programs, PSI was not based on formal multinational negotiations. Instead, it represents a "coalition of the willing" focused on promoting compliance with treaties and export control agreements that already exist but lack formal enforcement mechanisms. As of March 2007, over eighty countries had endorsed PSI's Statement of Interdiction Principles. Furthermore, seven had signed bilateral ship-boarding agreements that remove any legal obstacles that might have existed to interdicting WMD shipments at sea. PSI has since demonstrated several successful interdictions and was hailed by the Bush administration as an important nonproliferation and counterterrorism accomplishment.

17.3   Next Steps: Policy and Technology Tools

There is now widespread international recognition of the need to strengthen international and domestic controls on WMD along with their related materials, technologies, and expertise. Furthermore, many countries support more formal enforcement mechanisms for existing treaties, agreements, and commitments. This section reviews logical next steps that the international community can take to further reduce the threat of WMD terrorism.

17.3.1   Nuclear Weapons

Nuclear security will become steadily more important in coming decades as more and more countries expand their domestic nuclear fuel cycles and/or ship more nuclear fuel and waste across international borders. Existing initiatives to reduce nuclear weapons material stockpiles, safeguard peaceful uses of nuclear technology, and improve physical security are a good start. However, implementation is still not consistent and universal. Filling this gap will require a multifaceted strategy that understands that other countries may see threats differently, have different levels of technical development, and/or possess limited funding. In general, U.S. diplomacy will have to address four types of countries:

Like-minded nations   These nations already possess reasonably effective security programs but could still improve their nonproliferation and nuclear security practices by making them more consistent. They can also work together by offering their experience and resources to third countries. In this regard, it would be logical for the United States and Russia to collaborate in helping third countries implement UNSCR 1540 when the current G8 Global Partnership ends.

Nations that lack resources   These nations are committed to nonproliferation and terrorism prevention but will need help to implement needed programs and improvements effectively. The CTR program shows that supplying training and funds can close existing gaps and increase the number of states adhering to global norms and best practices. UNSCR 1540 would be an excellent vehicle for engaging these countries in efforts to improve nonproliferation and nuclear security measures.

Uncommitted countries   These states are indifferent to counterterrorism and nonproliferation issues but are potentially susceptible to diplomatic pressure to observe global norms and best practices. In a few cases, education and scientific engagement can help persuade governments and technical leaders that genuinely misunderstand the risks of WMD proliferation. Ferguson and Potter (2004) cite Pakistan as a prime example of country where greater engagement would likely improve nuclear security.

Defiant or "rogue" states   These states are largely indifferent to diplomatic pressure, conduct or support proliferation, and/or promote terrorism (Walt 2000). Improved technical means for detecting clandestine activities or shipments are essential to making existing initiatives and institutions (e.g., PSI, IAEA) effective. The world community should also make every effort to bring these countries under global nonproliferation and security norms at every opportunity. Current examples include Libya and potentially North Korea.

In principle, these approaches are not new and can be implemented using existing agreements, initiatives and treaties. UNSCR 1540, the G8 Global Partnership, IAEA, and NSG are among the most obvious frameworks for continuing the fight against nuclear terrorism. Improved detection of clandestine activities will be indispensable until rogue states and terrorists can be persuaded to accept global nonproliferation and counterterrorism norms. Conversely, the failure of these and other measures to stem nuclear proliferation would have a profoundly adverse effect on U.S. interests and international stability (Utgoff 2000).

17.3.2 Chemical Weapons

Existing treaties, agreements, and legislation have been reasonably successful in slowing the spread of traditional chemical weapons. Because the CWC has been signed by all but six nations, it is almost always possible to track official production and export of chemical weapons and/or their precursors. While the Australia Group is smaller, nonsignatories like China are at least publicly careful to adhere to its rules. For this reason, chemical weapons equipment and technology exports are similarly well controlled. This suggests that terrorists would find it hard to acquire chemical weapons or their immediate precursors from commercial markets.

The same level of tracking and control cannot be said to exist for TICs. Indeed, TICs are too ubiquitous and have too many civilian uses for such strategies to work. Instead, the only feasible response is to increase security systems around their storage and transport. In order to be effective, such systems will have to be worldwide and this will require additional agreements between nations.

Emerging industrial powers like India and China are problematic in other ways. Because their chemical industries are growing at an explosive pace, host countries may not be able to track the construction and operation of individual plants. Under these circumstances, terrorists might be able to obtain chemical weapons precursors without the host government's knowledge in much the same way that Aum Shinrikyo operated its disguised weapons factory in Japan. This danger could be reduced if nations shared more information. For example, an international agreement to share shipping receipts could help host nations identify unregulated plants operating within their borders. Such an agreement would also make it harder for host nations to turn a blind eye toward rogue factions like the A. Q. Khan network.

17.3.3 Biological Weapons

We have seen that biological weapons production is characterized by multiple, individually small but collectively important failure modes. A coherent security policy must carefully target these points.

Enhancing Detection   Compared to other forms of WMD, biological weapons labs and factories have few physical signatures. This means that authorities must be sensitive to unusual patterns of commercial transactions, communications, and tips from the general public. This suggests that policies should be aimed at increasing transparency and visibility wherever possible. Existing regulatory regimes for commercial and university biotech facilities in the developed world are a good start. Minor changes in these regimes could make bioterrorism significantly harder, with relatively little impact on legitimate research. Biosecurity policy can also take advantage of business models in which equipment suppliers typically continue selling support services, advice, and consumables for the life of their products. Encouraging suppliers and distributors to watch for and report suspicious behavior would create a significant security risk for terrorists.

More formal measures are also possible. One possibility is to implement a registration system for domestic equipment, technical support, and supplies so that the Australia Group requirements could be extended to domestic transactions. Registration would also simplify efforts to monitor equipment sales on secondary markets. Regulations requiring more government officials and corporate officers to countersign transfers of dangerous pathogens would similarly complicate covert transactions without placing an excessive burden on legitimate activities.

Finally, current Australia Group guidelines were designed in an era when the principal threat was battlefield-scale production by state programs. However, laboratory-scale processes may often be sufficient to support terrorist attacks. Cutting Australia Group exemptions from, say, twenty-liter fermenters down to ten would be relatively easy.[18] This comparatively modest change would force terrorists to extend production runs, potentially aggravating other problems involving safety, shelf life, and risk of discovery. In some cases, terrorists could decide to scale back or cancel attacks altogether.

Inhibiting Recruitment   We have emphasized that bioterrorists will often need to recruit outside experts or, at a minimum obtain advice from researchers working on biotechnology, infectious disease, or biodefense. Shrewd policy interventions can increase the chance that recipients will recognize such request for what they are and report them. One way to do this is to promote professional *codes of ethics* that reinforce researchers' existing norms against weapons work and create a duty to investigate (and possibly report) suspected violations. Recent proposals that would require researchers to seek institution-level review before performing certain experiments (NSABB 2006a) would similarly raise awareness and increase transparency. One natural corollary to this approach would be to establish "whistleblower" procedures at the national level to detect cases where review was bypassed. Such structures should be housed in national public health/research agencies instead of law enforcement so that the information does not routinely lead to prosecutions that would deter scientists from becoming whistleblowers in the first place.[19]

Finally, oversight and monitoring of the United States's roughly 1,400 BSL-3 facilities is currently spread across multiple, poorly coordinated agencies. Consolidating authority within one or two agencies would markedly improve the government's ability to detect suspicious activities (GAO 2007a).

Limiting Access to Pathogens   U.S. pathogen controls are based on the CDC's very comprehensive "Select Agent" list of microorganisms that can be used to make weapons. By comparison, most international controls tend to be uneven and incomplete. Diplomatic initiatives under the BWC or Australia Group could potentially improve the situation by making the CDC list universal. Furthermore, the CDC list could itself be improved by prioritizing agents according to their contagiousness and/or by whether they exhibit moderate to high morbidity and lethality. This would allow the CDC to impose more stringent controls on the comparatively small number of pathogens that are most likely to be useful in developing an effective weapon.

17.4   Conclusion

Preventing WMD terrorism will require the international community to work together to stop the spread of WMD expertise and technology, secure existing weapons and materials, and detect and intercept illicit trafficking. Fortunately, the need to strengthen and implement international and domestic controls is widely recognized and has already produced many useful treaties, agreements, initiatives, and high-level political statements. The task now is to fill the remaining gaps in political commitment, technical means and resources. Better implementation of existing mechanisms will go a long way toward preventing proliferation and terrorism. Improved coordination among the various international efforts and/or between international efforts and domestic security programs would also help.

Even so, complex political environments will continue to make effective enforcement difficult. Future diplomatic efforts can go some distance toward bolstering the international community's willingness to enforce existing treaties, agreements, and commitments. In the near term, the most critical challenges will almost certainly turn on whether Western sanctions and incentives are effective in persuading North Korea and Iran to relinquish their nuclear weapons programs and, beyond this, agree to intrusive and sustained international inspections. As this book goes to press, both states are still conducting nuclear weapons proliferation activities.[20] If today's complex U.S., multilateral, and international measures fail, North Korean and Iranian successes could trigger a cascade of state proliferators. This, in turn, would greatly increase the chances that terrorists could gain access to nuclear materials and even nuclear weapons themselves.

In the long run, it is reasonable to hope that the current patchwork of treaties, programs, and agreements may lead to comprehensive international verification regimes for preventing proliferation. Until then, improved technical methods will be needed to detect noncompliance. This task will often fall to the developed nations.

Notes

1. A. Q. Khan, the father of Pakistan's nuclear weapons program, clandestinely operated an international nuclear weapons technology trafficking network (Langewiesche 2005, 2007). Khan was released from house arrest in 2009.

2. Nuclear material has reportedly been seized from Russia and neighboring countries more than a dozen times since the early 1990s. Interested readers should consult Moody et al. 2005 for a detailed history of these events and detailed trend data. So far, however, the total amount of stolen fissionable material has been insignificant (NRC/Committee on Science and Technology 2002; Coll 2007). Readers interested in the current state of Russian nuclear security should consult Matthew Bunn's ongoing status reports—for example, Bunn 2007.

3. An additional source of uncertainty comes from the fact that the term "WMD" embraces a wide variety of possible weapons. As a result, a precise risk assessment will normally depend on the types of attacks being considered. These, in turn, must be compared against terrorists' existing capabilities and ability to call on outside suppliers for materials and/or technical expertise.

4. Special Nuclear Material (SNM), also known as weapons-usable fissile material, is either highly enriched uranium (U-235) or plutonium (Pu-239).

5. Mark Rowland, scientist at Lawrence Livermore National Laboratory, personal communication.

6. Some have questioned Chechen rebel leader Shamil Basayev's claims that the container was attached to an explosive device. Whether or not this is true, adding explosives would have been trivial. The capability clearly existed.

7. The legislation was sponsored by Senators Sam Nunn and Richard Lugar.

8. "Commoditized knowledge," for which standard training is widely available either within institutions or on the open market, represents a kind of middle-ground between explicit and tacit knowledge.

9. There is little evidence that Al Qaeda's program progressed beyond the "conceptual level" (Leitenberg 2004).

10. Aum's chemist successfully synthesized all of the major chemical weapons agents, including nitrogen mustard, sarin, and VX (Lifton 1999), most likely by finding and using recipes from publicly available journals and patents.

11. Chemical warfare agents are markedly more hazardous than most toxic industrial chemicals (Senior 1958) and would be dangerous to handle. It is worth noting that the (Provisional) IRA lost 120 members to accidental bomb accidents and shootings between 1970 and 1978 (Jackson 2001). This figure was only slightly lower than the 135 lost to British security forces in the same period (Fay, Morrisey, and Smyth 1998). Additionally, some (though not all) groups may have observed the chemical weapons taboo for political reasons. For example, the Tamil Tigers used TICs against a Sri Lankan military camp in 1990 but have refrained since then, at least in part because they wanted to appeal to an international audience (Jackson 2001).

12. The challenge has been understood for decades (Ikle 1961).

13. By creating a separate initiative, DOE consolidated the management of the Russian Research Reactor Fuel Return, the Reduced Enrichment for Research and Test Reactors, the Foreign Research Reactor Spent Nuclear Fuel Acceptance, and the Radiological Threat Reduction programs.

14. Equivalent to more than 30,000 nuclear weapons.

15. In addition to Russia, the ISTC funds scientists in Armenia, Belarus, Georgia, Kazakhstan, Kyrgyzstan, and Tajikistan. The U.S. side of the program is run by the State Department. For more on the history of the ISTC, see Schweitzer 1996.

16. The Group of Eight (G8) includes the United States, United Kingdom, Canada, France, Germany, Italy, Japan, and Russia.

17. The Iraqi program was eventually able to scavenge fermenters from an old vaccine factory. However, this work-around delayed the program and, in any case, would not have been available to terrorists (Pearson 2006).

18. Fermenters of less than twenty liters' capacity are already included in the Australia Group's awareness-raising guidelines.

19. The main challenge for such national-level whistleblower structures would be to remain focused on bioterrorism instead of broadening their mandate to enforce safety, best practices, or scientific ethics. Punishing simple sloppiness or attempts to shortcut red tape will quickly

erode scientists' willingness to report transgressions. Most agencies do not have enough bio-defense experts to staff a whistleblower function and would have to recruit them.

20. North Korea announced that it had suspended its plutonium reprocessing program and demolished its symbolic cooling tower at Yong Byon in mid-2008. As this is being written, however, it still had not met U.S. demands to document all of its nuclear activities (including uranium enrichment and reprocessing) despite promises that this would lead to the lifting of sanctions and the normalization of economic relations (Cooper 2008). Similarly, a U.S. National Intelligence Estimate written in 2007 found that Iran continues to maintain active enrichment even though it has apparently halted its weapons design program (Linzer and Warrick 2007).

18
Summing Up

Stephen M. Maurer

Eight years after September 11, no one should think that the United States knows everything it needs to know about the WMD terrorism problem, let alone what to do next. Still, readers who have come this far will appreciate just how much has been learned. The country has made a good beginning.

There is no avoiding the fact that WMD terrorism is different from other public policy subjects. Part of this is cultural. Unlike, say, housing policy, the idea of WMD terrorism is eye-catching—and Hollywood works hard to keep it that way. In the popular imagining, "WMD" has never been a set of specific, nuts-and-bolts technologies so much as a modern myth. Today's public sees every CBRN threat, regardless of type (or even scale), in terms of unlimited devastation (chapter 16). The fact that this is not even true for nuclear weapons—remediation clearly matters and much more could be done (chapter 12)—is neither here nor there. As Herman Kahn (1962) remarked more than forty years ago, people find the idea that everyone will die peculiarly comforting. By comparison, thinking about survival opens the door to a series of unpleasant discussions. WMD's dark glamour is seductive precisely because it makes these conversations unnecessary. Yet we have also seen that civil defense is a potentially powerful lever for minimizing casualties (chapters 3, 10, 12). Given how much our political classes talk about WMD terrorism, the absence of any practical information that would allow the public to protect itself is astonishing. How hard would it be to send civil defense information to every home in America? To broadcast public service messages urging the public to see past its passivity and fatalism? Or even return to the schoolyard drills of the 1950s?

As usual in a democracy, the fault is mostly our own. In the psychobabble of day-time television, we the public are "in avoidance," and politicians who know what's good for them had better "facilitate" us. Worse, Washington partisans can be reliably counted on to ridicule any leader who suggests that a WMD attack could actually happen, let alone admits that federal help might not arrive for hours or even days. Still, one can imagine politicians limiting partisanship long enough to teach the public how to protect itself, just as an earlier generation boasted that the country's internal political quarrels "stopped at the water's edge." The deeper problem is that most politicians believe the myth of all-destroying CBRN just as much as their constituents do. To talk of WMD terrorism as an "existential threat" and "unbounded risk,"[1] as academics too often do, is a profoundly disabling conceit. Infinite threats, after all, seem to call for infinite solutions. All sensible public policy starts by characterizing (and bounding) the problem.

This, of course, is exactly the sort of clear thinking that academics are supposed to do. While quantitative cost-benefit analyses (chapter 7) are still in their infancy, certain observations seem safe. The fact that great powers have developed a wide variety of CBRN weapons shows that WMD is possible; on the other hand, the fact that these programs have usually cost billons of dollars suggests that it is hard. Furthermore, we have seen that terrorists would have to succeed at multiple R&D tasks to acquire genuine WMD capabilities (chapters 3, 4) and that even the largest terrorist organizations have limited budgets, limited expertise, limited time horizons, and above all limited tolerance for technical risk (chapters 1, 2). These simple observations already offer an important insight: In a world where even middle-tier state programs (e.g., Iraq) take years, terrorist leaders will think long and hard before committing themselves to expensive multiyear development programs that may never come to anything or, worse still, invite ridicule. WMD is not nearly as good an investment as, naively, it might seem to be.

Furthermore, those terrorists who do go forward will continue to have doubts and may, quite rationally, abandon their R&D at the first setback. Critics like to complain that "a determined terrorist" can surmount, say, efforts to restrict access to ex-Soviet nuclear materials or American dual-use technologies (chapter 17), screen commercial orders for artificial DNA (chapter 4), or inspect cargo shipments at U.S. ports (chapter 6). This is true but irrelevant. If we grant that terrorist WMD involves a long chain of steps each of which has some modest possibility of failure, adding a few more hurdles—even minor ones—will often be sensible policy. It is not enough for would-be WMD terrorists to reassure themselves that they might possibly succeed. They must also consider how easy it is to fail. Policy initiatives that add even modest additional risk could easily persuade them that this already-marginal option is not worth pursuing.

The other side of the coin is that governments, too, should act as if WMD was a limited threat. Of course, in a practical sense this is true already—the federal budget, unlike politicians' "unbounded threats" rhetoric, is finite. Still, it would be good for politicians to admit the fact. It is not hard to find examples of projects—for example, civil defense and nuclear recovery technologies (chapter 12)—that seem grossly underfunded. Conversely, it is hard to resist the conclusion that some spending has been more symbolic than rational (chapter 8). In principle, reallocation should be obvious and easy. But this is exactly where America's homeland defense rhetoric makes it hard for politicians to cut any WMD defense program, ever. Recognizing that the total budget is fixed, and that defense programs really do compete with each other, would be a much healthier discussion.

None of this addresses the deeper question of whether government is spending its dollars wisely. Projects like stabilizing insurance markets (chapter 9), creating incentives for vaccine development (chapter 15), and setting cleanup standards that minimize the cost of an anthrax or radiological attack (chapter 13) are so unlike earlier challenges that business-as-usual approaches are bound to fail. Shortly after September 11, it looked like Washington politicians really would start with a blank sheet of paper. The picture today is very different. Airport screening has become a fight over federal unions, cleanup standards are entangled with fossilized arguments about nuclear power (chapter 6), and Congress conducts innovation policy by asking the drug companies which incentives they prefer (chapter 8). These are significant problems and the danger of failure is real. Even in the pharmaceutical business, the Bioshield program's $5.6 billion budget should have produced several products by now. Instead, there is almost nothing to show for it and no particular reason to expect more from Bioshield II. Similarly, we have seen that cleanup costs and economic disruptions will almost certainly dominate damages from a radiological attack (chapter 14). In this environment, seemingly minor changes in which areas are placed off limits and for how long can make a large difference in society's bottom line. One would think that authorities would want to have this information before setting standards, but this has not happened.

It would be easy to dismiss these results as "political," except that the deeper problem looks very much like a lack of imagination. Washington bureaucrats routinely point out that terrorists can get know-how and materials from the world's vast network of academic science and commercial firms, and then complain that these are impossible to regulate. This is foolish for at least two reasons. First, the WMD terrorism threat is, by any reasonable measure, far smaller than the Soviet Union's multiton stockpiles of nuclear, chemical, and biological weapons. If the Soviet Union did not buy what it needed from Western companies and universities, it was because they already had an entire continent to exploit. Can it really be that Washington has grown nostalgic for such an enemy? More importantly, no one ever said that the old Cold War methods of regulation and treaty were right for every problem. Sixty years ago, U.S. academic scientists stopped publishing atomic experiments and crippled Germany's atomic bomb program (Weart 1976). Twenty years ago, U.S. companies refused and later reported legal-but-suspicious orders from customers like Saddam Hussein and Aum Shinrikyo (chapter 17). Government can and should encourage such private-sector behavior again, even if it means making citizens partners—and, less conveniently, giving them a voice in their own security.

Reaching out to the public is, at least, is a familiar activity. Policymakers have far fewer precedents when it comes to intervening in markets. Government is right to worry that commercial know-how has begun to threaten its traditional WMD monopoly, but the story should not end there. The fact that markets reach across national borders also offers enormous opportunities. To take just one example, we have seen that terrorists may soon be able to resurrect otherwise-unobtainable diseases like 1918 influenza and smallpox from artificial DNA (chapter 4). Clearly, the world's eighty or so gene synthesis companies should screen orders before filling them. In the old way of doing things, this would require years of treaty negotiation and (witness black-market music sales in China) might not work even then. But suppose NIH told its grant recipients to stop buying from gene synthesis companies that failed to screen orders? Suddenly, screening would become a profit center—and in a global market that would be true everywhere, even in China (Maurer and Zoloth 2007). For this problem, at least, market interventions seem to be both quicker and more effective than any plausible treaty.

The old Cold War days when governments could safely ignore the private sector are gone, and it will take time for policymakers to learn how to manipulate the new levers (chiefly markets) effectively. But they have made a start. The influential National Science Advisory Board for Biosecurity has embraced the idea of using NIH's market power to promote responsible screening (NSABB 2006b), and this has made government policymakers noticeably more receptive to the idea than they were even a few years ago. Meanwhile, private sector gene synthesis companies have launched their own voluntary measures to make screening more powerful and uniform (IASB, 2008), and government is paying close attention. The challenge now is to generalize these small and tentative steps into a strategy broad enough to cope with the global biotechnology industry. Persuading companies to take biotechnology seriously— and sometimes even alter their services and products to avoid abuse—will clearly demand imaginative new tactics. That said, there is no need for government to reinvent the wheel. Economists and social scientists have thought about incentive design for years. Why not ask them?

Terrorism has always been a marginal strategy (chapter 1), even if the world's young people tend to forget—and then relearn—this lesson every generation or so. Convincing people to die for a glorious vision is depressingly easy, but it gets much harder when nothing changes and the martyrs start to look like suckers and jerks. However motivational, Bin Laden's goal of a pan-Arab Caliphate, let alone an Islamic planet, is ludicrously unachievable. Once the followers catch on, Al Qaeda will have to settle for something less or else disappear entirely. WMD is clearly the wild card in the deck, yet it, too, is a long shot. The task now is to find clever, cost-effective public policy interventions to make it even more remote. It is customary to end a book like this by saying that more study is needed, and the preceding chapters have identified many questions where this observation is justified. At the same time, scholars have learned a great deal about WMD terrorism in the years since September 11. Unlike, say, astronomy or German literature, there is no particular interest in studying homeland security for its own sake. However imperfect, our current understanding of WMD terrorism already offers U.S. leaders powerful levers for making society safer and happier. America needs to start using what it knows.

Note

1. See, for example, "Managing the Unbounded Risk," http://gspp.berkeley.edu/iths/conference.html.

Table of Abbreviations

ANI	American Nuclear Insurers. An insurance pool for U.S. nuclear power plants.
APHIS	U.S. Agricultural and Plant Health Inspection Service
ASP	Advanced Spectroscopic Portal. A type of large cargo-screening portal.
BARDA	HHS Biomedical Advanced Research and Development Authority
CBD	Los Angeles Central Business District
CBP	U.S. Customs and Border Patrol
CBRN	Chemical, biological, radiological, and nuclear weapons
CDC	U.S. Centers for Disease Control and Prevention, formerly the U.S. Centers for Disease Control
CEA	California Earthquake Authority
CIA	U.S. Central Intelligence Agency
C-TPAT	Customs Trade Partnership Against Terrorism Project
DARPA	DoD Defense Advanced Research Projects Agency
DHS	U.S. Department of Homeland Security
DMORT	Disaster Mortuary Operational Response Teams
DNDO	U.S. Domestic Nuclear Detection Office
DNI	U.S. Director of National Intelligence
DoD	U.S. Department of Defense
DOE	U.S. Department of Energy
E2E	End to End Innovation Incentives. Innovation incentive schemes that rely on a single reward payable on completion of the project.
EMAC	Emergency Mutual Assistance Compact. Agreement governing federal-state disaster assistance and cooperation.

EPA	U.S. Environmental Protection Agency
ERT-A	Emergency Response Team—Advance Element
ESAR-VHP	Emergency System for Advance Registration of Volunteer Health Professionals
ESF	Emergency Support Functions
FBI	U.S. Federal Bureau of Investigation
FCC	U.S. Federal Communications Commission
FEMA	U.S. Federal Emergency Management Agency
FMD	Foot-and-mouth disease
GAO	U.S. General Accountability Office, formerly the U.S. General Accounting Office.
GIS	Geographic Information System. A computerized system for storing and analyzing geographic data.
GPS	Global Positioning System. A satellite-based system for determining location on the surface of the earth.
HAN	Health Alert Network
HEICS	Hospital Emergency Incident Command System
HEU	Highly Enriched Uranium
HHS	U.S. Department of Health and Human Services
HRSA	Health Resources and Services Administration
HSARPA	DHS Homeland Security Advanced Research Projects Agency
ICS	Incident Command System
ILS	Insurance Linked Securitization
INS	Incident of National Significance
INS	U.S. Immigration and Naturalization Service
JCAHO	Joint Commission on Accreditation of Healthcare Organizations
JIC	Joint Information Center
JOC	Joint Operations Center
LC_{50}	Lethal concentration–50. The concentration of poison in air needed to kill half of all exposed victims.
LCCS	London Congestion Charging Scheme
LD_{50}	Lethal dose–50. The total amount of poison (in grams) needed to kill half of all exposed victims.

LIBOR	The London Interbank Offered Rate. A benchmark interest rate against which other interest rates are measured.
LRN	Laboratory Response Network
MRC	Medical Reserve Corps
NBHPP	National Bioterrorism Hospital Preparedness Program
NCTC	National Counterterrorism Center
NDMS	National Disaster Medical System
NEDSS	National Electronic Disease Surveillance System
NFI	National Flood Insurance program
NIEMO	National Interstate Economic Model
NIMS	National Incident Management System
NNDSS	National Notifiable Diseases Surveillance System
NRC	U.S. Nuclear Regulatory Commission
NRP	National Response Plan
OSHA	U.S. Occupational Safety and Health Administration
PA Act	Price Anderson Act. U.S. legislation limiting nuclear power plant liability.
PaYG	Pay as you go. Innovation incentive schemes offering rewards at multiple points along the R&D process.
PTSD	Post-Traumatic Stress Disorder
R_0	Reproduction number. The number of new persons who would be infected by a single infectious host absent control measures.
R&D	Research and development
RDD	Radioactive dispersion device. A weapon that spreads radioactive contaminants in the open air, sometimes informally referred to as a "dirty bomb."
SCPM	Southern California Planning Model
SNS	U.S. Strategic National Stockpile of drugs and medical supplies.
T_G	Generation time. The time that a primary case takes to infect secondary cases.
TAZ	Traffic Analysis Zone. Los Angeles County geographic designation similar to a census tract.
TICs	Toxic industrial chemicals. Commercially available chemicals that are potentially usable as weapons.

TOPOFF	Congressionally mandated series of WMD exercises involving top state and federal leaders
TRIA	Terrorism Risk Insurance Act of 2002
TRIEA	Terrorism Risk Insurance Extension Act
WMD	Weapon(s) of mass destruction

References

9/11 Commission. *See* National Commission on Terrorist Attacks upon the United States.

AAAS. *See* American Association for the Advancement of Science.

Abadie, Alberto, and Sofia Dermisi. 2006. Is Terrorism Eroding Agglomeration Economies in Central Business Districts? Lessons from the Office Market in Downtown Chicago. National Bureau of Economic Research Working Paper no. 12678.

ACA. *See* Arms Control Association.

ACGIH. *See* American Conference of Industrial Hygienists.

Ackerman, Gary A., and Jeffrey M. Bale. *Al-Qāʿida and Weapons of Mass Destruction*. CNS Research Report, 2002. http://www.cns.miis.edu/pubs/other/alqwmd.htm.

ACS. *See* American Cancer Society.

Adamovicz, Jeffrey J., Erica P. Wargo, and David M. Waag. 2006. "Tularemia." In James R. Swearengen, ed., *Biodefense: Research Methodology and Animal Models*, 137–162. Boca Raton, FL: CRC/Taylor & Francis Group.

Advanced Markets Working Group. 2002. *Making Markets for Vaccines: A Practical Plan to Spark Innovation for Global Health*. Washington, D.C.: Center for Global Development & Global Health Policy Research Network. http://www.who.int/intellectualproperty/news/en/SubmissionBarder1.pdf.

AFRRI. *See* Armed Forces Radiobiology Research Institute.

Agence France Presse. 2005. "US Senate Leader Urges 'Manhattan Project' against Bio-Terror Threat." January 27. http://findarticles.com/p/articles/mi_kmafp/is_200501/ai_n13263152.

Agency for Healthcare Research and Quality. 2005. *National Hospital Available Beds for Emergencies and Disasters (HAvBED) System: Final Report*. AHRQ Publication no. 05-0103. http://www.ahrq.gov/research/havbed/.

Aghassi, Michelle, and Dimitris Bertsimas. 2006. "Robust Game Theory." *Mathematical Programming (B)* 107: 231–273.

Agranoff, Robert. 1989. "Managing Intergovernmental Processes." In J. L. Perry, ed., *Handbook of Public Administration*, 131–147. San Francisco: Jossey-Bass.

AHA. *See* American Hospital Association.

AHRQ. *See* Agency for Healthcare Research and Quality.

Aiba, Suichi, Arthur E. Humphrey, and Nancy F. Millis. 1973. *Biochemical Engineering*. 2nd ed. San Diego, CA: Academic Press.

AIHA. *See* American Industrial Hygiene Association.

Aitken, Martin J. 1985. *Thermoluminescence Dating*. New York: Academic Press.

Albright, David, Cory Hinderstein, and Holly Higgins. 2002. "Does Al Qaeda have Nuclear Materials? Doubtful, But. . . ." Institute for Science and International Security Web Page. http://www.isis-online.org/publications/terrorism/doubtful.html.

Aldhouse, Peter. 2005. "The Bioweapon Is in the Post: Firms That Make DNA to Order Could Unwittingly Find Themselves Doing Business with Terrorists." *New Scientist*, November 12, 8–9.

Aldis, Geoffrey K., and M. G. Roberts. 2005. "An Integral Equation Model for the Control of a Smallpox Epidemic." *Mathematical Biosciences* 195: 1–22.

Alexander, David A., and Susan Klein. 2003. "Biochemical Terrorism: Too Awful to Contemplate, Too Serious to Ignore." *British Journal of Psychiatry* 183: 491–497.

Alexander, George A., Harold M. Swartz, Sally A. Amundson, William F. Blakely, Brooke Buddemeier, Bernard Gallez, Nicholas Dainiak, Ronald E. Goans, et al. 2007. "EPR–2006 Meeting: Acute Dosimetry Consensus Committee Recommendations on Biodosimetry Applications in Events Involving Uses of Radiation by Terrorists and Radiation Accidents." *Radiation Measurements* 42: 972–977.

Alexander, Martin. 2001. *Biodegradation and Bioremediation*. 2nd ed. San Diego, CA: Academic Press.

Alibek, Ken, and C. Bailey. 2004. "Bioshield or Biogap?" *Biosecurity and Bioterrorism: Strategy, Practice, and Science* 2: 132.

Alibek, Ken, and Stephen Handelman. 1999. *Biohazard: The Chilling True Story of the Largest Covert Biological Weapons Program in the World—Told from Inside by the Man Who Ran It*. New York: Random House.

Allanach, J., Haiying Tu, S. Singh, P. Willett, and K. Pattipati. 2004. "Detecting, Tracking, and Counteracting Terrorist Networks via Hidden Markov Models." *Proceedings of the 2004 IEEE Aerospace Conference* 5: 3246–3257.

Allison, Graham. 2001. "Could Worse Be Yet to Come?" *The Economist*, November 1.

Allison, Graham. 2004. *Nuclear Terrorism: The Ultimate Preventable Catastrophe*. New York: Henry Holt.

Aloise, Gene. 2007. *Combating Nuclear Smuggling: DHS's Decision to Procure and Deploy the Next Generation of Radiation Detection Equipment Is Not Supported by Its Cost-Benefit Analysis*. GAO Report no. GA0–07–581T. http://www.gao.gov/new.items/d05840t.pdf.

Alvarez, Luis W., Jared A. Anderson, F. El Bedewi, James Burkhard, Ahmed Fakhry, Adib Girgis, Amr Goenied, Fikhry Hassan, et al. 1970. "Search for Hidden Chambers in the Pyramids." *Science* 167: 832–839.

American Academy of Actuaries. 2006. "Public Comment to President's Working Group on Financial Markets." April 21. http://www.actuary.org/pdf/casualty/tris_042106.pdf.

American Association for the Advancement of Science. 2007. "AAAS R&D Funding Update on DHS R&D in FY 2008 House Appropriations." http://www.aaas.org/spp/rd/dhs08h .htm#tb.

American Cancer Society. 2007. "Cancer Facts & Figures 2007." Atlanta, GA: ACS. http:// www.cancer.org/downloads/STT/CAFF2007PWSecured.pdf.

American Conference of Governmental Industrial Hygienists. 2003. *TLVs and BEIs, Based on the Documentation of the Threshold Limit Values for Chemical Substances and Physical Agents and Biological Exposure Indices.* Cincinnati, OH: ACGIH.

American Enterprise Institute. 2007. *America and the War on Terrorism.* Washington, DC: American Enterprise Institute. http://www.aei.org/docLib/20050805_terror0805.pdf.

American Hospital Association. n.d. "Fast Facts on US Hospitals." http://www.aha.org/aha/ resource-center/Statistics-and-Studies/fast-facts.html.

American Industrial Hygiene Association. 2004. *Emergency Response Planning Guidelines & Workplace Environmental Exposure Level Guides.* Fairfax, VA: AIHA.

Anderson, Elizabeth. 2002. Special Issue: "Assessing the Risks of Terrorism: A Special Collection of Perspectives Articles by Former Presidents of the Society for Risk Analysis." *Risk Analysis* 22, no. 3.

Anderson, Patrick L., and Ilhan K. Geckil. 2002. "Flash Estimate: Impact of West Coast Shutdown." Lansing, MI: Anderson Economic Group, October 15. http://www .andersoneconomicgroup.com/modules.php?name=Content&pa=display_aeg&doc_ID=545.

Anderson, Roy M., and Robert M. May. 1991. *Infectious Diseases of Humans: Dynamics and Control.* Oxford: Oxford University Press.

Andersson, Kasper G., and Jorn Roed. 1999. "A Nordic Preparedness Guide for Early Cleanup in Radioactively Contaminated Residential Areas." *Journal of Environmental. Radioactivity* 46: 207–223.

Angulo, Elena, and Ben Gilna. 2008. "When Biotech Crosses Borders." *Nature Biotechnology* 26: 277–282.

Anno, G. H., R. W. Young, R. M. Bloom, and J. R. Mercier. 2003. "Dose Response Relationships for Acute Ionizing-Radiation Lethality." *Health Physics* 84: 565–575.

Aon Group. 2006. "Response to US Treasury Final Report." Unpublished. http://www.aon.com/ us/busi/risk_management/risk_transfer/terrorism/AonFinalTreasuryReportResponseApril2006 .pdf.

Aparicio, Juan Pablo, and Mercedes Pascual. 2007. "Building Epidemiological Models from R_0: An Implicit Treatment of Transmission in Networks." *Proceedings of the Royal Society (B)* 274: 505–512.

Apostolakis, George E., and Douglas Lemon. 2005. "A Screening Methodology for the Identification and Ranking of Infrastructure Vulnerabilities Due to Terrorism." *Risk Analysis* 25: 361–376.

Argonne National Laboratory. 2005. "Human Health Fact Sheet: Radiological Dispersal Device (RDD)." http://www.mipt.org/pdf/Radiological-Dispersal-Device-RDD.pdf.

Armed Forces Radiobiology Research Institute. 2003. *Medical Management of Radiological Casualties Handbook.* 2nd ed. Bethesda, MD: AFRRI, 2003. http://www.afrri.usuhs.mil/www/outreach/pdf/2edmmrchandbook.pdf.

Arms Control Association. 2005. "The 2005 NPT Review Conference: Can It Meet the Nuclear Challenge?" http://www.armscontrol.org/act/2005_04/duPreez.asp.

Arms Control Association. 2006. "The 1997 IAEA Additional Protocol at a Glance." http://www.armscontrol.org/factsheets/IAEAProtocol.asp.

Arnon, Stephen, Robert Schechter, Thomas V. Inglesby, Donald A. Henderson, John G. Bartlett, Michael S. Ascher, Edward Eitzen, et al. 2001. "Botulinum Toxin as a Biological Weapon: Medical and Public Health Management." *Journal of the American Medical Association* 285: 1059–1070.

Arrow, Kenneth. 1965. *Essays in the Theory of Risk Bearing.* Chicago: Markham Publishing Co.

Arterbery, V. Elayne, William A. Pryor, Long Jiang, Shelley S. Sehnert, W. Michael Foster, Ross A. Abrams, Jerry R. Williams, Moody D. Wharam, and Terence H. Risby. 1994. "Breath Ethane Generation during Clinical Total Body Irradiation as a Marker of Oxygen-Free-Radical-Mediated Lipid Peroxidation: A Case Study." *Free Radical Biology and Medicine* 17: 569–576.

ASPR. *See* Department of Health and Human Services/Assistant Secretary for Preparedness and Response.

Assim, Jabari. 2005. "African-Americans and the AIDS Conspiracy." *Washington Post*, January 31. http://www.washingtonpost.com/wp-dyn/articles/A51120-2005Jan31.html.

Association of State and Territorial Health Officials. 2005. "Intrastate Coordination of Mass Prophylaxis Caches." ASTHO Issue Brief. http://www.astho.org/pubs/MassProphylaxsis.pdf.

ASTHO. *See* Association of State and Territorial Health Officials.

Atkinson, Robert. 2001. *How Technology Can Help Make Air Travel Safe Again.* Progressive Policy Institute Report. http://www.ppionline.org/documents/Airport_Security_092501.pdf.

Atuhaire, Bernard. 2003. *The Uganda Cult Tragedy: A Private Investigation.* London: Janus.

Australia Group. 2007. "The Origins of the Australia Group." http://www.australiagroup.net/en/origins.html.

Bailer, Uri. 1980. *The Shadow of the Bomber: The Fear of Air Attack and British Politics, 1932–39.* London: Royal Historical Society.

Bailey, Norman T. J. 1967. *The Mathematical Approach to Biology and Medicine.* London: Wiley.

Bailey, Norman T. J., and J. Duppenthaler. 1980. "Sensitivity Analysis in the Modeling of Infectious Diseases Dynamics." *Journal of Mathematical Biology* 10: 113–131.

Balch, Robert W. 1995. "Waiting for the Ships: Disillusionment and the Revitalization of Faith in Bo and Peep's UFO Cult." In James Lewis, ed., *The Gods Have Landed: New Religions from Other Worlds*, 137–166. Albany: State University of New York Press.

Balch, Robert W., and David Taylor. 2002. "Making Sense of the Heaven's Gate Suicides." In David G. Bromley and J. Gordon Melton, eds., *Cults, Religion, and Violence*, 209–228. New York: Cambridge University Press.

Baldassare, Mark, Christopher Hoene, and Jonathan Cohen. 2006. *Local Homeland Security in California: Surveys of City Officials and State Residents.* Public Policy Institute of California Research Report.

Bale, Jeffrey M. 2001. "Terrorism, Right-Wing." In Bernard A. Cook, ed., *Europe since 1945: An Encyclopedia*, vol. 2, 1238–1240. New York: Garland.

Bale, Jeffrey M. 2004a. "Islamism." In Richard F. Pilch and Raymond Zilinskas, eds., *Encyclopedia of Bioterrorism Defense*, 296–298. New York: Wiley.

Bale, Jeffrey M. 2004b. "Responses to Questions Concerning CBRN Terrorism." Unpublished ms.

Bale, Jeffrey M. 2006. "South Africa's Project Coast: 'Death Squads,' Covert State-Sponsored Poisonings, and the Dangers of CBW Proliferation." *Democracy and Security* 2: 27–59.

Bale, Jeffrey M., and Gary Ackerman. 2005. *Recommendations on the Development of Methodologies and Attributes for Assessing Terrorist Threats of WMD Terrorism.* CNS Research Report.

Bale, Jeffrey M., Anjali Bhattacharjee, Eric Croddy, and Richard Pilch. 2003. *Ricin Reportedly Found in London: An al-Qā'ida Connection?* CNS Research Report. http://cns.miis.edu/pubs/reports.ricin.htm.

Ball, Deborah Yarsike, and Theodore P. Gerber. 2005. "Russian Scientists and Rogue States: Does Western Assistance Reduce the Proliferation Threat?" *International Security* 29: 50–77.

Barbera, Joseph, Anthony Macintyre, Larry Gostin, Thomas Inglesby, Tara O'Toole, Craig DeAtley, Kevin Tonat, and Marci Layton. 2001. "Large-Scale Quarantine Following Biological Terrorism in the United States: Scientific Examination, Logistic and Legal Limits, and Possible Consequences." *Journal of the American Medical Association* 286: 2711–2717.

Bard, Jonathan F. 1998. *Practical Bilevel Optimization: Algorithms and Applications.* Netherlands: Kluwer.

Bardach, Eugene. 1998. *Getting Agencies to Work Together: The Practice and Theory of Managerial Craftsmanship.* Washington, DC: Brookings Institution Press.

Bardach, Eugene. 2008. "Developmental Processes: A Conceptual Exploration." In Sandford Borins and Rizvi Gowher, eds., *Innovations in Government: Research, Recognition, and Replication*, 113–137. Washington, DC: Brookings Institution Press.

Bardach, Eugene, and Robert A. Kagan. [1982] 2002. *Going by the Book: The Problem of Regulatory Unreasonableness.* Somerset, NJ: Transaction Publishers.

Barrett, John A., William M. Jackson, Imran A. Baig, Amy L. Coverstone, Craig E. Harfield, Richard D. Arcilesi, James Butler, William Burton, and Charles W. Williams. 1999. *Wide Area Decontamination: CB Decontamination Technologies, Equipment and Projects.* Chemical and Biological Defense Information Analysis Center Report no. CR-99-10.

Barrett, Ronald. 2006. "Dark Winter and the Spring of 1972: Deflecting the Social Lessons of Smallpox." *Medical Anthropology* 25: 171–191.

Barry, John M. 2005. *The Great Influenza: The Epic Story of the Deadliest Plague in History.* New York: Penguin.

Bartholomew, Robert E., and Simon Wessely. 2002. "Protean Nature of Mass Sociogenic Illness." *British Journal of Psychiatry* 180: 300–306.

Barzilai, Amnon. 2002. "1.7 Million Have Wrong Gas Mask." *Haaretz* (Tel Aviv, Israel), December 31.

Basich, Anthony. 2006. "Where's the Pork? How Lawmakers Have Limited Earmarks in Homeland Security—So Far." *News21*, July 20, 2006. http://newsinitiative.org/story/2006/07/20/wheres_the_pork.

Bassetti, Stefano, Werner E. Bischoff, and Robert J. Sherertz. 2005. "Are SARS Superspreaders Cloud Adults?" *Emerging Infectious Diseases* 11: 637–638.

BBC News. 2002. "Anthrax Scare at Salt Lake City." February 13. http://news.bbc.co.uk/1/hi/world/americas/1817831.stm.

Beck, Earl R. 1986. *Under the Bombs: The German Home Front 1942–45.* Lexington, KY: University Press of Kentucky.

Becker, Naomi M., Julie Ann Canepa, James R. Gattiker, Thomas D. Kunkle, Maureen A. McGraw, Marjorie G. Snow, Tammy P. Taylor, and Giday WoldeGabriel. 2002. *Assessment of Particle Penetrations and Decontamination Options.* Los Alamos National Laboratory Report no. LA-UR-02-6614.

Becker, Steven M. 2004. "Emergency Communication and Information Issues in Terrorist Events Involving Radioactive Materials." *Biosecurity and Bioterrorism: Biodefense Strategy, Practice, and Science* 2: 195–207.

Bedat, Arnaud, Gilles Bouleau, and Bernard Nicolas. 2000. *L'Ordre du temple solaire: Les Secrets d'une manipulation.* Paris: Flammarion.

Beers, Rand, and Richard A. Clarke. 2006. *The Forgotten Homeland.* Washington, DC: Brookings Institution Press.

Behrens, Carl, and Mark Holt 2005. Report for Congress: *Nuclear Power Plants: Vulnerability to Terrorist Attack.* Congressional Research Service. February. http://www.globalsecurity.org/military/library/report/crs/rs21131.pdf.

Beir, Vicki. 2006. "Game Theoretic and Reliability Models in Counterterrorism and Security." In Alyson G. Wilson, Gregory D. Wilson, and David H. Olwell, eds., *Statistical Methods in Counterterrorism: Game Theory, Modeling, Syndromic Surveillance, and Biometric Authentication,* 23–42. New York: Springer.

Belkacemi, Yazid, Myriam Labopin, Jean-Paul Vernant, Hans G. Prentice, Andre Tichelli, Anton Schattenberg, Marc A. Boogaerts, Peter Ernst, et al. 1998. "Cataracts After Total Body Irradiation and Bone Marrow Transplantation in Patients with Acute Leukemia in Complete Remission: A Study of the European Group for Blood and Marrow Transplantation." *International Journal of Radiation Oncology, Biology and Physics* 41: 659–668.

Belke, James C. 2000. *Chemical Accident Risks in US Industry—A Preliminary Analysis of Accident Risk Data from US Hazardous Chemical Facilities.* EPA Report. http://www.epa.gov/ceppo/pubs/stockholmpaper.pdf.

Bell, William C., and Cham E. Dallas. 2007. "Vulnerability of Populations and the Urban Health Care Systems to Nuclear Weapon Attack—Examples from Four American Cities." *International Journal of Health Geographics* 6: 5.

Bellamy, Patrick. 2002. "TruTV Crime Library: False Prophet: The Aum Cult of Terror." http://www.crimelibrary.com/terrorists_spies/terrorists/prophet/1.html.

Bender, M. A., and P. C. Gooch. 1966. "Somatic Chromosome Aberrations Induced by Human Whole-Body Irradiation: The 'Recuplex' Criticality Accident." *Radiation Research* 29: 568–582.

Benjamin, Daniel, and Steven Simon. 2005. *The Next Attack: The Failure of the War on Terror and a Strategy for Getting It Right*. New York: Times Books.

Berger, Alan, Carolyn Kousky, and Richard J. Zeckhauser. 2006. Obstacles to Clear Thinking About Natural Disasters: Five Lessons for Policy. University of Pennsylvania Working Paper. http://www.law.upenn.edu/academics/institutes/regulation/papers/Zeckhauser_paper.pdf.

Berndt, Ernst R., Rachel Glennerster, Michael Kremer, Jean Lee, Ruth Levine, George Weizsacker, and Heidi Williams. 2005. Advanced Markets for a Malaria Vaccine: Estimating Costs and Effectiveness. National Bureau of Economic Research Working Paper no. 11288. http://www.cgdev.org/doc/books/vaccine/Berndt,%20E.%20et%20al.%20'Advance%20purchase%20commitments%20for%20a%20malaria%20vaccine.'.pdf.

Bernstein, A., Y. Wang, G. Gratta, and T. West. 2002. "Nuclear reactor safeguards and monitoring with antineutrino detectors." *Journal of Applied Physics* 91: 4672–4676.

Bhattacharjee, Yudhijit, and Martin Enserink. 2008. "FBI Discusses Microbial Forensics—But Key Questions Remain Unanswered." *Science* 321: 1026–1027.

Bigley, Gregory A., and Karlene H. Roberts. 2001. "The Incident Command System: High Reliability Organizing for Complex and Volatile Tasks." *Academy of Management Journal* 44: 1281–1299.

Biotechnology Industry Association. 2007. *BIO 2007 Guide to Biotechnology*. Washington, DC: Biotechnology Industry Association. http://www.bio.org/speeches/pubs/er/BiotechGuide.pdf.

Birkland, Thomas A. 2006. *Lessons of Disaster: Policy Change After Catastrophic Events*. Washington, DC: Georgetown University Press.

Blackett, P. M. S. 1949. *Fear, War, and the Bomb: Military and Political Consequences of Atomic Energy*. New York: McGraw-Hill.

Blakely, William F., Pataje G. S. Prasanna, Marcy B. Grace, and Alexandra C. Miller. 2001. "Radiation Exposure Assessment Using Cytological and Molecular Biomarkers." *Radiation Protection Dosimetry* 97: 17–23.

Blanchard, Janice C., Yolanda Haywood, Bradley D. Stein, Terri L. Tanielian, Michael A. Stoto, and Nicole Lurie. 2005. "In Their Own Words: Lessons Learned from Those Exposed to Anthrax." *American Journal of Public Health* 95: 489–495.

Bleich, Avraham, Marc Gelkopf, and Zahava Solomon. 2007. "Exposure to Terrorism, Stress Related Mental Health Symptoms, and Coping Behaviors among a Nationally Representative Sample in Israel." *Journal of American Medical Association* 290: 612–620.

Blixen, Samuel. 1994. *El vientre del Cóndor: Del archivio del terror al caso Berrmos*. Montevideo: Brecha.

Block, Seymour S., ed. 2001. *Disinfection, Sterilization, and Preservation*. 5th ed. Philadelphia: Lippincott, Williams, and Wilkins.

Block, Steven M. 1999. "Living Nightmares: Biological Threats Enabled by Molecular Biology." In Sidney D. Drell, Abraham D. Sofaer, and George D. Wilson, eds., *The New Terror:*

Facing the Threat of Biological and Chemical Weapons, 39–75. Palo Alto, CA: Hoover Institution Press.

Blomberg, S. Brock, and Stephen Sheppard. 2007. "The Impacts of Terrorism on Urban Form." *Brookings-Wharton Papers on Urban Affairs*. 257–290.

Blum, Manfred, and Merill Eisenbud. 1967. "Reduction of Thyroid Irradiation from ^{131}I by Potassium Iodide." *Journal of the American Medical Association*. 200: 1036–40.

Blumenthal, Sidney. 2004. "The 'Terminator' of Baghdad." *Salon.com*, December 9.

Bonetta, Laura. 2006. "Microarrays: Branching Out from Expression Analysis." *Nature Methods* 3: 571–578.

Borio, Luciano, Thomas V. Inglesby, Alan L. Schmaljohn, James M. Hughes, Peter B. Jahrling, Thomas Ksiazek, Karl M. Johnson, et al. 2001. "Hemorrhagic Fever Viruses as Biological Weapons: Medical and Public Health Management." *Journal of the American Medical Association* 285: 1059–1070.

Borjas, George J. 2003. "The Labor Demand Curve Is Downward-Sloping: Reexamining the Impact of Immigration on the Labor Market." *Quarterly Journal of Economics* 118: 1335–1374.

Borowitz, Albert. 2005. *Terrorism for Self-Glorification: The Herostratos Syndrome*. Kent, OH: Kent State University.

Borozdin, Konstaintin, N., Gary E. Hogan, Christopher Morris, William C. Priedhorsky, Alexander Saunders, Larry J. Schultz, and Margaret E. Teasdale. 2003. "Radiographic Imaging with Cosmic-Ray Muons." *Nature* 422: 277.

Borrie, John. 2006. "The Limits of Modest Progress: The Rise, Fall, and Return of Efforts to Strengthen the Biological Weapons Convention." http://www.armscontrol.org/act/2006_10/BWC.asp?print.

Bosco, Joseph. 1996. *A Problem of Evidence: How the Prosecution Freed O. J. Simpson*. New York: Morrow.

Boske, Leigh B. 2006. Port and Supply Chain Security Initiatives in the United States and Abroad. University of Texas/Lyndon B. Johnson School of Public Affairs Report no. 150. http://www.utexas.edu/lbj/pubs/isbn/0–89940–763–3/.

Boswell, Clay. 2003. "InnoCentive and Web-Based Collaborative Innovation." *Chemical Market Reporter*, April 14.

Boulad, Farad, S. Sands, and Charles Sklar. 1998. "Late Complications after Bone Marrow Transplantation in Children and Adolescents." *Current Problems in Pediatrics* 28: 277–297.

Boulet, Cam. 2003. Unpublished lecture, DHS Workshop on "Homeland Security: New Challenges for Decision-Making under Uncertainty," Livermore, CA, November 13–14.

Bourne, Christopher M. 1998. "Unintended Consequences of the Goldwater-Nichols Act." *Joint Forces Quarterly* 18: 99–108. http://www.dtic.mil/doctrine/jel/jfq_pubs/1818.pdf.

Bozzette, Samuel A., Rob Boer, Vibha Bhatnagar, Jennifer L. Brower, Emmett B. Keeler, Sally C. Morton, and Michael A. Stoto. 2003. "A Model for a Smallpox-Vaccination Policy." *New England Journal of Medicine* 348: 416–425 and Supplementary Appendix 1.

Bracken, Paul. 1983. *The Command and Control of Nuclear Forces*. New Haven, CT: Yale University Press.

Brainard, Jeffrey, and Karin Fischer. 2007. "Agency Halts Risky Research on Microbes at Texas A&M." *Chronicle of Higher Education*, July 13, A-1. http://chronicle.com/weekly/v53/i45/45a00101.htm.

Breeze, Roger G., Bruce Budowle, and Steven E. Schutzer, eds. 2005. *Microbial Forensics*. Amsterdam: Elsevier Academic Press.

Bregman, Joel G., and Donald A. Henderson. 2002. "Diagnosis and Management of Smallpox." *New England Journal of Medicine* 346: 1300–1308.

Brinkley, Douglas. 2006. *The Great Deluge: Hurricane Katrina, New Orleans, and the Mississippi Gulf Coast*. New York: HarperCollins.

Broad, William J. 2001. "Pandora's Box of Germ Warfare?" *International Herald Tribune*, January 25.

Brode, Harold L., and Richard D. Small. 1986. "A Review of the Physics of Large Urban Fires." In Fred Marston and Robert Q. Marston, eds., *The Medical Implications of Nuclear War*, 15–72. Washington, DC: National Academies Press.

Brzezinski, Matthew. 2005. *Fortress America: On the Front Lines of Homeland Security*. New York: Bantam.

Buck, Richard A., Joseph E. Trainor, and Benigno E. Aguirre. 2006. "A Critical Evaluation of the Incident Command System and NIMS." *Journal of Homeland Security and Emergency Management* 3: 1–27.

Bullock, Barbara F. 2002. *Surveillance and Detection: A Public Health Response to Bioterrorism*. U.S. Air Force Counterproliferation Center Future Warfare Series, no. 12. http://www.au.af.mil/au/awc/awcgate/cpc-pubs/bullock.pdf.

Bumiller, Elisabeth. 2004. "Kerik, Bush Saw Values Crucial to Post-9/11 World." *New York Times*, December 18.

Bunn, Matthew. 2002. "Stabilizing Employment for Nuclear Personnel: The Nuclear Cities Initiative." Nuclear Threat Initiative, Washington, DC. http://www.nti.org/e_research/cnwm/stabilizing/nci.asp.

Bunn, Matthew. 2003. "Reducing Excess Stockpiles: US-Russian HEU Purchase Agreement." Washinton, DC: NTI. http://www.nti.org/e_research/cnwm/reducing/heudeal.asp.

Bunn, Matthew. 2006. "A Mathematical Model of the Risk of Nuclear Terrorism." *Annals of the American Academy of Political and Social Sciences* 607: 103–120.

Bunn, Matthew. 2007. *Securing the Bomb: An Agenda for Action*. Cambridge, MA: Harvard University. http://www.nti.org/e_research/securingthebomb07.pdf.

Burke, Jason. 2003. *Al-Qaeda: Casting a Shadow of Terror*. London: I. B. Tauris.

Burl, Michael C., Brian C. Sisk, Thomas P. Vaid, and Nathan S. Lewis. 2002. "Classification Performance of Carbon Black-Polymer Composite Vapor Detector Arrays as a Function of Array Size and Detector Composition." *Sensors and Actuators (B)* 87: 130–149.

Burma, S., and D. J. Chen. 2004. "Role of DNA-PK in the Cellular Response to DNA Double-Strand Breaks." *DNA Repair* 3: 909–918.

Cabral, Luis, Guido Cozzi, Vincenzo Denicolò, Giancarlo Spagnolo, and Matteo Zanza. 2006. "Procuring Innovation." In Nicola Dimitri, Gustavo Piga, and Giancarlo Spagnolo, eds., *Handbook of Procurement*. Cambridge: Cambridge University Press.

Calabrese, Edward J. 1991. *Principles of Animal Extrapolation*. Chelsea, MI: Lewis Publishers.

Caldwell, Stephen L. 2007. Testimony before the US House Subcommittee on Border, Maritime, and Global Counterterrorism: *Maritime Security: Observations on Selected Aspects of the SAFE Port Act*. GAO Report GA0–08–86T. http://www.gao.gov/new.items/d0886t.pdf.

Cameron, Gavin. 1999a. "Multi-track Microproliferation: Lessons from Aum Shinrikyo and Al Qaida." *Studies in Conflict and Terrorism* 22: 277–309.

Cameron, Gavin. 1999b. *Nuclear Terrorism: A Threat Assessment for the 21st Century*. New York: Palgrave Macmillan.

Cameron, Gavin. 2000. "WMD Terrorism in the United States: The Threat and Possible Countermeasures." *Nonproliferation Review* 7: 162–179.

Cameron, Gavin, and Jason Pate. 2001. "Covert Biological Weapons Attacks against Agricultural Targets: Assessing the Impact against US Agriculture." *Terrorism and Political Violence* 13: 39.

Campbell, James K. 2000. "On Not Understanding the Problem." In Brad Roberts, ed., *Hype or Reality? The "New Terrorism" and Mass Casualty Attacks*, 17–45. Alexandria, VA: Chemical and Biological Arms Control Institute.

Campos-Outcault, D., R. England, and B. Porter. 1991. "Reporting of Communicable Diseases by University Physicians." *Public Health Reports* 106: 579–583.

Canada Border Services Agency. 2007. "Canada's New Government Invests over $430 Million for Smart, Secure Borders." http://www.cbsa-asfc.gc.ca/media/release-communique/2007/0112windsor-eng.html.

Canada Border Services Agency. n.d. "Security and Prosperity Partnership of North America." http://www.cbsa.gc.ca/agency-agence/spp-psp-eng.html.

Canberra Cryo-Pulse. n.d. Home page. http://www.canberra.com/products/438024.asp.

Carafano, James Jay. 2007. "Homeland Security Spending for the Long War." Lecture, The Heritage Foundation, Washington, DC, February 2. http://www.heritage.org/Research/HomelandSecurity/hl989.cfm.

Carafano, James Jay, and Paul Rosenzweig. 2005. *An Agenda for Increasing State and Local Government Efforts to Combat Terrorism*. Heritage Foundation *Backgrounder* no. 1826. http://www.heritage.org/Research/HomelandSecurity/bg1826.cfm.

Carlsen Tina, M., Robert Fischer, Jessie Coty, Hank Kahn, Karen Folks, and Sandy Mathews. 2004. "Strategies for Weapons of Mass Destruction (WMD) Decontamination." UCRL-TR-208085.

Carlsen, Tina M., D. H. MacQueen, and P. W. Krauter. 2001. *Sampling Requirements for Chemical and Biological Agent Decontamination Efficacy Verification*. Lawrence Livermore National Laboratory Report no. UCRL-AR-143245.

Carr, Matthew. 2006. *The Infernal Machine: A History of Terrorism from the Assassination of Tsar Alexander II to Al-Qaeda*. New York: New Press.

Carroll, Lewis. [1872] 2000. *Through the Looking Glass*. New York: Signet Classic.

Carroll, Stephen J., Tom LaTourrette, Brian G. Chow, Gregory S. Jones, and Craig Martin. 2005. *Distribution of Losses from Large Terrorist Attacks under the Terrorism Risk Insurance Act*. Santa Monica, CA: RAND Center for Terrorism Risk Management Policy. http:// rand.org/pubs/monographs/2005/RAND_MG427.pdf.

Carter, Ashton B., Michael M. May, and William J. Perry. 2007. Workshop Report: "The Day After: Action in the 24 Hours Following a Nuclear Blast in an American City." http:// iis-db.stanford.edu/pubs/21872/DayAfterWorkshopReport.pdf.

Carus, W. Seth. 2000a. "The Rajneeshees." In Jonathan Tucker, ed., *Toxic Terror: Assessing Terrorist Use of Chemical and Biological Weapons*, 115–137. Cambridge, MA: MIT Press.

Carus, W. Seth. 2000b. "R.I.S.E (1972)." In Jonathan Tucker, ed., *Toxic Terror: Assessing Terrorist Use of Chemical and Biological Weapons*, 55–70. Cambridge, MA: MIT Press.

Carus, W. Seth. 2006. Defining "Weapons of Mass Destruction." National Defense University Center for the Study of WMD Occasional Paper no. 4.

Casani, Julie, Diane L. Matuszak, and Georges C. Benjamin. 2003. "Under Siege: One State's Perspective on the Anthrax Events of October/November 2001." *Biosecurity and Bioterrorism: Biodefense Strategy, Practice, and Science* 1: 43–45.

Caudle, Sharon. 2005a. "Homeland Security: Approaches to Results Management." *Public Performance and Management Review* 28: 352–375.

Caudle, Sharon. 2005b. "Homeland Security Capabilities–Based Planning: Lessons from the Defense Community." *Homeland Security Affairs* 1: Article 2.

Caudle, Sharon L., and Randall Yim. 2006. "Homeland Security's National Strategic Position: Goals, Objectives, Measures Assessment." In David G. Kamien, ed., *The McGraw-Hill Homeland Security Handbook*, 225–262. New York: McGraw-Hill.

Cave-Brown, Anthony. 1978. *Dropshot: The American Plan for World War III against Russia in 1957*. New York: Dial Press.

CBO. *See* Congressional Budget Office.

CBS News. 2002. Television Transcript: "Fallon Cancer Cluster Probed." January 9. http:// www.cbsnews.com/stories/2002/01/09/60II/main323782.shtml.

CBS News. 2003. "Commando Solo." n.d. http://www.cbsnews.com/elements/2003/01/29/ iraq/whoswho538410_0_2_person.shtml.

CBP. *See* Customs and Border Protection Service.

CBSA. *See* Canada Border Services Agency.

CDC. *See* Centers for Disease Control and Prevention.

Cello, Jeronimo, Aniko V. Paul, and Eckard Wimmer. 2002. "Chemical Synthesis of Poliovirus cDNA: Generation of Infectious Virus in the Absence of Natural Template." *Science* 297: 1016–1018.

Center for Nonproliferation Studies. 2003. "Russia: DOE MPC&A Program." http://www .nti.org/db/nisprofs/russia/forasst/doe/mpca.htm.

Center for Nonproliferation Studies. 2005. "Nuclear Terrorism." http://www.nti.org/ h_learnmore/nuctutorial/chapter02_06.html.

Centers for Disease Control and Prevention. 1992. *Principles of Epidemiology: An Introduction to Applied Epidemiology and Biostatistics*. Atlanta, GA: CDC. http://www2a.cdc.gov/phtn/catalog/pdf-file/Epi_Course.pdf.

Centers for Disease Control and Prevention. 2001. *The Public Health Response to Biological and Chemical Terrorism: Interim Planning Guidance for State Public Health Officials*. Washington, DC: HHS. http://emergency.cdc.gov/Documents/Planning/PlanningGuidance.PDF.

Centers for Disease Control and Prevention. 2003a. "Summary of Notifiable Diseases—United States, 2001." *Morbidity and Mortality Weekly Report* 50: 1–108. http://www.cdc.gov/mmwr/PDF/wk/mm5053.pdf.

Centers for Disease Control and Prevention. 2003b. "Final Recommendations for Protecting Human Health from Potential Adverse Effects of Exposure to Agents GA (Tabun), GB (Sarin), and VX." *Federal Register* 68: 58348–58351.

Centers for Disease Control and Prevention. 2004a. "Continuance Guidance—Budget Year 5, Attachment A, Focus Area A—Preparedness Planning and Readiness Assessment." http://www.bt.cdc.gov/planning/continuationguidance/pdf/readiness-attacha.pdf.

Centers for Disease Control and Prevention. 2004b. "Continuation Guidance for Cooperative Agreement on Public Health Preparedness and Response for Bioterrorism—Budget Year Five Program Announcement 99051." http://www.bt.cdc.gov/planning/continuationguidance/pdf/guidance_intro.pdf.

Centers for Disease Control and Prevention. 2004c. "Interim Recommendations for Airborne Exposure Limits for Chemical Warfare Agents H and HD (Sulfur Mustard)." *Federal Register* 69: 24164–24168.

Centers for Disease Control and Prevention. 2004d. "Syndromic Surveillance: Reports from a National Conference." *Morbidity and Mortality Weekly Report* 53 (Supp.): 1–268. http://www.cdc.gov/mmwr/PDF/wk/mm53SU01.pdf.

Centers for Disease Control and Prevention. 2007a. "Biosense." http://www.cdc.gov/biosense/.

Centers for Disease Control and Prevention. 2007b. "Frequently Asked Questions about the Laboratory Response Network (LRN)." http://www.bt.cdc.gov/lrn/faq.asp.

Centers for Disease Control and Prevention. n.d.(a). "Bioterrorism Agents/Diseases." http://www.bt.cdc.gov/agent/agentlist-category.asp#a.

Centers for Disease Control and Prevention. n.d.(b). "Chemical Agents." http://www.bt.cdc.gov/agent/agentlistchem.asp.

Centers for Disease Control and Prevention. n.d.(c). "Radiation Emergencies." http://www.bt.cdc.gov/radiation/.

Centers for Disease Control and Prevention. n.d.(d). "Centers for Public Health Preparedness." http://www.bt.cdc.gov/training/cphp/.

Centers for Disease Control and Prevention. n.d.(e). "Strategic National Stockpile." http://www.bt.cdc.gov/stockpile/.

Central Intelligence Agency. 1996. "Stability of Iraq's CW Stockpile." Unpublished. http://www.fas.org/irp/gulf/cia/960715/72569.htm.

Central Intelligence Agency. 2003. "Terrorist CBRN: Materials and Effects." https: //www.cia.gov/library/reports/general-reports–1/terrorist_cbrn/terrorist_CBRN.htm.

Chatzandroulis, S., E. Tegou, D. Goustouridis, S. Polymenakos and D. Tsoukalas. 2004. "Capacitive-Type Chemical Sensors Using Thin Silicon/Polymer Bimorph Membranes." *Sensors and Actuators* 103: 392–396.

Chee, Mark, Robert Yang, Earl Hubbell, Anthony Berno, Xiaohua C. Huang, David Stern, Jim Winkler, David J. Lockhart, Macdonald S. Morris, and Stephen P. A. Fodor. 1996. "Accessing Genetic Information with High-Density DNA Arrays." *Science* 274: 610–614.

Cheremisinoff, Nicholas P. 1995. *Handbook of Emergency Response to Toxic Chemical Releases—A Guide to Compliance*. Park Ridge, NJ: Noyes Publications. http://www.knovel.com/knovel2/Toc.jsp?BookID=419&VerticalID=0.

Cherepy, Nerine J., Joshua D. Kuntz, Thomas M. Tillotson, Derrick T. Speaks, Stephen A. Payne, B. H. T. Chai, Yetta Porter-Chapman, and Stephen E. Derenzo. 2007. "Single Crystal and Transparent Ceramic Lutetium Aluminum Garnet Scintillators." *Nuclear Instruments and Methods in Physics Research (A)* 579: 38–41.

Chernobyl Forum. 2005. "Chernobyl's Legacy: Health, Environmental and Socio-Economic Impacts." http://www.chernobyl.info/resources/resource_en_131.pdf.

Chess, Caron, Jeff Calia, and Karen M. O'Neill. 2004. "Communication Triage: An Anthrax Case Study." *Biosecurity and Bioterrorism: Biodefense Strategy, Practice, and Science* 2: 106–111.

Chyba, Christopher F. 2006. "Biotechnology and the Challenge to Arms Control." http://www.armscontrol.org/act/2006_10/BioTechFeature.asp.

Claridge, David. 1999. "Exploding the Myths of Superterrorism." *Terrorism and Political Violence* 11: 133–148.

Claridge, David. 2000. "The Baader-Meinhof Gang (1975)." In Jonathan Tucker, ed., *Toxic Terror: Assessing Terrorist Use of Chemical and Biological Weapons*, 95–106. Cambridge, MA: MIT Press.

Clark, J. G., J. A. Hansen, M. I. Hertz, R. Parkman, L. Jensen, and H. H. Peavy. 1993. "NHLBI Workshop Summary: Idiopathic Pneumonia Syndrome After Bone Marrow Transplantation." *American Review of Respiratory Disease* 147: 1601–1606.

Clarke, Lee. 1999. *Mission Improbable: Using Fantasy Documents to Tame Disaster*. Chicago: University of Chicago Press.

Clemen, Robert T. 2005. *Making Hard Decisions: An Introduction to Decision Analysis*.

Clutterbuck, Richard. 1993. "Trends in Terrorist Weaponry." *Terrorism and Political Violence* 5: 130–139.

CMA. *See* U.S. Army/Chemical Materials Agency.

CNN. 2002. "Disturbing Scenes of Death Show Capability with Chemical Gas." http://archives.cnn.com/2002/US/08/19/terror.tape.chemical/.

CNS. *See* Center for Nonproliferation Studies.

Coaffee, Jon. 2003. *Terrorism, Risk and the City: The Making of a Contemporary Urban Landscape*. Aldershot, UK: Ashgate Publishing.

Cohen, Eric P. 2000. "Radiation Nephropathy After Bone Marrow Transplantation." *Kidney International* 58: 903–918.

Colbeck, Ian. 1998. *Physical and Chemical Properties of Aerosols*. London: Blackwood Scientific.

Coleman, C. Norman, William F. Blakely, John R. Fike, Thomas J. MacVittie, Noel F. Metting, James B. Mitchell, John E. Moulder, R. Julian Preston, et al. 2003. "Molecular and Cellular Biology of Moderate-Dose (1–10 Gy). Radiation and Potential Mechanisms of Radiation Protection: Report of a Workshop at Bethesda, Maryland, December 17–18, 2001." *Radiation Research* 159: 812–834. http://www3.niaid.nih.gov/research/topics/radnuc/PDF/NCI2001RadReport.pdf.

Coleman, C. Norman, Chad Hrdina, Judith Bader, Ann Norwood, Robert Hayhurst, Joseph Forsha, and Ann Knebel. 2007. "Medical Response to a Radiological/Nuclear Event: Integrated Plan from the Office of the Assistant Secretary for Preparedness and Response." Washington, DC: DHHS.

Coleman, C. Norman, Helen B. Stone, John E. Moulder, and Terry C. Pellmar. 2004. "Modulation of Radiation Injury." *Science* 304: 693–694.

Coll, Steven. 2007. "The Unthinkable: Can the United States Be Made Safe from Nuclear Terrorism?" *New Yorker*, March 12, 48–57.

Combellack, J. H., C. R. Tuck, P. C. H. Miller, and C. B. Christian. 2004. Performance Characteristics of a Double Chamber Twin Fluid Nozzle. *Aspects of Applied Biology* 64: 1–6. http://www.micron.co.uk/file_uploads_en/perfchartwinfluid.pdf.

Confessore, Nicholas. 2005. "Mayor Says It's Best to Let Police Control Terror Scenes." *New York Times*, April 23. http://www.nytimes.com/2005/04/23/nyregion/23respond.html?_r=1&pagewanted=print&position%20=&oref=slogin.

Congressional Budget Office. 2004. "Homeland Security and the Private Sector." http://www.cbo.gov/ftpdocs/60xx/doc6042/12-20-HomelandSecurity.pdf.

Congressional Budget Office. 2006. "The Economic Cost of Disruptions in Container Shipments." http://www.cbo.gov/ftpdocs/71xx/doc7106/03-29-Container_Shipments.pdf.

Congressional Budget Office. 2007. "Federal Reinsurance for Terrorism Risks: Issues in Reauthorization." http://www.cbo.gov/ftpdocs/85xx/doc8520/08-02-TRIA.pdf.

Coogan, Tim Pat. 2000. *The IRA*. New York: Palgrave.

Cooke-Deegan, Robert M. 1996. "Does NIH Need a DARPA?" *Issues in Science and Technology*, winter. http://issues.org/13.2/cookde.htm.

Cooper, Ben. 2006. "Poxy Models and Rash Decisions." *Proceedings of the National Academy of Sciences* 103: 12221–12222.

Cooper, Helene. 2008. "Bush Rebuffs Hard-Liners to Ease North Korea Curbs." *International Herald Tribune*, June 27. http://www.iht.com/articles/2008/06/27/asia/27nuke-korea.php.

Cooper, Robert G., Scott L. Edgett, and Elko J. Kleinschmidt. 2001. *Portfolio Management for New Products*. Cambridge, MA: Perseus.

Cordesman, Anthony. 2001. *Defending America: Asymmetric and Terrorist Attacks with Radiological and Nuclear Weapons*. Washington, DC: Center for Strategic and International Studies.

Couch, Robert B., Thomas R. Cate, R. Gordon Douglas, Peter J. Gerorne, and Vernon Knight. 1966. "Effect of Route of Inoculation on Experimental Respiratory Viral Disease in Volunteers and Evidence for Airborne Transmission." *Bacteriological Reviews* 30: 517–529.

Couffer, Jack. 1992. *The Bat Bomb: World War II's Other Secret Weapon.* Austin: University of Texas Press.

Covert, Norman M. 2000. "Cutting Edge: A History of Fort Detrick." Fort Detrick, MD: US Army/Fort Detrick Public Affairs Office. http://www.detrick.army.mil/detrick/cutting_edge/index.cfm?chapter12.

Crapo, James D., Elaine D. Smolko, Frederick J. Miller, Judith A. Graham, and A. Wallace Hayes, eds. 1987. *Extrapolation of Dosimetric Relationships for Inhaled Particles and Gases.* San Diego, CA: Academic Press.

Crenshaw, Martha. 1998. "The Logic of Terrorism: Terrorist Behavior as a Product of Strategic Choice." In Walter Reich, ed., *Origins of Terrorism: Psychologies, Ideologies, States of Mind,* 7–24. Washington, DC: Woodrow Wilson Center Press.

Crockett, Christopher S., Charles N. Haas, A. Fazil, J. B. Rose, and C. P. Gerba. 1996. "Prevalence of Shigellosis in the U.S.: Consistency with Dose-Response Information," *International Journal of Food Microbiology.* 30: 87–100.

Croddy, Eric, Clarissa Perez-Armendariz, and John Hart. 2002. *Chemical and Biological Warfare: A Comprehensive Guide for the Concerned Citizen.* New York: Springer.

Crowley, Philip J. 2007. *Time to Act: 14 Steps in 2007 to Further Implement the 9/11 Commission Recommendations.* Center for American Progress Research Report. http://www.americanprogress.org/issues/2007/01/pdf/911.pdf.

Cruz-Cruz, Norma E., Gary A. Toranzos, Donald G. Ahearn, and Terry C. Hazen. 1988. "In Situ Survival of Plasmid-Bearing and Plasmidless *Pseudomonas aeruginosa* in Pristine Tropical Waters." *Applied and Environmental Microbiology* 54: 2574–2577.

Cruz-Smith, Martin. 2006. *Wolves Eat Dogs.* New York: Simon & Schuster.

Cullison, Alan. 2004. "Inside Al-Qaeda's Hard Drive." *Atlantic Monthly,* September. http://www.theatlantic.com/doc/200409/cullison.

Cummins, J. David, Christopher M. Lewis, and Richard D. Phillips. 1999. "Pricing Excess-of-Loss Reinsurance Contracts Against Catastrophic Loss" in K. A. Froot, ed., *The Financing of Catastrophe Risk.* Chicago: University of Chicago Press.

Customs and Border Protection Service. 2004a. "National Border Patrol Strategy." http://www.au.af.mil/au/awc/awcgate/dhs/national_bp_strategy.pdf.

Customs and Border Protection Service. 2004b. "Securing the Global Supply Chain: Customs-Trade Partnership against Terrorism (C-TPAT). Strategic Plan." http://www.cbp.gov/xp/cgov/about/mission/cbp_plans_reports.xml.

Customs and Border Protection Service. 2005. "Combating the Threat of Nuclear Smuggling at Home and Abroad."

Customs and Border Protection Service. 2006. *Securing America's Borders at Ports of Entry, Office of Field Operations, Strategic Plan FY 2007–2011.* Washington, DC: U.S. Customs and Border Protection Service. http://www.cbp.gov/xp/cgov/about/mission/cbp_plans_reports.xml.

Customs and Border Protection Service. 2007. "News Report: US, Mexican Officials Announce Grand Opening of Brownsville SENTRI Lane." http://www.govtech.com/gt/118396?topic=117691.

Dainiak, N. 2002. "Hematologic Consequences of Exposure to Ionizing Radiation." *Experimental Hematology* 30: 513–528.

Dando, Malcolm. 2001. *The New Biological Weapons: Threat, Proliferation, and Control.* Boulder, CO: Lynne Rienner.

Daniels, Ted, ed. 1999. *A Doomsday Reader: Prophets, Predictors, and Hucksters of Salvation.* New York: NYU Press.

Danzig, Richard. 2003. *Catastrophic Bioterrorism—What Is to Be Done?* Center for Technology and National Security Policy Report. http://biotech.law.lsu.edu/blaw/general/danzig01.pdf

DARPA. *See* Defense Advanced Research Projects Agency.

Dausey, David J., Nicole Lurie, and Alexis Diamond. 2005. "Public Health Response to Urgent Case Reports." *Health Affairs* 24: 412.

Davis, James, and Barry Schneider. 2002. *The Gathering Biological Storm.* US Air Force Counterproliferation Center: Maxwell AFB Alabama. http://www.au.af.mil/au/awc/awcgate/cpc-pubs/biostorm/index.htm.

Davis, Lois M., and Janice C. Blanchard. 2002. *Are Local Health Responders Ready for Biological and Chemical Terrorism?* RAND Issue Paper no. IP-221. http://rand.org/pubs/issue_papers/IP221/index2.html.

Davis, Lois M., Louis T. Mariano, Jennifer E. Pace, Sarah K. Cotton, and Paul Steinberg. 2006b. *Combating Terrorism: How Prepared Are State and Local Response Organizations?* Santa Monica, CA: RAND.

Davis, Lois M., Jeanne S. Ringel, Sarah K. Cotton, Belle Griffin, Elizabeth Malcolm, Louis T. Mariano, Jennifer E. Pace, Karen A. Ricci, Molly Shea, Jeffrey Wasserman, and James Zazzali. 2006a. *Public Health Preparedness: Integrating Public Health and Hospital Preparedness Programs.* RAND Technical Report TR–317-DHHS. http://rand.org/pubs/technical_reports/TR317/.

Davis, Lynn E., Tom LaTourrette, David E. Mosher, Lois M. Davis, and David R. Howell. 2003. *Individual Preparedness and Response to Chemical, Radiological, Nuclear, and Biological Terrorist Attacks.* Santa Monica, CA: RAND.

Davis, Paul K. 2002. *Analytic Architecture for Capabilities-Based Planning, Mission-System Analysis, and Transformation.* Santa Monica, CA: RAND.

DeArmond, Paul. 2002. "The Anthrax Letters: Five Deaths–Five Grams–Five Clues." *Albion Monitor* (Sebastapol, CA), August 16. www.monitor.net/monitor/0208a/anthrax.html.

DeChema, E. V. 2003. Press release: "Microreactor Technologies on the Upswing." May 18. http://www.dechema.de/en/Press+Information/ACHEMA+2003/Press_Informations/Trend+Reports/8+_+Microreactor.print.

Defence Research and Development Canada. n.d.(a). "Priorities." http://www.css.drdc-rddc.gc.ca/crti/priorit/index-eng.asp.

Defence Research and Development Canada. n.d.(b). "Risk Portfolio." http://www.css .drdc-rddc.gc.ca/pstp/priorities-priorites/risk-risques-eng.asp.

Defense Advanced Research Projects Agency. n.d. "DARPA Grand Challenge." http:// www.darpa.mil/grandchallenge/.

Defense Advanced Research Projects Agency. n.d. *Defense Advanced Research Projects Agency—Technology Transition*. http://www.darpa.mil/body/pdf/transition.pdf.

Delahanty, Randolph. 2006. "Waiting for the Resurrection: New Orleans in the Aftermath." *Museum News*, May/June. http://www.aam-us.org/pubs/mn/MN_MJ06_NewOrleans.cfm.

Dennis, David T., Thomas V. Inglesby, Donald A. Henderson, John G. Bartlett, Michael S. Ascher, Edward Eitzen, Anne D. Fine, et al. 2001. "Tularemia as a Biological Weapon: Medical and Public Health Management." *Journal of the American Medical Association* 285: 2763–2773.

Department of Defense. 2008. *Dictionary of Military and Associated Terms*. Washington, DC: Government Printing Office. http://www.fas.org/irp/doddir/dod/jp1_02.pdf.

Department of Energy/National Nuclear Security Administration. n.d.(a). Home page. http:// www.nnsa.doe.gov/na–20/sitemap.shtml.

Department of Energy/National Nuclear Security Administration. n.d.(b). "Radiological Assistance Program (RAP)." www.nv.doe.gov/library/factsheets/RAP.pdf.

Department of Health and Human Services. 2005a. *HHS Pandemic Influenza Plan*. Washington, DC: HHS. http://www.hhs.gov/pandemicflu/plan/pdf/HHSPandemicInfluenzaPlan.pdf.

Department of Health and Human Services. 2005b. *Terrorism and Other Public Health Emergencies: A Reference Guide for Media*. Washington, DC: HHS. http://www.hhs.gov/ disasters/press/newsroom/mediaguide/HHSMedisReferenceGuideFinal.pdf.

Department of Health and Human Services. 2005c. "National Bioterrorism Hospital Preparedness Program." http://www.ncttrac.org/Documents/NBHPP%20Compliance%202005 .pdf.

Department of Health and Human Services. 2007. "Disaster Medical Assistance Teams." http://www.oep-ndms.dhhs.gov/teams/dmat.html.

Department of Health and Human Services. n.d. "Radiation Event Medical Management: Guidance on Diagnosis and Treatment for Health Care Providers." http://www.remm.nlm .gov/.

Department of Health and Human Services/Agency for Toxic Substances and Disease. 2006. *Medical Management Guidelines for Acute Chemical Exposures*. Atlanta, GA: HHS. http:// www.atsdr.cdc.gov/MHMI/mmg.html.

Department of Health and Human Services/Assistant Secretary for Preparedness and Response. Home page. n.d. http://www.hhs.gov/aspr/.

Department of Health and Human Services/Health Resources and Services Administration. 2000. "The Public Health Workforce Enumeration 2000." http://www.bhpr.hrsa.gov/ healthworkforce/reports/default.htm.

Department of Health and Human Services/Public Health Service. 1994. *The Public Health Workforce: An Agenda for the Twenty-First Century*. Washington, DC: Government Printing Office.

Department of Homeland Security. 2006. "Quick Reference Guide for the National Response Plan (Version 4.0)." http://watersc.org/pdf/QuickReferenceGuide.pdf.

Department of Homeland Security. 2008. *National Response Framework*. http://www.fema .gov/pdf/emergency/nrf/nrf-core.pdf.

Department of State. *See* State Department.

de Rugy, Veronique. 2005. What Does Homeland Security Spending Buy? American Enterprise Institute for Policy Research Working Paper. http://www.aei.org/docLib/ 20050408_wp107.pdf.

Devadoss, Stephen, David Holland, Leroy Stodick, and Joydeep Ghosh. 2006. "A General Equilibrium Analysis of Foreign and Domestic Demand Shocks Arising from Mad Cow Disease in the United States." *Journal of Agricultural and Resource Economics* 31: 441–453.

DHS. *See* Department of Homeland Security.

Dietz, Klaus. 1993. "The Estimation of the Basic Reproductive Number for Infectious Diseases." *Statistical Methods of Medical Research* 2: 23–41.

Digger History. n.d. "Boer War." http://www.diggerhistory.info/pages-conflicts-periods/other/ boer_war.htm.

Dillingham, G. 2001. Testimony before the U.S. Senate Committee on Commerce, Science and Transportation: "Aviation Security: Terrorist Acts Demonstrate Urgent Need to Improve Security at the Nation's Airports." GAO 01-62-1162T. http://www.gao.gov/new.items/ d011162t.pdf.

DiMasi, Joseph, Ronald Hansen, and Henry Grabowski. 2003. "The Price of Innovation: New Estimates of Drug Development Costs." *Journal of Health Economics* 22: 151–185.

Dixon, Cyril W. 1962. *Smallpox*. London: J. & A. Churchill.

Dixon, Lloyd, Robert Lempert, Tom LaTourette, Robert T. Reville, and Paul Steinberg. 2007. *Trade-Offs among Alternative Government Interventions in the Market for Terrorism Insurance: Interim Results*. Santa Monica, CA: RAND Center for Terrorism Risk Management Policy. http://www.rand.org/pubs/documented_briefings/2007/RAND_DB525.pdf.

DoD. *See* Department of Defense.

DOE/NRC Interagency Working Group on Radiological Dispersal Devices. 2003. "Radiological Dispersal Devices: An Initial Study to Identify Radioactive Materials of Greatest Concern and Approaches to Their Tracking, Tagging, and Disposition." http://www.nti.org/ e_research/official_docs/doe/DOE052003.pdf.

Doherty, Neil, Esther Goldsmith, Scott Harrington, Paul Kleindorfer, Howard Kunreuther, Erwann Michel-Kerjan, Mark Pauly, Irv Rosenthal, and Peter Schmeidler. 2005. *TRIA and Beyond: Terrorism Risk Financing in the US*. Wharton Decision Risk Management and Decision Processes Report. August. http://knowledge.wharton.upenn.edu/papers/1299.pdf.

Dollery, Brian E., and Andrew C. Worthington. 1996. "The Empirical Analysis of Fiscal Illusion." *Journal of Economic Surveys* 10: 261–308.

Dolnik, Adam. 2004. "All God's Poisons: Re-evaluating the Threat of Religious Terrorism with Respect to Non-conventional Weapons." In Russell D. Howard and Reid L. Sawyer, eds., *Terrorism and Counterterrorism: Understanding the New Security Environment*. Guilford, CT: McGraw-Hill.

Dolnik, Adam, and Rohan Gunaratna. 2006. "On the Nature of Religious Terrorism." In Andrew T. H. Tan, ed., *The Politics of Terrorism: A Survey*, 80–88. London: Routledge.

Downs, Anthony. 1960. "Why the Government Budget Is Too Small in a Democracy." *World Politics* 12: 541–563.

DRDC. *See* Defence Research and Development Canada.

Drennan, Matthew P. 2007. "The Economic Cost of Disasters: Permanent or Ephemeral?" In Harry W. Richardson, Peter Gordon, and James E. Moore, eds., *The Economic Costs and Consequences of Terrorism*, 159–181. Cheltenham, UK: Edward Elgar.

Dudoit, Sandrine, Yee Hwa Yang, Matthew J. Callow, and Thomas P. Speed. 2002. "Statistical Methods for Identifying Differentially Expressed Genes in Replicated cDNA Microarray Experiments." *Statistica Sinica* 12: 111–139.

Dunn, Neville. n.d. "Application Technique." Dunn Aviation. http://www.dunnav.com.au/staff.htm.

Durodie, William, and Simon Wessely. 2002. "Resilience or Panic? The Public and Terrorist Attack." *The Lancet* 360: 1901–1902.

Eckerman, Ingrid. 2005. *Bhopal: Causes and Consequences of the World's Largest Industrial Disaster*. Hyderbad: Universities Press.

Ecobichon, Donald J. 1998. "Toxicity, Acute." In Philip Wexler, ed., *Encyclopedia of Toxicology*. San Diego, CA: Academic Press.

Eden, Lynn. 2004. *Whole World on Fire: Organizations, Knowledge, and Nuclear Weapons Devastation*. Ithaca, NY: Cornell University Press.

Edmunds, Thomas, Richard Wheeler, James Gansemer, and Alix Robertson. 2004. "Department of Homeland Security Defensive Architectures Analysis for the Food Contamination Threat." UCRL-TR-208391, December 2004.

Edwards, S. L., and R. F. Stern. 1998. *Building and Sustaining Community Partnerships for Teen Pregnancy Prevention: A Working Paper*. Cornerstone Consulting Group, Inc.

Edwards, Ward, Ralph F. Miles Jr., and Detlof von Winterfeldt. 2007. *Advances in Decision Analysis*. New York: Cambridge University Press.

Eichner, Martin, and Klaus Dietz. 2004. "Transmission Potential for Smallpox: Estimates Based on Detailed Data from an Outbreak." *American Journal of Epidemiology* 158: 110–117.

Eidelson, Benjamin M., and Ian Lustick. 2004. "VIR-POX: An Agent-Based Analysis of Smallpox Preparedness and Response Policy." *Journal of Artificial Societies and Social Simulation* 7: 1–20.

Eisenman, David P., Cheryl Wold, Claude Setodji, Scot Hickey, Ben Lee, Bradley D. Stein, and Anna Long. 2004. "Will Public Health's Response to Terrorism Be Fair? Racial/Ethnic Variations in Perceived Fairness during a Bioterrorism Event." *Biosecurity and Bioterrorism: Biodefense Strategy, Practice, and Science* 2: 146–156.

Elderd, Bret D., Vanja M. Dukic, and Greg Dwyer. 2006. "Uncertainty in Predictions of Disease Spread and Public Health Responses to Bioterrorism and Emerging Diseases." *Proceedings of the National Academy of Sciences* 103: 15693–15697.

Ellison, D. Hank. 2000. *Handbook of Chemical and Biological Warfare Agents*. Boca Raton, FL: CRC Press.

Ellsberg, Daniel. 1961. "Risk, Ambiguity, and the Savage Axioms." *Quarterly Journal of Economics* 75: 643–669.

Elsayed, Nabil M., and Harry Salem. 2006. "Chemical Warfare Agents and Nuclear Weapons." In Harry Salem and Sidney A. Katz, eds., *Inhalation Toxicology*, 2nd ed., 521–542. Boca Raton, FL: CRC/Taylor & Francis Group.

EMAC. *See* Emergency Management and Assistance Compact.

Emergency Management and Assistance Compact. n.d. Home page. http://www.emacweb .org/.

Engel, Charles C., Steven Locke, Dori B. Reissman, Robert DeMartino, Ilan Kutz, Michael McDonald, and Arthur J. Barsky. 2007. "Terrorism, Trauma, and Mass Casualty Triage: How Might We Solve the Latest Mind-Body Problem?" *Biosecurity and Bioterrorism: Biodefense Strategy, Practice, and Science* 5: 155–163.

Environmental Protection Agency. 1996. "EPA Region III Risk-Based Concentration Table, Background Information, Development of Risk-Based Concentrations." Revised version available at http://www.epa.gov/reg3hwmd/risk/.

Environmental Protection Agency. 2002. *Challenges Faced during the Environmental Protection Agency's Response to Anthrax and Recommendations for Enhancing Response Capabilities: A Lessons Learned Report*. Washington, DC: EPA.

Environmental Protection Agency. 2005. "Region 9 Preliminary Remediation Goals (PRGs), Region 9 PRGs 2004 Table." http://www.epa.gov/region09/waste/sfund/prg/index.htm.

Environmental Protection Agency. 2006a. "Emergency Response (ER). Program." http:// www.epa.gov/superfund/programs/er/index.htm.

Environmental Protection Agency. 2006b. *Integrated Risk Information System: Phosgene*. CASRN 75-44-5. http://www.epa.gov/iris/index.html.

Environmental Protection Agency. 2006c. *Integrated Risk Information System (IRIS): Glossary*. http://www.epa.gov/iris/gloss8.htm.

Environmental Protection Agency/Office of Emergency and Remedial Response. 1991. *Risk Assessment Guidance for Superfund, Volume 1: Human Health Evaluation Manual (Part B, Development of Risk-Based Preliminary Remediation Goals)*. EPA Publication no. 9285.7-01B. Washington, DC: EPA.

Environmental Protection Agency/Office of Emergency and Remedial Response. 1996. *Soil Screening Guidance: Technical Background Document*. EPA Report no. EPA/540/R–95/128. Washington, DC: EPA.

Environmental Protection Agency/Office of Radiation Programs. 1992. *Manual of Protective Action Guides and Protective Actions for Nuclear Incidents*. Washington, DC: EPA. http:// www.epa.gov/radiation/rert/pags.html.

Environmental Protection Agency/Office of Radiation Programs. n.d. "Protective Action Guides." http://www.epa.gov/radiation/rert/pags.html.

Environmental Protection Agency/Region 9 Superfund Program. 2004. *Preliminary Remediation Goals*. http://www.epa.gov/region09/waste/sfund/prg/index.html.

EPA. *See* Environmental Protection Agency.

Espinosa, G., J. I. Golzarri, J. Bogard, and J. García-Macedo. 2004. "Commercial Optical Fibre as TLD Material." *Proceedings of the 14th International Conference on Solid State Dosimetry* 119: 197–200.

Eubank, Stephen, Hasan Guclu, V. S. Anil Kumar, Madhav V. Marathe, Aravind Srinivasan, Zoltan Toroczkai, and Nan Wang. 2004. "Modeling Disease Outbreaks in Realistic Urban Social Networks." *Nature* 429: 180–184.

Evans, Richard J. 1987. *Death in Hamburg: Society and Politics in the Cholera Years, 1830–1910*. Oxford: Clarendon.

Falkenrath, Richard A. 1998a. "Confronting Nuclear, Biological and Chemical Terrorism." *Survival* 40: 43–65.

Falkenrath, Richard A. 1998b. "Unknowable Threats, Prudent Policies." In Karl-Heinz Kamp, Joseph F. Pilat, Jessica Stern, and Richard A. Falkenrath, "WMD Terrorism: An Exchange." *Survival* 40: 179–183.

Falkenrath, Richard A., Robert D. Newman, and Bradley A. Thayer. 1998. *America's Achilles' Heal: Nuclear, Biological, and Chemical Terrorism and Covert Attack*. Cambridge, MA: MIT Press.

Farlow, Andrew. 2004. "An Analysis of the Problems of R&D Finance for Vaccines and an Appraisal of Advance Purchase Commitments." Unpublished. http://www.economics.ox.ac.uk/members/andrew.farlow/VaccineRD.pdf.

Fay, Marie Therese, Mike Morrisey, and Marie Smyth. 1998. *Mapping Troubles-Related Deaths in Northern Ireland 1969–1998*. 2nd ed. Belfast, UK: INCORE.

FBI. *See* Federal Bureau of Investigation.

Federal Bureau of Investigation. 2004. "Our Post 9/11 Transformation." http://www.fbi.gov/aboutus/transformation.htm.

Federal Bureau of Investigation. 2006. "FBI Transformation: Director Reflects on Tenure Since 2001." http://www.fbi.gov/page2/september06/mueller090806.htm.

Federal Emergency Management Agency. n.d. "FEMA Disaster Response Assets and Enhancements." http://www.fema.gov/media/archives/2007/061207.shtm.

FEMA. *See* Federal Emergency Management Agency.

Fenimore, Edward E. 1978. "Coded Aperture Imaging: Predicted Performance of Uniformly Redundant Arrays." *Applied Optics* 17: 3562–3570.

Fenner, Frank, Donald A. Henderson, Isao Arita, Zdenek Jezek, and Ivan Danilovich Ladnyi. 1988. *Smallpox and Its Eradication*. Geneva: World Health Organization. http://whqlibdoc.who.int/smallpox/9241561106.pdf.

Ferguson, Charles D., Tahseen Kazi, and Judith Perera. 2003. Commercial Radioactive Sources: Surveying the Security Risks. CNS Occasional Paper. http://cns.miis.edu/pubs/opapers/op11/op11.pdf.

Ferguson, Charles D., and William C. Potter. 2004. *The Four Faces of Nuclear Terrorism*. Washington, DC: Center for Nonproliferation Studies.

Ferguson, Neil M., Matt J. Keeling, W. John Edmunds, Raymond Gani, Bryan T. Grenfell, Roy M. Anderson, and Steve Leach. 2003. "Planning for Smallpox Outbreaks." *Nature* 425: 681–685.

Fernet, Marie, and Janet Hall. 2004. "Genetic Biomarkers of Therapeutic Radiation Sensitivity." *DNA Repair* 3: 1237–1243.

Finkel, Elizabeth. 2001. "Engineered Mouse Virus Spurs Bioweapons Fears." *Science* 291: 585.

Fire Prevention and Engineering Bureau of Dallas, Texas, and National Board of Fire Underwriters. n.d. "Texas City, Texas Disaster: April 16, 17, 1947." http://www.local1259iaff.org/report.htm.

Fischhoff, Baruch. 2005. Testimony before the U.S. House Science Committee: "Scientifically Sound Pandemic Risk Communication." December 14. http://www.healthsystem.virginia.edu/internet/ciag/conference/articles/s2006/fischhoff_pandemic_risk_communication.pdf.

Fischhoff, Baruch. 2006. "Risk Management, Perception, and Communication." In David G. Kamien, ed., *The McGraw-Hill Homeland Security Handbook*, 463–492. New York: McGraw-Hill.

Fischhoff, Baruch, Roxana M. Gonzalez, Deborah A. Small, and Jennifer S. Lerner. 2003. "Evaluating the Success of Terror Risk Communications." *Biosecurity and Bioterrorism: Biodefense Strategy, Practice, and Science* 1: 255–258.

Fischhoff, Baruch, Paul Slovic, Sarah Lichtenstein, Stephen Read, and Barbara Combs. 2004. "How Safe Is Safe Enough? A Psychometric Study of Attitudes toward Technological Risks and Benefits." In Paul Slovic, ed., *The Perception of Risk*. London: Earthscan.

Fitch, J. Patrick., Ellen Raber, and Dennis R. Imbro. 2003. "Technology Challenges in Responding to Biological or Chemical Attacks in the Civilian Sector." *Science* 302: 1350–1354.

Flamini, Gianni. 1981–1985. Il partito del golpe: Le strategie della tensione e del terrore dal primo centrosinistra organico al sequestro Moro. Ferrara: Bovolenta.

Fleischer, Robert L. 2002. "Serendipitous Radiation Monitors." *American Scientist* 90: 324–331.

Fleming, Ian. [1959] 2002. *Goldfinger*. New York: Penguin.

Fliedner, Theodore M., I. Friesecke, and K. Beyrer. 2001. *Medical Management of Radiation Accidents: Manual on the Acute Radiation Syndrome*. Oxford: British Institute of Radiology.

Flint, S. Jane, L. W. Enquist, and V. R. Rancaniello. 2004. *Principles of Virology: Molecular Biology, Pathogenesis, and Control of Animal Viruses*. 2nd ed. Washington, DC: American Society of Microbiology.

Flynn, Stephen. 2004. *America the Vulnerable*. New York: HarperCollins.

Folly, Martin H. 2004. *Palgrave Concise History of the Second World War*. New York: Palgrave Macmillan.

Foray, Dominique, and L. Hilaire-Perez. 2005. "The Economics of Open Technology: Collective Organization and Individual Claims in the 'Fabrique Lyonnaise' during the Old Regime." In Cristiano Antonelli, Dominique Foray, Bronwyn Hall, and W. Edward Steinmueller, eds., *Essays in Honor of Paul A. David*. Cheltenham, UK: Edward Elgar.

Ford, James L. 1998. Radiological Dispersal Device: Assessing the Transnational Threat. National Defense University Strategic Forum Paper no. 136. March. http://www.ndu.edu/inss/strforum/SF136/forum136.html.

Fornace, Albert J., S. A. Amundson, Michael L. Bittner, T. G. Myers, Paul S. Meltzer, John N. Weinsten, and Jeffrey M. Trent. 1999. "The Complexity of Radiation Stress Responses: Analysis by Informatics and Functional Genomics Approaches." *Gene Expression* 7: 387–400.

Fox News. 2004. "Sarin, Mustard Gas Discovered Separately in Iraq." May 17. http://www.foxnews.com/story/0,2933,120137,00.html.

Foxell, Joseph W. Jr. 1999. "The Debate on the Potential for Mass-Casualty Terrorism: The Challenge to US Security." *Terrorism and Political Violence* 11: 94–109.

Fradkin, Philip L. 2005. *The Great Earthquake and Firestorms of 1906: How San Francisco Nearly Destroyed Itself.* Berkeley: University of California Press.

Frank, Richard B. 1999. *Downfall: The End of the Imperial Japanese Empire.* New York: Random House.

Frank, W. J. ed. 1967. *Summary Report of the Nth Country Experiment.* Lawrence Livermore Radiation Laboratory Report no. URCRL-50249. http://www.gwu.edu/~nsarchiv/nsa/NC/nuchis.html.

Freeh, Louis. 1999. Statement before the Senate Committee on Appropriations: "President's Fiscal Year 2000 Budget." http://www.milnet.com/domestic/freehct2-0299.htm.

Freeh, Louis. 2001. Statement before the U.S. Senate Appropriation and Armed Services Committees: "Threat of Terrorism to the United States." http://www.fbi.gov/congress/congress01/freeh051001.htm.

Frey, Bruno S., and Simon Leuchinger. 2007. "Terrorism: Considering New Policies." In Harry W. Richardson, Peter Gordon, and James E. Moore, eds., *The Economic Costs and Consequences of Terrorism*, 17–37. Cheltenham, UK: Edward Elgar.

Friedman, James W. 1986. *Game Theory with Applications to Economics.* New York: Oxford University Press.

Friedrich, Jorg. 2006. *The Fire: The Bombing of Germany 1940–1945.* New York: Columbia University Press.

Frist, William. 2002. "Public Health and National Security: The Critical Role of Increased Federal Support." *Health Affairs* 21: 117–130.

Fung, Eric T., George L. Wright Jr., and Enrique A. Dalmasso. 2000. "Proteomic Strategies for Biomarker Identification: Progress and Challenges." *Current Opinion in Molecular Therapeutics* 2: 643–650.

Gani, Raymond, and Steve Leach. 2001. "Transmission Potential of Smallpox in Contemporary Populations." *Nature* 414: 748–751.

GAO. *See* General Accountability Office.

Gallup, Inc. 2008. "Obama Wins on the Economy, McCain on Terrorism." October 14. http://www.gallup.com/poll/111130/Obama-Wins-Economy-McCain-Terrorism.aspx.

Gao, Ting, Marc D. Woodka, Bruce S. Brunschwig, and Nathan S. Lewis. 2006. "Chemiresistors for Array-Based Vapor Sensing Using Composites of Carbon Black with Low Volatility Organic Molecules." *Chemistry of Materials* 18: 5193–5202.

Garrett, Laurie. 2001. "The Nightmare of Bioterrorism." *Foreign Affairs* 80: 76–89.

Garrett, Thomas A. 2007. *Economic Effects of the 1918 Influenza Pandemic: Implications for Modern-day Pandemic*. Federal Reserve Bank of St. Louis Report. November 2007. http:// stlouisfed.org/community/assets/pdf/pandemic_flu_report.pdf.

Garrick, B. John. 2002. "Perspectives on the Use of Risk Assessment to Address Terrorism." *Risk Analysis* 22: 425–426.

Garrison, Dee. 2006. *Bracing for Armageddon: Why Civil Defense Never Worked*. Oxford: Oxford University Press. http://www.oxfordscholarship.com/oso/public/content/history/ 9780195183191/toc.html.

Garth, Jeff, and Sheryl Gay Stolberg. 2000. "Drug Makers Reap Profits on Tax-Backed Research." *New York Times*, April 23.

Geller, David. 2002. "New Liquid Aerosol Devices: Systems That Force Pressurized Liquids through Nozzles." *Respiratory Care* 47: 1392–1404.

General Accountability Office. 1992. *Integrating Human Services: Linking At-Risk Families with Services More Successful Than System Reform Efforts*. GAO Report no. GAO/HRD-92-108. http://archive.gao.gov/d35t11/147772.pdf.

General Accountability Office. 2003a. *Capitol Hill Anthrax Incident, EPA's Cleanup Was Successful. Opportunities Exist to Enhance Oversight, Publication*. GAO Report no. GAO-03-686. http://www.gao.gov/new.items/d03686.pdf.

General Accountability Office. 2003b. *Container Security: Expansion of Key Customs Programs Will Require Greater Attention to Critical Success Factors*. GAO Report no. GA0-03-770. http://www.gao.gov/new.items/d03770.pdf.

General Accountability Office. 2003c. *US Postal Service: Issues Associated with Anthrax Testing at the Wallingford Facility*. GAO Report no. GAO-03-787T. http://www.gao.gov/ new.items/d03787t.pdf.

General Accountability Office. 2004a. *FBI Transformation: Human Capital Strategies May Assist the FBI in Its Commitment to Address Its Top Priorities*. GAO Report no. GAO-04-817T. http://www.gao.gov/htext/d04817t.html.

General Accountability Office, 2004b. *Further Action Needed to Promote Successful Use of Special DHS Acquisition Authority*. GAO Report no GA0-05-136. http://www.gao.gov/new .items/d05136.pdf.

General Accountability Office. 2005a. *Cargo Security: Partnership Program Grants Importers Reduced Scrutiny with Limited Assurance of Improved Security*. GAO Report no. GAO-05-404. http://www.gao.gov/new.items/d05404.pdf.

General Accountability Office. 2005b. *Information Technology: Federal Agencies Face Challenges in Implementing Initiatives to Improve Public Health Infrastructure*. GAO Report no. GAO-03-308. http://www.gao.gov/htext/d05308.html.

General Accountability Office. 2005c. Report to Congressional Committees: *Cooperative Threat Reduction: DOD Has Improved Its Management and Internal Controls, but Challenges Remain*. GAO Report no. GAO-05-329. http://www.gao.gov/new.items/d05329.pdf.

General Accountability Office. 2006a. *Combating Nuclear Smuggling: DHS Has Made Progress Deploying Radiation Detection Equipment at US Ports-of-Entry, but Concerns Remain*. GAO Report no. GAO-06-389. http://www.gao.gov/new.items/d06389.pdf.

General Accountability Office. 2006b. *DNDO's Cost-Benefit Analysis to Support the Purchase of New Radiation Detection Portal Monitors Was Not Based on Available Performance Data and Did Not Fully Evaluate All the Monitors' Costs and Benefits.* GAO Report no. GAO-07-334R. http://www.gao.gov/new.items/d07133r.pdf.

General Accountability Office. 2006c. *Border Security: US-Visit Program Faces Strategic, Operational, and Technological Challenges at Land Ports of Entry.* GAO Report no. GAO-07-248. http://www.rfidjournal.net/PDF_download/GAO_US_VISIT%20Program_Challenges .pdf.

General Accountability Office. 2006d. *Report to Congressional Requesters: Homeland Security: Recommendations to Improve Management of Key Border Security Program Need to be Implemented.* Report no. GA0-06-296. http://www.gao.gov/new.items/d06296.pdf.

General Accountability Office. 2006e. *Terrorism Insurance: Measuring and Predicting Losses from Unconventional Weapons Is Difficult, but Some Industry Exposure Exists.* GAO Report no. GAO-06-1081. www.gao.gov/new.items/d061081.pdf.

General Accountability Office. 2007a. *High-Containment Biosafety Laboratories: Preliminary Observations on the Oversight of the Proliferation of BSL-3 and BSL-4 Laboratories in the United States.* GAO Report no. GAO-08-108T. http://www.gao.gov/new.items/ d08108t.pdf.

General Accountability Office. 2007b. *Homeland Security Grants: Observations on Process DHS Used to Allocate Funds to Selected Urban Areas.* GAO Report no. GAO-07-381R. http://www.gao.gov/new.items/d07381r.pdf.

General Accountability Office. 2007c. Letter to Congressional Requesters: *Radiation Detection Equipment: DNDO Has Not Yet Collected Most of the National Laboratories' Test Results on Radiation Portal Monitors in Support of DNDO's Testing and Development Program.* GAO Report no. GAO-07-347R. http://www.gao.gov/new.items/d07347r.pdf.

General Accountability Office. 2007d. *Quadrennial Defense Review: Future Reviews Could Benefit from Improved Department of Defense Analyses and Changes to Legislative Requirements.* GAO Report no. GAO-07-709. http://bulk.resource.org/gpo.gov/gao/reports/d07709 .html.

General Accountability Office. 2008. *Border Security: Security Vulnerabilities at Unmanned and Unmonitored U.S. Border Locations.* GAO Report no. GAO-07-884T. http://www.gao .gov/new.items/d07884t.pdf.

General Accountability Office. 2008. Border Security "Summary of Covert Tests and Security Assessments for Senate Committee on Finance, 2003–2007." http://www.gao.gov/products/ GAO-08-757.

General Accounting Office. *See* General Accountability Office.

Gerber, Theodore P., and Deborah Yarsike Ball. Forthcoming. "Scientists in a Changed Institutional Environment: Subjective Adaptation and Social Responsibility Norms in Russia." *Social Studies of Science* 39.

Gibbons, Robert. 1992. *Game Theory for Applied Economists.* Princeton, NJ: Princeton University Press.

Gibson, Daniel G., Gwynedd A. Benders, Cynthia Andrews-Pfannkoch, Evgeniya A. Denisova, Holly Baden-Tillson, Jayshree Zaveri, Timothy B. Stockwell, Anushka Brownley, et al.

2008. "Complete Chemical Synthesis, Assembly, and Cloning of a Mycoplasma Genitalium Genome." *Science* 319: 1215–1220.

Gilmore Commission. *See* Advisory Panel to Assess Domestic Response Capabilities for Weapons of Mass Destruction.

Gilmore, James, and Janet Lynch Lambert. 2005. "Eight Strategies to Engage Industry in Biosecurity." *Biosecurity and Bioterrorism: Biodefense Strategy, Practice, and Science*, 3: 357–362.

Glaeser, Edward, and Jesse Shapiro. 2002. "Cities and Warfare: The Impact of Terrorism on Urban Form." *Journal of Urban Economics*, 51: 205–224.

Glass, Thomas A., and Monica Schoch-Spana. 2002. "Bioterrorism and the People: How to Vaccinate a City against Panic." *Clinical Infectious Diseases* 34: 217–223.

Glasstone, Samuel, and Philip J. Dolan. 1977. *The Effects of Nuclear Weapons*. Washington, DC: Government Printing Office.

Glazer, Amihai, and Lawrence S. Rothenberg. 2001. *Why Government Succeeds and Why It Fails*. Cambridge, MA: Harvard University Press.

Gledhill, B. L., and F. Mauro, eds. 1991. *New Horizons in Biological Dosimetry*. New York: Wiley-Liss.

Glik, Deborah, Kim Harrison, Mehrnaz Davoudi, and Deboraph Riopelle. 2004. "Public Perceptions and Risk Communications for Botulism." *Biosecurity and Bioterrorism: Biodefense Strategy, Practice, and Science*, 2: 216–223.

Global Alliance for TB Drug Development. 2001. *Economics of TB Drug Development*. Global Alliance for TB Drug Development Report. http://www.tballiance.org/downloads/publications/TBA_Economics_Report.pdf.

Goans, R. E., and J. H. Cantrell Jr. 1978. "Ultrasonic Characterization of Thermal Injury in Deep Burns." In *Proceedings of the Third International Symposium on Ultrasonic Imaging and Tissue Characterization*. Gaithersberg, MD: National Bureau of Standards.

Goans, Ronald E., and Jamie K. Waselenko. 2004. Unpublished lecture at NCRP Annual Meeting, Arlington VA.

Goda, Norman J. W. 1998. *Tomorrow the World: Hitler, Northwest Africa, and the Path Toward America*. College Station: Texas A&M University Press.

Godfrey-Smith, Dorothy I., and Barry A. Pass. 1997. "A New Method of Retrospective Biophysical Dosimetry: Optically Stimulated Luminescence and Fluorescence in Dental Enamel." *Health Physics* 72: 390–396.

Goldsmith, Stephen, and William D. Eggers. 2004. *Governing by Network: The New Shape of the Public Sector*. Washington, DC: Brookings Institution Press.

Goodwin, Peter. 1981. *Nuclear War: The Facts on Our Survival*. New York: Routledge.

Gordon, Peter, James E. Moore II, Ji Young Park, and Harry W. Richardson. 2007. "The Economic Impacts of a Terrorist Attack on the US Commercial Aviation System." *Risk Analysis* 27: 505–512.

Goss, Thomas. 2005. "Building a Contingency Menu: Using Capabilities-Based Planning for Homeland Defense and Homeland Security." *Homeland Security Affairs* 1: Article 5.

Gould, Chandre, and Peter Foll. 2002. *Project Coast: Apartheid's Chemical and Biological Warfare Programmes*. Geneva: United Nations Institute for Disarmament Research/Centre for Conflict Resolution.

Gould, Chandre, and Alastair Hay. 2006. "The South African Biological Weapons Program." In Mark Wheelis, Lajos Rozsa, and Malcolm Dando, eds., *Deadly Cultures: Biological Weapons Since 1945*, 191–212. Cambridge, MA: Harvard University Press.

Graff, Gordon. 2004. "Custom Chemical Manufacturing." *Purchasing*, March 4, 24C3.

Greenbaum, Stephen B., and Jaime B. Anderson. 2006a. "Botulinum Toxins." In James R. Swearengen, ed., *Biodefense: Research Methodology and Animal Models*, 259–274. Boca Raton, FL: CRC–Taylor & Francis Group.

Greenbaum, Stephen B., and Jaime B. Anderson. 2006b. "Ricin." In James R. Swearengen, ed., *Biodefense: Research Methodology and Animal Models*, 275–290. Boca Raton, FL: CRC–Taylor & Francis Group.

Greenspan, Alan. 2004. "Risk and Uncertainty in Monetary Policy." Remarks at American Economic Association Meeting, San Diego, CA, January 3.

Gregory, Nina. 2006. "Homeland Security's 'Procurement' Predicament." *News21*, July 25. http://newsinitiative.org/story/2006/07/25/homeland_securitys_procurement_predicament-oultn.

Gressang, Daniel S. IV. 2001. "Audience and Message: Assessing Terrorist WMD Potential." *Terrorism and Political Violence* 13: 83–106.

Griffith, Kevin S., Paul Mead, Gregory L. Armstrong, John Painter, Katherine A. Kelley, Alex R. Hoffmaster, Donald Mayo, et al. 2001. "Bioterrorism-Related Inhalational Anthrax in an Elderly Woman, Connecticut, 2001." *Emerging Infectious Disease* 9: 681–688.

Grigsby, Richard G. 1997. *Chemical Engineering for Chemists*. Washington, DC: American Chemical Society.

Gronvall, Gigi Kwik, Dennis Trent, Luciana Borio, Robert Brey, and Lee Nagao. 2008. "The FDA Animal Efficacy Rule and Biodefense." *Nature Biotechnology* 25: 1084–1087.

Group of Eight. 2003. Statement by G8 Leaders: "The G8 Global Partnership against the Spread of Weapons and Materials of Mass Destruction." http://www.g8.gc.ca/2002Kananaskis/kananaskis/globpart-en.asp.

Group of Eight. 2005. Gleneagles Meeting Statement: "G8 Statement on Counter-Terrorism." http://www.g8.gc.ca/pdf/g8_Gleneagles_CounterTerrorism-en.pdf.

Group of Eight. 2006. "G8 Summit Declaration on Counter-Terrorism." http://www.g8.gc.ca/declar_counter_terr-en.asp.

Grover, Will. 2005. "All the Easy Experiments: A Berkeley Professor, Dirty Bombs, and the Birth of Informed Consent." *Berkeley Science Review* 5: 41–45. http://sciencereview.berkeley.edu/articles/issue9/plutonium.pdf.

Grunwald, Michael, and Susan B. Glasser. 2005. "Brown's Turf Wars Sapped FEMA's Strength." *Washington Post*, December 23. http://www.washingtonpost.com/wp-dyn/content/article/2005/12/22/AR2005122202213.html.

Guillemin, Jeanne. 1999. *Anthrax: The Investigation of a Deadly Outbreak*. Berkeley: University of California Press.

Guillemin, Jeanne. 2005. *Biological Weapons: From the Invention of State-Sponsored Programs to Contemporary Bioterrorism.* New York: Columbia University Press.

Gunaratna, Rohan. 2003. *Inside Al Qaeda: Global Network of Terror.* New York: Berkley.

Gurr, Nadine, and Benjamin Cole. 2002. *The New Face of Terrorism: Threats from Weapons of Mass Destruction.* London: I. B. Tauris.

Gursky, Elin, Thomas V. Inglesby, and Tara O'Toole. 2003. "Anthrax 2001: Observations on the Medical and Public Health Response." *Biosecurity and Bioterrorism: Biodefense Strategy, Practice, and Science* 1: 97–110.

Guy Carpenter & Co. 2007. "Global Terror Insurance Market: The World Continues on High Alert." http://gcportal.guycarp.com/portal/extranet/popup/pdf_2007/GCPub/Terror%20Report%202007.pdf?vid=2.

Guy Carpenter & Co., and MMC Securities. 2007. "The Catastrophe Bond Market at Year-End 2006." http://www.guycarp.com/portal/extranet/pdf/GCPub/Cat%20Bond%202006.pdf;jsessionid=GDScflxLvCZj78N8GpywnDHrNSyCp82tt2yKts73VvKQZDs6psKM!1252222885?vid=1.

Haas, Charles N. 2002. "On the Risk of Mortality to Primates Exposed to Anthrax Spores," *Risk Analysis* 22: 189–193.

Haas, Charles N., Christopher S. Crockett, J. B. Rose, C. P. Gerba, and A. Fazil, "Infectivity of *Cryptosporidium parvum* Oocysts." 1996. *Journal of the American Water Works Association.* 88: 131–136.

Haas, Charles N., J. B. Rose, and C. P. Gerba. 1999. *Quantitative Microbial Risk Assessment,* New York: Wiley.

Haas, Charles N., Aadithya Thayyar-Madabusi, J. B. Rose, and C. P. Gerba. 2000. "Development of a Dose-Response Relationship for Escherichia coli O157:H7," *International Journal of Food Microbiology* 56: 153–159.

Hall, John R., ed. 2000. *Apocalypse Observed: Religious Movements and Violence in North America, Europe, and Japan.* London: Routledge.

Hall, John R., and Philip D. Schuyler. 2000. "The Mystical Apocalypse of the Solar Temple." In John R. Hall, ed., *Apocalypse Observed,* 111–148. London: Routledge.

Hall, Molly J., Anne E. Norwood, Robert J. Ursano, and Carol S. Fullerton. 2003. "The Psychological Impacts of Bioterrorism." *Biosecurity and Bioterrorism: Biodefense Strategy, Practice, and Science* 1: 139–144.

Halloran, M. Elizabeth. 1998. "Concepts of Infectious Disease Epidemiology." In Kenneth J. Rothman and Sander Greenland, eds., *Modern Epidemiology,* 2nd ed., 520–544. Philadelphia: Lippincott-Raven.

Hamburg, Margaret A. 2001. Testimony before the House Subcommittee on National Security, Veterans Affairs and International Relations. http://www.bioterrorism.slu.edu/bt/official/congress/hamburg072301pdf.pdf.

Hanson, Robin D. 2006. "Designing Real Terrorism Futures." *Public Choice* 128: 257–274.

Harclerode, Peter. 2001. *Secret Soldiers: Special Forces in the War against Terrorism.* London: Cassell.

Harris, Robert, and Jeremy Paxman. 2002. *A Higher Form of Killing*. New York: Random House.

Hart, John. 2006. "The Soviet Biological Weapons Program." In Mark Wheelis, Lajos Rozsa, and Malcolm Dando, eds., *Deadly Cultures: Biological Weapons Since 1945*, 132–156. Cambridge, MA: Harvard University Press.

Hartwig, Robert P. 2006. "September 11 and Insurance: The Five Year Anniversary." Insurance Information Institute. http://server.iii.org/yy_obj_data/binary/773375_1_0/September%2011%20Anniversary.pdf.

Havelaar, Arie H., and Johan Garssen. 2000. *Dose Response Relationships for Gastrointestinal Pathogens in an Animal Model*. Bilthoven, NL: National Insitute for Public Health and the Environment (RIVM).

Haveman, Jon D., Howard J. Shatz, and Ernesto I. Vilchis. 2005. "An Overview of US Port Security Programs." In Harry W. Richardson, Peter Gordon, and James E. Moore II, eds., *The Economic Impacts of Terrorist Attacks*, 242–261. Northampton, MA: Edward Elgar.

Heal, Geoffrey, and Howard Kunreuther. 2007. "Environmental Assets & Liabilities." Paper presented at "Measuring and Managing Federal Financial Risk," NBER Conference, Northwestern University, February 8–9.

Health Resources and Services Administration. n.d. "Home page." http://www.hrsa.gov/esarvhp/.

Heifetz, Ronald A. 1994. *Leadership Without Easy Answers*. Cambridge, MA: Belknap Press.

Heikkinen, Maire S. A., Mervi K. Hjelmroos-Koski, Max M. Haggblom, and Janet M. Macher. 2005. "Bioaerosols." In Lev S. Ruzer and Naomi H. Harley, eds., *Aerosols Handbook: Measurement, Dosimetry, and Health Effects*, 291–342. Boca Raton, FL.: CRC Press.

Helfand, Ira, Andy Kanter, Michael McCally, Kimberly Roberts, and Jaya Tiwari. 2006. *The US and Nuclear Terrorism: Still Dangerously Unprepared*. Physicians for Social Responsibility Report. http://www.psr.org/site/DocServer/PSR_NuclearTerr_rpt_full.pdf?docID=781.

Helfenstein, Reiner, and Thomas Holzheu. 2006. *Securitization: New Opportunities for Insurers and Investors*. Swiss Re *Sigma* Report no. 7/2006. http://www.swissre.com/resources/fc02f680455c6b548a5fba80a45d76a0-sigma7_2006_e.pdf.

Heller, Arnie. 2002. "This Model Can Take the Heat." *Science and Technology Review*, November.

Heller, Arnie. 2009. "Sniffing the air with an electronic 'nose.'" *Science and Technology Review*, January.

Henderson, Donald A. 1999. "The Looming Threat of Bioterrorism." *Science* 283: 1279–1283.

Henderson, J. Neil, L. Carolyn Henderson, Gary E. Raskob, and Daniel T. Boatwright. 2004. "Chemical (VX). Terrorist Threat: Public Knowledge, Attitudes, and Responses." *Biosecurity and Bioterrorism: Biodefense Strategy, Practice, and Science* 2: 224–228.

Hersey, John. [1946] 2001. "Hiroshima." In Samuel Hynes, Anne Matthews, Nancy Caldwell Sorrel, and Roger J. Spiller, eds., *Reporting World War II: American Journalism 1938–1946*. New York: Library of America.

Heyes, Anthony, and Catherine Liston-Heyes. 2000. "Capping Environmental Liability: The Case of American Nuclear Power." *Geneva Papers on Risk and Insurance* 25: 196–202.

HHS. *See* Department of Health and Human Services.

Himfar v. United States. 1966. 355 *Federal Reporter* 2d. 606. US Court of Claims.

Hittle, James D. 1944. *The Military Staff: Its History and Development.* Harrisburg, PA: Military Service Publishing Co.

Hitz, Frederick P., and Brian J. Weiss. 2004. "Helping the CIA and FBI Connect the Dots in the War on Terror." *International Journal of Intelligence and Counterintelligence* 17: 1–41.

Hobijn, Bart. 2002. "What Will Homeland Security Cost?" *Federal Reserve Bank of New York, Economic Policy Review*, November, 21–33. http://www.newyorkfed.org/research/epr/02v08n2/0211hobi.pdf.

Hobijn, Bart, and Erick Sager. 2007. "What Has Homeland Security Cost? An Assessment: 2001–2005." *Federal Reserve Bank of New York, Current Issues in Economics and Finance* no. 13. http://www.newyorkfed.org/research/current_issues/ci13-2.pdf.

Hoffman, Bruce. 1993a. *Holy Terror: The Implications of Terrorism Motivated by a Religious Imperative.* Santa Monica, CA: RAND.

Hoffman, Bruce. 1993b. "Terrorist Targeting: Tactics, Trends, and Potentialities." *Terrorism and Political Violence* 5: 12–29.

Hoffman, Bruce. 1997. "Terrorism and WMD: Some Preliminary Hypotheses." *Nonproliferation Review* 4: 45–50.

Hoffman, Bruce. 1998. *Inside Terrorism.* New York: Columbia University Press.

Hoffman, Bruce. 2000. "The American Perspective." In Olivier Roy, Bruce Hoffman, Reuven Paz, Steven Simon, and Daniel Benjamin, "America and the New Terrorism: An Exchange." *Survival* 42: 161–166.

Hogarth, Robin, and Howard Kunreuther. 1989. "Risk, Ambiguity and Insurance." *Journal of Risk and Uncertainty* 2: 5–35.

Hogg, Ian V. 2002. *German Secret Weapons of the Second World War: The Missiles, Rockets, Weapons, and New Technology of the Third Reich.* Mechanicsburg, PA: Stackpole Books.

Holcomb, D. L., M. A. Smith, G. O. Ware, Y. C. Hung, R. E. Brackett, and M. P. Doyle. 1999. "Comparison of Six Dose-Response Models for Use with Food-Borne Pathogens," *Risk Analysis* 19: 1091–1100.

Homeland Security Council. 2005. "National Planning Scenarios: Created for Use in National, Federal, State and Local Preparedness Activities." Draft 20.1. http://www.ap.org/california/planningscenarios.pdf.

Homeland Security National Preparedness Task Force. 2006. "Civil Defense and Homeland Security: A Short History of National Preparedness Efforts." http://training.fema.gov/EMIWeb/edu/docs/DHS%20Civil%20Defense-HS%20-%20Short%20History.pdf.

House Committee on Government Reform/Minority Staff/Special Investigations Division. 2006. "Dollars, Not Sense: Government Contracting under the Bush Administration." http://oversight.house.gov/documents/20061211100757-98364.pdf.

Hoyt, Edwin. 2000. *Inferno: The Firebombing of Japan, March 9–August 15, 1945.* Lanham, MD: Madison Books.

HRSA. *See* Health Resources and Services Administration.

HSC. *See* Homeland Security Council.

Hsu, Spencer S. 2007. "Job Vacancies at DHS Said to Hurt US Preparedness." *Washington Post*, July 9, 2007, A01.

Hsu, Spencer S., and Mary Beth Sheridan. 2007. "D.C., New York Get Biggest Increases in Counterterroism Aid." *Washington Post*, July 19, 1.

Hull, G., J. J. Roberts, J. D. Kuntz, S. E. Fisher, R. D. Sanner, T. M. Tillotson, Alexander D. Drobshoff, Stephen A. Payne, and Nerine J. Cherepy. 2007. "Ce-doped Single Crystal and Ceramic Garnets for γ-Ray Detection." *Society of Photo-Optical Instrumentation Engineers (SPIE) Proceedings*, 6706171–6706175.

Hume, Claudia, and William Schmitt. 2001. "Pharma's Prescription." *Chemical Week*, April 11, 21.

Huntley David J., Dorothy I. Godfrey-Smith, and Michael L. W. Thewalt. 1985. "Optical Dating of Sediments." *Nature* 313: 105–107.

Hyams, Kenneth C., Frances M. Murphy, and Simon Wessely. 2002. "Responding to Chemical, Biological, or Nuclear Terrorism: The Indirect and Long-Term Health Effects May Present the Greatest Challenge." *Journal of Health Politics, Policy, and Law* 27: 273–291.

IAEA. *See* International Atomic Energy Agency.

IASB. *See* International Association Synthetic Biology

Ibragimov, Rustam, Dwight Jaffee, and Johan Walden. 2008. "Non-Diversification Traps in Markets for Catastrophic Risk." *Review of Financial Studies*. 21. Advance copy posted March 28. http://rfs.oxfordjournals.org/cgi/content/full/hhn021v1.

ICRP. *See* International Commission on Radiation Protection.

Ikeya, M., and H. Ishii. 1989. "Atomic Bomb and Accident Dosimetry with ESR: Natural Rocks and Human Tooth *in Vivo* Spectrometer." *Applied Radiation and Isotopes* 40: 1021–1027.

Ikle, Fred. 1961. "After Detection, What?" *Foreign Affairs* 39: 208–220.

IMAAC. *See* Interagency Modeling and Atmospheric Assessment Center.

Industry Association Synthetic Biology. 2008. Workshop Report: "Technical Solutions for Biosecurity in Synthetic Biology." http://www.ia-sb.eu/wp-content/uploads/2008/09/iasb _report_biosecurity_syntheticbiology.pdf.

Inglesby, Thomas V., David T. Dennis, Donald A. Henderson, John G. Bartlett, Michael S. Ascher, Edward Eitzen, Anne D. Fine, Arthur M. Friedlander, et al. 2000. "Plague as a Biological Weapon: Medical and Public Health Management." *Journal of the American Medical Association* 283: 2281–2290.

Inglesby, Thomas V., Rita Grossman, and Tara O'Toole. 2001. "A Plague on Your City: Observations from TOPOFF." *Clinical Infectious Diseases* 32: 436–445.

Inglesby, Thomas V., Donald A. Henderson, John G. Bartlett, Michael S. Ascher, Edward Eitzen, Arthur M. Friedlander, Jerome Hauer, et al. 1999. "Anthrax as a Biological Weapon: Medical and Public Health Management." *Journal of the American Medical Association* 281: 1735–1745.

Inglesby, Thomas V., Tara O'Toole, Donald A. Henderson, John G. Bartlett, Michael S. Ascher, Edward Eitzen, Arthur M. Friedlander, et al. 2002. "Anthrax as a Biological Weapon, 2002: Updated Recommendations for Management." *Journal of the American Medical Association* 287: 2236–2252.

Inoue, Y., and Y. Kawakami. 2004. "Factors Influencing Tabloid News Diffusion: Comparison with Hard News." *Keio Communication Review* 26: 37–52.

Institute of Medicine/Committee on Assuring the Health of the Public in the 21st Century. 2002. *The Future of the Public's Health in the 21st Century*. Washington, DC: National Academies Press.

Insurance Information Institute. 2007a. "Catastrophe: Insurance Issues." http://www.iii.org/media/hottopics/insurance/catastrophes/.

Insurance Information Institute. 2007b. "Terrorism Risk and Insurance." http://www.iii.org/media/hottopics/insurance/terrorism/.

Insurance Information Institute. n.d. "Facts and Statistics: Terrorism." http://www.iii.org/media/facts/statsbyissue/terrorism/.

INTAS. See International Association for the Promotion of Cooperation with Scientists from the Commonwealth of Independent States and the Former Soviet Union.

Interagency Modeling and Atmospheric Assessment Center. 2005. "Introduction to the IMAAC." http://orise.orau.gov/emi/scapa/files/05mtg/AppM-Dillon.pdf.

International Association for the Promotion of Cooperation with Scientists from the Commonwealth of Independent States and the Former Soviet Union. n.d. "INTAS in Liquidation as of 1 January 2007." http://www.intas.be/liquidation.html.

International Atomic Energy Agency. 1970. *Treaty on the Non-Proliferation of Nuclear Weapons*. IAEA Information Circular INFCIRC/140. http://www.iaea.org/Publications/Documents/Infcircs/Others/infcirc140.pdf.

International Atomic Energy Agency. 1988. *The Radiological Accident in Goiania*." Vienna: IAEA.

International Atomic Energy Agency. 2005. *Generic Procedures for Medical Response during a Nuclear or Radiological Emergency*. Vienna: IAEA.

International Commission on Radiation Protection. 1980. *Biological Effects of Inhaled Radionuclides*. Oxford: Pergamon Press.

International Commission on Radiation Protection. 1986. *The Metabolism of Plutonium and Related Elements*. Oxford: Pergamon Press.

International Commission on Radiation Protection. 1988. *Individual Monitoring for Intakes of Radionuclides by Workers: Design and Interpretation*. Oxford: Pergamon Press.

International Commission on Radiation Protection. 1989–1996. *Age Dependent Doses to Members of the Public from Intake of Radionuclides, Parts 1–5*. Oxford: Pergamon Press.

International Commission on Radiation Protection. 1994a. *Dose Coefficients for Intakes of Radionuclides by Workers*. Oxford: Pergamon Press.

International Commission on Radiation Protection. 1994b. *Human Respiratory Tract Model for Radiological Protection*. Oxford: Pergamon Press.

International Commission on Radiation Protection. 1996. *Conversion Coefficients for Use in Radiological Protection against External Radiation.* Oxford: Pergamon Press.

International Commission on Radiation Protection. 1997. *Individual Monitoring for Internal Exposure of Workers: Replacement of ICRP Publication 54.* Oxford: Pergamon Press.

International Science and Technology Center. 2007. "Nonproliferation through Science Co-operation." http://www.istc.ru.

IOM. *See* Institute of Medicine.

Israeli, Eitan, and R. Kevin Wood. 2002. "Shortest-Path Network Interdiction." *Networks* 40: 97–111.

Issaq, Haleem J., Thomas P. Conrads, Darue A. Prieto, Radhakrishna S. Tirumala, and Timothy D. Veenstra. 2003. "SELDI-TOF MS for Diagnostic Proteomics." *Analytical Chemistry* 75, 148A–155A.

ISTC. *See* International Science and Technology Center.

Jackson, Brian A. 2001. "Technology Acquisition by Terrorist Groups: Threat Assessment Informed by Lessons from Private Sector Technology Adoption." *Studies in Conflict and Terrorism* 24: 183–213.

Jacobs, Stanley S. 1998. The Nuclear Threat as a Terrorist Option. *Terrorism and Political Violence* 10: 149–63.

Jaffee, Dwight. 2005. "The Role of Government in the Coverage of Terrorism Risks." In Organization for Economic Co-Operation and Development, *Terrorism Risk Insurance in OECD Countries.* Policy Issues in Insurance no. 9. Paris: OECD Publishing, 2005. http://faculty.haas.berkeley.edu/jaffee/Papers/091DJOECD.pdf.

Jaffee, Dwight. 2006. "Commentary." *Federal Reserve Bank of St. Louis Review*, July/August, 381–385. http://research.stlouisfed.org/publications/review/06/07/Jaffee.pdf.

Jaffee, Dwight, and Thomas Russell. 1997. "Catastrophe Insurance, Capital Markets, and Uninsurable Risks." *Journal of Risk and Insurance* 64: 205–230.

Jaffee, Dwight, and Thomas Russell. 2006. "Should Governments Provide Catastrophe Insurance?" *The Economists' Voice* 3, no. 5, article 6. http://www.bepress.com/ev/vol3/iss5/art6/.

Jaffee, Dwight, and Thomas Russell. 2007a. "CBRN Terrorism: Who Should Bear the Risk?" Unpublished conference paper.

Jaffee, Dwight, and Thomas Russell. 2007b. "Financing Catastrophe Insurance: A New Proposal." In John Quigley and Larry Rosenthal, eds., *Risking Housing and Home: Disasters, Cities, Public Policy.* Boalsburg, PA: Public Policy Press.

Jahrling, Peter B., and John W. Huggins. 2006. "Orthopox Viruses." In James R. Swearengen, ed., *Biodefense: Research Methodology and Animal Models*, 207–225. Boca Raton, FL.: CRC–Taylor & Francis Group.

Jain, Kewal K. 2002. "Proteomics-Based Anticancer Drug Discovery and Development." *Technology in Cancer Research and Treatment* 1: 231–236.

JCAHO. *See* Joint Commission on Accreditation of Healthcare Organizations.

Jenkins, Brian M. 1986. "Defense against Terrorism." *Political Science Quarterly* 101: 773–786.

Jenkins, Brian M. 1997. "Understanding the Link between Motives and Methods." In Brad Roberts, ed., *Terrorism with Chemical and Biological Weapons: Calibrating Risks and Responses*, 121–140. Alexandria, VA: Chemical and Biological Arms Control Institute.

Jenkins, Brian M. 2000. "The WMD Terrorist Threat—Is There a Consensus View?" In Brad Roberts, ed., *Hype or Reality: The "New" Terrorism and Mass Casualty Attacks*, 241–251. Alexandria, VA: Chemical and Biological Arms Control Institute.

Jentleson, Bruce A., and Christopher A. Whytok. 2005. "Who 'Won' Libya: The Force-Diplomacy Debate and Its Implications for Theory and Policy." *International Security* 30: 47–86.

JIWG. *See* Joint Interagency Working Group.

Johnson, E., Nancy Jaax, J. White, and Peter B. Jahrling. 1995. "Lethal Experimental Infections of Rhesus Monkeys by Aerosolized Ebola Virus." *International Journal of Experimental Pathology* 76: 227–236.

Joint Commission on Accreditation of Healthcare Organizations. 2005. *Standing Together: An Emergency Planning Guide for America's Communities*. Washington, DC: JCAHO. http://www.jointcommission.org/NR/rdonlyres/FE29E7D3-22AA-4DEB-94B2-5E8D507F92 D1/0/planning_guide.pdf.

Joint Commission on Accreditation of Healthcare Organizations. 2006. *Surge Hospitals: Providing Safe Care in Emergencies*. Washington, DC: JCAHO. http://www.jointcommission .org/NR/rdonlyres/802E9DA4-AE80-4584-A205-48989C5BD684/0/surge_hospital.pdf.

Joint Interagency Working Group. 2005. *Technology Assessment and Roadmap for the Emergency Radiation Dose Assessment Program*. Lawrence Livermore Report UCRL-TR–21587. http://www3.niaid.nih.gov/research/topics/radnuc/PDF/TechAssessment.pdf.

Jordan, Lara Jakes. 2006. "Physicians Group Says No Medical Plans Ready for Nuclear Explosion." *San Diego Tribune*, August 31.

Juergensmeyer, Marc. 1996. "The Worldwide Rise of Religious Nationalism." *Journal of International Affairs* 50: 1–20.

Kahn, Herman. 1962. *Thinking about the Unthinkable*. New York: Horizon Press.

Kaibao, L., C. Jindi, Z. Qixin, and Z. Zhizhao. 1986. "Investigations on the TL Properties of Chemical Reagent NaCl." *Radiation Protection. Dosimetry* 17: 411–414.

Kaiser, Jocelyn. 2003. "How Much Are Human Lives and Health Worth?" *Science* 299: 1836–1837.

Kamp, Karl-Heinz. 1998. "Nuclear Terrorism Is Not the Core Problem." In Karl-Heinz Kamp, Joseph F. Pilat, Jessica Stern, and Richard A. Falkenrath, "WMD Terrorism: An Exchange, *Survival* 40: 168–171.

Kaplan, David E. 2000. "Aum Shinrikyo (1995)." In Jonathan Tucker, ed., *Toxic Terror: Assessing Terrorist Use of Chemical and Biological Weapons*, 207–226. Cambridge, MA: MIT Press, 2000.

Kaplan, David E., and Andrew Marshall. 1996. *The Cult at the End of the World*. New York: Crown.

Kashparov, V. A., S. M. Lundin, A. M. Kadygrib, V. P. Protsak, S. E. Levtchuk, V. I. Yoschenko, V. A. Kashpur, and N. M. Talerko. 2000. "Forest Fires in the Territory Contaminated as a Result of the Chernobyl Accident: Radioactive Aerosol Resuspension and Exposure of Fire Fighters." *Journal of Environmental Radioactivity* 51: 281–298.

Kasperson, Roger E., Ortwin Renn, Paul Slovic, Halina S. Brown, Jacque Emel, Robert Goble, Jeanne X. Kasperson, and Samuel Ratick. 2004. "The Social Amplification of Risk: A Conceptual Framework." In Paul Slovic, ed., *The Perception of Risk*, 232–245. London: Earthscan.

Katz Aaron, Andrea B. Staiti, and Kelly L. McKenzie. 2006. "Preparing for the Unknown, Responding to the Unknown: Communities and Public Health Preparedness." *Health Affairs* 25: 946–957.

Keasling, Jay. 2007a. Video Lecture: "Has Synthetic Biology Changed the Security Threat— And Will It?" http://wiki.coe.berkeley.edu/biosecurity/Syllabus.doc.

Keasling, Jay. 2007b. Video Lecture: "Introduction to Synthetic Biology." http://wiki.coe .berkeley.edu/biosecurity/Syllabus.doc.

Keeney, Ralph L., and Howard Raiffa. 1976. *Decisions with Multiple Objectives*. New York: Wiley.

Kelle, Alexander, and Annette Schaper. 2001. *Terrorism Using Nuclear and Biological Weapons: A Critical Analysis of Risks after 11 September 2001*. Peace Research Institute Frankfurt Report no. 64. http://www.hsfk.de/downloads/prifrep64.pdf.

Kellman, Barry. 2006. "Notes from a BWC Gadfly." *Biosecurity and Bioterrorism: Biodefense Strategy, Practice, and Science* 4: 231–236.

Kelly, Rich. 1996. "The Nunn-Lugar Act: A Wasteful and Dangerous Illusion." Cato Institute Foreign Policy Briefing no. 39. http://www.cato.org/pubs/fpbriefs/fpb-039es.html.

Kennedy, Paul. 1999. *Freedom from Fear: The American People in Depression and War*. New York: Oxford.

Kepel, Gilles. 1994. *The Revenge of God: The Resurgence of Islam, Christianity, and Judaism in the Modern World*. University Park: Pennsylvania State University Press.

Kettl, Donald F. 2007. *System under Stress: Homeland Security and American Politics*. Washington, DC: CQ Press.

Keys, David. *Catastrophe: An Investigation into the Origins of the Modern World*. New York: Ballantine, 1999.

Khan, Ali S. 2003. Testimony before the House Select Committee on Homeland Security: "Public Health Assessment of Potential Biological Terrorism Agents." http://www.hhs.gov/ asl/testify/t030606b.html.

Khan, H. M., and Delincée, H., 1995. "Detection of Radiation Treatment of Spices and Herbs of Asian Origin Using Thermoluminescence of Mineral Contaminants." *Applied Radioactivity and Isotopes* 46: 1071–1075.

Kharitonov, Sergei A., and Peter J. Barnes. 2001. "Exhaled Markers of Pulmonary Disease." *American Journal of Respiratory and Critical Care Medicine* 163: 1693–1722.

Kingdon, John W. 1995. *Agendas, Alternatives, and Public Policies*. 2nd ed. New York: HarperCollins.

Koch, Andrew. 2004. "The Nuclear Network—Khanfessions of a Proliferator." *Jane's Security News*. http://www.janes.com/security/international_security/news/jdw/jdw040226_1_n .shtml

Koopman, Jim. 2003. "Controlling Smallpox." *Science* 298: 1342–1344.

Kraus, Nancy, Torjorn Malmfors, and Paul Slovic. 2004. "Intuitive Toxicology: Expert and Lay Judgments of Chemical Risks." In Paul Slovic, ed., *The Perception of Risk*, 285–315. London: Earthscan.

Kremer, Michael, and Rachel Glennerster. 2004. *Strong Medicine: Creating Incentives for Pharmaceutical Research on Neglected Diseases*. Princeton, NJ: Princeton University Press.

Krieg, R. C., F. Fogt, T. Braunschweig, P. C. Herrmann, V. Wollscheidt, and A. Wellmann. 2004. "ProteinChip Array Analysis of Microdissected Colorectal Carcinoma and Associated Tumor Stroma Shows Specific Protein Bands in the 3.4 to 3.6 kDa Range." *Anticancer Research* 24: 1791–1796.

Kukar, Thomas, S. Eckenrode, Y. Gu, W. Lian, M. Megginson, J. X. She, and D. Wu. 2002. "Protein Microarrays to Detect Protein-Protein Interactions Using Red and Green Fluorescent Proteins." *Analytical Biochemistry* 306: 50–54.

Kunreuther, Howard, Robin Hogarth, and Jacqueline Meszaros. 1993. "Insurer Ambiguity and Market Failure." *Journal of Risk and Uncertainty* 7: 71–89.

Kunreuther, Howard, and Geoffrey Heal. 2003. "Interdependent Security." *Journal of Risk and Uncertainty* 26: 231–249.

Kunreuther, Howard, and Mark Pauly. 2004. "Neglecting Disaster: Why Don't People Insure against Large Losses?" *Journal of Risk and Uncertainty* 28: 5–21.

Kurz, Ebba U., and Susan P. Lees-Miller. 2004. "DNA Damage-Induced Activation of ATM and ATM-Dependent Signaling Pathways." *DNA Repair* 3: 889–900.

Lakdawalla, Darius, and Eric Talley. 2006. Optimal Liability for Terrorism. NBER Working Paper 12578.

Landauer, Michael R., Venkataraman Srinivasan, and Thomas M. Seed. 2003. "Genistein Treatment Protects Mice from Ionizing Radiation Injury." *Journal of Applied Toxicology* 23: 379–385.

Landers, Peter. 2004. "Drug Industry's Big Push Into Technology Falls Short." *Wall Street Journal*, February 24. p. A-1.

Langewiesche, William. 2005. "The Wrath of Khan: How A. Q. Khan Made Pakistan a Nuclear Power—and Showed That the Spread of Atomic Weapons Can't Be Stopped." *The Atlantic*, November, 62–85.

Langewiesche, William. 2007. *The Atomic Bazaar: The Rise of the Nuclear Poor*. New York: Farrar, Straus & Giroux.

LaPorte, Todd R. 2007. "Critical Infrastructure in the Face of a Predatory Future: Preparing for Untoward Surprise." *Journal of Contingencies and Crisis Management* 15: 60–64.

Laqueur, Walter. 1999. *The New Terrorism: Fanaticism and the Arms of Mass Destruction*. New York: Oxford University Press.

Laqueur, Walter. 2002. *A History of Terrorism*. New York: Transaction Publishers.

Laqueur, Walter. 2004. *No End to War: Terrorism in the Twenty-First Century*. New York: Continuum.

Larence, Eileen R., and David A. Powner. 2007. Testimony before the House Subcommittee on Homeland Security: "Critical Infrastructure: Challenges Remain in Protecting Key Sectors." GAO Report no. GAO-07-626T. http://www.gao.gov/new.items/d07626t.pdf.

Lasker, Roz D., Christopher G. Atchison, Lester Breslow, Gert H. Brieger, Sherry Glied, Charles C. Hughes, Bonnie J. Kostelecky, et al. 1997. *Medicine and Public Health: The Power of Collaboration*. New York: New York Academy of Medicine.

Last, John M. 1995. *A Dictionary of Epidemiology*. 3rd ed. Oxford: Oxford University Press.

Laster, David, and Christian Schmidt. 2005. "Innovating to Insure the Uninsurable." Swiss Re *Sigma* Study no. 4/2005. http://www.swissre.com/resources/1340e800455c566c9753bf80a45d76a0-sigma_4_2005_e_rev.pdf.

Lave, Lester, Jay Apt, A. Farrell, and M. Granger Morgan. 2005. "Increasing the Security and Reliability of the US Electricity System." In Harry W. Richardson, Peter Gordon, and James E. Moore, eds., *The Economic Impacts of Terrorist Attacks*, 57–69. Cheltenham, UK: Edward Elgar.

Lave, Lester, Jay Apt, and M. Granger Morgan. 2007. "Worst-Case Electricity Scenarios: The Benefits and Costs of Prevention." In Harry W. Richardson, Peter Gordon and James E. Moore, eds., *The Economic Costs and Consequences of Terrorism*, 257–272. Cheltenham, UK: Edward Elgar.

Lawrence Livermore National Laboratory. 2007. *Remediation Guidance for Major Airports After a Bioterrorist Attack*. LLNL Report no. UCRL-TR-210178-DRAFT Rev. 2, 2007. To be issued as a joint Department of Homeland Security and US Environmental Protection Agency document (forthcoming).

Leamer, Edward E., and Christopher Thornberg. 2006. "Ports, Trade, and Terrorism: Balancing the Catastrophic and the Chronic." In Jon D. Haverman and Howard Shatz, eds., *Protecting the Nation's Seaports: Balancing Security and Cost*. San Francisco: Public Policy Institute of California.

Leavitt, Judith Walzer. 2003. "Public Resistance or Cooperation? A Tale of Smallpox in Two Cities." *Biosecurity and Bioterrorism: Biodefense Strategy, Practice, and Science* 1: 185–192.

Lee, Bumsoo, Peter Gordon, and James E. Moore II. 2007. Simulating the Economic Impacts of Various Hypothetical Bio-Terrorist Attacks. Working Paper, Center for Risk and Economic Analysis of Terrorist Events, University of Southern California, Los Angeles.

Lee, Bumsoo, Peter Gordon, James E. Moore II, and Harry W. Richardson. 2008. "Simulating the Economic Impacts of a Hypothetical Bio-Terrorist Attack: A Sports Stadium Case," *Journal of Homeland Security and Emergency Management* 5: Issue 1, Article 39. http://www.bepress.com/jhsem/vol5/iss1/39.

Leffel, Elizabeth K., and Douglas S. Reed. 2004. "Marburg and Ebola Viruses as Aerosol Threats." *Biosecurity and Bioterrorism: Biodefense Strategy, Practice, and Science* 2: 186–191.

Lehr, Ray. 2006. "Emergency Response: An Overview." In David G. Kamien, ed., *The McGraw-Hill Homeland Security Handbook*, 665–676. New York: McGraw-Hill.

Leiper, A. D. 1995. "Late Effects of Total Body Irradiation." *Archives of Disease in Childhood* 72: 382–385.

Leite, Marco Antonio Sperb, and L. David Roper. 1988. "The Goiania Radiation Incident—A Failure of Science and Society." http://arts.bev.net/roperldavid/GRI.htm.

Leitenberg, Milton. 1999. "Aum Shinrikyo's Efforts to Produce Biological Weapons: A Case Study in the Serial Propagation of Misinformation." *Terrorism and Political Violence* 11: 149–158.

Leitenberg, Milton. 2004. *The Problem of Biological Weapons*. Stockholm: Swedish National Defense College. http://www.strategicstudiesinstitute.army.mil/pdffiles/PUB639.pdf.

Leitenberg, Milton. 2005. *Assessing the Biological Weapons and Bioterrorism Threat*. Carlisle, PA: U.S. Army War College/Strategic Studies Institute. http://www.strategicstudiesinstitute.army.mil/pubs/display.cfm?pubID=639.

Lemyre, Louise M., Melanie Clement, Wayne Corneil, Lorraine Craig, Paul Boutette, Michael Tyshenko, Nataliya Karyankina, Robert Clarke, and Danie Krewski. 2005. "A Psychosocial Risk Assessment and Management Framework to Enhance Response to CBRN Terrorism Threats and Attacks." *Biosecurity and Bioterrorism: Biodefense Strategy, Practice, and Science* 3: 316–330.

Leonard, Herman B., and Arnold M. Howitt. 2006. "Katrina as Prelude: Preparing for and Responding to Katrina-Class Disturbances in the United States—Testimony to U.S. Senate Committee, March 8, 2006." *Journal of Homeland Security and Emergency Management* 3, no. 2, article 5. http://www.hks.harvard.edu/taubmancenter/emergencyprep/downloads/katrina_prelude.pdf.

Lewis, Christopher M., and Kevin C. Murdock. 1996. "The Role of Government Contracts in Discretionary Reinsurance Markets for Natural Disasters. *Journal of Risk and Insurance* 63: 567–597.

Leventhal, Paul, and Yonah Alexander. 1987. *Preventing Nuclear Terrorism*. Lexington, MA: Lexington Books.

Levin, David B., and Giovana Valdares de Amorim. 2003. "Potential for Aerosol Dissemination of Biological Weapons: Lessons from Biological Control of Insects." *Biosecurity and Bioterrorism: Biodefense Strategy, Practice, and Science* 1: 37–42.

Levinthal, Daniel A., and James G. March. 1993. "The Myopia of Learning." *Strategic Management Journal* 14: 95–112.

Lia, Brynjar. 2004. Unpublished lecture: "Al-Qaida's CBRN Programme: Lessons and Implications." Norwegian International Defense Seminar, October 12.

Lia, Brynjar. 2007. *Architect of Global Jihad: The Life of Al Qaeda Strategist Abu Mus'ab al-Suri*. New York: Columbia University Press.

Lieberman, Joseph L. 2004. "Testimony before Senate Judiciary and HELP Committees." http://www.senate.gov/comm/judiciary/general/member_statement.cfm?id=1327&wit_id=3892.

Lifton, Robert J. 1999. *Destroying the World to Save It: Aum Shinrikyo, Apocalyptic Violence, and the New Global Terrorism*. New York: Holt.

Linzer, Dafna, and Jodi Warrick. 2007. "US Finds That Iran Halted Nuclear Arms Bid in 2003." *Washington Post*, December 4. p. A01.

Lipshutz, Robert J., Stephen P. A. Fodor, Thomas R. Gingeras, and David J. Lockhart. 1999. "High Density Synthetic Oligonucleotide Arrays." *Nature Genetics* 21: 20–24.

Lipton, Eric. 2006. "Bid to Stockpile Bioterror Drugs Stymied by Setbacks." *New York Times*, September 18. http://www.nytimes.com/2006/09/18/washington/18anthrax.html?ex =1316232000&en=d524b8f658a33e43&ei=5088&partner=rssnyt&emc=rss.

Litovkin, Viktor. 2007. "Russia Destroys Chemical Weapons on Schedule." *Spacewar*, March 27. http://www.spacewar.com/reports/Russia_Destroys_Chemical_Weapons_On_Schedule _999.html.

Little, Richard G. 2007. "Cost-Effective Strategies to Address Urban Terrorism: A Risk Management Approach." In Harry W. Richardson, Peter Gordon, and James E. Moore, eds., *The Economic Costs and Consequences of Terrorism*, 98–115. Cheltenham, UK: Edward Elgar.

LLNL. *See* Lawrence Livermore National Laboratory.

Lloyd-Smith, J. O., S. J. Schreiber, P. E. Kopp, and Wayne M. Getz. 2005. "Superspreading and the Effect of Individual Variation on Disease Emergence." *Nature* 438: 355–359.

Locher, James R. III. 2002. *Victory on the Potomac: The Goldwater-Nichols Act Unifies the Pentagon*. College Station: Texas A&M University Press.

Lockhart, David J., Helin Dong, Michael C. Byrne, Maximillian T. Follettie, Michael V. Gallo, Mark S. Chee, Michael Mittmann, Chunwei Wang, Michiko Kobayashi, Heidi Norton, and Eugene L. Brown. 1996. "Expression Monitoring by Hybridization to High-Density Oligonucleotide Arrays." *Nature Biotechnology* 14: 1675–1680.

Lombardo, Joseph S., H. Burkom, and J. Pavlin. 2004. "Essence II and the Framework for Evaluating Surveillance Systems." *Morbidity and Mortality Weekly Report* 53 (Supp.): 159–163. http://www.cdc.gov/mmwR/preview/mmwrhtml/su5301a30.htm.

Loonsk, John W. 2004. "BioSense—A National Initiative for Early Detection and Quantification of Public Health Emergencies." Special syndromic surveillance issue, *Morbidity and Mortality Weekly Report* 2004 (Suppl): 53–55.

Loui, Albert, Timothy V. Ratto, Thomas S. Wilson, Scott K. McCall, Erik V. Mukerjee, Adam H. Love, and Bradley R. Hart. 2008. "Chemical Vapor Discrimination Using a Compact and Low-Power Array of Piezoresistive Microcantilevers." *Analyst* 133: 608–615.

Lowe, James K. 2006. "Homeland Security: Operations Research Initiatives and Applications." *Interfaces* 36: 483–485.

Lucas, Keith. 2006. Physics Modeling of Airborne Weapons: Estimates of Outdoor Attacks Using a Gaussian Plume Model. UC Berkeley/Goldman School of Public Policy Working Paper. http://gspp.berkeley.edu/iths/UC%20White%20Paper.pdf.

Luce, R. Duncan, and Howard Raiffa. 1957. *Games and Decisions: Introduction & Critical Survey*. New York: Wiley.

Lujaniene, G., V. Lujanas, A. Mastauskas, R. Ladygiene, B. I. Ogorodnikov, and K. Stelingis. 1998. "Influence of Physico-Chemical Forms of Radionuclides on Their Migration in the Environment." *Radiochimica Acta* 82: 305–310.

Lurie, Nicole, Jeffrey Wasserman, and Christopher D. Nelson. 2006. "Public Health Emergency Preparedness: Evolution or Revolution?" *Health Affairs* 25: 935–945.

Lyman, Edwin S. 2004. *Chernobyl on the Hudson: The Health and Economic Impacts of a Terrorist Attack at the Indian Point Nuclear Plant.* Union of Concerned Scientists Report. http://www.secureindianpoint.org/downloads/IPhealthstudy.pdf.

Lynn, Laurence E. Jr. 1997. "Innovation and the Public Interest: Insights from the Private Sector." In Alan A. Altshuler and Robert D. Behn, eds., *Innovation in American Government: Challenges, Opportunities, and Dilemmas,* 83–103. Washington, DC: Brookings Institution Press.

MacCoun, Robert. 2005. "A Psychological Analysis of Possible Public and Official Responses to a Nuclear Detonation in Moscow." Unpublished ms.

Machalaba, Daniel. 2001. "US Ports Are Losing the Battle to Keep Up with Overseas Trade." *Wall Street Journal,* July 9, A1, A13.

Macler, Bruce A., and Stig Regli. 1993. "Use of Microbial Risk Assessment in Setting United States Drinking Water Standards," *International Journal of Food Microbiology.* 18(4), 245–256.

Magnuson, Stew. 2007. "Trouble Shooter: Cohen Puts Imprint on Beleaguered Homeland Security Technology Arm." *National Defense,* May 1.

Mahle, Melissa Boyle. 2004. *Denial and Deception: An Insider's View of the CIA from Iran-Contra to 9/11.* New York: Nation Books.

Mahler, Julianne. Forthcoming. *Organizational Learning at NASA: The Challenger and the Columbia Accidents.* Washington, DC: Georgetown University Press.

Malik, John. 1985. *The Yields of the Hiroshima and Nagasaki Nuclear Explosions.* Los Alamos National Laboratory Technical Report LA–8819, UC–34. September 1985. http://www.fas.org/sgp/othergov/doe/lanl/docs1/00313791.pdf.

Mandel, Jan, Lynn S. Bennethum, Jonathan D. Beezley, Janice L. Coen, Craig C. Douglas, Minjeong Kim, and Anthony Vodacek. 2007. *A Wildland Fire Model with Data Assimilation.* National Center for Atmospheric Research/Mesoscale and Microscale Meteorology Division Technical Report. March.

Mangold, Tom, and Jeff Goldberg. 1999. *Plague Wars: The Terrifying Reality of Biological Warfare.* New York: St. Martin's.

Mann, Jessica M., and Nancy D. Connell. 2006. "Emerging Biothreats: Natural and Deliberate." In Harry Salem and Sidney A Katz, eds., *Inhalation Toxicology,* 2nd ed., 933–944. Boca Raton, FL: CRC–Taylor & Francis Group.

Marek, Angie C. 2006. "The Toxic Politics of Chemicals." *US News and World Report,* January 15.

Marier, R. 1977. "The Reporting of Communicable Disease." *American Journal of Epidemiology* 105: 587–590.

Mark, J. Carson, Theodore Taylor, Eugene Eyster, William Maraman, and Jacob Wechsler. 1987. "Can Terrorists Build Nuclear Weapons?" In Paul Leventhal and Yonah Alexander, eds., *Preventing Nuclear Terrorism: Report and Papers of the International Task Force on Prevention of Nuclear Terrorism,* 55–65. Lanham, MD: Rowman & Littlefield.

Markle Foundation. 2002. *Protecting America's Freedom in the Information Age.* Washington, DC: Markle Foundation.

Marlo, Francis H. 1999. "WMD Terrorism and US Intelligence Collection." *Terrorism and Political Violence* 11: 53–71.

Martin, James W. 2006. "The History of Biological Weapons." In James R. Swearengen, ed., *Biodefense: Research Methodology and Animal Models*, 1–12. Boca Raton, FL: CRC–Taylor & Francis Group.

Martinson, Karin. 1999. *Literature Review on Service Coordination and Integration in the Welfare and Workforce Development Systems*. Urban Institute Report. http://www.urban.org/url.cfm?ID=408026.

Matheny, Jason, Michael Mair, Andrew Mulcahy, and Bradley T. Smith. 2007. Incentives for Biodefense Countermeasure Development. *Biosecurity and Bioterrorism: Biodefense Strategy, Practice, and Science* 5: 228–238.

Maurer, Stephen M. 2003. "New Institutions for Doing Science: From Databases to Open Source Biology." Unpublished conference paper. http://www.merit.unimaas.nl/epip/papers/maurer_paper.pdf.

Maurer, Stephen M. 2005a. "The Right Tool(s): Designing Cost-Effective Strategies for Neglected Disease Research." World Health Organization/WHO Commission on Intellectual Property Rights, Innovation, and Public Health. http://www.who.int/intellectualproperty/studies/S.Maurer.pdf.

Maurer, Stephen M. 2005b. Video lecture: "The Third Wave." http://www.cs.washington.edu/education/courses/csep590/05au/lectures/slides/Maurer_Sept7.pdf.

Maurer, Stephen M. 2006. Video lecture: "Computing 1940–1970." http://www.cs.washington.edu/education/courses/csep590/CurrentQtr/lectures/.

Maurer, Stephen M., Richard B. Firestone, and Charles Scriver. 2000. "Science's Neglected Legacy." *Nature* 405: 117–120.

Maurer, Stephen M., Keith V. Lucas, and Starr Terrell. 2006. From Understanding to Action: Community-Based Options for Improving Safety and Security in Synthetic Biology. UC Berkeley/Goldman School of Public Policy Working Paper. http://gspp.berkeley.edu/iths/UC%20White%20Paper.pdf.

Maurer, Stephen M., and Suzanne Scotchmer. 2004. "Procuring Knowledge." In Gary D. Libecap, ed., *Intellectual Property and Entrepreneurship*. Amsterdam: Elsevier.

Maurer, Stephen M., and Laurie Zoloth. 2007. "Synthesizing Biosecurity." *Bulletin of the Atomic Scientists* (November/December): 16–18.

May, Peter J. 1992. "Policy Learning and Failure." *Journal of Public Policy* 12: 331–354.

Mayer, Jean-Frangois, and Elijah Siegler. 1999. "'Our Terrestrial Journey Is Coming to an End': The Last Voyage of the Solar Temple." *Nova Religio* 2: 172–96.

Mayer-Schonberger, Viktor. 2003. "Emergency Communications: The Quest for Interoperability in the United States and Europe." In Arnold M. Howitt and Robyn L. Pangi, eds., *Countering Terrorism: Dimensions of Preparedness*. Cambridge, 299–342. Cambridge, MA: MIT Press.

McCloud, Kimberly, Gary Ackerman, and Jeffrey M. Bale. 2003. *Al-Qā'ida's WMD Activities*. CNS Report. http://www.cns.miis.edu/pubs/other/sjm_cht.htm.

McConnell, Allan, and Lynn Drennan. 2006. "Mission Impossible? Planning and Preparing for Crisis." *Journal of Contingencies and Crisis Management* 14: 59–70.

McCormick, Gordon H. 2003. "Terrorist Decision Making." *Annual Reviews in Political Science* 6: 473–507.

McDonald, L. Clifford, Andrew E. Simor, Ih-Jen Su, Susan Maloney, Marianna Ofner, Kow-Tong Chen, James F. Lando, Allison Greer, Min-Ling Lee, and Daniel B. Jernigan. 2004. "SARS in Healthcare Facilities, Toronto and Taiwan." *Emerging Infectious Diseases* 10: 777–781.

McKenna, Maryn. 2007. "Syndromic Surveillance: Faulty Alarm System or Useful Tool?" *CIDRAP News*, May 16. http://www.cidrap.umn.edu/cidrap/content/influenza/panflu/news/may1607surveil.html.

Meade, Charles, and Roger C. Molander. 2006. *Considering the Effects of a Catastrophic Terrorist Attack*. Santa Monica, CA: RAND Center for Terrorism Risk Management Policy. http://www.rand.org/pubs/technical_reports/2006/RAND_TR391.pdf.

Meckler, Laura, and Susan Carey. 2007. "US Air Marshal Service Navigates Turbulent Times." *Wall Street Journal*, February 9, 2007, A1, A9.

Medalia, Jonathan. 2008. *Detection of Nuclear Weapons and Materials: Science, Technologies, Observations*. Congressional Research Service Report No. 7-5700.

Medema, G. J., Peter F. M. Teunis, Arie H. Havelaar, and Charles N. Haas. 1996. "Assessment of the Dose-Response Relationship of *Campylobacter jejuni*," *International Journal of Experimental Pathology* 30: 101–112.

Medical Reserve Corps. n.d. Home page. http://www.medicalreservecorps.gov/HomePage.

Meek, David W. 2004. "The p53 Response to DNA Damage." *DNA Repair* 3, 1049–1056.

Mendelsohn, Mortimer L., Lawrence C. Mohr, and John P. Peeters, eds. 1998. *Biomarkers: Medical and Workplace Applications*. Washington, DC: Joseph Henry Press.

Merari, Ariel. 2003. "Israel's Preparedness for High Consequence Terrorism." In Arnold M. Howitt and Robyn L. Pangi, eds., *Countering Terrorism: Dimensions of Preparedness*, 345–370. Cambridge, MA: MIT Press.

Merridale, Catherine. 2000. *Night of Stone: Death and Memory in Twentieth-Century Russia*. New York: Penguin.

Messelson, Matthew, Jeanne Guillemin, Martin Hugh-Jones, Alexander Langmuir, Ilona Popova, Alexis Shelokov, and Olga Yampolskaya. 1994. "The Sverdlovsk Anthrax Outbreak of 1979." *Science* 266: 1202–1208.

Messner, M. J., C. L. Chappell, and P. C. Okhuysen. 2001. "Risk Assessment for *Cryptosporidium*: A Hierarchical Bayesian Analysis of Human Dose-Response Data," *Water Resources* 35: 3934–3940.

Mettler, Fred A., and Arthur C. Upton, eds. 1995. *Medical Effects of Ionizing Radiation*. 2nd ed. Philadelphia: Saunders.

Metzger, Norman. 2005. "Oppenheimer's Bomb and His Falling Out." *Chemical and Engineering News* 83: 55–57. http://pubs.acs.org/cen/books/83/8346books.html.

Meyers, Deborah Waller. 2003. "Does 'Smarter' Lead to Safer? An Assessment of the US Border Accords with Mexico and Canada." *International Immigration* 41: 5–54.

Meyers, Lauren Ancel, M. E. J. Newman, Michael Martin, and Stephanie Schrag. 2003. "Applying Network Theory to Epidemics: Control Measures for Mycoplasma Pneumoniae Outbreaks." *Emerging Infections Diseases*, 9: no. 2. http://www.cdc.gov/ncidod/eid/vol9no2/pdfs/02-0188.pdf.

Micron Sprayers. n.d. Home page, Micron Sprayers, Ltd. http://www.micron.co.uk/home.

Middlebrook, Martin. 1980. *The Battle of Hamburg: Allied Bomber Forces against a German City in 1943*. New York: Scribner.

Miller, Judith. 2001. "Next to Old Rec Hall, a 'Germ-Making' Plant." *New York Times*, September 4. http://query.nytimes.com/gst/fullpage.html?res=9C07E5D91639F937A3575AC0A9679C8B63.

Miller, Judith, Stephen Engelberg, and William Broad. 2002. *Germs*. New York: Touchstone Press.

Miralbell, R., S. Bieri, B. Mermillod, C. Helg, G. Sancho, B. Pastoors, A. Keller, J. M. Kurtz, and B. Chapuis. 1996. "Renal Toxicity After Allogeneic Bone Marrow Transplantation: The Combined Effects of Total-Body Irradiation and Graft-versus-Host Disease." *Journal of Clinical Oncology* 14: 579–585.

Miyake, Minoru, Ke J. Liu, Tadeusz M. Walczak, and Harold M. Swartz. 2000. "*In vivo* EPR Dosimetry of Accidental Exposures to Radiation: Experimental Results Indicating the Feasibility of Practical Use in Human Subjects." *Applied Radiation and Isotopes* 52: 1031–1038.

Moody, Kenton J., Ian D. Hutcheon, and Patrick M. Grant. 2005. *Nuclear Forensic Analysis*. Boca Raton, FL: Taylor & Francis.

Moon, John Ellis van Courtland. 2006. "The US Biological Weapons Program." In Mark Wheelis, Lajos Rozsa, and Malcolm Dando, eds., *Deadly Cultures: Biological Weapons Since 1945*, 9–46. Cambridge, MA: Harvard University Press.

Moran, Mary, Anne-Laure Ropars, Javier Guzman, Jose Diaz, and Christopher Garrison. 2005. *The New Landscape of Neglected Disease Drug Development*. London: Wellcome Trust Publications Department. http://www.bvgh.org/documents/MMoranTheNewLandscape.pdf.

Moreau, Ron, and Michael Hirsh. 2007. "Where the Jihad Lives Now." *Newsweek*, October 29. http://www.newsweek.com/id/57485/output/print.

Morrall, John F. III. 2003. "Saving Lives: A Review of the Record." *Journal of Risk and Uncertainty* 27: 221–237.

Moses, William W., and Kanai Shah. 2005. "Potential of $RbGd_2Br_7$: Ce, $LaCl_3$: Ce, $LaBr_3$: Ce, and LuI_3: Ce in Nuclear Medical Imaging." *Nuclear Instruments and Methods in Physics Research (A)* 537: 317–320.

Moss, David A. 2002. *When All Else Fails*. Cambridge, MA: Harvard University Press.

Moulder, John E. 2004. "Post-Irradiation Approaches to Treatment of Radiation Injuries in the Context of Radiological Terrorism and Radiation Accidents: A Review." *International Journal of Radiation Biology* 80: 3–10.

Moulder, John E., Brian L. Fish, Kevin R. Regner, and Eric P. Cohen. 2002. "Angiotensin II Blockade Reduces Radiation-Induced Proliferation in Experimental Radiation Nephropathy." *Radiation Research* 157: 393–401.

MRC. *See* Medical Reserve Corps.

Mueller, John. 2006. *Overblown: How Politicians and the Terrorism Industry Inflate National Security Threats and Why We Believe Them.* New York: Free Press.

Mueller, Jochen Schubert, Albert Benzing, and Klaus Geiger. 1998. "Method for Analysis of Exhaled Air by Microwave Energy Desorption Coupled with Gas Chromatography–Flame Ionization Detection-Mass Spectrometry." *Journal of Chromatography B* 716: 27–38.

Mueller, John. 2007. "Reacting to Terrorism: Probabilities, Consequences, and the Persistence of Fear." Unpublished. http://psweb.sbs.ohio-state.edu/faculty/jmueller/ISA2007T.PDF.

Murray, Christopher L., Alan D. Lopez, Brian Chin, Dennis Feehan, and Kenneth H. Hill. 2006. "Estimation of Potential Global Pandemic Influenza Mortality on the Basis of Vital Registry Data from the 1918–20 Pandemic: A Quantitative Analysis." *Lancet* 368: 2211–2218.

NACCHO. *See* National Association of County and City Health Officials.

Nagao, Masataka, Takehiko Takatori, Yukimasa Matsuda, Makato Nakajima, Hirotaro Iwase, and Kimiharu Iwadate. 1997. "Definitive Evidence for the Acute Sarin Poisoning Diagnosis in the Tokyo Subway." *Toxicology and Applied Pharmacology* 144: 198–203.

Nasstrom, John S., Gayle Sugiyama, Ron Baskett, Shawn Larsen, and Michael Bradley. 2005. *The National Atmospheric Release Advisory Center (NARAC): Modeling and Decision Support System for Radiological and Nuclear Emergency Preparedness and Response.* Lawrence Livermore National Laboratory Report no. UCRL-JRNL–211678. https://narac.llnl.gov/uploads/Nasstrom_et_al_2006_IJRAM_NARAC_211678_hdbde.pdf.

National Aeronautics and Space Administration. n.d. "Centennial Challenges." http://www.centennialchallenges.nasa.gov.

National Association of County and City Health Officials. 2007. *Federal Funding for Public Health Emergency Preparedness: Implications and Ongoing Issues for Local Health Departments.* Washington, DC: NACCHO.

National Commission on Terrorist Attacks upon the United States. 2004. *The 9/11 Commission Report: Final Report of the National Commission on Terrorist Attacks upon the United States.* New York: Norton.

National Conference of State Legislatures/AFI Health Committee. 2002. "Summary: Public Health Threats and Emergencies Act." http://www.ncsl.org/statefed/health/PHTEAS.htm.

National Council on Compensation Insurance/Workers Compensation Terrorism Impact and Education Study Group. 2006. "Issues Paper." https: //www.ncci.com/NCCI/Media/PDF/TRIA_Study_Group_Jan_06.pdf.

National Council on Radiation Protection and Measurements. 2001. *Management of Terrorist Events Involving Radioactive Material.* Bethesda, MD: NCRP.

National Institute for Occupational Safety and Health and Occupational Safety and Health Administration. 2006. *OSHA/NIOSH Interim Guidance, Chemical-Biological-Radiological-Nuclear (CBRN), Personal Protective Equipment Selection Matrix for First Responders.* http://www.osha.gov/SLTC/emergencypreparedness/cbrnmatrix/index.html.

National Research Council/Committee on Advances in Biotechnology and the Prevention of Their Application to Next Generation Bioterrorism and Biowarfare Threats. 2006. *Globaliza-*

tion, Biosecurity, and the Future of the Life Sciences. Washington, DC: National Academies Press.

National Research Council/Committee on the Biological Effects of Ionizing Radiation. 1990. *BEIR V: Health Effects of Exposure to Low Levels of Ionizing Radiation.* Washington, DC: National Academies Press.

National Research Council/Committee on the Design of an NSF Innovation Prize. 2007. *Innovation Inducement Prizes at the National Science Foundation.* Washington, DC: National Academies Press.

National Research Council/Committee on Materials and Manufacturing Processes for Advanced Sensors. 2004. *Sensor Systems for Biological Agent Attacks: Protecting Buildings and Military Bases.* Washington, D.C.: National Academic Press.

National Research Council/Committee on Methodological Improvements to the Department of Homeland Security's Biological Agent Risk Analysis. 2007. *Interim Report on Methodological Improvements to the Department of Homeland Security's Biological Agent Risk Analysis.* Washington, DC: National Academies Press.

National Research Council/Committee on the Remediation of Buried and Tank Wastes. 2000. *Long-Term Institutional Management of US Department of Energy Legacy Waste Sites.* Washington, DC: National Academies Press.

National Research Council/Committee on Research Standards and Practices to Prevent the Destructive Application of Biotechnology. 2004. *Biotechnology Research in an Age of Terrorism: Confronting the Dual Use Dilemma.* Washington, DC: National Academies Press.

National Research Council/Committee on Risk Perception and Communication. 1989. *Improving Risk Communication.* Washington, DC: National Academies Press.

National Research Council/Committee on Science and Technology for Countering Terrorism. 2002. *Making the Nation Safer: The Role of Science and Technology in Countering Terrorism.* Washington, DC: National Academies Press.

National Research Council/Committee on Standards and Policies for Decontaminating Public Facilities Affected by Exposure to Harmful Biological Agents: How Clean Is Safe? 2005. *Reopening Public Facilities after a Biological Attack: A Decision Making Framework.* Washington, DC: National Academies Press.

National Research Council/Committee on Toxicology. 1999. *Review of the US Army's Health Risk Assessment for Oral Exposure to Six Chemical Warfare Agents.* Washington, DC: National Academies Press.

National Research Council/Committee on Toxicology. 2001. *Standing Operating Procedures for Developing Acute Exposure Guideline Levels for Hazardous Chemicals.* Washington, DC: National Academies Press.

National Research Council/Committee on Toxicology. 2002. *Acute Exposure Guideline Levels for Selected Airborne Chemicals.* Vol. 2. Washington, DC: National Academies Press.

National Research Council/Committee on Toxicology. 2003. *Acute Exposure Guideline Levels for Selected Airborne Chemicals.* Vol. 3. Washington, DC: National Academies Press.

National Research Council/U.S. and Russian Committees on Strengthening U.S. and Russian Cooperative Nuclear Nonproliferation. 2005. *Strengthening US-Russian Cooperation on Nuclear Nonproliferation.* Washington, DC: National Academies Press.

National Science Advisory Board for Biosecurity. 2006a. *NSABB Draft Guidance Documents*. http://www.biosecurityboard.gov/pdf/NSABB%20Draft%20Guidance%20Documents.pdf.

National Science Advisory Board for Biosecurity. 2006b. "Addressing Biosecurity Concerns Related to the Synthesis of Select Agents." http://www.upmc-biosecurity.org/website/resources/govt_docs/science_biosecurity/hhs/nsabb_addressing_biosecurity_concerns_related_to_the_synthesis_of_select_agents.html.

National Telecommunications and Safety Administration. n.d. "Digital Television Transmission and Public Safety." http://www.ntia.doc.gov/psic/.

Natural Resources Defense Council. 2003. "The ABC News Nuclear Smuggling Experiment: The Sequel." http://www.nrdc.org/nuclear/furanium.asp.

Nature Biotechnology. 2007. Editorial: "US Biodefense—Shocking and Awful." *Nature Biotechnology* 25: 603.

NCCI. *See* National Council on Compensation Insurance.

NCRP. *See* National Council on Radiation Protection and Measurements.

Nelson, Christopher, Nicole Lurie, Jeffrey Wasserman, and Sarah Zakowski. 2006. "Conceptualizing and Defining Public Health Preparedness." *American Journal of Public Health* 8: 449–471.

Nerine J. Cherepy, Giulia Hull, Alexander D. Drobshoff, Stephen A. Payne, Edgar van Loef, Cody M. Wilson, Kanai S. Shah, Utpal N. Roy, et al. 2008. "Strontium and Barium Iodide High Light Yield Scintillators." *Applied Physics Letters* 92: 083508-1–083508-3.

New York Jewish Times. 2006. "5 Years Later: The FBI's Transformation Since 9/11." *New York Jewish Times*, September 11.

Nguyen, Tuan H. 2005. "Microchallenges of Chemical Weapons Proliferation." *Science* 390: 1021.

Nicogossian, Arnauld, Karen N. Metscher, Thomas Zimmerman, Dan Hanfling, and Rosann Wise. 2007. "Community Training in Bioterror Response." *Journal of Homeland Security and Emergency Management* 4: article 10. http://www.bepress.com/jhsem/vol4/iss3/10/.

Nicolaus, Dan. n.d. *A Unique Twin-Fluid Water Mist Nozzle Creates an Exceptionally High Velocity, Fire Spray*. CFD Research Corp. Report. http://www.bfrl.nist.gov/866/HOTWC/HOTWC2004/pubs/R0000238.pdf#search='micron%20and%20nozzle'.

Nikitin, Mary Beth. 2006. "Global Initiative to Combat Nuclear Terrorism Launched in Morocco." *Commentary* (Center for Strategic and International Studies), October 30. http://www.csis.org/media/csis/pubs/061030_nikitin_commentary.pdf.

NIOSH. *See* National Institute for Occupational Safety and Health.

Nixdorff, Katheryn, Neil Davidson, Piers Millett, and Simon Whitby. 2004. *Technology and Biological Weapons: Future Threats*. University of Bradford (UK)/Department of Peace Studies Science and Technology Report no. 2. http://www.brad.ac.uk/acad/sbtwc/ST_Reports/ST_Report_No_2.pdf.

NNSA. *See* Department of Energy/National Nuclear Security Administration.

Noble, Kerry. 1998. *Tabernacle of Hate: Why They Bombed Oklahoma City*. Prescott, Ontario: Voyageur.

Norman, Eric B., Stanley G. Prussin, Ruth-Mary Larimer, Howard Shugart, Edgardo Browne, Alan R. Smith, Richard J. McDonald, Heino Nitsche, Puja Gupta, Michael I. Frank, and Thomas B. Gosnell. 2004. "Signatures of Fissile Materials: High-Energy γ Rays Following Fission." *Nuclear Instruments and Methods in Physics Research: A* 521: 608–610.

Norris, Philip. 2003. *Pharmaceutical Technology Europe*, March 1, 15.

NRC. *See* National Research Council.

NRDC. *See* Natural Resources Defense Council.

NSABB. *See* National Science Advisory Board for Biosecurity.

NSG. *See* Nuclear Suppliers Group.

NTIA. *See* National Telecommunications and Safety Administration.

Nuclear Regulatory Commission. 1975. *Reactor Safety Study: An Assessment of Accident Risks in U.S. Commercial Nuclear Power Plants*. Report no. WASH–1400 (NUREG–75/014).

Nuclear Suppliers Group. n.d. "History of the NSG." http://www.nuclearsuppliersgroup.org/history.htm.

Oak Ridge National Laboratory. n.d. *The Risk Assessment Information System*. http://rais.ornl.gov/cgi-bin/tox/TOX_select?select=rad.

Oates, Wallace E. 1972. *Fiscal Federalism*. New York: Harcourt Brace Jovanovich.

ODNI. *See* Office of Director of National Intelligence.

OECD. *See* Organization for Economic Cooperation and Development.

Office of the Director of National Intelligence. 2007. "Director McConnell Signs Instructions to Implement Joint Duty." ODNI News Release 17-07, June 26. http://www.dni.gov/press_releases/20070626_release.pdf.

Office of Technology Assessment. 1993a. *Pharmaceutical R&D: Costs, Risks and Rewards*. Washington, DC: Government Printing Office.

Office of Technology Assessment. 1993b. *Technologies Underlying Weapons of Mass Destruction*. Office of Technology Assessment Report no. OTA-BP-ISC–115. Washington, DC: Government Printing Office.

O'Hanlon, Michael. 2006. "Preface: The Bush Administration's 2007 Budget Request." In M. d'Arcy, M. O'Hanlon, P. Orszag, J. Shapiro, and J. Steinberg, eds., *Protecting the Homeland 2006/2007*. Washington, DC: Brookings Institution Press.

Olson, Mancur. 1982. *The Rise and Decline of Nations: Economic Growth, Stagflation, and Social Rigidities*. New Haven, CT: Yale University Press.

OMB. *See* U.S. Office of Management and Budget.

OPCW. *See* Organization for the Prohibition of Chemical Weapons.

Opresko, Dennis, Robert Young, Rosemarie A. Faust, S. Talmage, Annetta P. Watson, Robert H. Ross, K. Davidson, and Joseph King. 1998. "Chemical Warfare Agents: Estimating Oral Reference Doses," *Reviews of Environmental Contamination and Toxicology* 156: 1–183.

Opresko, Dennis M., Robert A. Young, Annetta P. Watson, Rosemarie A. Faust, S. S. Talmage, Robert H. Ross, Kowetha A. Davidson, Joseph King, and Veronique Hauschild.

2001. "Chemical Warfare Agents: Current Status of Oral Reference Doses." *Reviews of Environmental Contamination and Toxicology* 172: 65–85.

Organization for Economic Cooperation and Development. 2002. *Chernobyl: Assessment of Radiological and Health Impact/2002 Update of Chernobyl: Ten Years On.* Paris: OECD Publishing. http://www.nea.fr/html/rp/chernobyl/c01.html.

Organization for the Prohibition of Chemical Weapons. 2007. "The Chemical Weapons Ban: Facts and Figures." http://www.opcw.org/factsandfigures/index.html.

ORP. *See* Environmental Protection Agency/Office of Radiation Programs.

Ortec. n.d. "Ortec Detective Homepage." http://www.ortec-online.com/papers/detective_paper.pdf.

OTA. *See* Office of Technology Assessment.

Otake M. 1998. "Review of Radiation-Related Brain Damage and Growth Retardation among the Prenatally Exposed Atomic Bomb Survivors." *International Journal of Radiation Biology and Related Studies in Physics, Chemistry and Medicine* 74: 159–171.

Otake, M., H. Yoshimaru, and W. J. Schull. 1987. *Severe Mental Retardation among the Prenatally Exposed Survivors of Atomic Bombing of Hiroshima and Nagasaki: A Comparison of the F65DR and DS86 Dosimetry Systems.* Radiation Effects Research Foundation (RERF), Technical Report no. 16–87.

Owens, Mackubin Thomas. 2006. "Conformity Needs Competition." *Joint Forces Quarterly* 43: 24–26. http://www.armedforcesjournal.com/2006/06/1813587.

Oyston, Petra C. F., Anders Sjostedt, and Richard W. Titball. 2004. "Tularemia: Bioterrorism Defense Renews Interest in *Franciscella tularensis*." *Nature Reviews Microbiology* 2: 967–978.

Pacific Maritime Association. 2007. *Annual Report.* http://www.pmanet.org/?cmd=main.content&id_content=2142606675.

Palfy, Arpad. 2003. "Weapon System Selection and Mass-Casualty Terrorism." *Terrorism and Political Violence* 15: 81–95.

Palmer, Helen. 2005. National Public Radio transcript: "Dealing With Dirty Bombs" January 5. http://marketplace.publicradio.org/display/web/2005/01/05/dealing_with_dirty_bombs/#.

Pan, Qisheng, Harry W. Richardson, Peter Gordon, and James E. Moore. 2007. The Economic Impacts of a Terrorist Attack on the Downtown Los Angeles Financial District. University of Southern California Center for Risk and Economic Analysis of Terrorist Events Working Paper.

Pandanell, Mark. n.d. "The Texas City Disaster—April 16, 1947." http://www.local1259iaff.org/disaster.html.

Pangi, Robyn L. 2003. "Consequence Management in the 1995 Sarin Attacks on the Japanese Subway System." In Arthur M. Howitt and Robyn L. Pangi, eds., *Countering Terrorism: Dimensions of Preparedness.* Cambridge, MA: MIT Press.

Panke, Sven, Victor deLorenzo, Arne Kaiser, Berhard Witholt, and Marcel Wubbolts. 1999. "Engineering of a Stable Whole-Cell Biocatalyst Capable of (S)-Styrene Oxide Formation for Continuous Two-Liquid-Phase Applications." *Applied and Environmental Microbiology* 65: 5619–5623.

Panofsky, Wolfgang. 2007. "The Non-Proliferation Regime under Siege." *Bulletin of the Atomic Scientists*, August. http://www.thebulletin.org/web-edition/features/the-nonproliferation-regime-under-siege.

Parachini, John. 2003. "Putting WMD Terrorism into Perspective." *Washington Quarterly* 26: 37–50.

Park, Jiyoung, Peter Gordon, James E. Moore II, Harry W. Richardson, and Lanlan Wang. 2007. "Simulating the State-by-State Effects of Terrorist Attacks on Three Major US Ports: Applying NIEMO (National Interstate Economic Model)." In Harry W. Richardson, Peter Gordon, and James E. Moore, eds., *The Economic Costs and Consequences of Terrorism*, 208–234. Cheltenham, UK: Edward Elgar.

Park, Yooki. 2006. *Essays in the Economics of Innovation Incentives*. Unpublished doctoral dissertation, Department of Economics, UC Berkeley.

Parker, Anne. 2006. "Monitoring Nuclear Reactors with Antineutrinos." *Science and Technology Review*, January https://www.llnl.gov/str/JanFeb06/Bernstein.html.

Partridge, Christopher. 2006. "The Eschatology of Heaven's Gate." In Kenneth C. G. Newport and Crawford Gribben, eds., *Expecting the End: Millennialism in Social and Historical Context*, 49–66. Waco, TX: Baylor University.

Pastel, Ross H. 2001. "Collective Behaviors: Mass Panic and Outbreaks of Multiple Unexplained Symptoms." *Military Medicine* 166: 44–46.

Pasteur Institute. n.d. "The History of the Pasteur Institute." http://www.pasteur.fr/english.html.

Pasztor, Andy, Rhonda L. Rundle, and Jonathan Karp. 2007. "Progress in California Fires." *Wall Street Journal*, October 25. http://online.wsj.com/article/SB119322395186169688.html?mod=hps_us_whats_news.

Pate-Cornell, Elisabeth, and Seth Guikema. 2002. "Probabilistic Modeling of Terrorist Threats: A Systems Analysis Approach to Setting Priorities among Countermeasures." *Military Operations Research* 7: 5–24.

Paz, Reuven. 2005. "Global Jihad and WMD: Between Martyrdom and Mass Destruction." In Hillel Fradkin, Husain Haqqani, and Eric Brown, eds., *Current Trends in Islamist Ideology*, vol. 2, 74–86. Washington, DC: Hudson Institute.

Pearson, Graham S. 2006. "The Iraqi Biological Weapons Program." In Mark Wheelis, Lajos Rozsa, and Malcolm Dando, eds., *Deadly Cultures: Biological Weapons Since 1945*, 169–190. Cambridge, MA: Harvard University Press.

Pepper, Ian L., and T. J. Gentry. 2002. Incidence of *Bacillus anthracis* in Soil. *Soil Science* 167: 627–635.

Perkins, Rodney, and Forrest Jackson. 1997. *Cosmic Suicide: The Tragedy and Transcendence of Heaven's Gate*. Dallas, TX: Pentaradial.

Perkovich, George, Jessica Tuchman Mathews, Joseph Cirincione, Rose Gottemoeller, and Jon Wolfsthal. 2005. *Universal Compliance: A Strategy for Nuclear Security*. Washington, DC: Carnegie Endowment for International Peace. http://www.carnegieendowment.org/publications/index.cfm?fa=view&id=16593.

Perl, Raphael. 2004. "Terrorism and National Security: Issues and Trends." *CRS Issue Brief for Congress.* Washington, DC: Congressional Research Service. http://www.fas.org/irp/crs/IB10119.pdf.

Perliger, Arie, Ami Pedahzur, and Yair Zalmanovitch. 2005. "The Defensive Dimension of the Battle against Terrorism—An Analysis of Management of Terror Incidents in Jerusalem." *Journal of Contingencies and Crisis Management* 13: 79–91.

Perrow, Charles. 2006. "Using Organizations: The Case of FEMA." Social Science Research Council. http://understandingkatrina.ssrc.org/Perrow/.

Perry, Ronald W., and Michael K. Lindell. 2003. "Understanding Citizen Response to Disasters with Implications for Terrorism." *Journal of Contingencies and Crisis Management* 11: 49–60.

Peters, C. J., and D. M. Hartley. 2002. "Anthrax Inhalation and Lethal Human Infection." *The Lancet* 359: 710–711.

Peterson, Leif E. 2002. "Factor Analysis of Cluster-Specific Gene Expression Levels from cDNA Microarrays." *Computer Methods and Progress in Biomedicine* 69: 179–188.

Peterson, Leif E. 2003. "Partitioning Large-Scale Microarray-Based Gene Expression Profiles Using Principal Component Analysis." *Computer Methods and Progress in Biomedicine* 70: 107–119.

Petro, James B., Theodore R. Plasse, and Jack A. McNulty. 2003. "Biotechnology: Impact on Biological Warfare and Biodefense." *Biosecurity and Bioterrorism: Biodefense Strategy, Practice, and Science* 1: 161–168.

Pew Research Center for People and the Press. 2004. "Survey: Kerry Wins Debate, but Little Change in Candidate Images." http://people-press.org/report/227/kerry-wins-debate-but-little-change-in-candidate-images.

Philips, Sally, and Anne Knebel, eds. 2007. *Mass Medical Care with Scarce Resources: A Community Planning Guide.* Rockville, MD: Agency for Healthcare Research and Quality. http://www.ahrq.gov/research/mce/mceguide.pdf.

Phillips, David P. 1974. "The Influence of Suggestion on Suicide: Substantive and Theoretic Implications of the Werther Effect." *American Sociological Review* 39: 340–354.

Phillips, Gary W., Jerrette E. Spann, James S. Bogard, Tuan VoDinh, Dimitris Emfietzoglou, Robert T. Devine, and Marko Moscovitch. 2006. "Neutron Spectrometry Using CR–39 Track Etch Detectors." *Radiation Protection Dosimetry* 120: 457–460.

Phillips, Zack. 2006. "Practice Doesn't Make Perfect." *Government Executive,* November 1.

Pilat, Joseph F. 1998. "Apocalypse Now—or Never?" In Karl-Heinz Kamp, Joseph F. Pilat, Jessica Stern, and Richard A. Falkenrath. "WMD Terrorism: An Exchange." *Survival* 40: 171–175.

Pillar, Paul R. 2001. *Terrorism and US Foreign Policy.* Washington, DC: Brookings Institution Press.

Pinkney, John. 2006. *Great Australian Mysteries.* Rowville, Victoria: Five Mile Press.

Pita, René. 2005. "Al-Qa'ida and the Chemical Threat." *Applied Science and Analysis Newsletter,* June 9. http://www.asanltr.com/newsletter/05-3/articles/053a.htm.

Pollack, Andrew. 2002. "Despite Billions for Discoveries, Pipeline of Drugs Is Far from Full." *New York Times*, April 19, p C1.

Poole, Robert W., Jr., and Jay J. Carafano. 2006. "Time to Rethink Airport Security." Heritage Foundation *Backgrounder* no. 1955, July 26, 2.

Posner, Richard A. 2006. *Uncertain Shield: The US Intelligence System in the Throes of Reform*. New York: Rowman and Littlefield.

Post, Jerrold M. 1987. "Prospects for Nuclear Terrorism: Psychological Motivations and Constraints." In Paul Leventhal and Yonah Alexander, eds., *Preventing Nuclear Terrorism*, 91–103. Lexington, MA: Lexington Books.

Postol, Theodore A. 1986. "Possible Effects from Superfires Following Nuclear Attacks on or Near Urban Areas." In Fred Marston and Robert Q. Marston, eds., *The Medical Implications of Nuclear War*, 15–72. Washington, DC: National Academies Press.

Powell, Robert. 2007a. "Defending against Terrorist Attacks with Limited Resources." *American Political Science Review* 101: 527–541.

Powell, Warren B. 2007b. *Approximate Dynamic Programming*. Hoboken, NJ: Wiley.

Powers, Michael J. 2001. "Deterring Terrorism with CBRN Weapons: Developing a Conceptual Framework." *CBACI Occasional Paper* 2.

Preston, Richard. 1998. "The Bioweaponeers." *New Yorker*, March 9, 52–65.

Priest, George. 1996. "The Government, the Market, and the Problem of Catastrophic Loss." *Journal of Risk and Uncertainty* 12: 219–237.

Prosnitz, Donald. 2005. "WMD Sensors—Search and Seizure." *Science* 310: 978.

Public Discourse Project. 2005a. *Final Report on 9/11 Commission Recommendations*. http://www.9–11pdp.org/press/2005-12-05_report.pdf.

Public Discourse Project. 2005b. *Report on the Status of 9/11 Commission Recommendations, Part II: Reforming the Institutions of Government*. http://www.9-11pdp.org/press/2005-10-20_report.pdf.

Public Discourse Project. 2005c. *Report on the Status of 9/11 Commission Recommendations, Part III: Foreign Policy, Public Diplomacy, and Nonproliferation*. http://www.9-11pdp.org/press/2005-11-14_report.pdf.

Purver, Ron. 1996. "Chemical and Biological Terrorism: New Threat to Public Safety." *Conflict Studies* 295. London: Research Institute for the Study of Conflict and Terrorism.

Quarantelli, E. L. 2006. "Catastrophes Are Different from Disasters: Some Implications for Crisis Planning and Managing Drawn from Katrina." http://understandingkatrina.ssrc.org/Quarantelli/.

Qureshi, Kristine, R. R. M. Gershon, M. F. Sherman, T. Straub, E. Gebbie, M. McCollum, M. J. Erwin, and S. S. Morse. 2005. "Health Care Workers' Ability and Willingness to Report to Duty during Catastrophic Disasters." *Journal of Urban Health* 82: 378–388.

Raber, Ellen, Tina Carlsen, Karen J. Folks, Robert Kirvel, J. Daniels, and K. Bogen. 2004. "How Clean Is Clean Enough? Recent Developments in Response to Threats Posed by Chemical and Biological Warfare Agents." *International Journal of Environmental Health Research* 14: 31–41.

Raber, Ellen, Joy Hirabayashi, Saverio P. Mancieri, Alfred L. Jin, Karen J. Folks, Tina Carlsen, and Pete Estacio. 2002. "Chemical and Biological Agent Incident Response and Decision Process for Civilian and Public Sector Facilities." *Risk Analysis* 22: 195–202.

Raber, Ellen, A. Jin, K. Noonan, Raymond McGuire, and Robert Kirvel. 2001. "Decontamination Issues for Chemical and Biological Warfare Agents: How Clean Is Clean Enough?" *International Journal of Environmental Health Research* 11: 128–148.

Raber, Ellen, and Raymond McGuire. 2002. "Oxidative Decontamination of Chemical and Biological Warfare Agents Using L-Gel." *Journal of Hazardous Materials* B93: 339–352.

Radiation Effects Research Foundation. 1983. *US-Japan Joint Workshop for Reassessment of Atomic Bomb Radiation Dosimetry*. Hiroshima, Japan: RERF.

Radovanovic, Zoran, and Zorana Djordjevic. 1979. "Mass Vaccination against Smallpox and Mortality in Yugoslavia in 1972." *Transactions of the Royal Society of Tropical Medicine and Hygiene* 73: 122.

Ramalingaswami, V. 2001. "Psychological Effects of the 1994 Plague Outbreak in Surat, India." *Military Medicine*, December. http://findarticles.com/p/articles/mi_qa3912/is_200112/ai_n9006232.

Ramsden, D., F. H. Passant, C. O. Peabody and R. G. Speight. 1967. "Radioiodine uptakes in the thyroid: Studies of the blocking and subsequent recovery of the gland following the administration of stable iodine." *Health Physics* 13: 633–646.

Ranstorp, Magnus. 1996. "Terrorism in the Name of Religion." *Journal of International Affairs* 50: 41–62.

Rapoport, David C. 1984. "Fear and Trembling: Terrorism in Three Religious Traditions." *American Political Science Review* 78: 658–677.

Rapoport, David C. 1999. "Terrorism and Weapons of the Apocalypse." *National Security Studies Quarterly* 6: 49–67.

Reader, Ian. 2000. *Religious Violence in Contemporary Japan: The Case of Aum Shinrikyo*. Honolulu: University of Hawaii Press.

Real, J., F. Persin, and C. Camarasa-Claret. 2002. Mechanisms of Desorption of ^{134}Cs and ^{85}Sr Aerosols Deposited on Urban Surfaces. *Journal of Environmental Radioactivity* 62: 1–15.

Redfearn, Christian L. 2005. "Land Markets and Terrorism: Uncovering Perceptions of Risk by Examining Land Price Changes following September 11." In Harry W. Richardson, Peter Gordon, and James E. Moore, eds., *The Economic Impacts of Terrorist Attacks*, 152–169. Cheltenham, UK: Edward Elgar.

Reed, Thomas. 2006. *At the Abyss: An Insider's History of the Cold War*. Amsterdam: Elsevier.

Reed, Thomas C., and Danny B. Stillman. 2009. *The Nuclear Express: A Political History of the Bomb and Its Proliferation*. Minneaopolis MN: Zenith Press.

Reich, Walter. 1998. "Understanding Terrorist Behavior: The Limits and Opportunities of Psychological Inquiry." In Walter Reich, ed., *Origins of Terrorism: Psychologies, Ideologies, Theologies, States of Mind*, 261–279. Washington, DC: Woodrow Wilson Center.

Reissman, Dori B., Patricia J. Watson, Richard W. Klomp, Terri L. Tanielian, and Stephen D. Prior. 2006. "Pandemic Influenza Preparedness: Adaptive Responses to an Evolving Challenge." *Journal of Homeland Security and Emergency Management* 3, no. 2.

Rennie, Gabriele. 2004. "Radiation Detection on the Front Lines." *Science and Technology Review*, September. https://www.llnl.gov/str/September04/Labov.html.

RERF. See Radiation Effects Research Foundation.

Rhodes, Keith. 2007. Testimony before the Senate Committee on Homeland Security and Governmental Affairs: *Project BioShield: Actions Needed to Avoid Repeating Past Mistakes.* GAO Report GAO-08-208T.

Richelson, Jeffrey. 2006. *Spying on the Bomb: American Nuclear Intelligence from Nazi Germany to Iran and North Korea.* New York: Norton.

Ricks, Thomas E. 2006. *Fiasco: The American Military Adventure in Iraq.* New York: Penguin Press.

Ridley, David B., Henry G. Grabowski, and Jeffrey L. Moe. 2006. "Developing Drugs for Developing Countries." *Health Affairs* 25: 313–324.

Riebling, Mark. 2004. *Wedge: From Pearl Harbor to 9/11—How the Secret War between the FBI and CIA Has Endangered National Security.* New York: Simon and Schuster.

Ringel, Jeanne, Anita Chandra, Kristin J. Leuschner, Yee-Wei Lim, Nicole Lurie, Karen A. Ricci, Agnes Gereben Schaefer, Molly Shea, Lisa R. Shugarman, and Jeffrey Wasserman. 2007. *Lessons Learned from the State and Local Public Health Response to Hurricane Katrina.* RAND Health Working Paper no. WR-473. http://www.rand.org/pubs/working _papers/2007/RAND_WR473.sum.pdf.

Rios, Maribel. 2004. "Bringing Formulations to Size: Strategies for Micro- and Nanoparticle Development." *Pharmaceutical Technology* 28: 40–53. November.

Risk Management Solutions, Inc. 2005. "A Risk-Based Rationale for Extending the Terrorism Risk Insurance Act." September. http://www.rms.com/Publications/A%20Risk%20Based% 20Approach%20for%20Extending%20TRIA.pdf.

Rissanen, Jenni. 2003. "Biological Weapons Convention." *NTI Issue Brief* (March). Nuclear Threat Initiative. http://www.nti.org/e_research/e3_28a.html.

RMS. *See* Risk Management Solutions, Inc.

Roberts, Brad. 1997. "Has the Taboo Been Broken?" In Brad Roberts, ed., *Terrorism with Chemical and Biological Weapons: Calibrating Risks and Responses*, 121–140. Alexandria, VA: Chemical and Biological Arms Control Institute.

Roberts, Brad. 2008. "Deterrence and WMD Terrorism: Calibrating its Potential Contributions to Risk Reduction." In Gary Ackerman and Jeremy Tamsett, eds., *Jihadists and Weapons of Mass Destruction.* Boca Raton, FL: Auerbach.

Roberts, Patrick S. 2005. "Shifting Priorities: Congressional Incentives and the Homeland Security Granting Process." *Review of Policy Research* 22: 437–449.

Roed, Jorn, and Kasper G. Andersson. 1996. "Clean-up of Urban Areas in the CIS Countries Contaminated by Chernobyl Fallout." *Journal of Environmental Radioactivity* 33: 107–116.

Rogerson, William P. 1994. "Economic Incentives and the Defense Procurement Process." *Journal of Economic Perspectives* 8: 65–90.

Ronfeldt, David F., and William Sater. 1981. *The Mindsets of High-Technology Terrorists: Future Implications from an Historical Analog.* Santa Monica, CA: RAND.

Rose, Adam. 2006. Economic Resilience to Natural and Man-Made Disasters: Multidisciplinary Origins and Contextual Dimensions. Center for Risk and Economic Analysis of Terrorism Events Working Paper.

Rose, Adam, Gbadebo Oladosi, and Shu-Yi Lao. 2007. "Regional Economic Impacts of a Terrorist Attack on the Water System of Los Angeles: A Computable General Disequilibrium Analysis," In Harry W. Richardson, Peter Gordon, and James E. Moore, eds., *The Economic Costs and Consequences of Terrorism.* Cheltenham, UK: Edward Elgar.

Rose, J. B., Charles N. Haas, and Stig Regli. 1991. "Risk Assessment and the Control of Waterborne Giardiasis." *American Journal of Public Health* 81: 709–713.

Rosenau, William. 2001. "Aum Shinrikyo's Biological Weapons Program: Why Did it Fail?" *Studies in Conflict and Terrorism* 24: 289–301.

Rosoff, Heather, and Detlof von Winterfeldt. 2007. "A Risk and Economic Analysis of Dirty Bomb Attacks on the Ports of Los Angeles and Long Beach." *Risk Analysis* 27: 533–546.

Rota, Paul A., M. Steven Oberste, Stephan S. Monroe, W. Allan Nix, Ray Campagnoli, Joseph P. Icenogle, Silvia Peñaranda, Bettina Bankamp, et al. 2003. "Characterization of a Novel Coronavirus Associated with Severe Respiratory Syndrome." *Science* 300: 1394–1399.

Rothwell, Geoffrey. 2002. "Does the US Subsidize Nuclear Power Insurance?" Stanford, CA: Stanford Institute for Economic Policy Research Policy Brief, April. http://siepr.stanford.edu/papers/briefs/policybrief_jan02.pdf.

Roy, Chad J., and Louise M. Pitt. 2006. "Infectious Disease Aerobiology: Aerosol Challenge Methods." In James R. Swearengen, ed., *Biodefense: Research Methodology and Animal Models*, 61–76. Boca Raton, FL.: CRC–Taylor & Francis Group.

Royal Society and Wellcome Trust. 2004. "Do No Harm: Reducing the Potential for the Misuse of Life Science Research." Report of a Royal Society/Wellcome Trust Meeting. http://www.royalsoc.ac.uk/displaypagedoc.asp?id=13647.

Rubin, Claire B., and John R. Harrald. 2006. "National Response Plan, the National Incident Management System, and the Federal Response Plan." In David G. Kamien, ed., *The McGraw-Hill Homeland Security Handbook*. New York: McGraw-Hill.

Russell, Thomas, and Jeffrey E. Thomas. 2008. "Government Support for the Terrorism Insurance Industry: Where Do We Go from Here?" http://www.law.northwestern.edu/searlecenter/papers/Russell-Thomas_Terrorism_Insurance.pdf.

Sagan, Scott D. 1993. *The Limits of Safety: Organizations, Accidents, and Nuclear Weapons.* Princeton, NJ: Princeton University Press.

Salama, Sammy, and Lydia Hansell. 2005. "Does Intent Equal Capability?" *Nonproliferation Review* 12: 615–653.

Salerno, Judith A., and Catherine Nagy. 2002. "Terrorism and Aging." *Journal of Gerontology: Medical Sciences* 57: 552–554.

Sandia National Laboratories. 1982. *Technical Guidance for Siting Criteria Development.* Sandia National Laboratories Report no. SAND81–1549.

San Francisco (California) Fire Department. 1995. *Incident Command System.* Unpublished training manual.

San Mateo County Health Services Agency/Emergency Medical Services. 1998. *HEICS: The Hospital Emergency Incident Command System.* 3rd ed. Vol. 1. Unpublished. http://www .emsa.cahwnet.gov/Dms2/HEICS98a.pdf.

Scales, Joyce, Lance Kim, and Ronaldo Carpio. 2005. "Encouraging Innovative Homeland Security Technologies." Unpublished. http://gspp.berkeley.edu/iths/Scales%20et%20al.pdf.

Scanlon, Joseph, Terry McMahon, and Coen van Haastert. 2007. "Handling Mass Death by Integrating the Management of Disasters and Pandemics: Lessons from the Indian Ocean Tsunami, the Spanish Flu and Other Incidents." *Journal of Contingencies and Crisis Management* 15: 80–94.

Schaper, Annette. 2003. "Nuclear Terrorism: Risk Analysis after 11 September 2001." *Disarmament Forum—Nuclear Terrorism* 2: 7–16. http://www.unidir.ch/bdd/fiche-article.php?ref _article=1907.

Scheer, Robert. 1983. *With Enough Shovels: Reagan, Bush, and Nuclear War.* New York: Vintage.

Schelling, Thomas C. 2005. Nobel Prize Lecture: "An Astonishing Sixty Years: The Legacy of Hiroshima." http://nobelprize.org/nobel_prizes/economics/laureates/2005/schelling-lecture .html.

Schmid, Alex P. 2001. "Chemical Terrorism: Precedents and Prospects." *Synthesis,* summer. www.opcw.org/synthesis/html/s6/p9prt.html.

Schmid, Alex P., and Albert J. Jongman. 1988. *Political Terrorism: A New Guide to Actors, Authors, Concepts, Data Bases, Theories and Literature.* Amsterdam: North-Holland.

Schneier, Bruce. 2003. *Beyond Fear.* New York: Copernicus.

Schoch-Spana, Monica. 2000. "Implications of Pandemic Influenza for Bioterrorism Response." *Clinical Infectious Diseases* 31: 1409–1413.

Schoch-Spana, Monica, Crystal Franco, Jennifer F. Nuzzo, and Christiana Usenza. 2007. "Community Engagement: Leadership Tool for Catastrophic Health Events." *Biosecurity and Bioterrorism: Biodefense Strategy, Practice, and Science* 5: 8–25.

Schonfelder, Volker, H. Aarts, K. Bennett, H. de Boer, J. Clear, W. Collmar, A. Connors, A. Deerenberg, et al. 1993. "Instrument Description and Performance of the Imaging Gamma-Ray Telescope COMPTEL aboard NASA's Compton Gamma-Ray Observatory." *Astrophysical Journal Supplement* 86: 657–692.

Schuler, Richard E. 2007. "Two-Sided Electricity Markets: Self-Healing Systems." In Harry W. Richardson, Peter Gordon and James E. Moore, eds., *The Economic Costs and Consequences of Terrorism.* Cheltenham, UK: Edward Elgar.

Schweitzer, Glenn E. 1996. *Moscow DMZ.* New York: M. E. Sharpe.

Science Service Inc. 1950. *Atomic Bombing: How to Protect Yourself.* New York: William H. Wise & Co. http://www.foody.org/atomic/atomic00.html.

Scientific Committee on Problems of the Environment. 1993. *Radioecology after Chernobyl— Biogeochemical Pathways of Artificial Radionuclides (SCOPE 50).* London: Wiley. http:// www.icsu-scope.org/downloadpubs/scope50/contents.html.

SCOPE. *See* Scientific Committee on Problems of the Environment.

Scotchmer, Suzanne. 2004. *Innovation and Incentives*. Cambridge, MA: MIT Press, 2004.

Seidman, Harold, and Robert Gilmour. 1986. *Politics, Position, and Power: From the Positive to the Regulatory State*. 4th ed. New York: Oxford University Press.

Selengut, Charles. 2003. *Sacred Fury: Understanding Religious Violence*. Walnut Creek, CA: AltaMira.

Senate Armed Services Committee. 2000. "The Department of Defense Antibiological Warfare Agent Vaccine Acquisition Program." Senate Hearing Report no. 106–1124.

Senior, James K. 1958. "The Manufacture of Mustard Gas in World War I." *Armed Forces Chemical Journal* 12: 12–14, 16–17, 29.

Seper, Jerry. 2001. "Secret Lab Built to Make Mock Anthrax." *Washington Times*, October 26.

Serber, Robert. [1943] 1992. *The Los Alamos Primer: The First Lectures on How to Build an Atomic Bomb*. Berkeley: University of California Press.

SFFD. *See* San Francisco (California) Fire Department.

Shah, Kanai, J. Glodo, M. Klugerman, W. M. Higgins, T. Gupta, and P. Wong. 2004. "High Energy Resolution Scintillation Spectrometers." *IEEE Transactions on Nuclear Science* 51: 2395–2999.

Shane, Scott, and Lowell Bergman. 2006. "F.B.I. Struggling to Reinvent Itself to Fight Terror." *New York Times*, October 10, 1.

Shea, Dana A. *The Global Nuclear Detection Architecture: Issues for Congress*. 2008. Congressional Research Service Report no. RL 34564.

Shea, Dana A., and Sarah A. Lister. 2003. *The BioWatch Program: Detection of Bioterrorism*. Congressional Research Service Report no. RL 32152.

Shepperd, James A. 2001. "The Desire to Help and Behavior in Social Dilemmas: Exploring Responses to Catastrophes." *Group Dynamics—Theory, Research and Practice* 5: 304–314.

Shiloach, Joseph, and Rephael Fass. 2005. "Growing E. Coli to High Cell Density—A Historical Perpsective on Method Development." *Biotechnology Advances* 23: 345–357.

Shubik, Martin. 1982. *Game Theory in the Social Sciences: Concepts and Solutions*. Cambridge, MA: MIT Press.

Simon, Steven, and Daniel Benjamin. 2000. "America and the New Terrorism." *Survival* 42: 59–75.

Sine, R. C., I. H. Levine, W. E Jackson, A. L. Hawley, P. G. Prasanna, M. B. Grace, et al. 2001. "Biodosimetry Assessment Tool: A Post-Exposure Software Application for Management of Radiation Accidents." *Military Medicine* 16: 85–87.

Skinner, Richard. 2006. Unpublished lecture, UC Berkeley, April 27.

Slovic, Paul. 2004a. "Informing and Educating the Public about Risk." In Paul Slovic, ed., *The Perception of Risk*, 182–198. London: Earthscan.

Slovic, Paul. 2004b. "Perception of Risk from Radiation." In Paul Slovic, ed., *The Perception of Risk*, 264–274. London: Earthscan.

Slovic, Paul, Baruch Fischhoff, and Sarah Lichtenstein. 2004a. "Facts and Fears: Understanding Perceived Risk." In Paul Slovic, ed., *The Perception of Risk*, 137–153. London: Earthscan.

Slovic, Paul, Baruch Fischhoff, and Sarah Lichtenstein. 2004b. "Rating the Risks." In Paul Slovic, ed., *The Perception of Risk*, 104–120. London: Earthscan.

Smith, Bradley T., Thomas V. Inglesby, and Tara O'Toole. 2003. "Biodefense R&D: Anticipating Future Threats, Establishing a Strategic Environment." *Biosecurity and Bioterrorism: Biodefense Strategy, Practice, and Science* 1: 193–202.

Smith, Clifford. 2005. "Managing Corporate Risk." In Bjorn Espen Eckbo, ed., *Handbook of Corporate Finance: Empirical Corporate Finance*. Amsterdam: Elsevier.

Smith, David L., F. Ellis McKenzie, Robert W. Snow, and Simon I. Hay. 2007. "Revisiting the Basic Reproductive Number for Malaria and Its Implications for Malaria Control." *PLOS Biology* 5: 42.

Smith, Jane S. 1990. *Patenting the Sun*. New York: Morrow.

Smith, V. Kerry, and Daniel G. Hallstrom. 2005. "Designing Benefit-Cost Analyses for Homeland Security Policies." In Harry W. Richardson, Peter Gordon, and James E. Moore, eds., *The Economic Impacts of Terrorist Attacks*. Cheltenham, UK: Edward Elgar.

Smithson, Amy E., and Leslie-Anne Levy. 2000. *Ataxia: The Chemical and Biological Terrorism Threat and the US Response*. Washington, DC: Henry L. Stimson Center.

Smyth, Henry D. 1945. *Atomic Energy for Military Purposes: A General Account of the Scientific Research and Technical Development That Went into the Making of the Atomic Bombs*. Princeton, NJ: Princeton University Press.

Sneath, P. H. A. 1962. "Longevity of Microorganisms." *Nature* 195: 643–646.

Soares, Christopher. n.d. "Same-Day Travel between the US and Canada and the US and Mexico by Transportation Mode, 2000–2004." Unpublished.

Sobsey, Mark D., and John Scott Meschke. 2003. "Virus Survival in the Environment with Special Attention to Survival in Sewage Droplets and Other Environmental Media of Fecal or Respiratory Origin." Unpublished.

Sokov, Nikolai. 2004. "Suitcase Nukes: Permanently Lost Luggage." James Martin Center for Nonproliferation Studies. http://cns.miis.edu/pubs/week/040213.htm.

Sopko, John, and Alan Edelman. 1995. *Global Proliferation of Weapons of Mass Destruction: A Case Study on the Aum Shinrikyo*. Report for Senate Government Affairs Permanent Subcommittee on Investigations. http://www.fas.org/irp/congress/1995_rpt/aum/part01.htm.

Sorensen, J. 2004. "Risk Communication and Terrorism." *Biosecurity and Bioterrorism: Biodefense Strategy, Practice, and Science* 2: 229–231.

Speckhard, Anne. 2007. "Prevention Strategies and Promoting Psychological Resilience to Bioterrorism through Communication." In Manfred S. Green, Jonathan Zenilman, Dani Cohen, Itay Wiser, and Ran D. Balicer, eds., *Risk Assessment and Risk Communication Strategies in Bioterrorism Preparedness*, 135–162. Dordrecht: Springer.

Spivey, Richard N., Louis Lasagna, Judith K. Jones, and William Wardell. 2002. "The US FDA in the Drug Development Evaluation and Approval Process." In John P. Griffin and John O'Grady, eds., *Textbook of Pharmaceutical Medicine*. London: BMD Books.

Spotswood, Erica. 2006. "Flood of Criticism." *Berkeley Science Review* 11: 33–37.

Sprang, Ginny. 1999. "Post-Disaster Stress Following the Oklahoma City Bombing: An Examination of Three Community Groups." *Journal of Interpersonal Violence* 14: 169–183.

Sprinzak, Ehud. 1998. "The Great Superterrorism Scare." *Foreign Policy* 112: 110–124.

Sprinzak, Ehud. 2000. "On Not Overstating the Problem." In Brad Roberts, ed., *Hype or Reality? The "New Terrorism" and Mass Casualty Attacks*, 17–45. Alexandria, VA: Chemical and Biological Arms Control Institute.

Sprinzak, Ehud, and Idith Zertal. 2000. "Avenging Israel's Blood (1946)." In Jonathan Tucker, ed., *Toxic Terror: Assessing Terrorist Use of Chemical and Biological Weapons*, 17–41. Cambridge, MA: MIT Press.

Staiti, Andrea B., Aaron Katz, and John F. Hoadley. 2003. "Has Bioterrorism Preparedness Improved Public Health? Issue Brief no. 65, Center for Studying Health System Change.

State Department. n.d. "Current Partner Nations to the Global Initiative to Combat Nuclear Terrorism." http://www.state.gov/t/isn/82787.htm.

State Department/Office of the Coordinator for Counterterrorism. 2007. "Country Reports on Terrorism." http://www.state.gov/s/ct/rls/crt/2007/index.htm.

Steele, Paul Thomas. 2004. *Bioaerosol Mass Spectrometry: Reagentless Detection of Individual Airborne Spores and Other Biological Particles Based on Laser Desorption/Ionization Mass Spectrometry.* Lawrence Livermore National Laboratory Report no. UCRL-TH-207560. http://www.llnl.gov/tid/lof/documents/pdf/309813.pdf.

Stein, Bradley D., Terri L. Tanielian, Gery W. Ryan, Hilary J. Rhodes, Shalanda D. Young, and Janice C. Blanchard. 2004. "A Bitter Pill to Swallow: Nonadherence with Prophylactic Antibiotics during the Anthrax Attacks and the Role of Private Physicians." *Biosecurity and Bioterrorism: Biodefense Strategy, Practice, and Science* 2: 175–185.

Steinbruner, John, Elisa D. Harris, Nancy Gallagher, and Stacy Okutani. 2007. *Controlling Dangerous Pathogens: A Prototype Protective Oversight System.* Center for International and Security Studies at Maryland Research Report. http://www.cissm.umd.edu/papers/files/pathogens_project_monograph.pdf.

Stern, Jessica. 1999. *The Ultimate Terrorists.* Cambridge, MA: Harvard University Press.

Stern, Jessica. 2000. "The Covenant, the Sword, and the Arm of the Lord (1985)." In Jonathan Tucker, ed., *Toxic Terror: Assessing Terrorist Use of Chemical and Biological Weapons*, 139–157. Cambridge, MA: MIT Press.

Sternhell, Zeev. 1976. "Fascist Ideology." In Walter Laqueur, ed., *Fascism: A Reader's Guide: Analyses, Interpretations, Bibliography*, 325–406. Berkeley: University of California Press.

Sternthal, E. L., B. Stanley Lipworth, C. Abreau, S. L. Fang, L. E. Braverman. 1980. "Suppression of Thyroid Radioiodine Uptake by Various Doses of Stable Iodide." *New England Journal of Medicine* 303: 1083–1088.

Stephenson, E. H., E. W. Larson, and J. W. Dominik. 1984. "Effect of Environmental Factors on Aerosol-Induced Lassa Virus Infection," *Journal of Medical Virology* 14: 295–303.

Stewart, George R. [1949] 1989. *Earth Abides.* New York: Fawcett Crest.

Stinson, Thomas F. 2007. "The National Economic Impacts of a Food Terrorism Event: Initial Estimates of Indirect Costs." In Harry W. Richardson, Peter Gordon, and James E.

Moore, eds., *The Economic Costs and Consequences of Terrorism*. Cheltenham, UK: Edward Elgar.

Stoto, Michael A. 2003. *Public Health Surveillance: A Historical Review with a Focus on HIV/AIDS*. RAND Health Report no. DRU-3074-IOM. http://rand.org/pubs/drafts/DRU3074/DRU3074.pdf.

Stoto, Michael A., David J. Dausey, Lois M. Davis, Kristin J. Leuschner, Nicole Lurie, Sarah Myers, Stuart S. Olmsted, Karen A. Ricci, M. Susan Ridgely, Elizabeth M. Sloss, and Jeffrey Wasserman. 2005. *Learning from Experience: The Public Health Response to West Nile Virus, SARS, Monkeypox, and Hepatitis A Outbreaks in the United States*. Santa Monica, CA: RAND. http://rand.org/pubs/technical_reports/2005/RAND_TR285.pdf.

Stoto, Michael A., Matthias Schonlau, and Louis T. Mariano. 2004. "Syndromic Surveillance: Is It Worth the Effort?" *Chance* 17: 19–24.

Stowsky, Jay. 2006. "Harnessing a Trojan Horse: Aligning Security Investments with Commercial Trajectories in Cargo Container Shipping." In J. D. Haveman and H. J. Shatz, eds., *Protecting the Nation's Seaports: Balancing Security and Cost*, 129–184. San Francisco: Public Policy Institute of California. http://www.ppic.org/content/pubs/report/R_606JHR.pdf.

Sunstein, Cass R. 2003. "Terrorism and Probability Neglect." *Journal of Risk and Uncertainty* 26: 121–136.

Sunstein, Cass R. 2006. *On the Divergent American Reactions to Terrorism and Climate Change*. AEI-Brookings Center for Regulatory Studies Working Paper no. 06-13. http://aei-brookings.org/admin/authorpdfs/redirect-safely.php?fname=../pdffiles/phpb6.pdf.

Swain, Robert J. 2007. "New Frontiers in Simulation: Biennial Survey of Discrete-Event Simulation Software Tools." *OR/MS Today*, October. http://lionhrtpub.com/orms/orms–10–07/frsurvey.html.

Swartz, Harold M., Akinori Iwasaki, Tadeusz Walczak, Eugene Demidenko, Ildar Salikov, Piotr Lesniewski, Piotr Starewicz, David Schauer, and Alex Romanyukha. 2004a. "Measurements of Clinically Significant Doses of Ionizing Radiation Using Non-Invasive In Vivo EPR Spectroscopy of Teeth in Situ." *Applied Radiation and Isotopes* 62: 293–299.

Swartz, Harold M., Tadeusz Walczak, and Aknori Iwasaki. 2004b. Abstract: "In Vivo EPR Dosimetry to Quantify Exposures to Clinically Significant Doses of Ionizing Radiation." In Proceedings of 14th International Conference on Solid State Dosimetry. *Radiation Dosimetry* 119: 53.

Swearengen, James R., ed. 2006. *Biodefense: Research Methodology and Animal Models*. Boca Raton, FL: CRC–Taylor & Francis Group.

Tadros, M. E., and M. D. Tucker. 2003. "Formulations for Neutralization of Chemical and Biological Toxants." US Patent no. 6566574. http://www.freepatentsonline.com/6566574.html.

Taubenberger, Jeffery K., Ann H. Reid, Amy E. Krafft, Karen E. Bijwaard, and Thomas G. Fanning. 1997. "Initial Genetic Characterization of the 1918 'Spanish' Influenza Virus." *Science* 275: 1793–1796.

Taubenberger, Jeffery K., Ann H. Reid, R. M. Lourens, R. Wang, G. Jin, and T. G. Fanning. 2005. "Characterization of the 1918 Influenza Virus Polymerase Genes." *Nature* 437: 889–893.

Taylor, Frederick. 2004. *Dresden: Tuesday, February 13, 1945.* New York: Harper Perennial.

Taylor, Tammy P., David E. Morris, Thomasin C. Miller, and Sandra L. Gogol. 2003. *Radionuclide Decontamination Science and Technology Workshop: Workshop Summary and Findings.* Los Alamos National Laboratory Report LA UR-03-8215.

Taylor, Terence, and Tim Trevan. 2000. "The Red Army Faction (1980)." In Jonathan Tucker, ed., *Toxic Terror: Assessing Terrorist Use of Chemical and Biological Weapons,* 106–113. Cambridge, MA: MIT Press.

Tenet, George. 2007. *At the Center of the Storm: My Years at the CIA.* New York: HarperCollins.

Teunis, Peter F. M., Cynthia L. Chappell, and Pablo C. Okhuysen. 2002. "*Cryptosporidium* Dose Response Studies: Variation between Hosts." *Risk Analysis* 22: 475–485.

Texas State Historical Association. n.d. "Texas City Disaster." http://www.tsha.utexas.edu/handbook/online/articles/TT/lyt1.html.

Thacker, Stephen B., and Ruth L. Berkelman. 1988. "Public Health Surveillance in the United States." *Epidemiology Review* 10: 164–190.

Thevenot, Brian, and Gordon Russell. 2005. "Rumors of Deaths Greatly Exaggerated." *Times-Picayune* (New Orleans), September 26. http://www.freerepublic.com/focus/f-news/1491317/posts.

Thomas, L. C. 2004. *Games: Theory and Applications.* New York: Dover.

Thompson, James. 1986. "Psychological Consequences of Disaster: Analogies for the Nuclear Case." In Fred Marston and Robert Q. Marston, eds., *The Medical Implications of Nuclear War,* 290–316. Washington, DC: National Academies Press.

Thompson, Larry H., and David Schild. 2001. "Homologous Recombinational Repair of DNA Ensures Mammalian Chromosome Stability." *Journal of Mutation Research* 477: 131–153.

Thornburgh, Richard. 2006. Statement before House Committee on Appropriations Subcommittee on Science, State, Justice, and Commerce, and Related Agencies. http://www.napawash.org/resources/testimony/Thornburgh%20-%209-14-06.pdf.

Tiedje, James M., Robert K. Colwell, Yaffa L. Grossman, Robert E. Hodson, Richard E. Lenski, Richard N. Mack, and Philip J. Regal. 1989. "The Planned Introduction of Genetically Engineered Organisms: Ecological Considerations and Recommendations." *Ecology* 70: 298–315.

Tierney, Kathleen. 2006. "Hurricane Katrina: Catastrophic Impacts and Alarming Lessons." UC Berkeley Program on Housing and Urban Policy Conference Paper Series. http://urbanpolicy.berkeley.edu/pdf/tierney.pdf.

Tietenberg, Thomas H. 2006. *Emissions Trading: Principles and Practice.* 2nd ed. Washington, DC: Resources for the Future.

Tinnin, David B. 1977. *The Hit Team.* New York: Dell.

Tirumalai, Radhakrishna S., King C. Chan, DaRue A. Prieto, Haleem J. Issaq, Thomas P. Conrads, and Timothy D. Veenstra. 2003. "Characterization of the Low Molecular Weight Human Serum Proteome." *Molecular and Cellular Proteomics* 2: 1096–1103.

Titball, Richard W. 2004. "An Elusive Serial Killer." *Nature* 430: 145–146.

Todd, R. W., J. M. Nightingale, and D. B. Everett. 1974. "A Proposed γ Camera." *Nature* 251: 132–134.

Trull, Melanie C., Tracey V. du Laney, and Mark D. Dibner. 2007. "Turning Biodefense Dollars into Products." *Nature Biotechnology* 25: 179–184.

Trust for America's Health. 2006. "Ready or Not? Protecting the Public Health's from Diseases, Disasters, and Bioterrorism." http://healthyamericans.org/reports/bioterror07/BioTerrorReport2007.pdf.

Tucker, Jonathan B. 2000a. "Lessons from the Case Studies." In Jonathan Tucker, ed., *Toxic Terror: Assessing Terrorist Use of Chemical and Biological Weapons*, 249–269. Cambridge, MA: MIT Press.

Tucker, Jonathan B., ed. 2000b. *Toxic Terror: Assessing Terrorist Use of Chemical and Biological Weapons*. Cambridge, MA: MIT Press.

Tucker, Jonathan B. 2001. *The Chemical Weapons Convention: Implementation Challenges and Solutions*. Monterey Institute for International Studies/Center for Nonproliferation Studies Report. http://cns.miis.edu/pubs/reports/tuckcwc.htm.

Tucker, Jonathan B. 2004. *Biosecurity: Limiting Terrorist Access to Deadly Pathogens*. United States Institute of Peace Report no. 52. http://www.usip.org/pubs/peaceworks/pwks52.pdf.

Tucker, Jonathan B. 2006. *War of Nerves: Chemical Warfare from World War I to Al-Qaeda*. New York: Pantheon.

Tucker, Jonathan B. 2007. "Verifying the Chemical Weapons Ban: Missing Elements." *Arms Control Today*, January/February. Washington, DC: ACA. http://www.armscontrol.org/act/2007_01-02/Tucker.asp.

Tucker, Jonathan B., and Amy Sands. 1999. "An Unlikely Threat." *Bulletin of Atomic Scientists* 55: 46–52.

Tumpey, Terrence M., Christopher F. Basler, Patricia V. Aguilar, Hui Zeng, Alicia Solorzano, David E. Swayne, Nancy J. Cox, et al. 2005. "Characterization of the Reconstructed 1918 Spanish Influenza Pandemic Virus." *Science* 310: 77–80.

Tusher, Virginia Goss, Robert Tibshirani, and Gilbert Chu. 2001. "Significance Analysis of Microarrays Applied to the Ionizing Radiation Response." *Proceedings of the National Academy of Sciences* 98: 5116–5121.

Tversky, Amos, and Daniel Kahneman. 1973. "Availability: A Heuristic for Judging Frequency and Probability." *Cognitive Psychology* 5: 207–232.

Uganda Human Rights Commission. 2002. *The Kanungu Massacre: The Movement for the Restoration of the Ten Commandments of God Indicted*. Kampala: Uganda Human Rights Commission.

U.K. Home Office. [1938] 2007. *Air Raid Precautions Handbook No. 1: Personal Protection* (2d ed.). In Campbell McCutcheon, ed. *Air Raid Precautions*. Tempus: Chalford Stroud UK.

Unger, Laurie, and D. K. Trubey. 1982. *Specific Dose Constants for Nuclides Important to Dosimetry and Radiological Assessment*. Oak Ridge National Laboratory Report no. ORNL/RSIC–45/R1. http://www.ornl.gov/info/reports/1982/3445603573381.pdf.

United Nations. 2005. *International Convention for the Suppression of Acts of Nuclear Terrorism*. http://untreaty.un.org/English/Terrorism/English_18_15.pdf.

United Nations/1540 Committee. 2004. *United Nations Security Council Resolution 1540.* http://disarmament2.un.org/Committee1540.

United Nations/Department of Disarmament Affairs. n.d.(a). *Convention on the Prohibition of the Development, Production, Stockpiling and Use of Chemical Weapons and on Their Destruction.* http://disarmament2.un.org/wmd/cwc/index.html.

United Nations/Department of Disarmament Affairs. n.d.(b). *Weapons of Mass Destruction: Convention on the Prohibition of the Development, Production and Stockpiling of Bacteriological (Biological) and Toxin Weapons and on their Destruction.* http://disarmament2.un.org/wmd/bwc/index.html.

United Nations Special Commission on Iraq. 2004. *Iran Survey Group Final Report.* http://www.globalsecurity.org/wmd/library/report/2004/isg-final-report/isg-final-report_vol3_bw-01.htm.

United States of America v. Usama bin Laden, et al., Docket no. S(7) 98 Cr. 1023 (Southern District of New York, 2001). http://cryptome.org/usa-v-ubl-dt.htm.

United States Geological Survey. *See* USGS.

UNSCOM. *See* United Nations Special Commission on Iraq.

USA Today. "Century-Old Smallpox Scabs in N.M. Envelope." December 26, 2003. http://www.usatoday.com/news/health/2003-12-26-smallpox-in-envelope_x.htm.

USAMRIID. *See* U.S. Army Medical Research Institute of Infectious Diseases.

U.S. Army. 1990. *Army Field Manual no. 3-9: Potential Military Chemical/Biological Agents and Compounds.* Washington, DC: U.S. Army. http://www.globalsecurity.org/wmd/library/policy/army/fm/3-9/fm3-9.pdf.

U.S. Army. 1994. *Field Manual 22–51: Leaders' Manual for Combat Stress Control.* Washington, DC: U.S. Army. http://www.globalsecurity.org/military/library/policy/army/fm/22–51/.

U.S. Army/Center for Health Promotion and Preventive Medicine. 1999. *Derivation of Health-Based Environmental Screening Levels for Chemical Warfare Agents: A Technical Evaluation.* Aberdeen, MD: U.S. Army Center for Health Promotion and Preventive Medicine.

U.S. Army/Chemical Materials Agency. 2006. "Highlights." October 19. http://www.cma.army.mil.

U.S. Army Medical Research Institute of Infectious Diseases. 2004. *Medical Management of Biological Casualties Handbook.* 5th ed. Frederick, MD: USAMRIID. http://www.usamriid.army.mil/education/bluebookpdf/USAMRIID%20Blue%20Book%205th%20Edition.pdf.

U.S. Environmental Protection Agency. *See* EPA.

U.S. Government. 2003a. "Homeland Security Presidential Directive 5 (HSPD–5)." http://www.whitehouse.gov/news/releases/2003/02/20030228-9.html.

U.S. Government. 2003b. *National Strategy for Combating Terrorism.*

U.S. Government. 2006a. "Fact Sheet: The Global Initiative to Combat Nuclear Terrorism." July 15. http://www.whitehouse.gov/news/releases/2006/07/20060715-3.html.

U.S. Government. 2006b. *The Federal Response to Hurricane Katrina: Lessons Learned.* Washington, DC: White House. http://www.whitehouse.gov/reports/katrina-lessons-learned.pdf.

U.S. Government. 2006c. *National Strategy for Combating Terrorism.* http://www.state.gov/s/ct/rls/wh/71803.htm.

U.S. Government Accounting Office. *See* U.S. General Accountability Office.

USGS. n.d. "Earthshots: Satellite Images of Environmental Change: Chernobyl, Ukraine, 1986, 1992." http://edcwww.cr.usgs.gov/earthshots/slow/Chernobyl/Chernobyl.

U.S. Office of Management and Budget. 2008. "Analytical Perspectives, Budget of the United States Governemnt, Fiscal Year 2009." Washington, D.C. http://www.whitehouse.gov/omb/budget/fy2009/pdf/spec.pdf.

U.S. Postal Service. 2005. "United States Postal System Bio Detection System." http://www.nemaweb.org/?1381.

USPS. *See* U.S. Postal Service.

USSBS. *See* U.S. Strategic Bombing Survey.

U.S. Strategic Bombing Survey. 1945. *Summary Report (European War).* Washington, DC: Government Printing Office. http://www.anesi.com/ussbs02.htm.

U.S. Strategic Bombing Survey. 1946a. *The Effects of Atomic Bombs on Hiroshima and Nagasaki.* Washington, DC: Government Printing Office.

U.S. Strategic Bombing Survey. 1946b. *The Effects of Strategic Bombing on German Morale.* Vol. 2. Washington, DC: Government Printing Office.

U.S. Strategic Bombing Survey. 1947a. *Civilian Defense Division Final Report.* Washington, DC: Government Printing Office.

U.S. Strategic Bombing Survey. 1947b. *The Effects of Atomic Bombs on Health and Medical Services in Hiroshima and Nagasaki.* Washington, DC: Government Printing Office.

U.S. Strategic Bombing Survey. 1947c. *The Effects of Strategic Bombing on German Morale.* Vol. 1. Washington, DC: Government Printing Office.

U.S. Strategic Bombing Survey. 1947d. *The Effects of Strategic Bombing on Japanese Morale.* Washington, DC: Government Printing Office.

U.S. Strategic Bombing Survey. 1947e. *Field Report Covering Air-Raid Protection and Allied Subjects in Kyoto, Japan.* Washington, DC: Government Printing Office.

U.S. Strategic Bombing Survey. 1947f. *Final Report Covering Air-Raid Protection and Allied Subjects in Japan.* Washington, DC: Government Printing Office.

U.S. Treasury Department/Office of Economic Policy. 2005. *Report to Congress: Assessment: The Terrorism Risk Insurance Act of 2002.* http://www.ustreas.gov/press/releases/reports/063005%20tria%20study.pdf.

Utgoff, Victor A., ed. 2000. *The Coming Crisis: Nuclear Proliferation, US Interests, and World Order.* Cambridge, MA: MIT Press.

Vanderford, Marsha L. 2004. "Breaking New Ground in WMD Risk Communication: The Pre-Event Message Development Project." *Biosecurity and Bioterrorism: Biodefense Strategy, Practice, and Science* 2: 193–194.

Van Der Pligt, Joop. 1996. "Prospect Theory." In Anthony S. R. Manstead and Miles Hewstone, eds., *The Blackwell Encyclopedia of Social Psychology.* Cambridge, MA: Blackwell.

Verton, Dan. 2003. *Black Ice: The Invisible Threat of Cyber-Terrorism.* New York: McGraw-Hill.

Vesley, William E. 2002. *Fault Tree Handbook with Aerospace Applications: Version 1.1.* Washington, DC: NASA. http://www.hq.nasa.gov/office/codeq/doctree/fthb.pdf.

Vesley, William E., F. F. Goldberg, N. H. Roberts, and D. F. Hasl. 1987. *Fault Tree Handbook.* Nuclear Regulatory Commission, Report no. NUREG-492. http://www.nrc.gov/reading-rm/doc-collections/nuregs/staff/sr0492/sr0492.pdf.

Vogel, Kathleen. 2006. "Bioweapons Proliferation: Where Science Studies and Public Policy Collide." *Social Studies of Science* 36: 659–690.

Von Basum, Golo, Hannes Dahnke, Daniel Halmer, Peter Hering, and Manfred Murtz. 2003. "Online Recording of Ethane Traces in Human Breath via Infrared Laser Spectroscopy." *Journal of Applied Physiology* 95: 2583–2590.

Wald, Priscilla. 2007. *Contagious: Cultures, Carriers, and the Outbreak Narrative.* Durham, NC: Duke University Press.

Walden, Johan, and Edward H. Kaplan. 2004. "Estimating Time and Size of Bioterror Attack." *Emerging Infectious Diseases* 7: 1202–1205.

Waldrop, Mitchell. 2001. *The Dream Machine: J. C. Licklider and the Revolution that Made Computing Personal.* New York: Viking.

Walker, Richard I., and T. Jan Cerveny, eds. 1989. *Medical Consequences of Nuclear Warfare.* Falls Church, VA: Office of the Surgeon General. http://www.afrri.usuhs.mil/outreach/mmoresources.htm#TMM.

Walt, Stephen M. 2000. "Containing Rogues and Renegades: Coalition Strategies and Counterproliferation." In Victor A. Utgoff, eds., *The Coming Crisis: Nuclear Proliferation, US Interests, and World Order,* 191–226. Cambridge, MA: MIT Press.

Walter, Katie. 1999. "Handling Fluids in Microsensors." *Science and Technology Review,* November. http://www.llnl.gov/str/Miles.html.

Wampler, Robert A., and Thomas S. Blanton. 2001. "The September 11 Sourcebooks, Volume V: Anthrax at Sverdlovsk, 1979." National Security Archive Electronic Briefing Book no. 61. http://www.gwu.edu/~nsarchiv/NSAEBB/NSAEBB61/.

Ward, Thomas. 2001. "Improving Container Transport Security." Unpublished ms., JWG Group, Oakland, CA.

Waselenko, J. K., T. J. MacVittiee, William F. Blakely, A. Pesik, A. L. Wiley, W. E. Dickerson, H. Tsu, D. L. Confer, et al. 2004. "Medical Management of the Acute Radiation Syndrome: Recommendations of the Strategic National Stockpile Radiation Working Group." *Annals of Internal Medicine* 140: 1037–1051.

Washington State Department of Health. 2002. "Washington State Reporting and Surveillance Guidelines: Ebola-Marburg Viral Diseases." http://www.doh.wa.gov/notify/guidelines/pdf/ebola.pdf.

Wasserman, Jeffrey, Peter Jacobson, Nicole Lurie, Christopher Nelson, Karen A. Ricci, Molly Shea, James Zazzali, and Martha I. Nelson. 2006. *Organizing State and Local Health Departments for Public Health Preparedness.* RAND Technical Report TR–318–DHHS. http://www.rand.org/pubs/technical_reports/2006/RAND_TR318.pdf.

Watanabe, Manabu. 1998. "Religion and Violence in Japan Today: A Chronological and Doctrinal Analysis of Aum Shinrikyo." *Terrorism and Political Violence* 10: 80–100.

Weapons of Mass Destruction Commission. 2006. *Final Report: Weapons of Terror: Freeing the World of Nuclear, Biological and Chemical Arms.* Stockholm: WMDC. http://www.wmdcommission.org/files/Weapons_of_Terror.pdf.

Weapons of Mass Destruction Terrorism Research Program. 2004. *Assessing Terrorist Motivations for Attacking Critical Infrastructure.* CNS Research Report.

Weart, Spencer. 1976. "Scientists with a Secret." *Physics Today* 29: 23–30.

Weart, Spencer. 1989. *Nuclear Fear: A History of Images.* Cambridge, MA: Harvard University Press.

Weber, Eugen. 1964. *Varieties of Fascism: Doctrines of Revolution in the Twentieth Century.* Princeton, NJ: Van Nostrand.

Wehrle, Paul Francis, J. J. Posch, K. H. Richter, and Donald A. Henderson. 1970. "An Airborne Outbreak of Smallpox in a German Hospital and Its Significance with Respect to Other Recent Outbreaks." *Bulletin of the World Health Organization* 43, 2230–2251.

Weimer, David L., and Aidan R. Vining. 2005. *Policy Analysis: Concepts and Practice.* 4th ed. Englewood Cliffs, NJ: Prentice-Hall.

Wein, Lawrence M., and Yifan Liu. 2005. "Analyzing a Bioterror Attack on the Food Supply: The Case of Botulinum Toxin in Milk." *Proceedings of the National Academy of Sciences* 102: 9984–9989.

Weiner, Sharon K. 2002. "Preventing Nuclear Entrepreneurship in Russia's Nuclear Cities." *International Security* 27: 126–158.

Weiss, Peter. 2005. "Ghost Town Busters." *Science News* 168: 282–284.

Werner, T. 2001. "Cluster Analysis and Promoter Modelling as Bioinformatics Tools for the Identification of Target Genes from Expression Array Data." *Pharmacogenomics* 2: 25–36.

Wesley, Robert. 2006. "LeT Threat to Indian Nuclear Facilities Remains a Serious Concern." *Terrorism Focus* 3. September 12. http://www.jamestown.org/terrorism/news/uploads/tf_003_035.pdf.

Wessely, Simon, Kenneth C. Hyams, and Robert Bartholomew. 2002. "Psychological Implications of Chemical and Biological Weapons." *British Medical Journal* 323: 878–879.

Wessinger, Catherine. 2000. *How the Millennium Comes Violently: From Jonestown to Heaven's Gate.* New York: Seven Bridges.

Wheeler, Richard M., Thomas Edmunds, and Susan M. Howarth. 2004. Final Report: *DHS Workshop on Homeland Security: New Challenges for Decision-Making under Uncertainty.* Lawrence Livermore National Laboratory Report no. UCRL-TR–202536.

Wheelis, Mark, and Masaaki Sugishima. 2006. "Terrorist Use of Biological Weapons." In Mark Wheelis, Lajos Rozsa, and Malcolm Dando, eds., *Deadly Cultures: Biological Weapons Since 1945,* 284–303. Cambridge, MA: Harvard University Press.

White, Matthew. n.d.(a). "Death Tolls for Major Wars and Atrocities of the Twentieth Century." http://users.rcn.com/mwhite28/warstat2.htm.

White, Matthew. n.d.(b). "Selected Death Tolls for Wars, Massacres and Atrocities Before the Twentieth Century." http://users.rcn.com/mwhite28/warstat0.htm.

Williams, Paul L. 2005. *The Al Qaeda Connection: International Terrorism, Organized Crime, and the Coming Apocalypse*. Amherst, NY: Prometheus.

Williams, Paul L. 2007. *The Day of Islam: The Annihilation of America and the Western World*. Amherst, NY: Prometheus.

Williams, R. E. O. 1966. "Epidemiology of Airborne Staphylococcal Infection." *Bacteriological Reviews* 30: 660–674.

Willis, Henry H., Andrew R. Morral, Terrence K. Kelly, and Jamison Jo Medby. 2005. *Estimating Terrorism Risk*. Santa Monica, CA: RAND Center for Terrorism Risk Management Policy.

Wilson, James Q. 1989. *Bureaucracy*. New York: Basic Books.

Winder, Robert. 2003. "An Early Start: Dow, DSM, Dugussa, Helsinn and Clariant Are All At It." *Chemistry and Industry*, June 2, 17.

WMDC. *See* Weapons of Mass Destruction Commission.

WMD Terrorism Research Program. *See* Weapons of Mass Destruction Terrorism Research Program.

Woloschak, Gayle E., and Tatjana Paunesku. 1997. "Mechanisms of Radiation-Induced Gene Response." *Stem Cells* 15: 15–25.

Woodruff, David L. 2003. *Network Interdiction and Stochastic Integer Programming*. Netherlands: Kluwer.

Wray, Ricardo, and Keri Jupka. 2004. "What Does the Public Want to Know in the Event of a Terrorist Attack Using Plague?" *Biosecurity and Bioterrorism: Biodefense Strategy, Practice, and Science* 2: 208–215.

Wylie, Philip. [1942] 1955. *Generation of Vipers*. New York: Pocket Books.

Wylie, Philip. 1957. *Tomorrow!* New York: Popular Library.

Yamanaka, C., M. Ikeya, and H. Hara. 1993. "ESR Cavities for *In Vivo* Dosimetry of Tooth Enamel." *Applied Radation and Isotopes* 44: 70–80.

Yanagida, T., H. Takahashi, T. Ito, D. Kasama, M. Kokubun, K. Makishima, T. Yanigatani, H. Yagi, and T. Shigeta. 2005. "Evaluation of Properties of YAG(Ce) Ceramic Scintillators." *IEEE Transactions on Nuclear Science* 52: 1836.

Yao, Yiming, T. Edmunds, D. Papageorgiou, and R. Alvarez. 2007. "Trilevel Optimization in Power Network Defense." *IEEE Transactions on Systems, Man and Cybernetics (C)* 37: 712–718.

Yassif, Jaime M. 2004. Presentation slides: "Decontamination in the Aftermath of a Radiological Attack." American Physical Society Annual Meeting, May 3. http://www.fas.org/terrorism/wmd/docs/rad_dcon.pdf.

Zaman, Rashed uz. 2002. "WMD Terrorism in South Asia: Trends and Implications." *Journal of International Affairs* 7: 134–139. http://www.sam.gov.tr/perceptions/Volume7/September-November2002/Perception_RashedUzZaman.pdf.

Zanders, Jean Paul. 1999. "Assessing the Risks of Chemical and Biological Weapons Proliferation to Terrorists." *Nonproliferation Review* 6: 17–34. http://www.sipri.org/contents/cbwarfare/Publications/pdfs/zander64.pdf.

Zanetti, Aurelia, Susana Schwartz, and Andreas Lindemuth. 2007. "Natural Catastrophes and Man-Made Disasters in 2006: Low Insured Costs." Swiss Re *Sigma* Report no. 2/2007. http://www.swissre.com/resources/ce8f6a80455c6b9f8b2bbb80a45d76a0-sigma2_2007_e.pdf.

Zanjani, George. 2006. Public versus Private Underwriting of Catastrophe Risk: Lessons from the California Earthquake Authority. UC Berkeley Program on Housing and Urban Policy Working Paper C06-002.

Zanzonico, P. B., and D. V. Becker. 2000. "Effects of Time of Administration and Dietary Iodine Levels on Potassium Iodide (KI) Blockade of Thyroid Irradiation by ^{131}I from Radioactive Fallout." *Health Physics* 78: 660–667.

Zegart, Amy B. 1999. *Flawed by Design: The Evolution of the CIA, JCS, and NSC.* Palo Alto, CA: Stanford University Press.

Zegart, Amy B. 2007. *Failure and Consequence: Understanding US Intelligence and the Origins of 9/11.* Princeton, NJ: Princeton University Press.

Zegart, Amy B., Matthew C. Hipp, and Seth K. Jacobson. 2006. "Governance Challenges in Port Security: A Case Study of Emergency Response Capabilities at the Ports of Los Angeles and Long Beach." In John D. Haveman and Howard J. Shatz, eds., *Protecting the Nation's Seaports: Balancing Security and Cost.* San Francisco: Public Policy Institute of California, 155–184. http://www.ppic.org/content/pubs/report/R_606JHR.pdf.

Zenko, Micah. 2007. "A Nuclear Site Is Breached: South African Attack Should Sound Alarms." *Washington Post*, December 20. http://www.washingtonpost.com/wp-dyn/content/article/2007/12/19/AR2007121901857.html.

Zilinskas, Raymond A. 1999. "Iraq's Biological Warfare Program: The Past as Future?" In Joshua Lederberg, ed., *Biological Weapons: Limiting the Threat*, 137–158. Cambridge, MA: MIT Press.

Zilinskas, Raymond A. 2006. *Technical Barriers to Successful Biological Attacks with Synthetic Organisms.* Report for Synthetic Biology 2.0 Conference, Berkeley, CA, May 20–22, 2006. http://gspp.berkeley.edu/iths/UC%20White%20Paper.pdf.

Zimmerman, Peter D. 2006. "The Smoky Bomb Threat." *New York Times*, December 19. http://www.nytimes.com/2006/12/19/opinion/19zimmerman.html?ex=1324184400&en=979716b0cc23738d&ei=5090&partner=rssuserland&emc=rss.

Zimmerman, Peter D., and Cheryl Loeb. 2004. "Dirty Bombs: The Threat Revisited." *Defense Horizons* 38: 1–11. http://www.ndu.edu/ctnsp/defense_horizons/DH38.pdf.

Ziock, Klaus-Peter, J. W. Collins, L. Fabris, S. Gallagher, B. K. P. Horn, R. C. Lanza, and N. W. Madden. 2006. "Source-Search Sensitivity of a Large-Area, Coded-Aperture, Gamma-Ray Imager." *IEEE Transactions on Nuclear Science* 53: 1614–1621.

Ziock, Klaus-Peter, and W. Goldstein. 2002. "The Lost Source, Varying Backgrounds and Why Bigger May Not Be Better." In Jacob I. Trombka, David P. Spears, and Pamela H. Solomon, eds., *AIP Conference Proceedings Vol. 632: Unattended Radiation Sensor Systems for Remote Applications*, 60–70. Melville, NY: American Institute of Physics.

Ziock, Klaus-Peter, and Karl E. Nelson. 2007. "Maximum Detector Sizes Required for Orphan Source Detection." *Nuclear Instruments and Methods in Physics Research (A)* 579: 357–362.

.

Selected Web Sites

Armed Forces Radiobiology Research Institute
Downloadable Defense Department manuals detailing medical management of radiation injuries.
http://www.afrri.usuhs.mil/outreach/mmoresources.htm

Biosecurity and Bioterrorism: Biodefense Strategy, Practice, and Science
Online scholarly journal addressing biological warfare and public health issues.
http://www.liebertonline.com/bsp/

Center for Biosecurity, University of Pittsburgh Medical Center (UPMC)
Research reports, news, fact sheets, and government documents related to biodefense.
http://www.upmc-biosecurity.org/

Center for Infectious Disease Research & Policy, University of Minnesota
Resources and journal articles on bioweapons and agroterrorism.
http://www.cidrap.umn.edu/cidrap/

Center for Nonproliferation Studies, Monterey Institute of International Studies
Nuclear nonproliferation news and publications.
http://cns.miis.edu/

Centers for Disease Control and Prevention
Emergency preparedness and response information related to bioterrorism, chemical emergencies, radiation emergencies, mass casualties, and natural disasters.
www.bt.cdc.gov

Centers for Disease Control and Prevention, Health Alert Network home page
Links to government reporting protocols and disease surveillance programs.
http://www2a.cdc.gov/han/Index.asp

Center for Risk and Economic Analysis of Terrorism Events (CREATE)
Research reports analyzing the economic impact of terrorism.
http://www.usc.edu/dept/create/research/reports.htm

Combating Terrorism Center at West Point
Comprehensive bibliography of WMD and terrorism articles for classroom use.
http://www.teachingterror.com/bibliography/index.html

Counter-Terrorism, Training and Resources for Law Enforcement
Border and port security publications.
http://www.counterterrorismtraining.gov/pubs/port.html

Federation of American Scientists
Documents and online courses related to chemical and biological weapons.
www.fas.org/biosecurity

George Washington University, The National Security Archive
Online depository of declassified government documents. Extensive coverage of terrorism and WMD.
http://www2.gwu.edu/~nsarchiv/

Goldman School of Public Policy, Information Technology & Homeland Security Project
Online courses, working papers, and video lectures on various WMD- and terrorism-related topics.
http://gspp.berkeley.edu/programs/iths.html

Government Accountability Office
Search engine for GAO reports addressing border control, FBI transformation, nuclear smuggling, cooperative threat reduction, DHS, and other federal antiterrorism programs.
http://www.gao.gov

Health Resources and Services Administration (HRSA)
Information on hospital preparedness and volunteer health-care worker registration systems.
http://www.hrsa.gov/healthconcerns/default.htm

Homeland Security Council, National Planning Scenarios
Detailed estimates and descriptions for a wide variety of WMD scenarios.
http://www.ap.org/california/planningscenarios.pdf

International Institute for Counter-Terrorism
Publications and online resources related to international terrorism.
http://www.ict.org.il/

Journal of Homeland Security and Emergency Management
Online scholarly journal.
http://www.bepress.com/jhsem/

MedlinePlus
Resources and journal articles on the prevention and treatment of biological weapons diseases.
http://www.nlm.nih.gov/medlineplus/biodefenseandbioterrorism.html

Monterey Institute of International Studies, James Martin Center for Non-Proliferation Studies Chemical & Biological Weapons Resource Page
Reports, op-ed pieces, and other publications related to chemical and biological weapons.
http://cns.miis.edu/research/cbw/index.htm

Monterey WMD Terrorism Database
Worldwide database of terrorism incidents. Access is limited to government employees except by special arrangement.
http://cns.miis.edu/wmdt/

National Association of City and County Health Officials (NACCHO)
Public Health Preparedness Publications and Seminars.
http://www.naccho.org/topics/emergency/index.cfm

National Conference of State Legislatures (NCSL)
Information about state public health preparedness programs.
www.ncsl.org/programs/health/health-menu.htm

National Conference of State Legislatures
Model antiterrorism statutes for U.S. state legislatures.
www.ncsl.org/programs/press/2001/freedom/stateaction.htm

Nuclear Threat Initiative (NTI)
Nuclear nonproliferation news and documents.
http://www.nti.org/

Office of Defense Nuclear Nonproliferation
U.S. government initiatives to limit the proliferation of nuclear weapons and other WMD.
http://www.nnsa.doe.gov/na-20/sitemap.shtml

Oklahoma City National Memorial Institute for the Prevention of Terrorism (MIPT), Public Health–Terrorism Information Center
Government and private reports on various homeland security issues.
http://www.terrorisminfo.mipt.org/Public-Health.asp

RAND Corporation, Center for Domestic and International Health Security
Public health and terrorism research papers.
http://www.rand.org/health/centers/healthsecurity/

RAND Corporation, Public Health Preparedness Database
Information about training programs and exercises for public health officials.
http://www.rand.org/health/projects/php/

RAND Corporation, Terrorism and Homeland Security
Terrorism and homeland security research papers.
http://www.rand.org/research_areas/terrorism/

St. Louis University School of Public Health, Institute for Biosecurity
Resources and links related to the treatment of CBRN injuries.
http://www.bioterrorism.slu.edu/index.html

Terrorism Information Center
Terrorism-related resources.
http://www.terrorisminfo.mipt.org/

U.S. Army Medical Research Institute of Infectious Diseases (USAMRIID)
U.S. Army manuals detailing defensive measures and treatment of biological and toxin weapons.
http://www.usamriid.army.mil/education/instruct.htm

U.S. Department of Health and Human Services (DHHS), Disaster and Emergencies
Preparedness and emergency response publications and web resources for CBRN and conventional terrorism.
http://www.hhs.gov/disasters/

U.S. Department of Health and Human Services, Office of the Assistant Secretary for Preparedness and Response (ASPR)
Detailed summary of current government biosecurity preparedness and R&D initiatives.
http://www.hhs.gov/aspr/

U.S. Department of Homeland Security
Press releases, speeches, and congressional testimony covering all aspects of U.S. federal homeland security programs.
http://www.dhs.gov/index.shtm

U.S. Food and Drug Administration
Publications and web links related to biological and agroterrorism.
http://www.fda.gov/oc/opacom/hottopics/bioterrorism.html

WMD First Responders
Publications and web links for first responders confronting CRBN.
http://www.wmdfirstresponders.com/

Contributors

Gary Ackerman is research director for the National Consortium for the Study of Terrorism and Responses to Terrorism. His research interests include potential terrorist use of chemical, biological, radiological, and nuclear weapons; government response and prevention programs; and threat assessment tools for anticipating terrorist attacks.

Jeffrey M. Bale is an assistant professor in the Graduate School of International Policy Studies at the Monterey Institute of International Studies and a Senior Research Associate in the Weapons of Mass Destruction Terrorism Research Program at the Center for Nonproliferation Studies. He has published numerous articles on terrorism, right-wing extremism, Islamism, and covert operations. His current research is focused on Islamist terrorist networks operating in Europe and North America, their potential collaboration with left- and right-wing radicals in the West, and the extent to which they may be interested in acquiring and using WMD.

Deborah Yarsike Ball is a political-military analyst at Lawrence Livermore National Laboratory, where she leads the Global Security Directorate's Dynamic Network Assessment and Political Science Groups. Her research has specialized in Russian military doctrine, security issues, civil-military relations, and programs for improving the safety and security of Russian WMD. Her current research interests focus on terrorism.

Eugene Bardach is a professor of public policy at the Goldman School of Public Policy at U.C. Berkeley. Trained as political scientist, his research focus includes policy implementation, public management, and strategies for improving interorganizational collaboration. He has extensive practical experience training high-level public managers and performing policy analysis for the U.S. Department of the Interior.

Tina Carlsen is a senior environmental scientist at Lawrence Livermore National Laboratory with over twenty years of experience in the field of environmental restoration. For the past ten years she has led teams of engineers, chemists, and biologists in various projects related to removing contaminants from the environment, environmental monitoring of pathogens, and restoring critical infrastructure after chemical, biological, or radiological events. She has a PhD in ecology from the University of California, Davis, and is author or coauthor of numerous journal publications and technical documents.

Jason Christopher is IT manager of the Goldman School of Public Policy and Technical Director of the Berkeley Synthetic Biology Security Program. His research interests include academic self-regulation in synthetic biology and other molecular biology disciplines. He currently operates an online portal where biologists can obtain expert, independent, and timely advice before proceeding on experiments of concern.

C. Norman Coleman is director of the National Cancer Institute's Radiation Oncology Sciences Program and Senior Medical Expert at the Department of Health and Human Services' Office of Public Health Emergency Preparedness. He routinely represents NIH on issues related to radiological and nuclear terrorism.

Lois Davis is a senior researcher at the RAND Corporation in Santa Monica, California, specializing in health policy. Her research interests include technology support for public safety and emergency preparedness for terrorism involving chemical or biological weapons.

Thomas Edmunds is chief scientist for Systems and Decision Sciences at Lawrence Livermore National Laboratory. Trained in nuclear engineering and operations research, his research interests include developing and applying quantitative and qualitative risk assessment methods to arms control treaties, security systems, asymmetric warfare, and energy systems. Edmunds is the author of numerous papers on decision analysis, optimization, and game theory.

Peter Gordon is a professor of Policy, Planning and Development, and Economics and a member of the Center for Risk and Economic Analysis of Terrorism Events (CREATE) at the University of Southern California. His research interests focus on applied urban economics. He and his colleagues use sophisticated computer models to explore the economics of the effects of terrorism, earthquakes and natural disasters. He is the coeditor with James Moore and Harry Richardson of *The Economic Costs and Consequences of Terrorism*.

Lucy M. Hair is a chemical engineer at Lawrence Livermore National Laboratory's Counterproliferation Analysis Section, where she is a member of the Chemistry Team and Special Projects groups. Her research interests include developing new catalysts for removing nitrogen oxide from automobile exhaust and ultra-low-density, nanopore polyethylene and resorcinol-formaldehyde foams for laser fusion energy research. Hair received her B.S. and doctorate in chemical engineering from Purdue University.

Blas Pirez Henrmquez is director of Executive and International Programs at the Goldman School of Public Policy at U.C. Berkeley. His research focuses on the use of information technologies to improve policymaking in migration, border control, and national security.

Dwight Jaffee is Willis Booth Professor of Banking, Finance, and Real Estate at the Haas School of Business at U.C. Berkeley. His research interests include real estate markets, financial institutions, and catastrophe insurance for terrorism and earthquakes.

Robert Kirvel is a research associate and senior science writer at Lawrence Livermore National Laboratory. Trained in chemistry, physiological psychology, and neurophysiology, his specialties include response and recovery strategies following biological and chemical agent attacks.

Simon Labov is a physicist at Lawrence Livermore National Laboratory. Since 1999, his Radiation Detection Center has provided a focus for detector development and nuclear security research throughout the laboratory. Labov's recent work includes developing an advanced room-temperature gamma ray imaging spectrometer as well as superresolving gamma ray detectors for nuclear forensics applications. His current research interests focus on technologies for modeling, analyzing, and fusing data from multiple radiation and non-radiation sources.

Bumsoo Lee is assistant professor of planning at the University of Illinois at Urbana-Champaign. Dr. Lee, who earned his PhD from the University of Southern California in 2006, conducts research on land use, travel behavior, transportation, and urban spatial structure, with a focus on how technological change is reshaping agglomeration economies and urban form. He is also involved in several research projects on extreme events, including analyses of economic impacts and transportation mode choice change after terrorism events.

Stephen M. Maurer is adjunct associate professor at U.C. Berkeley's Goldman School of Public Policy and Boalt School of Law. He is also Director of the Goldman School's Information Technology and Homeland Security Project. Trained as an intellectual property lawyer, Maurer's research interests include innovation economics, government drug development incentives, and biological weapons policy. He is currently working with leading members of the gene synthesis industry on a series of initiatives to improve the screening of incoming orders, provide expert advice to scientists contemplating experiments of concern, and construct an industrywide database of virulence-confering genes.

Thomas McVey is a process engineer attached to the Global Security Directorate at Lawrence Livermore National Laboratory. Trained as a chemical engineer at Cambridge, he also holds an MBA from U.C. Berkeley. Before joining the Global Security Directorate, he worked as a management consultant specializing in process economics and conceptual design of new chemical and industrial biotechnology processes for SRI Consulting, a subsidiary of SRI International. His current research interests center on chemical weapons, biological weapons, and signature analysis for detecting proliferation.

James E. Moore II is professor of Industrial and Systems Engineering at the University of Southern California. His research interests focus on mathematical programming and connectionist models for studying the effects of natural disasters on transportation network performance and control. He has conducted numerous studies of the economic impacts of terrorism and is coeditor with Peter Gordon and Harry Richardson of *The Economic Costs and Consequences of Terrorism*.

Michael Nacht is Aaron Wildavsky Professor of Public Policy at the Goldman School of Public Policy at U.C. Berkeley. He formerly served as assistant director for Strategic and Eurasian Affairs of the U.S. Arms Control and Disarmament Agency, where he directed nuclear arms negotiations with Russia and China. Nacht recently chaired an advisory panel to the Secretary of Defense on combating terrorist use of weapons of mass destruction and serves on committees advising both the Lawrence Livermore and Los Alamos National Laboratories on homeland security issues.

Michael O'Hare is professor of Public Policy at the Goldman School of Public Policy at U.C. Berkeley. Trained as an architect and engineer, his research interests include environmental policy, facility siting, and public perception of risk.

Qisheng Pan is an associate professor in the Department of Urban Planning and Environmental Policy at Texas Southern University. His research interests include freight transportation modeling, socioeconomic impacts of transportation projects, transit planning, and the economic impacts of terrorist attacks in large metropolitan areas.

JiYoung Park is assistant professor in the Department of Urban and Regional Planning at the State University of New York (SUNY) at Buffalo. He holds a PhD in Urban Planning from the University of Southern California's School of Policy, Planning, and Development. His research interests are in urban economics and transportation modeling. He has also worked to develop modeling applications for the study of natural environmental disasters and national security problems. Dr. Park has published several peer-reviewed journal papers and book chapters in the regional science and risk analysis areas. He is the coauthor of two books in applied econometrics.

Ellen Raber is department head of the Environmental Protection Department at Lawrence Livermore National Laboratory. Her research interests focus on decontamination systems for chemical and biological warfare agents.

Harry W. Richardson holds the James Irvine Chair in Urban and Regional Planning and is a professor of economics at the University of Southern California. His primary research interests are in the economic impacts of terrorism, travel behavior, and metropolitan spatial structure. He has authored or edited twenty-six books, including most recently *The Economic Consequences and Costs of Terrorism* with Peter Gordon and James Moore.

Jeanne Ringel is senior economist and deputy director of the Public Health Preparedness program at RAND. Her research interests include pandemic influenza preparedness, incorporating vulnerable populations into public health preparedness planning, applying quality improvement methods to public health preparedness, health-care financing and organization, substance abuse, and mental health.

Thomas Russell is associate professor of economics at Santa Clara University. He has written extensively on the topic of catastrophe insurance in general and terrorism insurance in particular. He has served on the board of the Asian Pacific Risk and Insurance Association. His work has been presented at a number of conferences on Security and Counter-Terrorism, most recently in Moscow in 2007.

George W. Rutherford is the Salvatore Pablo Lucia Professor of Preventive Medicine, vice chair of the Department of Epidemiology and Biostatistics, and director of the Institute for Global Health at the University of California, San Francisco. Rutherford previously served as State Epidemiologist and State Health Officer for the State of California. His current work focuses on HIV and AIDS, tuberculosis, sexually transmitted diseases, and coccidioidomycosis.

Christine Hartmann Siantar is deputy program leader for Nuclear and Radiological Countermeasures at Lawrence Livermore National Laboratory and a Response and Recovery Thrust Area Leader for the Department of Health and Human Services. Trained as a medical physicist, she has authored more than eighty articles related to radiation detection, dosimetry, and radiation oncology.

Tom Slezak is associate program leader for Informatics in the Lawrence Livermore National Laboratory's Global Security Program. Trained as a computer scientist, he led LLNL (and subsequently DOE's) contributions to the Human Genome Project from 1987 to 2000. In 2000 he started a new bioinformatics team to develop DNA-based pathogen signatures based on a novel whole-genome approach. This work provided the intellectual foundations for the BASIS and BioWatch pathogen surveillance systems. Slezak's current research interests include human and agricultural pathogens and developing improved signatures for virulence, antibiotic resistance, and genetic engineering.

Tammy P. Taylor is a technical staff member in the Chemistry Division of Los Alamos National Laboratory. Trained as an environmental engineer, her research interests center on developing new homeland defense countermeasures against nuclear and radiological weapons.

Michael Thompson is an acting captain in the San Francisco Fire Department. He holds a Master of Public Policy degree from the Goldman School of Public Policy at U.C. Berkeley. His research interests focus on how advanced information technology can help first responders manage a WMD event.

Richard Wheeler is with the Nonproliferation, Arms Control, and International Security Program at Lawrence Livermore National Laboratory. Trained as an electrical engineer, he has a long-standing interest in decision making under uncertainty in complex systems. His research focuses on detection and response systems for national security, counterterrorism, and homeland security applications.

Index